FIFTH EDITION

Teaching Students in Inclusive Settings

Adapting and Accommodating Instruction

Judy W. Wood

Virginia Commonwealth University

PEARSON

Merrill
Prentice Hall

Upper Saddle River, New Jersey
Columbus, Ohio

Library of Congress Cataloging in Publication Data

Wood, Judy W.
  Teaching students in inclusive settings : adapting and accommodating instruction / Judy
W. Wood — 5th ed.
    p. cm.
  Rev. ed. of: Adapting instruction to accommodate students in inclusive settings. 4th ed. c2002.
  Includes bibliographical references and index.
  ISBN -13-118132-7
    1. Inclusive education—United States. 2. Students with disabilities—Education—United
States. 3. Children with social disabilities—Education—United States. 4. Mainstreaming in
education—United States. 1. Wood, Judy W. Adapting instruction to accommodate
students in inclusive settings. II. Title.

LC1201.W66 2006

2005043307

Vice President and Executive Publisher: Jeffrey W. Johnston
Acquisitions Editor: Allyson P. Sharp
Editorial Assistant: Kathleen S. Burk
Production Editor: Sheryl Glicker Langner
Production Coordination: Ann Mohan, WordCrafters Editorial Services, Inc.
Design Coordinator: Diane C. Lorenzo
Photo Coordinator: Valerie Schultz
Cover Designer: Linda Sorrells-Smith
Cover Image: Corbis
Production Manager: Laura Messerly
Director of Marketing: Ann Castel Davis
Marketing Manager: Autumn Purdy
Marketing Coordinator: Brian Mounts

This book was set in Helvetica by Carlisle Communications, Ltd. It was printed and bound by Courier Kendallville, Inc. The cover was printed by The Lehigh Press, Inc.

Photo Credits: Scott Cunningham/Merrill, pp. 36, 77, 122, 226; Laimute E. Druskis/PH College, p. 460; Larry Hamill/Merrill, p. 172; Richard Hutchings/PhotoEdit, p. 56; KS Studios/Merrill, pp. 2, 162; Anthony Magnacca/Merrill, pp. 26, 108, 133, 184, 244, 269, 272, 307, 400, 466; Barbara Schwartz/Merrill, p. 196; Anne Vega/Merrill, pp. 16, 88, 320, 378, 480; Tom Watson/Merrill, p. 206.

Pearson Education Ltd.
Pearson Education Singapore Pte. Ltd.
Pearson Education Canada, Ltd.
Pearson Education—Japan

Pearson Education Australia Pty. Limited
Pearson Education North Asia Ltd.
Pearson Educación de Mexico, S.A. de C.V.
Pearson Education Malaysia Pte. Ltd.

10 9 8 7 6 5 4 3 2 1
ISBN: 0-13-118132-7

This book is lovingly dedicated to the following persons who exhibit courage for life, love for others, and an endless drive for making a difference in the lives of all persons.

My special friend and assistant, *Paula Friedrich.*

My talented and gifted colleague, *Dr. Michelle Arant.*

My lifelong friends and sisters of choice: *Dr. Cynthia Bryant, Carolyn Tomlin, Carolyn Hamada, Dr. Jennifer Kilgo, Dr. Cherritta Matthews, Patsy Glover, Kay Christian Morse, Ginny C. Padgette, Carlo Jo Christian Looney, and Debra L. Gibson.*

My adopted mother, *Maxine Christian.*

My wonderful brother and his wife, *Dr. Ford Walker and Elaine Walker.*

My ever-growing family, *Ashley Wood, Melissa Wood, Clay Alexa Wood, Tanner Walker Wood, Camden Shay Wood, and Emma Elizabeth Friedrich.*

My sons, who have provided me inspiration for life and the vision for all of my works: *Eddie Wood, Scott Wood, and Jason Wood.*

To the memory of my parents, *Ford and Ercyle Walker.*

And last, but always first, to my best friend and loving husband, who made this work possible, *David A. Duncan.*

EDUCATOR LEARNING CENTER: AN INVALUABLE ONLINE RESOURCE

Merrill Education and the Association for Supervision and Curriculum Development (ASCD) invite you to take advantage of a new online resource, one that provides access to the top research and proven strategies associated with ASCD and Merrill—the Educator Learning Center. At www.educatorlearningcenter.com, you will find resources that will enhance your students' understanding of course topics and of current educational issues, in addition to being invaluable for further research.

HOW THE EDUCATOR LEARNING CENTER WILL HELP YOUR STUDENTS BECOME BETTER TEACHERS

With the combined resources of Merrill Education and ASCD, you and your students will find a wealth of tools and materials to better prepare them for the classroom.

Research

- More than 600 articles from the ASCD journal *Educational Leadership* discuss everyday issues faced by practicing teachers.
- A direct link on the site to Research Navigator™ gives students access to many of the leading education journals, as well as extensive content detailing the research process.
- Excerpts from Merrill Education texts give your students insights on important topics of instructional methods, diverse populations, assessment, classroom management, technology, and refining classroom practice.

Classroom Practice

- Hundreds of lesson plans and teaching strategies are categorized by content area and age range.
- Case studies and classroom video footage provide virtual field experience for student reflection.
- Computer simulations and other electronic tools keep your students abreast of today's classrooms and current technologies.

LOOK INTO THE VALUE OF EDUCATOR LEARNING CENTER YOURSELF

A four-month subscription to Educator Learning Center is $25 but is **FREE** when packaged with any Merrill Education text. In order for your students to have access to this site, you must use this special value-pack ISBN number **WHEN** placing your textbook order with the bookstore: 0-13-155989-3. Your students will then receive a copy of the text packaged with a free ASCD pincode. To preview the value of this website to you and your students, please go to **www.educatorlearningcenter.com** and click on "Demo."

PREFACE

Since the beginning of my career, I have maintained a simple vision that has developed into a driving mission. This vision is founded in four basic beliefs: We must begin teaching all children where they are instructionally, yet expose them to the general education curriculum; help students reach as high as they are capable instructionally, emotionally, and physically; provide love and support along the way; and maintain positive attitudes. Every child has extraordinary potential, and we must remove the societal boundaries for exceptional lives to develop to the fullest.

During my career, I have been fortunate to see many educational and emotional boundaries that prevent a child with disabilities from reaching his or her full potential unlocked. However, we still have work to do. We must assist students with disabilities, as well as those at risk who now struggle alongside them. Our journey is not yet completed, but the path has fewer obstacles. I do believe that our system will continue to open for all students. And each one of you will be a part of this incredible journey.

ORGANIZATION OF THE BOOK

Chapter 1 provides the foundation for the remaining chapters in the book. The history of special education, supporting legislation and services, and the rights of individuals with disabilities are presented. Chapter 2 continues to build on this foundation, sharing tips for collaboration between professional educators and families. Chapters 3, 4, and 5 describe the students we serve within America's classrooms: those with disabilities, those at risk, and those who have unique gifts. Chapter 6 examines the process of delivering special education and related services. The remaining chapters, 7 through 13, provide extensive information on assessing and teaching students with disabilities and students at risk. These chapters represent a lifetime of research, field testing, and implementation of interventions for all aspects of the classroom.

CHAPTER FORMAT

All chapters have the same format, one that aligns with effective teaching and presents a model for all educators.

- *Learner Objectives.* All chapters begin with learner objectives that explain what each learner will have accomplished upon completion of the chapter.
- *Key Terms.* Each chapter provides a list of terms and concepts that the author has deemed critical, with corresponding page numbers indicating where they are defined.

- *Vignettes.* Each chapter begins with a vignette, a short glimpse of a real student or educational situation that sets the stage for the chapter. Each vignette will be used on the Companion Website for further student learning and activities.

- *Chapter at a Glance.* Each chapter has a Chapter at a Glance illustration to help the reader see the complete structure of the chapter and how all sections of the chapter are connected.

- *Resources and Suggested Readings.* Each chapter concludes with lists of resources and suggested readings that the reader may find helpful.

- *Websites.* Websites for further exploration are also listed at the end of each chapter. These websites are hyperlinked on the Companion Website for student convenience.

- *Student Knowledge Check.* At the conclusion of each chapter, a student knowledge check with questions is provided. This serves to help students reflect on the information covered.

INFORMATION FOR SPECIAL EDUCATION AND GENERAL EDUCATION TEACHERS

To better serve all students and our readers, each chapter includes information on diversity, technology, and practical applications, as well as collaboration tips. Each of these features relates to the chapter's content.

- *Accommodating Diversity.* This section prepares teachers to teach the diverse populations in their classrooms. Ideas and research are presented based on differences in language, ethnicity, race, and socioeconomic status.

- *Accommodating Technology.* Information is presented on the latest technology for working with the chapter's population or for enhancing the chapters that cover instructional content.

- *Collaboration Tips.* Professionals must work together to provide quality education for all students. This need for collaboration is growing in importance. Each chapter's collaboration tips relate specifically to the chapter's content.

- *Practical Applications.* Each chapter presents practical teaching ideas for teachers to use with students.

- *Standards-Based Education.* Chapters 7 through 12 present interventions within the concept of a standards-based educational system. Chapter 9, "Adapting Lesson Plans," is developed around standards and where interventions "fit" into a standards-based lesson plan. Chapters 10, 11, and 12 incorporate standards. Chapter 12, "Adapting Assessment, Evaluation, and Grading," presents a model for incorporating classroom-embedded assessment within a standards-based lesson.

SUPPLEMENTS TO ACCOMPANY THE FIFTH EDITION

The fifth edition of *Teaching Students in Inclusive Settings: Adapting and Accommodating Instruction* has expanded supplements for both instructors and students. These include a comprehensive Instructor's Resource Manual and a Companion Website.

For Students

New! Companion Website with On-Line Practice Tests

Now students can benefit from the Companion Website, which is full of supplementary materials that aid in understanding the material in the text. Students have access to downloaded outlines, handouts for student activities, case studies with reflection questions, and interactive self-assessments. The self-assessments consist of multiple-choice, true/false, and short-answer questions that allow students to check their knowledge of chapter material. After answering the questions, students receive immediate feedback that helps in preparation for the chapter tests. The Companion Website also contains *web links* that provide additional material about chapter content. Other related resources for student investigation include the appendices referenced in the text. The Companion Website may be found at **http://www.prenhall.com/wood/.**

For Professors

Instructor's Resource Manual

The on-line Instructor's Resource Manual is located on the Prentice Hall website at **www.prenhall.com** on the book's description page. The on-line manual includes a message from the author, chapter objectives, and professor presentation outlines for each chapter. The presentation outline ties all of the ancillary components together in a cohesive package. Student activities and corresponding handouts for the activities are included in the Instructor's Resource Manual.

A comprehensive test file, presented in a variety of formats, includes multiple-choice, true/false and short-answer/essay items. Answer keys for these questions are provided along with the page numbers of the text where the topic is discussed in the chapter. The assessment questions can also be found at **www.prenhall.com** under the book's description.

New! PowerPoint Slide Package

The PowerPoint package, accessible at **www.prenhall.com,** contains approximately 150 slides organized by chapter and helps explain core information presented in each chapter. You may download these and use as a PowerPoint slide presentation or print them out as handouts. The slides coincide with the student outline that students may download from the book's Website. For instructors who prefer transparencies, the slides may easily be printed onto acetates. To add a little humor, 50 cartoons are included that may be inserted into a PowerPoint presentation or used separately during class lectures.

ACKNOWLEDGMENTS

It truly takes a team effort to write and produce a book. The journey is long and winds down many paths before finally reaching the planned destination. So many people have been on my team pulling me along and cheering at every turn. Many obstacles fell into the path: tragic deaths of family members, a critical illness of one family member, and, believe it or not, I broke "off" my right elbow just as the final deadline arrived. My team kept encouraging me and provided the options that made this book possible. My appreciation is extended to so many team members.

At Merrill/Prentice Hall, my publisher since the early 1990s, one of my teammates was Allyson Sharp, executive editor. Allyson was introduced to me in 2003. First, I was impressed at her youth and graceful beauty. As I listened to her speak and her vision, I realized that this young lady was unusually bright and indeed "sharp." Thank you, Allyson, for the encouragement and kindness you extended to me and to my family.

Through the development of the fifth edition of this text, several associate editors have been involved: Emily Wilson, Amy Nelson, and Amy Amspaugh. All have been wonderful to work with. Vice president and executive publisher Jeff Johnston has always supported my work, and for that I'm grateful. Others who worked hard to see this book to the end are Valerie Schultz, photo coordinator; Kathy Burk, editorial assistant; Sheryl Langner, production editor; Diane C. Lorenzo, design coordinator; Linda Sorrells-Smith, cover designer; and Ann Mohan, production editor at WordCrafters Editorial Services. One last person who actually was first is Ann Davis. Ann and I go back many years. Even though she has moved on to be director of marketing for Merrill/Prentice Hall, she was the one who kept the text moving along over many editions. Ann is a very gifted person and a tireless worker.

Many reviewers assisted with the long process of reading chapters, reviewing outlines, reading more chapters, and so on. For their valuable comments and new vision for this mission I am indebted: Elizabeth Altieri, Radford University; Gail Peterson Craig, University of Wisconsin, Superior; Linda Schwartz Green, Centenary College; and Elizabeth B. Keefe, University of New Mexico.

Very talented contributors joined my team to see that this work was developed to include all students and many perspectives. Some are friends of many years and others are newfound friends. They have all met deadlines, put their hearts into the work, and remained focused on the vision. To each of you, thank you. Dr. Paul Wehman, an international figure in the field of special education and rehabilitation services and a distinguished professor at Virginia Commonwealth University; Dr. Michael D. West, Virginia Commonwealth University; Dr. Bryan G. Cook, Dr. Lisa Audet, Dr. David L. Cameron, and Dr. Melody Tankersley, Kent State University; Dr. Elizabeth Evans Getzel and Dr. Colleen A. Thoma, Virginia Commonwealth University; and Debra L. Gibson.

The first string on the team worked endlessly, typing, researching, outlining, seeking permissions, and seeing that all the endless tasks finally came to an end. I forever thank Paula Friedrich, my assistant, and David A. Duncan, my husband, for their contribution to this work. No doubt without their endless late hours and forever positive attitudes, our book would not have made it to the finish line.

Ann Parkinson provided significant expertise in the research for the technology and diversity sections of the book. Detroit City Schools provided the setting for the videos, prayers for my family, and endless encouragement to me. These great educators include Dr. Aleatha H. Kimbrough; Dr. Emmalee S. Barham, Dr. Diane Jackson, Arezell Brown; Dr. Sandra J. Screen, Deletha Motley, Hariett Kirk, Elaine Brown, Doloris Nicholas, Dale Moss, and Deborah Williamson. A special thanks to Betty Blackwell, Chelle Furst, and Anne Burris of Akron, Ohio, Ohio City Schools.

The team of unsung heroes, the thousands of educators who go to work every day and stay late into the evening, truly make all hard work an honor. These professionals never stop believing in our students. I have had the privilege of meeting thousands of these true heroes who provide America's children with hope for the future.

BRIEF CONTENTS

CONTENTS

Note: Every effort has been made to provide accurate and current Internet information in this book. However, the Internet and information posted on it are constantly changing, so it is inevitable that some of the Internet addresses listed in this textbook will change.

Teaching Students in Inclusive Settings

1

Foundations

LEARNER OBJECTIVES

After you read this chapter, you will be able to:

- Understand the legal and social changes leading to the Education for All Handicapped Children Act (EAHCA).

- Understand the basic requirements of EAHCA (later the Individuals with Disabilities Education Act, IDEA) related to eligibility, services, and settings.

- Describe the characteristics of special education students, including distributions by age, race, sex, and disability.

- Describe the differences among the terms *least restrictive environment (LRE), mainstreaming,* and *inclusion.*

- Describe methods for achieving physical, social, and emotional inclusion of children with disabilities in general education classes.

CHAPTER AT A GLANCE

```
                    ┌─────────────────────┐
                    │   The History of    │
                    │  Special Education  │
                    └─────────────────────┘
```

| Early History: A Brief Review | The Modern Era: Setting the Stage | Section 504: Civil Rights for Citizens with Disabilities | The Education for All Handicapped Children Act | Disability Legislation Post-IDEA |

```
                    ┌─────────────────────┐
                    │      Inclusion      │
                    └─────────────────────┘

                    ┌─────────────────────┐
                    │     IDEA and        │
                    │     Access to       │
                    │     General         │
                    │     Education       │
                    └─────────────────────┘

                    ┌─────────────────────┐
                    │   Five Faces of     │
                    │     Inclusion       │
                    └─────────────────────┘
```

KEY TERMS

*D*eborah Nickerson had spent 2 years preparing to file a due process complaint with the Virginia Department of Education to have her 9-year-old daughter, Ashley, educated in a year-round program in her local education agency (LEA). Ashley has congenital deafness and only limited vision in one eye. She was enrolled in a preschool program at age 2½. By age 7, she was learning to communicate with sign language, and the school system provided her with a full-time interpreter. She was progressing academically, learning the alphabet, state capitals, and geometric shapes.

Problems with the school system began when Ashley was preparing to enter the second grade. Ms. Nickerson tried to convince the LEA that Ashley could benefit educationally from enrollment in a summer program. She videotaped Ashley at home signing complete sentences. She requested and received an independent evaluation of Ashley's academic progress that she believed buttressed her claim that Ashley needed to continue in an educational environment over the summer. When the LEA still declined to add the summer program to Ashley's individualized education program (IEP), Ms. Nickerson prepared for battle. She took out a loan on her home, hired a lawyer, and requested a due process hearing.

After months of preparation for the hearing, the LEA contacted Ms. Nickerson and negotiated an agreement with her. Ashley would attend school for 8 weeks over the summer, 5 days a week.

Adapted from Johnson (2004).

*D*eborah and Ashley Nickerson's story illustrates how far U.S. society has progressed regarding children with disabilities. Before 1975, when the Education for All Handicapped Children Act (EAHCA, PL 94–142) was signed into law, a school system would have been unlikely to even consider enrolling and providing educational services for children like Ashley. Parents of such children had little recourse other than private schools or institutional care. In contrast, Ashley receives not only a publicly funded education, but also a full-time interpreter and extended-year program so that her progress can continue uninterrupted.

EAHCA was only one link in a long chain of social and legislative changes in the United States, but it was an event of tremendous and far-reaching impact for children like Ashley and their families, schools, and indeed all of society. Since the act was passed, many state and local educational agencies (SEAs and LEAs) have challenged the law's core concept, that *all* children are to be provided a publicly funded education. But both Congress and the court system have held firm that every child is due this basic civil right, regardless of the nature or severity of the child's disabilities, or even whether there are observable benefits to the student (e.g., *Timothy W. v. Rochester N. H. School District,* 1989).

In this opening chapter, we will explore the events leading to the passage of this historic legislation, the main components of the legislation, and current information regarding students receiving special education and the types of services they receive. Finally, we will explore one of the most challenging and controversial aspects of special education today, inclusion of students with disabilities in classes with children who are not educationally handicapped.

HISTORY OF SPECIAL EDUCATION

Early History: A Brief Review

The history of special education spans several centuries. The development of sign language for deaf children and adults in the early 1600s was the first known attempt to devise specialized training programs based on disability. In 1760 the National Institute for the Deaf, the first special education school, was established in Paris. In 1799 French physician Jean-Marc Gaspard Itard began teaching a feral child using techniques adapted from deaf education. He subsequently published the first textbook on systematic teaching techniques for children with special learning needs (1801/1962).

Edouard Sequin, an educator, applied Itard's methods to children with mental retardation and developed a teaching system that emphasized sensory and motor development. His first school, founded in 1847 in Paris, had approximately 30 students. Sequin's work was highly influential worldwide and inspired Italian educator Maria Montessori and Americans such as Samuel Howe and Thomas Gallaudet, who founded the first schools for the blind and deaf, respectively, in the United States. The early part of the 20th century was marked by the use (and misuse)[1] of intelligence tests and the publication of J. E. Wallace Wallin's seminal special education textbook, *The Education of Handicapped Children* (1924).

Despite these milestone events, however, children and adults with disabilities have generally not fared well in society. For much of recorded history, they were shunned, isolated, persecuted, exploited, used for entertainment, and, in some ancient cultures, exterminated. Even in recent history, there have been efforts to remove individuals with disabilities from society. For example, the eugenics movement, which flourished in Europe and America from the 1880s until the 1930s, resulted in legal restrictions on immigration, marriage, childbearing, and other freedoms for "undesirables," including individuals with disabilities (Black, 2003). For much of the 20th century, children and adults with disabilities were, for the most part, unwanted elements of society.

---

[1] For an excellent summary, see Gould, 1981.

The Modern Era: Setting the Stage

Special education as we know it today—a publicly funded and legally mandated service—had its origins in the landmark *Brown v. Board of Education of Topeka* Supreme Court decision in 1954. Although *Brown* was a school desegregation case and did not include students with special needs, its impact cannot be minimized. As Chief Justice Earl Warren wrote in the unanimous decision:

> Today, education is perhaps the most important function of state and local governments. Compulsory school attendance laws and the great expenditures for education both demonstrate our recognition of the importance of education to our democratic society. It is required in the performance of our most basic public responsibilities, even service in the armed forces. It is the very foundation of good citizenship. Today it is a principal instrument in awakening the child to cultural values, in preparing him for later professional training, and in helping him to adjust normally to his environment. In these days, it is doubtful that any child may reasonably be expected to succeed in life if he is denied the opportunity of an education. Such an opportunity, where the state has undertaken to provide it, is a right which must be made available to all on equal terms.

The Supreme Court's affirmation of the value of education and equity in publicly funded services not only brought about major changes in America's schools, but also was the impetus for other far-reaching social and legislative changes. The principles laid down by the Supreme Court would lead to the Civil Rights Act of 1964, the Voting Rights Act of 1965, and ultimately, the inclusion of children with disabilities in the public schools. In fact, the preceding excerpt from Chief Justice Warren's decision was quoted verbatim in a landmark special education case, *Mills v. Board of Education of the District of Columbia* (1972).

President John F. Kennedy played a major role in this progression. Because he had a sister with mental retardation, he and the Kennedy family were very interested in developing and improving services for children and adults with this disability. In 1961 Kennedy established the President's Committee on Mental Retardation to advise him on ways the federal government could best meet the needs of this population. The committee's recommendations led to many new federal initiatives, including encouraging school systems to open their doors to students with disabilities.

The Elementary and Secondary Education Act (ESEA) Amendments of 1965 (PL 89–313) authorized the first state-level grant program specifically for children and youth with disabilities. The 1967 ESEA (PL 90–170) established the Bureau of the Handicapped within the U.S. Department of Education to administer funds for research, education, and training in special education.

These laws, however, did not require that states provide special education; they only provided funding if a state chose to require or encourage school systems to provide it. Best estimates available from this period suggest that less than half of America's children with disabilities were involved in appropriate educational programs. Out of more than 8 million children in need of special education, an estimated 3.9 million were receiving an appropriate education. Some 1.75 million children with disabilities were receiving no education at all, and 2.5 million were receiving what was considered an inappropriate education (Legislative History, 1975).

At the same time that educational laws were encouraging school systems to adopt special education, several court cases played a role as well. For example, *Wyatt vs. Stickney* (1971) and *Pennsylvania Association for Retarded Children v. Commonwealth of Pennsylvania* (1972) addressed deinstitutionalization and the right to treatment. However, the rulings in those cases included requirements that later became integral parts of EAHCA, including individualized planning, least restrictive environment, and due process. *Mills v. Board of Education of the District of Columbia* (1972) affirmed these rights for children with disabilities. The *Mills* case was a class action suit successfully brought on behalf of seven children with different types of disabilities who were denied admission to schools and provided no alternative means of receiving education.

In addition to these court cases, parent and advocacy groups such as the Association for Retarded Children (now The Arc) began grassroots efforts to pressure states and Congress to take action. Their efforts were aided by two forces: (a) the growth of the independent living and self-advocacy movements, predominantly spearheaded by adults with physical disabilities such as Ed Roberts (1935–1995), and (b) exposés of inhumane conditions in U.S. institutions for children and adults with mental retardation such as the 1966 photographic essay *Christmas in Purgatory* (which was widely distributed but not published commercially until 1974) by Burton Blatt and Fred Kaplan, and Geraldo Rivera's live television broadcast of the horrific conditions inside the Willowbrook State School on Staten Island, New York, in 1972. Together, these events led to the awakening of America's national conscience toward the plight of its citizens with disabilities.

Section 504: Civil Rights for Citizens with Disabilities

Although several pieces of disability-related legislation were passed in the 1960s and early 1970s, the most significant in this time period was the Rehabilitation Act Amendments of 1973 (PL 93–112). Dating to 1918, this legislation created and funded the federal/state Vocational Rehabilitation Program initially for wounded soldiers, then for injured workers, and finally for citizens with all types of disabilities affecting employment. When the Rehabilitation Act was reauthorized in 1973, it included the first civil rights protections for individuals with disabilities, including the right to education, in a new section, Section 504.

This addition to the act was strongly and bitterly contested because of its potential social impact and costs (Scotch, 2001). Section 504 mandated that no person with a disability could be excluded from or denied benefits of any program receiving federal financial assistance, which would include public elementary, secondary, and postsecondary schools. Congress required that schools covered by the act make their programs and activities accessible to and usable by all individuals with disabilities. In addition, Section 504 regulations required recipients of federal funding to provide a free appropriate public education (FAPE) to each qualified person with a disability in the recipient's jurisdiction. This mandate was designed to meet the individual educational needs of persons with disabilities as adequately as the needs of nondisabled persons were met.

Although groundbreaking in its purpose, Section 504 applied only to entities receiving federal funding, so its impact was intended to be limited.[2] Further limiting the impact of this section, regulations for implementing Section 504 were not released by the U.S. Department of Health, Education, and Welfare until April 1977, 4 years after the act was signed into law, following lawsuits and demonstrations by disability advocacy groups and supporters.

Moreover, the first Supreme Court test of Section 504 was a major setback for disability rights. *Southeastern Community College v. Davis* (1979) concerned a woman

---

[2] Later court decisions expanded the scope of the nondiscrimination mandates to businesses, schools, and other entities that received federal funds indirectly, as in contracts, loans, scholarships, and other means.

with hearing impairments who was excluded from a nursing program because the school felt that she could not complete the clinical requirements because of her disability, and that the hiring of a hearing impaired nurse could create safety issues. Not only did the Supreme Court rule in favor of the college, but its majority opinion stated that courts should give "little deference" to the 504 regulations. With that guidance, it would be unlikely that any organization would be required to accomodate citizens with disabilities. Another 504 case did not come before the Supreme Court until 1984, when it reversed itself in *Consolidated Rail Corporation v. Darronne* and required that courts give the regulations "great deference."

Section 504 survives today in coexistence with special education. Many SEAs and LEAs use Section 504 accommodation plans for students who have impairments but who would not be eligible for special education because the impairment is not considered a substantial impediment to education. Unlike special education, responsibility for Section 504 compliance typically falls under the responsibility of the general education program and is monitored at the federal level by the Office of Civil Rights in the U.S. Department of Education.

The Education for All Handicapped Children Act

Purposes and General Provisions

With Section 504, the *Mills* decision, and other societal influences described previously, the time was right for Congress to mandate educational services for children with disabilities. The Education for All Handicapped Children Act (EAHCA, PL 94–142) mandated that children with disabilities have access to public schools, and provided several safeguards and minimum standards for their participation. States were required to follow those minimum standards in order to receive federal financial assistance. Congress defined the purposes of the act as follows:

- "To assure that all children with disabilities have available to them . . . a free appropriate public education which emphasizes special education and related services designed to meet their unique needs"

- "To assure that the rights of children with disabilities and their parents . . . are protected"

- "To assist States and localities to provide for the education of all children with disabilities"

- "To assess and assure the effectiveness of efforts to educate all children with disabilities"

The main components of EAHCA are as follows:

Special Education.   Special education was defined by EAHCA as specially designed instruction, at no cost to parents, to meet the unique needs of a child with a disability from age 3 to age 21. Subsequent amendments to EAHCA added children from birth to age 3. It is important to note that children whose impairments do not limit their educational progress do not qualify for special education. In addition, to qualify for services, a child's educational needs must be related to his or her disability.

Related Services.   This term refers to supplemental services that may be required to assist a child with a disability to benefit from special education. Eligibility for related services is linked to eligibility for special education and is individually determined. EAHCA listed some possible related services, including transportation, speech-language pathology and audiology services, psychological services, physical and occupational therapy, therapeutic recreation, social work services, counseling services, orientation and mobility services, and diagnostic medical services.

Free Appropriate Public Education (FAPE).   FAPE means special education and related services that (a) are provided at public expense, under public supervision and direction, and without charge; (b) meet the standards of the SEA; (c) include preschool, elementary school, or secondary school education in the state; and (d) are provided in conformity with an individualized education program (IEP). The IEP is developed annually by a child's IEP team, which includes special and general education teachers, parents, related service providers, the student, and others as appropriate to each student's situation.

Due Process.   The EAHCA required that states implement a process for assuring parental rights and resolving disputes between the schools and parents or guardians of special education students. These requirements include appropriate notice for meetings, testing, changes in placement, and so forth; the right to attend and contribute to educational planning meetings; and the right to appeal decisions related to placement and services.

Least Restrictive Environment.   **Least restrictive environment (LRE)** is the legal requirement from EAHCA for integration of students with educational handicaps in general education classrooms. To the maximum extent appropriate, children with disabilities are educated with nondisabled children. Special classes, separate schooling, or other removal of children with disabilities from the general education environment occurs only when the disability is so severe that education in general classes with the use of supplementary aids and services cannot be achieved satisfactorily.

Zero Reject.   Students cannot be excluded from educational services based on their disability, severity of disability, contagious conditions, or costs of services.

Since it was first passed in 1975, the EAHCA has undergone many significant changes, including a change of name to the Individuals with Disabilities Education Improvement Act (IDEA). Table 1.1 provides a summary of the major changes to date.

Who Receives Services?

EAHCA includes two main programs, the Early Intervention Program for Infants and Toddlers and Special Education and Related Services. The following sections will describe the different populations served by these two programs.

Early Intervention.   The 1986 amendments of EAHCA established the Early Intervention Program for Infants and Toddlers with Disabilities under Part H (now Part C). The purpose of the Early Intervention Program was to assist states in developing and implementing a statewide, comprehensive, coordinated, multidisciplinary, interagency system that makes early intervention services available to all children with disabilities from birth to age 3. Full implementation of the program in all states and outlying areas was achieved by September 30, 1994 (U. S. Department of Education, 2000).

TABLE 1.1
Summary of major changes to the Education for All Handicapped Children Act (EAHCA).

Year	Major Changes
1983 (PL 98–199)	• Allowed transitional services for students with disabilities preparing to exit school • Provided funding for transition demonstration projects
1986 (PL 99–372)	• Created the Part H (now Part C) early intervention program for infants and toddlers • Clarified that parents and students have rights under both EAHCA and Section 504 of the Rehabilitation Act Amendments of 1973 • Authorized preschool incentive grants • Authorized interagency agreements between schools and state vocational rehabilitation agencies for transitioning students
1990 (PL 101–336)	• Name changed to Individuals with Disabilities Education Act (IDEA) • Mandated transition services for special education students beginning at least by age 16 • Added autism and traumatic brain injury as distinct disability groups • Strengthened least restrictive environment (LRE) requirements
1997 (PL 105–17)	• Redefined LRE to include "access to general curriculum" • Required consideration of assistive technology devices and services, orientation and mobility services • Modified transition age requirements to include consideration of a student's educational program beginning at least by age 14 • Created exceptions to the "stay-put" rule regarding disputed educational placement • Allowed state and local education agencies to use the term *developmental delay* for children up to age 9

Since 1994 the number of infants and toddlers served under Part C has grown by 40%, from 165, 351 on December 1, 1994, to 230, 853 on December 1, 2000, the date at which the most recent information was available. In 2000, 16% of the total number of children served under Part C were infants up to age 1, 32% were ages 1 through 2, and 53% were between 2 and 3 years of age. According to the 2000 child count, 63% of the children served under Part C were classified as White (non-Hispanic); 17% were Hispanic; 16% were Black (non-Hispanic); 4% were Asian/Pacific Islander; and 1% were American Indian/Alaska Native. There has been little racial or ethnic change in the distribution of children since these data were first collected in 1998 (U. S. Department of Education, 2002).

Infants and toddlers served under Part C do not receive a categorical diagnosis of disability, as do children served under Part B. Instead, Part C uses a designation of *developmental delay* for infants and toddlers. This term refers to ongoing major delays in reaching typical developmental milestones (Kilgo, et al., 1996; McLean, Smith, McCormick, Schakel, & McEvoy, 1991). IDEA also allows states to include infants and toddlers who are at risk for developmental delays even if those delays are not yet in evidence, in the hope that early intervention services will help to prevent or mitigate later impairments.

The term *developmental delay* has several advantages over categorical disability labels for very young children. First, categorical classification during these years would be premature and potentially inaccurate because of limited reliability of standardized and norm-referenced assessments for the identification of problems in very young children. In addition, the early years are a period of acculturation within day care, preschool, and school settings. For many children, the use of diagnostic categories could result in stigma and even segregation from these environments and opportunities. Because of these potential disadvantages, IDEA currently allows state and local educational agencies to use the developmental delay classification for children up to age 9, although it is rarely used for children older than 5.

Special Education and Related Services.   Special education and related services are provided under a preschool program, often referred to as Early Childhood Special Education (ECSE) for children ages 3 through 5, and school programs for children ages 6 through 21. These groups will be described separately.

Initially, EAHCA did not mandate services for preschoolers with disabilities; instead, children with disabilities ages 3 through 5 were served under an incentive grants program. In 1986 Congress amended section 619 of the law to include a new program, Preschool Grants for Children with Disabilities (U.S. Department of Education, 2000). All states currently participate in this program. To be eligible to receive funding under the program, states are required to make FAPE available to all children with disabilities between the ages of 3 and 5. States may also provide services, at the state's discretion, to 2-year-old children with disabilities who will turn 3 during the school year. States were required to serve all eligible preschoolers by the 1991–92 school year (U.S. Department of Education, 2000).

For the 2000–01 school year, the most recent year for which data were available, states reported serving 599,678 children with disabilities ages 3 through 5 under IDEA, up from 589,134 in 1999–2000. This number represents an increase of 144,229 preschoolers, or a 31.7% growth in the number of children served between the 1992–93 and 2000–01 school years.

Table 1.2 presents information regarding preschoolers' diagnostic categories during the 2000–01 school year from data provided by the U.S. Department of Education (2002). This table indicates that more than half of preschoolers served were classified as having speech and language impairments. The next largest category consisted of those students classified as developmentally delayed. The table also shows that the older the age group, the less likely the school system is to use the developmental delay classification.

Since 1997 IDEA has required states to submit racial and ethnic data as a part of their reporting requirements. The U.S. Department of Education reported that in the 2000–01 school year, White non-Hispanic preschoolers were overrepresented in the Part B population compared to their presence in the general school population. Asian American/Pacific Islander and, especially, Hispanic children were underrepresented among the preschoolers served under IDEA.

Students with disabilities ages 6 through 21 have been included in special education services since its origins in EAHCA. In 2000–01, states reported 5,775,722 students ages 6 through 21 under IDEA, a growth of 28.4% over the 10-year period since 1991–92. Students ages 6 through 17 with disabilities made up 11.5% of the estimated student enrollment, which is comparable to previous years.

STUDENT KNOWLEDGE CHECK

What are the advantages of classifying a young child as "developmentally delayed" as opposed to using a disability-specific classification? Are there any disadvantages?

TABLE 1.2
Disability categories of preschoolers served in 2000–2001 (percentages).

Disability Category	Age 3	Age 4	Age 5	All Preschoolers
Specific learning disabilities	2.6%	2.9%	4.1%	3.3%
Speech or language impairments	46.3	52.1	61.9	55.2
Mental retardation	4.1	3.7	4.8	4.3
Emotional disturbance	1.2	1.3	1.6	1.4
Multiple disabilities	2.4	2.0	2.0	2.1
Hearing impairments	1.6	1.3	1.3	1.4
Orthopedic impairments	2.3	1.7	1.6	1.8
Other health impairments	2.5	2.0	2.2	2.2
Visual impairments	0.8	0.6	0.5	0.6
Autism	2.6	2.4	2.8	2.6
Deaf-blindness	0.0	0.0	0.0	0.0
Traumatic brain injury	0.2	0.1	0.2	0.1
Developmental delay	33.4	29.9	17.0	24.9

ACCOMMODATING DIVERSITY

Is statistical overrepresentation of culturally and linguistically diverse children in special education good or bad? Some writers point to these statistics as evidence of bias in assessment or eligibility decision making on the part of schools and teachers, resulting in students being misidentified and misclassified. Other writers believe that overrepresentation may not be the result so much of bias as it is of efforts to ensure that children from culturally and linguistically diverse backgrounds who are having problems at school receive the supports and services needed to achieve academically. What do you think?

Table 1.3 presents the numbers of students served and their disability categories for the 1991–02 and 2000–01 school years. The large increases for traumatic brain injury and autism were because these two categories were added in IDEA in 1990, and

TABLE 1.3
Disability categories of students aged 6 through 21 served under IDEA.

Disability	Number 1991–92	Percent 1991–92	Number 2000–01	Percent 1991–92	Percent change
Specific learning disabilities	2,247,004	49.9%	2,887,217	50.0%	28.5%
Speech or language impairments	998,904	22.2	1,093,808	18.9	9.5
Mental retardation	553,262	12.3	612,978	10.6	10.8
Emotional disturbance	400,211	8.9	473,663	8.2	18.4
Multiple disabilities	98,408	2.2	122,559	2.1	24.5
Hearing impairments	60,727	1.3	70,767	1.2	16.5
Orthopedic impairments	51,389	1.1	73,057	1.3	42.2
Other health impairments	58,749	1.3	291,850	5.1	396.8
Visual impairments	24,083	0.5	25,975	0.4	7.9
Autism	5,415	0.1	78,749	1.4	1,354.3
Deaf-blindness	1,427	0.0	1,320	0.0	−7.5
Traumatic brain injury	245	0.0	14,844	0.3	5,958.8
Developmental delay	—		28,935	0.5	—
All disabilities	4,499,824		5,775,722		28.4

many students with these disabilities were continuing to be misclassified in the years immediately following. The large increase in students with other health impairments (OHI) may be due to a surge in the diagnosis of attention deficit disorder (ADD) and attention-deficit/hyperactivity disorder (ADHD), which are typically classified at the school level as OHI.

Table 1.3 also shows the continuation of long-running trends in special education students. Four disability categories (specific learning disabilities, speech or language impairments, mental retardation, and emotional disturbance) accounted for the majority of students served under IDEA. Together, these four categories represented 87.7% of all special education students ages 6 through 21. In 1991–92, these four groups accounted for 93.3% of students served.

In the early years of special education, the majority of students served were classified with mental retardation. The number and percentage of students with learning disabilities grew rapidly during the 1980s and 1990s, eventually encompassing half of all special education students in the 6-to-21 age group. Although the number of students with mental retardation has increased, as a proportion of all students served, their proportion has declined. The reasons for this trend are many: First, the incidence rate of mental retardation is declining nationwide as a result of the availability of prenatal care, genetic screening, therapeutic abortion, and early intervention services. Second, there is greater emphasis on culturally nonbiased assessment, which avoids misclassification resulting from cultural differences. Finally, diagnosis and assessment tend to follow social awareness patterns. Recent social and congressional awareness of the symptoms and consequences of emotional disturbances, autism, ADD and ADHD, and traumatic brain injury may have contributed in part to increasing numbers of diagnoses of children with these disorders.

Despite efforts to eliminate cultural bias in assessment and identification, there are racial and ethnic differences across diagnostic categories. In 2000–01, the rank ordering of the top five disability categories was nearly identical for all racial and ethnic groups; however, some racial and ethnic groups were overrepresented or underrepresented in specific disability categories when compared with the student population as a whole. For example:

- White, non-Hispanic children are overrepresented in the OHI group.
- American Indian/Alaska Native and Hispanic children are overrepresented in the specific learning disabilities group.
- Asian American/Pacific Islander children are overrepresented in the speech or language impairment group.
- African American children are overrepresented in the mental retardation group.

Conversely, the percentages of Asian American/Pacific Islander and Hispanic children receiving services for emotional disturbance and the percentage of Hispanic children receiving services for other health impairments were lower than the percentages for all IDEA students.

It is of interest to note that over two thirds (68%) of students served under IDEA are males, another long-standing phenomenon in special education. Harmon and colleagues (1992) identified five possible reasons for male overrepresentation in special education: (a) biological differences between boys and girls are responsible for some impairments and behavioral patterns being more prevalent in males (i.e., autism, Fragile X syndrome, Down syndrome); (b) learned differences between boys and girls result in different behavioral patterns; (c) boys and girls have different reactions to school; (d) teachers react differently to boys in comparison to girls; and (e) criteria, procedures, and tests overclassify boys as being in need of specialized instruction.

What Are These Services?

Early Intervention.   Services delivered in early intervention (i.e., infants and toddlers) programs are individually determined and documented in an individual family service plan (IFSP). Table 1.4 presents a list of services that are included under this program.

There are several important differences between the IFSP and the individualized education program (IEP) required under Part B. First, the IFSP focuses on the needs of the family, whereas the IEP is child focused. Many of the services that are allowed under Part C include interventions, training, counseling, and support to parents and siblings that are designed to enable them to provide for a child with disabilities, mitigate the effects of the child's disabilities, prevent worsening of the disabilities, and prevent out-of-home placement for the child with disabilities (Kolberg, Gustafson, & Ekblad, 1999).

Another difference relates to the fact that early intervention services in many localities were initially provided by noneducational agencies, such as private nonprofit agencies. IDEA regulations require that a service coordinator be identified to coordinate implementation of the IFSP. This coordinator need not be associated with the school system, but would instead be from the profession most relevant to the family's and child's needs.

The steps to development of the IFSP include (a) a multidisciplinary assessment of the unique strengths and needs of the infant or toddler and the identification of services appropriate to meet those needs and (b) a family-directed assessment of the resources, priorities, and concerns of the family and the supports

TABLE 1.4
Early intervention services under IDEA Part C.

Services	Examples
Family training, counseling, and home visits	Instructing parents on methods of behavior management or coping strategies
Special instruction	Enhancing cognitive skills through direct instruction
Speech-language pathology and audiology services	Communication instruction, hearing tests
Occupational therapy	Developing self-feeding skills
Physical therapy	Minimizing effects of cerebral palsy or other mobility deficits
Psychological services	Assessment and consultation for cognitive, social, or maturational issues
Service coordination	Assisting families with accessing needed services, eligibility requirements
Medical services	Only for diagnostic or evaluation purposes
Early identification, screening, and assessment services	Testing and assessment to determine eligibility for services under IDEA
Health services necessary to enable the infant or toddler to benefit from the other early intervention services	Preventive measures for control of diseases or conditions
Social work services	Assisting the family with other needs, such as housing, employment assistance, etc.
Vision services	Vision testing and correction
Assistive technology devices and assistive technology services	A prosthetic device to increase motor function or mobility
Transportation and related costs	Necessary to enable an infant or toddler and the infant's or toddler's family to receive another service described above

and services necessary to enhance the family's capacity to meet the developmental needs of the child. From these two activities, the multidisciplinary team (which includes the parents) develops a written IFSP. The content of the IFSP is detailed in IDEA as follows:

- A statement of the infant's or toddler's present levels of physical development, cognitive development, communication development, social or emotional development, and adaptive development, based on objective criteria
- A statement of the family's resources, priorities, and concerns relating to enhancing the development of the infant or toddler with a disability
- A statement of the major outcomes expected to be achieved for the infant or toddler and the family, and the criteria, procedures, and time lines used to determine the degree to which progress toward achieving the outcomes is being made and whether modifications or revisions of the outcomes or services are necessary
- A statement of specific early intervention services necessary to meet the unique needs of the infant or toddler and the family, including the frequency, intensity, and method of delivering services

Systems are mandated to serve young children. Why is it important to provide special education services to the very young child?

- A statement of the natural environments in which early intervention services will appropriately be provided, including a justification of the extent, if any, to which the services will not be provided in a natural environment
- The projected dates for initiation of services and the anticipated duration of the services
- The identification of the service coordinator from the profession most immediately relevant to the infant's or toddler's or family's needs (or who is otherwise qualified to carry out all applicable responsibilities under this part) who will be responsible for the implementation of the plan and coordination with other agencies and persons
- The steps to be taken to support the transition of the toddler with a disability to preschool or other appropriate services.

To assess the outcomes for children and families served under the infants and toddlers program, the Office of Special Education Programs (OSEP) commissioned the National Early Intervention Longitudinal Study (NEILS). NEILS is following a nationally representative sample of 3,338 infants and toddlers who received early intervention services for the first time between September 1997 and November 1998. A 1-year follow-up study (U.S. Department of Education, 2002) documented numerous positive results for both children and their families. One year after entry in early intervention, many children had mastered additional developmental milestones and had shown behavioral improvements. Families reported that their children's communication and motor skills had improved, and more than two thirds of families reported that early intervention had significant impact on their children's development. Most families were satisfied with numerous facets of their early intervention experience and were optimistic about their children's future development.

Special Education and Related Services.   As mentioned previously, special education services are prescribed by an individualized education program, or IEP. To be deemed eligible for special education services, a student must receive an initial assessment. This assessment can include psychological assessments, tests of intelligence or achievement, functional skills assessments, observation of the student, medical evaluations, or other information necessary for the educational team to determine, first, that an impairment exists and second, that it constitutes an educational handicap.

Once a determination is made that the student is eligible, the IEP team begins developing an IEP. The IEP team comprises the following:

1. The parents of the child with a disability
2. At least one regular education teacher of such child (if the child is, or may be, participating in the general education environment)
3. At least one special education teacher or, where appropriate, at least one special education provider of such child
4. A representative of the local education agency who is qualified to provide, or supervise the provision of, specially designed instruction to meet the unique needs of children with disabilities; is knowledgeable about the general curriculum; and is knowledgeable about the availability of resources of the local educational agency
5. An individual who can interpret the instructional implications of evaluation results
6. At the discretion of the parent or the agency, other individuals who have knowledge or special expertise regarding the child, including related services personnel as appropriate
7. The child with a disability, whenever appropriate

The content of the IEP is also specifically proscribed by IDEA. In brief, those requirements include the following:

1. A statement of the child's present levels of educational performance, including how the child's disability affects the child's involvement and progress in the general curriculum
2. A statement of measurable annual goals, including benchmarks or short-term objectives
3. A statement of the special education and related services and supplementary aids and services to be provided to the child
4. An explanation of the extent, if any, to which the child will not participate with nondisabled children in the regular class and in the activities described in clause (iii)
5. A statement of any individual modifications in the administration of state- or district-wide assessments of student achievement that are needed in order for the child to participate in such assessment
6. If the IEP team determines that the child will not participate in a particular state- or district-wide assessment of student achievement (or part of such an assessment), a statement of why that assessment is not appropriate for the child and how the child will be assessed
7. The projected date for the beginning of the services and modifications and the anticipated frequency, location, and duration of those services and modifications

8. A statement of how the child's progress toward the annual goals will be measured

9. An explanation of how the child's parents will be regularly informed of the child's progress toward the annual goals and the extent to which that progress is sufficient to enable the child to achieve the goals by the end of the year

In addition to these requirements, there are special requirements for students age 14 and over related to transition from school to adulthood. These additional requirements are described in chapter 13.

The core service of special education is specially designed instruction to meet the unique needs of a student with disabilities. This instruction can be delivered in the school, at home, or in a hospital or other setting. IDEA also requires that students receive related services, defined as those that are necessary for a child to benefit from specially designed instruction. Figure 1.1 provides a list of ways instruction can be specially designed to meet a student's unique needs. Figure 1.2 provides a list of related services commonly used to support students with disabilities.

IDEA and its regulations contain many additional requirements related to parental notification, grievance procedures, participation of students with disabilities in state- and district- wide testing, disciplinary procedures, and many other areas. A full description of these issues is beyond the scope of this chapter. Resources for locating additional information about IDEA are provided at the end of the chapter.

- Modified instructional materials
- Alternative presentation modes
- Alternative response modes
- Alternative instructional settings
- Individual or small-group instruction (e.g., resource room)

FIGURE 1.1
Specially designed instruction for students with disabilities.

Audiology	Recreation and therapeutic recreation
Counseling services	Rehabilitation counseling
Medical services (diagnostics only)	School health services
Nutrition services	Social work services
Occupational therapy	Speech-language pathology
Physical therapy	Transportation
Psychological services	Assistive technology

FIGURE 1.2
Common related services for special education students.

Disability Legislation Post-IDEA

Americans with Disabilities Act

The Americans with Disabilities Act (ADA) of 1990 was a landmark in disability rights legislation. The ADA extended the nondiscrimination protections under Section 504 of the Rehabilitation Act to other areas of society. Title I of the ADA prohibits discrimination in the areas of recruitment, hiring, advancement, and termination of individuals with disabilities. Title I also requires that businesses make reasonable accommodations for qualified applicants or employees with disabilities. Title II of the ADA relates to access and nondiscrimination based on disability with regard to public services, such as transportation systems and public buildings. Title III addresses issues related to public accommodations by private organizations, and Title IV addresses access to telecommunications.

The ADA is relevant to schools in many ways. First, school design, construction, and remodeling must take into account physical accessibility for students with disabilities. This relates most directly to those with mobility, health, or visual impairments, and would include elevators, wheelchair ramps, braille or audio signage, handrails, accessible bathrooms, modified workstations, and other accessibility features. Second, the ADA, like IDEA, requires that services be delivered to individuals with disabilities in the most integrated setting appropriate to the needs of the individual. Segregated options can be available, but persons with disabilities cannot be forced to participate in the segregated options.

A recent Supreme Court decision, *Olmstead v. L.C.* (1999), shows the impact that the ADA has had and will continue to have for citizens with disabilities. In that case, two women with cognitive and psychosocial disabilities, both residents in a psychiatric hospital, successfully sued under the ADA to be allowed to live in the community and receive community-based services. The Olmstead decision required states to administer their services, programs, and activities "in the most integrated setting appropriate to the needs of qualified individuals with disabilities."

Another area in which the ADA influences special education is in the Title I employment protections. Students now exiting special education enter a society that is far more aware and accommodating of disability than it was in previous generations. During the transition years, as teachers and transition specialists assist students with locating jobs, they can also assist employers with accommodating their work-related needs. Students and their families should be informed of the protections and remedies that are available under the ADA so that they can address discrimination and prejudice as the students enter adulthood.

The No Child Left Behind Act

The No Child Left Behind (NCLB) Act was the 2001 reauthorization of the ESEA. It included new requirements for states to develop standards for grades 3 through 8 and high school in key academic areas—reading/language arts, science, and mathematics—and implement annual assessments related to those standards.

Standards-based testing did not originate with the NCLB for either general or special education; many states, including Texas, New York, and Virginia, had already developed state standards and assessment systems prior to NCLB. A time line was included in NCLB that allowed states to either develop their standards-based system or bring existing systems into alignment with NCLB. In addition, states were required to establish goals for student and school proficiency and to

ACCOMMODATING TECHNOLOGY

IDEA supports the use of assistive technology as a related service for students with disabilities. Assistive technology is defined as "any item, piece of equipment, or product system, whether acquired commercially off the shelf, modified, or customized, that is used to increase, maintain, or improve the functional capabilities of a child with a disability." Assistive technology devices can be used to help the student with needs such as the following:

- Movement within or between areas of the school
- Communication with the teacher or other students
- Organizing classroom materials
- Memorization and learning

provide documentation of annual yearly progress (AYP) toward meeting those goals. There are significant repercussions for those systems that repeatedly fail to show AYP.

NCLB reinforces the inclusion of children with disabilities in state- or district-wide testing. For those students with the most severe disabilities, states can develop alternative assessment methods, such as portfolios based on achievement of IEP objectives completed or life skills mastered. However, NCLB limits the percentage of special education students who can be counted toward AYP using alternative assessments to 1%. This restriction was established to ensure that as many students with disabilities as possible are included in the general education testing program.

INCLUSION

Inclusion is a concept that is often misunderstood and perhaps just as often misapplied. To begin, it would be beneficial to define terminology related to inclusion and related concepts. Rogers (1993) provides a useful set of definitions.

Least restrictive environment (LRE) is the legal requirement from the Education for All Handicapped Children Act for integration of students with educational handicaps in general education classrooms and the general curriculum. This act states that, to the maximum extent appropriate, children with disabilities should be educated with nondisabled children. Special classes, separate schooling, or other removal of children with disabilities from the general education environment can occur only when the nature or severity of the disability requires that education in general education classes with the use of supplementary aids and services cannot be achieved satisfactorily.

Mainstreaming refers to the selective placement of special education students in one or more general education classes with commensurate expectations for the special education students. Mainstreaming can occur for both academic and nonacademic segments of the school day. Proponents of academic mainstreaming generally agree that a student must demonstrate an ability to keep up with the work performed by nondisabled students. This concept is closely linked to traditional forms of special education service delivery—that is, the "cascades" model of services described by Deno (1970) that included educational settings of progressively increasing integration and involvement in general education.

Inclusion is a term that expresses a commitment to educate each child in the school and classroom he or she would otherwise attend if he or she did not have a disability. Inclusion typically involves bringing the support services to the child in the general education classroom rather than moving the child to services or to a different educational setting, whenever feasible. Inclusion requires only that the child will benefit from being in the class, rather than that the child keep up with the other students.

Full inclusion means that all students, regardless of disabling condition or severity, are in a general education classroom or program full time. All services must be taken to the child in that setting.

IDEA AND ACCESS TO GENERAL EDUCATION

Mainstreaming, inclusion, and full inclusion are all efforts to operationalize the legal mandate for providing educational services to students with disabilities in the least restrictive environment, or LRE. However, LRE, mainstreaming, and inclusion differ both philosophically and conceptually. Mainstreaming implies that a child with disabilities first "belongs" in the special education environment and must earn his or her way into the general education environment. In contrast, inclusion implies that the child always should begin in the general education environment and be removed only when appropriate services cannot be provided in the general education classroom. In full inclusion, the child is not removed for any reason. Thus, inclusion appears to be the method for implementing LRE that is closer to the "integration imperative" of the EAHCA and subsequent legislation, the option that promotes general education classroom placement as the first choice.

Just how well are state and local education agencies (SEAs and LEAs) implementing LRE? The U.S. Department of Education, in its *Twenty-Fourth Annual Report to Congress on the Implementation of the Individuals with Disabilities Education Act* (2002), presented updates on educational placements for students with disabilities. In the 1999–2000 school year, 95.9% of students with disabilities were served in general education school buildings. Of those students, 47.3% were served outside of the general education classroom for less than 21% of the school day. Approximately 3% of students were educated in separate schools and other facilities, 0.7% of students were educated in residential facilities, and 0.5% of students were educated in home or hospital settings. The proportion of students with disabilities served in general education classrooms for all or most of the school day has increased slowly but steadily over the years.

However, this report also showed discrepancies across different student groups. For example, younger children with disabilities were educated more often in general education classrooms than were high school–age students with disabilities. In addition, students with mental retardation, emotional or behavioral disturbances, and multiple disabilities were far more likely to be educated in segregated classrooms and schools. Moreover, this report showed extreme differences among states. For example, many states reported that few or no students with mental retardation were in separate schools or classrooms. Other states reported that most of their students with mental retardation were educated in separate schools or classrooms. Similar discrepancies were seen with other disability groups as well, and undoubtedly tremendous variance occurred across LEAs within the states as well.

Danielson and Bellamy (1988) first raised this issue and questioned how SEAs and LEAs could implement the same legal requirement and obtain such wildly

COLLABORATION TIPS

One effective way to promote inclusion and LRE is through team teaching (also known as co-teaching). Using this strategy, two or more teachers or other professionals provide substantive instruction in the same classroom to children with diverse learning needs, including those with disabilities. This approach can increase instructional options for all students, reduce stigmatization of students with disabilities, and increase the skills of general education teachers to teach students with disabilities. Team teaching programs require planning, teacher preparation, and administrative support to be successful.

divergent results. There are many possible explanations, but the most plausible is that economic and political factors may influence the placement decisions made in students' IEP meetings. For example, many school districts have had separate facilities for different types of students for many years, perhaps even predating EAHCA. School systems may cluster related services in those separate schools for efficiency, or may feel the need to fill available classrooms to lower costs. Or school systems may place students with particular types of impairments in specific schools or classrooms because "that's how we've always done it." These are factors that should not influence educational decisions for individual students, but might anyway. Sadly, for many special education students, access to general education may depend not on educational needs or benefits, but on where they happen to live.

FIVE FACES OF INCLUSION

Physical inclusion refers to the placement of children with disabilities in general education classrooms. Physical inclusion also demands that the student with disabilities be separated from the classroom and classmates as infrequently as possible. Support services, such as speech and language therapy or tutoring, should be provided in the general education classroom rather than in separate rooms.

The physical organization of the classroom may need to be considered in the IEP meeting. Many students with disabilities may need few or no modifications; others may benefit from preferential seating or a second work area that has few distractions. Others may benefit from seating that is surrounded by other students as a means of promoting interactions with others.

As much as possible, classroom environments should incorporate principles of universal design. **Universal design** is the design of products and environments to be usable by all people, to the greatest extent possible, without the need for adaptation or specialized design. More information about universal design can be obtained from the Center for Universal Design, listed in the Resources section at the end of this chapter.

Physical inclusion is an important step for schools and teachers, but it is only the first step of the inclusion process. Other aspects of inclusion are often overlooked or expected to occur naturally. It is critical to plan for these aspects as well.

PRACTICAL APPLICATIONS

Shawn is a fourth-grader with Down syndrome in an inclusive classroom. His academic functioning is at kindergarten to first-grade level, and he has some physical limitations with fine motor skills and gait. What are some strategies you could use to help Shawn be involved with his classmates in the following areas?

- Academic periods (math, reading, etc.)
- Lunch and recess
- Physical education
- School clubs and events

Social inclusion refers to the nature and number of personal interactions with classmates. Positive interactions help to develop relationships between the student with disabilities and other students, even those that are planned and arranged by the teacher. Social inclusion can be fostered in both academic and nonacademic areas, such as recess, lunch, school clubs, and other areas.

Peer Connections is an example of a model program for social inclusion of students with significant disabilities in academic areas (Keachie, 1997). In this program, students work together in and out of class on activities designed to build relationships and mutual understanding and to assist those with disabilities in developing social skills. The class meets daily with a focus on learning about disabilities and removing some of the barriers to social inclusion. Guest speakers, videotapes, and a variety of activities are used to provide opportunities for students to learn about each other. Students with severe disabilities and identified as the "target peers." The other students in the class with mild disabilities or without disabilities are considered the "peer facilitators" who support those inclusion efforts.

Emotional inclusion refers to the student with disabilities feeling that he or she has purpose and value within the class and therefore is "connected" to others. This connection will help to ensure that students with disabilities have a stake in the welfare and general functioning of the class as a whole and act accordingly, such as by following rules and being respectful of others (which are components of **behavioral inclusion,** or the student having behavioral expectations that are consistent with others in the class).

Emotional inclusion can be fostered by the teacher's ensuring that the student with disabilities is treated as "special" or different as little as possible. For example, the student should have classroom roles and responsibilities along with other students. The teacher should also identify the strengths and interests of the student with disabilities and allow him or her to use them with others. For example, students with disabilities can be peer tutors to other students whose deficits match their strengths.

Academic inclusion refers to the extent of involvement in learning activities with general education students. As noted previously in this chapter, students with disabilities do not need to function on the same academic levels as their nondisabled classmates in order to be physically located in the general education classroom. However, the student with disabilities can be academically included by maintaining consistency between the work being performed by both. For example, while most of the students are learning multiplication or division, a student with cognitive disabilities can work on counting, pairing, or other math concepts.

Another strategy for academic inclusion is *paired learning.* This is a generic term for a group of carefully designed and well-evaluated methods for use by peer, parent, and volunteer tutors. Using a paired learning approach, the student with disabilities is paired with a nondisabled student, who provides assistance as needed.

SUMMARY

This chapter has provided a basic overview of the histroy and structure of special education, characteristics of special education students, and key issues related to special education. Integration of students with disabilities has progressed significantly over the years, but many SEAs and LEAs have far to go before realizing EAHCA's mandate for education in the least restrictive environment for all students. Inclusion is a giant step in that direction.

RESOURCES

Office of Special Education Programs (OSEP), U.S. Department of Education. Legislation, regulations, guidance, and grants for special education programs. www.ed.gov/about/offices/list/osers/osep/index.html.

Council for Exceptional Children (CEC). The largest international professional organization dedicated to improving educational outcomes for individuals with exceptionalities, students with disabilities, and/or the gifted. www.cec.sped.org.

Center for Universal Design (CUD). Located at North Carolina State University, the Center for Universal Design develops principles and resources for universal design elements. www.design.ncsu.edu:8120/cud/univ_design/princ_overview.htm.

SUGGESTED READINGS

Pierangelo, R. (2004). *The special educator's survival guide.* San Francisco: Jossey-Bass.

Rainforth, B., & Kugelmass, J. W. (Eds.). (2004). *Curriculum and instruction for all learners: Blending systematic and constructivist approaches in inclusive elementary schools.* Baltimore: Brookes.

Ryndak, D. L., & Alper, S. (2003). *Curriculum and instruction for students with significant disabilities in inclusive settings.* Boston: Allyn & Bacon.

U.S. Department of Education. (2004). *Twenty-fourth annual report to Congress on the implementation of the Individuals with Disabilities Education Act.* Available online at www.ed.gov.

WEBSITES TO VISIT

IDEA Practices, Council for Exceptional Children. Online resources for school districts and families related to the Individuals with Disabilities Education Act. www.ideapractices.org.

Special Education Resources on the Web. A collection of information resources of interest to those involved in the fields related to special education. www.seriweb.com.

Wrightslaw. Accurate, up-to-date information about special education law, regulations, court cases, and advocacy for children with disabilities. www.wrightslaw.com.

REFERENCES

Americans with Disabilities Act of 1990, 42 U.S.C. 12204 *et seq.* (PL 101–336).

Black, E. (2003). *War against the weak: Eugenics and America's campaign to create a master race.* New York: Four Walls Eight Windows.

Blatt, B., & Kaplan, F. (1974). *Christmas in purgatory: A photographic essay on mental retardation.* Syracuse, NY: Human Policy Press.

Brown v. Board of Education of Topeka, 347 U.S. 483 (1954).

Consolidated Rail Corp. v. Darrone, 465 U.S. 624, 635–36 (1984).

Danielson, L. C., & Bellamy, G. T. (1988). State variation in placement of children with handicaps in segregated environments. *Exceptional Children, 55,* 448–455.

Deno, E. (1970). Special education as developmental capital. *Exceptional Children, 37,* 229–237.

Dunn, L. M. (1986). Special education for the mildly retarded: Is much of it justifiable? *Exceptional Children, 35,* 5–22.

Education for All Handicapped Children Act of 1975, 20 U.S.C. 1400 et seq. (PL 94–142).

Education for All Handicapped Children Act Amendments of 1986, 20 U.S.C. 1400 et seq. (PL 99–457).

Gould, S. J. (1981). *The mismeasure of man.* New York: Norton.

Harmon, J. A., Stockton, T. S., & Construcci, V. J. (1992). *Gender disparities in special education.* (ERIC Document Reproduction Service No. ED 3358 631).

Individuals with Disabilities Education Act of 1990, 20 U.S.C. § 1400 et seq.

Individuals with Disabilities Education Act of 1997, 20 U.S.C. § 1400 et seq.

Itard, J. M. G. (1962). *The wild boy of Aveyron.* (G. Humphrey & M. Humphrey, Trans.). New York: Appleton-Century-Crofts. (Original work published 1801)

Johnson, N. (2004, June 15). Due processes can be grueling: Legal system designed to settle disputes of parents, schools. *Richmond Times-Dispatch,* p. A7.

Keachie, J. (1997). Social inclusion in a high school: The Peer Connections/Yes I Can Program. *Impact, 10*(3).

Kilgo, J., Danaher, J., McLean, M., McCormick, K., Smith, B., & Schakel, J. (1996). *Developmental delay as an eligibility category. A concept paper of the Division for Early Childhood of the Council for Exceptional Children.* Arlington, VA: Council for Exceptional Children.

Kolberg, J., Gustafson, K, & Ekblad, A. (1999). *Early childhood special education for children with disabilities ages three through five: Transition.* Bismarck, ND: North Dakota Department of Public Instruction, Division of Special Education.

Legislative History. (1975). *United States Code Congressional and Administrative News 1975,* p. 1432.

McLean, M., Smith, B., McCormick, K., Schakel, J., & McEvoy, M. (1991). *Developmental delay: Establishing parameters for a preschool category of exceptionality.* Position paper for Division of Early Childhood, Council for Exceptional Children. Arlington, VA: Council for Exceptional Children.

Mills v. Board of Education of the District of Columbia, 348 F.Supp. 866 (D. DC 1972).

Olmstead v. L. C. (98–536) 527 U.S. 581 (1999) 138 F.3d 893.

Rehabilitation Act Amendments of 1973 (PL 93–112).

Rogers, J. (1993, May). *The inclusion revolution* (Research Bulletin No. 11). Bloomington, IN: Phi Delta Kappa Center for Evaluation, Development, and Research. Available online at http://www.pdkintl.org/edres/resbul11.htm.

Scotch, R. K. (2001). *From good will to civil rights: Transforming federal disability policy* (2nd ed.). Philadelphia: Temple University Press.

Southeastern Community College v. Davis, 442 U.S. 397 (U.S. Supreme Court, 1979).

Timothy W. v. Rochester N. H. School District, 875 F.2d (1989).

U.S. Department of Education. (2000). *Twenty-second annual report to Congress on the implementation of the Individuals with Disabilities Education Act.* Washington, DC: U.S. Government Printing Office.

U.S. Department of Education. (2002). *Twenty-fourth annual report to Congress on the implementation of the Individuals with Disabilities Education Act.* Washington, DC: U.S. Government Printing Office.

Wallin, J. E. W. (1924). *The education of handicapped children.* Boston: Houghton Mifflin.

Wyatt vs. Stickney, 325 F. Supp 781 (M.D.Ala. 1971). Pennsylvania Association for Retarded Children v. Commonwealth of Pennsylvania, 334 F. Supp. 1257 (E.D. PA 1972).

2

Collaboration Between Professional Educators and Families

I do and I understand.
(Chinese Proverb)

LEARNER OBJECTIVES

After you read this chapter, you will be able to:

- Define collaboration and explain how collaboration differs from consultation, co-teaching, and teams.
- Discuss the skills necessary for an effective collaboration process.
- List and provide examples of the five levels of listening.
- Explain why a classroom teacher cannot devote the majority of time to any one student for any length of time.
- Explain the key to the teacher consultant's success.
- Define the role of the special education consultant.
- Explain the job of a paraeducator.
- Discuss the various types of teacher support teams and their uses.
- Explain how administrative support can promote successful collaboration.
- Provide strategies needed for successful parent conferences.

CHAPTER AT A GLANCE

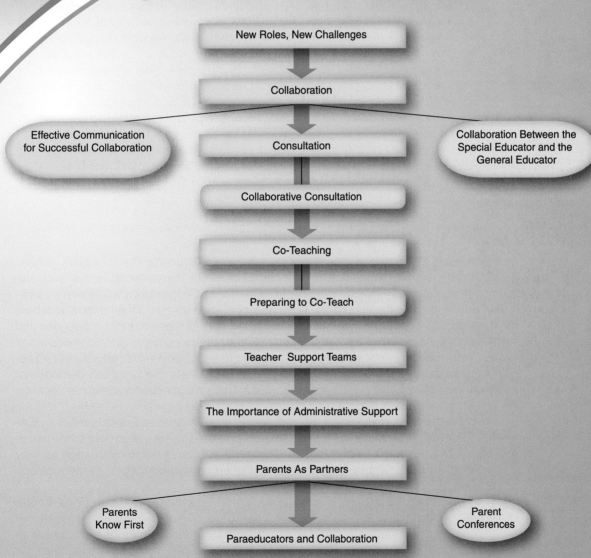

New Roles, New Challenges

Collaboration

Effective Communication for Successful Collaboration

Consultation

Collaboration Between the Special Educator and the General Educator

Collaborative Consultation

Co-Teaching

Preparing to Co-Teach

Teacher Support Teams

The Importance of Administrative Support

Parents As Partners

Parents Know First

Parent Conferences

Paraeducators and Collaboration

KEY TERMS

*M*r. Moody, the principal of Mattie Middle School, has just received a memo stating that educators within the building will be in total inclusive classrooms for the next school year. Mrs. Hanover, a seventh-grade English teacher, has successfully worked with at-risk students in the past. Mr. Moody approaches Mrs. Hanover regarding the possibility of beginning the inclusive program this school year to develop a model for the school. Mr. Hamada, the special education teacher, is asked to participate in a conversation about where to begin the inclusive process. Beginning with the standards for seventh-grade English, Mrs. Hanover and Mr. Hamada select several standards to be covered in the spring and brainstorm strategies that could be used to teach all students. The class schedule is developed to allow Mr. Hamada to work within the English class. The development of a model allows other educators to see inclusion in action.

*T*he call for shared responsibility in educating all students (full inclusion) echoes across educational America. The neat compartment of "my students" versus "your students" no longer prevails. "Our students" is the focus. Children as a whole move somewhat freely during the school day, receiving instruction unique to their needs. Teachers seek a quick answer to student educational diversity and look to other colleagues and the community for answers and support. Parents seek a common ground in education for their children with special needs. Children strive to blend in with peers and find acceptance in all school activities. With the federal mandate (No Child Left Behind) that "all children have their right to learn," students without a special education designation are moving to the forefront in education.

With the 1997 revisions of the Individuals with Disabilities Education Act (IDEA-97), PL 105-17, partnerships and collaboration within the education field continued to expand. As this happened, the roles of general educators began to change as they were called to participate in teams that included special educators, paraeducators, parents, administrators, and sometimes students.

This chapter presents the issue of, as well as ongoing discussions about, equal opportunities for all and the shared responsibility for the educational outcomes of all students. We will examine the emerging roles of participants in collaboration, the components of school-based delivery systems (consulting, co-teaching, and teams), the importance of administrative support, and parent and paraeducator relationships.

ACCOMMODATING TECHNOLOGY

Educators rarely disagree about the importance of including families in their students' learning, but they may struggle with the optimal way to achieve such collaboration. Many have used, often successfully, parent conferences, school events, and classroom newsletters to inform parents of and involve them in classroom goings-on. Today's high-tech world provides additional options, including websites, for communicating with parents and families.

Classroom websites are becoming more and more popular. Websites exist for school districts as a whole, single schools, specific teachers or courses, and even for individual students. These can be supported and updated by the administration, teachers, and the students themselves and include information on events, announcements, assignments, spelling words, contact information, and anything else the instructor wants to communicate to families. Some sites can notify parents when information is updated on the site. A Missouri teacher who included a guestbook on her classroom webpage found that this feature created "a great medium for parent and family feedback and support" (Sumner). If the site is secure, grades and other similar information can be accessed using a student number and password. This allows parents to stay connected with and involved in their child's learning, even if the child doesn't always share the information. Teachers can print copies of online newsletters and communications for families without Internet access.

Several Internet services offer classroom webpage hosting if your district or school does not support such sites, including www.schoolnotes.com, www.schoolmotion.com, www.classroomwebsites.com, and www.myteacherpages.com, the first two of which are free. No computer programming or html knowledge is needed to create the personalized webpages, and they can be updated fairly quickly and easily. Parents and families are able to access the information through any Internet connection, thereby staying informed from just about any location.

Source: Sumner, S. *Parent Communication? Try a classroom web page.* Retrieved September 2, 2004, from www.4teachers.org/testimony/sumner/index.shtml.

NEW ROLES, NEW CHALLENGES

To provide equal educational opportunities for students with disabilities and those at risk, those in the education field must alter traditional roles and responsibilities. No longer can general educators direct their teaching efforts to the middle level of the class, using standardized teaching techniques, curricula, testing procedures, and grading systems. Special educators must also modify their views of themselves, particularly their role as entities separate from the rest of the school. Their new roles (Bauwens & Hourcade, 1995) require that they consult with general educators about strategies to use with students with special needs within the context of the general education classroom (Gersten, Darch, Davis, & George, 1991). The pullout program models of the past have not been found to benefit children (Walther-Thomas, Korinek, McLaughlin, & Williams, 2000). Building administrators can no longer follow traditional grouping, placement, and scheduling practices, nor can they expect to meet students' needs using the lockstep sequence of the traditional curriculum within the structure of a graded system. District administrators must realize that maintaining separate budgets for general and special education is not cost efficient and therefore not fiscally defensible. Increasingly, parents are realizing that they can no longer leave their children's education in the hands of the experts; they, too, are now considered expert members of their children's educational teams. Finally, students with disabilities and those at risk must assume some responsibility for their educational outcomes, as much as their abilities allow. They must let their teachers and parents know when they need modifications in the general environment, which modifications are successful, and which ones are not.

The reality of education is that no individual can or should assume full responsibility for a student's success in inclusive settings. Teachers, parents, administrators, related services personnel, counselors, students, and the general school community must accept and share responsibility to provide equal educational opportunities to all students, regardless of the diversity of the population. (For a complete discussion of inclusion, see chapter 1.)

COLLABORATION

The concept of inclusion, a special philosophy defined by school districts, is the core of collaboration and school-based delivery systems. According to Lombardi (1994), "it is generally agreed that inclusion involves a commitment to educate each student with a disability in the school and, when appropriate, in the class that child would have attended had the child not had a disability. . . [The] guiding principle behind inclusion is to bring the services to the student, rather than the student to the services" (p. 7). This definition parallels our definition of special education: a service, not a place. Figure 2.1 presents an overview of the inclusive concept and how it is supported by collaboration and school-based delivery systems.

Inclusion is a process or a delivery system and involves collaboration, which is "how people work together, not what they do" (Friend & Bursuck, 2002, p. 77). Think of **collaboration** as an ongoing interaction that occurs when stakeholders are planning for students, solving student-related problems, or making student-related or school decisions. When educators are sharing responsibilities for a student, effective collaboration is crucial. Collaboration is present in school-based delivery systems such as consultation, co-teaching, and teaming.

Effective Communication for Successful Collaboration

Collaboration requires effective **communication,** skills, both verbal and nonverbal. Verbal communication consists of the words said, whereas nonverbal communication consists of how the words are said or the attitude of the speaker or listener. Nonverbal responses can alter verbal responses. Consider Mrs. Hanover from the opening vignette in this chapter. If she says, "I would love to try co-teaching," but her face is blank, her shoulders are slumped, and she is glancing away, her body language is sending a different message than her words are. Differences in cultures must also be considered when interpreting body language. For example, not looking directly at the person one is addressing is considered appropriate in some cultures.

Listening, another crucial component of effective communication, occurs at five different levels. *Organic listening* consists of actually hearing sounds, such as the highs or lows of the voice. *Informational listening* refers to understanding the literal

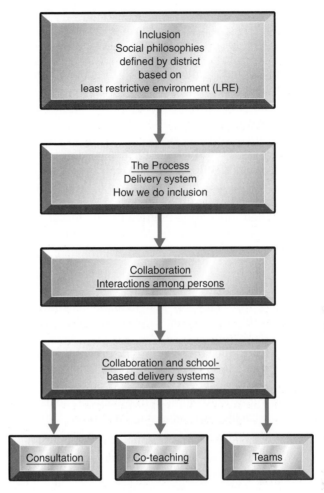

FIGURE 2.1
Relationship of collaboration and school-based delivery models.

meaning of what is said—the who, what, where, when, and how. *Inferential listening* involves grasping the "hidden agenda" or interpreting what is said. Inferential listening is referred to as listening "between the lines." *Empathic listening* is the ability to place yourself in the other's point of view. Empathic listening requires abandoning your own ego to truly "hear" the other. *Appreciative listening* is the ability to pull all the parts together and appreciate what is being said. It is the integration of all the listening levels.

Collaboration Between the Special Educator and the General Educator

Special educators and general educators must strive to acknowledge that they both have specialized skills, but that their experiences, values, and knowledge bases are different. Both are stakeholders in a student's educational process, and both will share a place on the student's team. As the team begins to develop, both educators take on new roles, and the ability to communicate becomes of greater importance.

ACCOMMODATING DIVERSITY

Embedding standards within the curriculum is a national focus. Educators have progressively learned how one concept can spread throughout different content subjects. Just as educators strive to integrate standards into the curriculum and students with disabilities into general education classrooms, so must they make multicultural education a central part of the school's curriculum. No longer can schools offer multicultural education as a separate entity such as in articles, units, or separate lessons. "Multicultural education is more than content; it includes policy, learning climate, instructional delivery, leadership, and evaluation" (see Banks, 1994; Bennett, 2003; Grant & Gomez, 2000).

When integrating multicultural content within the decision-making process in the class, teachers might do the following:

- Create learning goals and objectives that incorporate multicultural aspects, such as "Developing students' ability to write persuasively about social justice concerns."
- Use a frequency matrix to ensure that the teacher includes a wide variety of ethnic groups in a variety of ways in curriculum materials and instructional activities.
- Introduce different ethnic groups and their contributions on a rotating basis.
- Include several examples from different ethnic experiences to explain subject matter concepts, facts, and skills.
- Show how multicultural content, goals, and activities intersect with subject-specific curricular standards (Gay, 2004, p. 32).

As the inclusive movement and the emphasis on collaboration grow, educators can work together on blending multicultural education within our schools. Perhaps this emphasis could become a planning format for inclusive educators.

Note: Adapted from Gay, G. (2004). The importance of multicultural education: *Educational Leadership, 61*(4), 30–34; Banks, J. A. (1994). *Multiethnic education: Theory and practice* (3rd ed.). Boston: Allyn & Bacon; Bennett, C. I. (2003). *Comprehensive multicultural education: Theory and practice.* Boston: Allyn & Bacon; and Grant, C. H., & Gomez, M. I. (2000). (Eds.). *Making school multicultural: Campus and classroom* (2nd ed.). Upper Saddle River, NJ: Merrill/Prentice Hall.

Special educators should recognize that the techniques of instructional and behavioral management used by general educators can be effective means of working with students with special needs. For instance, teachers in regular classrooms must respond rapidly to the needs of many students every day. The special education teacher should acknowledge that placing a student with special needs in a general classroom does not relieve the teacher of his or her responsibilities to the other students. The special educator must realize that no classroom teacher can devote the majority of time to any student for any length of time. Finally, the special education teacher must strive to recognize that teaching techniques or programs that may be a success in a separate special education class may not be appropriate for the general classroom environment.

General educators must strive to understand that special educators may be responsible for a large number of students in a variety of settings and therefore have a limited amount of time to devote to each student. General educators should accept that a new intervention strategy or instructional approach may not have an immediate effect and that a fair trial must be given before a technique is judged ineffective. Finally, general educators should be familiar with each student's IEP, sharing responsibility with special educators for determining how goals and objects can be reinforced during the course of general education activities.

CONSULTATION

Consultation is the key to the successful integration of students at risk and those with disabilities into the general education environment. In the past, consultation between special and general educators occurred on a limited basis outside of the required team meetings during the steps of the special education identification and placement process (see chapter 6). Consultation has most often been linked to existing special education resource programs, whereby the resource room teacher operates in a limited consultative function with general education teachers (Kauffman & Pullen, 1989). In many school districts, resource room teachers by definition are allowed to serve only those students with valid IEPs. In practice, consultative services under this model are typically delivered in the resource room as opposed to the general education classroom. In many instances, resource room teachers are unable to carry out their responsibilities as consultants because their activities are limited to assessment and instruction in the resource room (Wiederholt & Chamberlain, 1990). Over the years consultation has evolved as a major classroom role.

Collaborative Consultation

A more responsive approach to collaboration between general and special educators emerged during the 1990s. **Collaborative consultation** is "an interactive process that enables people with diverse expertise to generate creative solutions to mutually defined problems" (Idol, Paolucci-Whitcomb, & Nevin, 1987, p. 1). West and Idol (1990) identified three major purposes of collaborative consultation: (a) to prevent learning and behavioral problems, (b) to remediate learning and behavioral problems, and (c) to coordinate instructional programs. Using a collaborative approach greatly enhances the likelihood of success because the proposed solutions or strategies are generated from a wider knowledge base than that of any individual team member. Burdette and Crocket (1999) stated that collaborative consultation is an integral part of supplementary aids and services as defined in IDEA 1997. Three questions arise:

1. How can teachers effectively provide an appropriate education to students with disabilities in heterogeneous classrooms and feel competent in the process?
2. Does teacher consultation provide support to teachers responsible for effective instruction?
3. What barriers and facilitators exist for the implementation of school-based consultative services? (pp. 432–433)

Consultation may be conducted without collaboration and teams. However, whenever collaboration and teams are involved, consultation is activated. In other words, a teacher may come to your classroom to share an idea and thus act as a consultant, but collaboration and teaming cannot occur unless you become involved.

The special education teacher consultant model was developed to address the learning difficulties of students with disabilities through support and consultation provided to their general classroom teachers (Greenburg, 1987). In contrast to traditional consultative services that typically involve calling in an outside expert for a one-time look at a program, classroom, or student, the teacher consultant model is built on the collaboration of school-based staff. Thus, ongoing consultation is available as staff members pool their resources and expertise to generate solutions to in-house problems and issues. This model provides benefits for all students (Phillips, Sapona, & Lubic, 1995).

The role of the special education teacher consultant encompasses several basic functions. One is to help general educators understand that students with special needs can successfully participate in inclusive settings (Lewis & Doorlag, 1987). Beyond this, the most important component of the role is to facilitate instructional or curricular decision making by the general classroom teacher or among team members regarding an individual student's educational needs. Key to the teacher consultant's success is establishing an atmosphere that encourages the exchange of ideas and advice rather than following a more traditional practice of giving advice to those seeking guidance.

Much of the decision making carried out by team members will concern adapting the general classroom environment to accommodate the needs of students with disabilities. Among the main functions of the special education consultant are gathering information, making observations, and facilitating discussion among team members that will result in instructional modifications at the appropriate level of the hierarchy.

Other duties of the special education consultant will depend in part on the type of consultation program in effect. Teacher consultative services usually take one of two forms: indirect or direct (Schulte, Osborne, & McKinney, 1990). Each form is used with approximately equal frequency (West & Brown, 1987).

In **indirect consultation,** the special educator provides technical assistance to the general class teacher. The consultant helps the general education teacher assess needs, arrange the physical environment, plan for instruction, prepare or adapt lesson plans and materials, and develop student evaluation and grading procedures for the students with disabilities. The consultant does not, however, deliver any direct instruction to students, a role that is maintained by the general education teacher. The main advantage to the indirect approach is that it allows the consultant to serve many students in a limited amount of time. A primary disadvantage is that it may be difficult to determine conclusively whether improved student performance is directly related to the intervention efforts of the consultant via the teacher (Heron & Harris, 1987). Another drawback is that the consultant may not have an adequate amount of time to spend addressing any one student's needs.

In **direct consultation,** the special education teacher carries out some direct instruction within the general classroom setting in addition to providing the technical assistance of indirect consultation. The main disadvantage of providing direct instruction to individual students is the added demand on the consultant's time, a factor that can be directly translated into increased costs (Heron & Harris, 1987). An obvious advantage is that it provides more opportunities for one-to-one instruction. The direct model also benefits the general classroom teacher by freeing up more time for other students and enabling more direct and consistent monitoring of the effects of the interventions.

Both direct and indirect consultation benefit students and teachers in many ways. Although there is limited research conclusively demonstrating the effectiveness of the consultative model (Schulte et al., 1990), a substantial amount of professional literature addresses the practical benefits of collaborative consultation (Idol & West, 1987; Lewis & Doorlag, 1987; Reynolds, Wang, & Walberg, 1987; Thousand & Villa, 1990). These benefits include the following:

- Reduced referrals to special education
- Maintenance of general education placements for students with disabilities, promoting inclusion with peers and reducing stigmatization
- Ongoing feedback and professional growth opportunities for teachers
- Increase in direct contact time between student and teacher
- Provision of needed resources that can be used with all students in the classroom
- Increased likelihood that all students' instruction will match the general education curriculum
- Potential for increasing teachers' accountability
- Potential for maximizing instructional outcomes
- Professional and personal satisfaction for teachers
- Improvement of staff morale
- Consistent availability of the consultant, which is not the case with outside consultants
- Availability of an effective vehicle for instructional decision making for all students with or without disabilities.

When we consider the many advantages of the consultative approach, we may wonder why it is not used for all students with special needs in all school districts. Some perceived disadvantages to this approach have interfered with its widespread implementation. One commonly cited drawback, especially by those not experienced in its use, is that it seems to eliminate or reduce a teacher's freedom and autonomy (Thousand & Villa, 1990). General education teachers may fear having another educator in their classrooms on a regular basis, assuming that it will interfere with their teaching styles and force them to modify the tried-and-true instructional approaches they have developed and refined during their professional careers. They may be concerned that having another adult in the classroom will be disruptive to the students. In addition, although general education teachers may welcome assistance for their students with special needs, they may have concerns about the performance and behavior of those students when the special education consultant is not there to provide individual support and instruction.

Special educators also have concerns about implementing the consultative model. Perhaps their greatest concern relates to schedule and caseload—whether they will have sufficient time to meet the needs of all students and their teachers or to carry out all the duties of the consultative role (Idol-Maestas & Ritter, 1985). Lack of administrative support is another factor that inhibits success in school consultant programs (Idol-Maestas & Ritter, 1985; Nelson & Stevens, 1981). Another concern relates to providing feedback to general educators. Observing on-the-job teaching performance can threaten even close relationships among colleagues (Rocha, Wiley, & Watson, 1982). It can be an uncomfortable task for the untrained consultant, especially if the general education teacher resists the consultant's role or does not enthusiastically endorse the inclusion of children with disabilities. A less obvious concern may involve the security of the consultant's role. Special education consultants may fear that they will no longer be needed if they do an outstanding job of helping general educators become skilled in meeting the needs of students with disabilities.

CO-TEACHING

Co-teaching, also known as cooperative teaching, is another model for integrating students with special needs into the general education classroom. As in direct consultation, the special educator participates in instruction in the general classroom. In co-teaching, however, the special educator has increased responsibility for classroom instruction. In most co-teaching situations, special educators continue to take the lead in activities such as child study, consulting with parents, and offering individual, intense instruction to students in need (Reynolds, 1989). Unlike a strict consultation model, co-teaching means that both teachers share equal responsibility for planning, instructing, evaluating, and monitoring all members of the class. A distinct advantage is the opportunity for co-teachers to combine their individual strengths and expertise to address particular student needs. Co-teaching is "two or more professionals delivering substantive instruction to a diverse or blended group of students in a single space (Cook & Friend, 1995, p. 2). Co-teaching is like having two cooks in one kitchen, each measuring, observing, adapting, sharing ideas, taking turns and sometimes doing tasks on their own.

Typically, minimal standards are set for co-taught programs; these limit the number of students in a class and prescribe an allowable ratio among teachers, general education students, and special education students. For example, a program might

The co-teaching model is used in many classrooms. What are some ideas that special and general educators may use to insure a smooth transition into co-teaching with their peers?

designate that two full-time teachers will be assigned to the class and that no more than one quarter of the class may be comprised of special needs students or identified high-risk students. Students also may need to meet certain standards, such as the ability to read content-area materials, before being placed in co-taught classes. Co-taught classes offer the obvious advantage of enabling students with disabilities to receive instruction in inclusive environments with necessary support without being singled out as the targets of special instruction.

Although co-teaching is a popular model for inclusion, research supporting it is scarce. Murawski and Swanson (2001) provided excellent research on the concept of co-teaching. The overall effect size of their study suggested "that co-teaching is a moderately effective procedure for influencing student outcomes" (p. 264). They stated:

> The fact that the research on co-teaching is lacking does not mean that co-teaching in schools should be eliminated altogether. In fact, for researchers to collect the needed data, teachers who are employing co-teaching as a service delivery option at all grade levels should open their classrooms for study. (p. 266)

Preparing to Co-Teach

When preparing for a co-teaching situation, the following factors should be addressed: the three stages of co-teaching and the relationship of the eight co-teaching components to each stage; issues related to co-teaching; and scheduling concerns and models to implement the process.

Stages of the Co-Teaching Process

Like most relationships, co-teaching has stages: the "honeymoon" or *beginning stage* moves into a *compromise stage* and then settles into a *collaborative stage* (Gately & Frank, 1997). Table 2.1 presents each stage and the transition continuum for each of the eight components of co-teaching that contribute to a successful collaborative learning environment.

As educators progress through each of the three stages, changes in their behaviors are reflected across eight components. *Interpersonal communication* moves from guarded to open and finally into a stage in which educators respond to each other's nonverbal behavior. *Physical arrangement* in materials and space develop. Initially, educators keep materials and students separate. Slowly, sharing begins. At the collaborative stage, both educators feel more comfortable during the co-teaching process and materials are used for all students. The students with disabilities are integrated within the general class seating, and more whole-group instruction occurs.

During the third component, *familiarity with the curriculum,* the special educator becomes comfortable with the general education content and both educators begin to appreciate their own competencies. The *curriculum goals and modifications* component moves from the issue of "no planning time" and a textbook, standards-driven program to both educators viewing the co-teaching process with a "bigger idea" of concepts taught. The fifth component, *instructional planning,* initially begins with the teaching of very separate curricula. As educators "give and take," continual planning inside and outside the classroom begins to transpire. As the sixth component, instructional presentation, develops, the process progresses to both teachers presenting, instructing, and structuring lesson activities.

TABLE 2.1
The three stages and the components for each stage of the co-teaching relationship.

Components of the Co-Teaching Classroom that Contribute to a Successful/Collaborative Learning Environment	1 Beginning Stage	2 Compromise Stage	3 Collaborative Stage
1 Interpersonal communication	Guarded communication.	Open and interactive.	Use more nonverbal communication and development of nonverbal signals.
2 Physical arrangement	Separateness of students and materials.	More sharing of space and materials.	Student seating more integrated. More whole-group lessons.
3 Familiarity with the Curriculum	Special education teacher is unfamiliar with content or methodology in general education.	Curriculum confidence of both teachers grows.	Both educators begin to appreciate the competencies they bring to the content.
4 Curriculum Goals and Modifications	"No planning time" an issue. Programs driven by textbooks, standards, tests. Special education teacher is viewed as a "helper."	Both teachers begin to see more ways to modify.	General educator may view modifications as "giving-up" or "watering down." Both educators begin to see the "big idea" of concepts taught.
5 Instructional Planning	District and separate curriculum taught.	Educators begin to show a more "give and take" in planning.	Continuous planning inside and outside the classrooms begins to transpire.
6 Instructional Presentation	One educator is the "boss" and one is perceived as the child.	Movement to mini-lessons or clarification of strategies.	Both teachers present, instruct, and structure learning activities.
7 Classroom Management	One teacher surfaces as the behavior enforcer and one as the teacher.	Mutual rule development. Discussion on behavior plans.	Both educators involved in rules and routines.
8 Assessment	Usually two assessment plans.	Exploration of various assessment measures.	A variety of assessments emerge.

Note: From "Understanding Co-teaching Components," by S. E. Gately & F. J. Frank, Jr., *Teaching Exceptional Children, 29*(6), (1997) pp. 40–47. Copyright 1997 by The Council for Exceptional Children. Reprinted with permission.

Classroom management is an ongoing issue. During the development of the co-teaching process, one educator surfaces as the enforcer and the other as the teacher. At the end of this progression, both educators become equally involved in the development and implementation of classroom management. The last component, *assessment,* begins with two different plans and develops into the exploration of a variety of assessment plans.

Co-Teaching Issues

Argüelles, Hugues, and Schumm (2000) listed seven factors that must be in place for a successful co-teaching process: a common planning time, flexibility among both teachers and administrators, risk taking, clarity of roles and responsibilities, compatibility, effective communication skills, and administrative support.

Bauwens and Hourcade (1995) listed eight issues expressed by educators as necessary when co-teaching. Six of these issues were reflected in Argüelles and colleagues' (2000) list of seven. Bauwens and Houreade added meeting individual student needs and measuring the effects of the co-teaching programs. See Figure 2.2 for suggestions for establishing successful co-teaching and collaboration.

Co-Teaching and Scheduling

The nature of elementary schools, middle schools, and high schools varies according to teacher training, physical building structure, and time frames of classes. Scheduling of co-taught classes also varies. The elementary school has extended time for language arts and math. Classes for other areas may be limited to 25- to 30-minute segments. Students enjoy specialties such as physical education, music, art, and drama. Many students with disabilities are removed from the classroom for speech and language, occupational therapy, physical therapy, or counseling. Scheduling becomes a "juggling act." However, bringing services inside the classroom benefits all students. Miss Robin, an occupational therapist from Ohio, visits lower elementary classes each week to assist the classroom teacher with correct positioning for student handwriting. This in-room consulting benefits all students, not only the student who has occupational therapy prescribed on the IEP. Mrs. Oats, a speech and language specialist, works daily with language within elementary classes. Both educators provide enriching experiences for all students. When educators work within one room, scheduling issues diminish.

Middle schools report fewer scheduling problems than elementary schools (Walther-Thomas, 1997). Middle schools frequently have one special educator shared by one team. A team planning time and a common planning period are frequently allowed. Unlike elementary schools, where special education teachers have large caseloads, middle schools find scheduling more manageable.

In high schools curricular materials are complex, the ability gap among students widens, and the teachers' attitudes change from "what will I give up?" to "what will I learn?" and "how many more will I help?"

Secondary educators are trained to be content centered. As students move into the secondary levels, the disability is often perceived as gone when, in fact, it is still present. What has to change is service delivery. Helpful options include hand scheduling students with disabilities instead of computer scheduling, and changing the schedule from the traditional six or seven blocks to a flexible system in which subjects are offered on a rotating schedule. For instance, students attend language classes on Monday and Wednesday and math and science classes on Tuesday and Thursday. Friday provides extra study or support time for all classes. When co-teaching at any level, specifically the secondary level, educators must also be sensitive to identifying students with disabilities. No one wants to be labeled.

Educators must be careful not to resort to segregated practices in the guise of co-teaching. An eighth-grade science class was reported to have an excellent co-teaching model with the scheduling running smoothly. On closer look, the special education teacher appeared with 10 students with disabilities at the beginning of the

1. Finding Planning Time:
   - Arrange for shared planning periods.
   - Schedule teacher cores/share students.
   - Develop shared team.
   - Share lesson plans with suggested "Help Me Here" tips.

2. Using Planning Time Effectively:
   - Develop objectives for each planning time.
   - Keep notes on who will develop/implement ideas.
   - Develop a follow-up plan for ideas suggested.
   - Make a brief list, before meeting ends, of objectives not completed or needed to be added for next meeting.

3. Meeting Individual Student Needs During Co-Teaching/Collaboration:
   - Acquire a knowledge base of curriculum alignment.
   - Decide the priority of skills to be taught.
   - List any prerequisite skills needed for present skill base.
   - Develop accommodations for teaching skills.

4. Balancing Time Across a Variety of Different Educational Activities:
   - Get organized.
   - Set priority of activities.
   - Before you become too stressed out, share concerns with supervisor (if possible).
   - Consult with the teacher who seems to balance everything well.

5. Communicating About Co-Teaching Activities:
   - Have more daily communication.
   - Have personal meetings/written communication.
   - Clarify role of teachers to each other, parents, and students.
   - Identify who will be primarily responsible for parent communications and who students should approach for adaptations, etc.

6. Resolving Conflicts with Co-Teaching Partners:
   - Take and discuss with your partner the Co-Teaching Personal Inventory.
   - Complete the inventory organizer list.
   - Be open to other points of view and ideas.
   - Have an agreed-upon third party sit with you during discussions.

7. Obtaining Support for Co-Teaching Programs:
   - Find successful models to observe.
   - State when you would like to begin your program.
   - Develop an outline of how your program will look.
   - Present your proposal to the administration. Be sure you have general educators and special educators involved.

8. Measuring the Effects of Co-Teaching Efforts:
   - Keep data on prereferral rate and pre/post co-teaching/collaborative efforts.
   - Have parents complete a "Parent Pleased" inventory.
   - Have other teachers complete a student progress report.
   - Evaluate your administration's reactions.
   - Don't forget to ask your students (pre/post).

FIGURE 2.2
Co-teaching/collaboration issues.

Note: Wood, J. W. (2002). *Reaching the Hard to Teach.* Richmond, VA: Judy Wood, Inc. Issues from: Bauwens, J., & Houreade, J. J. (1995). *Cooperative teaching: Rebuilding teaching: Rebuilding the schoolhouse for all students.* Austin, TX: Pro-Ed.

class, marched them in, and then moved up and down the aisle observing only those students. This is an example of physical inclusion that is not full inclusion. Separating the students and emphasizing the students with disabilities resulted.

Co-Teaching Models

What does the concept of co-teaching physically look like? Frequently, educators do not know where to go or what to do within the class. The following models (see Figure 2.3) may be used in any co-taught class. They include ideas for large groups and small groups. Each day or during the week's planning, co-teachers should decide which model best fits the lesson. Naturally, more than one model can be used.

Large-group models include tag teaching and direct teaching/support teaching. With tag teaching both educators deliver subject content. This requires that the special educator knows the content and that both educators are comfortable with sharing the content. Tagging is excellent when combining different content classes. For example, a literature lesson might coincide with a certain historical era. The class meets jointly, and the class information is delivered by both teachers.

Direct teaching/support teaching requires that one teacher provides direct teaching of content and the second teacher provides student support. Support could include employing classroom-embedded assessment, checking classroom assessments, answering questions one on one, recording questions for class discussion, observing students for needed preplanned interventions or spontaneous interventions, and managing student behavior. In this model teachers can trade roles.

An important benefit of a large-group model is that it provides time for the special education teacher to become more comfortable with the content. Students benefit from having an "extra" teacher, and behavior issues may be handled without class or task interruption.

Small-group models of co-teaching include academic stations/shared teaching and academic stations/support teaching. The first model, academic stations/shared teaching, has three variations. In split groups/same content, the group is split into two sections and each teacher teaches one group. With split groups/flip groups, the group is split into two sections and the subject matter is divided in half. Each teacher teaches one half of the lesson and "flips" the groups to reteach the content to the other group. Splitting groups based on students' styles of learning or abilities allow one teacher to teach to most of the class while the second teacher teaches the same lesson focusing on learning modalities or material that may be at a different instructional level.

With academic stations/support teaching the class is divided into groups or stations with one teacher direct teaching and the second supporting. The support station could include test review, homework, projects, or reteaching what was learned during direct teaching.

Benefits of the small-group models include smaller class size, immediate support for student needs, and providing new co-teachers time to adjust to the general education curriculum. Working in small groups allows students to move around to prevent too much "seat time." With small groups, student problems may be more readily seen, and the student–teacher ratio is reduced.

Co-Teaching Inventories

Figures 2.4 and 2.5 present co-teaching inventories for special educators and general educators to use to establish a positive beginning to their working relationship. Frequently teachers in a co-teaching situation are unaware of the needs and concerns of the other teacher. The inventories provide a starting point for a positive relationship.

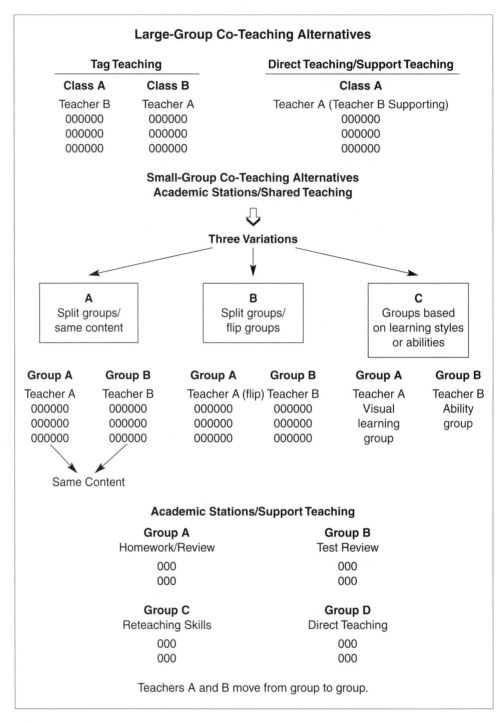

FIGURE 2.3
Co-teaching alternatives.

Level	Description	Yes	No	N/A
1	Comfortable with all class duties including direct instruction.			
2	Comfortable with all class duties including some direct teaching.			
3	Comfortable with all class duties.			
	Willing to learn subject matter for sharing direct teaching.			
4	Comfortable with all class duties. Not ready for direct teaching.			
5	Comfortable with the following class duties:			
	• Take class roll			
	• Collect monies			
	• Provide direct class instruction			
	• Conduct large-group activities after direct instruction			
	• Conduct small-group activities after direct instruction			
	• Assist with guided practice			
	• Assist with direct practice			
	• Provide one-on-one instruction to any student			
	• Assign homework			
	• Explain homework			
	• Check homework			
	• Assign class work			
	• Explain class work			
	• Check class work			
	• Ask questions			
	• Answer questions			
	• Design accommodations/interventions			
	• Develop accommodations/interventions			
	• Implement accommodations/interventions			
	• Give grades on papers			
	• Assign grades to report cards			
	• Discipline students			
	• Develop daily lesson plans			
	• Participate in parent conferences			
	• Administer end-of-year standardized testing			
	• Serve as the student case manager			
	• Serve as the student co-case manager			
	• Discuss class issues with other co-teachers			
	• See classroom as a shared environment			
	• See students as a shared responsibility			

FIGURE 2.4
Co-teaching inventory for special educators.

Note: From Wood, J. W. (2002). *Reaching the Hard to Teach.* Richmond, VA: Judy Wood, Inc. Reprinted with permission.

Level	Description	Yes	No	N/A
1	Comfortable with sharing all class duties including direct instruction.			
2	Comfortable with sharing all class duties including some direct teaching.			
3	Comfortable with sharing all class duties. Willing to learn subject matter for sharing direct teaching.			
4	Comfortable with sharing all class duties. Not ready for direct teaching.			
5	Comfortable with sharing the following class duties:			
	• Take class roll			
	• Collect monies			
	• Provide direct class instruction			
	• Conduct large-group activities after direct instruction			
	• Conduct small-group activities after direct instruction			
	• Assist with guided practice			
	• Assist with direct practice			
	• Provide one-on-one instruction to any student			
	• Assign homework			
	• Explain homework			
	• Check homework			
	• Assign class work			
	• Explain class work			
	• Check class work			
	• Ask questions			
	• Answer questions			
	• Design accommodations/interventions			
	• Develop accommodations/interventions			
	• Implement accommodations/interventions			
	• Give grades on papers			
	• Assign grades to report cards			
	• Discipline students			
	• Develop daily lesson plans			
	• Participate in parent conferences			
	• Administer end-of-year standardized testing			
	• Serve as the student case manager			
	• Serve as the student co-case manager			
	• Discuss class issues with other co-teachers			
	• See classroom as a shared environment			
	• See students as a shared responsibility			

FIGURE 2.5

Co-teaching inventory for general educators.

Note: From Wood, J. W. (2002). *Reaching the Hard to Teach.* Richmond, VA: Judy Wood, Inc. Reprinted with permission.

Do List	My List	Your List	Our List	Gray List
List all tasks to be completed. • lunch money • direct instruction • grading papers, etc.	We *both* agree that these are your tasks.	We *both* agree that these are my tasks.	These are the tasks we can share.	Tasks we cannot agree on immediately. List and act on these last.

FIGURE 2.6
Judy's list.

Before beginning a co-teaching relationship, both educators complete individual inventories. (Figure 2.4 is for general educators; Figure 2.5 is for special educators.) When they have completed their inventories, both educators sit down and review the results. This information is transferred to a chart with columns labeled "Do List," "My List," "Your List," "Our List," and "Gray List" (See Figure 2.6). In the first column, "Do List," the educators list all the tasks that will be completed within the classroom. These come from the class duties listed in the inventories. Under "My List," they list the tasks they both agree that the general education teacher will be doing. "Your List" will contain the tasks that both agree that the special educator will be doing. "Our List" contains tasks both educators will share, and the "Gray List" includes tasks that both educators cannot immediately agree on. The gray list tasks are set aside for later review and discussion. This process often demonstrates that there are more points of agreement than disagreement.

Here are some additional co-teaching tips:

1. During inclusionary procedures, one teacher can position him- or herself in the corner of the room. If that teacher cannot hear a question or an answer, he or she may raise a hand for a repeat. It is quite possible that students also did not hear.

2. Students can suggest strategies that work best for them. Sometimes we forget the most important player in the IEP, the student.

3. Support personnel can provide a one-page handout listing their students' strengths, needs, successful techniques, and so on. This will be extremely helpful for the general classroom teacher.

4. Students who are auditorially distracted in a large classroom can use earplugs when they do their work. Older students like the smaller earplugs; younger students like the big ones.

5. For parallel programming, teachers who are particularly good at this type of assignment can lead. A peer helper also may be assigned to the student receiving the parallel lesson. (*Parallel programming* means teaching the same subject but on different levels.)

6. A major step toward a successful co-teaching program is the ability of team teachers to work together.

In many areas of our country, the concept of "push-in" is applied to the co-teaching model. This is when the student at risk or with special needs is "pushed into" the general education classroom. Most frequently, a co-teaching model is used. Gerber and

STUDENT KNOWLEDGE CHECK

Amy, a special education teacher, would like to participate in a co-teaching model. She has listened to other teachers in the teachers' lounge and has heard many negative comments regarding the extra effort teachers must put out because so many students they serve have disabilities. Amy realizes that co-teaching would be a helpful approach to this issue.

- If you were Amy, how would you begin to establish a co-teaching situation?
- Who would you approach first?

Popp (1999) found a high level of satisfaction among students and parents with the co-teaching model. However, parents were concerned with the lack of communication between parents and the school and with the loss of continuity between grade levels.

To reduce parental concerns about co-teaching, schools can provide orientation programs on the co-teaching process in which they explain how this process will affect the students. Ongoing parental support can include parent–teacher conferences in which teachers explain the specific times and subjects when co-teaching will take place. Teachers can also reinforce the benefits of co-teaching and the specific models being used. Notes to parents stating how their child is reacting and progressing can also be very helpful. Parents may ask for this information.

TEACHER SUPPORT TEAMS

A third school-based approach to meeting the needs of all students in inclusive settings is **teacher support teams.** Several types of team arrangements have proven successful in promoting collaborative consultation between special and general educators. Perhaps the most broad-based type of support is provided by teacher coaching teams. In general, the purpose of coaching teams is "to build communities of teachers who continuously engage in the study of their craft" (Showers, 1985, p. 63). These teams are often organized during training activities designed to promote the use of a certain instructional strategy or curriculum approach. Teachers then have the support of their peers as they try to implement new strategies in their classrooms after the training.

Intervention assistance teams and school-based resource teams are similar in that both are formed to address a particular type of problem. Intervention assistance teams are formed as needed, and members may come from within or outside of the school building. Each member will have expertise in a particular intervention strategy. In contrast, school-based resource teams are always formed by personnel within the building. A variety of professionals, including teachers, administrators, and support staff, may serve as members (West & Idol, 1990).

The teacher assistance team (TAT) is the most strictly defined type of teacher support team. Like the models just described, TAT promotes the use of a school-based problem-solving team to generate intervention strategies for individual students or groups. A team is usually comprised of a core of three members representing various grade levels or disciplines, with the classroom teacher who has requested assistance serving as the fourth member. The team may address a wide variety of issues, including intervention strategies for a particular student, modification of the curriculum, or communication with parents. A distinguishing characteristic of a TAT is that it is teacher oriented rather than child oriented because its main purpose is to support teachers. Another distinctive aspect is the importance that training plays in the ultimate effectiveness of team members.

Establishing clear channels of communication among team members can address and possibly prevent many of the concerns surrounding the collaborative consultation and co-teaching models. There are predetermined occasions in the special education process when team members need to communicate. However, the less formal, daily communication may be of greater concern to educators and parents, who are assuming a wide variety of duties in a limited amount of time.

Pugach and Johnson (1995) conducted a study on the benefits of collaboration and described a four-step problem-solving process. The purpose of the process is to enable classroom teachers to develop a clearer understanding of problems they encounter in the classroom and create potential solutions to those problems (p. 107). The steps include (a) clarifying questions, (b) summarizing the information generated in the first step, (c) generating at least three interventions for the problem and predictions of possible results, and (d) developing an evaluation plan to measure the accuracy of the intervention plan and the outcome of the implementation. Pugach and Johnson found that the teachers in the intervention group, compared to a control group, became more confident in intervention planning and showed a higher degree of affect. A structured approach to problem solving in the classroom assists in developing successful solutions.

With the emphasis on intervention plans for students at risk, collaboration and school-based service delivery models such as consultation, co-teaching, and teams become more important. The numbers of students being served in special education are increasing as a result of the addition of the at-risk population. Working together and sharing our knowledge will be an educational must in the years to come.

THE IMPORTANCE OF ADMINISTRATIVE SUPPORT

Administrators are in a unique position to promote successful collaboration between special and general educators. Because of their dual roles of instructional leader and building administrator, principals are central to the implementation and maintenance of effective collaborative arrangements. Not only can they enact the necessary administrative procedures to accommodate students with special needs in inclusive settings, but they can also provide access to necessary training opportunities for staff members who are implementing classroom adaptations. District-level administrators, who play more central roles in the allocation of resources and the development of district-wide policies, can also have a direct influence on the implementation of integrated programming at the building level.

PARENTS AS PARTNERS

Being a parent of a child with a disability is not easy. If the disability is mild, parents may have difficulty explaining their suspicions to teachers. Some parents have no background in child development and simply think that their child could do their schoolwork if they "tried harder," paid attention to the teacher, played less after school, and so on. When a disability is more severe, parents know that "everyone is watching." Parents may feel that they are being punished or, oddly enough, that they are being blessed. The ever-tiring struggle to obtain services becomes a life focus. Many parents shop from resource to resource to find solutions, wondering why their child is like this, asking why their child has to work so hard, or wishing that the problem would simply go away.

Parents Know First

Although some parents may be reluctant to become members of a team comprised mainly of professionals, all parents possess a wealth of information that can be extremely helpful in promoting the success of their children in inclusive classrooms. Parents can observe their children in a variety of settings and have the unique advantage of being able to assess a child's performance over time. Thus, parents may be the first to notice that a child is having difficulty in the general classroom environment. This may be especially true for children with mild disabilities or those at risk, whose problems in the classroom may be initially manifested as emotional or behavioral difficulties at home. In these instances, parents may request a conference with the teacher to discuss proactive classroom adaptations. They can be very helpful in providing information about the child's learning style and past educational experiences.

Parent Conferences

Before the Conference

Being invited to a conference or trying to initiate a conference may be uncomfortable to parents. Perhaps the parent experienced difficulty in school as a child or left school at an early age. You can help the parent prepare for the conference by providing a list of academic classroom, nonacademic classroom, and nonacademic social concerns (see Figure 2.7).

Be flexible regarding when you are available to meet with the parent because many parents may be at work during your scheduled hours. Make every attempt to work with the parent in establishing the meeting time. Consider the physical setting of the conference room. Is the room too warm or too cold? Watch out for noisy areas, close your class door, reserve the school conference room and turn off your cell phone. Arrange the furniture for everyone's comfort. Trying to sit in a "pint-sized" chair does not help a parent feel at ease. Many times parents must bring other children to the meeting. Have a toy area available or arrange for a responsible person to have a supervised child care room available. Inform parents ahead of time of the arrangements you have made and request their suggestions. Remember that some parents may not read or read so poorly that a written list could be intimidating.

During the Conference

Sit on an equal basis with parents. Do not sit behind your desk (a sign of power) or place parents at the head of the table. Some parents may be divorced but both may wish to attend the conference. If possible, find out which parent has the authority to sign papers for the student. Carefully observe the parents' behaviors to see if tension is present. Parents sometimes cry. Let them cry and provide tissues. Some parents have anger and blame others. Remember that this is normal and not about the teacher. Remain calm. Ask what you can do for the parent, offer support and know prior to the conference a parent group and contact you can provide. Have all educators who have

Academic Classroom

- In which subject is my child having particular difficulty?
- Is my child having difficulty in all or most subject areas or only in certain subjects?
- Are there any medical concerns (such as seizures, hearing loss, visual impairments) that should be looked into as possible causes of my child's difficulties?
- Does my child's performance vary significantly between the morning and afternoon or on certain days of the week?
- What is my child's current level of performance in this skill area in comparison to the performance of others at this age level and in the class?
- What modifications in course content, pacing, and materials have been tried with my child? Which ones have proven successful? Which of these modifications should I carry out at home?
- How will I know when homework has been assigned? Is my child aware of the penalty for late or incomplete work?
- What appears to be my child's favorite subjects in school?

Nonacademic Classroom

- Does my child stay in his or her seat?
- Does my child raise his or her hand and wait to be acknowledged?
- Does my child walk quietly in line and follow other school rules in the cafeteria, library, gym, and so on?
- Is my child's behavior significantly different from that of other children in the class? If so, exactly what does my child do or not do that is considered inappropriate?
- What do you do when my child behaves inappropriately?
- Does my child understand the classroom rules? Are they posted in a place where students can refer to them as needed?
- Does my child's behavior vary significantly between the morning and afternoon or on certain days of the week?
- What can I do to provide a consistent approach to behavior management between school and home?
- How many times a day is my child leaving the classroom for support services?
- Does my child have difficulty reorienting to the classroom upon return?
- Is my child able to keep track of his or her belongings? Is there a system in place in the classroom for storing belongings?
- What leadership responsibilities does my child have? Are they carried out successfully?

Nonacademic Social

- Does my child have friends in the classroom?
- Does my child initiate contact with other students? Does he or she respond appropriately when others initiate contact?
- Does my child interact appropriately with other students on the playground, in the cafeteria, on the bus, and during other free times?
- Is my child being teased or ridiculed by other students? If so, are there any adjustments we can encourage in behavior, appearance, or manner to improve this situation?
- What are my child's favorite activities during the school day?
- Does my child appear to be happy at school most of the time?

FIGURE 2.7
Questions for parents when preparing for a parent–teacher conference.

responsibility for the child present. Allow the parent to have a "support friend" present. Naturally, not all conferences are difficult. Always remember that they are the parents and it is always easier to hear good news than bad. So start off with good things about the child and praise work samples. Thank parents for their interest in their child's educational experience.

After the Conference

Send a note to the parents thanking them once again for attending the meeting. Restate the points discussed, actions to be taken, and time lines for the actions. Send a brief note or e-mail to other educators who did not attend the meeting but have a legal right to the information. Keep your records of the meeting in a file to prompt your memory before the next meeting.

According to Evans (2003), the first contact with parents regarding a student's learning problem is crucial. Following are several suggestions:

- Meet in person, face to face, so that you can use body language to see how the parents receive your message.
- Emphasize the child's strengths and describe your concerns specifically.
- Be patient. Several meetings may be needed before the parent can listen and respond in a calm, constructive way. Parents may go through many emotions before reaching acceptance. They may experience these feelings every time you adjust the child's program.
- Try to meet with both parents so that your message does not get changed or misinterpreted as it is passed on, leading to more stress at home.
- Encourage questions and answer them frankly.
- Remain firm in your position that the student needs extra help.

PARAEDUCATORS AND COLLABORATION

Paraeducators, also referred to as **paraprofessionals,** are noncertified personnel who are assigned to assist teachers and other certified personnel in developing and implementing educational programs for students. The paraeducator is a fast-growing field. Many "paras" are being trained to assist not only in special education but also in general education classes.

Initially, paraeducators could be hired and trained on the job. Today No Child Left Behind mandates that paraeducators in some environments (Title I) have at least two years of college credit or an associate's degree. Therefore, when considering hiring a paraeducator, remember that their training will be continuous, as is training for all educators. According to Giangreco (2003), points to consider when collaborating with paraeducators include the following:

- Hiring the most talented, caring, and competent paraeducators available
- Demonstrating appreciation and respect for their work by treating them well
- Orienting them to the school, classroom, and students
- Clarifying their roles and assigning them tasks that align with their skills
- Providing initial and ongoing training that matches their roles
- Giving them professionally prepared plans to follow

- Directing their work through ongoing, supportive supervision
- Providing opportunities for them to be contributing team members (pp. 50–51)

Even though paraeducators are receiving more training, the teacher can provide on-the-job, ongoing training. Morgan and Ashbaker (2001) provided excellent suggestions for educators: First, treat your paraeducator as an adult learner. Second, be sure that the para has the necessary skills when given an assignment. Third, monitor how paras interact with students. Fourth, provide opportunities for paras to practice new skills. Fifth, encourage questions (pp. 52–53).

Morgan and Ashbaker (2001) also suggested that educators make professional resources available to paraeducators. Share professional publications, inform paraeducators of the journals and magazines the school subscribes to, and ask other educators to share any professional information they feel would be helpful to the paraeducators (p. 54).

An excellent way to teach any behavior is to model it. This would be no different for the teacher and paraeducator. Morgan and Ashbaker (2001) suggested that educators model a behavior prior to having the paraeducator practice it. Have the paraeducator observe you teach and collect data on critical skills. Review what the para observed. Have the paraeducator practice while you observe and provide feedback (p. 55).

PRACTICAL APPLICATIONS

The following checklist gives the paraprofessional an indication of the extent to which worksite policy and procedure information is needed. The checklist should be thoroughly studied initially and reviewed periodically for any changes. Although some of the suggestions may not seem very important, they can be helpful in improving the effectiveness with which the paraprofessional's job is performed.

Checklist of Things the Paraprofessional Needs to Know

✔ Phone numbers of supervisor, teacher(s), and/or colleagues.
✔ Fire evacuation routes and other emergency procedures.
✔ Building layout.
✔ Chain of command.
✔ Daily/weekly schedule.
✔ Names of building personnel and location of pertinent offices.
✔ Transportation system and personnel involved with student's class or program.
✔ Location of fire/safety equipment and first aid supplies.
✔ Location and operation of equipment.
✔ Location of and procedures for obtaining supplies.
✔ Appropriate playground rules and procedures.
✔ Lunchroom procedures and special event procedures.
✔ Procedure for notifying appropriate persons in case of illness.
✔ Policies regarding school records.
✔ Current update of the paraprofessional's specific responsibilities.

Note: From *A resource guide for administrators, educators, and paraprofessionals.* Montana Office of Public Instruction, September 2001. Reprinted with permission.

SUMMARY

The traditional roles and responsibilities of educators are being altered. Special educators are no longer separate from the rest of the school. General educators are developing and using new strategies within their classes, and administrators are no longer maintaining separate budgets. Parents are now considered experts on their children's educational teams and partners with educators. Collaboration is now a reality between educators and families. The field of education is now pulling together for all students. This chapter has examined this amazing process of everyone working together to provide the best education for all. The remainder of the text will look at what we now can do when teaching the children.

RESOURCES

Supporting Students with Disabilities in Inclusive Schools: A Curriculum for Job-Embedded Paraprofessional Development, by G. Ghere, J. York-Barr, and J. Sommereness. Published by the Institute on Community Integration, this new curriculum is a tool for special educators to use in training paraeducators who provide direct instructional and social support to students. Available from the Institute on Community Integration, University of Minnesota, 612/624–4512 or http://ici.umn.edu.

Strategies for Paraprofessionals Who Support Individuals with Disabilities Curriculum Series. The six modules in this curriculum series for training paraprofessionals in educational settings address the following topics: The Paraprofessional—An Introduction; Providing Cross-Cultural Support Services to Individuals With Disabilities and Their Families; Positive Behavior Strategies for Paraprofessionals; Early Childhood—The Role of the Paraprofessional; Transition—The Role of the Paraprofessional; and Supporting Students With Autism Spectrum Disorders. Available from the Institute on Community Integration, University of Minnesota, 612/624-4512 or http://ici.umn.edu.

National Resource Center for Paraprofessionals. The center offers training events and materials for paraprofessionals, teachers, and administrators; offers technical assistance to facilitate development of state and local systems and infrastructures that support the work of paraprofessionals; publishes a newsletter and website; and sponsors an annual national conference. For more information visit the website at www.nrcpara.org or call 435/797-7272.

National Clearinghouse for Paraeducator Resources. This resource operated by the Center for Multilingual, Multicultural Research at the University of Southern California offers an extensive collection of full-text online articles addressing various aspects of the paraeducator role in education, abstracts from the ERIC database on paraeducators, a description of numerous paraeducator-to-teacher career ladder programs, additional paraeducator resources, and an opportunity to subscribe to a listserv electronic discussion forum on paraeducators. www.usc.edu/dept/education/CMMR/Clearinghouse.html.

National Clearinghouse for Professions in Special Education. The website contains information on the nature of paraeducator work, education required, personal qualities, job outlook and advancement, preparation, and additional resources. www.special-ed-careers.org.

SUGGESTED READINGS

Downing, J. E., Ryndak, D., & Clark, D. (2000). Paraeducators in inclusive classrooms: Their own perspectives. *Remedial and Special Education, 23*(2), 157–164.

Giangreco, M., & Doyle, M. (2002). Students with disabilities and paraprofessional supports. *Focus on Exceptional Children, 34*(7), 1–12.

Giangreco, M., Edelman, S., Broer, S., & Doyle, M. (2001). Paraprofessional support of students with disabilities: Literature from the past decade. *Exceptional Children, 68,* 45–63.

Killoran, J., Templeman, T., Peters, J., & Udell, T. (2001). Identifying paraprofessional competencies for early intervention and early childhood special education. *Teaching Exceptional Children, 34*(1), 68–73.

Pickett, A. (1969). *Restructuring the schools: The role of paraprofessionals.* Washington, DC: Center for Policy Research, National Governor's Association.

Pickett, A., Likins, M., & Wallace, T. (2002). *The employment and preparation of paraeducators: The state of the art—2002.* Logan, UT: National Resource Center for Paraprofessionals, the University of Utah and the University of Minnesota.

Riggs, C., & Mueller, P. (2001). Employment of and utilization of paraeducators in inclusive settings. *Journal of Exceptional Children, 35*(1), 54–62.

WEBSITES TO VISIT

Council for Exceptional Children IDEA Practices Website. A site designed to answer questions and provide information about the Individuals with Disabilities Education Act, and support efforts to help all children learn. www.ideapractices.org

University of Vermont Paraeducator Support, Paraeducator and Supervisor Training. Contact Stephen Doll. www.uvm.edu/~cdci/paraprep/.

Washington Education Association. Addresses paraeducator issues. Contact Judith Sccardo, Director. www.wa.nea.org.

Utah Paraprofessional Website. Provides information for the paraprofessional on federal legislation, standards, guidelines and other issues. Contact Marilyn Likins. www.utahpara.org.

National Resource Center for Paraprofessionals. A center for paraprofessional activities and information. www.nrcpara.org

REFERENCES

Argüelles, M. E., Hughes, M. T., & Schumm, J. S. (2000). Co-teaching: A different approach to inclusion. *Principal,* 48–51.

Bauwens, J., & Houreade, J. J. (1995). *Cooperative teaching: Rebuilding teaching: Rebuilding the schoolhouse for all students.* Austin, TX: Pro-Ed.

Burdette, P. J., & Crockett, J. B. (1999). *An exploration of consultation approaches and implementation in heterogeneous classrooms. Research to practice in the 21st century. MRDD, 34*(4), 432–452.

Cook, L., & Friend, M. (1995). Co-teaching: Guidelines for creating effective practices. *Focus on Exceptional Children, 28*(3), 1–6.

Evans, A. (2003). Empowering families, supporting students. *Educational Leadership, 61*(2), 35–37.

Friend, M., & Bursuck, W. D. (2002). *Including students with special needs: A practical guide for classroom teachers.* Boston: Allyn & Bacon.

Gately, S. E., & Frank, F. J. Jr. (1997). Understanding co-teaching components. *Teaching Exceptional Children, 29*(6), 40–47.

Gerber, P. J., & Popp, P. A. (1999). Consumer perspectives on the collaborative teaching model. *Remedial and Special Education, 20*(5). Austin, TX: Pro-Ed.

Gersten, R., Darch, C., Davis, G., & George, N. (1991). Apprenticeship and intensive training of consulting teachers: A naturalistic study. *Exceptional Children, 57*(3), 226–236.

Giangreco, M. F. (2003). Working with paraprofessionals. *Education Leadership, 61*(2), 50–53.

Greenburg, D. E. (1987). *A special educator's perspective on interfacing special and regular education: A review for administrators.* Arlington, VA: Council for Exceptional Children.

Heron, T. E., & Harris, K. C. (1987). *The educational consultant.* Austin, TX: Pro-Ed.

Idol, L., & West, J. F. (1987). Consultation in special education. Part 2: Training and practice. *Journal of Learning Disabilities, 20*(8), 474–494.

Idol, L., Paolucci-Whitcomb, P., & Nevin, A. (1987). *Collaborative consultation.* Austin, TX: Pro-Ed.

Idol-Maestas, L., & Ritter, S. (1985). A follow-up study of resource/consulting teachers: Factors that facilitate and inhibit teacher consultation. *Teacher Education and Special Education, 8*(3), 121–131.

Kauffman, J. M., & Pullen, P. L. (1989). An historical perspective: A personal perspective on our history of service to mildly handicapped and at-risk students. *Remedial and Special Education, 10*(6), 12–14.

Lewis, R. B., & Doorlag, D. H. (1987). *Teaching special students in the mainstream.* Upper Saddle River, NJ: Merrill/ Prentice Hall.

Lombardi, T. P. (1994). *Responsible inclusion of students with disabilities.* Fastback 373. Bloomington, IN: Phi Delta Kappa Educational Foundation.

Morgan, J., & Ashbaker, B. Y. (2001). *A teacher's guide to working with paraeducators and other classroom aides.* Alexandria, VA: Association for Supervision and Curriculum Development.

Murawski, W. W., & Swanson, H. L. (2001). A meta-analysis of co-teaching research: Where are the data? *Remedial and Special Education, 22*(5), 258–267.

Nelson, C. M., & Stevens, K. B. (1981). An accountable consultation model for mainstreaming behaviorally disordered children. *Behavioral Disorders, 6*(12), 82–91.

Phillips, L., Sapona, R. H., & Lubic, B. L. (1995). Developing partnerships in inclusive education: One school's approach. *Intervention in School and Clinic, 30,* 262–272.

Pugach, M. C., & Johnson, L. J. (1995). Unlocking expertise among classroom teachers through structured dialogue: Extending research on peer collaboration. *Exceptional Children, 62*(2), 101–110.

Reynolds, M. C. (1989). An historical perspective: The delivery of special education to mildly disabled and at-risk students. *Remedial and Special Education, 10*(6), 7–11.

Reynolds, M. C., Wang, M. C., & Walberg, H. J. (1987). The necessary restructuring of special and regular education. *Exceptional Children, 53*(5), 391–398.

Rocha, R. M., Wiley, D., & Watson, M. J. (1982). Special subject teachers and the special educator work to mainstream. *Teaching Exceptional Children, 14*(4), 141–145.

Schulte, A. C., Osborne, S. S., & McKinney, J. D. (1990). Academic outcomes for students with learning disabilities in consultation and resource programs. *Exceptional Children, 57*(2), 162–172.

Showers, B. (1985). Teachers coaching teachers. *Educational Leadership, 42*(7), 63–68.

Thousand, J. S., & Villa, R. A. (1990). Sharing expertise and responsibilities through teaching teams. In W. Stainback & S. Stainback (Eds.), *Support systems for educating all students in the mainstream.* Baltimore: Brookes.

Walther-Thomas, C. S. (1997). Co-teaching experiences: The benefits and problems that teachers and principals report over time. *Journal of Learning Disabilities, 30,* 395–407.

Walther-Thomas, C., Korinek, L., McLaughlin, V. L., & Williams, B. T. (2000). *Collaboration for inclusive education: Developing successful programs.* Boston: Allyn & Bacon.

West, J. F., & Brown, P. (1987). State departments of education policies on consultation in special education: The state of the states. *Remedial and Special Education, 8*(3), 45–51.

West, J. F., & Idol, L. (1990). Collaborative consultation in the education of mildly handicapped and at-risk students. *Remedial and Special Education, 11*(1), 22–31.

Wiederholt, J. L., & Chamberlain, S. P. (1990). A critical analysis of resource programs. *Remedial and Special Education, 10*(6), 15–37.

3

Students with Low-Incidence Disabilities

LEARNER OBJECTIVES

After you read this chapter, you will be able to:

- Describe the basic characteristics associated with mental retardation and explain some instructional techniques and other strategies that can help the student learn academic, vocational, and social skills.

- Describe the basic characteristics associated with autism spectrum disorder and explain some instructional techniques and other strategies that can help the student learn academic, vocational, and social skills.

- Describe the basic characteristics associated with orthopedic and other health impairments and explain some instructional techniques and other strategies that can help the student learn academic, vocational, and social skills.

- Describe the basic characteristics associated with sensory impairments (deaf and hard of hearing and visual impairments) and explain some instructional techniques and other strategies that can help the student learn academic, vocational, and social skills.

- Explain why it is important to work with families and describe some strategies for success.

CHAPTER AT A GLANCE

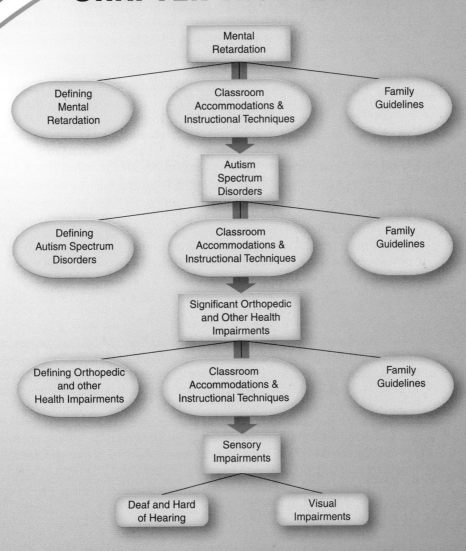

Mental Retardation

Defining Mental Retardation

Classroom Accommodations & Instructional Techniques

Family Guidelines

Autism Spectrum Disorders

Defining Autism Spectrum Disorders

Classroom Accommodations & Instructional Techniques

Family Guidelines

Significant Orthopedic and Other Health Impairments

Defining Orthopedic and other Health Impairments

Classroom Accommodations & Instructional Techniques

Family Guidelines

Sensory Impairments

Deaf and Hard of Hearing

Visual Impairments

KEY TERMS

Sarah is assessed as having mental retardation, which requires substantial supports. She has been tested using the Stanford-Binet Intelligence Scale, which measured her as having an IQ of 39. The 1992 AAMR definition would have placed her in the severe mental retardation range. Sarah also has cerebral palsy resulting in decreased fine motor functioning and a slow, unsteady gait pattern. She has low muscle tone, which gives her poor endurance and makes her appear very weak. Sarah is very outgoing and can speak in unclear sentences. She often exhibits immature social behaviors and inappropriate nonsensical vocalizations such as "yabadabadoo" and "look at me." She can recognize some symbols, has no number skills, and is unaware of time. Sarah attends a segregated school for students with severe disabilities.

Mickey is diagnosed with Fragile X syndrome and needs substantial supports. Earlier he was classified with mental retardation, with an IQ score of 24. He exhibits multiple repetitive behaviors such as rocking, hand flipping, covering his ears, and sticking his fingers down his throat. Mickey has difficulty dealing with change and is often violent and self-abusive when introduced to a new situation. He communicates using single words and occasional short phrases. Mickey has no motor, ambulation, or sensory impairments. He is unaware of time and has no number or word recognition skills. Mickey follows simple commands and responds well to verbal praise. He is enrolled in a special class for students with severe disabilities in a regular education setting.

*I*n this chapter we discuss young people like Sarah and Mickey, as well as other children with significant disabilities who are low incidence in number. There are a number of different types of disability low-incidence categories in special education, but the good news is that through creative adaptations and environmental modifications many of these challenges can be overcome.

In the not too distant past, individuals like Sarah and Mickey were considered so severely handicapped that they could not learn skills as basic as eating, toileting, or dressing, let alone hold a job. Imagine how severe the level of mental retardation must be for young adults to be unable to eat independently or to do even simple jobs such as sweeping or wiping off a table. Because of these perceived limitations, these individuals were relegated to state institutions and frequently abused and neglected. However, as a result of wonderful advances in educational and behavioral research in the 1970s and 1980s, students with mental retardation that require substantial supports (Herr, 1995), such as Sarah and Mickey, are now afforded opportunities to learn and demonstrate their potential. Despite persistent negative perceptions by many about the ability of people like Sarah and Mickey, a lack of learning on their part is more often the result of low expectations by others, inappropriate instructional techniques, or a lack of individualized supports rather than their own skills and abilities. The goal

- Very impaired learning ability and capacity is a major characteristic of people with severe mental retardation, as are impaired receptive and expressive language abilities.
- People with severe mental retardation do not typically develop many of the activities of daily living such as eating or dressing without special help.
- People with significant retardation are unlikely to develop sufficient abilities to achieve complete self-direction without significant levels of support or help.
- Most people with severe retardation receive assistance from their immediate families.
- Individualized help or support for those with severe retardation is critical in defining how mentally retarded they actually are.

FIGURE 3.1
A quick glimpse of severe mental retardation.

of teaching students with significant intellectual disabilities is to provide the skills and supports that will allow them to function as independently as possible in their adult roles. Teachers who follow this guideline while using state-of-the art practices, technologies, and supports can make dramatic differences in the postschool outcomes of students who need substantial supports (Shapiro, 1993). Figure 3.1 offers a quick glimpse of the characteristics presented by students like Sarah and Mickey.

MENTAL RETARDATION

Defining Mental Retardation

In addition to this aspect of the definition, the nature and intensity of individualized help or supports received is important in defining a person's intellectual disabilities. In other words, people labeled as having significant intellectual disabilities can reduce or even lose this label if they receive sufficient supports and good instruction. **Mental retardation** refers to substantial limitations in present functioning. It is characterized by significantly subaverage intellectual functioning existing concurrently with related limitations in two or more of the following applicable adaptive skill areas: communication, self-care, home living, social skills, community use, self-direction, health and safety, functional academics, leisure, and work. Mental retardation manifests before age 18 (American Association on Mental Retardation, 2002).

So what are these wonderful supports that can make such a terrific difference? Supports can be categorized as resources or functions. Support resources include (a) personal support, (b) other people, (c) technology, and (d) outside services; support functions include (a) befriending, (b) financial planning, (c) behavioral support, (d) employee assistance, and so forth. The accompanying Practical Application box lists a large array of supports.

Classroom Accommodations and Instructional Techniques

The key to good instruction for students with mental retardation is selecting a curriculum that is individualized and functional and uses instructional techniques that match the unique learning styles of each student. The basic elements of effective instruction for students with severe multiple and orthopedic impairments are task analysis, individualized supports, assistive technology, and instructional modifications.

PRACTICAL APPLICATIONS
SUPPORT FUNCTIONS AND REPRESENTATIVE ACTIVITIES

Support Functions		Representative Activities	
Befriending	Advocating Carpooling Supervising Instructing	Evaluating Communicating Training Giving feedback	Befriending Associating Collecting data Socializing
Financial planning	Working with SSI-Medicaid Advocating for benefits	Assisting with money management Protection and legal assistance	Budgeting Income assistance and planning/considerations
Employee assistance	Counseling Procuring/using assistive technology devices	Supervisory training Job performance enhancement	Crisis intervention/ assistance Job/task accommodation and redesigning job/work duties
Behavioral support	Functional analysis Multicomponent instruction Emphasis on antecedent Manipulation	Manipulation of ecological events Teaching adaptive behavior	Building environment with effective consequences and minimizing the use of punishers
In-home living assistance	Personal maintenance/ care Transfer and mobility Dressing and clothing care Architectural modifications	Communication devices Behavioral support Eating & food management Housekeeping	Respite care Attendant care Home health aides Homemaker services and med alert devices
Community access and use	Carpooling/rides program Transportation training	Recreation/leisure involvement Community awareness opportunities Vehicle modification	Community use opportu- nities and interacting with generic agencies Hazard awareness
Health assistance	Medical appointments Medical interventions Supervision Med alert devices	Emergency procedures Mobility (assistive devices) Counseling appointments Medication taking	Safety training Physical therapy and related activities Counseling interventions

Note: From *Mental Retardation: Definition, Classification, and Systems of Support* (p. 104) by American Association on Mental Retardation, 1992. Washington, DC: Author. Copyright 1992 by American Association on Mental Retardation. Reprinted with permission.

Curriculum

The basic foundation for learning is the development of relevant curricula that will enhance teaching and ensure the usefulness of the content. This can best be accomplished by developing curricula that are individualized, age appropriate, functional, and community referenced.

Individualized.   Too often decisions about what to teach are based on what the professional feels the student should learn or on standardized instructional materials developed for a certain age or disability label with little regard for individual needs. When this happens, students and their families can feel frustrated because what is being taught has little relevance to them, their lives, or their objectives. The family and the student must be involved in decisions about what to teach, and their needs and preferences must be reflected in the curriculum content.

Age Appropriate. The curriculum content for individuals with mental retardation should be appropriate for their chronological age—that is, similar to what their same-age peers are learning. This includes vocational, domestic, leisure, and community skills representative of what someone of the same chronological age without a disability would be taught regardless of the level of functioning of the person with mental retardation. For example, an adolescent learning to cook and prepare meals would use a real stove, refrigerator, sink, utensils, and food rather than a make-believe preschool toy designed to allow toddlers to practice cooking the way they see adults doing. This is the case even if the individual with a disability is reported to be at a 2-year-old level.

Functional. A functional curriculum is important for the development of skills that prepare an individual with severe mental retardation to function in a variety of community environments (Wehman & Kregel, 2004). This involves the training of such skills as grooming, using a telephone, grocery shopping, telling time, preparing a meal, and riding a bus. For example, a young man would be taken to a grocery store to learn how to pick up items off a shelf, interact with the public, go to the checkout counter, and pay for his purchases rather than staying in the classroom looking at pictures of food, role-playing with the teacher, and counting money in preparation for real grocery shopping experiences. Similarly, a young woman could be taught to use a key to exit or enter a vehicle or residence (Ivancic & Schepis, 1995).

Community Referenced. The criteria for developing and evaluating curricula should be based on the demands and expectations of the community in which the students will be living (Falvey, 1989; Sowers & Powers, 1995). Before teaching any skill, teachers should first find out how it is performed, under what circumstances, the characteristics of the environment, and the expected outcomes. This can only be accomplished by going out in the community and visiting a variety of settings such as businesses, stores, restaurants, movie theaters, homes, and public transportation systems.

Strategies for Intervention

Task Analysis. A task analysis is the breakdown of a specific task into smaller components or steps (Snell, 1993). Most people are familiar with a task analysis and probably have used one sometime in their lives even though they may not be aware of the term. For example, commercially bought food, such as a can of soup or frozen dinner, will often provide detailed instructions about how to prepare the item—for example, (a) open the can, (b) pour contents into pan, (c) turn stove on, and (d) heat on stove until hot. Similarly, an overwhelming day is often made more manageable by breaking it down into a daily "to do" list of all the chores that need to be completed that day.

A task analysis starts with the first step needed to begin the task and ends when all of the steps required to complete the task have been outlined in sequential order (Moon, Inge, Wehman, Brooke, & Barcus, 1990). Figure 3.2 shows a task analyses for riding a bus, including transferring to another bus.

1. Select change for bus ride before leaving work.
2. Go to bus stop—stand 2 feet from curb at bus stop.
3. Motion to approaching bus.
4. When bus door opens, ask driver "Is this the Mononu bus?"
   a. If answer is "no," say "Thank you, this is not my bus" and wait for next bus (step 3).
   b. If answer is "yes," proceed to step 5.
5. Holding rail, enter bus and pay fare.
6. Say to bus driver "I need a transfer please."
7. Wait for and take transfer.
8. Say to bus driver "Would you please tell me when we get to the Buckeye bus?"
9. Thank driver.
10. Walking toward back of bus while grasping seat or overhead rail, sit in first front facing window seat in empty left row (left is facing back of bus).
11. Watch for landmarks on right of bus (facing forward).
    a. Walgreens
    b. McDonald's
    c. West Town Mall sign
12. When West Town Mall sign comes into view, ring bell to signal driver to stop by pushing signal button or pulling signal cord (depending on bus type).
    a. If sitting in aisle seat while next to someone, say "Excuse me" and reach up or over to signal driver.
    b. If driver says "Mononu," prepare to leave.
13. Wait for bus to stop.
14. Exit bus by back door.
    a. If sitting by window and next to someone, say "Excuse me" before standing to exit bus.
15. Repeat steps 3 to 10 except:
    a. When bus door opens, ask driver "Is this the Buckeye bus?"
    b. Holding rail, enter bus and hand driver the transfer pass.
16. Watch for landmarks on right of bus.
17. When Speedway sign comes into view, signal driver to stop.
18. Repeat steps 12a to 14 (for 12, landmark is Speedway station, and for 12b, driver will say "Buckeye").
19. Turn right after exiting bus (toward Speedway service station).
20. Walk to corner.
21. Turn left.
22. Walk to next intersection.
23. Turn right and cross street (separate task analysis).
24. Walk home (fourth house).

FIGURE 3.2
Task analysis for riding and transferring to and from a bus from work to home using landmarks.

Note: From "Community Living" by T. Clees, in *Developmental Disabilities: A Handbook for Best Practices* (p. 258), edited by P. J. McLaughlin and P. Wehman, 1992, Austin, TX: Pro-Ed, Inc. Reprinted with permission.

Individualized Supports. Individualized supports can significantly influence the real and perceived functioning level of people with severe mental retardation. Most people, regardless of the severity of their disability, can perform more tasks and activities, and look more independent while doing them, when they are given the necessary and appropriate supports. For example, someone may be learning a new job and rely on a coworker to teach them how to do it, another individual may need a ride to the mall and call on a friend or neighbor to drive them, and another person may have difficulty in math class and advertise for a tutor to provide one-on-one instruction. The accompanying Practical Applications box provides a number of key tips for teaching and providing community supports.

Assistive Technology. For individuals with severe mental retardation, assistive technology opens up a vast array of opportunities for increased independence that not too long ago may have been considered impossible (Inge, Flippo, & Barcus, 1995). **Assistive technology** can be low- or high-tech devices designed to remove barriers or provide practical solutions to common everyday problems. Although most devices are designed for individuals with orthopedic impairments (see Sowers & Powers, 1991, 1995), much of the technology can be beneficial to someone with severe mental retardation who has limitations from the primary disability or perhaps a secondary disability that may result in mobility, speech, or sensory impairments. Assistive technology devices can be applied in the classroom to assist a student with learning curriculum content or in a community setting to promote skill development and participation.

Assistive technology (Inge, Flippo, & Barcus, 1995) can include such complex devices as (a) an environmental control unit to allow people with little or no mobility to control their environment (e.g., turn on the lights, television, air conditioning, etc.), (b) a voice-activated computer to allow people with mobility or sensory impairments to use computers, (c) augmentative communication systems to allow those with poor speech to communicate with others (e.g., electronic communication aids), and (d) microswitches to allow people to perform more complex tasks by reducing the number of steps to one press on the switch or to allow those with poor motor skills to access something by touching a very large switch pad as opposed to a small button or lever.

Instructional Modifications. Many tasks can be completed in a variety of ways. Most people can think about an activity that they perform and also remember another person, such as a friend, relative, or fellow student, who completes the activity in a very different way with the final outcome being identical. For example, one person may handwrite his homework and another with poor penmanship may type all assignments. Similarly, a confident cook may pour all the ingredients of a recipe into a bowl by just looking at the amounts, whereas another person may need to use measuring cups and spoons to be sure the right amount of each ingredient is added.

Family Guidelines

The issue of the family is an important thread that runs throughout the instructional process. If the child is from a home of poverty, the family challenge is compounded. The family, whether rich or poor, must be an integral part of the student's educational program. Teachers must work with and for the family, sharing ideas, concerns, setbacks, and triumphs. Building the program around the family presents a challenge but provides a base for potential success for the child.

PRACTICAL APPLICATIONS
TIPS FOR TEACHING AND PROVIDING COMMUNITY SUPPORTS

- Get to know your community and find out what opportunities and resources are available to all people regardless of whether they have a disability.
- Meet with the student and his or her family on a regular basis to share information about employment, community living, and recreational options available in their locality.
- Take the student to visit places of interest and observe firsthand what they have to offer.
- Ask the student what he or she would like to do. Be sure to ask questions in a way that he or she can understand by rewording them, trying different formats (e.g., multiple choice, open-ended, yes or no), and using alternative communication devices (e.g., sign language, communication boards, computers).
- Use creative strategies to find out what the student's preferences are, such as observing him or her in a familiar setting performing an enjoyable activity, asking the family what kinds of things their son or daughter likes to do, or exposing the student to different environments and activities and noting his or her reaction.
- Let the student try out the kinds of work, independent living, leisure, and community activities that he or she would like to do. These tryouts should also include different but related activities that the student has expressed an interest in (e.g., someone who would like to become a famous rock star may find that working in a record store, a shop that sells musical instruments, or a theater where concerts are held would be personally gratifying). Be creative in exploring a wide range of options.
- Ask the student if he or she likes an activity. Remember to move beyond broad questions, such as, Did you like working at the grocery store? Did you like going out to lunch with your schoolmates? Often, students' experiences will be very limited so that just doing anything is more enjoyable than what they were doing before even though they may not truly like it. Break the activity down into small parts and ask a variety of questions about it to find out just what the student may or may not have liked. For example, he or she may not have enjoyed working in a fast food restaurant but really liked the hours, location, and coworkers.
- Help the student learn how to express choices to other people, particularly other service providers such as rehabilitation counselors, case managers, and job coaches through role-playing and self-advocacy skills training.

The overriding problems educators face in working with the families are many, but two emerge as significant: (a) professionals do not always do a very good job of listening to what parents are saying, and (b) for so long the family has not seen the potential of the child. Families may have a hard time imagining their son or daughter riding a bus alone, shopping, holding a job, and so on, especially if the child has never performed competently. These are skills that are now possible with good long-term instruction, but it is not hard to see why families might be very skeptical if their son or daughter is incontinent or noncompliant at home or is acting out noisily all the time.

AUTISM SPECTRUM DISORDERS

Mark is a 17-year-old student with autism. His autism has affected both his language abilities and his ability to establish and maintain relationships with others. He is fluent in his speech; however, he has serious problems with abstract communications. Mark interprets everything that is said to him in a literal, concrete manner. His intelligence measures in the low average range. When others speak to him, they must be very specific. Mark is also very sensitive to changes in tone, and he becomes easily upset if his parents, teachers, or siblings are upset. Although he enjoys being with others, when he speaks he does not easily demonstrate his interest in other people. His conversations are usually centered on specific events that occurred during his day. Mark does not have many friends his age because his social skills are far below those of his peers. He might ask questions such as "How was your day?" but the question sounds rote and appears to lack real interest or curiosity.

Mark's autism has affected his learning and school achievement. He can read at a ninth-grade level, but his reading comprehension is at a first-grade level. He can do math at a third-grade level. He has an excellent memory for facts and can still remember the color of the carpet in the house he lived in when he was 3 years old. He also is quite good with dates and can tell you the day of the week on which you were born if you tell him your birthdate. He can also remember the dates of seemingly trivial events from years past. Mark is good at typing. He can do word processing and data entry.

Mark has had autism since birth, but did not receive the diagnosis until age 4. Although his mother noticed that he was not quite like other children, the doctor advised that he was merely slow. By age 4, his language was still delayed, and his behavior patterns were unlike those of the average 4-year-old. At that time, he was diagnosed with autism.

Figure 3.3 provides a quick look at the characteristics of autism spectrum disorders.

- Severe language deficits and limited ability to communicate are very common characteristics associated with autism.

- The majority of children with autism also have mental retardation; it is currently estimated that between 70 and 80% of children with autism score in the significant intellectual disabilities range on standardized intelligence tests.

- People with autism can have dramatic strengths coexisting with dramatic weaknesses.

- People with autism may exhibit a wide range of behavior problems that present a significant challenge to educating them.

- One of the most troublesome aspects of educating students with autism is the frequent lack of spontaneous generalization and the retention of skills learned previously.

- Social deficits such as acting-out behavior or excessive self-stimulatory actions are frequently seen in children who have autism.

- People with autism often insist on doing tasks exactly the same way each time, usually the way they learned it the first time, and may be resistant to doing it a different way even if it is more efficient.

FIGURE 3.3
A quick glimpse of autism.

Defining Autism Spectrum Disorders

According to the DSM-IV (*Diagnostic and Statistical Manual of Mental Disorders,* fourth edition), **autism** is one of five disorders under Pervasive Developmental Disorders (PDD), a category of neurological disorders characterized by "severe and pervasive impairment in several areas of development," including social interaction and communication skills (DSM-IV; American Psychiatric Association, 1987). It's a developmental disability that is thought to have an age of onset before 30 months (American Psychiatric Association, 1994). It is estimated that four or five children with autism are born for every 10,000 births. Children with autism are four to five times more likely to be males than females. Most researchers agree that autism is probably present from birth. Although some parents report that their newborn child did not respond normally to being held and cuddled, other parents become aware of the disability only when the child fails to achieve developmental milestones such as learning to talk on time. Many parents report that their child had a period of relatively normal development that was interrupted by the emergence of autistic behaviors. For instance, some parents report that their children with autism began speaking in either words or sentences and then abruptly stopped speaking, never to speak again.

Because autism does not have a known cause, it is identified by the presence of a cluster of observable behaviors. Most diagnostic systems recognize three primary symptoms:

1. *Deficits in language and nonverbal communication.* Approximately 50% of children with autism fail to develop speech at all. Those who do talk have limited receptive and expressive language skills. They may have difficulty following instructions and may not comprehend abstract concepts or emotional content.

2. *Impaired social relatedness.* Children with autism display a dramatic lack of attachment to others at an early age. They fail to establish social relationships and may appear oblivious to other people. Some children with autism may treat their parents as objects and cling to them without any apparent emotional attachment.

3. *Abnormal responses to sensory stimulation.* Children with autism have difficulty processing sensory stimulation. They may fail to react to sights or sounds. They often seem oblivious to their surroundings to such a degree that their parents suspect they are visually or hearing impaired.

Classroom Accommodations and Instructional Techniques

A wide array of instructional and behavioral techniques have been shown to help the student with autism overcome the deficits associated with the disability and to learn academic, vocational, and social skills. They give reason for great optimism about the educational outcomes of children with autism.

Strategies for Improving Generalization

When working with students with autism, teachers should use specific strategies to achieve generalization. A lack of ability to perform skills in different places is a critically defining characteristic of students with autism. To help students with autism transfer a new skill to the home and community, the teacher will need to help the stu-

ACCOMMODATING DIVERSITY

Culture helps us shape our beliefs and practices and define ourselves. However, it is not the only characteristic that determines an individual's or family's attitudes, values, beliefs, and behavior. Socioeconomic status, educational level, identification with one's heritage, the language spoken, reasons for immigration, and length of time in the United States are also important variables that shape an individual's and family's beliefs and desires. Although knowledge and understanding, sensitivity, and respect for cultural differences can significantly enhance the effectiveness of educators, they should be cautioned about forming stereotypes. Too often, people gain knowledge about a specific culture and then generalize that information to the entire group. For example, people cannot assume that attending a workshop about Latino values, watching programs on Latino roots, reading a book about their beliefs associated with child rearing and causation of disability can be then be applied to all individuals from that particular cultural group. Doing so is not only inaccurate but dangerous. Such generalizations greatly diminish rather than enhance cultural competence.

A prerequisite to understanding other cultures is an appreciation of one's own culture and ethnic background and the values and beliefs that one holds about those who are different. Educators should also acknowledge that although people are influenced by their ethnic, language, and cultural backgrounds, they are not fully defined by them. Teachers should embrace the words of the famous anthropologist Margaret Meade: "Always remember that you are absolutely unique. Just like everyone else."

dent practice it in different settings and with different people. These different situations require the teacher to be flexible about where teaching takes place. Instruction in the classroom alone will be insufficient.

Generalization from the teaching setting to other settings can be promoted by instructing in a variety of places. For example, when Mark learns how to order lunch, he should be taught in numerous restaurants ranging from McDonald's to Shoney's. Generalization across people can be promoted by using several instructors.

Strategies for Improving Maintenance

Remembering what the teacher teaches must be an essential education goal. In many instances, after instruction has ended, previously learned skills or knowledge gradually disappears. The reasons for the lack of maintenance are uncertain. However, one possibility is that the learned skill was reinforced during instruction, but reinforcers are not available in the postinstruction environment. For example, a young child with autism might be given candy each time she ties her shoes. After teaching is successful, the candy stops and so does shoe tying.

Language Remediation Techniques

Children with autism vary considerably in their ability to use language. Although many students with autism are nonverbal, other students range from using single words to using relatively complex sentences. However, in addition to generalization difficulties, another defining characteristic of autism is the failure to use speech in a truly interactive fashion. Improving this and other language impairments is essential if other life activities are to improve, such as shopping in the community or working at a job.

Prizant (1983) suggested that autistic language serves a communicative function for the autistic child, just as conventional language serves a communicative function for the normal child. He recommends analyzing aspects of autistic speech, such as echolalia, to determine the function that the speech serves and then capitalizing on existing speech to expand communication. For a child with autism, echolalia may serve the function of requesting favorite food or activities. A child with this behavior can be taught to functionally request things through incidental interactions. Prizant suggested that normal children learn language through incidental interactions with others and that language should be taught to students with autism in a similar fashion.

Developing Social Skills

Although highly related to language use, social skills encompass a wide range of interactive behaviors that may or may not require language. Students with autism are often withdrawn and seem uninterested in social interactions. They may require intensive instruction in order to learn social skills (Pierce & Schreibman, 1995). Social skills training packages have proven effective in teaching a variety of social skills including greeting others, sharing toys, and engaging in cooperative play. The traditional instructional package consists of instruction, modeling, role play, feedback, rehearsal, social reinforcement, and generalization training. These components are defined in the accompanying Practical Applications box.

Strategies for Managing Challenging Behavior

Destructive behaviors and other behavioral challenges can be major impediments to autistic students learning useful skills and must be significantly reduced through behavior management procedures. Although punishment procedures such as time-out were once common, research and multiple examples from clinical experience now suggest that such procedures are no longer necessary (Carr et al., 1994; Koegel, Koegel, & Dunlap, 1996). Positive approaches work and must be emphasized as the way to help students overcome inappropriate behavior.

Effective behavior management follows an established sequence of steps. Taken together, these steps result in an individualized behavior plan that can create successful educational experiences, both within and outside the classroom. Positive behaviors make autistic students feel better and increase acceptance in the school and the community.

Target Behavior for Change.   The first step in the behavior change process is to pinpoint the behaviors in need of change. These behaviors might be specific to the educational activity being planned or might represent a pervasive problem in the life of the individual. Elmer has severe self-injury such as head banging, which occurs intermittently throughout the day. His behavior change plan targets reducing self-injury as a goal. Joan has problems darting into the street. Changing this behavior is very important for class field trips.

Functional Assessment.   Once the behavior is targeted for change, a functional assessment is done to determine the purpose the behavior serves for the individual. This

---

PRACTICAL APPLICATIONS

SOCIAL SKILLS INSTRUCTION SEQUENCE

Support Functions	Representative Activities
Instruction	Teacher explains the nature and importance of the social skill.
Modeling	Teacher models the social skill.
Role play	Student practices the social skill.
Feedback	Teacher provides corrective feedback if necessary.
Rehearsal	Student rehearses the social skill several times.
Social reinforcement	Teacher praises student for displaying the social skill.
Generalization	Teacher provides general instruction on when to use the social skill. Teaching occurs with multiple exemplars. Peers are used in teaching social skills.

---

assessment can be done through naturalistic observations, structured observations, and data collection. People often misbehave for purposes such as obtaining attention; obtaining assistance; obtaining desired objects or activities; or avoiding certain tasks, activities, or people. Once the purposes of the behavior are determined, behavior change strategies can be selected.

Family Guidelines

Helping families understand how to manage and cope with challenging behaviors is imperative. This starts by having family members understand the environment in which different behaviors occur and why they occur. Communication with school personnel will help facilitate improvement of behavior.

SIGNIFICANT ORTHOPEDIC AND OTHER HEALTH IMPAIRMENTS

Teddy is a young man about to exit high school. He has severe spastic diplegia cerebral palsy. He has difficulty with ambulation and uses a walker (preferred) or a wheelchair for mobility. His speech is very difficult to understand, and he tends to drool a lot. He requires assistance with eating, drinking, and dressing, but is able to transfer himself to the toilet and take care of his own toileting needs. He has normal intelligence, but because of his motor problems, he is often mistakenly believed to have intellectual disabilities as well.

During his elementary school years, Teddy attended a special school for students with disabilities, most of whom had significant intellectual disabilities. His early educational program focused on improving his communication and self-help skills, with little emphasis on academic preparation. When he was about to enter junior high school, his parents objected to further placement in the special school, believing that his academic potential would not be achieved unless he were taught the same courses as his nondisabled peers. Although most of the other members of the IEP team disagreed that he would be "better off" (even doubting Teddy's educational potential), they agreed to a trial in a general education classroom at the local junior high school.

- Children with orthopedic and other health impairments exhibit a wide range and array of physical characteristics.
- Children with orthopedic and other health impairments have intellectual capabilities that range from profound mental retardation to gifted.
- Many children with orthopedic and other health impairments will have problems with incontinence, accidents, catheterization, transferring to a toilet, using a handheld urinal, etc., and require assistance in toileting and other personal needs.
- Orthopedic and other health impairments can range from very mild to very severe, depending on the degree of physical or motor impairment, functional limitations, and the impact of the impairment on educational participation and progress.

FIGURE 3.4
A quick glimpse of orthopedic and other health impairments.

Teddy's school system had little experience with mainstreaming children with severe disabilities, so Teddy's initial junior high experiences were far from ideal. Little time was spent preparing him, teachers and other staff, or other students for the difficulties they would all encounter. He had trouble keeping up with his classmates in most subject areas, and his teachers had trouble communicating with him. Lunch, recess, gym, and moving through the hallways between classes all posed significant challenges for Teddy. It was only through the tenacity of his parents and his homeroom teacher that the IEP team agreed to continue his general class placement.

In this section we will address the critical issues the educational team needs to concentrate on when helping children like Teddy, as well as the best way to formulate an educational plan for such children. Figure 3.4 offers a quick glimpse of issues related to orthopedic and other health impairments.

Defining Orthopedic and Other Health Impairments

Common orthopedic and other health impairments are listed in Figure 3.5. Not all students with any of these problems are automatically considered educationally handicapped. An individual determination must be made that the condition adversely affects the student's educational performance and that special education or related services are required for the student to receive an appropriate education.

Incidence and Prevalence

Data compiled through the National Health Interview Survey (Ficke, 1992) found approximately 6,987,000 cases of **orthopedic impairments** among the general population, most of which were back and other musculoskeletal disorders. Other high-prevalence physical problems identified by this study include arthritis (6,130,000 cases), absence of one or more appendages (373,000 cases), multiple sclerosis (171,000 cases), cerebral palsy (274,000 cases), and complete or partial paralysis (1,195,000 cases). This survey also found that among children, approximately 1,241,000, or 2%, had a physical impairment, with an additional 130,000 (0.2%) having a physical impairment in conjunction with a mental or emotional impairment.

Orthopedic Impairments	Other Health Impairments
Amputation	Acquired immune deficiency syndrome (AIDS)
Bone tuberculosis	AIDS-related complex (ARC)
Cerebral palsy	Asthma
Athetosis	Cardiac defects
Dystonia	Aortic valve stenosis
Hypotonia	Atrial septal defects
Mixed	Pulmonary valve stenosis
Rigidity	Ventricular septal defects
Spasticity	Cystic fibrosis
Clubfoot	Diabetes mellitus
Congenital limb absence	Epilepsy
Contractures	Hemophilia
Curvatures of the spine	Lead poisoning
Kyphosis	Leukemia
Lordosis	Metabolic disorders
Scoliosis	Hurler syndrome
Hip conditions	Phenylketonuria (PKU)
Congenital dislocation	Nephritis
Legg-Perthes disease	Other childhood cancers
Muscular dystrophy	Rheumatic fever
Poliomyelitis	Sickle cell anemia
Rheumatoid arthritis	Tuberculosis
Spina bifida	
Spinal cord injury	

FIGURE 3.5

Common orthopedic and other health impairments.

Note: From "Designing and Implementing Individual Transition Plans: Applications for Students with Orthopedic and Other Health Impairments" by M. West, M. Mast, R. Cosel, and M. Cosel, in *Life Beyond the Classroom: Transition Strategies for Young People with Disabilities* (p. 383) edited by P. Wehman, 1992, Baltimore: Paul H. Brookes Publishing Co. Adapted with permission.

As is the case with virtually all educational handicaps, a slight majority of students with orthopedic and other health impairments are male. Many of the hereditary and metabolic disorders that cause orthopedic and health impairments affect males more frequently than females. Certain disorders are also more prevalent among specific races. As examples, cystic fibrosis is much more common among Caucasians than among ethnic minorities, and sickle cell anemia is primarily found among African Americans.

Classroom Accommodations and Instructional Techniques

Adaptation and Support

In general, students with orthopedic and other health impairments tend to learn best when instructed with the same materials and methods used with nondisabled students. When students' motor problems, physical limitations, or performance deficits affect their academic performance, modifications can be made to (a) the instructional methods of the teacher, (b) the response mode of the student, (c) the environment, or (d) the student.

PRACTICAL APPLICATIONS

INSTRUCTIONAL ADAPTATIONS FOR STUDENTS WITH ORTHOPEDIC AND OTHER HEALTH IMPAIRMENTS

1. Prevent paper and objects from slipping by using pads of paper, tape, clipboards, magnets, photo album pages with sticky backing, etc.
2. Place a rubber strip on the back of a ruler or use a magnetic ruler to measure or draw lines.
3. Use calculators to perform computations.
4. Use felt tip pens and soft lead pencils that require less pressure. Improve grip on pencils and pens with rubber bands or sponge rubber.
5. Permit use of electric typewriters or word processors on written tests or assignments.
6. Use lap desks or a tabletop easel with cork that allows work to be attached with push pins.
7. Use a table that can be adapted to varying positions and angles and has elastic straps to hold books and other objects.
8. Use tables that adjust to wheelchair heights.
9. Provide two sets of books or workbooks—one for school and one for home.
10. Tape assignments, lectures, and activities that require extensive writing.
11. Allow a peer to photocopy class notes.
12. Design alternative worksheets or tests that allow students to respond in their preferred modes.
13. Use color-coded objects that are easy to handle to indicate responses to polar questions: true/false, same/different, agree/disagree/don't know.
14. Select materials that are available on cassette tapes for students unable to hold books or turn pages.
15. Use communication boards with pictures, symbols, numbers, or words.
16. Extend testing or assignment time and/or allow oral responses.

Note: From "Physically Challenged Students" by D. Knight & D. Wadsworth, 1993, *Childhood Education, 69*, p. 215. *Council for Exceptional Children.* Adapted with permission.

Many strategies are available to teachers who are willing to experiment and be creative. The accompanying Practical Applications box provides tips that general and special education teachers can use to adapt environments and materials.

Teachers should always keep in mind that the ultimate purpose of adaptation is to increase the student's active participation in age-appropriate activities, whether social, recreational, vocational, or academic. When adaptations are determined necessary, the IEP/ITP team should consider potential adaptions via a hierarchical selection process:

1. First consider adaptations in the *way* the student is performing the activity (i.e., eliminate difficult steps, devise alternate methods, use alternative response modes).
2. Next, consider adaptations of *materials* that are used in the activity (i.e., adapted tools, velcro fasteners, joy sticks, etc.).

3. Then, consider adaptations to the *setting* in which the activity is performed (i.e., adapt or rearrange the environment, reposition tools, develop alternative environmental cues).

4. Finally, consider adaptations to the *individual,* such as prosthetics or other assistive devices.

Handling, Positioning, and Safety Precautions

As noted earlier, individuals with orthopedic and other health impairments frequently exhibit varying degrees of limitations in physical movement, muscle tone, and body control, and may need assistance from another person to perform everyday functions. Special handling and positioning techniques are needed to (a) provide mobility within and among environments; (b) promote normal physical development; (c) reduce or prevent problems with circulation, respiration, digestion, infections, sores, or physical deformities; (d) reduce the risk of injury or infection to the student or the person assisting him or her; and (e) improve the academic performance of the student.

PRACTICAL APPLICATIONS
POSITIONING, HANDLING, AND SAFETY GUIDELINES

- Many students with severe physical impairments cannot move themselves and may develop pressure sores if left in the same position for extended periods of time. Identify a "menu" of positioning options and rotate among them during a day's activities.
- Select adaptive equipment that assists the student in completing an activity in as normal a position as possible.
- Eliminate excessive environmental noise and distractions. Overstimulation can increase muscle tone and facilitate abnormal movement patterns.
- Learn to feel muscle tone changes. *Stop* if you are increasing abnormal patterns.
- Avoid quick movements when positioning and handling individuals because rapid or jerky movement can stimulate spasticity. Slow, steady movement is important.
- Learn the key points of body control: the head, trunk, shoulders, hips, and pelvis.
- Never pull on a body part that is flexed. This will increase spasticity.
- Never carry the child like an infant because this limits his or her visual field and he or she will never learn head or body control.
- Provide the least amount of assistance and encourage the individual to participate whenever possible. Providing too much support or control does not allow the individual to develop muscle control. Always require the individual to assist based on his or her capabilities. Assess needs often and change as indicated.
- Never try to lift someone by yourself if the person is over one fourth of your total body weight. *If in doubt, seek assistance!* If you do injure your back, be sure to have it checked by a physician.

(continued)

- Keep the weight you are lifting as close to your body as possible. The farther away the person is, the "heavier" he or she will be.
- Always keep your knees bent when lifting and your back straight. *Never* lift using your back. The leg muscles are much stronger, and will allow you to lift the maximum amount of weight.
- Never twist or rotate at the waist when lifting. Move your body as one unit. To change directions, step around and turn your body without twisting at the waist or lower back.
- Never lift an individual with cerebral palsy by taking an arm and leg while someone else takes an arm and leg. This is especially true of an individual with hemiplegia because weight and tone will be different on the two sides of the person's body.
- Always lock wheelchair brakes prior to moving an individual to or from a wheelchair. Make sure all seatbelts and straps have been unfastened prior to lifting. Detach removable armrests and legrests from the wheelchair and get them out of the way.
- Clear the environment of all extraneous materials, i.e., toys that you may trip over during lifting.
- If the individual has more involvement on one side of the body than the other, make the transfer in the direction of the stronger side. For example, if the person has left hemiplegia, transfer him or her to the right whenever possible.
- Movements should be slow and smooth. The individual being lifted should be aware of what is going to occur and what is expected of him or her.

Note: Adapted from "Cerebral Palsy" by K. Inge. In P. J. McLaughlin and P. Wehman (Eds.), *Mental Retardation and Developmental Disabilities*, pp. 147–172. Austin TX: PRO-ED, 1992. Reprinted with permission.

Augmentive Communication

Neurological disease or damage that impairs motor movements can affect areas of the brain that control speech mechanisms or receptive and expressive language capabilities. Consequently, communication problems are frequently found in students with orthopedic and other health impairments (Copeland & Kimmel, 1989). With many students, speech and language therapy can improve communication abilities; when communication cannot be improved through therapy, augmentive communication systems can be developed and employed.

Augmentive communication can include any combination of the following: (a) refinement of the student's existing vocal and gestural capabilities into meaningful communication; (b) training in the use of manual signs; (c) training in the use of static symbols or icons, such as Blissymbols or Minspeak; and (d) manual or electronic communication devices that allow the student to communicate through pictorial cues, electronic printouts, or synthetic speech (Mirenda, Iacono, & Williams, 1990).

Communication Boards and Computers. These systems typically require a pointing response, although communication boards using eye glances can be designed. Pointing can be enhanced by adding various types of head wands, mouth sticks, or splintered arm–hand devices. Head and mouth devices usually include wooden or metal dowels from 4 to 12 inches in length that extend from the forehead or are held between the teeth. Instead of head wands, direct focus headlights, such as those used by doctors and dentists, can be used.

Electronic Communicators. Many students with severe communication disabilities need nonvocal systems of communication, such as communication boards, computers, or electronic devices such as the Zygo or Auto-Com. These systems can be adapted electronically or mechanically for students with limited motor skills. They can also be adapted by adding switches that allow independent use by those with motor or coordination difficulties.

Consider Teddy's communication needs. How can a therapist help him? A communication therapist, recognizing that his new school and regular class had different communication demands than the old, began to experiment with augmentive systems. Teddy eventually had a manual communication board that included the names of teachers, the names of other students, locations, daily activities, common phrases (*yes, no, please, thank you,* etc.) and letters for spelling out words not on the board. Teddy also used speech and gestures when he could. As Teddy became more communicative, his teachers were better able to see his academic strengths and weaknesses and were able to address them. Students were solicited to help Teddy with difficult tasks, and many responded. Gradually, the other students did not have to be asked to help Teddy, but instead thought of including and assisting him on their own. Although he was occasionally teased at school by some students, he was also defended and befriended by others. Perhaps best of all, his new friends began including him in their activities after school as well, such as sporting events, dances, and just hanging out.

Personal Assistance in School and Beyond

Personal assistance services are defined as "assistance from another person with activities of daily living to compensate for a functional limitation" (Nosek, 1991, p. 2) and could include assistance with personal hygiene, medical needs, meal preparation, housekeeping and household chores, community mobility, and other areas. Personal assistants allow people with severe physical or other health impairments to participate more fully in integrated settings, including education, employment, recreation and social activities, and independent living. During childhood and adolescence, the personal assistance needs of students with orthopedic and other health impairments are typically filled by teachers and aides in school, and by parents and other family members away from school. However, involving other students in personal care and assistance can be one way of orchestrating positive experiences between the student with the impairment and his or her classmates.

Family Guidelines

The family plays a uniquely major role with persons who have significant orthopedic and other health impairments. They often must play the role not only of advocate but also of caretaker and custodian. The amount of physical labor involved in the care, management, feeding, transfer, and mobility of young people with disabilities is enormous. Without the assistance of a personal aide or nurse assistant, many of these children will need to be unnecessarily institutionalized.

STUDENT KNOWLEDGE CHECK

Next semester, one of your students, Juanita, will be participating in a computer course and lab that is offered as part of the general education curriculum. Juanita is an upbeat young lady who has cerebral palsy and is legally blind. Because of her disabilities she cannot see, has limited use of her right hand, uses a wheelchair for mobility, and those who do not know her well find her speech difficult to understand. Juanita has never used a computer, but she has listened to her brother play games on the one at home. The computer course instructor, Mr. Robertson, is very concerned about how Juanita will access the computer equipment and is not sure about the best way to provide instruction. Although he will not come right out and admit it, he really believes that Juanita's deficits are so severe that she should not be allowed to participate in the class.

1. What would you do to help Mr. Robertson overcome his fears and concerns?
2. What tips would you give him on the instructional design process?
3. Provide three examples of some assistive technology that Juanita may find useful in the classroom.

SENSORY IMPAIRMENTS

Carolyn is a 17-year-old high school student with profound deafness and mental retardation who requires intermittent support. She lives in a suburban area with her parents, and she attends a public high school. Carolyn is included in general classes with her peers without disabilities for about half of the school day, where she uses an interpreter to help her with spoken information and class participation. Carolyn also uses a teacher's aide to assist her with content learning. For the other half of her school day, Carolyn is enrolled in a vocational training program sponsored by her school district. She works as a food service assistant in a local hospital cafeteria, and she is accompanied by a job coach. Her supervisor at the cafeteria is fluent in sign language, which enables her to provide direct feedback as Carolyn receives on-the-job training.

Carolyn has several friends who attend her state's school for the deaf, but she is not active in the local Deaf community. She enjoys swimming, arts and crafts, and bicycling. She independently uses public transportation to travel to and from familiar locations, including the mall and the hospital where she works. Carolyn's short-term goals are to graduate from high school, move from her parents' house into a group home and eventually into her own apartment, and secure employment in the food service field. She also wants to expand her network of friends and acquaintances, both within and outside of the Deaf community.

Another of Carolyn's goals is to increase her technology skills. She sometimes uses a teletypewriter (TTY) to communicate via telephone, and she is learning to operate the cash register at the cafeteria. She does not have typing or other computer skills, but she has expressed an interest in learning to use the Internet (especially e-mail).

Defining Sensory Impairment

Defining **sensory impairments** is a complicated task because of the wide range of effects that people with visual and auditory impairments experience.

Students Who Are Deaf or Hard of Hearing

Hearing loss is classified according to sensitivity to sound at various frequencies. These frequencies are termed hertz (Hz) and are measured according to loudness, or decibels (dB). An individual is considered to have typical hearing if he or she is first able to detect sound at 25dB or lower. Hearing within the 25–40dB range is considered to be a mild loss; within the 40 to 55dB range a moderate loss; within the 55 to 70dB range a moderately severe loss, within the 70 to 90dB range a severe loss; and more than 90dB a profound loss (Moores, 1996; Scheetz, 1993). An audiogram provides a graphic representation of the person's hearing levels in both ears and visually notes the decibel level across several frequencies.

Another important variable in hearing is the ability to understand speech and language, which is measured by the Speech Reception Threshold (SRT) and a speech discrimination score. Both of these are reported on the audiogram, usually next to or below the graphic notation of hearing loss. A high SRT indicates that the person needs speech to be amplified in order to understand it correctly. A low discrimination score indicates that regardless of amplification level, the person is unable to understand common spoken words. Such a person is likely to have substantial difficulties in communicating with others. This may occur despite a hearing loss level within the mild or even normal range of hearing.

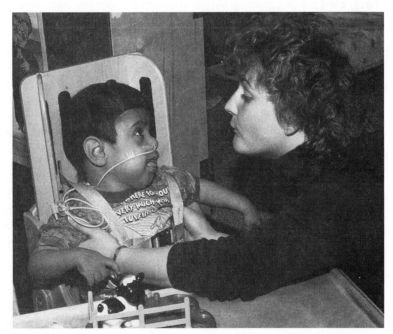

Students with severe disabilities are being served within the general education setting. What are the advantages for nondisabled peers when students with severe disabilities are placed into general education classrooms?

Several terms are used to describe people with hearing loss according to the amount of loss and their preferred communication modalities. The use of these terms may have little to do with the audiometric measurement of their hearing loss. These terms are defined here:

1. *Deaf.* Loss of hearing from severe to profound in which speech and language is not generally learned through the auditory mode, with or without the use of hearing aids.

2. *Hard of hearing.* A loss of hearing in which speech and language are learned through the auditory mode, with or without the use of hearing aides. This person typically feels more comfortable with the typically hearing world and uses auditory (residual hearing) and visual (speech reading) information to communicate successfully in most situations.

3. *Hearing impaired.* The Deaf community finds this term culturally offensive because it labels individuals with hearing loss as a disability group with implications of a "lessened" quality of life.

4. *Person with a hearing disability.* Appropriate "people first" language to which the Deaf community does not subscribe, just as a person from an ethnic minority does not identify himself or herself as "a person of Hispanic ethnicity" (Lane, Hoffmeister, & Bahan, 1996; Moores, 1996; Scheetz, 1993).

Classroom Accommodations and Instructional Techniques. As Mather (1990) noted, effective techniques for teaching students with hearing impairments are a function of the communication competence of the teacher and the student. This section will discuss a number of issues related to communication and instruction, including tips for classroom seating and instructional presentations, hearing aid evaluation and fitting, the use of assistive listening devices, auditory habilitation, and planning for adulthood.

Classroom seating and instructional presentation It is vitally important that students with hearing impairments receive both the auditory and visual aspects of classroom presentations. Obvious issues include good acoustics in a room, giving directions slowly, frequently checking the accuracy of hearing aids or other assistive devices, and correct positioning by the teacher. For students with hearing impairments to have a chance at success in general education classes, the learning environment must be set appropriately.

Assistive listening devices The selection of the proper hearing aid is one of the first critical tasks in helping a child with a hearing impairment. Parents and teachers must know what hearing aids will and will not do for a child. The hearing aid, though essential, is only an aid that takes advantage of the child's residual hearing. It is not a cure. It will not permit the child to hear "normally." For a hearing aid to work optimally, it must

- amplify sounds to a level that the child can hear;
- be tailored to the child's hearing loss so that frequencies that need to be louder to be heard are amplified more than frequencies that can be heard at softer levels;
- be designed to wear comfortably and at the same time be protected from damage; and
- be powerful enough to be useful, but avoid excessive loudness that can further damage hearing.

PRACTICAL APPLICATIONS

*FACILITATING LEARNING FOR THE HEARING IMPAIRED
CHILD IN THE CLASSROOM*

1. Provide optimal seating to allow full visual access to the teacher.
2. Use FM to achieve improved reception of the primary sound source in typical classroom noise.
3. Maintain full view of the teacher's face during lessons. Avoid speaking with back to class.
4. Use written support materials, such as outlines, key words, and assignments.
5. Use additional visual aids/media to supplement verbal information.
6. Assign a buddy/classmate who can help maintain child's attention to tasks.
7. Engage a notetaker to write down pertinent information discussed by class members or included in lectures, freeing the hearing impaired child to maintain visual contact with the speaker.
8. Allow previews and reviews of content material in academic support sessions.
9. Install sound-absorbing surfaces (carpeting, corkboard).
10. Check personal and classroom amplification daily. Keep extra batteries or other necessary spare equipment on hand.
11. The audiologist and classroom teacher should coordinate to ensure mastery of academic material.
12. Avoid simultaneously speaking and calling attention to a visual aid to allow student full access to speechreading clues and visual display.

Note: From *The Hearing Impaired Child: Infancy Through High School Years* (p. 192) by A. Maxon and D. Brackett, 1992, Boston: Andover Medical Publishers. Adapted with permission.

The selection of a hearing aid should involve the thoughtful decisions of a team directed by an audiologist. The team should include an otolaryngologist, a teacher, a hearing aid dealer, and the parents. This team effort should result in the best possible selection of a hearing aid for the child.

Once the hearing aids are fitted to the child, there is still much to do. The parents must learn, with the help of hearing aid dealers, the audiologist, and teachers, how to maintain and monitor the aids. Whether the child is fitted with a body aid or an ear-level aid, similar responsibility for care falls on parents.

Following is a daily checklist for the basic care and maintenance of a child's hearing aid:

- Check battery with battery tester.
- Check volume setting.
- Check earmold for clogging, cracks, or rough spots.
- Check tubing for clogging, cracks, hardening.
- Check case for damage.
- Check microphone for clogging.
- Check dials and switches for ease of movement or breakage.

PRACTICAL APPLICATIONS
TIPS FOR TEACHING STUDENTS WITH HEARING IMPAIRMENTS

1. Acknowledge that communication can come in many forms. Try to facilitate communication in the mode of communication preferred by the student who is hearing impaired. Structure settings and situations in which students who are deaf can initiate and respond easily.

2. Teach peers to initiate and respond to communication attempts. Make sure nondisabled students know how to communicate with their peers with hearing impairments. Incorporate the student's communication system within the classroom (e.g., sign and give verbal directions simultaneously). This will enable nondisabled students to become knowledgeable in the communication method and see it as an integral part of the classroom.

3. Teachers and peers should position themselves near the student to maximize the use of any residual hearing. Sit beside or in front of the student when interacting (versus behind) so that the student will understand that this is the way individuals typically interact.

4. Be aware that students differ in their ability to use their hearing. Individual abilities should be capitalized on.

5. Frequently check to verify that hearing aids or other prosthetic devices are working properly.

6. Avoid excessively prompting a student to wear hearing aids or glasses as this may increase the student's resistance to use them and/or signal that the device is not working properly.

7. The acoustics of the classroom should be noted and individualized for each student. Hard surfaces such as glass, chalkboards, and tiled floors reflect sound and produce extraneous sound. Soft materials such as carpet, fabric, and paper absorb and reduce sound. Desks that are staggered rather than in a row also reduce sound (as the bodies reflect the noise).

8. Locate classrooms away from high-noise areas such as cafeterias, gyms, or places with high traffic patterns.

9. Use functional activities and incorporate community settings into instruction. Community-based instruction can better enable students to unify concepts and apply their skills to new settings.

Note: From *Exceptional Individuals in School, Community, and Work* by P. Wehman, 2003, Richmond, VA: Richmond Consulting Group. Reprinted with permission.

- Check cords on body aids for breaks or interruption of amplification when cords are moved around.

In addition to the conventional hearing aid, the use of assistive listening devices (ALDs) can benefit the hearing impaired in a variety of ways. The term ALD refers to all systems designed to improve the communication ability of people with hearing impairments or to alert them to the presence of environmental sound (Kaplan, 1987). Sometimes ALDs have advantages over hearing aids in noisy environments and reverberative areas, or in hearing from a distance because of improved signal-to-noise ratios that facilitate understanding of speech and music. The impact of ALDs on independent performance and social integration can be dramatic, indeed.

ACCOMMODATING TECHNOLOGY

As time passes, assistive technology devices for students with disabilities continue to grow in power, usefulness, and affordability. These supports can provide practical solutions to common classroom problems. The range of high- and low-tech devices to help students with low-incidence disabilities complete an activity and make life easier is virtually endless. What follows is a selective overview of some assistive technology that may be useful for students with low-incidence disabilities. Many of these devices are commercially available or can be easily fabricated by any interested person who is resourceful and creative.

- Environmental control systems allow a student with little or limited mobility to control various things in the environment such as air conditioning, electronic games, and lighting.
- Augmentative communication systems are electronic and nonelectronic devices that allow a student with poor speech to communicate meaningfully with others.
- Portable note-taking devices allow a student to store material that can later be printed when connected to a computer.
- Computer access may be enhanced for a student by using special or modified keyboards or alternative input devices such as speech recognition programs, trackball mouse or touch screen, or pointers. Wheelchair or other seating systems can be customized to provide the student with greater body stability and upright position.
- Screen enlargement software can increase the size of objects appearing on a student's computer monitor.
- Audiotaped instruction allows a student to have access to the instructions, directions, or classroom materials in a usable format that can be repeated as needed.

Students with Visual Impairments

The question of defining the student with a visual impairment is very complex because there are many more differences than similarities. In fact, there are widely varying types and effects of visual impairment, and only approximately 10% of people with visual impairments are completely blind. The terminology used to describe the range and level of visual impairments varies widely. The generic term *blind,* as used by the general public, implies that the person receives no information through vision and learns mainly through touch or listening. The term *legal blindness* is quite different. It is used by many agencies and educational systems to determine whether an individual qualifies for services. People considered legally blind have a visual acuity of less than 20/200 with best correction (meaning that they can see at 20 feet what a person with normal vision can see at 200 feet) or a field loss of at least 20°. Regular unbiased assessments are needed to make decisions about appropriate interventions to enhance the academic performance and determine the effectiveness of previous instructional strategies of students with visual impairments. A systematic method of using whatever residual vision the student has (often enhanced by magnification) while providing alternative formats (e.g., braille, voice) for information the person cannot access visually enables the educational system to maximize the development of learning.

Incidence and Prevalence.   Prevalence data have been collected through the American Foundation for the Blind, Human Health Services, the National Institute of Disability Related Research, the National Association for the Visually Handicapped, and various university research and demonstration programs. U.S. prevalence rates determined from these data collection efforts vary dramatically based on disability definition and the age ranges studied. Data based on the definition of legal blindness and considering all age ranges yield a count of 600,000 persons. Perhaps the best estimation for the purposes of this discussion comes from data gathered in the Health Interview Survey administered by the National Center for Health Statistics (NCHS). NCHS estimated that 95,410 children under the age of 17 experience a severe visual impairment—often referred to as a "print disability" (Nelson & Dimitrova, 1993). Print disability implies that an individual, despite best correction, is unable to read typical print. Researchers from the National Center for Health Statistics contend that this figure will continue to increase in small increments, in part because of better medical technology that can save the lives of premature infants.

When referring to the amount and range of vision that a person has, terminology may vary. The generic term *blind,* as used by the general public, implies that a person receives no information through vision and learns mainly through touch or listening. However, legal blindness is very different. This term is used by some agencies and educational systems to decide whether an individual qualifies for services. People with legal blindness have an acuity of less than 20/200 with best correction or a field loss of 20° or more. Although a person whose acuity is 20/200 has difficulty resolving fine visual detail, he or she recognizes and identifies objects and learns a great deal through vision. Many people with legal blindness are very visual learners; those who are blind have little usable vision.

Several terms are used to describe vision that is significantly different from that of an unimpaired person. The term *low vision* describes a person who is "still severely visually impaired after correction, but who may increase visual functioning through the use of optical aids, nonoptical aids, environmental modifications and/or techniques" (Corn, 1980, p. 3). In some regions of the country, the term *partially seeing* refers to people who have a relatively mild vision difference that falls within the corrected range of 20/70 and 20/200 and does not qualify the person for services as legally blind.

Classroom Accommodations and Instructional Techniques.   The teacher's role in meeting the unique needs of the child with a visual disability is that of a mediator as well as one who can help the student overcome many challenges. For example, because the student may not be able to access information in standard ways, the teacher must be flexible and creative in determining how a student can most efficiently acquire information and skills.

Low vision devices   Many students will use special optical devices to assist them in using their vision efficiently. These devices should be individually prescribed by a low vision specialist, which is an optometrist or ophthalmologist who is trained in work with people who have low vision.

The most common low vision device is the student's own glasses or contact lenses. Some students' vision can be improved through glasses or contact lenses; for others, glasses do not make a difference. Although most students will wear their glasses or contacts all the time, there are exceptions to this. A child with extreme nearsightedness (myopia), for example, will often remove glasses to read material that is very small. This should be allowed if it facilitates reading.

Other optical devices may improve both near and distance visual function regardless of whether glasses are worn. For near vision tasks such as reading, hand magnifiers are the most widely used devices. Many shapes and sizes are available that are adaptable for individual needs: sturdy magnifiers that sit directly on the page may be useful for young children, and a small contemporary magnifier with a handle may be preferred for a high school student to carry in her purse. Sometimes magnification can be placed in a pair of glasses to free the hands for work such as sewing.

Let's take a look at how these devices have positively affected Maria. Until fourth grade, Maria wore glasses nearly all the time because they improved her visual acuity. Her glasses had tinted lenses, which helped to control sunlight because her eyes are especially sensitive to bright light. When she was in fourth grade, her ophthalmologist suggested that she try contact lenses, and she liked the idea. Not only did they make her visual difference less noticeable, but they also were colored blue, which helped make her eyes darker and control the sunlight. Now she uses a special pair of light-absorbing sunglasses when she goes outdoors. These glasses make it easier to adjust to increases in lighting.

Maria also has a condition called *nystagmus,* which refers to a rapid back-and-fourth movement of the eyes. Many people with low vision have this condition. Maria's sometimes increases when she is trying to concentrate. Sometimes people think that it is painful or uncomfortable. Maria's fourth-grade teacher would make her stop reading when she noticed the nystagmus, and Maria enjoyed this because then a friend would be assigned to read to her. When the teacher for children with visual handicaps told the classroom teacher that the nystagmus was not harmful or uncomfortable, Maria had to go back to doing her own reading!

Low vision devices offer a wide range of options to the student. They can facilitate normalization because the student maintains control of the visual environment rather than enlisting the assistance of others to enlarge or alter the material.

PRACTICAL APPLICATIONS

CHALLENGES TO TEACHERS IN HELPING STUDENTS WITH VISUAL IMPAIRMENTS

- Adopt a flexible attitude to allow for student accommodations.
- Maintain a consistently arranged classroom.
- Be creative in modifying or adapting curricula, activities, tools, and supplies.
- Stay as up-to-date as possible on technology advancements.
- Make use of school and community resource personnel.
- Listen to and incorporate student suggestions regarding adaptations that they need.
- Encourage opportunities for group work or shared activities that facilitate student interaction with peers.
- Cultivate support from the principal and other support personnel.

Orientation and mobility   For most people, the thought of having a visual disability raises concerns about movement and safety. Teachers often fear that a blind child in their classroom will be injured by running into furniture, or will require constant supervision when moving from place to place. This misconception occurs because people with vision are often not aware of how much information can be gathered through other senses. Some students will gather information automatically; others will need carefully planned instruction to maintain orientation and travel confidently. Most students who are blind and many who have low vision will benefit from specific instruction in orientation and mobility.

Some teachers wonder whether students who are blind will use dogs to travel within the school building and grounds. Dog guides are provided through private training schools across the country. Most training schools require that dog guide users be at least 16 years of age. In order to use a dog guide, a person must have developed independent travel skills through the use of a long cane. The student must be able to direct a dog appropriately and to understand concepts related to independent travel. Only about 3% of adults who are blind choose dogs as a travel aid because dogs require regular care and frequent activity. A student is unlikely to use a dog guide during her school years, although she may choose this option after she leaves secondary school.

Braille   Most students who are blind who have the ability to become readers will use braille, which is a system of reading and writing that uses combinations of raised dots based on a six-dot cell. This system was originally devised by Louis Braille in the early 1800s. Braille devised his system based on a tactile code called "night writing," which had been developed in the French army to send messages under the cover of darkness. The braille code includes symbols for the letters of the alphabet as well as more than 200 contractions and special forms that facilitate reading. In addition, there are specialized codes for music and mathematics.

The classroom teacher whose class includes a braille reader may be puzzled about her role in teaching braille. She is usually relieved to know that she is not expected to be the primary instructor for the braille reader: A teacher of visually handicapped children will work with the student to provide regular braille instruction. This is usually done through itinerant teaching several times a week. In some cases, the child who is blind will go to a resource room within the school building to work on reading skills with a teacher who is skilled in this area.

Most students who are braille readers will participate in reading instruction with their classes after early elementary school. After the student has mastered the major letters and contractions in braille during first and second grade, he can participate in the regular classroom for his major reading instruction. The itinerant teacher will continue to work with him on supplementary activities related to the braille code. It may take the braille reader longer to decode and read material than it does for the print reader. A very competent adult braille reader reads at 150 to 200 words per minute, in contrast with the print reader who reads 400 to 500 words per minute when reading silently.

Like their peers, children who are blind should have choices in reading material. There are several sources of children's books in both print and braille. These books usually consist of transparent plastic pages of braille bound into the printed book. These should be available in the regular classroom as well as in the school library so that the blind child is not restricted to textbooks. The National Library Service for the Blind and Physically Handicapped, which produces listening materials on cassette

COLLABORATION TIPS

There are numerous ways to enhance inclusion for students with low-incidence disabilities. For example:

- Participation in lunchroom with nondisabled peers and a peer model assigned to help facilitate inclusion.
- Participation in academic settings with a collaborative teacher helping to modify curriculum.
- Participation in academic settings through use of computer technology to facilitate new information.
- Participation in after-school activities as a helper, assistant, or participant similar to the way the young man helped manage the high school football team in the movie *Radio*.

The key is **participation,** along with training and modeling for nondisabled youth in the ways to be a good friend, helper, and coach.

tape, also circulates braille books for recreational reading. This federally funded agency loans materials at no cost to anyone with a disability that prevents him or her from reading printed matter. The teacher of children with visual disabilities can make sure that they have access to this and other supplementary resources.

SUMMARY

Teaching students with low-incidence disabilities can be very frustrating to some educators, particularly those who are not familiar with the vast array of classroom accommodations and instructional strategies that can help these students succeed. Supports and services must begin early in the educational experience of these students and continue into the community. Both special and regular education teachers can teach students with low-incidence disabilities by gaining knowledge on how to best meet each student's unique learning needs. This knowledge can be gained by working with families and keeping abreast of state-of-the-art practices specifically related to assistive technology, instructional strategies, and other classroom supports.

RESOURCES

The Center for Applied Special Technology (CAST) is a not-for-profit organization whose mission is to expand opportunities for individuals with disabilities through the development and innovative use of technology. CAST is accessible at www.cast.org. The resources available through CAST include universal design for access and for learning at www.cast.org/concepts/concepts_unaccess.htm, teaching strategies including adapting curricula at www.cast.org/strategies, and teaching tools at www.cast.org/tools.

Individual Transition Plans by P. Wehman. Austin, TX: Pro-Ed. This resource provides information on Social Security reform, assistive technology, vocational assessment, and programming and presents a number of transition plans.

SUGGESTED READINGS

Koegel, L. K., Koegel, R. L., & Dunlap, G. (Eds.). (1996). *Positive behavioral support: Including people with difficult behavior in the community.* Baltimore: Brookes.

Nolet, V., & McLaughlin, M. (2000). *Accessing the General Curriculum.* Thousand Oaks, CA: Corwin.

Wehman, P., & Kregel, J. (1997). *Functional curriculum for elementary, middle, and secondary age students with special needs.* Austin, TX: Pro-Ed.

WEBSITES TO VISIT

The Alexander Graham Bell Association for the Deaf and Hard of Hearing (AG Bell) is the world's oldest and largest membership organization promoting the use of spoken language by children and adults with hearing loss. Through advocacy, publications, financial aid and scholarships, and numerous programs and services, AG Bell promotes its mission: Advocating Independence Through Listening and Talking! www.agbell.org.

The American Foundation for the Blind —to which Helen Keller devoted her life—has been eliminating barriers that prevent the 10 million Americans who are blind or visually impaired from reaching their potential, since 1921. AFB is dedicated to addressing the most critical issues facing this growing population: independent living, literacy, employment, and technology. www.afb.org.

The Autism Society of America (ASA) site provides links to various organizational, university, library, government agency, and chapter World Wide Web sites. These links should not be construed as an endorsement, explicit or implied, either of the organization, university, library, government organization, chapter, method of treatment, or facility itself and/or the information contained within each World Wide Web site. www.autism-society.org.

The National Association of the Deaf (NAD), established in 1880, is the oldest and largest constituency organization safeguarding the accessibility and civil rights of 28 million deaf and hard of hearing Americans in education, employment, health care, and telecommunications. www.nad.org.

The National Multiple Sclerosis Society and its network of chapters nationwide promote research, educate, advocate on critical issues, and organize a wide range of programs—including support for the newly diagnosed and those living with MS over time. www.nmss.org.

The National Spinal Cord Injury Association (NSCIA), founded in 1948, is the nation's oldest and largest civilian organization dedicated to improving the quality of life for hundreds of thousands of Americans living with the results of spinal cord injury and disease (SCI/D) and their families. This number grows by 30 newly injured people each day. www.spinalcord.org.

The United Cerebral Palsy Association offers a clearinghouse of information on disability issues. Included are valuable resources on assistive technology for people with disabilities, families, and educators. www.ucp.org.

Closing the Gap, Inc., an organization that focuses on computer technology for people with special need through its bimonthly newspaper, annual international conference, and extensive website. www.closingthegap.com.

The National Technical Assistance Center on Positive Behavior Interventions and Supports is funded by OSEP of the U.S. Department of Education. www.pbis.org.

Rehabilitation Engineering Society of North America is an interdisciplinary association for the advancement of rehabilitation and assistive technologies (AT). This site provides contact information for the Technical Assistance programs authorized under the Assistive Technology Act of 1998 (PL 105-394), as well as numerous AT links. www.resna.org/.

Rehabilitation Research and Training Center on Workplace Supports. Sponsored by Virginia Commonwealth University's Rehabilitation Research and Training Center, this site is the gateway on disability and employment information. www.worksupport.com.

Research and Training Center on Positive Behavior Supports is funded by the National Institute on Disability and Rehabilitation Research of the U.S. Department of Education. www.rrtcpbs.org.

The Trace Center, located at the University of Wisconsin—Madison, focuses on making standard information technology and telecommunication systems more accessible to people with disabilities. www.trace.wisc.edu/.

REFERENCES

American Psychiatric Association. (1994). *Diagnostic and statistical manual of mental disorders* (4th ed.). Washington, DC: Author.

Augmentative Communication News. (1988, September). *1* (4), 14.

Carr, E. G., Levin, L., McConnachie, G., Carlson, J. I., Kemp, D. C., & Smith, C. E. (1994). *Communication-based intervention for problem behavior: A user's guide for producing positive change.* Baltimore: Brookes.

Copeland, M. E., & Kimmel, J. R. (1989). *Evaluation and management of infants and young children with developmental disabilities.* Baltimore: Brookes.

Corn, A. (1980). *Development and assessment of an inservice training program for teachers of the visually handicapped:*

Optical aids in the classroom. Unpublished doctoral dissertation, Teachers College, Columbia University, New York, NY.

Falvey, M. A. (1989). *Community-based curriculum: Instructional strategies for students with severe handicaps* (2nd ed.). Baltimore: Brookes.

Ficke, R. C. (1992). *Digest of data on persons with disabilities.* Washington, DC: U.S. Department of Education, National Institute on Disability and Rehabilitation Research.

Herr, S. S. (1995). Maximizing autonomy: Reforming personal support laws in Sweden and the United States. *Journal of the Association for Persons with Severe Handicaps, 20* (3), 213–223.

Inge, K. (1992). Cerebral palsy. In P. J. McLaughlin & P. Wehman (Eds.), *Mental retardation and developmental disabilities* (pp. 147–172). Austin, TX: Pro-Ed.

Inge, K., Flippo, K., & Barcus, M. (1995). *Assistive technology.* Baltimore: Brookes.

Ivancic, M. T., & Schepis, M. M. (1995). Teaching key use to persons with severe disabilities in congregate living settings. *Research in Developmental Disabilities, 16* (5), 415–423.

Kaplan, H. (1987). Assistive devices for the hearing impaired. *The Hearing Journal, 40 (5),* 13–18.

Knight, D., & Wadsworth, D. (1993). Physically challenged students. *Childhood Education, 69,* 211–215.

Koegel, L. K., Koegel, R. L., & Dunlap, G. (Eds.). (1996). *Positive behavioral support: Including people with difficult behavior in the community.* Baltimore: Brookes.

Lane, H., Hoffmeister, R., & Bahan, B. (1996). *A journey into the Deaf world.* San Diego, CA: Dawn Sign Press.

Mathur, S. M. (1990). Home and classroom communication. In D. F. Moores and K. P. Meadow-Orlans (Eds.), *Educational and developmental aspects of deafness* (pp. 232–254). Washington, DC: Gallaudet University Press.

Mirenda, P., Iacono, T., & Williams, R. (1990). Communication options for persons with severe and profound disabilities: State of the art and future directions. *Journal of the Association for Persons with Severe Handicaps, 15,* 3–21.

Moon, M. S., Inge, K. J., Wehman, P., Brooke, V., & Barcus, J. M. (1990). *Helping persons with severe mental retardation get and keep employment.* Baltimore, MD: Brookes.

Moores, D. F. (1996). *Educating the deaf: Psychology, principles, and practices* (4th ed.). Boston: Houghton Mifflin.

Nelson, K. A., & Dimitrova, E. (1993). Severe visual impairment in the United States, 1990. *Journal of Visual Impairment and Blindness, 87* (3), pp. 80–85.

Neisworth, J. T., & Wolfe, P. S. (2005). *The Autism Encyclopedia.* Baltimore: Brookes.

Nosek, M. A. (1991). Personal assistance services: A review of the literature and analysis of policy implications. *Journal of Disability Policy Studies, 2* (2), 1–17.

Pierce, K., & Schreibman, L. (1995). Increasing complex social behaviors in children with autism: Effects of peer-implemented pivotal response training. *Journal of Applied Behavior Analysis, 28* (3), 285–295.

Prizant, B. M. (1983). Language acquisition and communicative behavior in autism: Toward an understanding of the "whole" of it. *Journal of Speech and Hearing Disorders, 48* (3), 296–307.

Scheetz, N. A. (1993). *Orientation to deafness.* Needham Heights, MA: Allyn & Bacon.

Shapiro, J. P. (1993). *No pity: People with disabilities forging a new civil rights movement.* New York: Times Books.

Snell, M. E. (1987). *Systematic instruction of persons with severe handicaps* (3rd ed.). Upper Saddle River, NJ: Merrill/Prentice Hall.

Snell, M. (1993). *Systematic instruction for individuals with severe disabilities* (4th ed.). Upper Saddle River, NJ: Merrill/Prentice Hall.

Sowers, J., & Powers, L. (1991). *Vocational preparation and employment of students with physical and multiple disabilities.* Baltimore: Brookes.

Sowers, J., & Powers, L. (1995). Enhancing the participation and independence of students with severe physical and multiple disabilities in performing community activities. *Mental Retardation, 33* (4), 209–220.

Wehman, P. (2003). *Exceptional individuals in school, community and work.* Richmond, VA: Richmond Consulting Group.

Wehman, P., & Kregel, J. (2004). Functional curriculum for elementary, middle, & secondary age students with special needs (2nd ed.). Austin, TX: Pro-Ed.

4

Students with High-Incidence Disabilities

LEARNER OBJECTIVES

After you read this chapter, you will be able to:

- Describe the characteristics associated with students with learning disabilities and explain some instructional techniques and strategies that can help them learn.

- Describe the characteristics associated with students with speech and language disabilities and explain some instructional techniques and strategies that can help them learn.

- Describe the characteristics associated with students with mild cognitive disabilities and explain some instructional techniques and strategies that can help them learn.

- Describe the characteristics associated with students with emotional and behavioral disorders and explain some instructional techniques and strategies that can help them learn.

- Explain important aspects of (a) working with families, (b) collaborating with other professionals, (c) technology, (d) diversity, and (e) assessment in relation to students with high-incidence disabilities.

CHAPTER AT A GLANCE

Learning Disabilities

- Definition
- Prevalence
- Characteristics
- Classroom Accommodations

Speech-Language Disabilities

- Definition
- Prevalence
- Characteristics
- Classroom Accommodations

Mild Cognitive Disabilities

- Definition
- Prevalence
- Characteristics
- Classroom Accommodations

Emotional and Behavioral Disorders

- Definition
- Prevalence
- Characteristics
- Classroom Accommodations

Working with Families

Assessment

- High Stakes Assessment

KEY TERMS

adaptive behavior skills   103

comorbidity   110

curriculum-based measurement   115

emotional or behavioral disorder   108

externalizing behaviors   110

frequency modulation (FM)
    systems   101

functional curriculum   106

generalization   105

high-incidence disabilities   90

internalizing behaviors   110

intraindividual differences   92

language disabilities   98

learned helplessness   106

learning disability   91

metacognition   95

mild cognitive disability   103

response-to-intervention (RTI)
    model   93

speech disability   99

*M*rs. Colegate was a fifth-grade teacher who had never taught an inclusive class. So she was apprehensive when her principal told her that she would have a few students with disabilities in her class the next year. The principal assured her that this would be easy for her because she was a very good teacher and she would only be given students with high-incidence disabilities. "These kids are just like the low achievers you have every year," her principal had said. On the first day of the new school year, Mrs. Colegate was sure to give Ben (who had a learning disability) and Jeremy (who had an emotional or behavioral disorder) lots of attention and praise. She was pleased that they seemed to do fine and that she couldn't tell that they had disabilities at all. She thought that maybe her principal had been right after all and this wouldn't be too bad.*

But by the end of the first 2 weeks both Ben and Jeremy had become problems. Although she knew that Ben's IQ was average, he refused to do work in almost any subject but math and had taken on the role of the class clown. Jeremy was always behind on his work, never seemed to pay attention, and had already been in two fights on the playground. Neither appeared to have any friends. Mrs. Colegate was worried. She tried to give both students extra attention, and it seemed to help when she worked with them one on one, but she just didn't have time to do that very often.

*A*s the term implies, **high-incidence disabilities** refers to disabilities that occur most often. According to the *Twenty-fourth Annual Report to Congress* (U.S. Department of Education, 2002), the four categories of disability that encompass the largest number of students are learning disabilities, speech or language impairments, mental retardation (cognitive disabilities), and emotional disturbance (see Table 4.1 for the numbers of students served and the proportion of all students with disabilities in each disability category). The 5,067,666 students served in these categories comprised 87.7% of students served in special education in the United States during the 2000–2001 school year—more than seven times the number of students in the other nine disability categories combined.

High-incidence disabilities are often equated with mild disabilities. This assumption holds some truth: Learning disabilities or speech and language disabilities, for ex-

TABLE 4.1

Number of students served and percentage of total population of students with high-incidence disabilities in the United States for the 2000–01 school year.

Disability Category	Number of Students Served[a]	Percentage of Total Population of Students With Disabilities[a]
Learning Disabilities	2,887,217	50.0
Speech or Language Impairments	1,093,808	18.9
Mental Retardation	612,978	10.6
Emotional Disturbance	473,663	8.2

[a]Age 6–21.

Note: From the *Twenty-Fourth Annual Report to Congress on the Implementation of the Individuals with Disabilities Education Act,* 2002, Washington, DC: U.S. Department of Education.

ample, certainly present less severe limitations and necessitate fewer and less intensive supports than low-incidence disabilities such as deaf-blindness or autism. However, individuals within each of the disability categories have different characteristics and needs, and it may be misleading to think of high-incidence disabilities as mild. Many students with high-incidence disabilities have important limitations imposed on them that significantly affect their performance and behavior in school.

One commonality shared by almost all students with high-incidence disabilities is that their disabilities can be thought of as hidden. That is, there are no obvious, visible cues indicating that the person has a disability (this is not true for students with severe cognitive disabilities, who are considered in chapter 3). Although the hidden nature of their disabilities might appear to benefit these students, it may in fact pose additional problems. Because teachers and peers (and even the students themselves) may not think of them as disabled, they are often expected to behave and perform like everyone else. When they perform poorly in class, behave inappropriately, and/or have trouble communicating, they violate classmates' and teachers' expectations, often resulting in rejection (Cook, 2001; Cook & Semmel, 1999)

LEARNING DISABILITIES

Learning disability (LD) is not a very well understood construct (Hallahan & Kauffman, 2003). In fact, many people do not believe that it is a real disability (a joke that we have heard in some teachers' lounges is that LD really stands for lazy and dumb). Although a multitude of students, parents, and teachers believe that LD is very real, it is indeed difficult to pin down what exactly LD is and to whom the term does and does not apply.

Defining Learning Disabilities

Samuel Kirk is generally credited with coining the phrase *learning disability* in the early 1960s (see Kirk & Bateman, 1962). Although the phrasing that Kirk used was new, the characteristics he was describing had been recognized as educationally important since at least the late 19th century and had been previously denoted by such terms as *minimally brain injured, slow learner, dyslexic, word-blindness,* and *perceptually disabled* (Hallahan & Kauffman, 2003; Hallahan & Mercer, 2002). Kirk emphasized the concept of **intraindividual differences** in describing LD (e.g., Kirk & Kirk, 1971). That is, in some academic areas the achievement of an individual with LD is in the average or above average range (in accordance with his or her general ability or intelligence); however, in one or more particular areas (e.g., reading), someone with LD performs significantly below average.

During the foundational years in the field of learning disabilities (i.e., 1960s and 1970s), it was assumed that intraindividual differences were caused by an underlying deficit related to how the brain processed information, especially in regard to language (Vaughn & Linan-Thompson, 2003). The early emphases on intraindividual differences and process deficits are reflected in the federal definition of LD. The definition that appears in the 1997 Individuals with Disabilities Education Act (IDEA), which follows, has changed little from that used in the original enactment of the legislation in 1975 (then called the Education for All Handicapped Children Act, or Public Law 94-142).

(a) GENERAL—the term "specific learning disability" means a disorder in one or more of the basic psychological processes involved in understanding or in using language, spoken or written, which may manifest itself in an imperfect ability to listen, think, speak, read, write, spell, or do mathematical calculations.

(b) DISORDERS INCLUDED—Such term includes such conditions as perceptual disabilities, brain injury, minimal brain dysfunction, dyslexia, and developmental aphasia.

(c) DISORDERS NOT INCLUDED—Such term does not include a learning problem that is primarily the result of visual, hearing, or motor disabilities, or mental retardation, or emotional disturbance, or of environmental, cultural, or economic disadvantage. (IDEA, S. 1248, 2003, sec. 602(29))

One of the central components of this definition, that LD involves impairment of one or more of the basic psychological processes, is not directly observable. Therefore, no straightforward procedure exists for measuring LD as defined (brain scans may provide evidence of LD [see Richards, 2001], but it is impractical to conduct such a procedure on the millions of children that have and are suspected to have LD). The typical method used for identifying the existence of LD is based on the notion of intraindividual differences and involves identifying one or more academic domains in which an individual achieves lower than would be expected based on his or her overall intelligence. Most states currently use some type of discrepancy formula to identify an individual as LD. For example, if an individual is measured as having an average IQ (e.g., standard score of 100) but achieves significantly below average in reading (e.g., standard score of 70), he or she is considered to have LD in the area of reading.

Problems with Definition and Proposed Solutions

A number of criticisms have been raised regarding the use of severe discrepancies to identify LD. Fuchs, Mock, Morgan, and Young (2003) noted the following prominent concerns:

1. States use different formulas to calculate a significant discrepancy, which are often applied inconsistently within states, leading to variations in the prevalence of LD. Such inconsistency regarding who is identified as LD has led many to question the validity of the disability.

2. Recent research (e.g., Fletcher et al., 1994) has suggested that those identified as LD through an IQ–achievement discrepancy perform and respond to interventions similarly to a much larger group of low achievers who do not evidence such a discrepancy on tasks related to reading. Thus, there may be no rationale for identifying only the former group for specialized services.

3. Because achievement scores must be significantly below measured intelligence for a student to be identified as LD using a discrepancy model, educators must wait until a student's performance falls far below expected levels. As such, the discrepancy model has been dubbed a "wait-to-fail" approach that does not identify children for special services in their earliest years, when those services are likely to have the greatest impact.

4. A discrepancy between intelligence and achievement may in some cases be the result of poor teaching rather than LD—resulting in "false positives" (the identification of children who do not really have LD).

5. The intelligence and achievement testing involved in the discrepancy model are expensive and time-consuming and have little to do with the work students actually do in classrooms.

One increasingly popular alternative that circumvents the need for the discrepancy model is the **response-to-intervention (RTI) model.** This defines LD as lack of student progress in the presence of increased instructional intensity and support. Although different versions of this model exist, Fuchs and colleagues (2003) described the general approach for identifying a student with LD using the RTI model as consisting of five basic steps:

1. Teachers provide all students with effective instruction.
2. Student progress is monitored.
3. Those students making inadequate progress receive additional and/or more intensive instruction in their area of deficit.
4. Student progress is monitored further.
5. Students who still do not respond may be eligible for special education.

As we write this chapter, reauthorization of IDEA is being debated in Congress. Although some change in the definition of and process for identifying students as LD is possible, it is not yet known if any amendments will occur and what such changes might look like.

Prevalence of Learning Disabilities

Students with LD are the largest group of students with disabilities in U.S. schools. In the 2000–2001 school year, the 2,887,217 students with LD accounted for approximately half of all students with disabilities in U.S. schools (ages 6–21; U.S. Department of Education, 2002). In fact, there are almost three times more students with LD than there are in the next largest disability category, speech-language disabilities.

The proportion of students with LD has climbed steadily over the past 25 years. Indeed, Hallahan and Kauffman (2003) noted that the number of students categorized as LD has more than doubled since 1976–1977, the first year the federal government gathered these data. It is probable that a number of environmental factors, such as increases in the number of children living in poverty, have contributed to the growth of

LD. Others suggest that the stigma associated with the label of mental retardation contributed to the increasing numbers of children with LD (MacMillan, Gresham, & Bocian, 1998). It appears that students who previously would have been labeled as mildly mentally retarded may now be identified as LD.

There are also approximately three times as many boys identified as LD as there are girls. Cultural factors might play a role in the overrepresentativeness of males in the LD category. For example, Lerner (2003) suggested that boys tend to exhibit more troublesome behavior, which leads teachers to refer them to special education at a higher rate. However, males also appear more biologically vulnerable than females to a number of disabling conditions (Hallahan, Kauffman, & Lloyd, 1999).

Characteristics of Students with Learning Disabilities

Learning Needs

One of the hallmarks of students with LD is their heterogeneous nature. Whereas one student with LD reads 3 years below grade level but performs well in other academic areas, another student with LD in the same class may be able to read just fine, but requires special help in math and writing. As such, although the characteristics discussed here provide a general description of the needs of students with LD, teachers must look at each student individually to determine his or her unique pattern of strengths and needs.

Academic deficits are a fundamental characteristic of individuals with LD. By definition, as Hallahan and Kauffman (2003) stated, "if there is no academic problem, a learning disability does not exist" (p. 162). The academic domain in which individuals with LD most frequently experience problems is reading (sometimes referred to as dyslexia). Indeed, Denton, Vaughn, and Fletcher (2003) indicated that more than 90% of students identified as LD before the fifth grade have reading problems as their primary academic deficit. It appears that for many individuals with LD, reading problems are the result of a lack of phonological awareness—the recognition that language is composed of smaller units (e.g., syllables, letter sounds) (see Edelen-Smith, 1997). In addition to problems in reading recognition—the ability to decode words—students with LD also frequently experience difficulties in reading comprehension or understanding what they have read. Although reading problems are the prototypical characteristic of individuals with LD, they may also exhibit learning problems and low achievement in other areas such as writing, mathematics, and spoken language.

In the area of writing, students with LD often demonstrate severe problems in spelling, in writing legibly, and in composing written products. Students with LD often create writing that is less imaginative, organized, and complex than that of typical students. Problematic writing is sometimes called *dysgraphia*. Students with LD who experience low achievement in the area of mathematics (sometimes called *dyscalculia*) typically have problems with basic computational skills (i.e., addition, subtraction, multiplication, and division) as well as in applying appropriate problem-solving strategies when engaged in word problems and other higher order mathematics tasks. When communicating via spoken language, students with LD may also use improper grammar (*syntax*), not know the meaning of many age-appropriate words (*semantics*), and not use language appropriately or functionally (*pragmatics*). For example, children with LD who have problems with the pragmatics of language may speak to their teachers using the same language and tone with which they talk with friends on the playground (Raymond, 2000).

Related to, and perhaps underlying, these academic deficits, students with LD demonstrate deficits in motor abilities, information processing, and cognition. Some children with LD exhibit difficulties with gross motor (behaviors using large muscles and movements, such as running and jumping) and/or fine motor (actions involving small muscles and movements, such as writing and using eating utensils) activities. Movement may be linked to learning because our earliest knowledge comes from exploring and physically manipulating the world around us. As such, motor activities help provide us with foundational understandings of the world that influence later learning.

Processing problems are integral to the current definition and many conceptions of LD. It is often assumed that people with LD have problems with effectively processing the information their brains receive from their sense organs. For example, students who have auditory processing problems have difficulty discriminating between sounds and may misunderstand the first line of the national anthem to be "José can you see?" (Henley, Ramsey, & Algozzine, 1999). Those with visual processing problems may have problems putting puzzles together (Lerner, 2003). Children with LD often have difficulty determining the saliency of different auditory and visual inputs and therefore often seem distracted and have trouble paying attention (indeed, Gargiulo [2003] estimated that between 20 and 40% of children with LD display characteristics associated with attention-deficit/hyperactivity disorder [ADHD]).

Students with LD also have problems in at least two important areas of cognition: metacognition and memory. **Metacognition** refers to "thinking about thinking." Skilled learners devise plans about how to solve problems and think about how they can best learn. Students with LD tend not to use metacognitive strategies frequently or appropriately and may just sit in frustration when they do not immediately know how to perform a task. Students with LD also have problems with both short- and long-term memory. Related to their processing and attentional deficits, individuals with LD often have trouble recalling information with which they were just working. Because students with LD do not often think strategically when storing information, they may also encounter difficulty retrieving information they stored some time ago.

Social-Emotional Needs

Students with LD often exhibit problematic social skills (Nowicki, 2003). Some of the characteristics of students with LD (e.g., inattention, distractibility, difficulty perceiving and using language) that contribute to their academic problems also seem to play a role in the low levels of social competence exhibited by many students with LD. Probably because of these low social skills—in combination with the academic problems and physical/motor deficits experienced by many children with LD—these students typically are not well accepted by their classmates (Conderman, 1995). Given their low peer acceptance and academic difficulties, it is not surprising that many students with LD also have lower self-concepts than nondisabled students, particularly as related to academic ability (Bear, Minke, & Manning, 2002).

Classroom Accommodations for Students with Learning Disabilities

The characteristics and needs of students with LD have a number of implications for inclusive teaching. Specifically, inclusive teachers need to consider (a) adapting the general curriculum when appropriate and (b) using instructional procedures and accommodations that are shown by research to work and meet the individualized needs of their students with LD.

Curriculum

The 1997 IDEA amendments emphasized that students with disabilities should take part in the general curriculum whenever possible. This focus seems particularly apt for students with LD, whose intelligence is, by definition, within or above the typical range. As such, they might be expected to take part in and progress in the general curriculum in most areas. However, it is important to recognize that students with LD do have significant learning deficits in one or more areas, most often in reading. Reading deficits are particularly problematic in that they affect students' work in other academic areas. For example, students whose LD is in reading will have problems understanding written directions and word problems in math. In other subjects, they will have trouble reading the textbook and the teacher's notes. As such, even though they have the ability to do well in areas such as science and math, their performance may suffer because of their problems in reading. Because of the profound impact of LD, teachers must often supplement the general curriculum with remedial instruction so that students with LD have the opportunity to catch up with their peers.

Instructional Accommodations

Among the adaptations that Mastropieri and Scruggs (2000) suggested that teachers make to accommodate the needs of included students with LD are adapting the classroom environment, materials, instruction, and evaluation. When adapting the *classroom environment,* teachers should consider accommodations such as placing students with LD near the front of the class (to facilitate communication and improve attention), removing unnecessary distractions, and seating students with LD near helpful peers (to encourage positive social relationships as well as assisting students with LD with schoolwork).

Adapting materials so that critical information is emphasized can be accomplished by using audiotapes, videotapes, and/or computers to supplement and repeat critical instruction, and by highlighting key words and concepts in notes and texts. Materials can also be adapted so that reading and writing requirements are reduced. By having students with LD read only the critical information in a passage, for example, the teacher diminishes their frustration level without reducing their exposure to important concepts.

One primary concern when *adapting instruction* is to maximize the amount of time that included students with LD are actively engaged in academic learning. Mastropieri and Scruggs (2000) recommended using SCREAM variables (s̲tructure, c̲larity, r̲edundancy, e̲nthusiasm, a̲ppropriate pace, and m̲aximized engagement). By focusing instruction on academics—while also taking care to be clear (especially while giving directions), to repeat critical concepts, to be enthusiastic, and not to be too fast or too slow—teachers maximize the likelihood that students with LD will profit from instruction. Other straightforward accommodations regarding instruction include modeling metacognition by thinking out loud when problem solving, varying the presentation format by including visual aids and concrete manipulatives, asking questions frequently to check for understanding, and periodically reviewing important ideas and facts.

One way to *adapt evaluation* is to conduct informal assessments frequently and regularly. By assessing students' progress by regularly examining their work and giving short quizzes, teachers will know how effective their instruction is with each student, and, accordingly, whether they need to change their teaching for particular students. When devising tests for students with LD, teachers should design their assessments so that students' scores are reflective of their real ability, not the presence of LD. For example, a teacher might allow a student with LD with very poor handwriting to type an essay test on the computer rather than write it by hand. Students with LD who have attentional problems may take tests at a study carrel to reduce distractions.

In addition to these basic accommodations, Vaughn and Linan-Thompson (2003) proposed a number of instructional approaches that, on the basis of recent reviews and meta-analyses of the research literature, have been found to constitute the most effective instruction for students with LD, including the following:

- *Control task difficulty.* Make sure that students are not given work that is too difficult (resulting in frustration) or too easy (resulting in boredom and a lack of challenge).

- *Teach in small, interactive groups.* In this way students with LD can still be motivated by interacting with peers without getting lost in the crowd.

- *Provide direct and explicit instruction.* If students with LD must discover how to read or problem-solve on their own, some will never do it.

- *Teach the basics.* Skills such as phonemic awareness and writing speed are critical foundations for improving performance.

- *Provide instruction in higher order problem-solving skills.* Teachers must be wary that they do not neglect having students with LD apply their basic skills in complex problems and projects.

- *Provide modeling and instruction in using metacognitive strategies* (see Figure 4.1 for a discussion of strategy instruction). Students with LD must be familiar not only with different metacognitive problem-solving strategies, but also with when, where, and how to apply them.

Traditional teaching related to reading comprehension often consisted of asking students questions about what they just read. However, little instruction was provided for students to gain new strategies on how to better understand their reading. Strategies for improving reader comprehension can be grouped into the following areas (Bos & Vaughn, 2002):

- Activating background knowledge
- Predicting
- Generating questions
- Clarifying
- Summarizing
- Using text structure (e.g., narrative, expository)
- Monitoring comprehension (checking for understanding)

One simple example of a reading comprehension strategy is known as KWL, in which students learn to think about three questions (two before they read, one after) to improve their understanding of reading material:

- What do I know? (activating background knowledge)
- What do I want to learn? (generating questions)
- What did I learn? (summarizing)

FIGURE 4.1
Strategy instruction for reading comprehension.

SPEECH-LANGUAGE DISABILITIES

Speech-language disabilities are classified as affecting either the language or speech production systems (Owens, 2001). Language refers to the code (i.e., sound and symbol combinations) used to communicate, whereas speech involves the physical production of language.

Defining Speech-Language Disabilities

According to the 1997 IDEA amendments, a speech or language impairment is "a communication disorder such as stuttering, impaired articulation, a language impairment, or voice impairment, which adversely affect a child's educational performance" (34 C.F.R. 300.7). Speech-language disabilities are typically characterized as either delays or disorders. A speech or language *delay* reveals a flat profile of skills within or across communication domains—in other words, when all aspects of speech or language are delayed. In contrast, a speech or language *disorder* is evident when only some aspects of speech and language are affected. For example, an articulation disorder is present when a student has trouble pronouncing certain sounds but does not demonstrate problems in other areas of speech and language.

Speech-language disabilities are different from communication differences associated with students who are English language learners (ELL). Although some ELL students may also possess a speech-language disability, the communication and language problems experienced by ELL students are typically due to lack of mastery of a new language. To determine whether ELL students have a speech-language disability, assessment must occur in the student's primary language (Owens, 2001).

Prevalence of Speech-Language Disabilities

During the 2000–2001 academic year, the 1,093,808 students with speech-language disabilities comprised 18.9% of those served in special education under IDEA (U.S. Department of Education, 2002). Of these, 87.5% received educational services within the general education context for 79% or more of the school day. These figures indicate that in addition to speech-language disabilities being a prominent difficulty affecting the education of many students, most of these students receive the majority of instruction within general education classes. Therefore, all educators must understand the nature of speech-language disabilities and practical accommodations that can facilitate successful academic and communication development for these students.

Characteristics of Students with Language Disabilities

Language disabilities may affect understanding language (receptive language), using language (expressive language), understanding the quality and purpose of communicating (social-pragmatic functioning), and processing language. Students with *receptive language disabilities* may demonstrate deficits in understanding verbal instruction (such as directions or lectures), oral and written stories, and abstract language such as metaphors and idioms (Milosky, 1994). A student with a receptive language disability most often also possesses an expressive language disability because is it unusual for people to express more than they comprehend (Snyder, 1984).

Characteristics of an *expressive language disability* include limited or incorrect use of vocabulary and grammar (in oral and written communication), as well as difficulties with story structure, temporal sequence, causality, and pronoun use (Bashir, Conte, & Heerde, 1998). Educators may initially identify expressive language disabilities because students are difficult to understand even though their speech is clear.

Social-pragmatic language disabilities refer to deficits that interfere with students' abilities to communicate for social purposes (Westby, 1999). They may have problems identifying or maintaining the topic of conversation; appropriately shifting tone, voice, or content depending on who they are communicating with; comprehending or using nonverbal communication such as eye contact, vocal intonation, and facial expressions; and initiating or responding to peers or adults (Brinton & Fujiki, 1989). In addition, these students often monopolize conversations and provide tangential responses. Teachers may notice that children with social-pragmatic language disabilities may have problems understanding the social norms or unspoken rules of the classroom, as well as with changes in rules across different settings (Westby, 1999). It is important to recognize that deficits in social-pragmatic functioning can exist in the presence of intact receptive and expressive language skills.

Language processing disabilities are evident when a student demonstrates average knowledge of vocabulary and grammar but still has significant difficulties comprehending spoken language. Some students will demonstrate difficulties with auditory figure-ground (Friel-Patti, 1994). In other words, they demonstrate normal hearing acuity and can comprehend language within a small, quiet area, yet confuse sounds, words, and directions when there is competing noise, such as in a classroom. Other students may have problems comprehending information when the rate or complexity of the information increases and visual cues are not provided (Lahey & Bloom, 1994). These children may exhibit auditory memory difficulties and have problems with retrieval, which results in the use of circumlocutions (i.e., talking around a topic or struggling to find the right word; German, 1994) and communications void of rich vocabulary. Delays in responding in class discussion or to direct questions are common for students with such problems.

Characteristics of Students with Speech Disabilities

Speech disabilities affect the actual mechanism of speech production, the oral and nasal cavity and/or respiration (Owens, 2001). Disabilities of this nature include articulation problems, stuttering, and voice problems. Each of these can occur in isolation or in combination with language disabilities. *Articulation disorders* can be pervasive and related to physical anomalies such as a cleft palate or neurological impairment that lead to conditions resulting in limited motor planning or motor strength, referred to as apraxia or dysarthria of speech (Nelson, 1993). Other students may demonstrate articulation problems specific to a particular sound (e.g., "s") or set of sounds (e.g., sounds produced in the back of the oral cavity such as "k" and "g").

Stuttering is characterized by difficulties with fluency of speech production (Shapiro, 1999). Individuals who stutter may demonstrate stressful prolongation, repetitions, or hesitations as they begin to speak. They may also persistently block or stop on words that contain certain sounds. Everyone demonstrates problems with fluency of speech at times, particularly in the preschool years, yet most do not experience stress related to speaking. An individual is considered to stutter when the behavior includes signs of stress, avoidance of communication, or awareness of the problem (Shapiro, 1999).

Voice disorders affect the quality of the voice as demonstrated through persistent hoarseness, nasality, or problems with breath control. At times, voice disorders are related to medical conditions such as allergies, upper respiratory infections, neurological disorders, cleft palate, or hearing loss (Andrews, 2000). Voice disorders can also be related to vocal abuse, which is the persistent misuse of voice (e.g., yelling). In all cases, voice disorders require an assessment by an otolaryngologist (ENT) to determine whether the condition has a medical origin. The etiology of the disorder will determine the type of intervention required.

Social-Emotional Needs

Deficits in the communication domain can significantly and negatively influence behavioral functioning. In fact, up to 80% of school-age children with communication disabilities also demonstrate characteristics of an emotional or behavioral disorder (Baker & Cantwell, 1987). Therefore, educators must understand the nature and severity of a speech-language disability so that they recognize the need for appropriate accommodations, which will reduce the likelihood that students' communicative frustrations will develop into emotional and behavioral problems (Audet & Tankersley, 1999).

Classroom Accommodations for Students with Speech-Language Disabilities

Although students whose sole diagnosis is a speech-language disability do not typically require teachers to make significant changes in their curriculum, teachers can use a number of instructional accommodations to optimize the success of students with speech-language disabilities in the general curriculum. For students who are dually diagnosed as having a speech-language disability in combination with another disability (e.g., a cognitive disability), teachers should adapt the curriculum as appropriate to meet the specific needs of the student.

Classroom Accommodations for Students with Language Disabilities

Educators can accommodate many needs of students with receptive language and language processing problems by using concrete methods and integrating multiple modalities into instruction. For example, use of visual supports, three dimensional objects, and physical participation can assist students in comprehending, storing, and retrieving information (Culatta & Merritt, 1998). When completing written work or tests, these students benefit from learning how to identify and highlight key terms (Nelson, 1993). Very often students with language disabilities ask vague questions, such as, "What am I supposed to do?" Teaching children with language disabilities to identify words they need defined and to formulate questions specific to the task can help them understand their own needs and develop greater independence (Wallach & Butler, 1994). When designing classroom assessments, multiple-choice, matching, and fill-in-the-blank tests with answer banks should be considered because they provide response options for students, thereby reducing the demand for language retrieval.

Accommodations that involve modifications to presentation include speaking slowly, emphasizing and defining key terms, avoiding abstract language and sarcasm, reducing extraneous language, and modeling the use of mnemonic and memory cues (Merritt & Culatta, 1998). Mnemonic and memory cues use acronymns, rhymes, phrases, jingles, and finger tapping to remember information (Nelson, 1993).

Study guides and study skill strategies provide students with a template for learning that increases independence and comprehension (Nelson, 1993). SQ4R is an example of a study skill strategy in which students survey a passage/section prior to reading it, review questions following the section and hypothesize answers, *read* the section, *review* the questions, *revise* their answers, and *recite* key concepts (Nelson, 1993). The physical structure of a classroom can also be modified to accommodate the needs of students with receptive language or language processing problems. Strategies to reduce ambient noise include using work areas that support silent, independent work; installing carpeting; and placing coverings such as tennis balls on the bottom of chair legs (Friel-Patti, 1994). Teachers can also strategically alter their voice by varying the volume and intonation to match the lesson's objective and size of the group.

Some students benefit from the use of technology, specifically classroom or individual **frequency modulation (FM) systems** (English, 2002). **FM systems** provide amplification of the teacher's voice, over either classroom speakers or an individual headset, greatly reducing competing auditory information. By increasing students' attention to auditory input, FM systems can increase comprehension and retention of information.

Students who demonstrate expressive language and retrieval problems require different types of modifications that can be classified as supporting organization or output. Organizational accommodations include extra time to answer questions or complete written projects (Merritt & Culatta, 1998). One way that educators can provide extra processing time without delaying a class discussion is by asking a student a question and instructing her to raise her hand when she has the answer. Organizational accommodations may include visual, verbal, or auditory cues that remind students of a particular context to aid in retrieval of the information. For example, the teacher may model the use of finger cues by holding up a finger for each step in an assignment, encouraging the children to do the same. If a child forgets a step, the teacher can encourage and model the use of the finger cues to recall it.

Output accommodations pertain to the quality of verbal or written production. For example, when a student uses incorrect grammar, the teacher can validate the content as she reformulates the response correctly, highlighting key words or parts of speech the student omitted or misused (Owens, 2001). For written tasks, it is recommended that teachers provide instruction in outlining and brainstorming strategies (Culatta & Merritt, 1998). Learning to use supports such as dictionaries, thesauruses, and spelling and grammar checks can increase students' independence in writing.

Classroom norms are understood by most students without the need for repeated instruction. For students with social-pragmatic deficits, however, classroom expectations must be explicitly taught (Merritt & Culatta, 1998). For example, most classrooms require that students raise their hands to speak. However, there are usually times when raising one's hand is not required. Educators need to directly teach students with social-pragmatic language difficulties these differences and model or rehearse proper behavior.

Classroom Accommodations for Students with Speech Disabilities

The accommodations recommended for students with speech disabilities are typically less complex that those required for students with language disabilities. In general, all students with speech disabilities benefit from being presented with a clear speech model from adults. It is also important that students with speech disabilities are aware that educators are interested in the content of their productions, not just the quality or accuracy of their speech. This is especially true for students with articulation or stuttering disorders. When a student's speech is not intelligible, the teacher should indicate that she is interested in knowing what the student is trying to say and actively attend as the student attempts to repair or self-correct (Shapiro, 1999). For students with severe speech disabilities, the teacher can offer alternative modes of communication such as showing, drawing, or writing.

Fear of teasing may lead to students who stutter being especially reluctant to participate in oral reading activities. They can benefit from engaging in choral reading and can be paired with supportive peers for this task (Shapiro, 1999). Encouraging and validating their participation in group projects and providing alternatives to oral presentations should be considered. Finally, when a student is actively stuttering, the teacher needs to simply wait patiently (Shapiro, 1999). The educator can model slow speaking but should avoid telling the student to slow down or take a breath.

Some students may have severe speech disabilities that require the use of assistive technology, which can include low-tech supports such as a picture communication system or high-tech supports such as voice output devices. Students with assistive technology devices should have access to them throughout the day. Teachers will need to consult with a speech-language pathologist to (a) identify relevant vocabulary, messages, pictures, or icons for use on the assistive technology device; and (b) program the device to facilitate participation in class. To learn more about using technology for teaching students with high-incidence disabilities, see the Accommodating Technology box.

ACCOMMODATING TECHNOLOGY

One of the most influential technological advances in modern schools has been the microcomputer. A variety of readily available software programs can provide students with high-incidence disabilities the repetition and reinforcement they need to master critical skills. Using the computer is often inherently reinforcing to children and youth, and many programs have gamelike features to enhance the attentiveness and motivation of students while they practice and learn. As with virtually any innovation, the advantages of computers are accompanied by a set of new problems and responsibilities. Computers should not be perceived as a panacea or a substitute for good teaching. Students with high-incidence disabilities often exhibit problems with reading, typing, and other fine motor skills required for many computer programs. Software must be selected carefully to make sure that it matches individual students' skill levels. Furthermore, working at the computer requires monitoring and assistance, especially for students with high-incidence disabilities. These students often have attentional problems, are frustrated easily, and have little experience using computers. Without appropriate monitoring and assistance, many students with high-incidence disabilities may just sit and stare at the screen during their computer time—or worse, become frustrated and upset with their lack of success.

1. Why should students with high-incidence disabilities become proficient with computers?
2. What additional instruction and monitoring are required for students with high-incidence disabilities using the Internet?

MILD COGNITIVE DISABILITIES

Many teachers imagine a student with a very severe disability when they think of cognitive disabilities, often known as mental retardation. In fact, the majority of students in this disability category have relatively mild rather than severe cognitive disabilities, and their disabilities are not readily apparent.

Defining Mild Cognitive Disabilities

At the forefront of concerns related to defining cognitive disabilities is selecting the appropriate term for describing this population. The phrase that is most prevalent and well established, *mental retardation,* has been criticized by many as stigmatizing. Many now use alternative terms such as *cognitive disabilities.* Whatever it is called, the disability refers to impairments that vary substantially in severity and the intensity of supports required, which may make the use of any single term and definition problematic.

Nonetheless, a definition is necessary for the purposes of identification and provision of services. The definitions provided by IDEA and the leading organization for persons with mental retardation, the American Association on Mental Retardation (AAMR), are most commonly employed.

IDEA definition: Mental retardation means significantly subaverage general intellectual functioning, existing concurrently with deficits in adaptive behavior and manifested during the developmental period, that adversely affects a child's educational performance. (Individuals with Disabilities Education Act of 1997, 34 C.F.R. 300.7)

AAMR definition: Mental retardation is a disability characterized by significant limitations both in intellectual functioning and in adaptive behavior as expressed in conceptual, social, and practical adaptive skills. This disability originates before age 18. (AAMR, 2002, p. 1)

These definitions are noticeably similar, particularly with respect to the two features that are of greatest relevance to teachers: intellectual functioning and adaptive behavior. An identification of limited (or subaverage) intellectual functioning is typically indicated by an intelligent quotient (IQ) score of or below 70. Although these boundaries are intended to be somewhat flexible, an IQ falling between 50–55 and 70–75 generally indicates a **mild cognitive disability. Adaptive behavior skills** refers to the abilities that a person needs to function independently in everyday life. Deficiencies in adaptive behavior may refer to difficulties in social, communication, self-direction, self-help, community use, health, safety, work, and leisure areas. Although intelligence and adaptive behavior skills are related, it is important to view them independently for the purposes of identification and instruction.

States use a range of terms and definitions for students with cognitive disabilities. For example, Denning, Chamberlain, and Polloway (2000) reported at least 12 different terms used by education agencies, including *mental retardation* (e.g., California), *cognitive impairment* (e.g., New Jersey), and *intellectual disability* (e.g., Utah). States also differ considerably in how they apply measures of IQ in defining cognitive disabilities, with several states not using an IQ cutoff score at all (Denning et al., 2000). Despite these variations, virtually all states adhere to the principles of the IDEA and AAMR guidelines, recognizing that limitations in adaptive behavior must be present in addition to low IQ for a child to be identified as having a cognitive disability.

Prevalence of Mild Cognitive Disabilities

The prevalence of cognitive disabilities in U.S. schools is in the range of 1 to 2%. Approximately 610,000 students with mental retardation (the term used by the federal government) were receiving services across the United States in the 2000–2001 school year (ages 6–21; U.S. Department of Education, 2002). After LD and speech-language disabilities, it is the third largest group of children served under IDEA, accounting for 10.6% of all children with disabilities (U.S. Department of Education, 2002). An estimated 75 to 90% of individuals with cognitive disabilities have disabilities in the mild range (Field & Sanchez, 1999). There are about three males with cognitive disabilities for every two females (Larson et al., 2000). An overrepresentation of minorities is another characteristic of this population. In 2000–2001, 18.9% of African American students with disabilities were classified as having mental retardation, as compared to just 9.3% of Caucasian children with special needs (U.S. Department of Education, 2002). For more information on the representation of diverse students in high-incidence disability categories, see the Accommodating Diversity box. The proportion of students labeled as having mental retardation/cognitive disabilities has decreased over the past decades, in part because of changes in states' definitions. It has also been suggested that some children have been (inappropriately) designated as having a disability other than mental retardation (e.g., LD) because of the stigma attached to the label (Baroff, 1999).

Characteristics of Students with Mild Cognitive Disabilities

Learning Needs

Although there are characteristics common to many students with mild cognitive disabilities, it is important to recognize that each child is unique. Every child with a disability has individual needs that require adjustments in instruction and supports that are specific to his or her abilities and learning environment. In general, however, it is reasonable to view the learning needs of this population from the main components of the definition: deficits in intellectual functioning and adaptive behavior.

Whereas children with LD experience deficits in one or more, but not all, academic domains, students with cognitive disabilities have global intellectual difficulties. For these children, learning problems are typically apparent across the board—in reading recognition and comprehension, written expression, mathematical computation, conceptual and abstract thinking, and a range of other areas. Thus, it is not surprising that children with mild cognitive disabilities perform more poorly than students with LD and low-achieving students without disabilities on measures of cognitive ability and academic achievement (Gresham, MacMillan, & Bocian, 1996).

The main cognitive processes in which difficulties arise can be grouped into five broad categories: (a) attention, (b) memory, (c) generalization, (d) language, and (e) metacognition. Attention problems often cause students with mild cognitive disabilities to engage in learning tasks for such brief periods that little is gained from the experiences. Students may also experience deficits in selective attention, or an ability to determine which aspects of the experience are most important and warrant their attention.

Deficiencies in memory may be related to short-term or long-term memory problems. Problems of this kind are characterized by limitations in the ability to selectively process and store information. It has been suggested that poor memory in persons

ACCOMMODATING DIVERSITY

Students from culturally and linguistically diverse backgrounds have traditionally been overrepresented in certain high-incidence disabilities categories. In other words, a higher proportion of students from diverse backgrounds have been identified for special education than would be expected by chance. Interestingly, this phenomenon varies by racial/ethnic group and by disability. For example, although students with LD comprised 50% of the population of students with disabilities in the United States in the 2000-01 school year, 60.3% of Hispanic students with disabilities were categorized as LD (U.S. Department of Education, 2002). In the category of mental retardation, however, Black students are overrepresented; whereas 10.6% of all students with disabilities were categorized as mentally retarded, 18.9% of Black students with disabilities were labeled as such. Black students were also overrepresented among students labeled as emotionally disturbed. Most experts agree that a complex interaction of many factors plays into this varied pattern of racial/ethnic representation (Hallahan & Kauffman, 2003). Among the factors that likely play a role is the assessment process. Identification for special education typically relies on norm-referenced tests that contain items that may not reflect the experiences of certain groups of students. Therefore, low scores on these tests for some students from diverse backgrounds may reflect cultural differences rather than the presence of a disability.

1. Why might minority students be overrepresented among high-incidence disabilities but not among low-incidence disabilities?
2. What factors besides assessment might lead to an overrepresentation of minority students in high-incidence disability categories?

with cognitive disabilities is in part due to failure to use effective rehearsal strategies, or the "unconscious cognitive strategies students use to remember" (Utley & Obiakor, 2000, p. 30). One straightforward example of rehearsal strategies is the act of silently repeating information, such as a phone number, over and over in one's mind until it is memorized.

Generalization refers to the capacity to apply what has been learned to other settings and conditions. Persons with cognitive disabilities often have difficulty generalizing skills and knowledge that they have acquired under one set of circumstances to other new conditions and environments. For example, students who are successful in completing basic computations in the classroom using a calculator may still have difficulty applying that skill when using money in the community.

Appropriate use of language, both spoken and written, is a major part of any classroom environment. Because of problems encountered in structuring, storing, and retrieving information from long- and short-term memory, students with mild cognitive disorders frequently experience language difficulties. Examples of the types of problems that these children face in reading include difficulties recognizing and processing the phonological aspects of words (Kabrich & McCutchen, 1996) and delays in the comprehension and acquisition of vocabulary (Utley & Obiakor, 2000).

Metacognitive processes refers to the mental strategies that people use to approach and accomplish new learning tasks. As is the case for students with other high-incidence disabilities, children with mild cognitive disabilities often do not use learning strategies; when they do use them, they do so ineffectively (Borkowski, Peck, & Damberg, 1983). Difficulties may occur for these children when selecting, implementing, monitoring, or evaluating the appropriate strategy when confronted with a new learning task.

Social-Emotional Needs

The social and emotional needs of students with mild cognitive disabilities differ from student to student just as much as their learning characteristics do. Yet, extensive social skill deficits and emotional problems do exist among this group of students. Research suggests that children with cognitive disabilities have fewer social interactions with their peers and often do not know how to interact appropriately (Phillips-Hershey & Ridley, 1996). It is not surprising, then, that studies have consistently found that these children are more frequently rejected and less frequently accepted than are their peers without disabilities (Gresham, & MacMillan, 1997).

Closely tied to the problems of social and behavioral skills are the emotional needs of children in relation to their academic progress. Loss of self-esteem, motivation, and personal control are a few of the problems that children with mild cognitive disabilities may experience as a result of repeated academic failure. As struggling students with mild cognitive disabilities turn to adults for assistance, personal control and independence may be affected. Out of concern over low confidence and performance, teachers may find themselves providing excessive praise for mediocre work, assigning unchallenging activities, and supplying answers rather than instruction. Without careful monitoring, efforts intended to bolster self-esteem may lead to dependence on adults and feelings of **learned helplessness** in students.

Classroom Accommodations for Students with Mild Cognitive Disabilities

Curriculum

Most students with mild cognitive disabilities in schools in the United States today are receiving some portion of their education in segregated classes alongside other children with special needs. However, since the early 1990s the percentage of students with cognitive disabilities receiving their education primarily in inclusive settings has more than doubled (U.S. Department of Education, 2002). In 2000–2001, over 14% of children with cognitive disabilities were educated in inclusive classrooms for greater than 79% of the school day; and half of all children with this disability were included for more than 30% of the school day (U.S. Department of Education, 2002). Perhaps the most challenging issue related to inclusion involves striking an appropriate balance between functional and academic-based curricula.

A **functional curriculum** focuses on concrete, practical skills including a range of adaptive behaviors. Examples include social skills, money use, technical or vocational training, and community and independent living skills (e.g., household management, mobility, safety and health maintenance). As children spend more time in inclusive classrooms, a larger proportion of their education is usually devoted to the academic domains of the general education curriculum (e.g., reading, writing, mathematics). Given the difficulties that children with cognitive disabilities face in generalizing abstract concepts to applied tasks, special and general educators must work closely to ensure that opportunities for instruction in functional curriculum areas are maintained. This is particularly true during adolescence, when students begin preparing for transition to postschool settings.

Instructional Accommodations

The deficits in metacognition experienced by children with mild cognitive disabilities illustrate the need for strategy instruction with these students. Cognitive behavior modification and instruction in reading comprehension and mnemonic strategies are examples of interventions involving metacognitive skills. Mnemonic strategies involve teaching students explicit techniques (e.g., use of rhymes and acronyms) for remembering information. Examples of cognitive behavior modifications include students self-monitoring and self-recording performance. A critical aspect of these techniques is the teacher's modeling of the procedures while verbally describing the steps.

Behavior modification and direct instruction both involve monitoring of progress combined with reinforcement. Whereas behavior modification relies heavily on reinforcements such as praise and rewards, in direct instruction the focus is in explicitly teaching carefully sequenced tasks, each building on previously learned skills. Recall that children with mild cognitive disabilities experience impairments in attention relating to their ability to discriminate between valuable and irrelevant information. Strategies such as direct instruction, which purposefully limit the amount of information or concepts presented at a given time, reduce external distractions—thereby increasing student attention.

A critical feature of computer-assisted instruction and peer tutoring is that they provide opportunities for students to repeatedly practice their skills. Class time devoted to students working together or individually in these activities also frees teachers from being the center of the learning process and allows them to spend more time assisting students who need it most. Small-group instruction has other advantages for students with mild cognitive disabilities. For example, students benefit by observing the instruction the teacher provides to all the other students in the group (Shelton, Gast, Wolery, & Wintering, 1991). Another benefit of small-group instruction and peer tutoring is the opportunity for students to interact and develop social skills. However, successful inclusion requires more than having students with and without disabilities simply sitting and working in close proximity. Teachers must plan activities to facilitate positive interactions between these children and their peers in integrated settings (File, 1994). Gazda (1989) suggested that teachers use the following techniques to promote positive social interactions: (a) instruction in social skills, (b) role-playing, (c) feedback and social reinforcement, (d) modeling, and (e) practice.

EMOTIONAL OR BEHAVIORAL DISORDERS

By most accounts, students with emotional and behavioral disorders (EBD) represent one of the most challenging groups of students (Walker et al., 1998). Their inappropriate behavior upsets and troubles those around them, including their teachers, peers, and parents. Although most children and youths identified with EBD engage in aggressive and acting-out types of behaviors (Walker, Ramsey, & Gresham, 2004), others are withdrawn, disinterested, or fearful. Because their interactions with others can be very problematic, students with EBD have significant problems establishing and maintaining close, satisfying personal relationships (Ialongo, Vaden-Kiernan, & Kellam, 1998).

Greater emphasis is being placed using more technology within classrooms. How can technology be helpful to populations with special needs and students at risk?

Defining Emotional or Behavioral Disorders

Like many areas of disability, defining EBD is not an easy task, and different professional groups use different terms and definitions to describe this population (Forness & Kavale, 1997, 2000). The federal special education laws and regulations use the term *emotionally disturbed,* although **emotional or behavioral disorder** has become the most widely and generally accepted term in the field (Forness & Knitzer, 1992).

Problems of Definition

Underscoring the complex nature of the disability, there are many reasons why it is difficult to precisely define EBD. First, identifying inappropriate emotions and behaviors is subjective (Gelfand, Jenson, & Drew, 1997). There is no universally agreed-upon defintion of "typical" emotions and behaviors. Therefore, people often apply their own standards, values, and beliefs when judging the appropriateness of behaviors and emotions. Without a point of reference for what is acceptable, identifying the unacceptable is highly problematic. Defining EBD is also difficult because emotions and behaviors typically change with age (Rubin & Balow, 1971). For example, a 2-year-old throwing a temper tantrum after being denied a treat might be considered normal, but a temper tantrum from a 12-year-old for the same reason is considered inappropriate. The potentially transient nature of some problematic behaviors must also be considered. For example, any child or youth may display inappropriate behaviors in relation to stressors or conflicts in their lives, but such behaviors typically disappear after sufficient time has passed.

Dimensions of Behavior

Most definitions of EBD refer to several dimensions (Kauffman, 2005). First, behavior must be extreme. The frequency with which the behavior occurs, the intensity of the behavior, and/or the duration of the behavior far exceeds what is considered usual. Second, the behavior must be persistent and not only in reaction to situational events. That is, the problem occurs in different circumstances and with different people, and the behavioral problem has not been responsive to general approaches to alleviate it. Third, the behavior must be inappropriate in relation to the developmental level of the student.

IDEA Definition

As previously noted, IDEA uses the term *emotional disturbance* to describe this same population of students. The federal definition (Individuals with Disabilities Education Act of 1997, 34 C.F.R. 300.7) of emotional disturbance is as follows:

(i) The term means a condition exhibiting one or more of the following characteristics over a long period of time and to a marked degree that adversely affects a child's educational performance:

(A) An inability to learn that cannot be explained by intellectual, sensory, or health factors;

(B) An inability to build or maintain satisfactory interpersonal relationships with peers and teachers;

(C) Inappropriate types of behavior or feelings under normal circumstances;

(D) A general pervasive mood of unhappiness or depression; or

(E) A tendency to develop physical symptoms or fears associated with personal or school problems.

(ii) The term includes schizophrenia. The term does not apply to children who are socially maladjusted, unless it is determined that they have an emotional disturbance.

The federal definition was built on one proposed by Eli Bower (1981) but includes clauses in part (ii) that were not part of his original work. There is some controversy surrounding the definition, and much of the criticism surrounds the clause that excludes students who are socially maladjusted (Cline, 1990; Forness & Kavale, 1997).

Prevalence of Emotional or Behavioral Disorders

A relatively small percentage of students with EBD are actually identified as such and receive special education and related services. Those who are identified as EBD tend to have the most severe problem behaviors (Kauffman, 2005). Researchers suggest that 6% to 10% of school-age children have EBD (Anderson & Werry, 1994; Costello, Messer, Bird, Cohen, & Reinherz, 1998). Yet the U.S. Department of Education (2002) reported that during the 2000–2001 school year, the 473, 663 students identified as emotionally disturbed constituted less than 1% of students. It is apparent, then, that many students who are believed to need special services in this area are not identified. Certainly, EBD represents the most underidentified and underserved category in special education (U.S. Department of Education, 1998).

Characteristics of Students with Emotional or Behavioral Disorders

As with other high-incidence disabilities, students with EBD represent an extremely diverse and heterogeneous group. Their behavioral problems are evidenced in many ways, and their intellectual achievement varies greatly. In general, though, students with EBD have trouble with behavior, social interactions, and academic achievement. By definition, students with EBD display more inappropriate behavior and fewer positive behaviors compared with students without behavior problems (Walker et al., 2004). Moreover, they tend to experience academic difficulties that are at least related, if not causally linked, to their behavioral excesses and deficits (Dishion, Patterson, Stoolmiller, & Skinner, 1991). These problems combine in a complex manner such that one problem area reinforces and/or maintains the other problem area (Kauffman, 2005).

Learning Needs

Students with EBD generally have difficulty achieving in school. They typically have an IQ in the low-average range, but do not achieve at levels expected given their abilities (Kauffman, 2005). These students generally perform more than one year below grade level, earn lower grades, fail more courses, are retained in grade more often, and pass minimum competency tests at lower rates than students without disabilities as well as students with other disabilities (Cullinan, Epstein, & Sabornie, 1992; Koyangi & Gaines, 1993). Perhaps one of the greatest challenges related to their performance is school attendance. Dropout rates and absenteeism among these students are high (U.S. Department of Education, 2002). It has been estimated, for example, that 43% to 56% of students with EBD drop out of school, a rate almost twice that for all students with disabilities (Marder, 1992).

Students with EBD may also have LD. In fact, more than 50% of students with EBD have been found to meet at least one definition of LD (Glassberg, Hooper, & Mattison, 1999). Certainly, problems with attention, metacognition, and motivation that are prevalent in students with LD are also common among students with EBD (Meese, 2001). However, unlike students with LD, most students with EBD have significant problems in all curricular areas. One of the most recent emphases in identifying learning needs for students with EBD is in the area of language and communication (Rogers-Adkinson & Griffith, 1999). Studies suggest that the difficulties many students with EBD have using and understanding language contribute to their problematic behaviors, emotions, and academic performance.

Social-Emotional Needs

The behaviors of students with EBD can be classified along two major dimensions: externalizing and internalizing (Achenbach, 1995). **Externalizing behaviors** are directed outwardly and include aggression, disruption, overactivity, and yelling. **Internalizing behaviors** are emotional or mental conflicts that are directed inwardly, such as social withdrawal, anxiety, fearfulness, and depression. Students may demonstrate behaviors associated with only one of these dimensions or both. In fact, **comorbidity**—"the co-occurrence of two or more conditions within the same individual" (Tankersley & Landrum, 1998, p. 154)—of disordered behavior is the rule rather than the exception.

The most common types of behavioral problems exhibited by students with EBD are externalizing (Epstein, Kauffman, & Cullinan, 1985). Overall, boys tend to exhibit more externalizing patterns of behavior than girls (Kazdin, 1997), which may influence the overrepresentation of boys in this disability category. Given the range of problematic behaviors that students with EBD display and their difficulty developing and maintaining relationships, it is not surprising that most of these students, especially those who exhibit aggressive behavior, are rejected by the peers and adults in their lives (Ialongo et al., 1998). When aggressive students do make friends, it is often with deviant peers (Farmer, Farmer, & Gut, 1999).

Classroom Accommodations for Students with Emotional or Behavioral Disorders

Classroom accommodations and techniques for students with EBD must be geared toward both the achievement problems and the behavioral characteristics that characterize this population.

Curriculum

In most ways, the academic curriculum of students with EBD is much like that of students without disabilities. The focus of the general curriculum not only is appropriate for most students in this population, but, to the greatest extent possible, is also required by IDEA. However, to successfully progress through the general education curriculum, students with EBD often need additional and specific instruction in learning strategies (see, e.g., Instructional Accommodations sections in this chapter for specific learning strategies for students with LD and with mild cognitive disabilities) and social skills. Social skills should be a standard part of any curriculum for students with EBD. It is important to note that the effectiveness of social skills curricula is not conclusive, and research does not provide overwhelming support for its use (Forness, Kavale, Blum, & Lloyd, 1997). Researchers suspect that one reason that social skills curricula are not more effective for students with EBD is the generic nature of most curricular programs (packaged curricula delivered to an entire class or school).

Gresham (2002) suggested that social skills curricula for students with EBD be based on carefully and individually targeted behaviors. Moreover, the curriculum should facilitate the generalization and maintenance of social skills. To be successful, students must employ positive social skills in various settings, with different people, and in changing circumstances. Also, social skills instruction should be accompanied with repeated practice opportunities as well as consistent correction and feedback on students' performance.

Instructional Accommodations

The instructional strategies that have been shown to work with students with EBD are not unique (Landrum, Tankersley, & Kauffman, 2003); they are effective with most learners and include techniques such as the following:

- Continually assessing and monitoring progress
- Providing repeated opportunities to engage in new skills through modeling, rehearsal, and guided practice
- Applying new skills to everyday situations
- Matching the intervention to the individual needs of the students

STUDENT KNOWLEDGE CHECK

You are teaching an inclusive fourth-grade classroom attended by three students with high-incidence disabilities. Throughout the first semester of the school year, you have made a number of adaptations to your typical teaching for each of these students and, as a result, they are each making satisfactory progress after a difficult first few weeks. Your principal informs you that you will co-teaching with Mrs. Smith, an experienced teacher whose classroom is next door, for language arts next semester. As you co-plan your first unit with Mrs. Smith, you tell her that you have three included students with high-incidence disabilities in your class. Mrs. Smith says, "I don't need to know about that. I don't believe in those disabilities, anyway. I think that those kids are really just like everyone else and that if they really try, they can do just as well as any other student. The problem is that most of them just don't try hard enough."

1. How would you respond to Mrs. Smith to convey to her that high-incidence disabilities are real?
2. What types of instructional adaptations would you suggest that Mrs. Smith consider adopting when she teaches these students with high-incidence disabilities?

- Providing multiple opportunities to transfer learning to new situations
- Sustaining interventions over time (Walker et al., 1998).

Although these instructional strategies are important for almost any learner, teachers of students with EBD must be particularly strident in their application. Instruction must be very structured, intense, precise, and relentless (Kauffman, Bantz, & McCullough, 2002).

Successful strategies for teaching academic and social skills to students with EBD are built on a behavioral foundation that includes arranging the environment to promote a desired behavior and then reinforcing its occurrence (see Alberto & Troutman, 2003). ClassWide Peer Tutoring (CWPT; see Delquadri, Greenwood, Whorton, Carta, & Hall, 1986) is a good example of how the classroom environment can be arranged to promote and reinforce positive academic and social behavior. CWPT is an instructional program that makes use of small groups of students working together (Greenwood, Carta, & Kamps, 1990). Students work in pairs in which one partner practices his or her own individualized instructional task while the other partner encourages and provides feedback regarding the accuracy of responses. All partners have the opportunity to practice, and their results contribute to a larger group reward.

The advantages of CWPT over other forms of instruction include students' increased academic engaged time, opportunities to respond, opportunities for error correction, opportunities for help and encouragement, and motivation. In addition to increasing student performance, CWPT is attractive to teachers because it is relatively easy to implement and can be used with the entire classroom (Kamps, Barbetta, Leonard, & Delquadri, 1994). Rather than supplanting the regular education curriculum, CWPT provides the flexibility for students to engage in tasks at different levels while working together—making it an excellent choice for intervening in inclusive environments.

WORKING WITH FAMILIES OF STUDENTS WITH HIGH-INCIDENCE DISABILITIES

In school, effective collaboration among teachers can help to optimize the education that students with disabilities receive (for tips on collaborating with other teachers, see the Collaboration Tips box). Teachers should also work well with parents to improve the behavior and performance of students with high-incidence disabilities. Unfortunately, parents and teachers often see each other as opposing forces in raising and educating a child. Teachers often blame parents for being the cause of the problems exhibited by students with high-incidence disabilities. This tendency to hold the parents responsible for the learning and social-emotional difficulties of these students is likely exacerbated by the hidden nature of these disabilities. In the absence of obvious signs of a disability, some teachers may be quick to blame parents for their child's transgressions. Alternatively, parents often see teachers and schools as a primary reason that their children are experiencing failure and "running with the wrong crowd." Parents often feel that if teachers and schools did a better job, many of the problems they see at home with their children would go away.

Although instances of poor parenting and ineffective schooling are all too common, we must recognize that blaming and finger-pointing does nothing but worsen the situation (Bos, Mahmias, & Urban, 1999). Special education and the individualized education program (IEP) that is required for each student receiving special services in the United States is predicated on the notion that parents and teachers working together design the best education for each individual child. Although parental participation in IEPs is recognized by IDEA as critical, many parents are often overwhelmed at IEP meetings and choose to stop attending or to attend only as passive participants. Thus, teachers need to make efforts to involve parents actively in the IEP process as well as in the day-to-day education of students with high-incidence disabilities.

Perhaps the most critical guideline for involving parents in IEP meetings is that teachers truly believe that parents and families (and the students themselves) should be the primary decision makers in a child's education. The following suggestions for conducting IEP meetings (see Gargiulo & Graves, 1991) naturally follow from this guiding principle:

- *Explain terminology and avoid jargon.* Teaching, special education, and testing involve unique terms and acronyms that parents and family members may not understand. Avoid using these terms when possible and explain what they mean when they are used.

- *Acknowledge feelings.* Although time is limited, parents need to express their feelings and frustrations and to have those feelings acknowledged and considered.

- *Listen.* Do not come to the meeting with preconceived notions about the outcome(s) of the meeting. Allow parents to have real input their child's education, not just affirm decisions that have already been made.

- *Respect diverse parenting styles.* Teachers can present their viewpoints and provide resources for parents and families to make informed decisions. However, they need to understand and respect that parents and families may hold different values and make decisions that do not accord with their personal perspective.

COLLABORATION TIPS

Because teachers are generally used to being in charge of their own classrooms, co-teaching can be a difficult process—even when teachers genuinely like each other (but especially if they do not). In addition to being stressful for teachers, and unsuccessful co-teaching experience fails to provide included students with high-incidence disabilities the instruction they need to succeed. Gargiulo (2003) provided eight tips for co-teaching (adapted from Friend & Cook, 1992):

1. *Take time to plan.* Time for mutual planning is critical. Make (and stick to) a schedule for frequent meetings to co-plan.
2. *Share your perspectives on teaching and learning.* It is important to understand your co-teacher's beliefs, which dictate how he or she will teach.
3. *Attend to the details.* Before you start teaching together, agree how you will handle classroom routines (e.g., turning in assignments, leaving the room), discipline, and grading.
4. *Prepare parents.* Explain to parents that there will be two teachers in the classroom and present the benefits this can provide to their child.
5. *Make the other teacher feel welcome.* Give the other teacher some space (e.g., a desk) and allow him or her to decorate part of the room.
6. *Make sure both co-teachers are really teaching.* Sometimes the special educator takes on the role of a paraprofessional, working only with students with disabilities.
7. *Talk out disagreements.* Disagreements will occur. Don't take them personally, but resolve them professionally.
8. *Go slowly.* Like any relationship, co-teaching develops over time. Spend time reviewing what is working and what needs to be changed.

By following these eight steps, co-teachers will enhance their ability to effectively collaborate, thereby increasing the potential impact of their instruction on students with (and without) high-incidence disabilities.

- Your co-teacher always seems to have to leave school right after the last bell rings. What are some ideas for finding time to co-plan?
- Your co-teacher deals with classroom discipline much differently than you do (e.g., she demands complete silence during classwork and you like students to be able to talk with one another about their work). How would you handle this situation?

School–home notes are one method for involving parents in their child's education (see Rathvon, 1999). First, a target behavior is selected—it could be completed homework, time on task during class, or a particular behavior such as raising one's hand before speaking. The parents, teacher, and student then agree on a reward and a criterion for earning the reward (e.g., 4 of 5 days exhibiting desired behavior in a week). Through notes or a journal that is brought home by the student each day, the teacher communicates with parents regarding the student's behavior and indicates whether the student demonstrated the desired behavior for that day. When the predetermined criterion is met, the parents deliver the reward. This system (a) keeps parents informed of their child's behavior, (b) involves an extra motivator for students to engage in a desired school-related behavior, (c) encourages parents to reward positive behaviors at home, thereby reinforcing the teacher's efforts during school. School–home notes can be expanded so that the student's behavior is also monitored at home. When using this system, teachers should be very clear with parents that they should never punish children if and when they do not exhibit the desired behavior or meet their goal.

ASSESSMENT OF STUDENTS WITH HIGH-INCIDENCE DISABILITIES

Norm-referenced tests are typically used to identify students as having a particular disability. These tests are called norm-referenced because test makers administer the assessment to a large and representative group of people. The score of any individual who subsequently takes the test is then compared to that of others in the "norming sample" at the same age or grade level. In this way, educators can determine where a student performs in relation to others at the same age or grade level. However, because norm-referenced tests typically contain only a few items at each grade level—which may not reflect what the student is actually learning in school—they provide little guidance for teachers seeking to determine the effectiveness of their instruction for students with high-incidence disabilities.

Curriculum-based measurement (CBM; Deno, 2003; Shinn, 1989) assesses the growth of students in basic skills (e.g., reading, mathematics, writing, and spelling). It involves short (e.g., 1- to 3-minute) "probes" or quizzes that are curriculum based, in that teachers generate them from grade-level curricula. In reading, for example, probes can be made from reading passages from grade-level basal readers with which students are not familiar. Students read a passage out loud for 1 minute, and the number of words read correctly in that time constitutes their score. Multiple probes are easily generated (different passages from one or more grade-level texts) so that students can be quizzed repeatedly without scores becoming inflated from repeated exposure to the same passage. Because of the brief nature of the probes, teachers can administer them frequently (e.g., two or more times per week) without significant interruption of their usual schedule. CBM scores are graphed for each individual student, illustrating their rate of progress in comparison to a predetermined goal.

By frequently administering CBM probes, teachers are provided immediate feedback on the improvement of each student in core academic areas. When a student shows little or no improvement over multiple probes, teachers know that they need to change their instruction in some way. Alternatively, if the CBM graph indicates that a student is making adequate progress (e.g., is on track to meet the IEP goals), then teachers know that their instruction is effective and need not be altered. By increasing teachers' awareness of student performance, CBM has been shown to be associated with improved achievement for students with high-incidence disabilities (Fuchs, Deno, & Mirkin, 1984).

High Stakes Assessments and Students with High-Incidence Disabilities

States have begun to administer tests to students for the purpose of academic accountability; that is, monitoring the progress of schools and teachers in promoting students' proficiency in core academic areas. These proficiency tests are often referred to as "high stakes" because rewards and consequences for high and low performance are involved. The 1997 IDEA amendments and the No Child Left Behind (NCLB) Act, signed into law in 2002, mandate that students with disabilities participate in state proficiency testing. Specifically, NCLB indicates that only 1% of students with disabilities are allowed to take alternative assessments in lieu of the typical state proficiency test. Because the students exempted from taking standard state proficiency tests will be those with the most severe disabilities, it is presumed that all students with high-incidence disabilities are administered typical state proficiency tests.

However, both NCLB and the 1997 IDEA amendments, specify that students with disabilities can take proficiency tests using accommodations. Accommodations are intended to compensate for student's disability so that the student's true ability is reflected in the test score—but without unfairly benefiting the student. For example, if a student with LD is very slow reader (as a result of his disability), having extra time to take a math test containing many word problems may "level the playing field" with nondisabled test takers.

Thurlow, Lazarus, Thompson, and Robey (2002) indicated that the determination of whether a student with a disability receives accommodations, and what accommodations are used, is most frequently made by the IEP team. Figure 4.2 presents the five categories into which most accommodations made for students with high-incidence disabilities can be grouped, with examples of specific accommodations in each category. How students with disabilities are provided with accommodations on high stakes tests, and whether those accommodations give these students an unfair advantage (which might encourage school officials to identify more students for special education in an effort to increase school performance) will be a prominent issue for educators and policy makers to consider in the coming years.

Presentation
- Directions and/or items read aloud

Equipment/material
- Use of calculator

Response
- Use of scribe (someone who writes responses that student provides orally), use of computer or typewriter instead of writing by hand

Scheduling/timing
- Breaks, extended time on test

Setting
- Test taken in small group, individually, or in a separate room

FIGURE 4.2
Categories and examples of common accommodations for students with high-incidence disabilities on proficiency tests.

SUMMARY

This chapter provided an overview of four high-incidence disabilities—learning disabilities, speech and language disabilities, mild cognitive disorders, and emotional or behavioral disorders. Students who are identified in these categories (a) make up the vast majority of students with disabilities in contemporary U.S. public schools, (b) typically spend a large part of their school day in inclusive classrooms, and (c) are often not perceived as having a disability because of their typical appearances. Students with high-incidence disabilities frequently experience problems with academic performance, communication and language, and behavior and social skills. Curricular and instructional accommodations that can be used to address these areas of need were presented. Although students who are identified as having high-incidence disabilities share many similarities, educators need to be aware of the differences among these disability categories. It is perhaps just as imperative, however, that teachers recognize the great variability within each disability category and that each student will have distinct needs and require a unique instructional approach.

RESOURCES

Textbooks

Lerner, J. W. (2003). *Learning disabilities: Theories diagnosis, and teaching strategies* (9th ed.). Boston: Houghton Mifflin. This comprehensive textbook provides a wealth of information on theories and instructional strategies related to students with learning disabilities.

Kauffman, J. M. (2005). *Characteristics of emotional and behavioral disorders of children and youth* (8th ed.). Upper Saddle River, NJ: Merrill/Prentice Hall. This seminal textbook provides an excellent overview of emotional and behavioral disorders.

Merritt, D. & Culatta, B. (1999). *Language intervention in the Classroom.* San Diego, CA: Singular. This text provides a theoretical understanding of language processing, comprehension, production abilities, and demands across curricular areas. It also provides practical considerations and interventions for teachers and speech-language pathologists working with students with speech and language disabilities.

McLaughlin, P. J., & Wehman, P. (Eds.). (1997). *Mental retardation and developmental disabilities* (2nd ed.). Austin, TX: Pro-Ed. This textbook includes information on best practices in mental retardation and developmental disabilities and uses case studies to bring the information to life.

Organizations

Council for Children with Behavioral Disorders. The Council for Children with Behavioral Disorders (CCBD) is the division of the Council for Exceptional Children (CEC) committed to promoting and facilitating the education and general welfare of children and youth with emotional or behavioral disorders. www.ccbd.net.

Division for Communicative Disabilities and Deafness. DCDD is a division of the Council for Exceptional Children whose primary mission is to promote the welfare, development, and education of infants, toddlers, children, and youth with communicative disabilities or who are deaf and hard of hearing. http://education.gsu.edu/dcdd

Division for Learning Disabilities. DLD is a division of the Council for Exceptional Children consisting of teachers, higher education professionals, administrators, parents, and others. The major purposes of DLD are to promote the education and general welfare of persons with learning disabilities, to provide a forum for discussion of issues facing the field of learning disabilities, to encourage interaction among the many disciplinary groups whose research and service efforts affect persons with learning disabilities, to foster research regarding the varied disabilities subsumed in the term *learning disabilities* and promote dissemination of research findings, to advocate exemplary professional training practices to ensure the highest quality of services in the field of learning disabilities, and to promote exemplary diagnostic and teaching practices in a context of tolerance for new and divergent ideas. www.teachingld.org.

Division on Developmental Disabilities. DDD is a division of the Council for Exceptional Children that focuses on individuals with cognitive disabilities/mental retardation, autism, and related disabilities. It mission is to advance the educational and general welfare of individuals with developmental disabilities, the competency of educators engaged in the field, public understanding of developmental disabilities, and legislation needed to help accomplish these goals. www.dddcec.org.

Journals

Behavioral Disorders. The quarterly publication of the Council for Children with Behavioral Disorders.

Communication Disorders Quarterly. A quarterly publication of Pro-Ed associated with the Division for Communicative Disabilities and Deafness.

Education and Training in Developmental Disabilities. The professional journal published quarterly by DDD.

Learning Disabilities Research & Practice. The quarterly publication of DLD.

SUGGESTED READINGS

Alberto, P. A. & Troutman, A. C. (1999). *Applied behavior analysis for teachers* (5th ed.). Upper Saddle River, NJ: Merrill/Prentice Hall.

American Association on Mental Retardation. (2002). *Mental retardation: Definition, classification, and systems of supports.* Washington, DC: Author.

Bradley, R., Danielson, L., & Hallahan, D. P. (2002). *Identification of learning disabilities. Research to practice.* Mahwah, NJ: Erlbaum.

Cook, B. G., & Semmel, M. I. (1999). Inclusion and students with mental retardation: Theoretical perspectives and implications. *Special Services in the Schools, 15,* 49–71.

Forness, S. R., Kavale, K. A., Blum, I. M., & Lloyd, J. W. (1997). What works in special education and related services: Using meta-analysis to guide practice. *Teaching Exceptional Children, 29* (6) 4–9.

Gartin, B. C., Murdick, N. L., Imbeau, M., Perner, D. E. (2002). *How to use differentiated instruction with students with developmental disabilities in the general education classroom.* Arlington, VA: Division on Developmental Disabilities of the Council for Exceptional Children.

Kauffman, J. M. (2005). *Characteristics of emotional and behavioral disorders of children and youth* (8th ed.). Upper Saddle River, NJ: Merrill/Prentice Hall.

Lerner, J. W. (2003). *Learning disabilities: Theories, diagnosis, and teaching strategies* (9th ed.). Boston: Houghton Mifflin.

McLaughlin, P. J., & Wehman, P. (Eds.). (1997). *Mental retardation and developmental disabilities* (2nd ed.). Austin, TX: Pro-Ed.

Merritt, D. & Culatta, B. (1999). *Language intervention in the classroom.* San Diego, CA: Singular.

Polloway, E., Smith, T., Patton, J., & Smith, J. (1996). Historical perspectives in mental retardation. *Education and Training in Mental Retardation and Developmental Disabilities, 31,* 3–12.

Rhode, G., Jensen, W. R., & Reavis, H. K. (1993). *The tough kid book: Practical classroom management strategies.* Longmont, CO: Sopris West.

Silliman, E. R., & Wilkinson, L. C. (2004). *Language and literacy learning in schools.* New York: Guilford.

Stone, C. A., Silliman, E. R., Ehren, B. J., & Apel, K. (2004). *Handbook of language and literacy: Development and disorders.* New York: Guilford.

Walker, H. M., Ramsey, E., & Gresham, F. M. (2004). *Antisocial behavior in school: Evidence-based practices* (2nd ed.). Belmont, CA: Wadsworth/Thomson.

WEBSITES TO VISIT

The American Association on Mental Retardation. This site contains such resources as *AAMR F. Y. I.,* a monthly e-newsletter that keeps you informed about recent developments in the developmental disabilities community and the latest AAMR initiatives. www.aamr.org.

Dr. Mac's Amazing Behavior Management Advice. This site offers a wide array of resources for teachers and other professionals working with children with problematic behavior. www.behavioradvisor.com.

Center for Speech and Language Disorders. This site contains information such as answers to frequently asked questions related to speech and language disorders. www.csld.com.

The Learning Disabilities Association of America. This site includes a "For Teachers" section offering resources for teachers of students with learning disabilities. www.ldanatl.org.

The National Center for Learning Disabilities (NCLD). This site provides resources such as fact sheets covering a number of topics related to learning disabilities and reports of research related to effective teaching practices for students with learning disabilities. www.ncld.org.

The Project for Parents of Children with Emotional or Behavioral Disorders. This site contains sections on such topics as, What is an emotional or behavioral disorder?, Does my child have an emotional or behavioral disorder?, and Preventing and treating challenging behavior in young children. www.pacer.org/ebd.

The National Center for Stuttering (NCS). This site provides factual information on stuttering (The NCS Model of Stuttering) and its treatment (The NCS Treatment Program). www.stuttering.com.

The Arc is a national organization of and for people with mental retardation and related developmental disabilities and their families. The Arc's website includes a "Know the System" section, which provides information on state and local policies related to people with mental retardation. www.thearc.org

REFERENCES

Achenbach, T. M. (1995). Empirically based assessment and taxonomy; Application to clinical research. *Psychological Assessment, 7,* 261–274.

Alberto, P. A. & Troutman, A. C. (2003). *Applied behavior analysis for teachers* (6th ed.). Upper Saddle River, NJ: Merrill/Prentice Hall.

American Association on Mental Retardation. (2002). *Mental retardation: Definition, classification, and systems of supports.* Washington, DC: Author.

Anderson, J., & Werry, J. S. (1994). Emotional and behavioral problems. In I. B. Pless (Ed.), *The epidemiology of childhood disorders* (pp. 304–338). New York: Oxford University Press.

Andrews, M. L. (2000). *Voice treatment for children and adolescents.* San Diego, CA: Singular.

Audet, L., & Tankersley, M. (1999). Implications of communication and behavioral disorders for classroom management: Collaborative intervention techniques. In D. Rogers-Adkinson & P. Griffith (Eds.), *Communication disorders and children with psychiatric and behavioral disorders* (pp. 403–440). San Diego, CA: Singular.

Baker, L., & Cantwell., D. (1987). Comparison of well, emotionally disordered, and behaviorally disordered children with linguistic problems. *Journal of the American Academy of Child and Adolescent Psychiatry, 26,* 193–196.

Baroff, G. S. (1999). General learning disorder: A new designation for mental retardation. *Mental Retardation, 3,* 68–70.

Bashir, A. S., Conte, B. M., & Heerde, S. M. (1998). Language and school success: Collaborative challenges and choices. In D. Merritt & B. Culatta (Eds.), *Language intervention in the classroom* (pp. 1–36). San Diego, CA: Singular.

Bear, G. G., Minke, K. M., & Manning, M. A. (2002). Self-concept of students with learning disabilities: A meta-analysis. *School Psychology Review, 31,* 405–427.

Borkowski, J. G., Peck, V. A., & Damberg, P. R. (1983). Attention, memory, and cognition. In J. L. Matson & J. A. Mulick (Eds.), *Handbook of mental retardation* (pp. 479–497). New York: Pergamon.

Brinton, B., & Fujiki, M. (1989). *Conversational management with language-impaired children: Pragmatic assessment and intervention.* Rockville, MD: Aspen.

Bos, C. S., Mahmias, M. L., & Urban, M. A. (1999). Targeting home-school collaboration for students with ADHD. *Teaching Exceptional Children, 31*(6), 4–11.

Bos, C. S., & Vaughn, S. (2002). *Strategies for teaching students with learning and behavior problems* (5th ed.). Boston: Allyn & Bacon.

Bower, E. M. (1981). *Early identification of emotionally handicapped children in school* (3rd ed.). Springfield, IL: Charles C. Thomas.

Cline, D. H. (1990). A legal analysis of policy initiatives to exclude handicapped/disruptive students from special education. *Behavioral Disorders, 15,* 159–173.

Conderman, G. (1995). Social status of sixth-and seventh-grade students with learning disabilities. *Learning Disability Quarterly, 18,* 13–24.

Cook, B. G. (2001). A comparison of teachers' attitudes toward their included students with mild and severe disabilities. *Journal of Special Education, 34,* 203–213.

Cook, B. G., & Semmel, M. I. (1999). Peer acceptance of included students with disabilities as a function of severity of disability and classroom composition. *Journal of Special Education, 33,* 50–61.

Costello, E. J., Messer, S. C., Bird, H. R., Cohen, P., & Reinherz, H. Z. (1998). The prevalence of serous emotional disturbance: A re-analysis of community studies. *Journal of Child and Family Studies, 7,* 411–432.

Culatta, B., & Merritt, D. (1998). Enhancing comprehension of discourse. In D. Merritt & B. Culatta (Ed.), *Language intervention in the classroom* (pp. 175–214). San Diego, CA: Singular.

Cullinan, D., Epstein, M. H., & Sabornie, E. J. (1992). Selected characteristics of a national sample of seriously emotionally disturbed adolescents. *Behavioral Disorders, 17,* 273–280.

Delquadri, J. C., Greenwood, C. R., Whorton, D., Carta, J. J., & Hall, R. V. (1986). Classwide peer tutoring. *Exceptional Children, 52,* 535–542.

Denning, C. B., Chamberlain, J. A., & Polloway, E. A. (2000). An evaluation of state guidelines for mental retardation: Focus on definition and classification practices. *Education and Training in Mental Retardation and Developmental Disabilities, 35,* 226–232.

Deno, S. L. (2003). Developments in curriculum-based measurement. *Journal of Special Education, 37,* 184–192.

Denton, C. A., Vaughn, A., & Fletcher, J. M. (2003). Bringing research-based practice in reading intervention to scale. *Learning Disabilities Research & Practice, 18,* 201–211.

Dishion, T. J., Patterson, G. R., Stoolmiller, M., & Skinner, M. L. (1991). Family, school, and behavioral antecedents to early adolescent involvement with antisocial peers. *Developmental Psychology, 27,* 172–180.

Edelen-Smith, P. (1997). How now brown cow: Phoneme awareness activities for collaborative classrooms. *Intervention in School and Clinic, 33,* 103–111.

English, K. (2002). Audiologic rehabilitation services in the school setting. In R. Schow & M. Nerbonne (Eds.), *Introduction to audiologic rehabilitation* (4th ed., pp. 247–274). Boston: Allyn & Bacon.

Epstein, M. H., Kauffman, J. M., & Cullinan, D. (1985). Patterns of maladjustment among the behaviorally disordered, II: Boys aged 6–11, boys aged 12–18, girls aged 6–11, girls aged 12–18. *Behavioral Disorders, 10,* 125–135.

Farmer, T. W., Farmer, E. M. Z., & Gut, D. (1999). Implications of social development research for school based intervention for aggressive youth with emotional and behavioral disorders. *Journal of Emotional and Behavioral Disorders, 7,* 130–136.

Field, M. A., & Sanchez, V. A. (1999). *Equal treatment for people with mental retardation: Having and raising children.* Cambridge, MA: Harvard University Press.

File, N. (1994). Children's play, teacher-child interactions, and teacher beliefs in integrated early childhood programs. *Early Childhood Research Quarterly, 9,* 223–240.

Fletcher, J. M., Shaywitz, S. E., Shankweiler, D. P., Katz, L., Liberman, I. Y., Stuebing, K. K., et al., (1994). Cognitive profiles of reading disability: Comparisons of discrepancy and low achievement definitions. *Journal of Educational Psychology, 86*(1), 6–23.

Forness, S. R., & Kavale, K. A. (1997). Defining EBD in school and related services. In J. W. Lloyd, E. J. Kameenui, & D. Chard (Eds.), *Issues in educating students with disabilities* (pp. 45–61). Mahwah, NJ: Erlbaum.

Forness, S. R., & Kavale, K. A. (2000). EBD: Background and current status of E/BD terminology and definition. *Behavioral Disorders, 25,* 264–269.

Forness, S. R., Kavale, K. A., Blum, I. M., & Lloyd, J. W. (1997). What works in special education and related services: Using meta-analysis to guide practice. *Teaching Exceptional Children, 29,* 4–9.

Forness, S. R., & Knitzer, J. (1992). A new proposed definition and terminology to replace "Serious Emotional Disturbance" in Individuals with Disabilities Education Act. *School Psychology Review, 21,* 12–20.

Friel-Patti, S. (1994). Auditory linguistic processing and language learning. In G. Wallach & K. Butler (Eds.), *Language learning disabilities in school-age children and adolescents: Some principles and applications* (pp. 373–392). New York: Merrill.

Friend, M., & Cook, L. (1992). The new mainstreaming: How it really works. *Instructor, 101*(7), 30, 32, 34, 36.

Fuchs, D., Mock, D., Morgan, P. L., & Young, C. L. (2003). Responsiveness-to-intervention: Definitions, evidence, and implications for the learning disabilities construct. *Learning Disabilities Research & Practice, 18,* 157–171.

Fuchs, L. S., Deno, S., & Mirkin, P. (1984). Effects of frequent curriculum-based measurement and evaluation on pedagogy, student achievement, and student awareness of learning. *American Educational Research Journal, 21,* 449–460.

Gargiulo, R. M. (2003). *Special education in contemporary society: An introduction to exceptionality.* Belmont, CA: Wadsworth/Thomson Learning.

Gargiulo, R., & Graves, S. (1991). Parental feelings: The forgotten component when working with parents of handicapped preschool students. *Childhood Education, 67,* 176–178.

Gazda, G. M. (1989). *Group counseling: A developmental approach* (4th ed.) Boston: Allyn & Bacon.

Gelfand, D. M., Jenson, W. R., & Drew, C. J. (1997). *Understanding child behavior disorders* (3rd ed.). New York: Holt.

German, D. (1994). Word finding difficulties in children and adolescents. In G. Wallach & K. Butler (Eds.), *Language learning disabilities in school-age children and adolescents: Some principles and applications* (pp. 323–347). New York: Merrill.

Glassberg. L. A., Hooper, S. R., & Mattison, R. E. (1999). Prevalence of learning disabilities at enrollment in special education students with behavioral disorders. *Behavioral Disorders, 25,* 9–21.

Greenwood, C. R., Carta, J. J., & Kamps, D. (1990). Teacher-mediated versus peer-mediated instruction: A review of educational advantages and disadvantages. In H. C. Foot, M. J. Morgan, & R. H. Shute (Eds.), *Children helping children* (pp. 177–205). Chichester, England: Wiley.

Gresham, F. M. (2002). Teaching social skills to high-risk children and youth: Preventive and remedial strategies. In M. R. Shinn, H. H. Walker, & G. Stoner (Eds.), *Interventions for academic and behavior problems II: Preventive and remedial approaches* (pp. 403–432).

Bethesda, MD: National Association of School Psychologists.

Gresham, F. M., & MacMillan, D. L. (1997). Social competence and affective characteristics of students with mild disabilities. *Review of Educational Research, 67,* 377–415.

Gresham, F. M., MacMillan, D. L., & Bocian, K. M. (1996). Learning disabilities, low achievement, and mild mental retardation: More alike than different? *Journal of Learning Disabilities, 29,* 570–581.

Hallahan, D. P., & Kauffman, J. M. (2003). *Exceptional learners: Introduction to special education* (9th ed.). Boston: Allyn & Bacon.

Hallahan, D. P., Kauffman, J. M., & Lloyd, J. W. (1999). *Introduction to learning disabilities* (2nd ed.). Boston: Allyn & Bacon.

Hallahan, D. P., Mercer, C. D. (2002). Learning disabilities: Historical perspectives. In R. Bradley, L. Danielson, L., & D. P. Hallahan (Eds.), *Identification of learning disabilities: Research to practice* (pp. 1–67). Mahwah, NJ: Erlbaum.

Henley, M., Ramsey, R. S., & Algozzine, R. F. (1999). *Characteristics of and strategies for teaching students with mild disabilities* (3rd ed.). Boston: Allyn & Bacon.

Ialongo, N. S., Vaden-Kiernan, N., & Kellam, S. (1998). Early peer rejection and aggression: Longitudinal relations with adolescent behavior. *Journal of Developmental and Physical Disabilities, 10,* 199–213.

Individuals with Disabilities Education Act Amendments of 1997, 20 U.S.C. 1400 *et seq.*

Kabrich, M., & McCutchen, D. (1996). Phonemic support in comprehension: Comparisons between children with and without mild disabilities. *American Journal on Mental Retardation, 5,* 510–527.

Kamps, D. M, Barbetta, P., Leonard, B., & Delquadri, J. C. (1994). Classwide peer tutoring: An integration strategy to improve reading skills and promote peer interactions among students with autism and general education peers. *Journal of Applied Behavior Analysis, 27,* 49–61.

Kauffman, J. M. (2005). *Characteristics of emotional and behavioral disorders of children and youth* (8th ed.). Upper Saddle River, NJ: Merrill/Prentice Hall.

Kauffman, J. M., Bantz, J., & McCullough, J. (2002). Separate and better: A special public school class for students with emotional and behavioral disorders. *Exceptionality, 10,* 149–170.

Kazdin, A. E. (1997). Conduct disorder. In R. J. Morris & T. R. Kratochwill (Eds.), *The practice of child therapy* (3rd ed., pp. 199–270). Boston: Allyn & Bacon.

Kirk, S. A., & Bateman, B. (1962). Diagnosis and remediation of learning disabilities. *Exceptional Children, 29,* 73–78.

Kirk, S. A., & Kirk, W. D. (1971). *Psycholinguistic learning disabilities: Diagnosis and remediation.* Urbana: University of Illinois.

Koyangi, C., & Gaines, S. (1993). *All systems failure: An examination of the results of neglecting the needs of children with serious emotional disturbance.* Washington, DC: National Mental Health Association.

Lahey, M., & Bloom, L. (1994). Variability and language learning disabilities. In G. Wallach & K. Bulter (Eds.), *Language learning disabilities in school-age children and adolescents: Some principles and applications* (pp. 354–372). New York: Merrill.

Landrum, T. J., Tankersley, M., & Kauffman, J. M. (2003). What's special about special education for students with emotional and behavioral disorders. *Journal of Special Education, 37,* 148–156.

Larson, S. A., Lakin, K. C., Anderson, L., Kwak, N., Lee, J. H., & Anderson, D. (2000). Prevalence of mental retardation and/or development disabilities: Analysis of the 1994/1995 NHIS-D. *MR/DD Data Brief, 1*(2). Minneapolis: University of Minnesota, Institute on Community Integration, Research and Training Center on Community Living.

Lerner, J. W. (2003). *Learning disabilities: Theories, diagnosis, and teaching strategies* (9th ed.). Boston: Houghton Mifflin.

MacMillian, D. L., Gresham, F. M. & Bocian, K. M. (1998). Discrepancy between definitions of learning disabilities and school practices: An empirical investigation. *Journal of Learning Disabilities, 31,* 314–326.

Marder, C. (1992). Education after secondary school. In M. Wagner, R. D'Amico, C. Marder, L. Newman, & J. Blackorby (Eds.), *What happens next? Trends in postschool outcomes of youth with disabilities. The second comprehensive report from the National Longitudinal Transition Study of Special Education Students* (pp. 3–39). Menlo Park, CA: SRI International.

Mastropieri, M. A., & Scruggs, T. E. (2000). *The inclusive classroom: Strategies for effective instruction.* Upper Saddle River, NJ: Merrill/Prentice Hall.

Meese, R. L. (2001). *Teaching learners with mild disabilities: Integrating research and practice* (2nd ed.). Belmont, CA: Wadsworth.

Merritt, D., & Culatta, B. (1998). Dynamic assessment, language processes, and curricular content. In D. Merritt & B Culatta (Eds.), *Language intervention in the classroom* (pp. 99–142). San Diego, CA: Singular.

Milosky, L. (1994). Nonliteral language abilities: Seeing the forest for the trees. In G. Wallach & K. Butler (Eds.), *Language learning disabilities in school-age children and adolescents: Some principles and applications* (pp. 275–303). New York: Merrill.

Nelson, N. (1993). *Childhood language disorders in context: Infancy Through adolescence.* New York: Merrill.

Nowicki, E. A. (2003). A meta-analysis of the social competence of children with learning disabilities compared to classmates of low and average to high achievement. *Learning Disability Quarterly, 26,* 171–188.

Owens, R. (2001). *Language development: An introduction* (5th ed.). Boston: Allyn & Bacon.

Phillips-Hershey, E. H., & Ridley, L. L. (1996). Strategies for acceptance of diversity with mental retardation. *Elementary School Guidance and Counseling, 30,* 282–291.

Rathvon, N. (1999). *Effective school interventions: Strategies for enhancing academic achievement and social competence.* New York: Guilford.

Raymond, E. B. (2000). *Learners with mild disabilities: A characteristics approach.* Boston: Allyn & Bacon.

Richards, T. L. (2001). Functional magnetic resonance imaging and spectroscopic imaging of the brain: Application of fMRI and fMRS to reading disabilities and education. *Learning Disability Quarterly, 24,* 189–203.

Rogers-Adkinson, D., & Griffith, P. L. (Eds.). (1999). *Assessment and intervention of communication and psychiatric disorders in children.* San Diego, CA: Singular.

Rubin, R. A., & Balow, B. (1971). Learning and behavior disorders: A longitudinal study. *Exceptional Children, 38,* 293–299.

Shapiro, D. (1999). *Stuttering intervention: A collaborative journey to fluency freedom.* Austin, TX: Pro-Ed.

Shelton, B. S., Gast, D. L., Wolery, M., & Wintering, V. (1991). The role of small group instruction in facilitating observational and incidental learning. *Language, Speech, and Hearing Services in the Schools, 22,* 123–133.

Shinn, M. R. (Ed.). (1989). *Curriculm-based measurement: Assessing special children.* New York: Guilford.

Slesaransky-Poe, G., & Bartel, N. R. (2003). Integrating technology in the classroom. In D. D. Hammill & N. R. Bartel (Eds.), *Teaching students with learning and behavior problems* (7th ed., pp. 369–402). Austin, TX: Pro-Ed.

Snyder, L. (1984). Developmental language disorders: Elementary school age. In A. Holland (Ed.), *Language disorders in children: Recent advances* (pp. 129–158). San Diego, CA: College-Hill.

Tankersley, M., & Landrum, T. J. (1998). Comorbidity of emotional and behavioral disorders. In J. W. Lloyd, E. J., Kameenui, and D. Chard (Eds.), *Issues in educating students with disabilities* (pp. 153–173). Mahwah, NJ: Erlbaum.

Thurlow, M. L., Lazarus, S., Thompson, S., & Robey, J. (2002). 2001 state policies on assessment participation and accommodations (Synthesis Report 46). Minneapolis: University of Minnesota, National Center on Educational Outcomes. Retrieved May 21, 2004, from http://education.umn.edu/NCEO/OnlinePubs/Synthesis46.html.

U.S. Department of Education. (1998). *Twentieth annual report to Congress on the implementation of the Individuals with Disabilities Education Act.* Washington, DC: Author.

U.S. Department of Education. (2002). *Twenty-fourth annual report to Congress on the implementation of the Individuals with Disabilities Education Act.* Washington, DC: Author.

Utley, C. A., & Obiakor, F. E. (2000). Students with cognitive disabilities. In F. Obiakor, S. Burkhardt, A. Rotatori, & T. Wahlberg, (Eds.), *Intervention techniques for individuals with exceptionalities in inclusive settings* (pp. 21–53). Stamford, CT: Jai Press.

Vaughn, S., & Linan-Thompson, S. (2003). What is special about special education for students with learning disabilities? *The Journal of Special Education, 37,* 140–147.

Walker, H. M., Forness, S. R., Kauffman, J. M., Epstein, M. H., Gresham, F. M., Nelson, C. M., et al., (1998). Macro-social validation: Referencing outcomes in behavioral disorders to societal issues and problems. *Behavioral Disorders, 24,* 7–18.

Walker, H. M., Ramsey, E., & Gresham, F. M. (2004). *Antisocial behavior in school: Evidence-based practices* (2nd ed.). Belmont, CA: Wadsworth/Thomson.

Wallach, G., & Butler, K., (1994). *Language learning disabilities in school-age children and adolescents: Some principles and applications.* New York: Merrill.

Westby, C. (1999). Assessment of pragmatic competence in children with psychiatric disorders. In D. Rogers-Adkinson & P. Griffith (Eds.), *Communication disorders and children with psychiatric and behavioral disorders* (pp. 177–258). San Diego, CA: Singular.

5

Students with Other Special Learning Needs

LEARNER OBJECTIVES

After reading this chapter, you will be able to:

- List the major features of Section 504 of the Rehabilitation Act.
- Explain the differences between Section 504 and IDEA.
- Explain tips for working with families of students who learn differently.
- List the major characteristics of students with attention-deficit/hyperactivity disorder.
- Describe the educational considerations for students with attention-deficit/hyperactivity disorder.
- List the major characteristics of students who are considered to be "at risk."
- Describe the educational considerations for students who are considered to be "at risk."
- List the major characteristics of students who come from culturally and/or linguistically diverse backgrounds.
- Describe the educational considerations for students who come from culturally and/or linguistically diverse backgrounds.
- List the major characteristics of students who are considered to be gifted and talented.
- Describe the educational considerations for students who are gifted and talented.

CHAPTER AT A GLANCE

```
                    Universal
                    Instructional
                    Design
                        │
                        ▼
                    Technology
                        │
                        ▼
                    Collaboration
```

Attention-Deficit/Hyperactivity Disorder (ADHD)	Gifted and Talented	Cultural and Linguistic Diversity	Students Who Are At Risk	Culture of Poverty
• Defining ADHD • Classroom Accommodations and Techniques • Learning Strategies and Techniques • Strategies for Intervention • Working with the family • Cultural Diversity	• Defining Gifted and Talented • Classroom Accommodations and Techniques • Strategies for Intervention • Working with the family	• Defining Cultural and Linguistic Diversity • Classroom Accommodations and Techniques • Strategies for Intervention • Working with the family	• Defining Students Who Are At Risk • Classroom Accommodations and Techniques • Strategies for Intervention • Working with the family	• Defining Poverty • Classroom Accommodations and Techniques • Strategies for Intervention • Working with the family

- List resources for teachers of students who have ADHD, come from culturally/linguistically diverse backgrounds, are at risk, and/or who are gifted.
- Describe major characteristics of students from a culture of poverty.
- List educational considerations for students from a culture of poverty.

KEY TERMS

acceleration   137

attention-deficit/hyperactivity
   disorder   128

enrichment   136

gifted and talented   132

novelty   137

positive reinforcement   130

resiliency   150

self-determination   151

sophistication   137

technology   127

universal instructional design   125

wraparound service   149

*J*oseph is a 16-year-old student at Kennedy High School. He has been identified as having attention-deficit/hyperactivity disorder. It is believed that his ADHD stemmed from lead poisoning. At the age of 4, he was tested for lead poisoning and it was determined that he had toxic levels of lead in his body, probably from eating paint chips. Joseph was diagnosed with attention-deficit/hyperactivity disorder in the first grade and was pre-scribed Ritalin. He still takes Ritalin with good results. Although he used to have significant difficulty with excessive activity level, causing him to be constantly moving around the room, now he is struggling with extreme fidgetiness, restlessness, and impulsive behavior. This is particularly a problem in his science class where the teacher uses a lecture format for the class. Joseph enjoys science class, but he does not have the attention span for a 50-minute lecture. About 10 minutes into class, he will start rocking in his chair, thumping out a beat on his desk, or fidgeting with his notes, book, or pencil. He also will distract others around him by talking to them. Joseph is currently failing the class, although science was always a sub-ject in which he excelled. He told his mother that he is thinking about drop-ping out of school because he doesn't see the point in being in school if he's going to fail anyway.*

Lena is a 15-year-old student at Jamestown High School. She has been in the gifted program since she was in kindergarten, when her IQ was de-termined to be 165. She has completed all requirements for graduation and has taken her college boards; she scored in the 99th percentile on both the SAT and ACT. Lena desperately wants to go to college next year, but her par-ents, Mr. and Mrs. Bursik, have refused to agree to this plan. She has been accepted into the medical biomechanics program of a prestigious univer-sity located in New York. She has also been offered a full scholarship by this university. Mr. and Mrs. Bursik have stated that they think their daughter is too immature to go off to school by herself. They seem to understand that Lena is a highly creative individual, but they don't appear to trust her. Lena's teachers, on the other hand, believe that she should go to college next year. They believe she is ready for the academic challenge, and believe it is a problem that she has finished all the courses that were suitable for her through a curriculum-compacting approach to instruction. The Bursiks responded, however, that they consider it to be the school's responsibility to provide her with whatever instruction she needs at whatever level is appropriate for her ability.

Juan is a 13-year-old student at Morristown Middle School. He and his family recently moved to town from California, where they had lived for 3 years. Prior to that, they lived in their native country, Guatemala. Juan's parents speak very little English, and Juan struggles with English as well. Juan is considered to be Spanish dominant for receptive language but English dominant for expressive language. He was tested in both Spanish and English for a special education evaluation. His academic testing did not reveal a disability. Yet Juan continues to struggle at school. He has a difficult time following directions and even when he does, his writing is so difficult to read that his teachers are not sure what he knows and understands. The teachers have sent home notes to his parents requesting a conference, but they do not receive a reply. Phone calls home during the day are not answered, and there is no answering machine on which to leave a message.

*T*his chapter will discuss adapting curricula for students with other special learning needs. The information presented in the following pages will cover students with attention-deficit/hyperactivity disorder served through Section 504 of the Rehabilitation Act, gifted and talented students, students who are culturally and linguistically diverse, students who are at risk of failing in school, and students who are from a culture of poverty. These are the students who tend to "fall through the cracks" because their academic needs are poorly understood.

The students discussed in this chapter are a very diverse group, with each category bringing its own unique characteristics, needs, and challenges. To help you better understand how to meet these students' needs, we will cover accommodations and strategies that can be incorporated into your classroom. Many of the ideas will focus on how the information is organized, incorporating different methods for presenting materials, including hands-on activities and other modes of learning, both visually and auditory.

It has been said that in today's education environment there is a need to build more of an emotional connection between students and their schools (Raspberry, 2004). In this chapter we offer several suggestions for how to build this connection. Our primary concern is that the students feeling detached from school are often not the ones we would consider to be potential dropouts. It is our hope that this chapter will provide an overview of some of the issues and concerns faced by these students and offer practical approaches to help students become more engaged in their learning and responsible for their educational success.

UNIVERSAL INSTRUCTIONAL DESIGN

The various groups of students discussed in this chapter all have varying academic skills and needs. An educational model that is gaining recognition in the field of education is **universal instructional design.** Initially the use of universal instructional design was applied to architectural barriers to people with disabilities. As a result of universal design techniques, things such as curb cuts and automatic doors are now

PRACTICAL APPLICATIONS
UNIVERSAL DESIGN

The students described in this chapter all have varying academic skills and needs. An educational model that is gaining more recognition in the field of education is universal design. This approach addresses individual learner differences through the use of multiple approaches helping them to demonstrate their learning in their preferred learning style. The principles of universal design (Bowe, 2000) are defined here along with examples of incorporating those principles in classroom settings.

Principle 1: Equitable use. Design is useful for learners with diverse abilities.

- Provide electronic version of text that allows students to access in multiple ways.
- Use charts, graphs, or other visual aids to assist students to "see" the materials during lectures.

Principle 2: Flexible in use. Design accommodates a wide range of students' preferences and abilities.

- Use alternate strategies to determine student's level of knowledge including oral presentations, written papers, and demonstrations of mastery.
- Develop tests that allow for differences in time limits or number of problems completed.

Principle 3: Simple and intuitive use. Use of design is easy to understand regardless of student's experience, knowledge, language skills, or concentration level.

- Use uncomplicated and direct statements when teaching students.
- Present new information at a slower pace allowing students to keep up with the content.

Principle 4: Perceptible information. Design communicates necessary information effectively to student.

- Introduce main points first allowing students to understand what important information will be covered.
- Use guided notes to highlight key topics from a lecture and/or readings.

Principle 5: Tolerance for error. Design minimizes hazards and the adverse consequences of accidental or unintended actions.

- Provide rubrics and exemplars so students understand requirements of assignments.
- Provide key guard so students do not unintentionally strike incorrect keys.

Principle 6: Low physical effort. Design can be used efficiently and comfortably with minimum fatigue.

- Ensure that materials are located on shelves that students can reach easily.
- Ensure that tables and chairs are provided to eliminate need for prolonged standing.

> **Principle 7: Size and space for approach and use.** Appropriate size and space are provided for approach, manipulation, and use regardless of student's body size, posture, or mobility.
>
> - Provide clear line of sight for any seated or standing student.
> - Ensure that students who use wheelchairs or other adaptive devices are able to maneuver easily around the classroom.

common sights in our communities, helping to make sidewalks and buildings accessible for everyone. This same concept is being applied to education. The "curb cuts" in education focus on making the curriculum or information accessible for all students—that is, meeting the learning needs and styles of all learners (Johnson & Fox, 2002). Universal instructional design addresses individual learner differences by offering alternative methods of representation, expression, and engagement (CAST, 2001). For example, one student could describe what he has learned through a research paper, whereas another student could give an oral report (Johnson & Fox, 2002). This model allows all students to demonstrate their learning using their preferred learning styles.

TECHNOLOGY

The presence of **technology** in education is helping to enhance student learning and understanding. Technology such as text-to-speech software for reading, writing, and test taking; speech recognition and word prediction software for writing; electronic organizers for time management and organization; and electronic graphic organizers for reading comprehension, writing, and studying can be used to address students' learning needs and strengthen their learning skills. For students who may have special learning needs, technology exposes them to alternate ways of learning, allowing them more independence with learning and providing flexibility in demonstrating what they have learned (Johnson & Fox, 2002).

Students who are diverse learners need to be exposed to available technology throughout their educational experience. All too often students are not exposed to technology during their middle and high school years, which leaves them unprepared for the employment or higher education environment.

As you read the sections describing the learning needs of students from diverse backgrounds or with specific learning challenges, think about how the curricula for these students can be made more accessible through alternate formats or through the use of technology.

COLLABORATION

Teachers must work with a variety of individuals to meet the learning needs of such a diverse group of learners. Collaborating with families and learning the cultural, ethnic, or religious framework of families in order to understand the goals and aspirations they have for their children can help these students succeed. Another critical group with whom teachers must collaborate is school personnel, including other teachers, social workers, school counselors, and administrators. Some students that we will discuss have serious life issues that they are dealing with while trying to go to school. Some students may be homeless, others may have significant behavioral issues, and some may be trying to straddle two worlds, that of their home and school. Working as a team to identify the supports and services students need to be successful in school will be critical.

Community service and resource providers represent a third group teachers will need to engage with to address the needs of their students. Community support groups that help families and students cope with disability issues or family problems are part of the educational process, helping give students the opportunity to focus on their learning. Becoming familiar with the services and supports both within the school and in the community will assist teachers in creating a learning environment that welcomes students and provides a place for them to gain the skills and knowledge to succeed.

STUDENTS WITH ATTENTION-DEFICIT/ HYPERACTIVITY DISORDER

Defining ADHD

Students with **attention-deficit/hyperactivity disorder**(ADHD) represent about 5% of the school-age population (Power, Karustis, & Habboushe, 2001). Generally, symptoms become evident during the preschool or early elementary school years. It was previously thought that the symptoms diminished when students reached adolescence; however, it is now known that ADHD can persist through these years and into adulthood. Boys are two to three times more often diagnosed with ADHD than girls (CHADD, 2004; Power et al., 2001; Waaland, David, & Wehman, 1997). Left untreated, these students can experience problems making friends or performing well in school.

What are the characteristics associated with ADHD? Three primary subtypes are used to categorize ADHD behaviors (CHADD, 2004; Power et al., 2001) Table 5.1 describes these subcategories, which are used as diagnostic criteria. To be diagnosed as ADHD, an individual must display at least six symptoms of inattention or hyperactivity, their symptoms must have persisted for at least 6 months resulting in behavior that is maladaptive and inconsistent with developmental levels, and the symptoms must exist in different environmental settings (Power et al., 2001; Smith, Polloway, Patton, & Dowdy, 2004; Waaland et al., 1997).

It is important to remember that we all show signs of inattention or restlessness from time to time. However, ADHD is a neurobiological disorder that is characterized by developmentally inappropriate impulsivity, inattention, and sometimes hyperactivity (Waaland et al., 1997). It is not the direct result of poor parenting, faulty education, or junk food (Power et al., 2001). Although ADHD is one of the most prevalent childhood behavior disorders, it can be one of the most misunderstood. Although students with ADHD may share certain characteristics, they are still individuals with different personalities, behaviors, and learning traits. Educators who understand the dynamics of ADHD and the educational and support needs of these students can enhance their school experience and the relationships they develop with their classmates and teachers.

Based on current educational trends, the regular education classroom teacher will have primary responsibility, more than the special education teacher, for teaching academics and behavior control to students with ADHD (Reid, Maag, Vasa, & Wright, 1994; Waaland et al., 1997). Therefore, they must understand the impact of medication if the student is taking it and how best to work with the family and other school personnel. Because most students with ADHD have a combination of symptoms (both inattention and hyperactivity), the ideas and suggestions presented here will encompass both of these areas.

TABLE 5.1
Subtypes of ADHD behaviors.

Subtypes of ADHD	ADHD Behaviors
Predominately Inattentive Type	• Fails to give close attention to details • Has difficulty sustaining attention • Struggles to follow through on instructions • Does not seem to listen • Loses things • Avoids tasks requiring sustained mental effort • Is easily distracted • Is forgetful in daily activities
Predominately Hyperactive-Impulsive Type	• Fidgets with hands or feet—squirms in chair • Has difficulty remaining seated • Runs or climbs excessively • Difficulty engaging in activities quietly • Talks excessively • Interrupts or intrudes on others • Blurts out answers before questions are completed • Difficulty waiting or taking turns
Combined Type	• Individual meets both sets of inattention and hyperative-impulsive criteria

Note: From *The disorder named AD/HD, CHADD fact sheet* #1. Retrieved June 17, 2004, from http://www.chadd.org/fs/fsl.pdf

Classroom Accommodations and Techniques

Special Education Services and Section 504

Students with ADHD can receive either special assistance or more specialized services if their behaviors prevent them from performing adequately in the classroom (Waaland et al., 1997). The accommodations and techniques described in this section are for students who are in the regular classroom. Students may receive special accommodations as a result of qualifying for special education services through the Individuals with Disabilities Education Act (IDEA). These students will have an individualized education program (IEP) that details the types of accommodations and supports that must be provided. Typically, students whose primary disability is ADHD will be categorized for services in the category of other health impairments (OHI). The rationale for using this category centered on the student's sensitivity or heightened awareness to environmental stimuli resulting in limited attentiveness to the educational environment (Smith et al., 2004; U.S. Department of Education, 2000).

However, a number of students with ADHD did not qualify for special education and yet were experiencing great difficulties in school (Smith et al., 2004). To help meet the needs of these students, the U.S. Department of Education determined that Section 504 of the Rehabilitation Act of 1973 could be a legal basis for providing assessment and services to students diagnosed with ADHD (U.S. Department of Education,

2000). Individuals with disabilities can qualify for services under Section 504 if their disability substantially limits one or more major life activities. Students with ADHD met the requirement of the law in that the one major life activity, in this case learning, was limited as a result of their disability. This law is not designed as a special education law, but is viewed as a civil rights law. IDEA and Section 504 are also different in their eligibility requirements and the benefits they provide. The definition of a disability is much broader in Section 504 than under IDEA. Therefore, all students under IDEA are covered under Section 504, but not all students protected under Section 504 qualify for special education services under IDEA (National Resource Center on ADHD, 2004.). Students who receive services under IDEA must have those services tailored to meet their needs, and these services must result in educational benefit. Services provided under Section 504 are based on the student's disability and do not have to result in academic improvement (help4adhd.org).

Learning Strategies and Techniques

Students with ADHD have difficulty concentrating, planning, and controlling impulses (Waaland et al., 1997; Power et al., 2001). To assist students in the classroom, educators must develop a plan that includes behavioral and educational interventions (Power et al., 2001). Medication in combination with an academic plan is often an approach used to help these students. Often the learning strategies and techniques focus on how information is delivered rather than what needs to be learned. For example, teachers may reduce the amount of material covered at a particular point during the instructional day. This does not mean that the material is watered down, but that the amount of information is broken down into smaller, perhaps more manageable pieces.

When assessing how best to teach students with ADHD, teachers should review the curriculum to determine how they are presenting information and whether they are using different learning modes. Figure 5.1 provides a list of suggested teaching tips to use in the regular classroom. Many of the suggestions can be helpful for all students because the basis of the tips is instructing students using all learning modalities or learning styles.

Strategies for Intervention

Students with ADHD will typically need assistance in developing time management and organizational skills, working effectively with their peers, and creating self-management strategies. The intervention strategies mentioned here are aimed at helping students work more independently and assess their own progress toward meeting their goals. Additionally, interventions should be based on **positive reinforcement** of students' behavior as much as possible. It is the concept of "catching them while they are good." This is not always easy, but it is important to recognize students who are working on meeting the educational expectations and not focus entirely on when the student misbehaves (Swanson, 1992). Positive reinforcements can enhance students' self-esteem and help them learn what behaviors are acceptable. This point refers to the instructional tip of providing feedback. Providing students information on how they are meeting their educational goals is critical along with feedback on their behavior. This feedback needs to be positive, highlighting strengths as well as areas that need improvement. Feedback enables students to see the bigger picture of how they are performing, and not just their areas of weakness.

Teachers should structure the classroom and activities to minimize the occurrence of problems as much as possible. Following are examples of strategies (Waaland et al.,

Break learning tasks down into a number of steps. Present students with one task at a time helping to reduce their anxiety of needing to cover several pages of material all at once.

Use charts, graphs, or other visual aids to assist students to "see" the material during lectures.

Use graph paper to help with math and handwriting. The graph paper provides more structure to help students line up their math problems or keep their handwriting more organized on a page.

Tape long passages of reading material to enable students to listen as they read along.

Let students highlight information in their text or highlight key phrases and sentences.

Provide manipulative objects to assist students who have difficulty solving math problems.

Slow down the pace of instruction to enable students to keep up with the content.

Introduce the main points first so that students can grasp what important information will be covered.

Use simple, direct statements when instructing students.

Provide frequent feedback to students so they can understand what they have successfully learned and where improvements are needed.

Make instructional objectives clear to students.

FIGURE 5.1
Instructional tips for teaching students with ADHD.

Note: Adapted from R. Waaland, C. David, & P. Wehman (1997). "Attention Deficit/Hyperactivity Disorder." In P. Wehman (Ed.), *Exceptional Individuals in School, Community, and Work* (pp. 207–241). Austin, TX: Pro-Ed; and M. Cherkes-Julkowski, S. Sharp, & J. Stolzenberg (1997). *Rethinking Attention Deficit Disorders.* Cambridge, MA: Brookline Books.

1997) for reinforcing good behavior or anticipating problems when instructing students with ADHD:

- Always use a positive, firm voice and language when interacting with students. Problems can escalate when frustration or anger becomes part of the interaction between teacher and student.

- Anticipate potential problem situations by arranging the classroom seating, placing a student in a group activity with peers who are task oriented, or developing contracts and rewards (reinforcers) for positive behaviors and completing assignments.

- Develop rewards or reinforcers that are meaningful to the student. The rewards should be varied to keep the student's interest. If the plan is not working, talk with the student, parents, and other teachers to revise the plan and determine what was effective and what proved ineffective.

Working with the Family

Maintaining a close working relationship with the family of a student with ADHD will help reinforce appropriate behaviors both in school and in the community. Working as a team will enhance the student's ability to perform in school because there is a consistent message between the school and home. Educators should communicate to family members about what is happening at school, both the progress the student is making and the areas that still need improvement. They should also be sure to listen to what families say is happening at home. Sometimes a divorce or death in the family can heighten behaviors of distraction, inattentiveness, or not completing homework assignments. Realistic goals for student progress need to be set and within the capabilities of the family (if reinforcements are to be made at school and home) to implement. The ultimate goal of both school personnel and the family is to promote in the student a sense of self-esteem and a positive attitude about school.

Cultural Diversity

When working with students with ADHD who are from different cultural or linguistic backgrounds, teachers should make an effort to understand the educational expectations of the family along with the cultural expectations for appropriate behavior (Swanson, 1992). It is also important to understand the assessments used to determine if the student has the characteristics associated with ADHD. Again cultural differences can play a role in parents' understanding of what the test results mean and what interventions the school believes are necessary. Additionally, teachers should listen to family members about the behaviors they are seeing at home. Sometimes students with ADHD exhibit specific behaviors in reaction to the structure of the school setting or classroom and the family does not see these types of behaviors as frequently in the home. Clear communication of what the school and home view as behaviors needing improvement is essential for ultimately helping the student to succeed.

GIFTED AND TALENTED

Defining Gifted and Talented

Our understanding of students who are **gifted and talented** continues to evolve. The earliest definitions were based on intellectual potential as measured by intelligence tests. More recently developed definitions focus not only on intellectual potential, but also on the many facets of talent as well. Regardless of the definition used, this section focuses on students whose giftedness and talents require services and supports not typically provided by schools.

The most widely used definition of gifted and talented students was developed by Marland (1972):

> Gifted and talented students are those identified by professionally qualified persons who by virtue of outstanding abilities are capable of high performance. These are students who require differentiated educational programs and services beyond those normally provided by the regular school program in order to realize their contributions to self and society. Students capable of high performance include those with demonstrated achievement and/or potential ability in any of the following areas singly or in combination:
>
> 1. General intellectual aptitude
> 2. Specific academic aptitude
> 3. Creative or productive thinking
> 4. Leadership ability
> 5. Visual and performing arts (p. 1)

Many students who are gifted and talented require different educational experiences than their age peers if they are to fully benefit from school experiences. If these

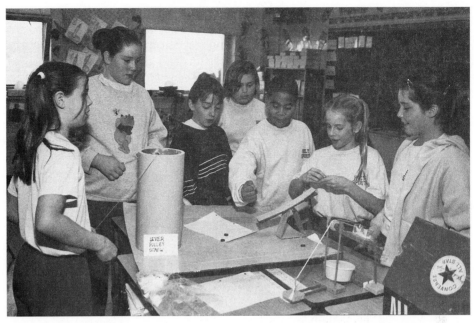

Students with disabilities work successfully with general education students. Have you experienced seeing collaboration between students with special needs and their nondisabled peers? What did you observe?

students are already proficient in areas of the curriculum, they have nothing to gain from the general education pathway. With the passage of PL 95-561 in 1978 and PL 100-297, the Jacob K. Javits Gifted and Talented Children's Education Act of 1988, Congress incorporated Marland's conceptualization into law. The U.S. Department of Education estimates that approximately 6% of the school population receives special education services through the Jacob Javits Act.

What are the characteristics of students who are gifted and talented? Because the definition covers a wide variety of possibilities, abilities, and skills, each occurring individually or in combination with others, a correspondingly wide variety of characteristics are applicable to students in this group. However, we can point to some common characteristics. Terman (1925, 1947, 1959) found that students who were gifted tended to be superior to their age mates in almost every measure he applied. As a group they were taller, heavier, stronger, more energetic, and healthier than their age mates. They were also more emotionally stable. Gallagher (1985) also reported that the students observed were socially and emotionally equal to or ahead of their age peer's developmental levels and above average in their concerns about moral and ethical issues and behaviors. They tended to be well liked by their peers, social leaders, and self-sufficient, and they demonstrated a wide variety of interests. Although not immune to problems, they were less prone to neurotic or psychotic episodes than their contemporaries (Piechowski, 1997; Smith, 2001; Van Tassel-Baska, 1998).

Students who are gifted and talented can show exceptional academic skills, and in general, they are able to grasp concepts, generalize, analyze, and synthesize new ideas or problems with greater facility than their age peers (Clark, 1997). Sometimes they have unusual aptitude in only a given area or areas. They sometimes learn to read easily before entering school, either teaching themselves or learning from minimal input from parents. Reading is often also a preferred leisure activity (Hardman, Drew, & Egan, 2002).

They learn a great deal of information quickly, retain and use what they learn, have an excellent command of language, enjoy acquiring and manipulating abstract material, and are excited by the learning process in general. Students who are gifted and talented characteristically do more than just absorb knowledge. They have the ability to see the "big picture" as evidenced by their ability to deal with a variety of concepts at a time and organize them into large, meaningful patterns. They have an intellectual curiosity that fires a need for mental stimulation and an intuitive sense of appropriateness reflected in good judgment (Clark, 1997; Gallagher & Gallagher, 1994; Piirto, 1994; Silverman, 1995). Table 5.2 is a summary of some of the characteristics of people who are gifted and talented and some potential concomitant problems.

Classroom Accommodations and Techniques

Working with students who are gifted and talented requires that teachers learn to differentiate instruction, individualizing the general education curriculum in ways that build on a student's strengths. This is not different from what is considered to be best practice in teaching students with any other special learning needs.

Individual Learning Contracts

One possibility for classroom accommodations is the individual learning contract. This contract, developed between the teacher and an individual student, clearly outlines expectations for learning and activities that the student will complete. Contracts that are exceptional include rubrics for grading as well as steps the student will follow to complete the assignment.

Promoting Inquiry and Independent Learning

An effective strategy for teaching students who are gifted and talented in general education classrooms is the use of independent learning activities. Because simultaneously teaching students at many different ability levels can be difficult, the use of independent learning activities can provide instruction to a small group of students while direct instruction is being delivered to the larger group. When students learn to work independently, they not only gain a great deal of knowledge and personal satisfaction by exploring topics in breadth and depth, but they also develop strategies for inquiry and knowledge acquisition that will help them become lifelong learners.

Winebrenner (1992) offered some general procedural tips for teachers and students working on individual activities. Specific planning for independent learning can be tricky and should include behavioral guidelines for students. Those behavioral guidelines should address such procedural issues as what to do when the student needs help but the teacher is working with a larger group and what voice level to use if a student needs to confer with a classmate. Behavioral guidelines should also address social interactional skills such as not bragging to classmates about one's participation in alternative activities and not calling attention to oneself.

Teaching Thinking Skills

Working with students who are gifted and talented presents teachers with an opportunity to teach more than simple memorization of facts or mastery of skills. Because these students excel cognitively, they have the ability to think creatively as well as

TABLE 5.2

Representative characteristics of people who are gifted and potential concomitant problems.

Domains	Differentiating Characteristics	Problems
Cognitive (thinking)	Extraordinary quantity of information, unusual retentiveness. High level of language development.	Boredom with regular curriculum; impatience with waiting for group.
		Perceived as showoff by children of the same age.
	Persistent, goal-directed behavior.	Perceived as stubborn, willful, uncooperative.
	Unusual capacity for processing information.	Resent being interrupted; perceived as too serious; dislike for routine and drill.
Affective (feeling)	Unusual sensitivity to the expectations and feelings of others.	Unusually vulnerable to criticism of others; high level of need for success and recognition.
	Keen sense of humor—may be gentle or hostile.	Use of humor for critical attack on others, resulting in damage to interpersonal relationships.
	Unusual emotional depth and intensity.	Unusual vulnerability; problem focusing on realistic goals for life's work. Intolerance of and lack of understanding from peer group, leading to rejection and possible isolation.
	Advanced levels of moral judgment.	
Physical (sensation)	Unusual discrepancy between physical and intellectual development.	Result in adults who function with a mind/body dichotomy; children are comfortable expressing themselves only in mental activity, resulting in a limited development both physically and mentally.
	Low tolerance for lag between standards and athletic skills.	Refusal to take part in any activities where they do not excel, limiting experience with otherwise pleasurable, constructive physical activities.
Intuitive	Early involvement and concern for intuitive knowing and metaphysical ideas and phenomena.	Ridiculed by peers; not taken seriously by elders; considered weird or strange.
	Creativity apparent in all areas of endeavor.	Seen as deviant; become bored with mundane tasks; may be viewed as troublemaker.
Societal	Strongly motivated by self-actualization needs.	Frustration of not feeling challenged; loss of unrealized talents. Lack of opportunity to use social ability constructively may result in its disappearance from child's repertoire or its being turned into a negative characteristic (e.g., gang leadership).
	Leadership.	
	Solutions to social and environmental problems.	Loss to society if these traits are not allowed to develop with guidance and opportunity for meaningful involvement.

Note: From M. L. Hardman, C. J. Drew, & M. W. Egan (1996). *Human Exceptionality: Society, School and Family* (5th ed.). Needham, MA: Allyn & Bacon.

identify and solve problems. By structuring classroom activities to emphasize thinking and problem-solving skills, teachers can enrich, sophisticate, or make novel the general education curriculum.

Thinking skills are vital for success in this information age. Students must learn how to access information, evaluate it, and make decisions about or act on that information. Students can also have opportunities to create new products, come up with fresh ideas, and synthesize the ideas of others in innovative ways.

Thinking skills can be taught directly through the use of a curriculum specifically designed to focus on creative or critical thinking or problem solving. It can also be taught indirectly. Throughout the school day and in all subject areas, teachers can encourage students to think critically or solve problems related to the subject matter or to consider issues in and beyond the classroom. Teachers can also increase students' awareness of and appreciation for creative people and creative ideas by talking about them and by involving students in creative activities (Vaughn, Bos, & Schumm, 2003).

Grading Strategies

Gifted students experience a great deal of pressure to earn good grades for all their work, but the criteria that are used to assign grades are often unclear. Often, students are given a more rigorous curriculum or extra assignments as part of their educational program and then are evaluated according a more rigorous grading system. This may cause gifted students to resent their participation in advanced work, and they may also request to be excused from such assignments. They might not see the advantage of working harder on extra assignments for the grades they receive (Hoctor & Kaplan, 1989).

One suggestion for avoiding these negative feelings is to formally evaluate students on grade-level assignments only. Enrichment activities should not be graded at all; they should serve as an opportunity for students to explore topics of interest and share what they have learned with their classmates (Winebrenner, 1992). Another grading strategy for gifted students is to give them an incentive to participate in more challenging tasks; for example, teachers could tell them that no one who completes a task will earn lower than a B provided they follow the steps outlined in their learning contract. Teachers can also use alternative or holistic methods of assessment, leading students to develop the ability to evaluate their own work according to a set of predetermined criteria and possibly comparing their own work with exemplars.

Curriculum

Currently, no nationally adopted curriculum or standardized set of instructional procedures exists for students who are gifted and talented (Culatta, Tompkins, & Werts, 2003). Although many states have mandated programs, some do not. Moreover, where those programs are administered vary from state to state, and in some instances from school to school. Programs for students who are identified as gifted and talented are usually composed of curriculum enrichment, acceleration, sophistication, and novelty (Gallagher & Gallagher, 1994).

Enrichment

Enrichment is an instructional approach that provides students with information, materials, and assignments that enable them to elaborate on concepts being presented as part of the regular curriculum (Gallagher & Gallagher, 1994). This option refers to attempts made within the classroom setting by the classroom teacher to add depth, detail, and challenges to the curriculum in place for students at a given grade level. The classroom teacher might provide students who are gifted and talented with special activities such as independent study with advanced texts, independent small-group projects, or access to computer programs or other activities that can replace drills. To be successful, enrichment activities need a purpose and specified outcomes. They should be systematic in extending student learning, stress higher order thinking skills, and be interdisciplinary to allow students to view a subject from different perspectives (Banks, 1993). Enrichment activities should be used in lieu of other classroom activities instead of as additional work, and teachers need to ensure that students have access to many learning resources both in and out of the classroom (Maker, 1993).

Acceleration

Acceleration is providing students with a curriculum that takes them from their current level of learning and moves them forward (Feldhusen, Van Winkle, & Ehle, 1996). For example, Chris is a middle school student in sixth grade who is gifted in math. Instead of taking the usual sixth-grade math, he was placed in an accelerated class in which he and other students were taught the curriculum typical of eighth-grade math. By the time he is a junior in high school, he will have completed the typical high school math classes and will be able to take math classes at the local university. Chris's program is an example of acceleration. Acceleration can focus on one academic area, or it can be total. Because offering an acceleration program in the typical general education classroom is more difficult, they are typically offered in separate classrooms or separate schools.

Sophistication

Sophistication is a strategy in which teachers help students to see the principles or systems that underlie the content the rest of the class is learning (Gallagher & Gallagher, 1994). For example, in a music class, a student who is gifted and talented in music might be encouraged to add harmony to a basic melody that other students are learning.

Novelty

Novelty is an approach in which teachers give students opportunities to explore traditional curriculum content in alternative and unusual ways (Gallagher & Gallagher, 1994). For example, in a science class, students who are gifted and talented might be required to develop a multimedia presentation that describes concepts taught in a unit on weather. Table 5.3 provides examples of content modifications for gifted students.

Strategies for Intervention

Social-Emotional Needs

Students who are gifted and talented must cope with a number of potential problems (Deisle, 1997; Kerr, 1997; Perrone, 1997). One problem is the expectations they have of themselves and those that have been explicitly imposed by parents, teachers, and others. Students who are gifted frequently feel an inordinate amount of pressure to achieve high grades or to select particular professions. They often feel obligated or duty bound to achieve and contribute to excellence in every area, a syndrome called perfectionism (Adderholdt-Elliott, 1987). Such pressure often fosters a kind of conformity,

TABLE 5.3
Sample content modification for gifted students.

Modification	Subject: Math	Subject: Science	Subject: Language Arts	Subject: Social Studies
Enrichment	Changing bases in number system	Experimentation and data collecting	Short story and poetry writing	Early introduction to world history
Acceleration	Algebra in fifth grade	Early chemistry and physics	Learning grammatical structure early	Early introduction to world history
Sophistication Novelty	Mastering the laws of arithmetic	Learning the laws of physics	Mastering the structural properties of plays	Learning and applying the principles of economics
	Probability and statistics	Science and its impact on society	Rewriting Shakespeare's tragedies with happy endings	Creating future societies and telling how they would be governed

Note: From J. J. Gallagher & S. A. Gallagher, *Teaching the Gifted Child* 4/e. Published by Allyn and Bacon, Boston, MA. Copyright © 1994 by Pearson Education. Reprinted by permission of the publisher.

preventing students from selecting avenues of endeavor that truly fit them and their personal interests.

Van Tassel-Baska (1989) identified a number of social-emotional needs of students who are gifted that differentiate them from their same-age peers, including the following:

- Understanding how they are different from and similar to their peers
- Appreciating and valuing their own uniqueness as well as that of others
- Understanding and developing relationship skills
- Developing and valuing their high-level sensitivity
- Gaining a realistic understanding of their own abilities and talents
- Identifying ways of nurturing and developing their own abilities and talents
- Adequately distinguishing between pursuits of excellence and pursuits of perfection
- Developing the behaviors associated with negotiation and compromise.

To begin to meet these social-emotional needs, students need access to adult role models who have interests and abilities that parallel theirs (Clasen & Clasen, 1997). Role models are particularly important for gifted students who come from diverse backgrounds.

Underachievement of Females

"Although the gap between numbers of girls and boys identified for gifted programs has narrowed over the years, at least two lingering concerns remain. First, girls tend to score lower than boys on mathematical ability assessments. Second, the early achievement of girls who have been identified as gifted appears to diminish during adolescence and beyond" (Vaugh, Bos, & Schumm, 2003, p. 318).

Many factors are believed to cause this gap between the achievement of girls and boys, including biological differences, differences in cultural expectations, differences in peer attitudes, and differences in self-expectations. For example, some researchers have proposed that mathematical ability may be linked to gender differences in how the brain learns (i.e., Armstrong, 1980; Benbow, 1986). Others propose that the differences in mathematical abilities may be the result of the cultural expectation that boys are more likely to excel in mathematics than girls are. For example, Sutton-Smith, Rosenberg, and Landy (1968) hypothesized that children learn mathematical problem-solving from their fathers. Hall (1980) attributed the strong math achievement of girls to a strong identification with their fathers. Peer expectations are even more critical; Parsons, Frieze, and Ruble (1978) found that females were more likely to excel in mathematics when they were encouraged by their male peers. Lastly, in relation to self-expectations, Noble (1989) reported that gifted females are often unaware of and/or frightened by their own potential, possibly fearing rejection by families, teachers, and peers.

Although many of these challenges are societal in nature, schools can have an impact by making changes in how they educate female students who are gifted and talented. Rimm (1986) recommended a six-step model for working with underachieving students, from underachieving female students to students from culturally diverse and/or low socioeconomic backgrounds. She found that underachievement can be effectively addressed when school and family collaborate in the implementation of her TRIFOCAL Model:

1. *Assessment.* Intelligence tests and creativity tests should be administered in addition to interviewing parents, teachers, and students.

2. *Communication.* Communication between teachers and parents is vital if gifted students are to reach their potential.

3. *Changing expectations.* Professional support may be necessary to change lower expectations, including counseling, family therapy, or supports to change environmental factors that prevent achievement.

4. *Role model identification.* Linking students with a strong role model, someone who has had similar experiences and succeeded despite these challenges, is a key factor in changing underachievement.

5. *Correction of deficiencies.* Addressing skill deficits that result from inattention in class and poor work and study habits can be helpful.

6. *Modifications of reinforcements.* Changing reinforcements to reward students when they work hard, and eliminating reinforcements that currently exist for poor performance and/or inattention in class, are also crucial.

Working with the Family

It's important to involve parents in the education of students who are gifted and talented. This should begin with the referral/identification process. Parents have the opportunity to observe their children in environments other than the classroom. They see their children during play and in community-related activities and witness involvement in academic and recreational activities beyond the more restrictive setting of the classroom. The information parents gather about their children is information that might not be readily apparent to the classroom teacher and is extraordinarily valuable in the referral process. A common myth that all parents think their children are gifted and entitled to special services is not the case (Feldhusen et al., 1989). However, many parents do not

STUDENT KNOWLEDGE CHECK

Mike, a special education teacher, meets with a student after school to discuss another failing test grade. He is very concerned about Juan because he knows he faces several challenges in his life including problems at home and difficulties with language comprehension. In spite of these challenges, Mike has seen some of Juan's artwork and believes he is very gifted. During the meeting, Juan expresses his frustration with school and is overwhelmed with all of the things happening in his life. He tells Mike he is seriously thinking about dropping out of school.

1. If you were Mike, what would be the first steps you would take to help Juan?
2. What learning strategies should Mike consider to ensure that Juan is fully accessing the curriculum?
3. Are there resources and supports that Mike should identify to help Juan?

take action when they believe the school is not meeting their child's educational needs (Feldhusen et al., 1989).

Parents play an important role in the continued achievement of students who are identified as being gifted and talented. For this reason teachers should help parents understand how their son or daughter is gifted and talented and provide resources for them to continue to enrich their learning. Teachers can also put parents in contact with other parents who have successfully raised children with similar gifts or talents.

Parents of children who are gifted can be encouraged to do the following:

- Provide toys for the child that may be used for a variety of activities
- Take trips to museums, exhibits, fairs, and other places of interest
- Provide out-of-school experiences that foster talent or skill development (i.e., artistic, physical, academic, leadership)
- Enroll the child in summer programs offered by universities or colleges
- Encourage the child's friendships and associations with other people who have like interests and aptitudes
- Provide access to tools (computers, video cameras) and resources (specialists, coaches, mentors) that contribute to the child's performance
- Expect variations in performance from time to time
- Provide opportunities for rest and relaxation from demanding schedules. (Hardman, Drew, & Egan, 2002)

CULTURAL AND LINGUISTIC DIVERSITY

Defining Cultural and Linguistic Diversity

The number of students in U.S. classrooms who speak a native language other than English has steadily increased over the past 10 years (Tinajero & Hurley, 2000). Today, one of five American students entering school knows a second language other than English (Wood & Tinajero, 2002). It is anticipated that by the year 2020, the number of such students will grow to 5 million and by 2030 language minority students will represent 40% of the school-age population (Berliner & Biddle, 1995). Although this chapter will discuss culturally or linguistically diverse students as a group, this does not mean that these students hold the same values or beliefs. As with all students, teachers should treat each as an individual and learn about his or her own unique characteristics.

Classroom Accommodations and Techniques

Students who are culturally diverse may experience a very different family lifestyle and different academic expectations than those of the mainstream educational system. Teachers should learn about the student(s) in their classrooms, including (a) the predominant language spoken at home, (b) the family's educational and career goals for their child, (c) the family's concept of their child's personal and social development in school, and (d) the family's level of assimilation into their community or society (Black, Mrasek, & Ballinger, 2003). This information will assist teachers in better understanding the framework that the student is operating from when entering the classroom.

Working with students from culturally or linguistically diverse backgrounds involves being sensitive to their culture or heritage and constructing a classroom learning environment that builds on their strengths and identifies areas of weaknesses. Inestroza (1990) suggested the following techniques when instructing these students:

- Allow students to provide information nonverbally (e.g., pointing to answers on graphs or charts).

- Use synonyms and antonyms, or paraphrase to convey classroom material. Redundancy is allowable when instructing these students.

- Use demonstrations or visual cues when instructing. Concrete examples are helpful when explaining material.

- Respond to students' intended meaning when answering questions. The instructor can rephrase what the student is saying to enable him or her to hear how to state an answer correctly. The teacher should build on the information already provided by the student.

- Do not correct a student's pronunciation more than three times consecutively. Excessive correction may make the student afraid to speak. Correction of grammar is best done through writing.

- Do not change students' names to make them sound more American. Doing so deprives students of their cultural identities.

Students from cultural or linguistically diverse backgrounds benefit from academic content that is elaborated and not simplified (Teemant, Bernhardt, Rodriguez-Muñoz, & Aiello, 2000). In other words, teachers should maintain the learning expectations of their class and not assume that these students need a watered-down version of the material. For example, Teemant and her colleagues (2000) suggested that in a science class if a student is unable to write well, the student may be allowed to illustrate the concepts in lab reports and journals. They recommend that in any classroom, students from multicultural backgrounds will benefit from academic content that is presented using multiple and varied forms of participation, materials, and instruction.

Strategies for Intervention

As a result of having to learn a second language (English) and become more as-similated into the larger society and into the school environment, students from culturally diverse backgrounds often feel isolated and disconnected from school (Clemente & Collison, 2000). These authors point out that students' isolation can stem from feelings of both physical and intellectual segregation from the rest of the school population. Strategies are needed to assist students to feel a sense of belonging in their academic environment. Steps can be taken to enable students to share their cultural heritage with other students, perhaps through preparing special foods or sharing about important holidays. Teachers can assist in creating a positive learning environment in which all differences are appreciated and ac-cepted, adding a richness to the learning experience and to the school as a whole (Scribner & Scribner, 2001). Students need opportunities to express their opinions or feelings about their school experience and how school personnel can assist in their adjustment. Today's high schools and even middle schools are becoming more complex with varying schedules, high demands on students performance, and larger numbers of students served within one building. Teachers who are sen-sitive to students' academic and personal needs and determine effective ap-proaches to addressing these needs can help students to advance within the learning environment.

Working with the Family

There are unique challenges in working with families from culturally and linguistically diverse backgrounds. First, the primary language used by such families may not be English. Communicating educational goals and objectives in a language unfamiliar to the family can be difficult. Second, families may not be able to be involved in the life of the school because of transportation, work schedules, or limited knowledge about the school as a whole. As stated previously, middle and high schools are more com-plex and function on varying schedules. Family members may feel uncomfortable coming to school because of language barriers or feelings of inadequacy.

Perhaps one of the most important aspects of working with culturally and lin-guistically diverse families is understanding the family dynamics and cultural be-liefs. Black and colleagues (2003) raised several points that need to be considered about family dynamics from individualist or collectivist cultures. Sometimes the be-lief systems that families have are in direct contradiction to the culture of the school. For example, students from collectivist cultures often interact with their families dif-ferently than they interact with people at school. They do not ask a great deal of questions or interact with their parents at home (Black et al., 2003). This can lead to a misunderstanding about a student in the classroom (Chattergy & Ongteco, 1991, and Losey, 1995, in Black et al., 2003). Individualism, which is highly re-garded in our educational system, creates conflicts for students who are from a col-lectivist environment in which the needs of the group are more important than those of the individual and competition to outperform others is not part of the culture (Black et al., 2003).

To help families understand the educational system and feel more welcome in this environment, schools can engage in outreach efforts to learn about the different

COLLABORATION TIPS

It is important for teachers to work with a variety of individuals to help meet the learning needs of such a diverse group of learners. Collaboration with families is critical to helping these students succeed in school and to understanding the cultural, ethnic, or religious framework of families and the goals and aspirations they have for their children. Another critical group is school personnel, including teachers, social workers, school counselors, and administrators. Some students are dealing with serious life issues while trying to go to school. Some students may be homeless; others may have significant behavioral issues; and some may be trying to straddle two worlds—their home and the school. Working as a team to identify the supports and services students need to be successful in school is critical.

Community service and resource providers is a third group that teachers need to engage with to address the needs of their students. Community support groups that help families and students cope with disability issues or family problems are part of the educational process because they help give students the opportunity to focus on their learning. Becoming familiar with the services and supports available in both school and community will assist teachers in creating a learning environment that welcomes students and provides a place for them to gain the skills and knowledge to succeed.

communities the school serves and how the economic, cultural, racial, and class factors interact with the school and community (Scribner & Scribner, 2001). Scribner and Scribner stressed that often communication goes beyond just the educational sphere, and includes best practices in community involvement around health, safety, and economic issues.

STUDENTS WHO ARE AT RISK

Who are the students considered to be at risk and for what, exactly, are they at risk? The term *at risk* denotes a student who is at risk for school failure. Although any student may fail at school, those who are considered to be more likely to fail are those who have been exposed to some condition that negatively affects their learning, such as poverty, pregnancy, homelessness, abuse and/or neglect, drug use, and alcohol abuse. Students who are at risk include students like Joseph, for whom school is a series of disappointments and failures. They also include students like Lena, who is bored with what's currently being taught and who fails to see a point in remaining in school. In addition, they include students like Juan, who struggles with learning English while trying to learn academic content such as math, science, English, and social studies. Students who are at risk of school failure include students with and without disabilities, so it makes sense that a book about students with disabilities would include information about this large, diverse group of students.

Defining Students Who Are at Risk

This group of students is as diverse as students in the general population, making it difficult to create a list of characteristics and/or needs. The term *at risk* was first used in the report *A Nation at Risk* (Gardner, 1983), which described an inadequate educational system in the United States, producing a large number of students who were likely to leave school without the skills they needed to help our country compete in a world market. What defines this group of students from others is the high likelihood that they will drop out of high school, or if they don't drop out, fail to learn the basic skills necessary for success in society. Some students determined to be at risk also share other characteristics, including noncompliance, difficulties in being self-determined in their learning, communication delays, struggles with establishing and maintaining social relationships, and problems understanding the consequences of their behaviors (Stephens & Price, 1992). Figure 5.2 lists some factors associated with being at risk.

Because so many factors can place a student at risk of dropping out of school, it is difficult to obtain reliable data on the prevalence of such students. Prevalence figures tend to focus on some of the underlying causes for being at risk, although not everyone who has one or more of these factors will have difficulties in learning or will drop out of school.

The consequences of students' dropping out of school are costly to both the individual and society. For example, dropouts have fewer options for employment and are usually employed in low-skilled, low-paying positions. Dropouts are more likely than high school graduates to experience health problems, engage in criminal activities, and become dependent on welfare and other government programs (Guagliardo, Huang, Hicks, & D'Angelo, 1998; Rumberger, 1995). The national average for high school completion was 85.7% (National Center for Education Statistics, 2002), and the states with the lowest rates included Alabama, Arizona, Colorado, Louisiana, Nevada, and Texas.

It cannot be denied that what happens in the home affects students in school. Home conditions that can potentially affect student academic performance include family poverty and family instability (Frymier, 1992). The Children's Defense Fund (2004) recently published their report on the state of our nation. In the report, they reported statistics about some of the factors that identify students who are at risk, including poverty, poor health, abuse and neglect, and problems with the law. Figure 5.3 summarizes their findings.

Classroom Accommodations and Techniques

The main focus of working with students who are at risk is to prevent them from dropping out of school. Attaining a high school diploma has been linked to postschool success, whereas students who drop out of high school have limited employment opportunities, fewer opportunities for advancement, and inadequate preparation for additional training (Rumberger, 1987). Finn (1993) described dropping out as a process and not an instantaneous decision or discrete occurrence. According to Finn, student participation in school activities over time leads to positive outcomes that, in turn, help students identify with their school and school-related goals. The importance of identifying with school, according to Finn, is that students are then more likely to remain engaged and on track to graduate. Finn's research suggests that most students who drop out are expressing an extreme sense of alienation or disengagement that was preceded by several alterable indicators of withdrawal and unsuccessful school experiences, such as failing classes, absenteeism, and behavior problems. Many students who have trouble "reading" the expectations of others,

1. Attempted suicide during the past year
2. Used drugs or engaged in substance abuse
3. Has been a drug "pusher" during the past year
4. Has a negative sense of self-esteem
5. Was involved in a pregnancy during the past year
6. Was expelled from school during the past year
7. Consumes alcohol regularly
8. Was arrested for illegal activity
9. Parents have negative attitudes toward education
10. Has several brothers or sisters who have dropped out
11. Was sexually or physically abused last year
12. Failed two courses last school year
13. Was suspended from school twice last year
14. Was absent more than 20 days last year
15. Parent drinks excessively and is an alcoholic
16. Was retained in grade
17. One parent attempted suicide last year
18. Scored below 20th percentile on a standardized test
19. Other family members used drugs during the past year
20. Attended three or more schools during the past 5 years
21. Average grades were below C last school year
22. Was arrested for driving while intoxicated
23. Has an IQ score below 90
24. Parents divorced or separated last year
25. Father is an unskilled laborer who is unemployed
26. Father or mother died during the past year
27. Diagnosed as being in special education
28. English is not the language used most often in the home
29. Mother is an unskilled laborer who is unemployed
30. Lives in an inner-city, urban area
31. Mother is only parent living in the home
32. Is a year older than other students in the same grade
33. Mother did not graduate from high school
34. Father lost his job during the past year
35. Was dropped from an athletic team during the past year
36. Experienced a serious illness or accident
37. Does not participate in extracurricular activities
38. Parent had a major change in health status
39. Had a close friend who died during the past year
40. Father did not graduate from high school
41. Changed schools during the year
42. Changed place of residence during the past year
43. Has three or more brothers or sisters
44. Is the youngest child in the family

FIGURE 5.2

Factors associated with being at risk.

Note: From "Special Education and Students at Risk: Findings from a National Study" by T. P. Lombardi, K. S. Odell, & D. E. Novotny, 1990, *Remedial and Special Education, 12*(1), 56–62. Copyright 1990 by PRO-ED, Inc. Reprinted with permission.

complying with the rules, and identifying strategies to successfully meet new standards of performance flounder in the high school setting and either leave or are pushed out.

Many different approaches have been shown to be effective in lowering dropout rates. The first focuses on providing an education that is directly tied to future careers, called a school-to-work or school-to-careers focus. A second approach concentrates on providing additional supports for students to meet higher academic achievement. This is typically accomplished through the use of peer tutors and/or adult mentors. The third approach focuses on the use of functional behavior analysis to identify the underlying problem and develop an individualized support plan based on the results

Family Income
- Three out of four children live in families where someone worked and one in three poor children lives with a full-time year-round worker. More than 5.1 million children live in extremely low-income households spending at least half of their income on housing.
- Twenty-two million adults and 13 million children live in households suffering form hunger or "food insecurity without hunger."
- The richest one-fifth of households made 10.7 times as much in median income as the poorest one-fifth, the widest gap on record from the U.S. Census Bureau.

Child Health
- 9.3 million children lack health insurance; yet six million of these uninsured children are eligible for Medicaid or the State Children's Health Insurance Program (CHIP) under current law.
- Infants born to Black mothers are more than twice as likely to die before their first birthday as infants born to white mothers.
- The number of overweight children has more than tripled since 1980. Almost nine million young people are overweight—over 15 percent of children and adolescents under age 19.

Child Care, Head Start, and School-Age Care
- Sixty-four percent of mothers with children under six and 78 percent of mothers with children ages six to 17 work outside the home.
- In 48 states, the cost of center-based child care for a four-year-old is greater than tuition at a four-year public college.
- The number of children participating in Head Start has more than doubled during the past three decades, but currently the program only serves three out of five three- and four-year-olds.

Education
- Seven out of ten fourth graders cannot read or do math at grade level.
- Ninety percent of the nation's children attend public schools. Children in the poorest families are six times as likely as children in more affluent families to drop out of high school.
- Three-quarters of the nation's public schools are in need of repairs, renovations, and modernization. The average school building is more than 40 years old. Yet states spend on average almost three times as much per prisoner as per public school pupil.

Children and Families in Crisis
- Three million children in a year are reported abused or neglected and referred for investigation or assessment; close to 900,000 of them are confirmed as victims of child maltreatment.
- Child abuse and domestic violence co-occur in an estimated 30 to 60 percent of the families where there is some form of family violence.
- The 51,000 children adopted from foster care in 2002 is almost double the number adopted in 1995, but more than 126,000 children in foster care continue to wait for permanent families.

Juvenile Justice and Youth Development
- The national crime rate has dropped nearly 25 percent since 1993, but more than one-quarter of violent crime victims known to police in the U.S. are juveniles. Youths ages 16 to 19 currently experience overall violence, including rape and general assault, at higher rates than people in all other age categories.
- Two-third of youths in the juvenile justice system have one or more diagnosable mental health disorders. Girls are the fastest growing segment of the juvenile justice population: The arrest rate for females under age 18 increased more than 14 percent between 1993 and 2002, while the rate for males under age 18 decreased.
- More than six million school-age children are left alone after school without supervision. The average child watches 28 hours of television a week and by age 18 will have seen more than 200,000 acts of violence and 16,000 simulated murders depicted on the TV screen.

FIGURE 5.3

Findings from *The State of America's Children.*

Note: From Children's Defense Fund, (2004). *The State of America's Children,* (pp. 1–202).

of the analysis. A fourth approach looks at the services available to support a student where he or she currently is. These are called wraparound services. The final approach, moving a student to an alternative school, is more restrictive but has been shown to be effective for some students who are at risk of dropping out.

School-to-Careers Approach

What works for dropout prevention? Many experts in the field believe that a school-to-work focus is the best prevention. The Carl D. Perkins Vocational-Technical Education Act of 1998 (Perkins III), designed to encourage collaborative efforts among schools, businesses, and community agencies, benefits a large number of students, including students at risk for dropout (Finch, 1999). The development of programs under this initiative necessitates that districts embrace new policies that address the logistics of implementing work-based experiences (e.g., transportation, time for school and community staff to meet). In addition, school administrators and employers must provide the leadership required for systems-level changes.

A majority of educators believe that "experiential learning"—ranging from internships to job shadowing—can effectively boost academic achievement and reduce dropout rates, according to the results of a new poll. In fact, in a survey conducted by Junior Achievement, about 9 of 10 respondents agreed that experiential learning was either "somewhat effective" or "very effective" at raising student achievement. In addition, 85% of those polled said that career-linked learning experiences get students somewhat interested in careers and higher education, and 79% said such methods can help to curtail dropout rates.

Academic Tutoring

Academic tutoring is one way that at-risk adolescents can improve their academic functioning. Researchers have shown that before- and after-school tutoring programs improve academic success by helping students with actual class assignments and teaching various strategies that students can generalize to other academic problems (Hock, Pulvers, Deshler, & Schumaker, 2001). The concept of academic tutoring has been applied to all ages, from elementary school to postbaccalaureate education. In

ACCOMMODATING TECHNOLOGY

Exploration and utilization of technology is an important part of preparing students for future education and employment pursuits. Technology software and devices include text-to-speech software for reading, writing, and test-taking; speech recognition software for writing; and electronic organizers for reading, comprehension, writing, and studying. It is important to determine the best "technology fit" for students based on their needs, strengths, weaknesses, and familiarity with technology. For example, a student with reading comprehension difficulties could benefit from a type of text-to-speech software with study skill features that can be individualized for the student by slowing down the speech, enlarging the text, highlighting the print, and using an electronic dictionary.

For further information about technology, a helpful resource might be www.abledata.com/Site 2. This website provides basic information as well as links for additional information.

most instances, students who attended frequent sessions of tutoring had positive out-comes. For instance, Wasik and Slavin (1990) reported results of research that eval-uated the effects of five primary grade reading programs. They found that one-to-one tutoring had positive effects on students' reading achievement in two of the programs, and had positive short-term effects in another. In a related study, Dennison (2000) im-plemented a program called Big Buddies to provide tutoring/mentoring for third- and fourth-graders by 11th- and 12th-grade honor students. Effects were positive, though not statistically significant, on self-esteem, attitudes toward school, and on-task class-room behavior. However, the majority of the elementary school students increased their skill levels by one grade level in the area in which they received tutoring.

In a study with direct implications for urban youth, Ginsburg-Block and Fantuzzo (1997) found that African American elementary school students highly benefited by reciprocal peer tutoring (RPT). RPT produced high rates of mathematics achieve-ment, positive self-reports of social acceptance, positive change in behavioral/con-duct, and improved teacher and student task-related behavior. Schinke, Cole, and Poulin (2000) showed that students' discussions with adults, along with specific other academic/cognitive tasks, were related to higher grades in major subject areas. Individual help from others has also been shown to help college-level students. A study of second- and third-year medical students revealed that regular and frequent meetings with tutors, as well as other social and academic involvement, were related to academic success (Malik, 2000).

Another study demonstrated that the use of peer tutoring has a positive impact on the decision of students to stay in school (Somers & Piliawsky, 2004). This interven-tion provided opportunities for at-risk youth to have peer tutoring and adult mentoring on a regular basis. Somers and Piliawsky (2004) found that at-risk students who re-ceived peer tutoring and adult mentoring were more likely to remain in school, had higher expectations for their own academic performance, and made the connection between academic achievement and long-term success on the job. Participants in this study indicated that the role models helped them understand the specific steps, one at a time in a sequence, involved in reaching their goals.

Functional Behavioral Assessment (FBA)

Students who have unexcused absences and serious behavior problems are already experiencing school failure, especially when attempts to correct the situation are puni-tive and exclusionary. Fortunately, recognition is growing that suspensions, expulsions, and homebound placements are inadequate responses to school discipline problems for many individuals (Jackson & Panyan, 2002; Morrison & D'Incau, 2000; Tobin & Sugai, 1999a, 1999b). Indeed, the Individuals with Disabilities Education Act (IDEA, 1997, 1999) addresses the use of functional behavioral assessment, which can be used to design positive behavior supports to reduce behavior or attendance problems (Dras-gow, Yell, Bradley, & Shriner, 1999; Fox & Conroy, 2000; Gable & Hendrickson, 2000; Kearney & Tillotson, 1998; Sugai, Lewis-Palmer, & Hagan, 1998; Tobin & Martin, 2001).

Typically, function-based support starts with interviewing staff and the student to determine the nature of the problem and identify events occurring before and after the behavior to identify the likely function(s) of the behavior. This should be followed by repeated direct observations of the student's actions in naturally occurring situations at school. The results of the FBA should lead to the formulation of an intervention plan, often involving several aspects, such as (a) teaching and reinforcing appropriate re-placement behaviors, (b) changes in curriculum and instruction, and (c) changes in the way other students and teachers respond to problem behavior. In most cases, the intervention must address the individual needs of the student to produce positive outcomes (Condon & Tobin, 2001; Doggert, Edwards, Moore, Tingstrom, & Wilczynski, 2001; Liaupsin, Scott, & Nelson, 2000; O'Neill et al., 1997; Witt, Daly, & Noell, 2000).

Wraparound Service

Often, students who are at risk of dropping out of school present behavioral challenges that require support and intervention across multiple domains. *Wraparound* is a term used when school staff and personnel from community agencies collaborate to provide services that "wrap around" the student and his or her family. Originally a plan for integrating community mental health and school services, the concept of **wraparound service** now includes other agencies and has been very effective in keeping students with multiple problems in school (Eber, 1996; Eber & Nelson, 1997). Wraparound planning typically leads to an individualized package of several types of support. Services that might be coordinated in a comprehensive plan include (a) student services (e.g., behavior change program, medication management, after-school tutoring); (b) school services (e.g., coverage for in-school respite to prevent out-of-school suspension, technical assistance for staff, substitutes to assure teacher participation in meetings); (c) family services (e.g., trained advocates to accompany parents and student to court, transportation to appointments, development of home behavior plans); and (d) community services (e.g., recreational coaching, partnerships with businesses, emergency funds to pay utilities).

Alternative Education

The use of alternative education is an increasingly popular way to address the needs of students at risk for leaving school early (Tobin & Sprague, 2000, 2002; Wetzel, McNaboe, Schneidermeyer, Jones, & Nash, 1997). Alternative education programs vary greatly, making it difficult to generalize positive reports from the limited studies available (Raywid, 1994). For example, some serve students who voluntarily select the program because it offers interesting activities or opportunities to work with teachers who are perceived as being less authoritarian than traditional teachers (Richardson & Griffin, 1994). Other alternative schools are more authoritarian than traditional schools, such as reform schools for students who have been expelled (Hill, 1998). Still other alternative programs meet specific needs, such as help in preparing to take the test for the GED and finding a job. Castleberry and Enger (1998) found that students in alternative programs with low teacher–student ratios reported that being able to frequently work one on one with teachers greatly improved their intention to graduate or receive their GED. However, Rumberger and Larson (1998) warned that the practice of transferring troublesome students to an alternative setting could increase the odds that students will not graduate from high school. In fact, one or more nonpromotional school changes between 8th and 12th grade can increase a student's odds of not graduating by 50% (Rumberger & Larson, 1998). Alternative programs represent only one available intervention in an array of effective possible strategies designed to meet the needs of at-risk students. Because of the broad array of philosophies and program designs, we must be careful about generalizing findings without considering the features of the settings in which the studies were conducted.

Curriculum

Educational policies are increasingly moving away from minimum competencies and toward higher performance standards (Education Commission of the States, 1996).

Although the goal is to improve students' skills, an unintentional outcome of the shift in policy may be an increase in the dropout rate, especially for students with disabilities (U.S. Department of Education, 2000). Teachers may feel pressured to increase the amount of material covered at the expense of instructional activities that might benefit learners at risk for school failure (Benz, Lindstrom, & Yovanoff, 2000). Policies that emphasize standards-based reform efforts must be accompanied by practices that afford all students opportunities to succeed. Sound educational policies are needed to ensure greater school engagement and retention of high-risk youth, particularly students with learning and behavioral difficulties (Rumberger, 1995; Sinclair, Christenson, Evelo, & Hurley, 1998).

Strategies for Intervention

Arroyo, Rhoad, and Drew (1999) identified the following variables as the 10 most strongly associated with underachievement of youth in urban settings (presented not in order of strength but in order of likelihood of school having an influence on change): teachers' demonstrations of caring, respect, and interest in children's growth; teacher expectations for children's achievement; curriculum relevance; class size; disengagement from school-related activities; students' own confidence in their abilities to achieve; high mobility in school attendance; parental expectations and involvement; level of parents' education; and poverty or low income.

Resiliency

Not every student who is at risk will have difficulty learning or decide to drop out of school. What differentiates those who are able to succeed in spite of these challenges from those who are not? **Resiliency** is the term that many are using to describe an ability to rise above adverse circumstances. Eisenberg and colleagues (2004) referred to high resiliency as "resourceful adaptation to changing circumstances and flexible use of problem-solving strategies, whereas low resiliency involves little adaptive flexibility, an inability to respond to changing circumstances, the tendency to perseverate or become disorganized when dealing with change or stress, and difficulty recouping after traumatic experiences" (p. 29).

Experts in the area of resiliency promote a focus on providing supports to students living in these high-risk settings and/or confronted with high-risk situations rather than on changing the situation or setting. This makes sense given that it is beyond a typical teacher's control to make changes in these factors. Through the support of teachers, students can learn to change the situation themselves, or at the very least, learn that a better future is possible. In a recent research study, at-risk adolescents were asked what factors would help them, and they overwhelmingly reported that supports and involved adults were crucial to their long-term success. "Despite the challenges they acknowledge they confront—guns, violence, the drug culture, even rape—the most striking finding of this teen-centered process is that the teenagers in this study hold the optimistic view that the protection offered by education and involved adults will help them overcome the odds" (Ginsberg-Block & Fantuzzo, 1997, p. 1140). They asked for supports such as help with getting into college, more job opportunities, and stronger punishments for serious criminals.

Self-Determination

The idea of promoting resiliency to prevent problems is parallel to another focus in the education of students with disabilities, self-determination. **Self-determination** refers to "acting as the primary causal agent in one's life free to make choices and decisions about one's quality of life, free from undue influence or interference" (Wehmeyer, 1992, p. 302). Wehmeyer, Agran, and Hughes (2000) described 12 component skills that are important to the emergence of self-determined behavior: "choice-making; decision-making; problem-solving; goal setting and attainment; independence, risk-taking and safety skills; self-observation, evaluation, and reinforcement skills; self-instruction; self-advocacy and leadership skills; internal locus of control; positive attributes of efficacy and outcome expectancy; self-awareness; and self-knowledge" (p. 11). Researchers have demonstrated that higher levels of self-determination are linked to improved outcomes in later life (Wehmeyer & Bolding, 1999; Wehmeyer & Kelchner, 1995, 1996; Wehmeyer, Kelchner & Richards, 1995, 1996), and to higher levels of independence in learning for students (Agran, 1997).

Adolescents live up to the expectations others hold for them. Teachers must provide opportunities, with options, and the supports to help students make their dreams a reality. Instruction and interactions that focus on increasing resiliency and/or self-determination skills will show students that they have the skills to overcome adversity themselves.

Extracurricular Activities

Finally, Mahoney and Cairns (1997) found that engaging at-risk students in extracurricular activities that are available to all students in school is an effective method of dropout prevention. They concluded that involvement in extracurricular activities helped students develop conventional social support networks and personal goals and interests. Mahoney and Cairns (1997) found that some extracurricular activities had a stronger impact on dropout rates than others. The extracurricular activities most closely associated with reduced dropout rates were athletic and vocational activities (e.g., Automobile Club, Career Club, Future Business Leaders, Future Farmers, Future Homemakers, and Vocational Industrial Club). Further support for extracurricular activities that encourage healthy peer relationships comes from a study of a dropout prevention program (Communities in Schools) by Walters and Bowen (1997), who found that peer group acceptance, which can be fostered through extracurricular activities, helps students avoid problem behaviors and improve academic performance

Working with the Family

Students who are at risk often find themselves living in less than ideal situations, and schools are not likely to provide interventions that will change those circumstances. However, teachers and other school personnel can understand the implications of these family factors and provide support and guidance to parents who are willing and able to make changes. As O'Shea and O'Shea stated, "most students bring their family issues with them to class and take their school issues home" (2001, p. 8), so it is imperative that schools and families learn to work together.

ACCOMMODATING DIVERSITY

When working with students from different cultural or linguistic backgrounds, understanding parents' educational expectations for their sons or daughters is important (Black et al., 2003; Yamauchi, 1998). Clear communication of what the school and home view as the value of education and a student's educational goals is critical. Otherwise, there is the potential of creating a conflict for students as they strive to meet the school's educational expectations and those of their families (Black et al., 2003).

It is particularly important that sensitivity to cultural values and attitudes be understood when teaching students with special needs. For example, families of students with ADHD may consider certain behaviors as appropriate and may not understand a school's concern (Swanson, 1992). Cultural differences can play a role in parents' understanding of what test results mean and what interventions a school believes are necessary. In addition, it is vital that the school and family members communicate what behaviors they are seeing. Sometimes students can exhibit specific behaviors in reaction to the structure of the school setting or classroom whereas these types of behaviors might not be seen as frequently in the home (Swanson, 1992).

Research clearly shows that the more parents are involved in the school, the better students do academically. However, many parents struggle to find time to be involved or are unsure of how to do that. The National PTA (1992) cited the following reasons parents fail to be involved in school activities:

- *Time.* Single and working parents reported that they were often unable to attend meetings, conferences, and school activities, particularly those held during the day.
- *Intimidation.* Parents reported that they often felt intimidated by school personnel.
- *Don't understand the system.* Parents reported that they did not understand how the general and special education systems worked.
- *Child care.* Parents reported that they did not have someone to watch their children when they attended school meetings, conferences, or activities.
- *Language.* Parents who speak English as a second language often have problems reading printed materials and/or understanding school personnel at meetings.
- *Cultural differences.* Parents reported that the differences in manners and courtesies may offend or embarrass them.
- *Transportation.* Some parents may lack transportation to attend meetings, conferences, and other school events.
- *Not welcomed.* Some parents reported that they did not feel welcome at school.

Despite the challenges in getting parents involved in schools, it is worth the effort. Schools that are successful at lowering dropout rates and increasing the academic performance of their students find innovative ways to reach out and involve parents. Epstein (1995) described six types of involvement teachers can use to partner with parents to support the academic achievement of at-risk students. Figure 5.4 outlines Epstein's work.

A combination of what O'Shea and O'Shea (2001) called direct and indirect family services should be used to both help parents ameliorate the risk factors and help students learn to deal with adverse situations. Indirect services include services that are provided directly to the student such as positive behavior support

Type of Involvement	Action
Type 1: Parenting	Help all families establish home environments to support children as students (i.e., show them how to provide work space for homework, how to acknowledge school achievement, etc.)
Type 2: Communicating	Design effective forms of school-to-home and home-to-school communication about school programs and children's progress (i.e., send notes home on a specific day regarding extracurricular/school-based activities so parents know when to look for that information in students' backpacks).
Type 3: Volunteering	Recruit and organize parent help and support (i.e., find ways that parents who find it difficult to travel to the school could help out by doing something at home or in their neighborhoods; also, provide specific tasks that parents can help with).
Type 4: Learning at home	Provide information and ideas to families about how to help students at home with homework and other curriculum-related activities, decisions, and planning (i.e., provide contact information about free or low-cost tutors who can help students and parents catch up with work).
Type 5: Decision making	Include parents in school decisions, developing parent leaders and representatives (i.e., not just having typical parent advisory groups, but also having a group address the issues for parents from culturally diverse backgrounds, or working parents).
Type 6: Collaborating with community	Identify and integrate resources and services from the community to strengthen school programs, family practices, and student learning and development (i.e., getting cultural groups involved in sharing their customs, getting business partnerships formed to help with fundraising and/or school-to-careers activities).

FIGURE 5.4
Epstein's Framework of Six Types of Involvement.

Note: Adapted from J. L. Epstein, (1995), "School/Family/Community Partnerships: Caring for the Children We Share." *Phi Delta Kappan, 76*(9), 704.

plans, Section 504 plans, and so forth, which were described elsewhere in this chapter. Direct family support services are described in further detail in chapter 3. Whatever approaches are used to support families, Henderson and Mapp (2002) suggested the following action steps to establish family engagement programs and services:

1. Recognize that all parents, regardless of income, education level, or cultural background, are involved in their children's education and want their children to do well in school.

2. Link family and community engagement efforts to student learning.

3. Create initiatives that will support families to guide their children's learning, from preschool through high school.

4. Develop the capacity of school staff to work with families.

5. Focus efforts to engage families on developing trusting and respectful relationships.

6. Embrace a philosophy of partnership and be willing to share power with families. Make sure that parents and school staff understand that the responsibility for children's educational development is a collaborative enterprise (Mapp, 2004).

Direct Family Support Services

Direct family support services provide specific supports to individual families in the home. These services are often supported by educational, human resources, and health agencies and are geared to focus on specific outcomes such as improving parenting skills, increasing family involvement in children's education, and/or academic remediation for parents.

Parent groups that are based in the school or are part of community, regional, and/or national organizations are great sources of support and information for parents. The underlying goals of such groups usually include helping parents overcome isolation, providing supports for each other, learn skills, and develop insights about children and themselves (Carter & Harvey, 1996).

Home–school partnerships such as those described in Figure 5.4 offer opportunities for parents to work with schools in addition to the typical parent–teacher organizations. At-risk parents often report that they do not participate because they lack time, resources, and interest in doing so (Epstein, 1995).

Whiteford (1998) described a school-based program aimed at retraining parents in skill areas to enable them to help their children with schoolwork at home. This program involved a series of seven hour-long workshops designed to deepen parents' conceptual knowledge and understanding of the mathematics their children would encounter during the elementary school years. Whiteford reported that as a result of their workshop, parents, felt more confident helping their children.

CULTURE OF POVERTY

Defining Poverty

It is estimated that more than 14 million children grow up in the United States in poverty (Smith et al., 2004). Poverty has been identified as the number one cause of putting students at risk for academic failure (Davis, 1993). Poverty is associated with causing learning, behavioral, and emotional problems. More research is needed to determine the impacts of poverty that contribute to some of the causes of disabilities such as learning disabilities or mental retardation (Smith et al., 2004; Wood, Lazzari, & Wehman, 1997).

Classroom Accommodations and Techniques

As with all of the groups that we have discussed in this chapter, each student brings unique learning strengths and weaknesses. Individualizing instruction or incorporating a variety of techniques into the learning process are important considerations. Because students who come from a culture of poverty bring a variety of issues to the education setting, each unique to their situation, readers should review other sections of this chapter or chapters in this book. It is possible that a student could have significant learning disabilities and live in a culture of poverty. It could be that the conditions where a student lives puts him or her at risk of succeeding in school. Understanding students' specific needs will assist in determining effective accommodations and techniques for these students.

Strategies for Intervention

Students from a culture of poverty bring to school a set of issues unique to their own situation. These students could come hungry, homeless, or in ill health (Smith et al., 2004). These situations can make it difficult for students to concentrate, be involved in school, or even see the meaning of receiving an education. Smith and colleagues (2004) suggested the following techniques to help these students in the classroom (additional intervention strategies or ideas are described in the at-risk section of this chapter):

- Help to make all students in the classroom feel important.
- Avoid putting students in situations where they cannot afford to pay for an activity, thus potentially leaving them out or bringing attention to the fact that they cannot afford to participate.
- Seek contingency funds or find a volunteer organization that can help provide needed school supplies that students might not be able to purchase on their own.

Working with the Family

Working with families who come from a culture of poverty presents several challenges. Difficulty reaching family members because of homelessness, lack of a telephone or computer, or scheduling conflicts resulting from working several jobs can make communication between the school and family difficult. Other factors could include a mistrust of the school, the fact that English is not the predominant language used at home, and being overwhelmed with daily living issues that do not include school. Teachers need to understand to the extent possible what is happening with the family and through outreach efforts connect the family with a school social worker or counselor to help the family seek needed assistance.

SUMMARY

Students with other special learning needs represents a wide spectrum of skills, abilities, interests, and weaknesses. This chapter has sought to provide an overview of some of the educational issues and concerns of these groups, and practical ideas and strategies to better meet their educational needs. Collaboration among families, students, school personnel, and community agencies plays a part in developing a team approach to educating students. Technology will continue to play a critical role in helping students access information and overcome some of their learning deficits through the use of software programs and devices.

It is hoped that an understanding of these diverse learners will help you better prepare your curriculum and class activities to provide alternate ways of learning and expression of students of the knowledge they have gained. The underlying goal of this chapter has been to help teachers create a welcoming environment for all students so that each can appreciate the learning strengths and weaknesses of others and respect the cultural or ethnic practices and beliefs of all students in their school or classroom. Schools should challenge all learners to expand their horizons and to think creatively and structure their learning experiences to meet their own personal educational goals.

RESOURCES

teachergrants. Provides a "related searches" box with information on obtaining a variety of grants. www.teachergrants.org.

National Dropout Prevention Centers. Provides knowledge and promotes networking for researchers, practitioners, policymakers, and families to increase opportunities for youth in at-risk situations to receive the quality education and services necessary to successfully graduate from high school. www.dropoutprevention.org.

Children's Defense Fund. Provides information on meeting children's needs, preventing poverty, advocating for children and engaging faith communities. www.childrensdefense.org.

National Center for Education Statistics. Provides information on collected and analyzed data on education in the United States and other nations nces.ed.gov.

EPMagazine. Provides information, support, ideas encouragement, and outreach for parents and families of children with disabilities and the professionals who work with them. www.eparent.com.

SUGGESTED READINGS

Arroyo, A. A., Rhoad, R., & Drew, R. (1999). Meeting diverse student needs in urban schools: Research-based recommendations for school personnel. *Preventing School Failure, 43*(4), 145–153.

Benz, M. R., Lindstrom, L., & Yovanoff, P. (2000). Improving graduation and employment outcomes of students with disabilities: Predictive factors and student perspectives. *Exceptional Children, 66,* 509–529.

Black, R. S., Mrasek, K. D., & Ballinger, R. (2003). Individualist and collectivist values in transition planning for culturally diverse students with special needs. *The Journal for Vocational Special Needs Education, 25*(2,3), 20–29.

Center for Applied Special Technology. (2001). *Universal design for learning.* [Online]. Available: www.cast.org.

Culatta, R. A., Tompkins, J. R.., & Werts, M. G. (2003). *Fundamentals of special education: What every teacher needs to know* (2nd ed.). Upper Saddle River, NJ: Merrill/Prentice Hall.

Finn, J. D., & Rock, D. A. (1997). Academic success among students at risk for school failure. *Journal of Applied Psychology, 82,* 221–234.

Gable, R. A., & Hendrickson, J. M. (2000). Strategies for maintaining positive behavior change stemming from functional behavioral assessments in schools. *Education and Treatment of Children, 23*(3), 286–297.

Hock. M. F., Pulvers, K. A., Deshler, D. D., & Schumaker, J. B. (2001). The effects of an after-school tutoring program on the academic performance of at-risk students and students with LD. *Remedial & Special Education* (Special Issue), *22*(3), 172–186.

Johnson, D., & Fox, J. (2002). Creating curb cuts in the classroom: Adapting universal design principles. In J. L. Higbee (Ed.), *Curriculum transformation and disability: Implementing universal design in higher education.* Minneapolis: University of Minnesota, Center for Research and Developmental Education and Urban Literacy.

Sinclair, M. F., Christenson, S. L., Evelo, D. L., & Hurley, C. M. (1998). Dropout prevention for youth with disabilities: Efficacy of a sustained school engagement procedure. *Exceptional Children, 65,* 7–21.

Smith, T. E., Polloway, E., Patton, J. R., & Dowdy, C. A. (2004). *Teaching students with special needs in inclusive settings* (4th ed.). Boston: Allyn & Bacon.

Sugai, G., Lewis-Palmer, T., & Hagan, S. (1998). Using functional assessments to develop behavior support plans. *Preventing School Failure, 43*(1), 6–13.

Tobin, T., & Sprague, J. (2000). Alternative education strategies: Reducing violence in school and the community. *Journal of Emotional and Behavioral Disorders, 8*(3), 177–186.

Wehmeyer, M. L., Agran, M., & Hughes, C. (2000). A national survey of teachers' promotion of self-determination and student-directed learning. *Journal of Special Education, 34*(2), 58–68.

WEBSITES TO VISIT

Center for the Improvement of Early Reading Achievement. This site is research oriented, looking to find answers to early childhood reading problems. It creates instructional materials based on the results of the research while also advancing knowledge in the area through the design and distribution of a variety of publications and presentations. Although the site may be of interest to parents, it is primarily geared toward educators, publishers, and school districts. www.ciera.org.

International Reading Association. This site promotes the primary goals of literacy around the world. The site, accessible to parents and educators alike, is a forum for a variety of information including current research on reading, international reading news and topics, current literature for children through young adults, and continuing education opportunities. Online membership and benefits are also discussed on the site. www.reading.org.

American Association for Gifted Children. This website describes the history and purpose of the American Association for Gifted Children. Serving as an advocacy organization, it promotes research of and research opportunities for gifted students, continuing education through workshops and meetings, and dissemination of information through publications. The site provides information regarding children from preschool through high school and is a resource for parents and educators alike. www.aagc.org

Neag Center for Gifted Education and Talent Development. This site is connected to the University of Connecticut in Storrs, Connecticut. It is a comprehensive resource providing information on the latest legislative news, hands-on projects and programs for gifted students in the community, research, and continuing and graduate-level educational opportunities. It is a website useful to K-12 students, parents, educators, and school districts. www.gifted. uconn.edu

The Rhode Island State Advisory Committee on Gifted and Talented Education. This website represents the work and efforts of an advisory committee in the state of Rhode Island formed to facilitate communication and advocacy on behalf of those involved with gifted and talented education. The advisory board consists of a broad membership of individuals from legislators to school administrators, teachers, business and community leaders, and parents and students. The site not only provides information on programs, events, and continuing education, but also provides practical information to parents and teachers of gifted children as well as suggestions for business involvement with the students. This website has gathered information regarding continued communication through listservs around the country and provides information on a speaker's bureau with active participants promoting the cause of gifted and talented education within the state of Rhode Island. www.ri.net/gifted talented/parents.html.

National Dropout Prevention Center/Network. This website serves as a research center and resource for at-risk K-12 youth in America. Its reach extends to practitioners, researchers, and policy makers. This website benefits the needs of both at-risk youth and their communities by providing information concerning statistics for at-risk youth; best practices for students, families, and educators; model programs across the country; journals disseminating the results of research studies; resources for families, teachers, and administrators; continued education through conferences and seminars; and evaluation of programs. Finally, the site offers membership information for interested parties. www.dropoutprevention.org.

Children and Adults with Attention-Deficit/Hyperactivity Disorder. This site provides information, advocacy, and support for all individuals with attention-deficit/hyperactivity disorder. Not only does it inform viewers of facts regarding attention-deficit/hyperactivity disorder, research results, and continuing education through conferences, but it also provides information on local chapters of the organization around the United States. www.chadd.org

REFERENCES

Adderholdt-Elliott, M. (1987). *Perfectionism: What's bad about being too good?* Minneapolis, MN: Free Spirit Publishing.

Agran, M. (1997). Teaching self-management. In M. Agran (Ed.), *Student directed learning: Teaching self-determination skills* (pp. 1–27). Pacific Grove, CA: Brooks/Cole.

Armstrong, J. M. (1980). *Achievement and participation of women in mathematics: An overview.* Denver, CO: Education Commission of the States. (ERIC Document Reproduction Service No. ED 184878)

Arroyo, A. A., Rhoad, R., & Drew, R. (1999). Meeting diverse student needs in urban schools: Research-based recommendations for school personnel. *Preventing School Failure, 43*(4), 145–453.

Banks, J. A. (1993). Multicultural education: Development, dimensions, and challenges. *Phi Delta Kappan, 75,* 22–28.

Benbow, C. P. (1986). SMPY's model for teaching mathematically precocious students. In J. S. Renzulli (Ed.), *Systems and models for developing programs for the gifted and talented* (pp. 2–25). Mansfield Center, CT: Creative Learning Press.

Benz, M. R., Lindstrom, L., & Yovanoff, P. (2000). Improving graduation and employment outcomes of students with disabilities: Predictive factors and student perspectives. *Exceptional Children, 66,* 509–529.

Berliner, D. C., & Biddle, B. J. (1995). *The manufactured crisis: Myths, fraud, and the attack on America's public schools.* Cambridge, MA: Perseus.

Black, R. S., Mrasek, K. D., & Ballinger, R. (2003). Individualist and collectivist values in transition planning for culturally diverse students with special needs. *Journal for Vocational Special Needs Education, 25*(2,3), 20–29.

Bowe, F. G. (2000). *Universal design in education: Teaching non-traditional students.* Westport, CT: Bergen & Garvey.

Carter, N., & Harvey, C. (1996). Gaining perspective on parenting groups. *Zero to Three, 16*(6), 1–8.

Center for Applied Special Technology. (2001). *Universal design for learning.* [Online]. Available: www.cast.org.

CHADD (2004). *The disorder named AD/HD, CHADD fact sheet #1.* Retrieved June 17, 2004, from www.chadd.org/fs/fsl.pdf.

Chattergy, V., & Ongteco, B. C. (1991). Education needs of Filipino immigrant students. *Social Process in Hawaii, 33,* 142–152.

Cherkes-Julkowski, M., Sharp, S., & Stolzenberg, J. (1997). Rethinking attention deficit disorders. Cambridge, MA: Brookline Books.

Children's Defense Fund (2004). *The state of America's children.* Washington, DC: Author.

Clark, B. (1997). *Growing up gifted: Developing the potential of children at home and at school* (5th ed.). Upper Saddle River, NJ: Merrill/Prentice Hall.

Clasen, D. R. & Clasen, R. E. (1997). Mentoring: A time-honored option for education of the gifted and talented. In N. Colangelo & A. D. Davis (Eds.), *Handbook of gifted education* (2nd ed., pp. 218–229). Boston: Allyn & Bacon.

Clemente, R., & Collison, B. B. (2000). The relationships among counselors, ESL teachers, and students. *Professional School Counseling, 3*(5), 339–349.

Condon, K. A., & Tobin, T. J. (2001). Using electronic and other new ways to help students improve their behavior: Functional behavioral assessment at work. *Teaching Exceptional Children, 34*(1), 44–51.

Culatta, R. A., Tompkins, J. R., & Werts, M. G. (2003). *Fundamentals of special education: What every teacher needs to know* (2nd ed.). Upper Saddle River, NJ: Merrill/Prentice Hall.

Davis, G. A. (1993). Identifying the creatively gifted. In J. Genshaft, M. Bireley, & C. L. Hollinger (Eds.), *A guidebook for serving the gifted and talented.* Washington, DC: National Association of School Psychologists.

Delisle, J. R. (1997). Gifted adolescents: Five steps toward understanding and acceptance. In N. Colangelo & A. D. Davis (Eds.), *Handbook of clinical and experimental neuropsychology.* Hove, UK: Psychology Press/Erlbaum (UK) Taylor and Francis.

Dennison, S. (2000). A win-win peer mentoring and tutoring program: A collaborative model. *Journal of Primary Prevention, 20*(3), 161–174.

Doggert, R. A., Edwards, R. P., Moore, J. W., Tingstrom, D. H., & Wilczynski, S. M. (2001). An approach to functional assessment in general education classroom settings. *School Psychology Review, 30*(3), 313–328.

Drasgow, E., Yell, M. L., Bradley, R., & Shriner, J. G. (1999). The IDEA Amendments of 1997: A school-wide model for conducting functional behavioral assessments and developing behavior intervention plans. *Education and Treatment of Children, 22*(3), 244–266.

Eber, L. (1996). Restructuring schools through the wraparound approach: The LADSE experience. *Special Services in the Schools, 11*(1/2), 135–149.

Eber, L., & Nelson, C. M. (1997). School-based wraparound planning: Integrating services for students with emotional and behavioral needs. *American Journal of Orthopsychiatry, 67,* 385–395.

Education Commission of the States. (1996). *Standards and education: A roadmap for state policymakers* (No. SI-96–3). Denver, Co: Author.

Eisenberg, N., Spinrad, T. L., Fabes, R. A., Reiser, M., Cumberland, A., Shepard, S. A., Valiente, C., Losoya, S. H., Guthrie, I. K., & Thompson, M. (2004). The relations of effortful control and impulsivity to children's resiliency and adjustment. *Child Development, 75,* 25–47.

Epstein, J. L. (1995). School/family/community partnerships: Caring for the children we share. *Phi Delta Kappan, 76*(9), 701–712.

Feldhusen, J. F., Hansen, J. B., & Kennedy, D. M. (1989). Curriculum development for GCT teachers. *Gifted Child Today, 12*(6), 12–19.

Feldhusen, J., Van Winkle, L., & Ehle, D. A. (1996). Is it acceleration or simply appropriate instruction for precocious youth? *Teaching Exceptional Children, 28*(3), 48–51.

Finch, C. R. (1999). School-to-work programs: Opportunities and issues. *School Business Affairs, 65*(5), 16–20.

Finn, J. D. (1993). *School engagement and students at risk.* Buffalo, NY: State University, U. S. Department of Education. National Center for Educational Statistics. (ERIC Document Reproduction Service No. ED 362322)

Finn, J. D., & Rock, D. A. (1997). Academic success among students at risk for school failure. *Journal of Applied Psychology, 82,* 221–234.

Fleming, J. L., & Monda-Amaya, L. E. (2001). Process variables for team effectiveness: A Delphi study of wraparound team members. *Remedial and Special Education, 22*(3), 158–171.

Fox, J. J., & Conroy, M. A. (2000). Current issues in FBA for children and youth with emotional-behavioral disorders [Special issue]. *Preventing School Failure, 44*(4), 182–194.

Frymier, J. (1992). Children who are hurt, children who fail. *Phi Delta Kappan, 74*(3), 257–259.

Gable, R. A., & Hendrickson, J. M. (2000). Strategies for maintaining positive behavior change stemming from functional behavioral assessments in schools. *Education and Treatment of Children, 23*(3), 286–297.

Gallagher, J. (1985). *Teaching the gifted child* (3rd. ed.). Boston: Allyn & Bacon.

Gallagher, J. J. & Gallagher, S. A. (1994). *Teaching the gifted child* (4th ed.). Boston: Allyn & Bacon.

Gardner, H. (1983). *Frames of mind: The theory of multiple intelligences.* New York: Basic Books.

Ginsburg-Block, M., & Fantuzzo, J. (1997). Reciprocal peer tutoring: An analysis of "teacher" and "student" interactions as a function of training and experience. *School Psychology Quarterly, 12*(2), 134–149.

Guagliardo, M. F., Huang, Z., Hicks, J., & D'Angelo, L. (1998). Increased drug use among old-for-grade and dropout urban adolescents. *American Journal of Preventive Medicine, 15*(1), 42–48.

Hall, E. G. (1980). Sex differences in IQ development for intellectually gifted students. *Roeper Review, 2*(3), 25–28.

Hardman, M. L., Drew, C. J., & Egan, M. W. (2002). *Human exceptionality: Society, school, and family* (7th ed.). Boston: Allyn & Bacon.

Henderson, A., & Mapp, K. (2002). *A few wave of evidence: The impact of school, family, and community connections on student achievement.* Austin, TX: Southwest Educational Development Laboratory.

Hill, D. (1998). Reform school. *Teacher Magazine, 9*(8), 34–35, 38–41.

Hock M. F., Pulvers, K. A., Deshler, D. D., & Schumaker, J. B. (2001). The effects of an after-school tutoring program on the academic performance of at-risk students and students with LD. *Remedial & Special Education* (Special Issue), *22*(3), 172–186.

Hoctor, M., & Kaplan, S. (1989). *Developing policies for a gifted/talented program: A handbook.* Canoga Park, CA: California Association of the Gifted.

Individuals with Disabilities Education Act Amendments of 1997, Public Law 105–17, 105th Congress, 1st Session.

Individuals with Disabilities Education Act of 1999, 20 U.S.C. [section] 1400 *et seq;* 34 C.F.R. [section] 300.1 *et seq.* (1999); 64 Fed. Reg. 12, 406–12, 672 (1999).

Inestroza, R. A. (1990). Integrating basic skills for IEPs in vocational education. *Journal for Vocational Special Needs Education, 13*(1), 41.

Jackson, L., & Panyan, M. V. (2002). *Positive behavioral support in the classroom: Principles and practices.* Baltimore: Brookes.

Johnson, D., & Fox, J. (2002). Creating curb cuts in the classroom: Adapting Universal Design principles. In J. L. Higbee (Ed.), *Curriculum transformation and disability: Implementing Universal Design in higher education.* Minneapolis: University of Minnesota, Center for Research and Developmental Education and Urban Literacy.

Kearney, C. A., & Tillotson, C. A. (1998). School attendance. In T. S. Watson & F. M. Gresham (Eds.), *Handbook of child behavior therapy* (pp. 143–161). New York: Plenum.

Kerr, B. A. (1997). *Smart girls: A new psychology of girls, women, and giftedness.* Scottsdale, AZ: Gifted Psychology Press.

Liaupsin, C. J., Scott, T. M., & Nelson, C. M. (2000). *Functional behavioral assessment: An interactive training module: User's manual and facilitator's guide,* (2nd ed.). Longmont, CO: Sopris West.

Mahoney, J. L., & Cairns, R. B. (1997). Do extracurricular activities protect against early school dropout? *Developmental Psychology, 33,* 241–253.

Maker, J. C. (1993). Gifted students in the general education classroom: What practices are defensible and feasible? In C. J. Maker (Ed.), *Critical issues in gifted education: Programs for the gifted in regular classrooms,* (Vol. 3, pp. 413–436). Austin, TX: Pro-Ed.

Malik, S. (2000). Students, tutors, and relationships: The ingredients of a successful student support scheme. *Medical Education, 34*(8), 635–641.

Mapp, K. (2004). Family engagement. In F. P. Schargel & J. Smink (Eds.), *Helping students graduate: A strategic approach to dropout preventivon* (pp. 99–113). Larchmont, NY: Eye on Education.

Marland, S. (1972). *Education of the gifted and talented.* Report to Congress by the U.S. Commissioner of Education. Washington, DC: U. S. Government Printing Office.

Morrison, G. M., & D' Incau, B. (2000). Developmental and service trajectories of students with disabilities recommended for expulsion from school. *Exceptional Children, 66,* 257–272.

National Center for Educational Statistics. (2002). *Dropout rates in the United States: 2000.* [Online]. Available: http://nces.ed.gov/

National PTA. (1992). *For our children: Parents and families in education* (Results of the National Parent Involvement Summit, April 1992). Chicago: Author.

National Resources Center on AD/HD (2004). *What is the difference between Section 504 and IDEA?* Retrieved May 10, 2004, from www.help4adhd.org

Noble, K. D. (1989). Counseling and gifted women: Becoming the heroes of their own stories. *Journal for the Education of the Gifted, 12*(2), 131–141.

O'Neill, R. E., Homer, R. H., Albin, R. W., Sprague, J. R., Storey, K., & Newton, J. S. (1997). *Functional assessment and program development for problem behavior: A practical handbook.* Pacific Grove, CA: Brooks/Cole.

O'Shea, D. J., & O'Shea, L. J. (2001). Why learn about students' families? In D. J. O'Shea, L. J. O'Shea, R. Algozzine, & D. J. Hammittee (Eds.), *Families and teachers of individuals with disabilities: Collaborative orientations and responsive practices* (pp. 5–24). Boston: Allyn & Bacon.

Parsons, J. E., Frieze, I. H. & Ruble, D. M. (1978). Intrapsychic factors influencing career aspirations in college women. *Sex Roles: A Journal of Research, 4,* 237–248.

Perrone, P. A. (1997). Gifted individuals' career development. In N. Colangelo & G. A. Davis (Eds.), *Handbook of gifted education* (2nd ed., pp. 398–407). Boston: Allyn & Bacon.

Piechowski, M. M. (1997). Emotional giftedness: The measure of intrapersonal intelligence. In N. Colangelo & G. A. Davis (Eds.), *Handbook of gifted education* (2nd ed., pp. 336–381). Boston: Allyn & Bacon.

Piirto, J. (1994). Precocity as a hallmark of giftedness. In W. L. Heward (Eds.), *Exceptional children: An introduction to special education.* Upper Saddle River, NJ: Merrill/Prentice, Hall.

Power, T. J., Karustis, J. L., & Habboushe, D. F. (2001). *Homework success for children with ADHD: A family-school intervention program.* New York: Guilford.

Rasberry, W. (2004). Emotional ties to school vital to success. Retrieved on September 17, 2004, from *The Seattle Times:* http://seattletimes.nwsource.com/html/opinion/2002034444_raspberry14.html.

Reid, R., Maag, J. W., Vasa, S. F., & Wright, G. (1994). Who are the children with attention deficit-hyperactivity disorder? A school-based survey. *The Journal of Special Education, 28,* 117–137.

Richardson, M. D., & Griffin, B. L. (1994). Alternative schools: Research implications for principals. *NASSP Bulletin, 78,* 105–111.

Rimm, S. B. (1986). *Underachievement syndrome: Causes and cures.* Watertown, WI: Apple.

Rumberger, R. W. (1987). High school drop outs: A review of issues and evidence. *Review of Educational Research, 57*(2), 101–121.

Rumberger, R. W. (1995). Dropping out of middle school: A multilevel analysis of students and schools. *American Educational Research Journal, 32,* 583–625.

Rumberger, R. W., & Larson, K. A. (1998). Student mobility and the increased risk of high school dropout. *American Journal of Education, 107,* 1–35.

Schinke, S. P., Cole, K. C., & Poulin, S. R. (2000). Enhancing the educational achievement of at risk youth. *Prevention Science, 1*(1), 51–60.

Scribner, A., & Scribner, J. D. (2001). *High-performing schools serving Mexican American students: What they can teach us.* ERIC Digest. (Report No. EDO-RC-01-4) Charleston, WV: ERIC Clearinghouse on Rural Education and Small Schools. (ERIC Document Reproduction Services No. ED 459048)

Silverman, L. K. (1995). Highly gifted children. In J. L. Genshaft, M. Bireley, & C. L. Hollinger (Eds.), *Serving gifted and talented students: A resource for school personnel.* Austin, TX: Pro-Ed.

Sinclair, M. F., Christenson, S. L., Evelo, D. L., & Hurley, C. M. (1998). Dropout prevention for youth with disabilities: Efficacy of a sustained school engagement procedure. *Exceptional Children, 65,* 7–21.

Smith, D. D. (2001). *Introduction to special education: Teaching in an age of challenge* (2nd ed.). Needham, MA: Allyn & Bacon.

Smith, T. E., Polloway, E., Patton, J. R., & Dowdy, C. A. (2004). *Teaching students with special needs in inclusive settings* (4th ed.). Boston: Allyn & Bacon.

Somers, C. L. & Piliawsky, M. (2004). Drop-out prevention among urban, African American adolescents: Program evaluation and practical implications. *Preventing School Failure, 48*(3) 17–22.

Stevens, L. J. & Price, M. (1992). Meeting the challenge of educating children at risk. *Phi Delta Kappan, 74,* 18–23.

Swanson, J. M. (1992). *School-based assessments and interventions for ADD students.* Irvine, CA: K.C. Press.

Sugai, G., Lewis-Palmer, T., & Hagan, S. (1998). Using functional assessments to develop behavior support plans. *Preventing School Failure, 43*(1), 6–13.

Sutton-Smith, B., Rosenberg, B. G., & Landy, F. (1968). Father-absence effects in families of different sibling compositions. *Child Development, 39,* 1213–1221.

Teemant, A., Bernhardt, E., Rodriguez-Muñoz, M., & Aiello, M. (2000). A dialogue among teachers that benefits second language learners. *Middle School Journal, 32*(2), 30–38.

Terman, L. M. (1959). Early signs of giftedness: Research and commentary. *Journal for the Education of the Gifted, 15,* 104–133.

Tinajero, J. V., & Hurley, S. (2000). Exemplary schooling for intermediate and middle school students acquiring English. In K. D. Wood & T. S. Dickinson, (Eds.), *Promoting literacy in grades 4–9: A handbook for teachers and administrators* (pp. 172–190). Boston: Allyn & Bacon.

Tobin, T. J., & Martin, E. (2001). *Can discipline referrals be reduced by functional behavioral assessments?* Poster Session presented April 20, 2001. Council for Exceptional Children Conference, Kansas City, MO. [Online as "Seven out of Eight"]. Available: http://darkwing.uoregon.edu/~ttobin. (ERIC Document Reproduction Service No. ED 346082)

Tobin, T., & Sprague, J. (2000). Alternative education strategies: Reducing violence in school and the community. *Journal of Emotional and Behavioral Disorders, 8*(3), 177–186.

Tobin, T. J., & Sprague, J. R. (2002). Alternative educational programs: Accommodating tertiary level, at-risk students. In M. R. Shinn, G. Stoner, & H. M. Walker (Eds.), *Interventions for academic and behavior problems: Preventive and remedial approaches* (pp. 961–992). Silver Spring, MD: National Association of School Psychologists.

Tobin, T. J., & Sugai, G. M. (1999a). Discipline problems, placements, and outcomes for students with serious emotional disturbance. *Behavioral Disorders, 24,* 109–121.

Tobin, T. J., & Sugai, G. M. (1999b). Using sixth-grade school records to predict violence, chronic discipline problems, and high school outcomes. *Journal of Emotional and Behavioral Disorders, 7*(1), 40–53.

U.S. Department of Education. (2000). *To assure the free appropriate public education of all children with disabilities: Twenty-first annual report to Congress on the implementation of the Individuals with Disabilities Education Act.* [Online]. Washington, DC: Author. Available: http://www.ed.gov/offices/OSERS/OSEP/.

Van Tassel-Baska, J. (1989). The role of the family in the success of disadvantaged gifted learners. *Journal for the Education of the Gifted, 13*(1), 22–36.

Van Tassel-Baska, J. (1998). *Gifted and talented learners.* Denver: Love.

Vaughn, S., Bos, C., & Schumm, J. S. (2003). *Teaching exceptional, diverse, and at-risk students in the general education classroom* (3rd ed.). Boston: Allyn & Bacon.

Waaland, P., David, C., & Wehman, P. (1997). Attention-deficit/hyperactivity disorder. In P. Wehman (Ed.), *Exceptional individuals in school, community, and work* (pp. 207–241). Austin, TX: Pro-Ed.

Walters, K., & Bowen, G. L. (1997). Peer group acceptance and academic performance among adolescents participating in a dropout prevention program. *Child and Adolescent Social Work Journal, 14*(6), 413–426.

Wasik, B. A., & Slavin. R. E. (1990). *Preventing early reading failure with one-to-one tutoring: A best-evidence synthesis.* Needham Heights, MA: Allyn & Bacon.

Wehmeyer, M. L. (1992). Self-determination and the education of students with mental retardation. *Education and Training in Mental Retardation, 27,* 302–314.

Wehmeyer, M. L., Agran, M., & Hughes, C. (2000). A national survey of teachers' promotion of self-determination and student-directed learning. *Journal of Special Education, 34*(2), 58–68.

Wehmeyer, M. L., & Bolding, N. (1999). Self-determination across living and working environments: A matched samples study of adults with mental retardation. *Mental Retardation, 37*(5), 353–363.

Wehmeyer, M. L., & Kelchner, K. (1995). Measuring the autonomy of adolescents and adults with mental retardation: A self-report from the autonomous functioning checklist. *Career Development for Exceptional Individuals, 18*(1), 3–20.

Wehmeyer, M. L., & Kelchner, K. (1996). Perceptions of classroom environment, locus of control and academic attributions of adolescents with and without cognitive disabilities. *Career Development for Exceptional Individuals, 19*(1), 15–30.

Wehmeyer, M. L., & Kelchner, K., & Richards, S. (1995). Individual and environmental factors related to the self-determination of adults with mental retardation. *Journal of Vocational Rehabilitation, 5*(4), 291–305.

Wehmeyer, M. L., & Kelchner, K., & Richards, S. (1996). Essential characteristics of self-determination behavior of individuals with mental retardation. *American Journal on Mental Retardation, 100,* 632–642.

Wetzel, M. C., McNaboe, K. A., Schneidermeyer, S. A., Jones, A. B., & Nash, P. N. (1997). Public and private partnership in an alternative middle school program. *Preventing School Failure, 41,* 179–184.

Winebrenner, S. (1992). *Teaching gifted kids in the regular classroom.* Minneapolis: Free Spirit.

Witt, J. C., Daly, E. M., & Noell, G. (2000). *Functional assessments: A step-by-step guide to solving academic and behavior problems.* Longmont, CO: Sopris West.

Whiteford, T. (1998). Math for moms and dads. *Educational Leadership, 55*(8), 64–66.

Wood, J. W., Lazzari, A. M., & Wehman, P. (1997). Mild mental retardation. In P. Wehman (Ed.), *Exceptional individuals in school, community, and work* (pp. 111–143). Austin, TX: Pro-Ed.

Wood, K. D., & Tinajero, J. (2002). Using pictures to teach content to second language learners. *Middle School Journal, 33*(5), 47–51.

Yamauchi, L. A. (1998). Individualism, collectivism, and cultural compatibility: Implications for counselors and teachers. *Journal of Humanistic Education and Development, 36,* 189–198.

6

A Process of Delivering Special Education and Related Services

LEARNER OBJECTIVES

After you read this chapter, you will be able to:

- Name the federal law that governs special education.
- Describe the complexity of today's classroom.
- Discuss the No Child Left Behind Act of 2001.
- Briefly describe prereferral.
- Explain the purpose of instructional support teams.
- Describe the referral and formal evaluation process.
- Discuss issues related to evaluation and eligibility.
- State the major components of an individualized education program.

CHAPTER AT A GLANCE

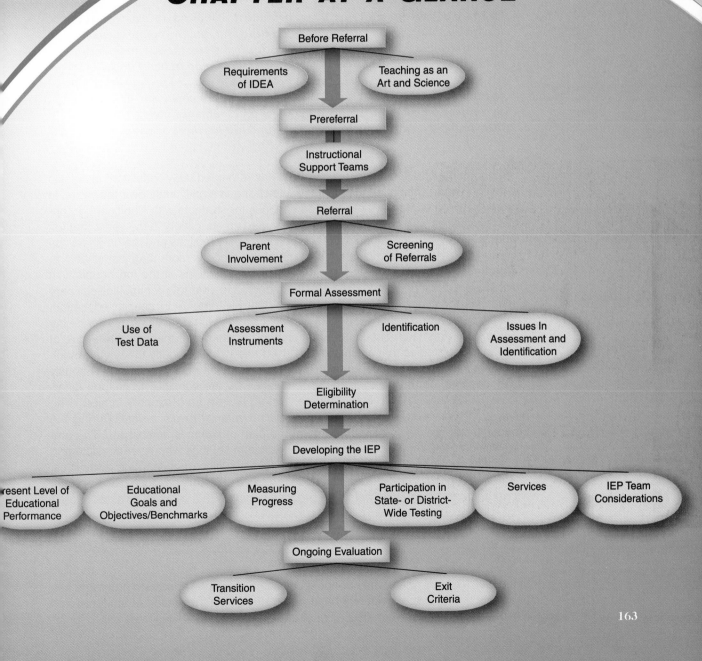

Before Referral

Requirements of IDEA

Teaching as an Art and Science

Prereferral

Instructional Support Teams

Referral

Parent Involvement

Screening of Referrals

Formal Assessment

Use of Test Data

Assessment Instruments

Identification

Issues In Assessment and Identification

Eligibility Determination

Developing the IEP

Present Level of Educational Performance

Educational Goals and Objectives/Benchmarks

Measuring Progress

Participation in State- or District-Wide Testing

Services

IEP Team Considerations

Ongoing Evaluation

Transition Services

Exit Criteria

KEY TERMS

child study team   169

curriculum-based assessment   167

eligibility determination   175

formal assessment   167

individualized education program
   (IEP)   176

informal assessment   167

instructional support teams   167

norm group   173

special education   175

*P*hoebe is a bright and athletic youngster in middle school. She managed to get by in school until fifth grade, when the demands of school, especially reading, caught up with her. When evaluated, Phoebe was determined to have a specific learning disability in reading and reading comprehension. Her performance is above average in math when given the accommodation of having word problems and lengthy directions read to her. Phoebe is in all general education classes except for language arts. A special education teacher co-teaches in her science and social studies class. She is learning to compensate for her learning differences and will most likely go on to college, probably continuing to need accommodations there as well.

*A*lthough the process for special services has remained fairly consistent at least in the last 30 years, special education itself has changed significantly over the years. In its early years, the intent was to provide services for students with significant or "obvious" disabilities who had previously been denied an education. In the years that followed, teacher attitudes, along with research into best practices and the emphasis on "access to the general curriculum," have made the process more than just what's required by law. This chapter discusses some of the intentions of the Individuals with Disabilities Education Act (IDEA, 1997) to decrease referrals for multidisciplinary evaluations for special education and ultimately placements in special education. These actions will prevent overidentification of children with disabilities by intervening early and with research-based interventions and strategies. If teachers are aware of intervention strategies that are research based and work to modify the environment, instruction, and testing procedures, this will reduce the chance of a child erroneously being identified as having a disability. Teachers who are sensitive to cultural differences will be less likely to inappropriately refer children from minority families. The process for delivering special services is called *referral to placement*. During the process a disability is identified (if any) and a plan of action is established. The emphasis is on providing services in general education settings whenever possible and on identifying "hidden" disabilities such as processing disorders, learning disabilities, or emotional disabilities. Special education is viewed as a service, not a place or room where students go for extra help. The process begins with a request for assistance.

BEFORE REFERRAL

Requirements of IDEA

In the last 10 years one of the strongest criticisms of special education programs has been the lack of use of evidence-based practices in the instruction of students with disabilities. Therefore, when (IDEA) was reauthorized in 1997, Congress called for increased efforts in this area. School districts must now use research-based educational practices and focus attention on accountability and improved results for students with disabilities. The reauthorization also provided for incentives for whole-school approaches and prereferral interventions to reduce the need to label children as disabled in order to address their learning needs.

From 1984 to 1997, high school graduation rates and employment rates among youth with disabilities increased by 14%. Postsecondary enrollments for students with disabilities have tripled since 1978 (U.S. Department of Education, 2003). However, many are still concerned that students with disabilities are more likely to drop out of school and to be unemployed than their nondisabled peers. Special education services continue to emphasize educational experiences and transition services that will prepare students for employment and independent living beyond school.

IDEA '97 is currently under revision in the U.S. Congress, having passed from the House of Representatives to the Senate. Preliminary indications are that the revision will continue to emphasize ensuring that research-based interventions are implemented and documented prior to evaluating children for special services.

Teaching as an Art and Science

It has been said that teaching is both an art and a science. In many ways, this is true. Teachers try many different techniques, seating arrangements, and testing methods (the science). They then add their creative spin (the art) to the things they try. A teacher may decide that the pace of instruction is too fast or slow for a particular group of students. A teacher may decide to teach a particular subject at a different time. Environmental assessments will give teachers insights that they can use in planning instruction. The general classroom teacher should also assess teaching methods to determine whether the strategies provide structure, guidance, and reinforcement of skills and content, and whether they are best for all students, particularly those who may be at risk for academic failure. A teacher may ask a peer, guidance counselor, or administrator to observe the whole classroom and to offer an objective view for improving general classroom organization, learning center management, or classroom behavior management. As opinions gather on ways to help a student at risk, the process of special education begins. Figure 6.1 illustrates the process from referral to placement for services.

PREREFERRAL

The complexity of today's classroom results in many challenges for even an experienced teacher. The call for reform has created greater demands for teacher performance and student achievement. The No Child Left Behind Act of 2001 has raised standards, expectations, and issues regarding highly qualified teachers.

> Schools are expected to add value to students' educational experience by providing effective instruction, and opportunities that enable them to achieve at the highest levels. This is a dramatic departure from the expectations of prior generations, and in stark contrast to the expectations that exist in many other countries. To further compound the challenge, at the same time that expectations for achievement have been sharply raised, the student population has changed dramatically, becoming increasingly diverse in many ways. For example, it is not unusual for schools to have students who speak many different languages. Many of these children are newly arrived immigrants from countries around the world, many of which are in the throes of war or economic disaster. With the changing family and workplace dynamics in the United States,

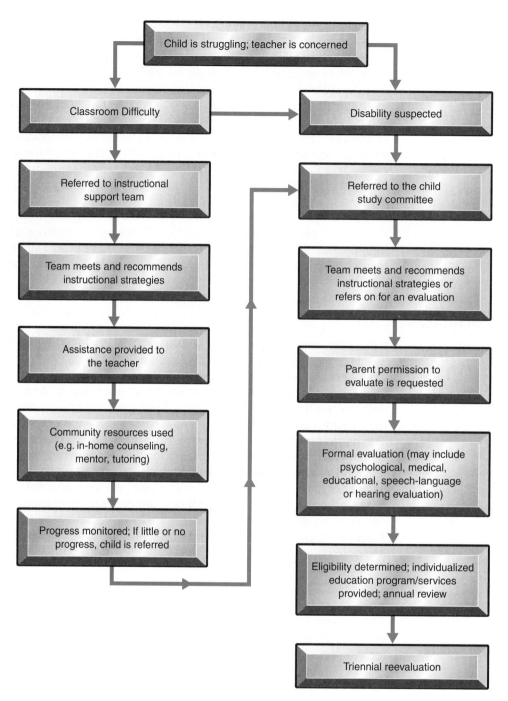

FIGURE 6.1
Flow chart of special education services.

and the stresses of difficult economic times and heightened work schedules, public schools are expected to fill existing voids and play an ever increasing role in the lives of many students. (Iervolino & Hansen, 2003, p. 7)

COLLABORATION TIPS

Many new teachers are paired with a mentor teacher for their first year. Most find this collaboration extremely helpful. Because teams, procedures, and processes work differently in each school district within a state as well as across states, the mentor teacher in essence has "been there, done that." New teachers can talk to them about their concerns regarding certain students and see what suggestions they might have. Mentor teachers will have a vested interest in having a teacher assigned to them succeed.

If a student continues to experience difficulty after the teacher has looked at classroom variables, instructional methods, and student variables (e.g., are the student's physical and personal needs being met at home?), the teacher takes a closer look at the student's ability to master the task or curriculum. For example, the teacher may notice that a student seems to do fine with math until the unit on division starts. Upon further investigation using **informal assessment,** the teacher notices that the student only minimally understood multiplication. Given additional reinforcement and instruction in multiplication, the student is able to move forward in division.

At times, a more **formal assessment** is necessary. When a student appears to have difficulty mastering content or skills at the appropriate grade level, the teacher may use a **curriculum-based assessment** to pinpoint the areas of difficulty. Curriculum-based assessment is used to determine what skills have been mastered and what skills were not mastered and may need to be retaught.

Good teachers differentiate instruction for all learners, not just those with special needs. At times, even after differentiating, a student may continue to struggle with learning or emotional issues. There are various teams in place in schools to assist teachers with strategies, interventions, or modifications depending on the level of support a student needs. Teachers should trust that a team approach could generate more possible solutions and provide greater support for a student who is having difficulty.

Instructional Support Teams

Many schools have recognized the need to provide teachers with assistance and resources to deal with the challenges of diverse learners in the classroom. Teams may take on many names, but *instructional support team* is probably the most commonly used. Other frequently used names include student intervention team, teacher support team, and student success team.

In 1990 Pennsylvania Special Education Regulations and Standards required that elementary schools in Pennsylvania develop instructional support teams. These teams were to be phased in over a 5-year period. Five hundred and one school districts initiated the initiative. **Instructional support teams** (ISTs) were to help schools develop a system within the school whereby teachers were provided ideas and suggestions through support teachers and teams to help students who were at risk for school failure. The philosophy of IST is based on seven principals:

- All students learn.
- The most crucial link is the student–teacher relationship within the general education classroom.
- A problem-solving community is the foundation for professional and student learning.
- The instructional match and setting is the focus of problem solving.
- Early intervention is preferable to waiting for failure.
- Teachers, as professionals, are entitled to the opportunity to consult and collaborate.
- Change is a process, not an event. (Pennell, 2001)

A support teacher is a must for an IST to work. The support teacher is specially trained and coordinates the process. He or she works with students to assess their needs and to model strategies in the classroom for teachers and others who provide services to the student. In a recent study of states using prereferral intervention processes, most included the following defining features:

1. A *process* that is preventive (i.e., interventions are developed and implemented before a formal special education evaluation) and a problem-solving approach that is team based (i.e., team members review data on a referred student, hypothesize causes to explain the student's difficulties, and develop strategies to remediate those difficulties).

2. An *approach* that is action-research-oriented (i.e., the team develops specific interventions that the referring teacher is expected to implement in his or her classroom—either with or without outside assistance—and then evaluate in terms of its effectiveness).

3. An *intervention* process that is centered on the enhanced success of students and teachers within the general education setting and using the general education curriculum (Buck, Polloway, Smith-Thomas, & Cook, 2003).

In some states, instructional support teams receive extensive training on how to work as a team. The training is skill oriented and is provided in five areas: (a) collaboration and team building, (b) instructional assessment, (c) instructional adaptation, (d) student discipline, and (e) student assistance for at-risk issues (Kovaleski, Tucker, & Duffy, 1995). Effective teams share common characteristics. Dee (1999) defined seven characteristics of high-performance teams: commitment, contribution, communication, cooperation, conflict management, change management, and connections. Teams celebrate their successes as well as participate in additional training as time goes on.

> The goal of instructional support is to assure that students are taught at their instructional levels and that they are reinforced at their independent level throughout the intervention period. Students' reaction to their instruction can be assessed according to their rates of acquisition and retention, leading to an analysis of the extent to which the regular classroom environment can accommodate and sustain their progress. Whenever student progress is sufficiently maintained in the regular classroom through instructional support so that the rates of acquiring and retaining skills and information meet the goals set by the intervention team, the student is not in need of special education services since the student does not display the need for special education to achieve success. (Kovaleski, Lowery, & Gickling, 1996 pp. 16–17)

In a review of the research on IST, DeFur (2001) found that

1. 85% of students screened via IST were successful in regular education placements and did not require further evaluations for special education;
2. the IST process led to a decrease in the number of students retained in a grade which led to instruction matched to student's needs and which led to a decrease in behavior problems; and
3. the IST process was perceived to be an effective pre-referral intervention strategy even for those students who were later referred and found eligible for special education. (p. 2)

Kovaleski, Tucker, and Stevens (1996) had the following suggestion for the makeup of the IST:

While team membership varies from school to school, most every IST includes the principal, the student's regular teacher, and a support teacher. Parents are encouraged to participate, and depending on the student's needs, school psychologists, remedial mathematics and reading specialists, guidance counselors, speech therapists, school nurses, and others also may be involved. (p. 3)

The two primary goals of the instructional support initiative were to reduce the number of students referred or needing special education services and to decrease student retentions. For the most part, ISTs seem to meet these goals while also preventing the overrepresentation of minority students in special education. However, at times, despite strong efforts, the IST is not enough. If the child has been through an instructional support team and interventions and strategies have been documented and the child still struggles, a **child study team** may determine that further evaluations are warranted. The child study team may also suggest that they reconvene after additional interventions are implemented. Figure 6.2 shows an example of part of a referral to a child study team.

REFERRAL

The next step in the special education process is referral. At this point all avenues to assist the student within the general education classroom have been exhausted. The child study team begins a more in-depth look at the child.

If the classroom teacher has referred the child to the IST, he or she should have significant documentation of interventions and strategies used. The teacher may use data, observations, or charts and graphs to demonstrate improvement or lack of improvement in an academic skill or behavior.

Parent Involvement

The reauthorization of IDEA strengthened the role of parents. Parents are encouraged to participate actively in their child's education. Parents are invited and encouraged to attend child study, eligibility, and IEP meetings. Many local schools have parent resource centers or lending libraries for parents. Parents are a vital part of their child's life and especially of their educational planning. As discussed in chapter 2, parents need support and assurance that they are a part of the team.

Request for Assistance
(Referral to Child Study Committee)

Student: _____

III. Description of referred student: Check each statement that describes the student.

Weaknesses

Academics/behavior		
☐ Difficulty concentrating	☐ Difficulty remembering facts	☐ Deficient in vocabulary
☐ Poor reading skills	☐ Deficient in mathematical calculations	☐ Difficulty in problem solving
☐ Poor memory for facts and details	☐ Achieves below grade level in content areas	☐ Difficulty following directions
☐ Frequent reversals of letters and numbers	☐ Talks excessively, attention seeking, disruptive	☐ Poor handwriting, organization, and legibility
☐ Poor self-concept	☐ Disorganized work habits	☐ Requires constant supervision
☐ Fights and/or bites	☐ Talks about morbid themes	☐ Overactive
☐ Makes excuses	☐ Physically aggressive	☐ Talks about hurting or killing self or others
☐ Fearful	☐ Provokes/aggravates others, defiant	☐ Excessive daydreaming
☐ Ritualistic behaviors—rocking, pacing, etc.	☐ Temper tantrums	☐ Perseveration
☐ Immature behaviors	☐ Appears depressed, withdrawn	☐ Difficulty making transition
☐ Irritable or moody	☐ Cries easily, oversensitive	
☐ Difficulty without written expression	☐ Consistent inappropriate emotional response	
☐ Destructive	☐ Blames others	
☐ Poor social skills	☐ Abandons difficult tasks	

FIGURE 6.2
Checklist of classroom concerns or behaviors.

Note: From King William County Public Schools, King William, VA. Reprinted with permission.

Request for Assistance
(Referral to Child Study Committee)

Student: _____

Weaknesses (continued)

Communication skills	Physical symptoms	
☐ Difficulty using and understanding language	☐ Physical complaints	☐ Bites nails
☐ Unable to communicate basic needs and wants	☐ Involuntary muscle spasms	☐ Lacks age-appropriate self-care
☐ Indistinct articulation—speech sounds omitted, substituted, distorted	☐ Seizures	☐ Lacks physical mobility
☐ Voice problems	☐ Poor gross motor skills	☐ Lacks fine motor coordination
☐ Nonverbal	☐ Difficulty copying—paper or board	☐ Chronic allergic conditions
☐ Slow, labored speech	☐ Impaired hearing	☐ Impaired vision
☐ Reluctant to communicate in groups	☐ Poor physical fitness	☐ Lethargic—tired and listless
☐ Difficulty with written expression	☐ Overweight	☐ Underweight
☐ Cannot understand spoken language	☐ Asthma	☐ Epilepsy
☐ Difficulty in oral expression	☐ Wets or soils clothes	☐ Frequently gets hurt
☐ Other (specify):	☐ Currently takes medication	☐ Other (specify):

Screening of Referrals

Every school must have a child study team in place. Teachers, parents, principals, even doctors or other concerned persons can make referrals to the child study team. This team must convene within 10 working days to discuss the referral and determine the appropriate course of action. When prereferral instructional strategies are not effective in changing the student's learning or behavioral difficulties, the committee may decide that a student needs to be evaluated to determine whether a disability exists that requires special services. The parents must give their permission for assessment components to be collected.

Many professionals collectively work together to decide the appropriate placement for a student. What role would you play in this team effort?

PRACTICAL APPLICATIONS

Some children start school "behind." The movement in education now is to provide more intervention prior to kindergarten and prior to special education referrals. The National Academy of Sciences is proposing that all children be screened early. This is a shift from the "wait for the child to fail" approach. Some at-risk students who receive early support may succeed with minimal effort. Educators can then spend the most time and effort on students who do not respond to traditional interventions and need more specialized instruction.

FORMAL ASSESSMENT

The primary purpose of the formal assessment is to obtain information that will be useful in determining whether a child has a disability. It also provides useful information as well for making education decisions about interventions that may be necessary for the student's success. If an evaluation is deemed appropriate, the team will also determine what evaluations are necessary. Typically, a psychological exam given by a licensed school psychologist will determine the child's ability level and learning style. As educational exam given by a trained special education teacher or diagnostician determines the child's academic level of functioning. Other evaluations can be given such as speech and language, occupational, or physical therapy evaluations. Hearing tests are a required component.

Use of Test Data

Schools are required to ensure that tests and other evaluation materials used to assess a child are not discriminatory in nature and are provided and administered in the child's native language or other mode of communication. The purpose of assessment is to obtain information that will be useful in determining whether the child has a disability. Assessment is also helpful in making educational decisions about intervention strategies or accommodations the child may need in the classroom to be successful. The test data obtained regarding the student's cognitive abilities, perceptual/processing abilities (best mode of learning, i.e., visual, auditory, multisensory), and academic functioning are assessed during this process.

Teachers and parents may feel more comfortable with scores that are reported as age or grade equivalents. However, it is important to remember that grade equivalents do not represent a grade level of functioning. These equivalents merely represent the number of items answered correctly by the **norm group** at each level rather than mastery of content at a particular grade. The norm group is selected by the testing company for comparison. The norm group is usually a randomly selected group of persons with whom the test was originally conducted. It should be a cross section of students, classrooms, school districts, states, and the nation. For example, a student who obtains a 4.5 (fourth-grade, fifth-month grade level) may not have mastered skills required of the mid-fourth-grade year. The score means that the student answered the same number of items correctly as did the norm group of fourth-graders. One should not assume, therefore, that the student has mastered half of the district's fourth-grade curriculum.

Often scores are reported as raw scores, scale scores, percentile ranks, standard scores, or standard deviations. Teachers and parents should have a basic working knowledge of scores. Many resources that explain scores are available. Although these will not be covered in detail in this text, one common resource is a session to explain scores held by directors of testing, guidance counselors, or school psychologists.

Assessment Instruments

Every year more commercially produced assessment instruments are available, and publishers are constantly updating test instruments. One of the most familiar, the Wechsler Intelligence Scale for Children (WISC), has recently been revised and is called the WISC-IV. Another commonly used achievement test, the Woodcock-Johnson Battery, is also in its third revision. The WISC-IV measures the child's ability in the areas of verbal comprehension, perceptual reasoning, working memory, and processing speed; the Woodcock-Johnson Battery assesses the student's achievement in the areas of reading, mathematics, and written language. Both provide valuable information for further assessing students.

In addition to formal testing, the student's school records are reviewed and all previous individual or group testing is collected for input into assessment.

Many tests are administered by a school psychologist, school diagnostician, or special education teacher. The purpose of the test and who is qualified to administer it will determine which professional actually administers the tests.

ACCOMMODATING DIVERSITY

As mentioned earlier in the chapter, many school districts, small and large, are seeing an influx of students from culturally diverse groups. It is important for teachers, instructional support teams, and child study teams to be sensitive to these groups. Children and their families may have different dialects, beliefs, customs, or traditions that should be valued. Educators must relate to the family and make an effort to understand how disabilities are viewed from their perspective. Many state departments offer copies of parents' procedural safeguards and rights in several languages. However, just as the English version is written in technical and legal language and at times needs to be explained to English-speaking parents, the rights may need to be explained to families who present with language diversities.

As expected, determining whether a child with English as a second language has a disability or is primarily struggling because of language obstacles is particularly difficult. Several companies have recognized this and developed tests in other languages. The Woodcock-Johnson III test mentioned in this chapter is available in a Spanish version. However, the evaluator would need to be fluent in Spanish. This is just one example of how the evaluation process can be tailored to adequately assess a non-English-speaking student and to prevent overrepresentation of minority students in special education.

Identification

IDEA identifies 12 disabling conditions under which a child could be identified as having a disability in need of special services. These conditions are listed in chapter 1 and are covered in detail in chapters 3, 4, and 5. As a review, these conditions include the following:

- Autism
- Deaf-blindness
- Emotional disturbance
- Hearing impairment, including deafness
- Mental retardation
- Orthopedic impairments
- Other health impairments
- Severe disability
- Specific learning disability
- Speech or language impairment
- Traumatic brain injury
- Visual impairment, including blindness

The anticipated reauthorization of IDEA is not expected to add more categories. The general education teacher may have students with mild, moderate, or more involved disabilities in her or his class for some part or all of the school day. Each child may have varying degrees of support outlined in the individualized education program (IEP), which is discussed later in the chapter in the section on eligibility. Minimal support such as accommodations may be provided, although some students require a personal aide, classroom assistant, or collaborative teacher (see chapter 2). Again, with each reauthorization of IDEA, there is more of a shift toward the concept of **special education** being a service, not a place. Emphasis is placed on providing help to students in general education classes and using the general education curriculum.

Issues in Assessment and Identification

One of the most critical issues in assessment and identification is the overrepresentation of a specific segment of the population in special education.

> In many cases, children are inappropriately referred and erroneously determined to require special education and related services, when in fact, they do not. When this happens repeatedly and primarily to one group of students in a school district—as in the case for African American students in many districts across the country—it results in a disproportionate percentage of group membership in special education. Overrepresentation in special education occurs when a group's membership in the program is larger than the percentage of that group in the educational system or within a given disability category (i.e., learning disability, mental retardation, emotional disturbance, etc.). Such population variance is rarely justifiable and is always a cause for significant concern. (Council for Exceptional Children, 2002, p. 1)

The Office of Civil Rights is continually monitoring this area. Schools districts are being identified as having "overrepresentation." These districts are in the process of reviewing identification procedures and processes. The prereferral intervention process is a natural point at which to ensure that this does not occur.

> The professional literature suggests that prereferral intervention process shows promise for preventing the overidentification of African American students for special education. Such processes may have the potential to identify and address systematic problems (e.g., inadequate instruction, irrelevant curriculum, lack of resources), and may, in turn, alleviate the source of the student's academic and/or behavior difficulties. (Council for Exceptional Children, 2002, p. 16)

Prior to the passage of special education laws (before the passage of PL 94-142 in 1975), students could be inappropriately identified by one person. As laws were passed, the process of special education referral developed more protective pathways for students. For example, multiple persons were required for making eligibility decisions, multiple assessment measures were provided, and multiple instructional options are constantly being developed. After thorough and well-regulated procedures, some students are found eligible to receive special services. A team begins this process.

ELIGIBILITY DETERMINATION

The eligibility team consists of qualified professionals and the parent. The team, by law, has 65 days to conduct evaluations and determine whether the child is eligible for special services. The initial evaluation consists of procedures that will determine whether the child has a disability and his or her educational needs. The team is responsible for reviewing the case study evaluation or reevaluation, determining

whether a disability exists that interferes with learning, identifying the adverse affects of the disability, identifying educational needs, and determining whether the child is eligible for special services.

DEVELOPING THE IEP

If the child is eligible for services, the team will develop an **individualized education program (IEP).** This may be done following eligibility. If not, it must be done with 30 calendar days from the date of eligibility. The IEP is a written statement designed to meet the child's unique needs, and it must be in effect at the beginning of each school year (if the child is already eligible) before special services and related services are provided for the child. The IEP should be written as soon as possible following the IEP meeting.

The IEP team includes the parent, at least one of the child's general education teachers, at least one special education teacher or related service provider of the child, and a person who is qualified to provide or supervise the provision of special education and is knowledgeable about the general curriculum and resources. A person who can interpret the test results is required to be present at the meeting. At times, it may be appropriate to have the child attend. This is required when the child turns 16, or in some instances 14, because planning for the child's educational future begins at these ages, depending on each state's requirements. IEPs should be performance based, legally correct, easily understood, and student centered, and show access to the general educational curriculum.

Present Level of Educational Performance

The present level of educational performance is the foundation of the IEP, and the information under this section will determine the goals and objectives in the IEP. The present level of performance must include information about how the student's disability affects his or her involvement in the general curriculum. It will include information about the student's strengths, weaknesses, and learning style. Depending on the student, it may include information about academic levels, motor skills, social skills, self-care, and independent skills. The present level of performance is measured most often by general curriculum benchmarks, pre/post testing, criterion-referenced testing, or teacher observation.

Educational Goals and Objectives/Benchmarks

The IEP includes goals that are intended to project a student's educational progress for one school year, while also serving as the bridge to the end result—transition to independent adult living, whether that be to college, trade school, or work. Goals are included for the weaknesses identified under the present level of performance. Goals must be measurable and broken down into steps (often called short-term objectives or benchmarks), or major milestones.

Today with educational standards and benchmarks at the forefront of education, IEP goals are linked to the stated standards. Figure 6.3 shows a sample IEP that demonstrates a student's present level of performance, projected annual goals, and the link to the standard or benchmark covered in the general curriculum. Standards or benchmarks will be covered in detail in chapter 9, "Adapting Lesson Plans."

Measuring Progress

The IEP is a lengthy document. In addition to the major components mentioned earlier, it will also include information about how the child's progress toward the annual goals will be measured, how parents will be informed of their child's progress, how often parents will be informed, and whether the progress is sufficient to meet the goals by the end of the year.

Participation in State- or District-Wide Testing

The IEP must include a statement explaining any accommodations or modifications for state- or district-wide tests; reasons for the child's nonparticipation in the tests; how the child's nonparticipation will affect promotion and graduation; and how the child will be assessed if he or she is not participating in the state- or district-wide tests.

Services

The IEP team (which includes the parent) will determine the type and amount of special education services the child needs to accomplish the established goals and objectives. The team will also determine what accommodations the student needs in the classroom to access the general curriculum.

At times a student may need other support or related services to benefit from special education. These include, but are not limited to, the following:

Counseling services

Medical services

Physical or occupational therapy

Speech-language pathology services

Transportation

Parent counseling or training

A child who is eligible for special education services is then eligible for related services, provided the related service is necessary for the child to benefit from special education.

Revised 4/2000

Present Level of Performance
(Continued on Justification Page)

Student: Heather Nicole Blakely

I.D. No.: 1779

Date of Assessment: 05/05/2003

Chronological Age: 8

SUBTEST	GR. EQUIV.	%	ST. SCORE
Reading			
Accelerated Reading	1.6	44%	N/A
Individual books read			
3/13/03	1.4	N/A	N/A
3/24/03	1.2	N/A	N/A
4/30/03	1.7	N/A	N/A
Arithmetic			
Stanford 9			
09/02	N/A	70%	N/A
Written Language			
Stanford 9			
09/02	N/A	28%	N/A

Strengths:

Heather is strong in math. She is an active participant in discussions in science and social studies. She enjoys reading and has good listening comprehension skills. She is very social and enjoys helping others.

Weaknesses:

Heather has a weakness in decoding and encoding skills. In language arts she is able to successfully work with one area at a time but has difficulty when there are multiple tasks. She has difficulty with written language in the area of writing machanics.

Learning Styles:

Auditory learner

Data Sources:

Stanford 9, Accelerated Reading, and teacher observations from regular and special educators

CONFIDENTIAL: The information on this page must be maintained in the student's confidential file.

FIGURE 6.3
Sample IEP.

Note: From King William County Public Schools, King William, VA. Reprinted with permission.

Revised 4/2000

Annual Goals and Objectives

GOAL: Heather will improve her decoding and comprehension skills up to a third-grade level with 85% accuracy.

LOCATION OF SERVICES: Special education room

Short-term objective	Criteria for mastery	Evaluation method
Read and spell multisyllabic words that use the closed syllable	85% proficiency	Work sample evaluation/ teacher-designed test
Read and spell vowel consonant e words including the exception to this syllable type	85% proficiency	Work sample evaluation/ teacher-designed test
Read and spell words using the open syllable in conjunction with closed and vowel consonant e syllables	85% proficiency	Work sample evaluation/ teacher-designed test
Read words with one and two suffixes added to unchanging basewords	85% proficiency	Work sample evaluation/ teacher-designed test
Read and spell words that are the consonant-le syllable type including the exception to this syllable type	85% proficiency	Work sample evaluation/ teacher-designed test
Demonstrate comprehension of a variety of literary forms	85% proficiency	Work sample evaluation/ teacher-designed test
Identify cause-and-effect relationships	85% proficiency	Work sample evaluation/ teacher-designed test

(continued)

Revised 4/2000

Modifications for the Regular Classroom

Student: Heather Nicole Blakely

Attending:
- Cue before instruction begins
- Cue before assignments/homework are given

Direction:
- Simplify directions
- Use verbal and written directions
- Give example by modeling or demonstrations involving student

Organization:
- Opportunity to make up missed assignments
- Daily and/or weekly organizational sheets

Handwriting:

Self-Esteem:
- Recognize acceptable parts of student's work

Academics:
- Prepared advanced organizers
- Provide definite feedback
- Allow extra time to complete tests and assignments
- Provide study guides

Tests:
- Read test to student
- Advance exposure to type of test given
- Type(s) of tests to be given:
  - multiple choice, completion, short answer, and matching

The special education teacher has reviewed this information with me.

Signature: ______________________________ **Date:** ____________________

CONFIDENTIAL: The information on this page must be maintained in the student's confidential file.

FIGURE 6.3
Continued.

ACCOMMODATING TECHNOLOGY

Technology has changed education in many ways. Within hours of a student transferring into a new district, a teacher can easily assess basic reading and math skills using programs such as Accelerated Reader or STAR Math assessments. A psychologist or educational diagnostician can run a computer-generated score report and not worry about making a computational or scoring error. Special education teachers can produce computer-generated IEPs that decrease the time spent hand writing them. Students can have books on tape or "talking books" to assist with reading.

Students who have significant difficulty copying notes from the board or during a lecture have several options to make this task easier. AlphaSmarts and Dana-Smarts, the latest version, make note taking much easier and quicker for students. Both are relatively small keyboards that later can be connected to a computer and print out the notes a student took.

Only time will tell what other advances will make teaching and learning easier.

IEP Team Considerations

The IEP team is also responsible for considering many other factors in an IEP and documenting this information, such as the following:

- What parents consider the strengths of the child and their concerns for enhancing their child's education
- The results of the first or most recent evaluation of the child
- The child's language needs if he or she uses a language other than English
- Behavior intervention strategies and supports or the need for a behavior intervention plan
- Instruction in braille and the use of braille, if the child is visually impaired
- The child's communication needs
- The needs of a student who is deaf or hard of hearing
- The need for any assistive technology
- Whether the child needs extended educational services beyond the normal school year

Clearly IEPs must be considered thoughtfully and in great detail to include all of the information that is required and to make them understandable to teachers and parents.

ONGOING EVALUATION

The reevaluation of a student with a disability is similar to the initial evaluation. Every three years, the IEP team will redetermine eligibility by reviewing existing data for the student (possibly state or local assessments) and determine whether additional information is necessary. If so, parental permission must be obtained again for evaluation. If additional information is not needed to determine the continued need for services, and if the parent agrees, the current information is used to determine the need for continued services.

Transition Services

For students who remain in special education through high school, special emphasis is placed on preparing them for the world of work or secondary education. These services are called transition services. The team must consider whether the student needs special instruction, related services, or community experiences. Agencies that can assist the student with the transition process include departments of rehabilitative services (DRS), community services boards (CSB), departments of social services (DSS), and employment commissions. The transition plan that is required in a student's IEP beginning at age 16 describes who is responsible for linking the student with other agencies.

Exit Criteria

The goal of special education is to prepare students with disabilities for employment and independent living. Ideally at the eligibility and IEP meeting, thoughts should center on looking to the time when the student will no longer need or receive special services. To prepare for this time, students should be taught compensatory strategies and how to advocate for their needs. When the student demonstrates that he or she does not need special education, he or she should be considered for dismissal. Some students may demonstrate a need to continue in special education services until they reach their 22nd birthday in order to reach the goals of employment and independent living. Services at that time will continue through an adult service provider, such as those mentioned earlier.

SUMMARY

This chapter provided a general overview of the possible steps to be taken when a concern about a child's education or behavior surfaces. Instructional support teams, which may be known by another name, are one way to request assistance and to document the interventions tried prior to referring a child to the special education process. When the team has exhausted all efforts, the process begins. The specific steps include the referral, the formal assessment, eligibility, and developing the individualized education program. Special education is a service, not a place. One of the main goals while the student is of school age is for the student to remain in the general education classroom with success. Ultimately, the goal is for the student to be prepared for secondary education, employment, and independent living.

SUGGESTED READINGS

Creating Collaborative IEPs: A Handbook. (2001). Richmond: Virginia Commonwealth University, Virginia Institute for Developmental Disabilities.

Downing, J. (1996). *Including students with severe and multiple disabilities in typical classrooms.* Baltimore: Paul H. Brookes.

Giangreco, M. (1997). *Quick guides to inclusion: Ideas for educating students with disabilities.* Baltimore: Paul H. Brookes.

MaGahee-Kovac, M. (1995). *A student's guide to the IEP.* Washington, DC: National Information Center for Children and Youth with Disabilities.

Power DeFur, L., & Orelove, F. P. (Eds.). (1997). *Inclusive education: A practical guide to the least restrictive environment.* Gaithersburg, MD: Aspen.

WEBSITE TO VISIT

U.S. Department of Education. This is the official website of the U. S. Department of Education with publications, links, and law reports. www.ed.gov/print/policy/speced/leg/idea/history/html.

REFERENCES

Buck, G. H., Polloway, E. A., Smith-Thomas, A., & Cook, K. W. (2003). Prereferral interventions processes: A survey of state practices. *Exceptional Children, 69,* 349–360.

Council for Exceptional Children. (2002). *Addressing over-representation of African-American students in special education: The prereferral intervention process, an administrator's guide* (pp. 1, 16). Arlington, VA: Author.

Dee, D. (1999). *The High Performance Team Series, 1, Everything you need to know to start a team . . . lead a team first team . . . and be a team* (pp. 14–15). Chicago: Dartnell.

DeFur, S. (2001). *Findings abstract/selected IST studies.* Williamsburg, VA: College of William & Mary.

Iervolino, C. W., & Hansen, H. M. (2003). *Differentiated instruction practice series.* Port Chester, NY: National Professional Resources.

Kovaleski, J. F., Lowery, P. E., & Gickling, E. E. (1996). School reform through instructional support: Instructional evaluation. *Communique, 24*(2), 14–17.

Kovaleski, J. F., Tucker, J. A., & Duffy, D. J. (1995). *School reform through instructional support: The Pennsylvania Initiative, Part I: The instructional support team (IST). Communique, 23*(8).

Kovaleski, J. F., Tucker, J. A., & Stevens, L. J. (1996). The instructional support team. *Educational Leadership, 23*(8), 44–47.

Pennell, D. (2001). Instructional support team effort. *T/TAC Link Lines.* Williamsburg, VA: The College of William & Mary Training & Technical Assistance Center.

U.S. Department of Education. (2003). *The history of IDEA.* Retrieved September 24, 2003, from www.ed.gov/print/policy/speced/leg/idea/history/html.

7

Systematic Assessment for Inclusion

The SAALE Model

LEARNER OBJECTIVES

After you read this chapter, you will be able to:

- Explain the use of the SAALE model.
- Explain how the SAALE model fits into the big picture of education.
- Define preplanned and spontaneous interventions.
- Explain how to use the intervention/transition checklist.
- Discuss the SAALE model's relationship to universal design.
- Discuss the SAALE model's history.

CHAPTER AT A GLANCE

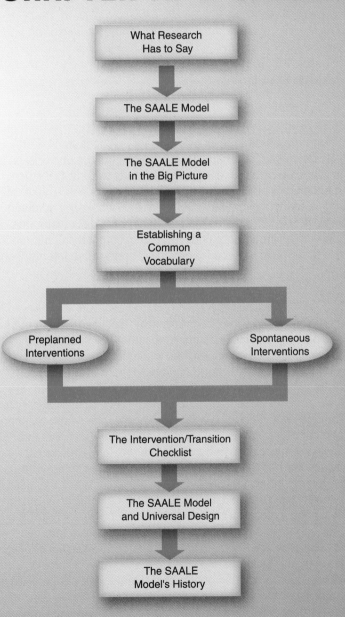

What Research
Has to Say

The SAALE Model

The SAALE Model
in the Big Picture

Establishing a
Common
Vocabulary

Preplanned
Interventions

Spontaneous
Interventions

The Intervention/Transition
Checklist

The SAALE Model
and Universal Design

The SAALE
Model's History

KEY TERMS

intervention/transition checklist   195   spontaneous interventions   195

preplanned interventions   195   universal design   201

SAALE model   188

*S*usi *is making the transition from elementary school to middle school. Because Susi is receiving special education services, the special education teacher completes the intervention checklist for Susi and sends the checklist with Susi's file. The receiving teachers at the middle school review the checklist and realize that Susi needs to work in small groups, has difficulty copying notes from lecture, has low self-esteem, and has difficulty following a series of directions. This information allows the middle school teachers to plan how they will help Susi make a smooth transition into their classes. The SAALE model and intervention checklist in this chapter will also assist you in planning for student success.*

*T*he future holds a great challenge for educators. Not only will students with disabilities be served in general environments, but "no child will be left behind." Our focus within classrooms on meeting diverse needs widens. Educators must begin to provide interventions for all students with educational needs. These interventions cannot occur in a random fashion, but must be *placed* where the educational need manifests, or at the point of what I call the mismatch. The SAALE (s̲ystematic a̲pproach for a̲dapting the l̲earning e̲nvironment) model and its accompanying Intervention/Transition Checklist is a systematic method for providing appropriate interventions for students.

WHAT RESEARCH HAS TO SAY

Problem solving in regard to children with special needs has been defined as "a systematic process that includes the assessment of children and their environments, identification of needs, development and implementation of supports to meet needs, and the monitoring and evaluation of outcomes" (Thomas & Grimes, 1995, p. V). The process generally progresses through four basic stages: (a) problem identification, (b) problem analysis, (c) plan implementation, and (d) problem evaluation (Bergan, 1995). Problem solving does not need to be a formal process; classroom teachers can informally identify a student's struggles and try out various interventions throughout the instructional day until one successfully addresses the problem. Problem solving, in part, is designed to "reduce the need for special education services by providing assistance to students in the general education classroom . . . [and] increase the abilities of teachers to educate students who are experiencing difficulties" (Nelson & Smith, 1991, p. 243).

Adopting a problem-solving approach such as the SAALE model described in this chapter can have several benefits. When educators intervene within general education classrooms, the stigmatization of a separate special education placement can often be avoided (McNamara & Hollinger, 2003). Additionally, a problem-solving model tends to focus on specific obstacles of immediate concern, which often reduces the length of time spent addressing a particular student's difficulties and helps contain costs (Bergan, 1995). Problem solving also fits well with recommendations made by the President's Commission on Excellence in Special Education in its 2002 report. The commission recommended implementing identification and intervention plans early, incorporating responses to interventions in planning and evaluation, and including a student's response to research-based instruction as part of the criteria for diagnosing a learning disability (President's Commission, 2002). The SAALE model, or a similar model, fulfills these recommendations.

Since the 1980s, a majority of states have required or recommended implementing interventions before referring students to special education services (Sindelar, Griffin, Smith, & Watanabe, 1992). Decades of research support this approach. Bergan stated, "An impressive body of evidence indicates that [a problem-solving model] is effective in promoting the learning and adjustment of children and youth" (1995, p. 121). The President's Commission refers to a National Research Council report that showed that early screening and effective interventions in the classroom actually prevented many disabilities (2002). Studies of early intervention programs found reduced special education referral rates; high satisfaction among teachers, parents, and students; and positive student behavior change (Sindelar et al., 1992). Another analysis found that "such interventions can increase the abilities of teachers to educate students who are experiencing difficulty and improve the attitudes of teachers toward such students" (Nelson & Smith, 1991, p. 243). Such results indicate the positive results that are possible with the adoption of a problem-solving process such as the SAALE model.

Research (Wood, 1989) has repeatedly shown that the use of the SAALE model provides significant educational gains in diverse populations. A 4-year longitudinal

ACCOMMODATING DIVERSITY

Just about any teacher will agree that our classrooms are full of students with diverse abilities and learning styles. Our students, even those found in the same general education classroom, vary on how well they read, compute, remember, listen, write, follow directions, communicate, complete work, and perform a host of other skills. Although much of this diversity is not formally recognized or reported, we do know that in the 2001–02 school year, 13% of public school students across the United States had an IEP, and 8% were English language learners (Hoffman, 2003). And these are only two of the differences teachers encounter every day.

It's no wonder that students differ in the ways they learn. Eight neurodevelopmental systems play a role in the learning process: the attention control system, the memory system, the language system, the spatial ordering system, the sequential ordering system, the motor system, the higher thinking system, and the social thinking system (Levine, 2002). Differences can occur in any or all of these areas that change how a particular student learns. Additional research on what happens in the brain during learning has led to the following conclusion: "The challenge for teachers is that they are faced with students who, at any given moment in class, may be processing the same piece of text or information in different ways" (American Youth Policy Forum, 2000, p. 2). Genetics, family life and stress level, cultural values, peer influence, physical health, temperament, and educational experience can also affect how an individual learns (Levine, 2002).

Teachers generally recognize this diversity and agree that they need to meet the needs of all learners; the difficulty lies in how to do that. The SAALE model and the suggestions found in the remainder of this book should help, providing interventions teachers can try with diverse learners.

study, begun in 2003, includes a stratified sample of schools using the SAALE model to determine its effects on student performance. The SAALE model is a growing concept, and any best practice fits somewhere within the model's pattern. Now let's take a look at this model, prepare a foundation for effective teaching, and get ready for the remainder of the text.

THE SAALE MODEL

The **SAALE model** is a framework for making decisions on how to teach students with special needs and all students served in an inclusive setting. This is the cornerstone for creating an inclusive classroom. The SAALE model is a process for differentiating instruction to ensure students' success.

Proponents of the SAALE model conceptualize the school day not as a whole but as several environments that interact continuously. The model provides a framework to help educators decide where in the instructional day (or in which environment) a student is having or will have a mismatch. Figure 7.1 demonstrates the components of the model.

According to the SAALE model, content and students interact in three major *environments:* the *learning environment,* which includes (socio-emotional, behavioral, and physical aspects; the *teaching environment,* in which educators plan, deliver, and assess instruction (teaching techniques and content), and the *evaluation and grading environment.* Each of the three environments is ongoing and includes technology. At any point a student may experience a "mismatch." When a mismatch occurs and is identified (using the checklist), the "point of intervention" is identified and the appropriate research-based strategy is implemented. Educators must identify mismatches and employ effective strategies based on the identified match. For example, if a student does not copy or cannot copy from a chalkboard, the educator must ensure that information written on the chalkboard is provided to the student. What is important within a classroom is that students *receive* the content and be *assessed* for content knowledge in a manner in which they learn. In the previous example it is important for the student to *learn,* not *copy.*

Understanding the concept of *mismatch* is crucial when using the SAALE model. Mismatches are not caused by the child or the teacher. A mismatch is simply a point at which the child cannot succeed because the teacher has expectations that are not compatible with the child's abilities. In the example of the student who cannot copy from the chalkboard, the teacher must understand that there is nothing wrong with requiring copying from the chalkboard or not being able to copy; the point is simply that a mismatch has occurred. No one is at fault. The teacher has identified a point of intervention.

I have changed my stand on who has the mismatch from the view previously expressed. With maturity I have grown to understand that what happens happens. No one is ever too old to learn. Teachers do the best they can; when they are not doing what is best for a student, it is usually because they simply do not know what to do. If they did, they would do it. However, because we are professionals, we must (a) find the mismatch and (b) develop and implement the appropriate intervention. Children are not going to adjust to the environment; the environment must be adjusted to the student. For too long we have tried to make students fit our molds, but we can no longer follow this reasoning.

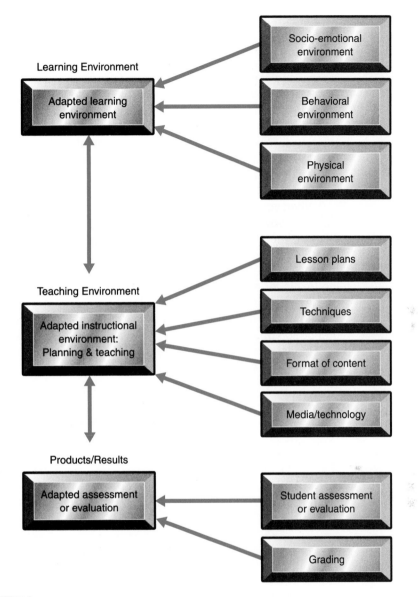

FIGURE 7.1

The SAALE model.

Note: From *Reaching the Hard to Teach, by* J. W. Wood, 2004, Richmond, VA: Judy Wood, Inc. Reprinted with permission.

Let me go one step further in explaining what I mean by a mismatch. Let's pretend that I've cut my finger. The doctor says, "I think a Band-Aid will be an appropriate intervention." Then the doctor puts the Band-Aid on my knee. My knee may feel better, but my problem is a cut finger. The next day I cut my finger again and return to the same doctor. The doctor says, "This time I will pour a Coke over your finger." I appreciate the intervention, but Coke has nothing to do with the problem. The intervention must fit the mismatch.

Logical Connections: Putting What You Know into the SAALE Model

To demonstrate how to place and use everything you know into the SAALE model, I would like to teach you the concept of *logical connections.* Let's pretend that I'm giving you one of my business cards. Now, what might be the purpose of your having one of my cards? Well, you can write to me, fax me, or perhaps e-mail me. But if I return in 3 months and ask if you still have my card, odds are that you will have lost it or at least left it at home.

Now let's pretend that I'm giving you one of my business cards and telling you that I'll return in 3 months. If you can produce my card at that time, you'll receive $10,000. Will you have the card when I return? You bet! You now have a logical connection between my card and a special reward.

When you are given something with no meaning (or logical connection), it has no value. However, if you have something and someone teaches you *why* it is important to learn, keep, or know, it has value. We often forget to provide logical connections for our students. For example, we issue textbooks and assume that the student realizes that the text has a connection with a specific course. But we must teach students what the text is for and how to use it. Throughout the year we should make those logical connections for the student.

Now that you understand what a logical connection is, let me use the term in reference to you. Figure 7.2 presents the SAALE model (see also Figure 7.1) in a filing cabinet format. Visualize the model as a large filing cabinet with nine drawers. Each drawer represents one of the blocks in the model. Everything you know and

FIGURE 7.2
How the SAALE model is like a filing cabinet.

Note: From *Reaching the Hard to Teach* by J. W. Wood, 2002, Richmond, VA: Judy Wood, Inc. Reprinted with permission.

everything you will know can be filed away in a drawer. Can you remember some of the college courses you took and simply did not understand why? Now you have a place (a mental drawer) to file away the information learned. For example, did you take a course about teaching reading? Well, what you learned fits neatly into the content drawer. You will begin to see how all the information you learn can be filed away. When a student has a mismatch, you can identify where within the model the mismatch is occurring, mentally pull out the drawer, and select an intervention for the mismatch. You see, an intervention is simply doing something that you have not tried. If one idea does not work, then try another. The remaining chapters in this book correspond with each block in the model. In this way, I will help you fill up the file drawers.

Now let's draw some logical connections between the SAALE model and your own knowledge.

Where the SAALE Model Fits Into the School Day

Many things go on during a school day. For our purposes, however, we are going to simplify the school day into three blocks: student outcomes (what we want the students to learn), the curriculum (what we will teach the students, based on student outcomes), and the students themselves (see Figure 7.3).

For students to reach selected or established outcomes, they must learn the curriculum. Therefore, teachers must teach the curriculum (which will be based on student outcomes and should be student appropriate) effectively to their students. The SAALE model provides a framework that helps teachers continually watch for mismatches so that they can more effectively deliver the curriculum to the students and thus reach the established outcomes. In this way they align the curriculum to the students.

Figure 7.4 expands on Figure 7.3 by visually explaining where interventions come into play.

The curriculum has been thought of as what we teach and interventions as "those things that are too much trouble to do." Often the curriculum takes so much time that no time is left for preparing and implementing interventions.

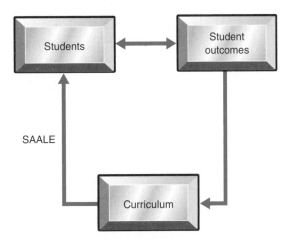

FIGURE 7.3

Where the SAALE model fits into the school day.

Note: From *Reaching the Hard to Teach* by J. W. Wood, 2002, Richmond, VA: Judy Wood, Inc. Reprinted with permission.

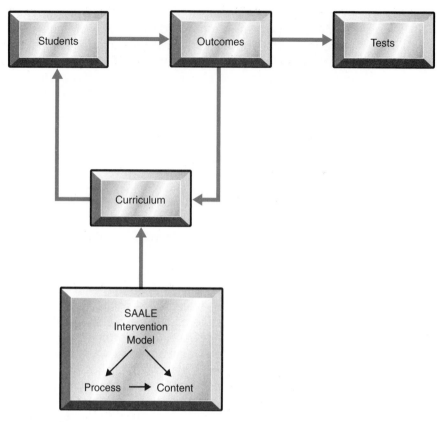

FIGURE 7.4
SAALE intervention model and curriculum.

Note: From *Reaching the Hard to Teach* by J. W. Wood, 2002, Richmond, VA: Judy Wood, Inc. Reprinted with permission.

By reconsidering how we think, we can make the intervention process an integral part of the curriculum. One does not function without the other. Figure 7.5 demonstrates what I mean. From now on let's become a new generation of teachers—ones who see curriculum and intervention as equal. However, remember that the interventions must be applied in an organized manner. The SAALE model provides the organization of identifying the mismatch, finding the correct intervention, and applying it as we teach the curriculum.

I would like to show you how the SAALE model fits into history. In the early years of education, only privileged males received an education. Women cooked, spun yarn, sewed, and did other household tasks. But as time passed, our country began to develop a two-track educational system: general education and special education. The systems were extremely separate, including facilities and curriculum. By the 1970s special education slowly began to move into general education buildings. However, the curriculum remained separate.

In the late 1970s I taught a special education class that met in the basement of the school even though there were empty rooms on the first and second floors. My students were as far removed from the other students as possible. We had to eat lunch and go out to recess at times separate from the general education students. We have really come a long way since then.

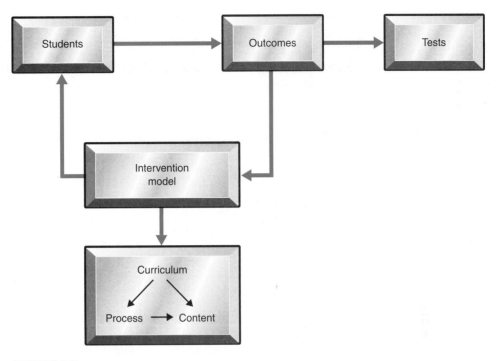

FIGURE 7.5

SAALE intervention model assists in delivery of curriculum to students.

Note: From *Reaching the Hard to Teach* by J. W. Wood, 2002, Richmond, VA: Judy Wood, Inc. Reprinted with permission.

In the 1980s students with special needs were gradually integrated into general education classes. Mostly you would see these students in art, music, and physical education classes. Resource or self-contained classes for students with disabilities were still major models for placement. Nonetheless, interventions for general class curricula were slowly surfacing. In the 1990s, we moved toward an inclusive environment within our schools.

As discussed in chapter 2, inclusion is our goal. But for our students to be included in general education classes, doors need to open and stay open. The 2000s are seeing a movement to serve all students, not only those with special needs. Students with special needs need to fit in socially, behaviorally, physically, and academically to be successful in general education classes. Imagine coming home late one evening and discovering you have the wrong door key in your hand. Will you remain outside all night or try another key? The logical answer is to try another key. This is exactly what we must do for students: try another key or intervention to unlock the door and keep it open.

I want you to think *SAALE model* when you see that a student is having difficulty with instruction. In other words, think about where the mismatch might be occurring. Then you will be on the right path toward identifying the problem.

THE SAALE MODEL IN THE BIG PICTURE

Before we move on, let's place the SAALE model into the big picture of education. (see Figure 7.6). For our purposes we are going to simplify the school day into four blocks: students, standards or outcomes (what we want the students to learn), curriculum

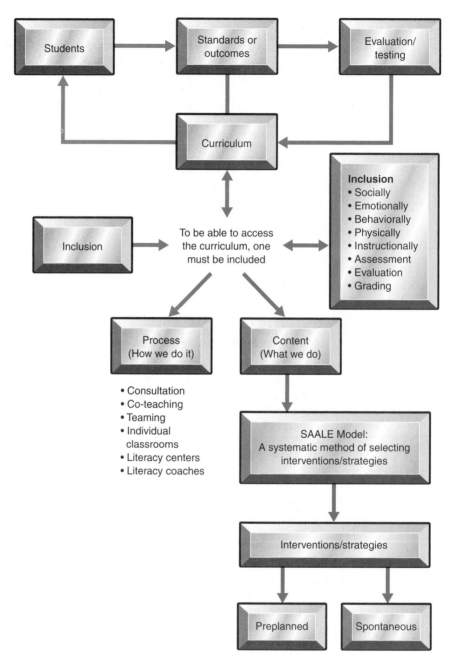

FIGURE 7.6

The SAALE model in the big picture.

Note: From *Reaching the Hard to Teach* by J. W. Wood, 2002, Richmond, VA: Judy Wood, Inc. Reprinted with permission.

(what we will teach the students), and evaluation (evidence of students' learning). These four blocks in Figure 7.6 represent what is happening in American education today. States establish standards, curricula must be aligned to the standards, and students must provide evidence of learning by evaluation measures.

For students to be able to access the curriculum, however, they must be included, thus the term *inclusion* in Figure 7.6. However, inclusion is a general term, not an educational one. We are either included or excluded in life. These inclusion or exclusion measures may be social, emotional, behavioral, physical, instructional, or through evaluation and grading. Students must be included in the curriculum to have access to it. They cannot move on to standards (or outcomes) or evaluation if they do not first have access to the curriculum.

Access is provided in two ways: the *process* (how we do it) and the *content* (what we do). The process of inclusion is displayed in Figure 7.6 and discussed in chapter 2. The content of inclusion (Figure 7.6) is what we do to get the curriculum to students. The SAALE process provides this access. The remaining parts of this chapter and of this text explain in detail how we get content to students.

ESTABLISHING A COMMON VOCABULARY

Now that we have studied the SAALE model and the checklist, we will begin discussing different strategies that may be stored in your mental filing cabinet. First, however, we need to establish a common vocabulary. We casually throw out the words *adapt, modify, intervene, accommodate,* and so on, yet we may not be thinking along the same lines.

Figure 7.6, The Big Picture, presents the relationship between the student, standards, evaluation, and curriculum. The curriculum must be accessible to all students. The SAALE Model provides this access. We have two ways to access: The process (collaboration) and the content (the Model). The term interventions is the secret to accessing or getting curriculum to students. Many terms appear when we speak of doing something differently: accommodations, modifications, adaptations, or supports. I like to use the term *interventions.*

Interventions: Trying what we have not yet tried.

There are two types of interventions: **preplanned interventions** and **spontaneous interventions.**

1. *Preplanned*—Interventions preplanned by the teacher during the lesson-planning stage.

   Example: Intervention required by the IEP or Section 504:

   Teacher establishes choices within the lesson based on ability levels, learning styles, interest, etc.

   Teacher establishes choices for assignments, projects, products, assessment measures, etc.

2. *Spontaneous*—Interventions implemented by the teacher when a student's needs for alternatives occur during instruction. This is an "on-your-feet" change in direction.

   Example: The teacher is giving oral directions (several at one time). A student can follow only one direction at a time. The teacher realizes the student is lost and quickly writes the main points on an overhead or chalkboard.

You will be referred back to preplanned and spontaneous interventions as we travel through the text. Using these two terms prepares us for differentiating instruction. Remember these terms!

Teacher observations serve as a valuable tool in collecting data on students. How could the intervention checklist discussed in this chapter serve as an effective instrument for teacher observations?

THE INTERVENTION/TRANSITION CHECKLIST

The key to success in any inclusive placement is the appropriate intervention to the learning environment. A major function of the school-based team that is guiding the student's learning outcomes is the identification of needed areas of interventions in the inclusive environment. The **intervention/transition checklist** is a helpful and practical method of identifying where adaptations or interventions in the learning environment may be needed. This simple device enables teachers and other team members to compare the characteristics of the general class setting with the performance levels of the student in that setting. The entire checklist appears in Appendix A on the companion website. However, the checklist, and how to use it, will be discussed here.

The intervention/transition checklist is divided into two parts, a checklist for the classroom and a checklist for the student. I encourage all classroom educators to complete the classroom checklist. This has to be done only once. When you review how you have responded to the checklist (rarely, sometimes, or most of the time), you will discover that you have normed yourself; that is, you have documented what you usually do or require in your classroom and how often you require a skill. This is your norm or standard. Perhaps you realize that when you give a test, you always use multiple-choice items. What about the student who does not respond well to multiple-choice questions? Do you have an accurate measure of this student's learning? When you have completed the classroom checklist, compare your responses to the responses on the student checklist. Remember, your answers are not right or wrong. If I completed the classroom checklist for a university class and then completed another for an in-service program, my norm would be different. Nothing would be wrong. I would simply know more about my "style" (norm).

Without comparing the classroom with the student, we *cannot* find mismatches. Identifying possible mismatches between a student's performance and the classroom learning environment is the first step to developing prereferral or postplacement interventions. For example, if the checklist reveals that a history teacher requires students to copy extensive notes from the board, and the student has difficulty copying, then a mismatch has occurred. The general and special education teachers can now work cooperatively to develop necessary accommodations for the student, perhaps by providing a graphic organizer for note taking. General educators can use this procedure for all students. The remaining chapters in this book provide numerous suggestions for ways to adapt each learning environment.

The checklist also assesses related environments. Completing this section of the checklist helps team members assess the student's performance during other academic portions of the school day.

Many times the high-risk student has difficulty within one or more of the related environments, resulting in his or her removal from the regular class. Although learning is going on in the classroom, the high-risk student is no longer participating. Therefore, the area of related environments becomes extremely important.

Figure 7.7 displays the sections of the checklist that assess the skill of directions. In this classroom students are expected to understand and follow oral directions. According to the notation on the student's checklist, the student is unable to understand and follow oral directions. For this skill area, there is a mismatch between the inclusive environment and the student's present skill level. The special and general educators and the student can now work together to develop accommodations that will enable the student to be successful in completing assignments that require note taking.

Beyond identifying needed areas for accommodations, the checklist can be used in several other ways. For students receiving instruction in a variety of classrooms, the checklist or appropriate subsections can be used to compare their performances across educational settings. Each of the student's teachers may complete a copy of the checklist, or the special education teacher consultant may complete the checklist while observing each classroom. This enables team members to compare observations about the student's learning environments and needs throughout the school day and develop consistent interventions.

The checklist can also be effective for students who are making a transition into the general education setting from a self-contained or resource placement. The special education teacher fills out the "student's present performance level" column and reviews the checklist with the general education teacher before the student joins the general classroom. This gives the general education teacher insight into the student's learning characteristics and special needs, enabling him or her to make accommodations in the learning environment to facilitate a smoother transition. For transitioning students who continue to be identified as students with special needs, the checklist can be used to generate objectives for the IEP.

Teachers can also make valuable use of the checklist in conferences with parents. Too often, teachers present the parents with test scores or grade reports that provide information about achievement and failure but offer no reasons for them. Using the checklist as a before-and-after comparison of the student's current level of performance (for example, at the beginning and midpoint of the school year), teachers can give parents concrete information about how the educational environment may be contributing to performance and which interventions have proven successful. Parents, in turn, can use the information to help structure an appropriate learning environment for the student at home. This will help prevent the frustration that often results when parents attempt to help students with homework but use inappropriate pacing, methods, or materials.

Section of Classroom Checklist

R (required **R**arely)   S (required **S**ome of the time)   M (required **M**ost of the time)

Format of Content

	RSM
Directions	
Oral directions	000
Written directions	000
Vocabulary study	
Understanding/learning vocabulary	000
Homework	
Homework listed on chalkboard	000
Homework shown on overhead projector	000
Homework listed on calendar/checklist	000
Homework assigned orally	000
Homework filed in notebook	000
Independent work required	000
Homework turned in	000

Section of Student Checklist

R (**R**arely demonstrates)   S (demonstrates **S**ome of the time)
M (demonstrates **M**ost of the time)

Format of Content

	RSM
Directions	
Understands and follows oral directions	000
Understands and follows written directions	000
Vocabulary study	
Understands/learns vocabulary	000
Homework	
Copies accurately from chalkboard	000
Copies accurately from overhead projector	000
Follows calendar/checklist	000
Understands and retains oral directions	000
Accurately files homework in notebook	000
Completes homework independently	000
Locates and turns in homework	000

FIGURE 7.7

Sample from intervention/transition checklist.

Note: From *Reaching the Hard to Teach* by J. W. Wood, 2004, Richmond, VA: Judy Wood, Inc. Reprinted with permission.

COLLABORATION TIPS

The SAALE model and the intervention/transition checklist are excellent tools for collaboration.

1. Before a student is placed into an inclusive environment, the special education teacher completes the checklist for the student to provide baseline information for the receiving teacher.

2. The special education teacher asks the receiving teacher to complete the classroom section of the checklist prior to the student with special needs entering the classroom. This allows time for the special education teacher to prepare an intervention plan for the student.

3. During a co-teaching partnership, both teachers could complete the classroom checklist and compare their expectations. These may differ.

4. The general education teacher completes the student section for all at-risk students moving to another grade level. The receiving teacher or teachers for next year will have baseline information for intervention planning.

5. The referring teacher can use the checklist to provide information for the referral team for intervention planning.

6. Teachers can use the checklist when conferencing with parents. Parents are excellent sources of student information.

7. After completing the checklist for the classroom and student, the classroom teacher can share the information with the teacher support team for intervention ideas.

The following list summarizes eight ways to use the intervention/transition checklist:

1. A special education teacher who is considering placing a student in an inclusive environment sends copies of the checklist to several general teachers and asks them to fill out the "characteristics of setting" column. The special education teacher fills out the "student's present performance level" column. The results of the checklist are used to make the best possible match between the general classroom and the student to be included. For example, if the science teacher uses small-group instruction almost exclusively in her class, and the student works best in a small-group setting, a possible match has been made. On the other hand, if assessment reveals that the history teacher requires students to copy extensive notes from the chalkboard, and the student has difficulty copying, educators will question the wisdom of placing the student in that class or consider interventions for copying. Remember, the history teacher is still doing an excellent job; teachers are simply matching the student to an inappropriate environment.

2. The special education teacher fills out the "student's present performance level" column and sends it to the general teacher either before or after a child has been placed into the general classroom. This gives the general classroom teacher information

James is experiencing difficulty in the general education classroom. From listening to his teacher, you realize that numerous "mismatches" are occurring. You have knowledge of the SAALE model and access to the intervention checklist. You realize that this information would be helpful to the teacher as well as James.

1. How would you approach the teacher?
2. Would you be prepared to offer suggestions for interventions for James?

about the student's learning characteristics and facilitates a closer match between teaching procedures and student learning style. For example, if the teacher uses the lecture approach and the included student has listening problems, a good match has not been made. However, if the teacher makes some simple adaptations to the lectures (such as using the overhead projector as a visual aid or providing a printed lecture outline), then the student's placement in the class may be appropriate.

3. The special education teacher observes the inclusive setting and fills out the checklist independently or together with the general education teacher. Results are then compiled by the special education teacher and shared with the general education teacher, helping to determine the appropriateness of the inclusive placement.

4. The special education teacher uses the checklist to identify skills that the student needs to master before entering an inclusive setting and includes these skills in the student's IEP. For example, if the teacher discovers that a student cannot accurately copy notes from the chalkboard, the IEP should include note-taking skills as an objective.

5. Multidisciplinary teams use the checklist to help them determine a student's readiness for inclusion.

6. The child study committee, teacher assistance team, and others use the checklist to assess a student before deciding on a special education evaluation or planning an IEP.

7. The classroom teacher completes the "student's present performance level" column and places it in the student's folder for next year's teacher to review.

8. The checklist is used to document appropriate prereferral interventions.

THE SAALE MODEL AND UNIVERSAL DESIGN

IDEA 1997 (the reauthorization of the Individuals with Disabilities Education Act, 1997) places a call to general education to provide even greater access to students with disabilities. In meeting the goal of IDEA, "teachers must provide useful alternatives in both curricular materials and instructional delivery." Nancy Safer, executive director of the Council for Exceptional Children, stated that "one size does not fit all." Teachers of students with special needs must recognize that the "design" of the curricular content may require a change to render it accessible. This goes back to the concept that it is not only *what* we teach but *how* we teach that opens doors for students who learn differently. Lou Danielson (1999) stated that the concept of **universal design** is one practice that helps students reach educational goals.

> In terms of learning, universal design means the design of instructional materials and activities that makes the learning goals achievable by individuals with wide differences in their abilities to see, hear, speak, move, read, write, understand English, attend, organize, engage, and remember. Universal design for learning is achieved by means of flexible curricular materials and activities that provide alternatives for students with differing abilities. These alternatives are built into the instructional design and operating systems—they are not added on after-the-fact. (p. 2)

Why the fuss about universal design? Answer: The SAALE model is truly universal design in action. The SAALE model has been around since the late 1970s, and universal design is presently emerging as a best practice. The SAALE model is a model for differentiating instruction for students based on learning styles, ability levels, and immediate educational needs. The model provides an organized method of selecting the appropriate intervention for the student's problem.

"Universal design for learning begins by assuming that students vary widely, even though they may all be in the same grade and same course, and is flexible in order to respond to a wide degree of student diversity from the very outset" (Turnbull, Turnbull, Shank, & Smith, 2004). SAALE also assumes that students have vast differences, yet are served in the same grades and same courses. SAALE is a problem-solving process for identifying the differences (or mismatches) between the student and the curriculum, instruction, and evaluation. According to Turnbull and colleagues, the principles of universal design can be applied to the curriculum, instruction, and evaluation of students.

There are two major ways to add flexibility to *curriculum:*

1. *Augmentation.* The teacher adds content to the general curriculum and/or raises performance levels to meet students' particular needs (for example, content enrichment for students whose achievement is significantly above grade level). (Turnbull et al., 2004, p. 56)

2. *Alteration.* The teacher teaches foundational content in the general curriculum and/or scales back performance levels (for example, a foundational curriculum for students whose achievement is significantly below grade level). (Turnbull et al., 2004, p. 56)

Universal design of *instruction* focuses on how to teach the curriculum so that teaching is consistent with each student's most effective way of learning (Turnbull et al., 2004, p. 57). According to Turnbull, the two major ways of enhancing flexible instruction are augmentation and adaptation. With augmentation the teacher teaches additional skills for generalization of information. For example, a student who does not speak English will be assisted with bilingual education. With adaptation the teacher (a) "changes how the content is presented during instruction" (p. 57) (for example, graphic organizers for delivery of information), (b) "changes how the environment is arranged" (p. 57) (for example, small-group work stations), and/or (c) "changes how the student is expected to respond" (p. 54) (for example, a student with written expression difficulties may use a tape recorder).

Universal design of *evaluation* provides for differentiation of student evaluation. (For example, a student may need a word bank for a fill-in-the-blank test.)

Figure 7.8 presents how SAALE finds mismatches within each of these components.

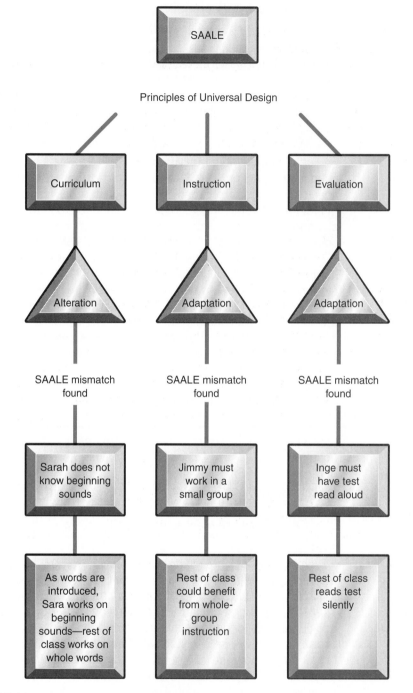

FIGURE 7.8

SAALE mismatches and universal design.

Note: From *Reading the Hard to Teach* by J. W. Wood, 2004, Richmond, VA: Judy Wood, Inc. Reprinted with permission.

THE SAALE MODEL'S HISTORY

SAALE model training has been conducted in every state and in several countries. Numerous sites/states have provided long-term SAALE training to educators (Texas, Hawaii, Ohio, Illinois, Tennessee, Michigan, Utah, Nebraska, Iowa, North Carolina, and Montana).

The SAALE model initially was an attempt to help educators in general education work more successfully with students who learn differently. Over a 24-year period the SAALE model training has gained national recognition for meeting its goals: helping educators change their pedagogical structure; helping educators remain longer in their fields; and, most important, helping students be more successful.

THE SAALE MODEL AND UPCOMING CHAPTERS

The SAALE model will be expanded throughout the remaining chapters of this text. "Adapting the Learning Environment," chapter 8, addresses student attitudes and ways of improving these attitudes as well as helping students develop appropriate social skills. How to work with mild to severe behavior problems and how to schedule and group students are covered in that chapter. The learning environment sets the stage for the teaching environment. Chapter 9 looks at lesson plans in the teaching process. Chapter 10, "Adapting Teaching Techniques," discusses the process of delivering instruction. Chapter 11, "Adapting the Format of Content," looks at ways to organize instruction and ideas for teaching subject matter. Chapter 12, "Adapting Evaluation and Grading," looks at how to provide classroom-embedded assessment, how to adapt tests, and numerous alternatives to assessment and grading. Chapter 13, "Transition," provides a total picture of the transition of students from the young years to postsecondary education.

SUMMARY

Making the transition from one educational setting to another can be either a positive experience or a frustrating one for a student with special needs or one who is at-risk for school failure. By assessing the setting and determining whether the student has the skills needed to enter the environment, educators can enhance the chances for successful learning.

Now that we have learned about two parts of the three-step process (the model and the checklist) and are using the same vocabulary, we will move ahead to step 3: strategies or interventions. Remember that everything you already know, and will learn, can be placed into your filing cabinet (our model). The rest of this book will suggest hundreds of ideas for you to consider.

RESOURCES

ERIC Clearinghouse on Handicapped
and Gifted Children
c/o Council for Exceptional Children (CEC)
1110 West Glebe Road

Suite 300
Arlington, VA 22201-5704
(703) 620-3660
www.cec.sped.org

SUGGESTED READING

McNamara, K., & Hollinger, C. (2003). Intervention-based assessment: Evaluation rates and eligibility findings. *Exceptional Children, 69,* 181–193.

REFERENCES

American Youth Policy Forum. (2000, November 3). *Accessing the general curriculum: Promoting a universal design for learning* (Forum Brief). Retrieved September 7, 2004, from www.aypf.org/forumbriefs/2000/fb110300.htm.

Bergan, J. R. (1995). Evolution of a problem-solving model of consultation. *Journal of Educational and Psychological Consultation, 6*(2), 111–123.

Danielson, L. (1999, Fall). Universal design: Ensuring access to the general education curriculum. *Research Connections, 5,* 2–3.

Hoffman, L. M. (2003, March). *Overview of public elementary and secondary schools and districts: School year 2001–02.* Washington, DC: National Center for Education Statistics.

Levine, M. (2002). *A mind at a time.* New York: Simon & Schuster.

McNamara, K., & Hollinger, C. (2003). Intervention-based assessment: Evaluation rates and eligibility findings. *Exceptional Children, 69,* 181–193.

Nelson, J. R., & Smith, D. J. (1991). Prereferral intervention: A review of the research. *Education & Treatment of Children, 14*(3), 243–254.

President's Commission on Excellence in Special Education. (2002). *A new era: Revitalizing special education for children and their families.* Jessup, MD: U.S. Department of Education.

Sindelar, P. T., Griffin, C. C., Smith, S. W., & Watanabe, A. K. (1992). Prereferral intervention: Encouraging notes on preliminary findings. *The Elementary School Journal, 92*(3), 245–259.

Thomas, A., & Grimes, J. (Eds). (1995). *Best practices in school psychology, III.* Washington, DC: National Association of School Psychologists.

Turnbull, R., Turnbull, A., Shank, M., & Smith, S. J. (2004). *Exceptional lives: Special education in today's schools* (4th ed.). Upper Saddle River, NJ: Merrill/Prentice Hall.

Wood, J. W. (1989). *Mainstreaming: A practical approach for teachers.* Upper Saddle River, NJ: Merrill/Prentice Hall.

8

Adapting the Learning Environment

LEARNER OBJECTIVES

After you read this chapter, you will be able to:

- Discuss how teacher attitudes affect student learning.
- List specific activities for teaching students social skills.
- Define and discuss the behavioral continuum.
- Discuss how scheduling affects learning.
- Explain various grouping techniques.
- List various designs for the classroom.

CHAPTER AT A GLANCE

Socioemotional
Adaptations for
the Classroom

Teacher Attitudes

Teachers with
a Heart

The Special Education Teacher's
Role in Preparing the General
Education Teacher

Communication

Student Attitudes
and Self-Esteem

Planning for Inclusion

Social Skills

Social Skill Categories

Adapting the
Behavioral
Environment

The Teacher
Sets the Tone

Preventive
Planning
Techniques

Providing Class
Structure

Motivating
Students

Surface
Behavior
Techniques

Positive Behavior
Supports

Adapting the
Physical Environment

Grouping for
Instruction

Classroom
Design

KEY TERMS

communication   212

functional assessment   231

risk-free environment   209

surface behaviors   225

*N*atasha was a premature baby and exhibited numerous medical, social, and academic problems throughout her educational history. As a
young child, Natasha had great difficulty making friends and joining into
play with other children. As Natasha developed into her teens, these problems continued and began to affect the classroom. Because Natasha could
not interact socially (social environment), her teachers had to carefully select how she would be placed in small-group settings (physical environment). If the group size was too large and a strong leader was not in the
group, Natasha would act out (behavior environment). Knowing that
Natasha had social issues, the teacher was able to control her behavior by
carefully arranging the physical environment (grouping) and thereby preventing outbursts from Natasha.

*T*he learning environment component of the SAALE (Systematic Approach for
Adapting the Learning Environment) process sets the stage for an effective classroom. It has a significant effect on a student's success or failure. Often when a student
is experiencing difficulty at school, teachers immediately focus on what the student
cannot do academically. However, the mismatch may lie within the learning environment. This chapter will enable you to begin to see "school" as a total picture, not just
a place for instruction. The three components of the learning environment are the socioemotional, the behavioral, and the physical environments. After reading this chapter, you will have a deeper understanding of the nature of the child as well as the role
of the teacher. You will be given many ideas (interventions) that will assist you in working with students in these critical areas.

SOCIOEMOTIONAL ADAPTATIONS FOR THE CLASSROOM

Our children come to school with much more than the latest tennis shoes, lunch
money, and backpacks. Because many come from homes in which the climate is much
different from that of the classroom, entering the classroom can require an emotional-
social adjustment. Educators need to establish a warm and accepting environment for
all children so they feel more comfortable and have a greater opportunity to learn. This
is what we call a risk-free environment. To understand this concept, let's think first
about *risk-filled* environments.

Recall a teacher you had in high school or perhaps a professor you've had in college. Have you ever waited with breathless anticipation for that person to ask you a
question, not knowing which question you would be expected to respond to or when
you would be called on? Perhaps the teacher called on students randomly to read
aloud. In such cases, your anticipation may have become almost too great.

During my undergraduate studies I had a professor who was unpredictable in this
way. I never knew when I would be called on, what types of items were going to be on

the tests, or how my papers or projects would be graded. I also had a teacher who took great pleasure in pointing out how wrong I was when I answered. In elementary school students in my class would take turns reading aloud. Because I was an extremely poor reader, I almost had a nervous breakdown before my turn arrived.

These were certainly not risk-free environments. An environment that is risk-free is one in which students are not afraid to take chances. A **risk-free environment** is a safe place for students, where mistakes are seen as stepping-stones to success. Before everyone runs to the playground, the teams are established. No one must stand anxiously waiting to be picked. When an answer is incorrect, the student is praised for trying. Everyone's efforts are appreciated. A risk-free environment is safe, relaxed, and nonthreatening to students.

A risk-free environment has many components. Two of the most important are positive teacher attitudes and honoring students' self-esteem.

TEACHER ATTITUDES

The classroom teacher plays an important role in the success of an included child. Establishing a warm socioemotional climate helps teachers to maximize student achievement. The teacher's attitude toward students is the major catalyst that affects interaction and achievement. "Whether in special or general education, there is growing evidence that the single most important school influence in a student's education is a well-prepared, caring, and qualified teacher" (Council for Exceptional Children, 2000).

When inclusion first became a reality, teachers generally expressed reservations about accepting students with special needs into the general classroom setting. Teachers were concerned about what they may have perceived as dumping students with special needs back into regular classrooms. Teachers felt unprepared to work with diverse special populations and feared that these students would demand too much of their time in classes that were already full. Teachers were also concerned about their roles, increased paperwork, possible conflict with special education teachers and related service providers, and fulfilling parent's expectations. The results of a study by Michele Wood indicated that "in the initial stages of inclusion, teachers maintained discrete role boundaries through a relatively clear, albeit division of labor. As the school year progressed, role perceptions became less rigid as the teaming became more cooperative" (Wood, 1998).

Many teachers who once felt isolated and alone in their classroom now see a network of resources if they are willing to be open to suggestions and to risk changing their presentation of material or how they might review or design a test. Many of the suggestions help not only the student with special needs in the classroom, but the at-risk student as well.

For inclusion to be successful, positive teacher attitudes are essential. Equally important, teachers need appropriate support and training. Meyen, Vergason, and Whelan (1993) suggested that teacher attitudes should be continually reassessed. Areas of assessment may include "opinions of perceived success or failure in providing curriculum content, increased learning for all students involved, student discipline, team efforts, and grading procedures" (p. 101).

More needs to be done to provide training for teachers and school staff on attitudes toward and acceptance of, not only students with special needs but the increasing number of students from culturally, racially, and ethnically diverse populations. Teachers need information on supports for maximizing student success and on appropriate interventions and accommodations when necessary.

COLLABORATION TIPS

Successful teachers are honest, realistic, and open about the learning abilities of all students. At the same time they present a friendly, positive attitude. Following are a few tips that may help teachers share the responsibility of educating all students:

1. Share knowledge on students' learning strengths and weaknesses. Awareness or understanding is a step toward growth.
2. Reassure each other that educators can teach diverse abilities.
3. Arrange for general educators to visit special education classes to observe students who will be included in general education classes.
4. Discuss openly strategies that can be used for large groups, small groups, and individual students.
5. Develop the attitude that all students may need different instructional supports and that learning becomes more effective when we incorporate different strategies into our teaching.
6. Model or demonstrate special strategies for each other.
7. Remember that good teaching reaches all children and every teacher has information to share.
8. Develop the mind-set of asking your colleagues when you are having difficulty with a student. The student does not have to be a "special" student.
9. Provide instructional materials and resources. Educators can reciprocate and share materials and resources.
10. Help each other to decide on support needed for students—i.e., consultation services, school psychology, etc. Some services are special education related and must be decided by committee. Others are not special education specific.
11. Understand that good communication is crucial to establishing a good working relationship between special and general education teachers.
12. Develop an understanding of self and a realization that others see and respond to others as they project self.
13. Listen, demonstrate, and understand others' concerns by acting in positive ways, respecting the problems of colleagues, and responding quickly to the needs of others.

Note: From *Reaching the Hard to Teach* by J. W. Wood, 2004, Richmond, VA: Judy Wood, Inc. Reprinted with permission.

Teachers with a Heart

Two wonderful articles appeared in the September 2003 issue of the journal *Educational Leadership:* "Hearts and Minds" by Steven Wolk and "Giving Students What They Need" by Jonathan C. Erwin. I was so moved by both articles that I wanted to include excerpts from both in this section. So many times we are busy writing about what to do and how to teach that we forget the most important aspect of a teacher—the heart "chip." We may know a lot of information, but we must never forget the heart chip. I can assure you that children know whether a teacher has this chip or not.

First let's look at some quotes from Dr. Wolk's article:

You have to make that social and emotional connection with kids in order to get inside their heads—the fact that you care makes them see you differently. (Brown, 2002, p. 67, cited in Wolk, 2003)

The late humanistic psychologist Carl Rogers (1969) wrote:

It is quite customary for teachers rather consciously to put on the mask, the role, the façade, of being a teacher, and to wear this façade all day, removing it only when they have left the school at night. (p. 107)

Dr. Wolk stated:

Teachers need to allow students to see them as complete people with emotions, opinions, and lives outside of school. A good way for a teacher to get students to treat him or her like a human is to act like one. (p. 18)

In "Giving Students What They Need," Dr. Erwin provided tips for teachers for meeting students' basic needs. To help students feel a source of power:

- Give students a voice in the classroom. Solicit their input regarding classroom rules and behavior guidelines; allow them to generate questions that guide the direction of the curriculum.
- Discover students' instructional levels and meet them where they are.
- Teach to a variety of learning styles.
- Hold regular discussion about the value of the curriculum to students' lives.
- Use research-based best practices, such as structured cooperative learning, authentic assessment, and brain-based teaching strategies.
- Instead of giving a student low or failing grades, allow them second and third chances to demonstrate their learning. (Bloom, 1971; Glasser, 2000; cited in Erwin, 2003, p. 21)

We can appeal to students' needs for freedom of choice by providing them with choices regarding the following:

- Their seating
- Team members for cooperative learning activities or projects.
- Assignments (topics for essays or class projects, outside reading, and odd- or even-numbered math problems).
- Performance tasks for assessments. There are dozens of ways in which student can demonstrate their understanding of course content. Provide them with a list and let them choose one that allows them to play to their strengths and talents. (p. 22)

Teachers can create the conditions for student to feel a sense of belonging and acceptance in dozens of ways. Consider the following:

- Learn each student's name as soon as possible, and engage student in activities that help them learn one another's names.
- Greet all students as they enter your classroom.
- Let students get to know you personally: your outside interests, what you stand for, and who you are.
- Regularly engage students in team-building activities.
- Teach students how to work cooperatively, and give them regular opportunities to learn in structured cooperative activities.

- Conduct class meetings on a regular basis for class-building, problem-solving, and content-related discussions.
- Smile *long* before Thanksgiving. (p. 21)

To gain and keep students' attention, we can do the following:

- Change location (the teacher's, the student's, or both).
- Introduce lessons with different kinds of music.
- Use a variety of instructional strategies.
- Change students' cooperative learning partners or team members regularly.
- Begin class with a variety of team-building activities.
- Go on field trips. (p. 21)

Take these tips from Wolk and Ervin, tuck them away, and remember to pull them out when you enter a classroom. Keep that "teacher heart chip" active.

The Special Education Teacher's Role in Preparing the General Education Teacher

Special educators are in a unique position to promote positive inclusive experiences as well as to offer support and expertise to their general education peers. General educators, in turn, have special expertise that will benefit special educators. Special personnel and general teachers of student with special needs need to work together to plan and implement inclusion. Table 8.1 presents issues and suggestions for the special education teacher's role in preparing the general class teacher.

Communication

Communication—the exchange of ideas, information, and suggestions—is crucial to establishing a good working relationship between special and general education teachers.

Because the general educator faces the task of accommodating instruction in inclusive classrooms, the special educator bears more, although not all, of the responsibility for making the communication process easier. To communicate better, special education teachers must understand themselves, realize that others see and respond to them as they project themselves, be able to listen, demonstrate an understanding of others' concerns by acting in positive ways, respect the problems and concerns of their colleagues, and respond quickly to the needs of others.

Understanding oneself leads to good communication. In addition, knowing and internalizing the role of special educator and then projecting that role in a positive way gives others guidelines for communication. If special educators project confidence in their abilities, others trust that competence. However, the reverse is also true. If special educators project a lack of confidence in their abilities, others may view them as incompetent.

Listening is the basis of all communication. Often we listen to others without actually hearing what they are saying. Special educators must not only listen but also hear the concerns of general educators. Then they can show evidence of hearing those concerns by reacting to their colleagues' needs in a positive manner. For example, special education teachers who quickly provide the appropriate instructional

TABLE 8.1

The special education teacher's role in preparing the general class teacher.

Issue	Suggestions
The student with special needs may not fit into the regular class setting.	1. Prepare the student with special needs as to class expectations prior to entry. 2. Arrange for the student with special needs to have short visits in the general education class prior to entry. 3. If the disability is severe, have someone explain to the class what is involved for the student.
The teacher is reluctant to have a student with special needs in her class.	1. Although today all children belong to all educators, some educators are still reluctant to serve students with special needs. This works both ways. Special educators resist "giving up" their students, and general educators resist "receiving" students with special needs. 2. Begin by seeing the advantages for all students and teachers when students are combined. 3. Start sharing materials, supplies, etc. Everyone benefits from this. 4. Discuss how having an extra teacher in the class will be a support for all students.
The teacher does not believe his training includes working with students with special needs or with general education students.	1. Begin cross training. Be sure that inservice programs serve all educators. 2. Teachers can begin to model skills and strategies for each other. 3. Involve literacy centers and coaches.
The teacher does not know how to develop and implement instruction to a diverse population.	1. Classrooms have always been diverse. Remember the one-room schoolhouse? Teaching to diverse populations requires organization and planning. When two work as one, this planning is possible. 2. Remember that when you teach a class or subject, everyone benefits. Learn to differentiate the subject. Not everyone will learn all. Some will learn more than others, but all will learn according to their abilities. 3. Draw on all of the school resources. Many times resources are untapped (for example, the literacy coach).

Note: From *Reaching the Hard to Teach* by J. W. Wood, 2004, Richmond, VA: Judy Wood, Inc. Reprinted with permission.

material, suggest an alternative teaching technique, or assist in designing a behavior management plan for an inclusive student show that the problems of others are important. Once general educators believe that the door of communication is open, effective inclusion becomes a reality. (See chapter 2 for information on collaborative consultation models.)

STUDENT ATTITUDES AND SELF-ESTEEM

Like adults, students develop a set of attitudes about themselves and their peers. Students who have been found eligible for special education services or who are at risk for school failure usually have experienced learning difficulty for a long time. Often educators wonder why students have low self-esteem or why they seem unmotivated. Failure is a cumulative process. It does not occur overnight, and the damage it causes cannot be repaired overnight. Students with disabilities often have lower positions of class status than their nondisabled peers do, and this pattern of rejection holds true in both general and special classrooms.

Following is an excerpt from a wonderful work by Anne F. Parkinson, Isabel Dulfano, and Carl E. Nink (2003) on student self-esteem:

> Self-esteem in increased when individuals are involved in activities they enjoy and at which they excel. "Students having trouble in the classroom need to be involved in something they do well, whether painting, baseball, or dancing. Otherwise, they may experience chronic success deprivation" (Levine, 1990). "When a student is experiencing academic stress and failure, art, music, mechanical pursuits, or sports may serve as venues in which he feels successful and can obtain longed-for positive recognition" (Levine, 2002, p. 186). Some students are better creators than learners; for these, opportunities to be creative and brainstorm enhance self-esteem and motivation. (p. 14)

Quotes from Levine are also included in this wonderful work and certainly address the issue of self-esteem:

> Most kids simply lack the insulation to handle repeated frustration and personal failure. Some simply surrender. Some become permanently anxious or depressed. Others act out, cause trouble, get themselves pregnant, or take drugs. Still others become transformed into conservative nonrisktakers, shutting down and decisively writing themselves off at an early age. Or else they keep criticizing and putting down whatever it is they can't succeed at. (p. 246)

> A student's enhanced insight into his or her learning disorders (and strengths) will engender hopefulness and ambition. (p. xi)

> Expertise kindles intellectual self-esteem. (p. 323)

Preparing for Inclusion

Even though we consider the general classroom to be the appropriate home base for the student with a disability, we need to make preparations to provide a smooth transition to that environment for all concerned. Some special students may spend a large portion of their day receiving services in alternative settings. Students with mild disabilities will spend most of their day within the general classroom in multi-age or multi-ability groupings. In either case, students as well as teachers need support.

Special students need many skills to function within the general class environment. Whether a student is new to the general class or has previously spent a large portion of time there, he or she needs skills to help smooth the transition.

The structure of the class can present major problems for students with special needs who must be taught the rules and routines. Even if teachers post and review rules, the students may not truly understand them. After reviewing the rules and routines, teachers should encourage students to discuss them and ask questions if a rule is unclear. To avoid embarrassment, older students can ask such questions after school or during a study break.

Figure 8.1 presents a checklist of classroom rules and routines. The teacher may complete the checklist and give it to the students, who can keep it in a notebook for reference. This checklist is also excellent for substitute teachers because it helps them clearly understand classroom expectations.

For younger children you may want to videotape last year's students modeling the rules. When fall arrives, and as you discuss each rule, you can show the rule modeled on the videotape. Tell the children that if they work very hard, they will be the movie stars for next year's children. However, be sure that you have administrative

Class _____ Teacher _____ Period _____

1. Seating arrangement:
   _____ Open seating
   _____ Assigned seating

2. Behavior for entering the class:
   _____ Visiting with friends allowed
   _____ Visiting with friends not allowed
   _____ Place personal belongings in desk, locker, or bookshelf, etc.
   _____ Place class materials on desk
   _____ Copy class work from board
   _____ Copy homework assignment from behind
   _____ Other

3. Behavior when leaving the class:
   _____ Leave when the bell is sounded
   _____ Leave only when dismissed by teacher

4. Format for heading papers:
   Model of format _____
   _____ Location on paper

5. Procedure for turning in completed work:
   _____ Will be discussed with each assignment
   _____ At beginning of each class
   _____ At end of each class
   _____ Only when requested by teacher

6. How to request a drink of water:

7. Procedure for going to the restroom:

8. Procedure for going to the clinic:

9. Procedure for going to the office:

10. Procedure for sharpening pencils and requesting supplies:

11. What to do when tardy for class:

12. Procedure for going to the locker:

13. Policy regarding book covers and jackets:

14. Policy on care of texts:

15. Materials needed for class:

16. Procedure if you do not have class materials:

17. What to do when you need to leave class or cannot cope:

18. Class policy for making up work:

19. Penalty for late work:

20. Grading policy:

21. Testing schedule:

22. Structure of class procedures:

23. Where to put trash:

24. Can I chew gum or have snacks?

25. How to ask for assistance:

26. When is talking allowed?

27. Procedure for asking questions:

28. Procedure for responding to questions:

29. Procedure if you are unsure about asking a question in front of peers:

30. Rules for attire—hats:

31. Rule of clothes that advertise:

32. Rules on cigarettes and alcohol.

FIGURE 8.1
Checklist of rules and routines.

Note: From *Reaching the Hard to Teach* by J. W. Wood, 2004, Richmond, VA: Judy Wood, Inc. Reprinted with permission.

PRACTICAL APPLICATIONS

1. Collect personal information on a card about each child. For example, ask each of them to write or tell you about his or her greatest accomplishment or a hobby he or she enjoys. This gives you an entry into the child's life. Use this information to start a quick, verbal exchange from time to time.
2. Use body language to show warmth and acceptance, such as extending palm of hands outward when greeting students, standing in close proximity, standing in front of the desk rather than behind it, and making eye contact during a discussion.
3. Let the student get to know you as a person, not just as a teacher.
4. Try to spend time every day with each student. A minute of individual attention from you can make a child's day.
5. Give students honest praise. Many have suffered much failure in school, and they need to know that they are capable of success.
6. Don't be afraid to tell students you love them. This may be the only time some will ever hear those words.
7. Take the pressure of grades off the students by marking them according to their own level, not the class level.
8. Provide 5 to 7 seconds for a student to answer a question. The average time a teacher waits is 0.9 seconds, which is much too short.
9. Establish a risk-free classroom. Mistakes are O.K.
10. Let students know that trying is important.

Note: From *Reaching the Hard to Teach* by J. W. Wood, 2004, Richmond, VA: Judy Wood, Inc. Reprinted with permission.

permission to videotape students. You may need written permission. Also, remember to show the modeled rules one at a time with practice sessions. Showing all the rules at one sitting may overwhelm young children.

SOCIAL SKILLS

Social Skill Categories

In addition to having difficulty understanding specific rules and class outlines, the student at risk or with special needs often displays a mismatch in the area of social skill development. Frequently, a student may fall behind academically, and the teacher will become concerned. When the student's social behavior is inappropriate, the concern increases. Social skills can and should be taught to students because many children with special needs or at risk do not have a repertoire of appropriate skills with which to respond to school-related events. Table 8.2 presents selected categories of social skills. For older students, the teacher may want to discuss these skills, add appropriate ones to the rules and routines checklist (Figure 8.1), and use the list as a student handout. For younger students, the teacher may prefer to use as classroom activities the suggestions for teaching social skills listed on the Companion Website.

TABLE 8.2
Social skills by categories.

Orientation skills	• Respecting cultural differences • Adapting to changes
Communication skills	• Following directions • Making eye contact • Requesting permission • Ignoring distractions • Interpreting facial clues and body language • Listening • Requesting clarification • Adjusting language to situational demands • Using greetings and farewells • Interrupting appropriately • Initiating conversations • Maintaining conversations • Joining ongoing conversations • Ending conversations • Talking on the telephone • Reading social environments
Managing emotions	• Changing activities • Expressing needs and wants • Disagreeing • Controlling anger • Accepting disappointment • Accepting criticism • Accepting praise • Coping with rejection • Responding to threats • Responding to embarrassment
Independent living	• Using free time wisely • Following rules
Responsibility (social and personal)	• Participating in class • Accepting responsibility • Making new friends • Sharing and taking turns
Critical thinking	• Solving problems
Relationships	• Understanding student/teacher roles • Respecting others' space • Working cooperatively in a group
Instructions with others	• Expressing appreciation • Apologizing • Helping others • Showing respect for others • Joining in

Note: From *Reaching the Hard to Teach,* by J. W. Wood, 2004, Richmond, VA: Judy Wood, Inc. Reprinted with permission.

The Companion Website includes all of the social skills found in Table 8.3 (on page 219) including words to be defined prior to teaching the social skill and suggested activities for teaching each skill. A note to remember: in the "words-to-be defined" column, I have listed *suggested* words for defining. The exact words must be selected for defining based on the developmental level of the student being taught. Defining words become a teaching prerequisite to teaching the social skill. For example, the skill of "understanding student/teacher roles" may need the word *role* defined when teaching young children. Some children may think that a role is something to eat (roll) or perhaps everyone is going to "roll" around on the floor. Therefore, the word *role* must be defined. A role is a duty or job. Helping students understand selected words provides a baseline for teaching a social skill.

ADAPTING THE BEHAVIORAL ENVIRONMENT

Managing student behavior is an ongoing process that occurs simultaneously with teaching. When teachers have assessed their student properly, have carefully adapted the physical environment, and have appropriately planned instruction to fit students' needs, most management problems will disappear. But no system is foolproof; sometimes problem behaviors distract from the positive instructional atmosphere that teachers have so carefully built.

Behavior has many faces, comes in different degrees, and presents itself in many environments. Figure 8.2 presents the continuum of behavior. From the onset educators may lay a foundation in the classroom to prevent "misbehaviors," structure the class to diminish "misbehaviors," motivate students, and manage those behaviors referred to as only surface behaviors. After a foundation has been established within the classroom, other behavior supports assist the teacher, such as universal or school-wide supports, group supports, and individual behavior supports. In this section we will look at each stage of the continuum beginning with the teacher setting the tone.

The Teacher Sets the Tone

The teacher sets the tone in the classroom. He or she adjusts the lighting, controls the temperature, arranges the seating, decides how to present lessons, elects when to give tests, and chooses what types of tests to administer. The teacher sets the affective atmosphere of the classroom and the stage for learning. The teacher alone has the power to invite or not invite each student to learn. The teacher's attentiveness, expectations, encouragement, attitudes, and evaluations strongly influence students' perceptions of themselves as learners. Thus, the teacher's behavior influences the students' behavior. To assess their potential influence on student behavior, teachers should ask themselves the following questions:

- Do I leave my personal problems at home?
- Am I in good physical and emotional health?
- Am I happy with my role in life?
- Does my voice convey confidence?
- Does my walk convey confidence?
- Do I have a positive self-concept?
- What is my attitude toward my peer group?

TABLE 8.3
Ten problem behaviors and strategies to deal with them.

Problem Behavior	Strategies
Impulsiveness	• Explain to the student what impulsiveness means. Provide examples of what impulsiveness is. Model problem solving. • Praise students when they have reflected on their behavior.
Inattention	• Use proximity and gently touching the student. • Use verbal clues such as "listen carefully" or "look what I am now writing." • Use colored chalk or large print. • Gently call the student's name. • Remove the distraction of objects or noises. • Seat the student by a student who pays attention.
Noncompletion of tasks	• Check to see if the student understands the task requirements. Clarify any misunderstandings. • Provide appropriate instruction if the student is missing prerequisite skills. • Provide a contract that states specific rewards for task completion.
Noncompliance	• Privately talk to the student to be sure that the student understands what to do and has the skills to complete the task. • Praise small steps made toward the goal. • After appropriate behavior is observed, even at a low rate, establish a contract with the student.
Out-of-seat	• Determine where out-of-seat behavior occurs. • Be sure that the student understands what you expect. • Be sure that the time for in-seat behavior is reasonable for the student. • Schedule stretch or movement breaks for the class. • Allow the student to self monitor in-seat behavior.
Talking without permission	• Discuss privately with the student the class rules for talking. • Reinforce appropriate behavior. • Use techniques such as ignoring or time-out.
Unmotivated to learn	• Privately talk with the student to find out his or her feelings about school and learning. • Be sure that the academic task required is an ability match for the student. • Involve the parents, if possible, in a reward system for home and/or school. • Let the student suggest tasks to be learned that are of interest.
Unprepared for class	• Privately discuss with the student why he or she is unprepared for class—family finances or a personal situation may be the cause. Get help from the appropriate services for the student. • Make sure that the student has the ability to prepare the necessary work. • Use contracting.
Unruly class	• Establish class rules. • Provide a rules checklist.
Unsatisfactory homework	• Make sure that homework is appropriate for the student. • Individualize homework. Same-for-all is not always best-for-all.

Note: From *Reaching the Hard to Teach* by J. W. Wood, 2004, Richmond, VA: Judy Wood, Inc. Reprinted with permission.

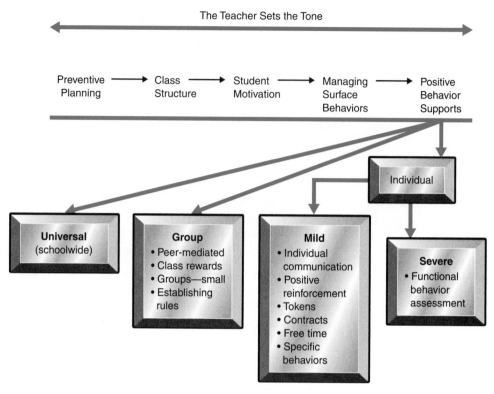

FIGURE 8.2
The behavior continuum.

Note: From *Reaching the Hard to Teach* by J. W. Wood, 2004, Richmond, VA: Judy Wood, Inc. Reprinted with permission.

- What is my attitude toward children?
- Do I accept the responsibility of students at risk?
- Do I feel comfortable about admitting mistakes?
- Will I change my opinion when someone presents a valid reason for doing so?
- Do I have a sense of humor?
- Can I laugh at myself?
- Am I an attentive listener?
- Do I teach subjects or children?

Figure 8.3 offers eight behavior suggestions for the teacher.

Preventive Planning Techniques

One way to manage behavior is to prevent misbehavior before it begins. The Utah State Board of Education (1992) has 12 tips for preventive planning:

1. *Appropriate and motivating curriculum.* The curriculum must be appropriate for the functional level of each child. Work that is too difficult or too easy is likely to increase inappropriate behavior. Testing and evaluation skills are important tools that help teachers discover these functional levels.

Fairness: Teachers must demonstrate fairness in assignments, giving help, etc., or they cannot expect students to begin to like them.

Appearance: Appearance is often mentioned by students when they describe teachers for whom they have high regard. Good grooming and a pleasant appearance are interpreted as a sign of respect.

Humor: William Glasser says humor is a form of caring. Teachers need not be joke tellers, but those who respond openly to humorous moments or who can kid lightheartedly with students seem to strike particularly responsive chords.

Courtesy: Courtesy in the classroom helps build personal relationships and is frequently responded to in kind.

Respect: Teachers show respect by encouraging students to express ideas without criticism, by valuing student products, or by not "putting down" a student. When respect is extended, it is usually returned.

Realness: Students see teachers as "real" only when the teacher allows them to do so. Teachers can share anecdotes with students from their own lives, integrating personal experiences into explanation and presentations.

Re-establishing Contact: After a student has been reprimanded, reestablishing contact by showing that a grudge is not held helps the student reenter the emotional flow of the classroom.

Active Listening: Teachers should listen carefully to the content, reflect back the message, and do so with feeling.

FIGURE 8.3
Behavior suggestions for the teacher.

Note: Adapted from *The Skillful Teacher: Building Your Teaching Skills,* 5th ed. (pp. 347–349), by J. Saphier and R. Gower, 1997, Carlisle, MA: Research for Better Teaching. Adapted with permission.

2. *Positive teacher response.* A high rate of positive teacher responses will reinforce students for appropriate and correct behavior. Teachers who provide more positive than negative responses have students who want to remain in the classroom rather than be removed to another environment.

3. *Structured daily schedule.* A structured daily schedule helps students remain on task—that is, be engaged in academic or other activities that demand their time and attention. This eliminates many behavior problems because unengaged time is likely to accelerate students' inappropriate behaviors. A daily schedule must maximize on-task behavior; and the schedule must be followed. A sufficient number of staff members must be present to make high rates of on-task behavior feasible.

4. *Staff training.* Staff training is essential. Formal and informal inservice classes must be conducted in order for all staff members to become and remain competent in the use of behavioral interventions.

5. *Environmental engineering.* Environmental engineering is the arrangement or manipulation of the physical environment and stimuli to facilitate appropriate responses and avoid disruption that can adversely affect students. Here are several examples:

- Divide the classroom into one area for quiet reading, another for seatwork, and another for small-group work.
- Create rules that state how loud or quiet students must be.

- Arrange the room so that students cannot easily look out windows or doorways into halls.
- Keep a teacher between the students and open areas if there are children who tend to run away in the class.

6. *Instructional pacing.* Instructional pacing refers to the rate at which the teacher presents instructional material to the learner. Proper instructional pacing is not too fast, which can frustrate students, nor is it too slow, which can bore them or make them vulnerable to distractions.

7. *Notes to home.* Notes to home can provide clear, precise communication between school and home. In order to work, they must be sent on a regular basis. Also, the majority of feedback to parents must be positive.

8. *Precise commands.* A teacher's precise verbal statements can enhance student compliance with appropriate behavior. For example, if a student will not sit down, the instructor says, "Bill, please sit down!" (5-second delay); "Bill, you *need* to sit down *now!*" (5-second delay). The behavior should have appropriate consequences for both compliance and noncompliance.

9. *Data collection.* Teachers should collect information about how well a child is doing in academic or behavior programs. Collecting information can help the teacher determine whether the program is effective. By evaluating the data, the teacher knows when to make changes.

10. *Parent conferences.* Parent conferences should be arranged so that parents may be notified of the student's difficulties. Teachers should also attempt to involve them in problem resolution. Parents may be involved through ongoing phone calls or school visits.

11. *Special equipment.* Adaptive equipment that students require to be successful is available and being used throughout the country. Equipment may involve items such as large-print materials, typewriters, computers, or augmentative communication devices.

12. *Supervision.* Schools provide adequate and appropriate supervision as needed for students to succeed or to prevent problems.

Providing Class Structure

When trouble occurs in the classroom, teachers should first assess themselves and the environment. If they are still having difficulty managing student behaviors, they should look at class structure.

Frequently, mild misbehaviors will disappear when the student is given structure within the class environment. Providing boundaries for students facilitates a risk-free environment and allows students the freedom to relax within the class, knowing what is and is not expected. Not knowing how to behave or being unclear about the teacher's expectations creates a confusing situation for many students.

By effectively introducing structured rules, teachers can control the environment of the class and prevent inappropriate behaviors. For example, the teacher should let all students, especially those with special needs, know what behaviors are permitted. Inappropriate behavior will often disappear when students know their limits. For teachers, setting rules for behavior establishes a structure for managing the classroom environment. For students, working within the boundaries of the rules establishes a structure for being responsible. Teachers can use the following guidelines when setting rules:

1. Involve students in formulating the rules.
2. Keep the list of rules short.
3. Keep the rules short and to the point.
4. Phrase the rules positively.
5. Don't just mention the rules when someone misbehaves; remind students about them at other times.
6. Post rules in a conspicuous place and review them regularly.
7. Record the number of times rules have been reviewed with the class.
8. Make different sets of rules for different activities. Let students know when those different rules apply.
9. Make only rules that can be enforced.
10. When a student first breaks a rule, review the rule together one on one.

Motivating Students

Students are motivated when they "buy into" what is being presented. This is intertwined with who you are as a teacher. If you're fair, empathetic, and willing to modify your approach when appropriate, you will gain an incredible edge with your students. They will respect you and want to do well. Moreover, they will be more receptive to redirection or private discussions about problems when these become necessary. The foremost characteristic they intuit is, are you *really* interested in them? Treating them with respect lays the foundation for motivation. As with all students, respecting the dignity of "reluctant learners" and students with behavioral challenges is still the cornerstone for developing rapport and the effective use of most strategies.

Following are good motivating actions teachers can use inside or outside the classroom:

1. Try not to react to the behavior of children at risk, but try to understand what they want to gain. Is it attention, power, or revenge?
2. Speak quietly when in a stressful situation with a student. Try not to yell—it doesn't help.
3. Send positive notes to parents.
4. Discipline with dignity.
5. Talk with students about the problem and ask how you might work together to solve it.
6. Treat all children the way you want to be treated.
7. Touch children on the elbows. This is the least intrusive part of a person.
8. Practice being a listener to problems.
9. Allow students to choose a "time-out" place or time if they feel the need for one.
10. Develop a behavior analysis/intervention.

Behaviors	Situation
Feelings	Thoughts

- Outline what happened in sequence, in the appropriate boxes.
- Determine what (in what area and in what specifics) would result in different outcomes.

Surface Behavior Techniques

When problems occur with students with mild disabilities, teachers often anticipate and fear long, involved management strategies, which can be both time consuming during the instructional period and last for a period of months. However, not all be-

ACCOMMODATING TECHNOLOGY

With the rising diversity in our classrooms, teachers are increasingly challenged with finding appropriate materials to use with students from different cultures and ethnicities, with different values, and who speak different languages. The federally funded Early Childhood Research Institute on Culturally and Linguistically Appropriate Services (CLAS) can help. Its website (http://clas.uiuc.edu) provides a database of nearly 2,000 early childhood/early intervention resources that have been developed for children with disabilities (Corso, Santos, & Roof, 2002). Much of the site is presented in both English and Spanish to make it accessible for more parents and families.

As part of the CLAS process, experts in the fields of early childhood education, early intervention/early childhood special education, and multicultural education review validated materials and strategies. The CLAS database includes those deemed both effective and culturally and linguistically appropriate. Visitors to the site can search the resources by subject, language, format, title, author, or project/publisher. The subject search includes 26 different topics, including behavior management, IFSPs/IEPs, inclusion, and transition. Along with a summary of the material, the CLAS site also lists whom the material is intended for, language (s) in which the material is available, the format of the material, how to order the material, and the cost (if any). Often the resource is immediately downloadable at no cost.

Although a goal of CLAS is to assist stakeholders in the education of diverse students by disseminating appropriate materials, the website warns against making generalizations about a certain group. Because intragroup differences can be large, site visitors should refrain from deducting that "practice X works with culture Y." Those using materials from the CLAS database still need to test them for appropriateness in their particular situations. But even so, the CLAS website can provide educators the assistance they need in effectively reaching a classroom full of diverse students.

havior problems are that serious. Long and Newman (1980) developed techniques for what they call **surface behaviors**—behaviors that merit attention but do not demand total management programs.

Teachers should think of surface behaviors as minor infractions. Many teachers already have techniques for handling surface behaviors in their repertoires and merely need to remember a few tricks for coping with certain minor behavior problems.

In some situations, the teacher cannot permit or overlook certain behaviors in the classroom. At these times, the teacher needs a systematic plan for intervention. Long and Newman (1980) discussed techniques they found to be successful in interventions with surface behaviors. These techniques can be used on a daily basis. The trick is to match the correct technique with the surface behavior and use it immediately when the behavior occurs.

Planned Ignoring

This simple technique requires little training but a great deal of patience. Research psychologists refer to this technique as extinction—that is, eliminating a behavior by ignoring it. Planned ignoring means that the teacher immediately rewards students when they act appropriately and totally ignores students as long as they behave inappropriately. But the teacher must be patient. When a behavior that was previously rewarded with attention is suddenly ignored, the inappropriate behavior usually increases before it decreases. The student cannot understand why the teacher is not paying attention to a behavior that has always elicited a response, albeit a negative one. Teachers should keep calm, grit their teeth (if necessary), and wait for the appropriate behavior.

Here is an example: A student pulls on the teacher's clothing for attention. The teacher ignores the student, which eventually causes the student to stop.

Signal Interference

Teachers use a nonverbal signal to let a student know that they see the inappropriate behavior occurring or about to occur. For example, a teacher may use hand gestures to say, "Be quiet," "Sit down," "Come here," or "Give it to me." Teachers may also snap their fingers, use eye gestures, flick the light switch, or turn their backs to the group. Frequently, by using signal interference, teachers can stop the inappropriate behavior or, better yet, never let it start.

Proximity Control

Proximity control means moving close to the student who is exhibiting inappropriate behavior. Often a teacher only needs to stand near the student or place a hand on the student's shoulder. This technique has a calming effect on some students and helps maintain control without interrupting the current activity.

Defusing Tension Through Humor

Humor can sometimes defuse a potentially explosive situation. For example, imagine that a teacher is reading a book about witches to a class of kindergarten students on Halloween. One bright young boy looks up at her and says, "You're a witch, aren't you?" The teacher immediately slams down the book and tells all the students to return to their seats and put their heads on the desk for 15 minutes.

Now imagine that the teacher laughs and replies, "And you should see how fast I can ride my broom!" She has eliminated the problem, and the story continues uninterrupted.

Support for Routine

A simple but effective technique for young children and students with mild disabilities involves providing support for the student's routine. Displaying a chart in a special place on the board to show the week's or day's schedule provides security for the student. Then the teacher can announce in advance whenever schedules need to change and what the new schedules will be. Such preparation gives the student consistency and avoids problems.

Here's an example: The school nurse appears at the door of a first-grade class and tells all the children to line up. A little boy begins to cry, and nothing can calm him. At last the nurse says, "I'm only going to check your eyes." The boy replies, "But I thought you were going to give me a shot!" Advance preparation for the change in the routine can prevent anxiety and save the class from disruption.

Interest Boosting

This technique involves taking an interest in the student who may be off task or on the verge of acting out. Walk up to the student and mention one of his or her hobbies or interests. After a brief conversation, walk away. Often the student will go back to work, and the inappropriate behavior will not recur. Sometimes a student may become interested in only one aspect of a lesson or in a topic unrelated to the lesson. The teacher can use interest boosting to channel interest and get the student back to work.

For example, a fourth-grade class is studying prehistoric animals, but one student, who is fascinated with dinosaurs, cannot attend to any other class assignments. The teacher, realizing the problem, suddenly becomes greatly interested in dinosaurs and decides to do a unit on them, putting the fascinated student in charge of the unit. The student can work on the dinosaur topic only during a selected period of the day and

Small group instruction assists students sharing information with peers. Can you list two methods of small grouping?

STUDENT KNOWLEDGE CHECK

Jamie has difficulty sharing and taking turns with his peers. His teacher would like to plan a few activities for working on this social skill.

- What activities would you suggest to Jamie's teacher? (See Appendix B on the Companion Website.)

Cherritta is having difficulty with the behavior of speaking without permission and being out-of-seat. Her teacher needs a plan to assist Cherritta with these behaviors.

- What activities would you suggest for Cherritta?

after other work is completed. Thus, interest boosting encourages the distracted student to learn more but allows the teacher to maintain the day's structure.

Removing Distracting Objects

Many well-planned and well-intentioned lessons have gone astray because the teacher failed to remove distracting objects from the classroom. To solve this problem, simply walk up to the student and remove the object from the desk or the student's hand. Or begin the lesson by saying, "I see some very tempting objects on some desks. I don't want to be tempted to stop our lesson to play with them, so please remove the objects by the time I have counted to 3."

Positive Behavior Supports

According to Sugai and colleagues, "positive behavior support is a good example of an intervention that was first developed to help students with more significant disabilities but that now has been applied to all students, even to those who do not have disabilities" (Sugai et al., 2000, cited in Turnbull, Shank, & Smith, 2004, p. 294). Positive behavior supports is based on the theory that once inappropriate behaviors are replaced by appropriate behavior, students will begin to benefit from the general education curriculum. Often a good and motivating curriculum will eliminate many "misbehaviors." Positive behavior supports may be developed as universal supports, group supports, or individual supports.

Universal Supports

Schoolwide areas where inappropriate behaviors may develop are looked at in advance and expectations are established early. Turnbull and colleagues (2004) listed five characteristics of universal support within a school; they:

1. Clearly define behavioral expectations.
2. Teach behavioral expectation.
3. Frequently acknowledge appropriate behaviors.
4. Evaluate programs and make adaptations on an ongoing basis through a team approach.
5. Target students who need more intense skill development and practice than that offered through universal support.

I had the opportunity to visit an elementary school in Ohio and watch their school-wide support system in action. All expectations were carefully listed and explained. (The chart placed in every room is presented in Appendix C on the Companion Website.) The children were clearly aware of all schoolwide expectations during school arrival, in the hallways, at lunch, on the playground and at recess, during dismissal, during assemblies, in the bathroom, riding the bus, and on field trips. All students benefited from the listed expectations. A student, class, and schoolwide reward system was established. This was a school smoothly run and one that ran smoothly.

Group Supports

Group supports are used most often in high-risk areas such as playgrounds, hallways, and so on. At these locations the expectations may be listed in the schoolwide list and further discussed within classes. When a high-risk area begins to develop problems, solutions are developed and implemented.

A Virginia high school was having difficulty with select groups between bells. When students used the lockers, they were slamming locker doors, leaving doors open, holding up other students, and blocking hall traffic. The situation was evaluated and discussed with students from each homeroom. A decision was made to extend the between-bell time at the start of the school day and at lunch from 3 to 5 minutes. Lockers could only be opened at these times and after school. Problem solved.

Class rewards are often used to encourage all students to use appropriate behaviors. One class worked together for a point system to receive weekly treats. Students encouraged each other to behave within the rules.

Clearly defined rules and procedures for the classroom need to be established. Rules identify expected behavior, and procedures explain the expectations for the behavior. Tips on classroom rules include classroom setup, rule setup, and rule review. When setting up the classroom, teachers should be sure that the physical organization is such that problems do not escalate. Teachers need direct access to students; they don't want to have to jump over hurdles to get to students. Classroom rules should be kept to a minimum—no more than five or six rules. All rules should be short and easily understood. Rules should represent the expected behavior in the classroom. All rules should be tight—no "loopholes." The behavior described in the rules should be clear and precise. Teachers should review rules after holiday breaks, when new students arrive, and during times of increased problem behaviors.

Individual Supports

Individual behavior supports may be developed for both mild and more severe behaviors. Mild supports include individual communication, positive reinforcement, tokens, contingency contracts, free time, and ideas for specific behavior problems. For students with severe behavior problems, a functional behavior assessment should be developed.

Individual Communications.   Speaking with a student on an individual basis and finding out more about the situation can be helpful to the teacher. Sometimes a quiet visit with a student prevents an escalating problem. One teacher in New York used a communication box where students could drop in concerns and the teacher would conference with the student in private at a later time. A teacher in Oregon used a folder for each student; students could write their concerns, and the teacher read them and wrote a comment or spoke with the student.

Positive Reinforcement.   Most people feel good when someone says, "Gee, you look nice today," or when they get paid, or when they overhear a compliment. Educators call this positive reinforcement. Positive reinforcement means giving a reward to increase or maintain a behavior. In the classroom, for example, a teacher smiles at the student who has satisfactorily completed an assignment or compliments a student for sharing nicely with a neighbor. When using positive reinforcement, teachers must be sure they have chosen the appropriate reinforcer because what reinforces one student may not reinforce another.

One way to find out what reinforces a student is to ask. In fact, some teachers develop a reinforcement menu for every student in their class. The teacher has a card indicating all the items that each student finds reinforcing. When it becomes obvious that a student has tired of a specific reinforcer, the teacher replaces it with another one. Students can even complete an interest inventory so that the teacher knows what reinforces the student (see Figure 8.4). Teachers can also observe students closely to find out what to use.

Reinforcers fall into three major categories: social (praise, a smile, a pat on the back), tangible (points, stars), and activity (word games). Because society basically functions on social reinforcement, such as praise for a job well done or a smile of

---

My favorite school subject is _____

Three of my favorite things are

1. _____

2. _____

3. _____

My favorite TV show is _____

I do not like to do _____

Three things I would like to have are

1. _____

2. _____

3. _____

Three places I would go are

1. _____

2. _____

3. _____

FIGURE 8.4
Student interest inventory.

acknowledgment, students need to learn to perform tasks related to their jobs or behave in a socially acceptable manner without tangible or activity reinforcements. However, teachers should use tangible or activity rewards when beginning a behavior management program.

After identifying and measuring target behaviors and selecting the appropriate type of reinforcer, the teacher can begin implementing a positive behavior support program following these guidelines:

- Select appropriate reinforcements for the student.

- Reinforce only those behaviors that need changing, modifying, or increasing.

- Reinforce the appropriate behavior *immediately.*

- At first, reinforce the desired behavior each time it occurs.

- Once the student has learned, changed, or modified a behavior, reinforce only intermittently (that is, on an alternating basis).

- If using a tangible or activity reinforcement, apply a social reinforcer simultaneously.

- Later, withdraw the tangible or activity reward slowly and keep reinforcing the student's behavior with social rewards.

It is important to use immediate, continuous, and consistent reinforcement when a behavior is being learned.

Contingency Contracts.   With a contingency contract, a student and teacher agree to accomplish a specific objective. Contracts formally apply "Grandma's Law", or the Premack Principle: "You get to do what you want to do after you do what I want you to do." To set up a contract, the teacher and student choose the behavior, task, or skill to work on; agree on how many times the behavior should occur or how long the student should spend on the task; determine how long the contract should be in effect; decide what the reinforcer should be if the student successfully completes the task; and sign the contract. Consequences of the contract should be realistic and understood: Students should know what to expect if they meet the criteria of the contract and what to expect if they do not. Regardless of whether students meet the contract's criteria, they and the teacher should eventually evaluate the contract and decide whether a new one is needed.

Contracts are fun to develop and design, and students should help the teacher create them. Contracting works well in inclusive classes because it provides structure for students with mild disabilities; they know what is expected of them socially and academically. The contract also provides a visual and ongoing progress report for the student. Most important, regular and special education teachers can develop the contract together.

Specific Behavior Problems.   Occasionally specific behavior problems will be exhibited in the classroom. At times like these the teacher needs a few tips to handle the behavior and keep the classroom running smoothly. Table 8.3 presents 10 specific problem behaviors that occur in the classrooms, including impulsiveness, inattention, noncompletion of tasks, noncompliance, out-of-seat behavior, talking without permission, being unmotivated to learn, being unprepared for class, being unruly in class, and turning in unsatisfactory homework. One behavior teachers of younger children express concern over is talking without permission. In addition to the teacher tips found in Table 8.4, teachers can hand out "talking" passes. When students speak

TABLE 8–4
Checklist for creating an effective classroom environment.

	Yes	No
Wall areas		
Walls clean to prevent distractions.	_____	_____
Bulletin boards neatly designed and seasonally up-to-date.	_____	_____
Bulletin boards available for students' use and display.	_____	_____
Windows clean or neatly covered.	_____	_____
Blackboards in view of all students, clean and undamaged.	_____	_____
Lighting		
Proper window lighting.	_____	_____
Ceiling lighting sufficient.	_____	_____
Floors		
Clean	_____	_____
Obstructive objects removed.	_____	_____
Barrier-free for wheelchairs, etc.	_____	_____
Room Area		
Appropriate chair sizes for age level.	_____	_____
Arrangements for left- as well as right-handed students.	_____	_____
Areas provided for small-group instruction.	_____	_____
Areas provided for independent instruction.	_____	_____
Areas in room designated for specific behaviors, such as quiet time, reading in twos, game areas, motor areas, art areas.	_____	_____
Learning centers provided.	_____	_____
Study carrels provided.	_____	_____
Areas designated for listening to tapes, such as recordings of lessons or chapters in books.	_____	_____

Note: From *Reaching the Hard to Teach* by J. W. Wood, 2004, Richmond, VA: Judy Wood, Inc. Reprinted with permission.

without permission, they give up a pass. Naturally one would expect very young children to speak out without permission until they have practiced the rule. Motivation ideas were covered early in this chapter. Homework issues will be addressed in detail in chapter 11.

Functional Behavior Assessment. Functional behavior assessments are conducted for students with severe behavioral problems. **Functional assessment** "identifies specific relationships between a student's behavior and the circumstances that trigger those behaviors" (Turnbull et al., 2004, p. 290). The authors list six basic steps to use when conducting a functional assessment:

1. Describe as precisely as possible the nature of the behaviors that are impeding the student's learning or the learning of others.
2. Gather information from teachers, family members, the student, related service providers, and any other individuals who have extensive firsthand knowledge

about the circumstances that are regularly associated with the occurrence and nonoccurrence of the problem behavior. Determine as specifically as possible the events that occur before, during, and after the student's appropriate and inappropriate behavior.

3. Determine why the student engages in the problem behavior. What is the student trying to accomplish through the problem behavior? What is the student communicating? For example, does the student want to obtain something positive, avoid or escape something unpleasant, or increase or decrease sensory stimulation?

4. Hypothesize the relationship between the problem behavior and the events occurring before, during, and after the behavior.

5. Incorporate the functional assessment information into the student's IEP. Focus on changing the environmental events and circumstances so that the student does not need to engage in problem behavior to accomplish his or her purposes.

6. Help the student develop alternative behaviors and new skills so that he or she can accomplish the same purpose in more socially acceptable ways. (pp. 290–292)

ADAPTING THE PHYSICAL ENVIRONMENT

Teachers instruct students within the tightly woven framework of the school day. For harmonious and structured management, schools design the day around various schedules and physical arrangements. This framework affects students and teachers because it affects the types of subjects taught, class size, resources, students' choice of subjects, and educational philosophy. Schedules and physical environments vary in different schools, districts, and states. Regardless of the framework used, however, educators want to be able to adapt it to make instruction easy and productive. The following sections consider grouping for instruction and classroom design.

Grouping for Instruction

Grouping procedures vary from school to school and from teacher to teacher. Many teachers feel that grouping within classrooms creates an even heavier workload. However, children do learn at different rates and in different ways and therefore do not always learn best in one large group.

In 2003 Smith, Molnar, and Zahorik conducted a study of the effects of class size on student achievement. Reducing the K–3 class size to 15 students (with one teacher), they found that by the end of the third grade, students entering the study at grade 1 increased in achievement at a level of one-third to one-half a year ahead of the students in larger classes.

Regretfully, schools across the nation are increasing class size because of financial cutbacks and teacher shortages. These increases in class size usually dictate whole-group instruction. But whole-group instruction does not provide the best benefits to students academically: Questions go unattended, easily distracted students remain off task, and students become lost in the masses. Instruction continues to move along, leaving students with special needs and those at risk lost and confused, which in turn means that many of these students drop out of school.

Fortunately, there are a variety of ways to group students that will help teachers individualize within whole-group situations. Following are some examples.

ACCOMMODATING DIVERSITY

Establishing an Accepting Classroom Atmosphere

1. Arrange for students to visit general education classrooms before placement to become acquainted with the teacher and class members.
2. Develop an understanding for all students regarding different abilities, cultures, etc. The following ideas may be useful:
   - Have class discussions to increase knowledge about diversities.
   - Hold discussions on how we are all different in selected ways.
   - Let students provide examples of how they are different.
   - Share feelings on being different. For example, a new student is different because he or she is new.
   - Discuss ways students may help other students feel part of the group.
3. Plan instruction around diversity.
   - Select guest speakers who are different in some special way.
   - Place pictures around the classroom walls of students depicting an array of differences—disabilities, gender, occupations, cultures, etc.
   - Provide suggestions for projects or book reports in which students could participate in developing a greater insight into differences.
   - Focus projects or reports on a person who was "different" in their environment. For example, focus on (a) background; (b) cause, if disabled; (c) person's accomplishments; (d) emotions felt by the person and his or her family; (e) PowerPoint presentations regarding diversity; etc.
4. Provide learning stations at which students can find activities or readings focusing on diversity.
   - Save newspaper articles showing achievements of persons who are diverse.
   - Have a list of comprehensive questions that students answer after reading articles or listening to recordings.
   - Provide a list of words that students can define in their own words or draw picture for definitions.
   - Provide blank paper on which students can write short essays or draw pictures describing their reaction to articles or pictures.

Creative Grouping

When teachers group students, students become labeled. This can present a problem: No matter what the teacher calls the group, all children know which ones are bright, average, and slow. Creative grouping, however, allows for a diversity of academic skills, thus eliminating labels and giving students the freedom to move among groups.

Creative grouping may be used at either the secondary or elementary level. Teachers set up the groups according to academic subject and then break the subject into specific objectives or skills. They assign a student to a creative group based on the specific skill that the student needs to work on. No one is locked into a group because each student moves into another group after mastering the skill. Figure 8.5 shows a chart for a creative mathematics group that allows a student to complete a skill, keep a personal record, and then move on.

	Tanner	Camden	Clay	Nora	Emma
Identifies penny, nickel, and dime by name.					
Identifies penny, nickel, and dime by value.					
Identifies quarter, half-dollar, and dollar by name.					
Identifies quarter, half-dollar, and dollar by value.					

FIGURE 8.5
Chart for a creative mathematics group.

Creative grouping may include at least three variations, all of which work simultaneously: a learning station, a seatwork station, and a small-group instructional station. When class begins, the teacher color codes or numbers the stations and gives each student a direction card or uses a list on the board to indicate the station the student should use first. Remember, a student who masters a given skill can enter a new creative group.

Interest Grouping

Interest grouping is a method of grouping students based on their specific interests. For example, in reading, students may select the same types of books to read. In social studies, students may be interested in the same period of history. These students may be grouped by interest and develop a series of questions, review a specific book, or research a certain period.

Research Grouping

Research groups can be established by giving each group a specific problem to research. Each group then reports back to the class with the results of the research. Teachers may give groups lists of specific research questions to be answered and possible sources to investigate.

Cooperative Learning

Cooperative learning, a worthwhile grouping strategy for heterogeneous student populations, is a method of class structure in which students work together to achieve a shared academic goal. Students are held accountable for their own academic behaviors as well as for those of their peers. Students with disabilities work well in cooperative settings and develop class behaviors such as asking questions. Additionally, they learn from their nondisabled peers. Groups are assigned a group task with individual duties. Grades may be given for individual task completion and group completion. The beginning teacher can use four basic formats to implement cooperative learning: peer teaching, project groups, the jigsaw, and the shield.

Teachers should not overlook one of a school's most valuable resources—its students. Within class groups, teachers can assign peer tutors to assist students who are having difficulty with the content of a lesson. For example, peer tutors may record assignments so that the student with mild disabilities can listen to the tape for extra reinforcement. Peer tutors can also work one on one using a flannel board, manipulating real or paper money, and helping a student with special needs at the computer. At the secondary level, peer tutors can help small groups of students with disabilities look up their chapter study questions, work on class work or homework assignments, and participate in study or review sessions. A peer can also call out words during group or individual spelling tests. Using peers and small groupings for spelling tests helps students with disabilities who may need to have their spelling words called out more slowly.

Peer tutoring has numerous advantages: facilitating the interaction between students without disabilities and students with disabilities; making use of children's insights about how to teach recently learned or newly presented content to other students; making learning more cooperative and less competitive; and providing experiences related to living in a democracy, to caring, and to being cared for.

In project groups, students share knowledge and skills to complete a task. All students are included in the process, and motivation is heightened. Each student contributes to the group project based on his or her skill level. But if the group project is not structured, the burden of task completion may be shouldered by only one or a few students.

The jigsaw format is an adaptation of the project group format in which group members are assigned specific tasks. The shield, another cooperative method, assists students in summarizing progress, summarizing learning, and formulating questions for feedback. The jigsaw and the shield are further developed in Figures 8.6 and 8.7 (Laham, 2000).

Classroom Design

The physical environment of a classroom should stimulate students if effective learning is to occur. Before developing a classroom design, teachers may use the checklist in Table 8.4 to evaluate the effectiveness of the classroom's physical environment. The physical environment includes all physical aspects of the room: wall areas, lighting, floors, and room area. Being aware of the classroom's physical organization can help teachers prevent classroom problems.

Classroom designs should be developed around the type of grouping strategies the teacher has selected. At both the secondary and elementary levels, classroom designs are important because they dictate whether a teacher uses small-group instruction, one-on-one instruction, or whole-class instruction. Once teachers decide which type of instructional design to use during a lesson, they can alter room arrangements to meet their needs. Because no one design works best for every student, teachers need to change from time to time. Students can often help to choose a viable design for the day's lesson.

Learning Centers

A learning station or learning center is a selected space in the classroom where students may go to work on a new assignment or on a skill or concept they have recently learned. The learning center approach to teaching or reinforcing skills saves the classroom teacher's time and energy. At the same time, it allows student freedom of choice in activities, successful completion of tasks, and immediate feedback for correct or

The Jigsaw

Step # 1: Personal Reflections

Individually   Write   _____ Minutes

Step # 2: Sharing Ideas—Small Groups

Same Color   Record on your number   _____ Minutes/Questions

Step # 3: Combining Ideas

Same Number   Review & Clarify   _____ Minutes   Charts

Step # 4: Reporting Out—Whole Group

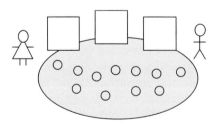

FIGURE 8.6
The jigsaw.

Note: From *Working Together: A Practical Guide for Facilitators,* by S. L. Laham (2000). Reprinted with permission.

Title:	**The Jigsaw**
Process Step:	Individual and group listening
Use:	Processing of information and issues presented to group
Time:	Process description 5 minutes Group formation 2–3 minutes Each question 4–6 minutes Compiling 10–20 minutes Reporting out/Processing 20 minutes +

Preparation:

I. Identify intent for jigsaw processing.
   A. Processing of information (what we heard individually and as a group).
   B. Implication/application of information (what this information means, how it applies to our situation).

II. Develop questions for jigsaw.

   A. Use three or five questions.
     1. Avoid fours in groups of questions.
     2. Discourage polarity.
   B. When processing information:
     1. The first two (or three) questions sample the same information.
       a. Allows for more discussion within the groups.
       b. Supports dialogue within the groups.
       c. Supports learning of listening skills.
     2. Focus final question(s) on missing items or areas.
       a. Allows the groups to capture concerns.
       b. May provide amplification of high interest or concern.
       c. When processing for implications/application, develop questions that sample for that area.

III. Determine the method to assign persons to small discussion groups.
   A. Random assignment.
     1. Count off by numbers.
     2. Use an energizer such as data processing to arrange members into a new sequence and break into groups.
   B. Card assignment.
     1. Distribute cards with number and color randomly.
     2. Arrange cards in categorical groups (e.g., grade level position).
       a. Arrange groups so all categories are represented in all groups.
       b. Self-selection.
       c. Assignment by facilitator.
   C. Announce them by:
     1. Posting on board.
     2. Pre-coding materials.
   NOTE: Do not reveal assignments prior to small groups.

IV. Prepare charts with:
   A. Overall charge to the group.
   B. Purpose of the discussion.
   C. Questions for the jigsaw process.
   D. Directions to the jigsaw process. (You may wish to distribute the process directions.)

	V.	Duplicate questions for group use.

       V. Duplicate questions for group use.
          A. Copy of all questions to all members.
          B. Recording sheet with one question on a sheet for small group work.

Operation:

I. Introduce activity by reviewing the purpose of the discussion.

II. Describe the process in general.
   A. Use small groups to discuss.
   B. Will allow everyone to discuss all questions.
   C. Will provide time to report to the whole group on the results of discussion.

III. Review questions with the group as a whole.
   A. Ask for questions about the questions.
   B. You may choose to have participants individually reflect on the questions and make notes for the discussion at this point.

IV. Assign participants to small groups.
   A. Have participants move to new locations.
   B. Distribute questions, if not distributed in step III, once all are seated.

V. Review the process and time frame:
   A. The process.
      1. Each person will record the groups' comments on one question.
      2. At the end of discussing all questions, new groups will be formed with like-items.
   B. The time frame.
      1. Give them a fixed time for each question.
      2. Adjust time frame based on discussion.

VI. Monitor group discussion:
   A. Move from group to group, answering questions regarding the focusing questions.
   B. Prompt discussion within small groups.
   C. Call "time" between questions.

VII. Reform groups into like-item groups:
   A. Review directions for the like-item small groups.
      1. The purpose is to compile and clarify responses.
      2. Give total time for like-item small groups.
      3. Prior to compiling them, suggest that they review responses from all groups for the item.
      4. Ask questions within the small group for clarification.
   B. May want to ask the group to review responses and prioritize them based on the similarities found.
   C. Distribute chart paper with question on top to each group.
      1. Give each group two markers for writing.
      2. Tell them whoever writes does not have to report.

VIII. Reporting Out.
   A. Have groups report out on the questions in order.
   B. Check for understanding of items as they are recorded.
      1. Ask: "Does this capture your discussion?".
      2. Prove for clarification on items.
         a. Want to clarify group ideas.
         b. Encourage discussion through the facilitator to clarify ideas.
         c. At the end of the processing, check for understanding.
            1. Ask: "How well does this capture the sense of the group?".
         d. Processing for patterns or trends in the responses *after* all groups have reported out can support the group in moving forward.

FIGURE 8.6
Continued.

The Group Shield

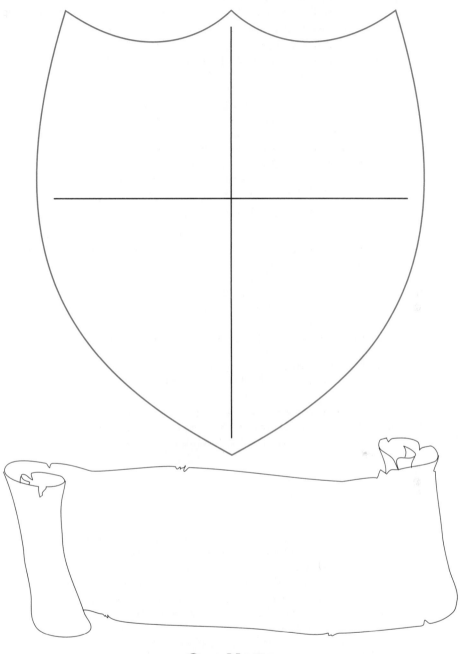

Our Motto

FIGURE 8.7
The shield.

Note: From *Working Together: A Practical Guide for Facilitators* by S. L. Laham (2000). Reprinted with permission.

Title:	**Group Shield**
Process Step:	Agreement
Use:	Summarize progress thus far
	Summarize learning thus far
	Feedback to group
Time:	Development of shield 10–5 minutes
	Presentation of shield 5–10 minutes
	Processing of activity 15 minutes +
Preparation:	I. Identify four summarization categories.
	A. To summarize progress thus far, consider:
	1. What we have accomplished thus far?
	2. What we have left to do?
	3. How we are working to accomplish our task?
	4. What is getting in the way of our work?
	B. To summarize learning, consider:
	1. What we have learned thus far.
	2. What we wish we had learned.
	3. Feedback to the instructor.
	4. Feedback to our fellow learners.
	C. To provide feedback to the group, consider:
	1. What the group has learned to do.
	2. What the group is working on.
	3. How we are doing as individuals.
	4. How we are doing as a group.
	II. Prepare individual shields to distribute to all.
	III. Prepare on chart paper.
	A. Group shields.
	B. Questions for four quadrants of the shield.
	1. Use a symbol to represent the question.
	IV. Have plenty of multicolor chart markers.
Operation:	I. Introduce the activity by reviewing its purpose.
	II. Break participants into groups of five to eight people.
	III. Present the shield and the quadrant questions.
	IV. Review the task.
	A. Develop a group shield and a one-word motto for our efforts.
	B. Represent the responses to the question in pictures.
	C. Ask for clarification.
	V. Give the groups the time frame for the development of the shield and begin.
	A. Distribute chart paper, shield, and markers.
	B. Monitor discussion and probe for clarity.
	VI. Have groups individually present shield to the group as a whole.
	A. Ask them to explain the symbols and motto.
	B. Ask questions for clarification only.
	C. Prompt applause at the end of each presentation.
	VII. Process the shields as a group of the whole.
	A. Ask for trends observed.
	B. Ask for patterns observed.
	C. Ask for inconsistencies/consistencies.
	D. Ask for discoveries or insights after seeing all shields.
	VIII. Summarize across comments.

FIGURE 8.7
Continued.

incorrect responses. The learning center gives the teacher a way to individualize instruction and work with specific educational objectives. Common in elementary schools, learning centers are rarely used in secondary classrooms. Nevertheless, they can give the secondary teacher a desirable instructional alternative.

Advantages of Learning Centers for Inclusion.   Learning centers serve multiple purposes in instructing students. For one thing, the teacher saves time during the day because a group or an individual can work alone at the center. In addition, learning centers in inclusive classrooms have the following specific advantages:

- Many students prefer to work alone, and the learning center gives them this option.

- Self-correcting learning centers provide immediate feedback about correct or incorrect responses without embarrassment.

- Students with special needs can work at their own pace without pressure.

- From a variety of activities, students can select the most appropriate.

- Because special needs students in inclusive environments may work below the level of other students in the general classroom, learning centers provide them with appropriate activities at their own levels.

- Activities at the learning center can reinforce the objectives specified in the student's IEP.

- Learning centers reinforce the mode of learning best suited to the student with a mild disability. For example, if the student learns better visually, the teacher can present more activities in a visual manner. If the student learns better auditorially, the teacher can put activities on tape recorders.

Learning Centers and Standards. With the emphasis on standards-driven curricula, learning centers may be developed to reteach standard strands. One elementary school in Ohio established an excellent procedure for doing so. The 10 strands for standards in math/language arts were reviewed for each student. Each student's strand with an 80% or lower score was identified, and then the three lowest strands were selected for reteaching in a learning center. Learning centers for each of the 10 strands were developed. One teacher was assigned three strands, one teacher was assigned four, and the third teacher was assigned three strands for center development. Activities were developed to reteach or reinforce the specific strands. During one 90-minute block each week, the students floated to the classroom that housed the center for the strand on which the student scored 80% or lower. Each student worked at three centers during the 90-minute block.

A Few Last Tips for Learning Centers.   Seats from an old SUV and a table on which to store records or tapes and headphones can make a great listening center. Floating centers, consisting of materials in boxes that can be moved to various locations, can be useful when room space and class size become issues. To start a learning center, the teacher should survey all of the materials available and ask peers for additional materials. Because centers are always a work-in-progress, teachers should add to centers as students' needs change.

Bulletin Boards

Most classrooms have at least one bulletin board. Teachers usually design bulletin boards as seasonal decorations or as special places to display work. However, bulletin

Language involvement bulletin board	This bulletin board is designed with round rotating disks that are used interchangeably for any subject or content.
Slide-study bulletin board	This bulletin board can be used for any subject area. Slides are taken related to the desired subject matter and stored in compartments attached to the bulletin board.
Auditory-action bulletin board	This bulletin board contains an activity mounted beneath the display on the bulletin board. A cassette is prepared by the teacher, which guides the students through the required lessons.
Lift panel bulletin board	These bulletin boards are made with pieces of construction paper folded in half. The outer flap of the panel contains a question or idea. The inner flap is secured to the bulletin board and contains the answer or solution.
Sentence strips bulletin board	Strips are attached to the bulletin board and may convey relevant printed information or questions. They may be changed frequently to maintain interest.

FIGURE 8.8
Types of bulletin boards.

Note: From "Instructional Games" by J. G. Greer, I. Friedman, and V. Laycock, 1978. In R. M. Anderson, J. G. Greer, & S. Odle (Eds.), *Individualizing Educational Materials for Special Children in the Mainstream* (pp. 267–293). Baltimore: University Park Press. Copyright 1978 by PRO-ED. Inc. Adapted by permission.

boards can also reflect a specific learning purpose. Bulletin boards designed for incidental learning are simply placed around the room with the hope that students will pick up a little extra learning. For example, in one school, the halls are painted to look like highways, street signs hang over classroom doors, and the ABCs run around the walls. It is hard to get a drink of water without learning a little multiplication. As children line the halls, incidental learning takes place in every direction they look. Many books have ideas that teachers can use to design bulletin boards for incidental learning.

In contrast, intentional learning is planned learning. Teachers can design bulletin boards based on a lesson or current events. One school has a "good morning news" bulletin board for the class. The teacher broadcasts the news, and each student brings an item for the bulletin board or the announcements. This method uses intentional learning effectively.

Figure 8.8 presents different types of bulletin boards with a brief description of each. Teachers may adapt the content format to match the individual needs of students.

SUMMARY

Establishing an effective learning environment requires a careful look at the socioe-motional, behavioral, and physical aspects of the classroom. When this foundation is laid, it is time to plan for the teaching environment, which includes lesson plans, teaching techniques, content, and evaluation.

RESOURCES

American Academy of Child and
Adolescent Psychiatry
Public Information Office
1615 Wisconsin Avenue NW
Washington, DC 20016
(202) 966-7300
www.aacap.org

American Psychiatric Association
1400 K St. NW
Washington, DC 20005
(202) 682-6000
www.psych.org

American Psychological Association
750 First St. NE
Washington, DC 20002
www.apa.org

Council for Children with Behavioral Disorders,
c/o Council for Exceptional Children (CEC)
1110 W. Glebe Road
Suite 300
Arlington, VA 22201-5704
www.cec.sped.org

SUGGESTED READINGS

Lewis, C., Schaps, E., & Watson, M. (1996). The caring classroom's academic edge. *Educational Leadership 54*(1), 15–21.

Zins, J. E., Travis, L. F., & Freppon, P. A. (1997). Linking research and educational programming to promote social and emotional learning. In P. Salovery & D. Syulter (Eds.), *Emotional development and emotional intelligence: Implications for educators.* New York: Basic Books.

WEBSITES TO VISIT

Coalition of Essential Schools. A website of the organization directed at improving schools and school systems. www.essentialschools.org.

National Center for Children in Poverty home site. www.nccp.org

REFERENCES

Bloom, B. S. (1971). *Master learning: Theory and practice.* New York: Holt, Rinehart, & Wilson.

Brown, D. (2002). *Becoming a successful urban teacher.* Portsmouth, NH: Heinemann.

Corso, R. M., Santos, R. M., & Roof, V. (2002). Honoring diversity in early childhood education materials. *Teaching Exceptional Children, 34*(3), 30–36.

Council for Exceptional Children. (2000). Bright futures for exceptional learners: An action agenda to achieve quality conditions for teaching and learning for every exceptional learner. *Teaching Exceptional Children, 32*(6), 56–69 [Online]. Available: www.cec.sped.org.

Erwin, J. C. (2003). Giving students what they need. *Educational Leadership, 61*(1), 19–23.

Glasser, W. (2000). *Every student can succeed.* Chula Vista, CA: Black Forest Press.

Laham, S. L. (2000). *Working together: A practical guide for facilitators.* Richmond, VA: Judy Wood Publishing Company.

Levine, M. (1990). *Keeping a head in school: A student's book about learning abilities and learning disorders.* Cambridge, MA: Educators Publishing Service.

Levine, M. (2002). *A mind at a time.* New York: Simon & Schuster.

Long, N. J., & Newman, R. (1980). Managing surface behaviors of children in schools. In N. J. Long, W. Morse, & R. Newman (Eds.), *Conflict in the classroom: The education of emotionally disturbed children* (4th ed.). Belmont, CA: Wadsworth.

Meyen, D., Vergason, H., & Whelan, C. (1993). "In my dreams": A second look at inclusion and programming. *Journal of the Association for Persons with Severe Handicaps, 18,* 296–298.

Parkinson, A. F., Dulfano, I., & Nink, C. E. (2003). *Removing barriers: Research-based strategies for teaching those who learn differently.* Centerville, UT: MTC Institute.

Rogers, C. (1969). *Freedom to learn.* Upper Saddle River, NJ: Merrill/Prentice Hall.

Sugai, G., Horner, R. H., Dunlap, G., Hienenan, M., Lewis, T. J., Nelson, C. M., et al. (2000). Applying positive behavior support and functional behavioral assessment in schools. *Journal of Positive Behavior Interventions, 2*(3), 131–143.

Sugai, G., & Lewis, T. J. (1999). *Developing positive behavioral support for students with challenging behavior.* Arlington, VA: Council for Children with Behavioral Disorders.

Turnbull, R., Turnbull, A., Shank, M., & Smith, S. J. (2004). *Exceptional lives: Special education in today's schools* (4th ed.). Upper Saddle River, NJ: Merrill/Prentice Hall.

Utah State Board of Education. (1992). *Special education rules.* Salt Lake City: Author.

Wood, M. (1998). Whose job is it anyway? Educational roles in inclusion. *Exceptional Children, 64,* 181–195.

Wolk, S. (2003) Hearts and minds. *Educational Leadership, 61*(1), 14–18.

9

Adapting Lesson Plans

CHAPTER AT A GLANCE

```
                    ┌──────────────────────┐
                    │   The Process of     │
                    │   Lesson Planning    │
                    └──────────────────────┘
         ┌──────────────┬──────────┬──────────────┬──────────────┐
    ╭─────────╮  ╭──────────────╮  │  ╭──────────────╮  ╭──────────────╮
    │Standards│  │Collaboration │  │  │Components of │  │General        │
    ╰─────────╯  │in Lesson     │  │  │a Lesson Plan │  │Principles of  │
                 │Planning      │  │  ╰──────────────╯  │Learning and   │
                 ╰──────────────╯  │                    │the Lesson Plan│
                                   ▼                    ╰──────────────╯
                    ┌──────────────────────┐
                    │ Research-Based        │
                    │ Categories of         │
                    │ Instructional         │
                    │ Strategies Affecting  │
                    │ Student Achievement   │
                    └──────────────────────┘
                                   │
                                   ▼
                    ╭──────────────────────╮
                    │ Standards-Based Lesson│
                    │ Plans: Where          │
                    │ Interventions Go      │
                    ╰──────────────────────╯
                                   │
                                   ▼
                    ┌──────────────────────┐
                    │ How the Saale Model   │
                    │ Fits into a           │
                    │ Standards-Based       │
                    │ Educational System    │
                    └──────────────────────┘
                                   │
                                   ▼
                    ╭──────────────────────╮
                    │   Lesson Delivery     │
                    ╰──────────────────────╯
```

KEY TERMS

*M*rs. Hang, a first-year teacher, was asked to develop lesson plans for each lesson she taught. Realizing that the lesson plan is the baseline for instruction, Mrs. Hang called on her mentor teacher, Mr. Confer, to provide input. One of the first tips Mr. Confer gave her was to create a yearly, monthly, weekly, and daily plan. He explained that teaching from day to day without seeing the big picture makes lesson planning a piecemeal process. Once she has the total picture, Mr. Confer explained, she can break it down into smaller parts. He also explained the importance of incorporating interventions into her lesson plans.

*T*his chapter offers simple techniques that both general and special education teachers can use when developing interventions for lesson plans. The following topics will be discussed: the lesson planning process as it relates to standards; lesson planning collaboration; components of the lesson plan; principles of learning; and the SAALE model and lesson planning.

This chapter also introduces a broad framework for managing transitions during the instructional process. As such, it has a direct bearing on the issues addressed in the remaining chapters of the text. Try to keep this chapter in mind as you read the remainder of the text.

THE PROCESS OF LESSON PLANNING AND STANDARDS

Before lesson planning begins, the nation and states have been busy developing guidelines for curricula selection for school districts. From the curricula educators begin to develop their units and resulting lessons. Let's back up and take a look at national and state preparation for curricula development.

National statements or standards are stated that include what all students should learn in schools. From these statements or standards, each state develops a list of what its students should learn from kindergarten to 12th grade. These statements are completed for math, language arts, and other subjects. After completion of the broad categories, what students should learn by grade level is developed.

Standards

Traditionally, educators within school districts were free to select what to teach and what materials to use. Across the nation attention was drawn to the diversity in the skills students were taught. Many felt that our students were capable of learning more. As a result, states began to develop **standards** for school districts to follow when developing curricula. These standards were further broken down into small steps, or **benchmarks,** and **indicators** were inserted into the benchmarks to establish a measuring point for educators. Figure 9.1 provides an overview of the relationship of standards to lesson planning.

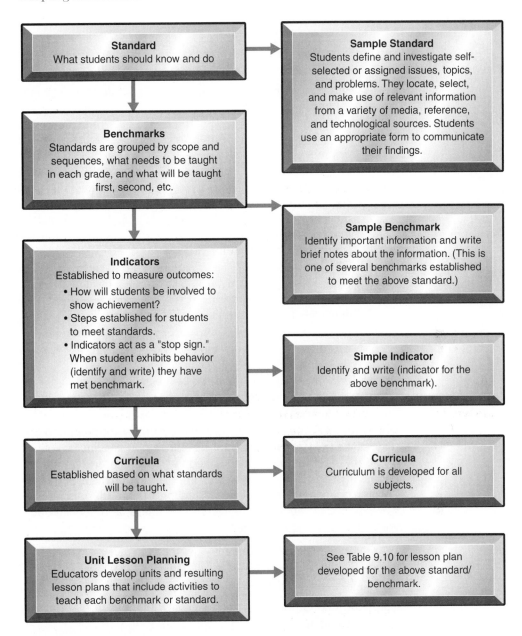

FIGURE 9.1

An overview of the relationship of standards to lesson planning.

Note: From *Reaching the Hard to Teach* by J. W. Wood, 2004, Richmond, VA: Judy Wood, Inc. Reprinted with permission.

Collaboration in Lesson Planning

Most often, the special education teacher becomes actively involved in the lesson planning process only when the general education teacher is in the last stage of planning: developing a daily lesson plan. However, it is more beneficial to the student with special needs if the special education teacher becomes involved in the first phase of planning: the yearly plan. A year's worth of learning outcomes as set forth in daily

COLLABORATION TIPS

1. When planning a lesson, be sure to search all resources (material as well as human) that may enhance the lesson.
2. Literacy centers and literacy coaches can provide numerous resources to support the lesson. Literacy coaches can come into classrooms and model strategies for helping implement the lesson.
3. Don't forget communication and language specialists. The information they can bring to the classroom serves all students. Many of these specialists are willing to teach part of the lesson to promote language development.
4. When planning the lesson, don't forget special education educators. They are a valuable resource for assisting in planning, developing, and implementing preplanned interventions.
5. Don't forget community resources that may be useful for the lesson.
6. Many parents have invaluable information to share on such topics as travel, food, and culture.

plans might be attainable for students without disabilities but difficult for students with special needs. It's a losing battle to try to keep a student in a general education class where the skills being taught are instructionally too advanced. A balance must be maintained between skills taught and those that are reasonably attainable.

Many students with special needs and those at risk can achieve success during general lesson plan activities when intervention points are identified and appropriate accommodations or modifications are provided. This process depends on careful, well-planned collaboration between the general and special education teachers. As teachers work together, they should follow several guidelines:

1. Realize that interventions may be necessary in the general class lesson.
2. Be specific in listing what will occur during each component of the lesson plan. Include an objective, strategies, resources, and evaluation.
3. Allow time for both teachers to review the lesson plan and develop appropriate interventions.
4. Be flexible when an adaptation or intervention does not work.
5. Be prepared to develop an alternative intervention.
6. Realize that when an intervention is made to the lesson plan, the plan is still valid and not watered down.

Components of a Lesson Plan

All lesson plans have several essential parts, although various authors may give these parts different names.

1. The *purpose* states instructional objectives, including what students should learn from the lesson based on the stated standard or benchmark.

2. The sequence of lesson *strategies,* or learning experiences, describes the work-study activities that will occur during the lesson.

3. The *learning process* lists the resources (learning materials, media, or technology) needed to teach the lesson.

4. The *evaluation* describes the activities designed to measure the lesson process. Evaluation is also an ongoing process.

Instructional Objectives

The instructional objective, which is based on the standards or benchmarks of the lesson, is a statement of specific learner outcomes that should result from the lesson. Objectives should be focused on the student, be clearly stated, express the intended behavior outcome, and identify how the behavior outcome will be measured. Objectives should be carefully written in the domain level appropriate for the student. These levels include knowledge, comprehension, application, analysis, synthesis, and evaluation. Objectives should be shared with learners so that they are aware of the purpose of the lesson. A teacher can explain to the learner how objectives spring from established standards and benchmarks. For younger students, the teacher may need to paraphrase the objective or provide a visual representation of the desired outcome to help them understand the objective. It may be helpful to show graphically how today's objective continues yesterday's objective and will tie into tomorrow's objectives. This provides a connection for students, who may not readily see the logical sequence of the skills being taught.

After selecting an appropriate objective, the teacher moves ahead to the next steps: (a) making a list of all subobjectives (breaking down the class objective), (b) analyzing the subobjectives by task (putting them into sequential order from simple to complex), (c) listing the necessary prerequisite skills students must have before they can master the objective, and (d) deciding the point of entry for students with special needs or those who are at risk. Instructional objectives are useful in the following situations:

- Planning lessons based on the benchmarks
- Selecting learning aids and appropriate technology
- Determining appropriate assignments for individual students
- Selecting and constructing classroom tests
- Determining classroom-embedded assessment measures
- Determining when to gather evaluation data
- Summarizing and reporting evaluation results
- Helping learners determine where they are and where they need to go as they strive to become independent

Table 9.1 has suggestions for adapting the objective component of lesson plans.

Strategies

After carefully selecting, writing, displaying, and explaining the objectives, the educator begins the second phase of lesson planning: developing strategies or learning experiences. The teacher must determine the instructional makeup of the lesson as well as the sequence the lesson should follow. While developing this section, the teacher should remember the stated objectives and carefully build strategies around the objectives. Unfortunately, it is common to find excellent objectives and excellent strategies that do not match. Such an instructional mismatch can result in a student not being able to reach the objectives.

TABLE 9.1
Interventions for lesson objectives.

Component	Considerations for Planning	Suggested Interventions
Objective/lesson purpose A statement of the specific learner outcomes that should result from the lesson. Objectives are based on standards or benchmarks. The lesson objective/purpose is obtained when the indicator has been reached.		Clearly state the objective to reflect the behavior outcome and how the behavior will be measured. Check to see that the objective is student oriented. Select instructional objectives for the lesson that are in the appropriate domain level for the learner. Graphically show the learner how today's objective fits into yesterday's lesson and will tie into tomorrow's lesson. Make a list of all possible subobjectives for the main objective. Put all subobjectives in the logical sequential order for teaching. Make a list of all prerequisite skills needed before the student can master the stated objective. Be prepared to alter any objective if it is not meeting the needs of the learner.

Note: From *Reaching the Hard to Teach* by J. W. Wood, 2004, Richmond, VA: Judy Wood, Inc. Reprinted with permission.

PRACTICAL APPLICATIONS

1. The purpose of the lesson should be clearly presented to the class. Because all lessons spring from the standards and benchmarks, these should be clearly displayed in the room. Place all standards on sentence strips in one color. As each benchmark is taught, place the benchmark on anther sentence strip (in a different color) under the standard. As lessons develop, add the appropriate benchmark.
2. Be sure to post each indicator by the benchmark and discuss how the assessment links to the indicator. For example, if the indicator says that students write, then the product (assessment) will be a writing product.
3. Connect the lesson plan to real-life events. Students are interested in and remember things that are meaningful to them.
4. Any class assignment or homework activity should be related to today's lesson or tomorrow's lesson (see chapter 11). Is the activity for preparation, practice, extension, or creativity? When students see *why* they are doing an assignment, the assignment has more meaning.

The strategies section of the lesson plan is developed around three major parts: the introduction, the lesson development, and the summary or closing activity.

Lesson Introduction.   In the lesson plan introduction, the teacher should state and/or demonstrate what students should learn; use a provocative question, artifact, or hands-on activity to stimulate student interest in the lesson; or link the present lesson to past lessons or student experiences. The teacher should follow these six steps during the introduction:

1. Review the relationship of the objective, or lesson purpose, to the standard or benchmark.
2. Review what is to be learned, including the major instructional objective and all subobjectives. Think in terms of preparing the student for the lesson itself, and make sure that instructional objectives are on the student's instructional level and are in sequential order. Also include an assessment of the students' prerequisite skills.
3. Demonstrate what the student should learn. This might include a whole-part-whole method using a lecture outline or organizer, or providing sequential written directions.
4. Use a mind capturer or activator such as a manipulative or hands-on activity to boost interest.
5. Link past lessons to students' current or past experiences, which make the lesson more meaningful for students.
6. Relate the lesson to a future event. Students can see the purpose in learning a lesson if it relates to them personally.

Lesson Development.   Here the teacher selects activities to achieve the lesson's purpose, describes these activities, and chooses an instructional model around which to organize the lesson. For each of the model's parts, the educator should plan the appropriate adaptation or intervention if needed. Frequently, by the time he or she is developing a lesson, the teacher may be aware of intervention points for specific students. For other students, however, the need for identifying an intervention point may emerge as the lesson progresses. The intervention/transition checklist is a useful tool for intervention point identification. (Appendix A on the Companion Website). As the lesson develops, the teacher should keep several major points in mind:

1. Select strategies for teaching for acquisition, retention, and generalization.
2. Select the appropriate activities for teaching for each part of the model.
3. Be sure that all activities are based on the appropriate objective level.
4. Sequence all activities.
5. Identify any necessary intervention points during the lesson for students experiencing difficulty.
6. Identify the areas that need modification or adaptation: technique, content, technology, or assessment/evaluation.
7. Develop the appropriate modification for the areas identified in item 6. (Each area will be discussed later in this text.)
8. Plan for an adapted learning environment.

Lesson Summary.   Here the major points of the lesson are summarized and the lesson's events are tied together. The teacher may choose to have students describe what they have learned by performing one of several activities, such as answering questions, taking part in a discussion, demonstrating something, or presenting a project. Table 9.2 presents the strategy component of the lesson plan and suggested interventions to consider for each stage.

TABLE 9.2
Interventions for lesson strategies.

Component	Considerations for Planning	Suggested Interventions
Strategies: The work-study activities that occur during the lesson		
Introduction: Setting the stage for the work-study activities that will occur during the lesson		
	• Review what is to be learned.	Review the instructional objectives before developing the lesson's activities.
		Modify the objective if necessary for student success.
		Reassess the students' prerequisite skill level.
		Explain to the student how today's lesson is related to yesterday's lesson.
	• Demonstrate what student should learn.	Provide a model of a completed assignment.
		Using the whole-part-whole method, review the assignment/task.
		Provide directions that are sequential, written, and reviewed orally.
	• Use mind-capture or activator.	Use a manipulative or hands-on activity to boost interest.
		Note whether students have prerequisite skills for mastering the objective.
	• Provide a link to past lessons or students' experiences.	Ask questions on students' taxonomy levels about past lessons.
		Provide example from own experience and relate to lesson (modeling technique).
		Ask students to share similar experiences; relate student comments to present lesson.
	• Relate lesson to a future life event or purpose for learning the lesson.	Show students how today's lesson will have meaning in their future.
		Let students provide examples of how or what they learn today will be helpful tomorrow.

Component	Considerations for Planning	Suggested Interventions
Development: The sequence of work-study activities that will occur during the lesson	• Select teaching strategies for acquisition, retention, and transfer.	*Acquisition:* The learning of a new skill Get the students' attention and explain the intent of the lesson. Use whole-part-whole activities (i.e., provide a lecture outline). Plan for practice and distribute the practice throughout the lesson. Cover only small segments of material if the lesson is long. Provide students with immediate feedback on their progress. Use multisensory approaches while teaching the activities. Point out specific details that you want the students to learn. Plan for appropriate note-taking procedures.
	• Select strategies for teaching for retention.	*Retention:* Remembering over an extended period of time Provide for overlearning by developing extended activities that teach the lesson. Help students see that how you teach relates to how you will test. Teach students the different types of retention measures. Point out specific information you will want student to recall at a later date. After a short rest from the material check for recall and retention. Reteach if the student has not retained the skills.
	• Select teaching strategies for acquisition, retention, and transfer.	*Generalization:* Transferring what is learned in one situation to another situation. Point out the similarities between the tasks learned. Show how the information learned will be useful in another situation.
	• Select the appropriate activities for teaching each part of the model.	Assist in overlearning by letting students participate in independent practice. Overlearning does not mean boredom. Carefully select appropriate activities for teaching for acquisition, retention, and generalization.

(continued)

TABLE 9.2
Continued.

Component	Considerations for Planning	Suggested Interventions
		Remember that each part of the three-part model must be mastered before the student begins the next step.
	• Assess that all activities are based on the appropriate objective level.	Check each activity to be sure that you are teaching the objective, and that you are teaching on the appropriate instructional level.
	• Sequence all activities.	Organize all activities from lowest to highest level of difficulty.
		Sequence the activities within each segment of the model.
	• Identify any necessary intervention points during the lesson for students experiencing difficulty.	Using the intervention checklist, identify any intervention point within the lesson at which a student is experiencing difficulty.
		Remember that continuing with the lesson when a student is lost defeats the lesson's purpose.
		The lesson must relate directly to the standard or benchmark.
	• Identify the necessary areas of intervention within technique, content, media, technology, and evaluation.	Identify the necessary areas of mismatch for the student (teaching technique, content, media, technology, and evaluation).
	• Develop the appropriate modification for the areas identified above.	Select the appropriate adaptation or modification for the identified area.
	• Plan for an adapted learning environment.	Assign peer tutors to students with disabilities if needed.
		Organize creative groups for instruction.
		Select grouping arrangements.
Summary/Closing: Tying together the lesson's events.		
	• Conclude the lesson.	Select closing activities on the students' instructional level.
		Assess students' mastery of the concepts.
	• Let students describe what they have learned.	Ask students to tell about what they have learned.
		Have students draw pictures of what they have learned.
		Invite students to present projects or assignments completed during lesson development.

Note: From *Reaching the Hard to Teach* by J. W. Wood, 2004, Richmond, VA: Judy Wood, Inc. Reprinted with permission.

TABLE 9.3
Interventions for resources.

Component	Considerations for Planning	Suggested Interventions
Resources: A list of the learning materials or technology needed to teach the lesson		
	• Develop all materials to be used in presenting the lesson.	Assess materials as to instructional level.
		Select a variety of materials that address different perceptual learning styles(i.e., visual, auditory).
	• Select appropriate media/technology to be used with the lesson.	Select a variety of media/technology and plan how to use them in lesson implementation.
		Match media to perceptual learning styles of students.
		Select bulletin boards for incidental and intentional learning.
		Design learning centers to enhance the instructional activities.

Note: From *Reaching the Hard to Teach* by J. W. Wood, 2004, Richmond, VA: Judy Wood, Inc. Reprinted with permission.

Resources

In the resources section of the lesson plan, the teacher identifies any materials, media, or technology to be used to achieve the lesson's purpose. Such resources may include pages or chapters in a pamphlet, text, or workbook; video or DVD; guest experts; field experience; special settings; art or cooking supplies; or audiovisual equipment. Table 9.3 lists suggested interventions for resources used. Assessing the instructional level of materials, matching perceptual learning styles with media, and using a variety of materials or media are all part of developing resources.

Evaluation

Evaluation, the final component of the lesson plan, is designed to measure student outcomes, identify a teacher's need to reorganize lesson plans, and target areas for reteaching. Evaluation may appear to be the last component in the lesson plan format, but actually it is an ongoing process.

During evaluation, the teacher assesses student learning and the success of the lesson. Teachers can assess students by checking behavioral objectives, using informal questions, administering formal pre- and posttests, or having students develop projects or products. A teacher may choose to have students check their own work by providing them with feedback, a model of a completed activity, or an illustration of the lesson's concept or process. Another method is to have students assess one another's work or self-assess. To determine the lesson's degree of success, a teacher may analyze students' reactions during the lesson, the value of the lesson as a learning experience, or the teacher's own teaching performance.

ACCOMMODATING TECHNOLOGY

Incorporating multiple teaching methods into a lesson plan to meet the needs of all of our learners is not always easy, but new technology often provides help. From electronic devices to computer programs, we can rely on some of these proven advances to help our students use multiple senses as they learn. Wiggleworks, a literacy program for young learners developed by the Center for Applied Special Technology and Scholastic, is a software program that does just that (see www.scholastic.com/wiggleworks/index.htm for more information).

Built around leveled trade books, the computer program provides instruction in phonemic awareness, phonics, fluency, vocabulary, and comprehension. It allows students to customize their learning experience. Users can enlarge, highlight, or change the color of the text; can have the program read a word, sentence, or passage more slowly; and can test how well they are reading by using a built-in microphone (U.S. Office of Special Education Programs, 1999). Wiggleworks also allows learners to write, draw, and record using a variety of starting points. For instance, "students can begin a composition by typing text, by recording themselves speaking or drawing, or by placing words from a word list into their text" (American Youth Policy Forum, 2000, p. 2). Using a program such as Wiggleworks can assist teachers as they try to meet the individual learning needs in their classrooms.

Student assignments are also a major component of evaluation. Assignments are part of the evaluation process as well as an extension of content mastery. They give the teacher an opportunity to see whether the student has mastered the skill and whether reteaching will be necessary. Table 9.4 offers suggestions for student evaluations and assignments. Additional information on assignments may be found in chapter 11. We will return to the subject of evaluation later in this book.

General Principles of Learning and the Lesson Plan

If teaching is the interaction between teacher and learner, then effective teaching is planning that interaction to incorporate the principles of learning. Teaching occurs in three steps: acquisition, retention, and transfer or generalization. When a teacher teaches a skill, the first stage is **acquisition**—learning a new skill, idea, or concept. When students "acquire" the skill, the teacher continues to teach for **retention,** or remembering the skill. Lastly, educators teach for transfer or **generalization,** which means using a learned skill in another situation. This three-stage teaching process can be facilitated with the use of specific teaching strategies (see Table 9.5).

Some students acquire a new skill and immediately retain the skill and can transfer it to other situations. Other students must be purposefully taught to acquire, retain, and transfer. Employing appropriate teaching strategies is a form of intervening. Interventions occur in different forms; one form is to constantly be aware of a student's learning within the cycle. Is the student in the acquisition, retention, or generalization stage?

TABLE 9.4
Interventions for assessment and evaluation.

Component	Considerations for Planning	Suggested Interventions
Evaluation: Checking for mastery and areas for reteaching.		
	• Assess student learning.	Check to see that the way you test reflects the way you taught for retention during the strategies/procedures component of the lesson plan.
	• Match lesson intent and indicator.	
	• Assess instruction.	Assess the effectiveness of the instructional objective.
	• Assist teachers in redesigning the lesson.	Assess activities not mastered and consider further adaptations of the lesson plan.
		Use a variety of assessment measures.
	• Provide for student self-assessment.	Give student self-correcting materials for immediate reinforcement.
		Provide models to which students can compare this work.
	• Allow students to assess each other.	Provide one-on-one peer tutors to give feedback.
		Oversee student assessment of peers (peers' criticism can harm self-concepts).
		Were all students included in the lesson activities?
	• Provide for teacher self-assessment.	Did each student experience success?
		Was I aware of the instructional level of each student?
		Did each student reach expected learning outcome?
		Did I effectively manage student behaviors?
		Was the learning environment adapted to meet student's learning needs?
	• Student assignments	Were assignments on the appropriate instructional level for students?
		Were students overwhelmed with too much of an assignment?
		Were assignments designed so that students experienced success?
		Were all assignments related to the lesson?
		Were assignments given for a specific reason?
		Were students informed of the purpose of assignments?

Note: From *Reaching the Hard to Teach* by J. W. Wood, 2004, Richmond, VA: Judy Wood, Inc. Reprinted with permission.

TABLE 9.5
General principles of learning and strategies for teaching each principle.

Principle	Definition	Strategy
Acquisition	The learning of a new skill, concept, or idea	• Attention and purpose • Demonstration of end results • Whole and parts methods • Amount of material • Sequenced steps • Knowledge of results • Multisensory presentation • Structure • Understanding psychological needs
Retention	Remembering over an extended period of time what was taught	• Overlearning • Distribution of practice • Recitation • Amount of practice • Type of retention measure • Reminiscence/review • Instructions to recall
Generalization	Taking what is learned in one situation and using it in a second situation	• Intertask similarity • Overlearning • Multiple career applications • Instructions to transfer

Note: From *Reaching the Hard to Teach* by J. W. Wood, 2004, Richmond, VA: Judy Wood, Inc. Reprinted with permission.

When employing a strategy for the teaching of a principle, the teacher must develop the strategy into an activity or practical application. Tables 9.6, 9.7, and 9.8 provide practical activities for each teaching strategy found in Table 9.5. For example, Mrs. Divi was beginning a lesson on the parts of a flower. For acquisition she used the teaching technique *attention and purpose.* Mrs. Divi displayed the flower parts on picture cards and then placed the "puzzle pieces" together. As the lesson developed, Mrs. Divi continued teaching the acquisition of flower parts employing sequenced steps by using a graphic organizer. When the class acquired the skill, Mrs. Divi continued to teach for retention using the teaching strategy *overlearning.* The students developed games for learning flower parts. For transfer, Mrs. Divi showed the students similarities between the parts of the flower and the parts of other plants.

TABLE 9.6
Strategies for facilitating student acquisition.

Strategy	Examples
Attention and purpose: Establishing attention and purpose for the task to be learned	• Explain or show pictures or a video of problem situations where concept or skill is needed. • State *what* student will be learning. • Tie what students will be learning to previous learning. Show a connection. • List and state the standard the learning activity will be addressing. • State the learning outcome. • Establish situations in life where problems/situations will be needed. • Focus students' attention to the task by using colors, bold print, etc. • Provide step-by-step directions, placing each direction on one 3-× 5-inch index card. • For younger children use picture cards. • Use tape recorders to give directions with a written checklist to watch as directions are presented orally. • Use wall charts with pictures and word clues. • Review class outlines prior to test. • Be clear with class objective and structures. • Use a "rule list."
Demonstration of end results: Establishing for students what the learning objectives will be and what they will look like	• Repeat objective/outcome/indicators. • Visually display objective/outcome indicators. • Have students explain what they think they are going to learn. • Have students discuss what products/examples they can create that will demonstrate the learning outcomes. • Show examples of prior products that demonstrate learning results.
Whole and parts methods: Whole method presents tasks as a whole; parts method presents tasks in parts	**Whole Method** • Present a word as a whole then break it down into specific sounds or parts. • Review the outline for the lesson as a whole. • Address a chapter with a brief summary. • Show the completed product before the student begins to work on the exercise. • Show the video of a novel before the student reads the novel. **Parts Method** • Break skills down into small steps, teaching from lowest to highest skills. • Place each step of an exercise in a checklist so the student can clearly see the parts in progressing order. • Number directions in order. • Tape short segments of a literary work so that the student may listen in parts. • Give tests in small sections. • Focus on parts of the outline or organizer that make up the whole. • Focus on specific steps or segments in a video.
Amount of material: The size of the task and the number of items in the task	• The amount of material may vary depending on the student's ability to handle specific amounts of material. • Worksheets may contain the same information but quantity should be monitored. • Spelling tests may be split in half. • If the student needs more material to learn the task, then the distribution of material should be monitored.

(continued)

TABLE 9.6
Continued.

Strategy	Examples
Sequenced steps: Placing steps of activity in sequential order	• Provide visual in handout format of the steps necessary for completing the task. • Place tasks on individual 3 × 5 cards. Give some students only a step or two at a time. • Place the sequence of activities on a bulletin board. • Number all sequences. • Use outlines and graphic organizers.
Knowledge of results: Providing immediate feedback on answers	• Instant feedback is necessary for students to know whether their responses are correct or incorrect. • It has been said that if a student learns the answer incorrectly, it will take 250 times hearing the correct answer to correct the error. • Use computers and/or self-correcting materials. • Provide math problems in puzzle format so that only the correct answer completes the puzzle. • Place the correct response on the reverse side of activity cards. • Develop overlays for tests, such as fill-in-the-blank, multiple-choice, or true-false. • Develop overlays for activities so that correct answers appear either beside or on top of the student's answer.
Multisensory presentation: Using all of the senses for teaching input	• Use outlines and organizers. • Present material visually as well as auditorily. • Let students manipulate objects for concrete learning. • Check the learning styles section in chapter 10 for an explanation of ideas for multisensory presentation. • Use brightly decorated bulletin boards. • Use large print on all transparencies. • Use flashcards, TV, video, filmstrips, games, and pictures. • Use tape recorders, radios, and recorders with earphones. • Provide recorded books. • Hang mobiles from the ceiling with new information to be learned. • Place information around drinking fountains.
Structure: Organizing the material to be learned so that the student understands the task.	• Use acquisition outlines. • Provide organizers. • Review the daily class procedure. • Provide "logical connections" for students between old and new information and explain where the new information fits into the old. • Remember that just because you understand the material's structure does not mean that the student understands; ask students to explain or demonstrate understanding.
Understanding psychological needs: Understanding what needs the learner has psychologically	• Learning is enhanced when the student's psychological needs are met through instructional/learning activities. • Provide appropriate attention to the student. • Help the student achieve in something. • Help the student feel secure and safe. • Be fair with all students.

Note: From *Reaching the Hard to Teach* by J. W. Wood, 2004, Richmond, VA: Judy Wood, Inc. Reprinted with permission.

TABLE 9.7
Strategies for facilitating student retention.

Strategy	Examples
Overlearning: Practicing beyond the point of acquisition the new skill learned	• Provide learning stations or centers with numerous activities designed to teach the newly acquired skill. • Overlearning does not mean boredom. • Let students create ways to practice new skills. • Develop games that reinforce the new skills.
Distribution of practice: The amount of practice required	• The amount of distribution of practice depends on the attention span of the student. • Practice may be mass practice: long periods of practice on a task, distributed practice, or practice in small segments. • Practice vocabulary or spelling words in sets of five. • Practice, rest, and return to practice. • Practice with a friend. • Changing the way information is presented, but not the information, will facilitate quicker learning.
Recitation: Practicing a new task after the teacher has removed the original material	• Have students review a new list of vocabulary words with definitions. Have the students use the words without viewing the list. • Present a new word orally and have the students repeat the word within a sentence into a recorder. • Let the students play games that use material previously presented by the teacher.
Amount of practice: The total number of practice sessions (the time) students spend to learn a task	• Use games to teach a concept. • Change to another activity teaching the same concept. • Point out practical uses of the concept being taught.

Type of retention measure: Refers to the retention measure a teacher uses to teach material	• The types of retention measures are
	    recognition (the selection of previously learned items from unlearned or false items, for example, a multiple-choice test);
	    structured recall (supplying items within a specific context, for example, essay tests or fill-in-the-blank test items); and
	    relearning (the time or effort required to relearn previously learned material).
	• Make a match between how you teach and how you test.
	• Provide study guides that clearly specify the type of items that will be on the test.

Reminiscence: After a long practice session and rest, the student should have an increase in performance	• Design short check-up tests for students to complete after rest and extended practice. • The practice-rest cycle may have to be repeated several times for some students. • Reward students for information learned even if it is only a small amount. • Students may keep a personal chart of progress.
Instructions to recall: Refers to directing the student to learn with the specific idea of recalling the material at a later time	• Use color-coded notes. • Use note-taking techniques emphasizing specific details. • Provide study guides. • Use outlines and highlight specific details.

Note: From *Reaching the Hard to Teach* by J. W. Wood, 2004, Richmond, VA: Judy Wood, Inc. Reprinted with permission.

TABLE 9.8
Strategies for facilitating student generalization/transfer.

Strategy	Examples
Intertask similarity: Showing the student the similarity between two different tasks	• Emphasize the similarity between manuscript writing and cursive writing. • Point out how addition and multiplication relate. • Show students how pasting leaves into a book is similar to keeping a notebook in the upper grades. • Explain how rules in the first or second grade may differ from those in the upper grades. However, rules are rules.
Overlearning: Practice beyond the point of mastery	• Remember that overlearning is not the same as boredom. • Return to skills taught to reinforce the skill. • Use new and creative ways to teach the same skill. • Allow mental and physical rest periods.
Multiple career applications: Generalizing the skills learned to a career choice	• Discuss life careers. • Discuss why one selects a career. • Discuss what careers the students are interested in. • List career interest or parent careers on board. • Show the connection of skill to the career of interest.
Instructions to transfer: Showing the student how learning in one situation will be useful in another	• Show how basic math facts will help the student keep a checkbook. • Point out how reading will help them fill out job forms. • Emphasize how learning to read relates to passing the driver's education class, leading to a driver's license. • Students plan and discuss where they will use what they learned. • Students choose and create a product that uses what they learned. • Relate products to outcomes initially established.

Note: From *Reaching the Hard to Teach* by J. W. Wood, 2004, Richmond, VA: Judy Wood, Inc. Reprinted with permission.

RESEARCH-BASED CATEGORIES OF INSTRUCTIONAL STRATEGIES AFFECTING STUDENT ACHIEVEMENT

A teacher level factor that affects student achievement is "instructional strategies." It is perhaps self-evident that more effective teachers use more effective instructional strategies. It is probably also true that effective teachers have more instructional strategies at their disposal (Marzano, 2003, p. 78).

This text has presented, and will continue to present, strategies that affect student achievement. Because the lesson plan is the starting point for planning and organizing strategies, this would be an appropriate place for discussing categories of research-based instructional strategies and how to incorporate these into lesson planning.

ACCOMODATING DIVERSITY

We all have distinct learning strengths and weaknesses, and we often understand and remember information more easily when it is presented in one way instead of another. This is often referred to as our preferred learning style, and many teachers try to build elements into their lesson plans that match their students' inclinations. Although many different categories and models of learning styles exist, the most common grouping is by visual, auditory, or kinesthetic preference. Many believe that attending to a student's particular learning style increases the likelihood that the student will construct meaning from the information and transfer the new knowledge to other applications (Thomson & Mascazine, 1997). Data even suggest that achievement test scores improve 55 to 59% when teachers instruct using students' preferred learning styles (Barkley & Bianco, 2002).

Other researchers recognize that our students come to us with unique learning strengths and weaknesses, but question the learning styles concept. These researchers cite a lack of evidence for why visual, auditory, or kinesthetic teaching methods would be particularly effective with any one type of student (Cromley, 2000). They also question the validity and reliability of tests that claim to diagnose a style.

Although agreement does not exist on the learning styles concept itself, research has proven that several teaching methods work for our diverse students. We all learn better when we learn through several senses instead of just one. Hearing, seeing, and doing something with new information all create different memory traces, or retrieval cues, that increase the ways students can recall what they learned (Cromley, 2000). Students who actively learn using multiple senses tend to remember better and longer than those who use just one sense. We can build various activities into our lesson plans that use multiple styles over a particular unit of study to increase our students' learning rather than simply relying on lecture and note taking or any other single method. Lesson plans can include various grouping arrangements, different visual aids, manipulatives, portfolios, and interviewing to help all students achieve mastery of the information.

Marzano (2003) reported nine categories of instructional strategies that affect student achievement, which he and his colleagues researched (Marzano, 1998a; Marzano, Gaddy, & Dean, 2000; Marzano, Pickering, & Pollock, 2001). These include identifying similarities and differences, summarizing and note taking; reinforcing effort and providing recognition; homework and practice; nonlinguistic representations; cooperative learning; setting objectives and providing feedback; generating and testing hypotheses; and questions, cues, and advanced organizers (p. 80). Marzano (2003) suggested that educators incorporate these strategies into an instructional framework for units so as not to constrain educators to a day-to-day lesson design. He suggested that general strategies be considered in three categories: "(1) those used at regular intervals in a unit; (2) those focusing on input experiences; and (3) those dealing with

Prior to Lesson

☐ Prepare a list of questions to help students identify prior knowledge.

☐ Prepare logical connections between new content and old content.

☐ Provide procedure for organizing new content or thinking about new content.

Goals

☐ Establish and identify clear teaming goals. Post standard, benchmark, and indicator.

☐ Have students establish self-learning goals.

Class Design

☐ Establish individual work based on student ability.

☐ Establish cooperative groups.

☐ Establish grouping design for lesson.
  • Ability groups
  • Interest groups
  • Creative groups

☐ Ask students to revise their mental images.

☐ Assign homework.
  • Develop homework and in-class activities requiring students to practice and process new skills.
  • Assign homework and in-class activities that assist students in comparing content with previous knowledge.

During and After Lesson

☐ Develop note-taking procedure. Several types may be presented.

☐ Have students verbally summarize content.

☐ Have students summarize content through written expression. (Some students may not be able to do a complete summary but only write a word summary or sentence summary.)

☐ Have students "represent the content as pictures, pictographs, symbols, graphic representations, physical models or dramatic enactments."

☐ Have students use their visual memory to create mental images for content learned.

Lesson Review, Practice, and Content Application

☐ Have students revise notes, correct errors, expand information, add details, etc.

☐ Ask students to revise graphic representations to correct errors, expand visuals, add details, etc.

Evaluation Measures

☐ Establish student self-tracking measures.

☐ Establish teacher method of providing student feedback.
  • Item test/reporting back
  • Conferencing
  • Rubric
  • Informal feedback

☐ Establish procedures for student comparison of self-evaluation to teacher evaluation.

FIGURE 9.2
Checklist for integrating best practice into lessons.

Note: From *What Works in Schools: Translating Research into Action* (pp. 85–87) by R. J. Marzano. Alexandria, VA: Association for Supervision and Curriculum Development. Copyright © 2003 by the Association for Supervision and Curriculum Development. Used with Permission. The Association for Supervision and Curriculum Development is a worldwide community of educators advocating sound policies and sharing best practices to achieve the success of each learner. To learn more, visit ASCD at www.ascd.org.

Develop Projects

☐ Assign projects that require students "to generate and test hypotheses through problem-solving tasks."

☐ Engage "students in projects that require them to generate and test hypotheses through decision-making tasks."

☐ Engage "students in projects that require them to generate and test hypotheses through investigation tasks."

☐ Engage "students in projects that require them to generate and test hypotheses through experimental inquiry tasks."

☐ Engage "students in projects that require them to generate and test hypotheses through systems analysis tasks."

☐ Engage "students in projects that require them to generate and test hypotheses through invention."

Homework

☐ Assign homework and in-class activities that assist students in classifying new content.

☐ Assign homework and in-class activities requiring students to create metaphors with content learned.

☐ Assign homework and in-class activities assisting students in creating analogies with content.

FIGURE 9.2
Continued.

reviewing, practicing, and applying content" (p 85). Marzano went on to list numerous suggestions for implementation. These suggestions have been developed into a checklist for educators, found in Figure 9.2. As they develop each lesson within a lesson, teachers can refer to this checklist to ensure that they have incorporated best practice into their unit or lesson.

Standards-Based Lesson Plans: Where Interventions Go

Where does an educator physically place interventions within the lesson plan? Table 9.9 presents a sample standard, benchmark, and indicator. Table 9.10 uses benchmark 4 from Table 9.9 and expands it into a sample standards-based lesson plan with preplanned interventions. As Table 9.10 shows, a standards-based lesson plan begins with the broad concept under investigation. Benchmarks are assessed by indicators.

In the "Learning activities/experiences" column in Table 9.10, the lesson purpose is listed, an introduction activity is planned, lesson activity is developed, and the lesson ends with a closing. As seen in the third column, preplanned interventions are inserted into the lesson plan. These interventions are organized according to the SAALE model: learning environment, technique/process, content, technology, and products/results. The interventions help the teacher implement the lesson described in the second column. The lesson is assessed according to the indicator listed with the benchmark.

TABLE 9.9
Standards-based lesson plan.

Broad Concept: Research	Collaboration Tips: Grade Level Two

Standard: Students define and investigate self-selected or assigned issues, topics, and problems. They locate, select, and make use of relevant information from a variety of media, reference, and technological sources. Students use an appropriate form to communicate their findings.

Benchmarks	Indicators
1. Create questions for investigation, assigned topics, or personal areas of interest	1. Create
2. Utilize appropriate searching techniques to gather information from a variety of locations (e.g., classroom, school library, public library, or community resources).	2. Locate, select, utilize
3. Acquire information, with teacher assistance, from multiple resources about the topic.	3. Acquire
4. Identify important information and write brief notes about the information.	4. Identify and write
5. Sort relevant information about the topic into categories with teacher assistance.	5. Sort
6. Report important findings to others.	6. Report, communicate

Note: From Ohio Department of Education. (2002). *Academic content standards: English language arts K–12* (pp. 132–133). Center for Curriculum and Assessment. Office of Curriculum and Instruction.

HOW THE SAALE MODEL FITS INTO A STANDARDS-BASED EDUCATIONAL SYSTEM

Chapter 7 presented the SAALE model. This section will show how the SAALE model fits into a standards-based educational system (see Figure 9.3).

Always starting with the standards, benchmarks, and indicators, educators begin to plan for instruction and assessment. Using the intervention checklist and other assessment measures of the SAALE model, they can look for student mismatches. Once they have identified mismatches, teachers can select appropriate interventions. These preplanned interventions are then incorporated into the lesson plan. The need for additional interventions may also become evident during instruction. At this point the educator does not have time to preplan. Spontaneous interventions now come into play as educators pull from their "bag of tricks" to help students.

Lesson Delivery

Intervention can be as simple as presenting the lesson effectively. Therefore, while planning lessons, teachers should think about how they will present those lessons to students. Cooper and colleagues (1977) suggested five stimulus variation techniques that teachers can use to deliver the lesson effectively: kinetic variation, focusing, shifting interaction, pausing, and shifting the senses.

TABLE 9.10
Standards-based lesson plan.

Broad Concepts: Research

Standard: See Table 9.9.

Grade Level: Two

Benchmark: No. 4—Identify

Lesson Prerequisites	Learning Activities/Experiences	Preplanned Interventions	Assessment Continuum
Key vocabulary:	**Lesson purpose:** What are we doing today? Benchmark/standard.	**Learning environment:** • Place in interest groups. • Add new words to word wall.	**Identify** • Self-assessment, student reflection.
Resources needed:	**Introductory activity:** Put a topic in PowerPoint with a list of short statements. Read and ask what statements are important to the topic.	**Technique/process:** • Post intro activity in room as a model. • Print and place model in interest groups.	• Identified list of important information/teacher observation. • Student highlight important information.
Hyperlinks:	**Lesson activity:** 1. List topic on an envelope. 2. Using information researched, place important information on small post-it notes.	**Content:** • Chop book. • For lesson activity, list activity steps.	• Using the activity list provided to students, make notes for each student for teacher purposes of reteach or back teach. • Completed white boards.
Literacy coach/room requests:	3. Drop ideas into envelope. 4. Peers may help. 5. Remove post-it notes and place on white boards. 6. With group/peer help, identify which is important to topic.	• Some students may use pictures with code words. **Media/technology:** • PowerPoint **Products/results:**	
	Closing activity: • Restate lesson purpose. • Using activity list created by teacher, students check what they have completed. • Star what student needs to rework or continue. • Students self-review.	• Some students may work alone or write information in phrases or sentences.	

Note: From *Reaching the Hard to Teach* by J. W. Wood, 2004, Richmond, VA: Judy Wood, Inc. Reprinted with permission.

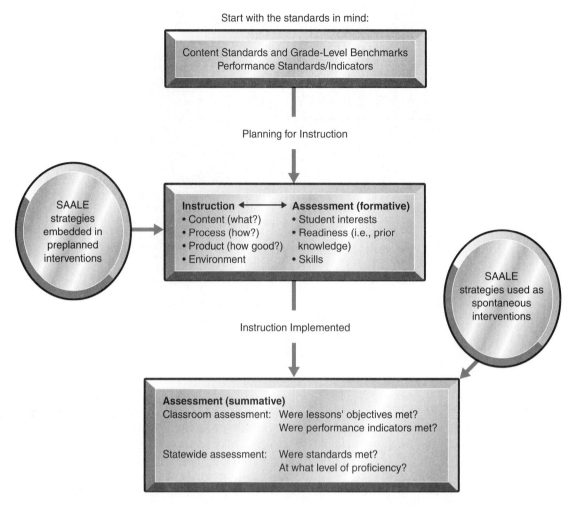

Start with the standards in mind:

Content Standards and Grade-Level Benchmarks
Performance Standards/Indicators

Planning for Instruction

SAALE
strategies
embedded in
preplanned
interventions

Instruction ←——→ **Assessment (formative)**
• Content (what?)   • Student interests
• Process (how?)   • Readiness (i.e., prior
• Product (how good?)   knowledge)
• Environment   • Skills

SAALE
strategies used as
spontaneous
interventions

Instruction Implemented

Assessment (summative)
Classroom assessment: Were lessons' objectives met?
                        Were performance indicators met?

Statewide assessment: Were standards met?
                        At what level of proficiency?

FIGURE 9.3
The SAALE model in a standards-based educational system.
Note: From *Reaching the Hard to Teach* by J. W. Wood, 2004, Richmond, VA: Judy Wood, Inc. Reprinted with permission.

Kinetic variation refers to changes in the teacher's position in the classroom. A teacher should move around the room to improve communication rather than sit behind a desk for the whole period. The teacher's movements should be smooth and natural, neither distracting from the lesson nor disturbing to the students. Kinetic variation includes one or a combination of the following motions: (a) moving freely from right to left and then from left to right in front of the classroom; (b) moving freely from front to back and then from back to front; and (c) moving freely among or behind students (Cooper et al., 1977). This technique also enables the teacher to use proximity control to intervene with problem behaviors.

Focusing is the "teacher's way of intentionally controlling the direction of student attention" (Cooper et al., 1977, p. 136). Focusing can be verbal, behavioral, or both. Teachers can focus students' attention verbally by asking specific questions or using accent words such as *for example, look, how,* or *find.* Behavioral focusing may involve using body language: for example, facial expressions, eye contact, or pointing or other hand gestures to attract or direct attention.

Lessons may be developed using listening stations. Can you think of ways a listening station may be used in general education classrooms?

Shifting interaction refers to the teacher's use of any one of the following interaction styles: teacher–group, teacher–student, or student–student. Teacher–group, interaction puts the teacher in control, lecturing and directing discussion as needed. Teacher–student interaction is also teacher directed, but the teacher becomes more of a facilitator, asking questions to clarify a story or answering questions raised by students after they have completed a lab assignment. Student–student interaction centers around students, with the teacher "redirecting student questions to other students for comment or clarification" (Cooper et al., 1977, p. 138). When planning a lesson, teachers should strive to include a variety of interaction styles.

Teachers can also use *pauses,* or moments of silence, effectively during a lesson. For example, a teacher can completely regain students' attention by becoming silent. Cooper and colleagues (1977) listed 10 effective uses of pausing (p. 139):

1. It can break informational segments into smaller pieces for better understanding. Reading oral problems or dictating material for transcription requires careful attention to the effective use of pausing.

2. It can capture attention by contrasting sound with silence (alternating two distinctly different stimuli). Remember that attention is maintained at a high level when stimuli are varied, not when one increases the intensity of a single stimulus.

3. It can be a signal for students to prepare for the next teacher action.

4. It can be used to emphasize or underscore an important point.

5. It can provide time for thinking about a question or formulating an answer.

6. It can prevent teachers from unconsciously dominating discussion.

7. It encourages teachers to listen to individual student responses. People do not listen well when they are talking.

8. It can create suspense or expectation. For all types of literature, the effective reader uses the pause to stir emotion and heighten anticipation in the listener.

STUDENT KNOWLEDGE CHECK

Sarah, a general education teacher, is beginning to prepare her yearly lesson plans for the new school year. Sarah wants to be sure that all students will be successful within each lesson.

Sarah approaches a special education teacher and requests support for her lesson planning.

1. If you were approached by Sarah, where would you begin?
2. Explain how preplanned interventions go into a lesson plan.

9. It can help provide a model of listening behavior for other students.

10. It can be used to show disapproval of undesired student behavior.

Shifting the senses means presenting information through more than one of the five senses—seeing, touching, hearing, smelling, and tasking. The importance of shifting senses for mainstreamed students cannot be overemphasized. Assimilating information through various perceptual modalities helps those students learn the information in as many ways as possible.

Teachers who use these stimulus variation techniques enhance their teaching. When teachers plan the lesson carefully, adapt it when necessary for mainstreamed students, and include techniques for adding variety to the presentation, they increase their chances of stimulating all students to learn.

SUMMARY

As teachers prepare lesson plans, they should take time to make adaptations for students with special needs and those at risk. By working collaboratively in the development and implementation of lesson plans, general and special education teachers can provide appropriate instruction for all students. This chapter looked at lesson planning and standards, collaboration during lesson planning, components of a lesson plan, lesson plans and the principles of learning, research-based strategies in lesson planning, interventions in a standards-based lesson plan, the SAALE model in a standards-based educational system, and simple techniques for lesson delivery. Teachers will discover that when they adapt their lesson plans to the specific needs of learners, students *can* learn the lessons.

RESOURCES

Reading Tree Publications
51 Avesta Street
Springfield, MA 01118-1239
(413) 782-5839
Fax: (413) 782-0862
www.trelease-on-reading.com

SUGGESTED READINGS

Brooks, J. G. (2004). To see beyond the lesson. *Educational Leadership, 62*(1) 8–12.

Hitchcock, C., Meyer, A., Rose, D., & Jackson, R. (2002). Providing new access to the general curriculum: Universal design for learning. *Council for Exceptional Children, 35*(2), 8–12.

Rose, D. (2000). Universal design for learning. *Journal of Special Education Technology, 15*(4), 47–51.

Saphier, J., & Gower, R. (1987). *The skillful teacher: Building your teaching skills*. Carlisle, MA: Research for Better Teaching.

Wong, H. K., & Wong, R. T. (1998). *The first days of school: How to be an effective teacher*. Mountain View, CA: Harry K. Wong.

WEBSITES TO VISIT

The Information Institute of Syracuse. Educators reference web page offers links to resources and services to the education community. www.eduref.org.

Columbia Educational Center Lesson Plans. Lesson plans that have been used successfully by teachers in the classroom. www.col-ed.org/lessons page.html.

Mid Continent Research for Education and Learning. Provides resources including lesson plans to educators. www.mcrel.org/resources/plus.

Teachers.net. Web page offering a Mentor Support Center. www.teachers.net/mentors.

REFERENCES

American Youth Policy Forum. (2000, November 3) *Accessing the general curriculum: Promoting a universal design for learning* (Forum Brief) Retrieved September 7, 2004, from www.aypf.org/forumbriefs/2000/fb110300.htm.

Barkley, S. & Bianco, T. (2002, Winter). Part digital training, part human touch. *Journal of Staff Development, 23*(1). National Staff Development Council.

Cooper, J., Hansen, J., Martorella, P., Morine-Dershimer, G., Sadker, M., Sokolove, S., et al. (Eds.). (1977). *Classroom teaching skills: A workbook*. Lexington, MA: Heath.

Cromley, J. (2000). *Learning to think, thinking to learn: What the science of thinking and learning has to offer adult education*. Washington, DC: National Institute for Literacy.

Marzano, R. J. (1998a). *A theory-based meta-analysis of research on instruction*. Aurora, CO: Mid-Continent Research for Education and Learning. (ERIC Document Reproduction Service No. ED 427087)

Marzano, R. J. (2003). *What works in schools: Translating research into action*. Alexandria, VA: Association for Supervision and Curriculum Development.

Marzano, R. J., Gaddy, B. B., & Dean, C. (2000). *What works in classroom instruction?* Aurora, CO: Mid-Continent Research for Education and Learning.

Marzano, R. J., Pickering, D. J., & Pollock, J. E. (2001). *Classroom instruction that works: Research-based strategies for increasing student achievement*. Alexandria, VA: Association for Supervision and Curriculum Development.

Tenbrink, T. (1997). Writing instructional objectives. In J. Cooper, J. Hansen, P. Martorella, G.Morine-Dershimer, D. Sadker, M. Sadker, et al. (Eds.), *Classroom teaching skills: A handbook*. Lexington, MA: Heath.

Thomson, B. S., & Mascazine, J. R. (1997). *Attending to learning styles in mathematics and science classrooms* (ERIC Digest No. ED 432440). Columbus, OH: ERIC Clearinghouse for Science, Mathematics, and Environmental Education.

U.S. Office of Special Education Programs. (1999, Fall). Ensuring access to the general education curriculum. *Research Connections, 5*. Retrieved September 7, 2004, from http://ericec.org/osep/recon5/rc5sec1.html.

10

Adapting Teaching Techniques

LEARNER OBJECTIVES

After you read this chapter you will be able to:

- Explain the importance of structure and student success.
- List six learning modalities and techniques for teaching each.
- List and discuss the four modes of teaching.
- List three teaching techniques for each mode and accommodations for each.
- Discuss other technique delivery systems.

CHAPTER AT A GLANCE

```
            ┌─────────────┐
            │ Structuring │
            │ for Student │
            │   Success   │
            └──────┬──────┘
                   │
                   ▼
            ┌─────────────┐
            │     How     │
            │  Students   │
            │    Learn    │
            └──────┬──────┘
```

```
  ┌──────────────┐   ┌────────────────┐   ┌──────────────┐   ┌───────────────┐
  │ Learning and │   │   Conditions   │   │   Learning   │   │   Gardner's   │
  │  Cognitive   │   │   Affecting    │   │   Styles     │   │    Frames     │
  │    Styles    │   │ Learning Styles│   │and Instruction│  │    of Mind    │
  └──────────────┘   └────────────────┘   └──────────────┘   └───────────────┘
```

```
            ┌─────────────┐
            │   Adapting  │
            │   Teaching  │
            │  Techniques │
            └──────┬──────┘
```

```
      ┌──────────────┐        ┌──────────────────┐
      │   Teaching   │        │    Additional    │
      │    Modes     │        │     Teaching     │
      │              │        │    Techniques    │
      └──────────────┘        └──────────────────┘
```

KEY TERMS

*M*r. Able, a fifth-grade math teacher, was trying to teach math angles to his students. His method was "chalk and talk." The students who learned differently in the class were having difficulty grasping the concept of angles. During his planning period, Mr. Able expressed his concerns to his mentor teacher, Mr. Franks, who suggested that he combine a linguistic and nonlinguistic approach to teaching angles. You will find this problem solved as you read this chapter.

*I*nstruction is a teacher's major responsibility to children, school, and community. Good instructional planning paves the way for an organized school day and for the smooth delivery of information vital to children's academic development. But instead of defining instruction as simply imparting specific content, teachers should think of instruction as an ongoing process; the teacher delivers information to children, who receive and assimilate it. Teachers who adapt instruction to meet the needs of all students, especially those with mild disabilities, discover that they deliver information more effectively and students learn it more easily. Instruction becomes a continuous process of presenting information, adapting information, representing information, and testing for concept mastery. Making adaptation a natural component of this continuum helps students succeed.

The teaching technique is the delivery system that transmits content from teacher to students. If the technique is not appropriate for a student, then the content will most likely never be delivered. This chapter examines the importance of structure in student's lives, learning styles, teaching techniques, and adaptations for specific modes of teaching.

STRUCTURING FOR STUDENT SUCCESS

"Many at-risk youngsters thrive in well-structured learning situations" (Carbo & Hughes, 1988, p. 57). A structured environment provides predictability, and predictability reduces anxiety. Students who have difficulty imposing structure on the learning process benefit greatly from the efforts of educators to incorporate structure within the instructional process.

Students who naturally do well in school appear to have the ability to reduce the chaos of disorganized information and impose their own structure on material. The second type of learner is the random learner. There is a natural tendency within our system to *avoid* imposing structure on random learners because "no one will do this when they leave school and move into adult life." In reality, however, if we help disorganized or random learners impose structure, then they will transfer those skills into adult life.

Lessons in which the pattern of organization reflects structure are effective for all learners. Structured lessons provide the following benefits:

1. Structure provides a pathway for organizing information.

2. The work effort is reduced for learners because they do not have to process the information first and then establish order or a connection to understand the information.

3. The patterns of thought in a structured lesson or class can be generalized into other learning situations.

Providing structure instructionally is imperative for many learners. We cannot wait for learners to figure out how to structure or organize information. Structuring must become a natural part of instruction. George, a successful young adult, defined structure as "the ability to organize oneself efficiently enough in order for one to remain self-sufficient." Perhaps by imposing instructional structure we can assist children and young adults such as George with this process.

ACCOMMODATING DIVERSITY

The way students learn best may be partly shaped by their culture and ethnicity. Researchers have found variations in learning styles among students from different cultures, possibly as a result of the characteristics most valued by each group. Awareness of variations that can exist among students can help teachers reach each one of their students.

Most Hispanic cultures deeply value family commitment, loyalty, and cooperation. This can be why some Hispanic students are uncomfortable with competition in the classroom and the traditional U.S. value on individualism (Griggs & Dunn, 1996). Based on such research, "teachers and counselors should expect larger numbers of Hispanic students to prefer: 1) a cool environment; 2) conformity; 3) peer-oriented learning; 4) kinesthetic instructional resources; 5) a high degree of structure; 6) late morning and afternoon peak energy levels; 7) variety as opposed to routines; and 8) a field-dependent cognitive style" (Griggs & Dunn, 1996, p. 3).

African American students, in general, prefer their own style of learning experiences. Many prefer kinesthic/tactile learning, subdued lighting, visual input, and cooperative learning (Project Personnel, 2004). They may also prefer to study with background music or conversation noise. African American students are likely to rely more on information from their surroundings and react intensely to praise or criticism.

Certain teaching techniques may work well with American Indian students. Many of these students learn best through a process of "observation, self-testing in private, and then demonstration of task for approval" (Swisher, 1991, p. 1). These cultures respect experiential learning without constant supervision and correction. Some educators have found American Indian students hiding academic competence to avoid seeming superior to other students. This may be due to the traditional respect they hold for personal humility. Because advancing oneself above another violates this value, cooperative learning may be best for these students.

Although this type of research assists educators in choosing appropriate teaching techniques for their students, they must recognize that great diversity can exist within a cultural group. Different subcultures within each of these groups can have significantly different customs, values, and educational orientations. Given this, teachers can use these research findings as a guide, but should avoid assuming that a particular teaching style will always work with students from a particular culture.

HOW STUDENTS LEARN

Students want to learn to acquire knowledge or skills. Designing and implementing effective instruction so that students learn to their fullest capacity challenges us all. If learning means the acquisition of knowledge or skills, and the teacher wants to help students with that acquisition, then the teacher needs to understand the process of learning in general.

This brings us back to the concept that learning, or the capacity to learn, is based on intellectual ability. The theories of intellect are numerous. Costa and Kallick (2000) presented the following influential theories of intelligence:

1. *Intelligence can be taught.* Arthur Whimbley (Whimbley, Whimbley, & Shaw, 1975, as cited in Costa & Kallick, 2000) introduced the concept that intelligence can be taught and therefore is not exclusively genetically inherited (p. 4).

2. *Structure of the intellect.* Guilford and Hoeptner (1971) reported 120 individual factors of intellect that could also be combined. Twenty-six factors related to school success. These authors asserted that interventions could amplify intelligence (pp. 4–5).

During one of my postgraduate classes, I had the wonderful opportunity to study under psychologist Raymond Muskgrove. Dr. Muskgrove taught a complete course on theories of intelligence, with the Guilford model being his favorite. It is a fascinating theory that I encourage readers to investigate further. I was impressed that Guilford identified early on the importance of interventions to learning. (Another note regarding my professor, Dr. Muskgrove. He was a colleague of B. F. Skinner and worked beside Skinner in the lab watching the rats scurry about. I was always fascinated with the old pictures of Dr. Skinner and Dr. Muskgrove standing in the lab. Both were so young, and history was written all over those pictures. I salute both great men and will forever be grateful for having the great opportunity to study with the late Dr. Raymond Muskgrove.)

3. *Theory of cognitive modifiability.* Feuerstein believed that intelligence is not fixed, but instead is a function of experience. This theory is the underlying thread of the modern theory that intelligence can be taught and that everyone is gifted to a degree and retarded to a degree (p. 5).

4. *Multiple forms of intelligence.* Howard Gardner (1983, 1999) reported many ways for learning to be expressed! The popular model lists the following intelligences: verbal, logical/mathematical, kinesthetic, musical, spatial, naturalistic, interpersonal, and intrapersonal. These intelligences may be developed throughout our lifetime.

5. *Intelligence as success in life.* Sternberg, Torff, and Grigorenko (1998) reported three intelligences, which grow throughout life: analytical, creative, and practical (p. 6).

6. *Learned intelligence.* David Perkins (1995) "further supports the theory that intelligence can be taught and learned" (p. 6). He believes that three important mechanisms underlie intelligence:

- *Neural intelligence* is "genetically determined, hard-wired original equipment" that one has inherited and that determines the speed and efficiency of one's brain. Neural intelligence cannot be altered much.
- *Experiential intelligence* is context-specific knowledge that is accumulated through experience. It means knowing one's way around the various set-

tings and contexts in which one functions. A person's reservoir of experiential intelligence can be expanded.

- *Reflective intelligence* is the "good use of the mind; the artful deployment of our facilities of thinking" (p. 264). It includes self-managing, self-monitoring, and self-modifying. Perkins referred to this capacity as "mindware," which can and should be cultivated (p. 6).

7. *Emotional intelligence.* Daniel Goleman (1995) simply stated that intelligence and emotions are intertwined. One develops with the other.

8. *Moral intelligence.* Robert Coles (1997) believes that inner character development through interactions with the environment and persons within one's environment produces a "moral archeology," a moral code of ethics (pp. 6–7).

Learning and Cognitive Styles

Learning styles are students' individual approaches to learning. Knowledge of the different ways students may approach a learning situation and awareness of the influences on these approaches pave the way for successful teaching. Some students with mild disabilities may use one learning style or another, but many reflect a composite of different styles, showing that children learn in many different ways.

In addition to having a distinctive learning style, each student has a **cognitive style.** According to Fuhrmann (1980), "The cognitive components create learning. . . . Each of us develops a typical approach in our use of our cognitive characteristics to perceive, to think, and to remember. This approach constitutes our cognitive learning style" (p. 2). Keefe (1979) placed the many cognitive styles into two major categories: reception styles, which involve perceiving and analyzing functions; and concept formation and retention styles, which pertain to generating hypotheses, solving problems, and remembering. According to Fuhrmann (1980), these two cognitive categories "can be described by a series of continua, with an individual style being found at any point" (p. 2). Table 10.1 shows individual differences in reception, concept formation, and retention styles.

Conditions Affecting Learning Styles

In addition to an awareness of learning and cognitive styles, teachers should understand the many other conditions affecting the way children learn. The relationships among teaching and learning styles, students' perceptual styles, time, sound, seating arrangements and place, class procedures, group size, and students' attention spans all influence the learning process.

Interaction Between Teaching and Learning Styles

How students respond, how well they respond, or why they do not respond at all often depends on the interaction between teaching and learning styles. Johnson (1976) described two student learning styles: the dependent and independent. The Fuhrmann-Jacobs model of social interaction (Fuhrmann, 1980) added a third: the collaborative style. A student may be learning in all three styles but prefer a certain style in a certain situation. Thus, if some students prefer the dependent style for learning new information, but the teacher presents the material in the independent style, the students may not learn as quickly or as well as they could otherwise. Teachers should try to match their teaching styles to their students' learning styles as often as

TABLE 10.1
Cognitive styles: Learner and teacher descriptions.

Learner Style	Learner Needs	Teacher Role	Teacher Behavior
Dependent: may occur in introductory courses, languages, some sciences when learners have little or no information upon entering course	• Structure • Direction • External reinforcement • Encouragement • Esteem from authority	• Expert • Authority	• Lecturing • Demonstrating • Assigning • Checking • Encouragement • Testing • Reinforcing content • Transmitting • Grading • Designing materials
Independent: may occur when learners have much more knowledge or skill upon entering the course and want to continue to search on their own; may feel instructor cannot offer as much as they would like	• Internal awareness • Experimentation • Time • Nonjudgmental support	• Facilitator	• Allowing • Providing requested feedback • Consulting • Listening • Negotiating • Evaluating
Collaborative: may occur when learners have knowledge, information, ideas, and would like to share them or try them out	• Interaction • Practice • Probing self and others • Observation • Participation • Peer challenge • Peer esteem • Experimentation	• Colearner • Environment setter	• Interacting • Questioning • Providing resources • Modeling to share • Providing feedback • Coordinating • Evaluating • Managing • Processing observer • Grading

Note: From *A Practical Handbook for College Teachers* (p. 115) by B. S. Fuhrmann and A. F. Grasha, 1983, Boston: Little, Brown. Adapted by permission.

possible or vary their teaching styles so that, in any given situation, each student can use the learning style he or she prefers.

Students in an inclusive classroom usually prefer the dependent learner style. However, when students with special needs have some information about the subject, they tend to use the collaborative style.

Perceptual Styles

A student's perceptual style refers to the sense through which the student best receives information: visual (seeing), auditory (hearing), or kinesthetic (touching). Most children tend to use one perceptual style more than the others. Visual learners learn best when they can see the information presented (for example, on the chalkboard, through overhead projectors, or with filmstrips).

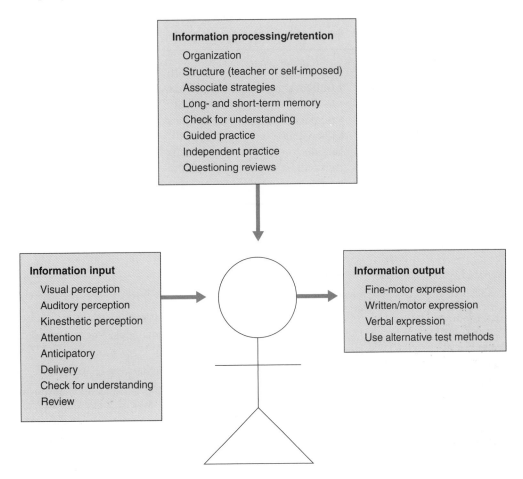

FIGURE 10.1

Perception, processing, and retention.

Note: From *Reaching the Hard to Teach* by J. W. Wood, 2004, Richmond, VA: Judy Wood, Inc. Reprinted with permission.

Auditory learners learn best when they can hear the information presented (for example, in a lecture). A classroom teacher who uses the lecture method can help visual learners by recording lectures for students to play back later.

Some students need kinesthetic feedback to learn. An example would be a teacher providing sandboxes so that students can draw or trace the letters of the alphabet in the sand and get kinesthetic feedback. Teachers need to plan instruction so that it addresses students' dominant perceptual modes.

Perception, Processing, and Retention

Figure 10.1 shows the impact of perception, processing, and retention on the learner. First, information enters the student through any one of three areas of perception: visual, auditory, or kinesthetic. Modifications in those areas help educators effectively impart information.

Next, information is processed and retained (which is the subject of this entire book). Students must organize information and impose some sort of structure or associate strategies. Long- and short-term memory are extremely important in the processing/retention component.

COLLABORATION TIPS

1. When team or co-teaching, both teachers should carefully review the lesson plan and identify the specific teaching techniques they will use.
2. Decide on the visualizations that will be used to support the lesson.
3. Develop outlines and organizers for the main lesson points.
4. Be sure to include all student modalities in the lesson delivery.

Characteristics

- Frequently loses place when reading or copying
- Has trouble discriminating among similar shapes, letters, and words
- Does not enjoy pictures, slides, or books
- Has difficulty reading and copying accurately from chalkboard
- Shows signs of eye strain such as squinting, blinking, and holding head close to page
- Has trouble following written directions from board or printed page
- Works slowly on printed assignments or tests
- Displays poor sight vocabulary
- May use fingers to keep place while reading
- Skips words or reverses words when reading aloud
- Cannot visualize things in mind
- Demonstrates erratic spelling or incorrect letter sequences
- Does not notice details on pictures, maps, and photographs
- Confused by work sheets containing a great deal of visual stimuli
- Has difficulty remembering what is seen
- May whisper to self while working with visual material

Accommodations for all subject areas

- Give the child the clearest copy of the photocopied work sheets.
- Make sure students are seated close to the teacher, board, or work area.
- Make an effort to write clearly and neatly on the board and on work sheets.
- Try always to give verbal information or an explanation along with a visual presentation.

FIGURE 10.2

Note: From *Promoting Successful Mainstreaming: Reasonable Classroom Accommodations for Learning Disabled Students* by S. A. Fagen, D. L. Graves, and D. Tessier-Switlick, n.d., Rockville, MD: Montgomery County Public Schools. Adapted with permission.

Accommodations for reading/literature

- Use color highlighting on work sheets to cue the student to important words and concepts.
- Introduce new vocabulary in context before a reading assignment.
- Allow students to use index cards to keep their place while reading.
- Pair students for reading assignments.

Accommodations for math

- Encourage students to verbalize the steps involved in solving a problem as they work through it on paper.
- Give practice in reading word problems just to identify the key words and determine the operation needed to solve the problem.
- Alert students to the importance of paying close attention to the signs of operation on randomly mixed problem work sheets; for example, in the written directions, write WATCH THE SIGNS!
- Exchange practice work sheets with another teacher, which gives each double materials without double work.

Accommodations for social studies/science

- Pause periodically during an oral presentation to ask for questions and give students a chance to add notes to their papers.
- Summarize at the end of the lecture and encourage students to ask questions about what they may have missed in their notes.
- Review the notes from the previous lesson before beginning a new presentation.
- Assign the student with learning disabilities to a reliable work group in lab situations.

FIGURE 10.2
Continued.

Finally, students express the information they have processed and retained, using any of three output components: fine-motor expression, written/motor expression, or verbal expression. Information output can be measured using numerous models. Modifications during the output stage help teachers get the most from the student.

Figures 10.2 through 10.7 provide information on characteristics that may prevail when a student has visual perception, auditory perception, kinesthetic perception, fine motor, written/motor, and verbal expression problems. Within each figure accommodations for assisting students within general education classrooms are included. These figures provide valuable information that may be helpful to all educators.

Seating Arrangements

When students first come into a classroom, where do they sit? Do they return to the same places the next day? Teachers attending a class or a meeting prefer certain places—by the window, next to the door, in the front row, or in the back of the room—and children also have such seating preferences. Teachers should try to provide students with a seating arrangement flexible enough for variety but structured enough for consistency.

Characteristics

- Has trouble distinguishing fine differences between sounds and words (such as *d-t* and *pin-pen*)
- Loses interest or concentration during lectures
- Has difficulty following a series of oral directions
- Cannot accurately record notes from oral presentations
- Displays poor receptive vocabulary
- Repeats what is told before acting or responding
- Often repeats the same question
- Asks questions about oral directions and facts previously given
- May watch the speaker's face intently or lean forward toward the speaker
- Does not enjoy listening to records or rhythmic activities
- Becomes irritated by extraneous noise
- Has difficulty learning and applying phonetic rules
- May have difficulty remembering what is heard

Accommodations for all subject areas

- Seat students in a location where sound is clear; avoid seating near distracting sounds or noises.
- Keep oral directions short and simple. Give one-step directions at first. Gradually increase to two-step directions and so on.
- Accompany oral directions with written directions. List them sequentially, using vocabulary appropriate for the students.
- Ask students to paraphrase your oral directions. Call upon different group members to do this.
- Alert the students when you are giving directions by setting the stage. ("This is important. I'll give you the directions now.") Alert an individual student through eye contact, teacher positioning, or a gentle touch.
- Be conscious of your rate of speech. Talk slower if students indicate they are having difficulty staying with you.
- Assist students to stay with you during instruction by using gestures and changes in the tone and pitch of your voice.
- Allow the students to move to a quiet place in the classroom to do their independent work.
- Write key points on the board for students to copy for studying during a lecture or oral presentation.
- Allow a classmate to use carbon paper to take notes for a student with learning disabilities during a lecture. This allows the student to concentrate on listening. After the lecture, the student can add to the notes his or her classmate took.
- Summarize the key points of your lesson with a visual prop. For instance, after a lesson, use the overhead projector to do a simple work sheet together. This work sheet may use a fill-in-the-blank, true-false, or multiple-choice format. Individual work sheets may or may not accompany the overhead.

FIGURE 10.3

Auditory perception problems and accommodations.

Note: From *Promoting Successful Mainstreaming: Reasonable Classroom Accommodations for Learning Disabled Students* by S. A. Fagen, D. L. Graves, and D. Tessier-Switlick, n.d., Rockville, MD: Montgomery County Public Schools. Adapted with permission.

Accomodations for all subject areas — *continued*

- Try to use visual support (pictures, photographs, charts, maps, films, filmstrips, overheads) with auditory presentations. Many audiovisual materials are available upon request from the school media center.
- Circulate about the room, inconspicuously repeating directions to those who need them. Assign a buddy to repeat directions.
- Take notes yourself or assign a student to take notes on the board, chart paper, overhead, or ditto master during class discussions. This frees the students with learning disabilities to concentrate on listening. Allow the class to copy the notes at the end of the period, or run copies from the ditto master for students who need them.
- Teach students how to listen. Emphasize the importance of correct listening posture, eye contact with the speaker, removal of distracters, and the intent to remember.

Accommodations for reading/literature

- Prepare students for listening by giving them an outline to follow and fill in during class presentations. The outline can be presented on the board or overhead or as an individual handout.
- Set up an audiovisual center with headsets to reinforce listening skills through high-interest visual materials— for example, cassette/book or filmstrip/cassette kits. Stories with repetitious words or phrases may be used.
- Break up oral presentations with visual or motor activities. It is difficult for a student with auditory problems to sit passively while listening for an entire period.

Accommodations for math

- When reading word problems aloud to students, give them a visual clue. Chart or graph the problem on the board, rewrite it simply, use manipulatives, or allow students to draw a picture.
- Show an example of how the problems are to be solved at the top of work sheets. Another option is to complete the first problem or two with the students before they complete the page independently.
- Make a basic problem-solving sequence chart to post in the room. Here is an example:

  1. Read the problem.
  2. Identify key words.
  3. Identify the operation.
  4. Write the number sentence.
  5. Solve the problem.

Accommodations for social studies/science

- Provide ample wait time for students who are having difficulty answering questions. Give a partial sentence, gesture, or visual aid as a clue, if necessary.
- Give students work sheets to follow along with a filmstrip or a film. Stop the film at appropriate points to allow students to fill in the work sheet. This will break up the listening activity into shorter segments. Summarize the film at its conclusion so that students do not lose sense of the whole.
- Use a film or a filmstrip to provide an overview when introducing new material. It can be shown again at the end of the unit to summarize.

Characteristics

- Tries things out; touches, feels, manipulates
- Expresses things physically; jumps for joy, pushes, tugs, stomps, pounds
- Gestures when speaking; is a poor listener; stands very close when speaking or listening; quickly loses interest in long verbal discourse
- Starts the day looking neat and tidy but soon becomes disheveled through physical activity
- Seems impulsive
- Prefers to attack problems physically; seeks solutions that involve the greatest activity
- Handwriting that appears good initially but deteriorates as space runs out on the paper and the student exerts more and more pressure on the writing instrument
- Prefers stories with lots of action, especially in the beginning; rarely an avid reader
- Fidgets a lot while handling books
- Often a poor speller; needs to write words to see if they look correct

Accommodations for all subject areas

- Provide opportunities for direct concrete physical involvement in activities.
- Allow opportunities for materials manipulation.
- Allow opportunities for writing on paper and the chalkboard, drawing, and hands-on activities with real objects that can be touched.
- Use hand signals, small-group discussions, and activities that involve emotions and feelings or enable students to move around.
- Play music as a good method of involving movement; sculpture and clay molding are preferable to painting.
- Plan field trips that enable students to dance or play percussion instruments or to touch items.
- Try activities that allow for gross-motor movement reinforced by visual stimulation.
- Avoid verbal lectures and sedentary classroom activities as much as possible.

FIGURE 10.4
Kinesthetic perception problems and accommodations.

Note: From *Promoting Successful Mainstreaming: Reasonable Classroom Accommodations for Learning Disabled Students* by S. A. Fagen, D. L. Graves, and D. Tessier-Switlick, n.d., Rockville, MD: Montgomery County Public Schools. Adapted with permission.

Some students lose interest in assigned tasks when they sit in the same seats day after day. Possible variations include having students sit on small mats on the floor, taking students to the library for class, or going outside for the lecture. One secondary school, for example, provides learning stations under the trees and uses logs for seating. Teachers then register for outside stations at the times they want.

When adapting classroom seating arrangements for students with mild disabilities, the teacher must consider any special needs the children may have. Also, many students with disabilities are easily distracted and need to be placed close to the teacher.

Characteristics

- Displays poor handwriting and has difficulty forming letters and numbers
- Has difficulty in activities requiring cutting or pasting
- Finds it hard to trace or color within given borders
- Has trouble with speed and neatness in taking notes
- Shows fatigue and restlessness during writing or drawing tasks
- Handwritten work often appears sloppy and disorganized
- Has difficulty manipulating or using small objects and tools
- Usually works slowly in completing written work
- Has trouble making straight lines for connecting points, matching answers, or labeling maps
- Displays poor copying skills

Accommodations for all subject areas

- Set a good handwriting example. A teacher's own handwriting serves as a model for students' writing.
- Place the paper to be copied directly at the top of students' papers rather than to one side or the other when copying is necessary.
- Teach students how to erase and make corrections without beginning over each time. This is a minor matter that can make a big difference in the appearance of students' papers. Students may be able to eliminate unclear, distracting erasures by using erasable pens.
- Minimize copying activities by providing the information or activities on work sheets or handouts. Introduce copying exercises slowly, gradually lengthening the amount of material to be copied.
- Assign follow-up activities that reduce students' writing requirement. Paired talking activities, cooperative small-group assignments, short-answer activity sheets, and instructional games all provide students with opportunities to review skills and knowledge without requiring lengthy written answers.
- Allow a peer with good note-taking skills to use carbon paper to make an extra set of notes for students with learning disabilities.
- Encourage students to acquire typing skills and to type homework assignments.
- Sometimes breaking crayons or pencils forces the child to grip the writing utensil in a more controlled and appropriate manner.

(continued)

FIGURE 10.5
Fine motor problems and accommodations.

Note: From *Promoting Successful Mainstreaming: Reasonable Classroom Accommodations for Learning Disabled Students* by S. A. Fagen, D. L. Graves, and D. Tessier-Switlick, n.d., Rockville, MD: Montgomery County Public Schools. Adapted with permission.

Class Procedures

Class procedures are more effective when they are based on the teacher's awareness of students' various learning styles. It is important to match assignments with learning styles when assigning students to projects, library work, reports, seatwork, or learning centers, especially because the average class assignment is usually too difficult for the student with mild disabilities. The teacher can divide the same assignment into several short segments and use a variety of techniques for presenting the information. Class evaluation procedures also should vary according to learning styles. For example, a teacher can evaluate the work of a student with mild disabilities by simply observing,

Accommodations for reading/literature

- Establish a routine for having students enter new vocabulary into a "word bank" on index cards. Cards can be color-coded for different subjects. Give students opportunities to use these cards to complete skills activities. (For example, ask students to use the cards for classifying activities, matching antonyms or synonyms, or identifying parts of speech.)
- Occasionally allow students to use manipulatives for composing words or sentences. You may use letter puzzle pieces or cubes from commercial materials.

Accommodations for spelling/writing

- Help students understand the importance of good handwriting. Show how correct answers may be marked as incorrect because of poor letter formation. Help students understand that good handwriting is a communication skill that allows others to understand their written ideas and thoughts.

Accommodations for math

- Begin with the easiest problems and add the harder problems in a progressive order on work sheets.
- Fold or divide math paper into fourths, sixths, eighths, and so on. Place one problem per box.

Accommodations for social studies/science

- Give students study guide questions or other advanced organizers for reading assignments.
- Teach students how to use the divided page method of note taking. To begin, students divide a sheet of dated notebook paper lengthwise into thirds by folding. On the left-hand side of the paper, students write key concepts in a word or short phrase. The center section is used to record important subpoints or supporting details relating to each key concept. The right-hand side is used to write a brief summary of the notes on the page. When studying, students refold the paper on the fold line so that their notes are on the outside. The student reads the key point and then tries to recall the important supporting data. To check, he or she turns to the other side of the notes.
- Help students to understand that their notes should serve as a study guide. It is important that they write down the key points, not every word in a lecture.
- Teach students to use abbreviations for note taking. It may be helpful to post abbreviations for specific subject matter vocabulary.
- Ask students to preview the text pages pertinent to your next lecture the night before. The preview may be accomplished by the SQ3R method or simply by skimming the material. This way the student will be ready for the lecture and more apt to recognize important points when mentioned.
- Give students plenty of opportunity to recall new information. Learning is promoted when students do more than just reread.

FIGURE 10.5
Continued.

collecting work samples, or using formative evaluation procedures. Matching the evaluation procedure to the student's learning style helps the teacher evaluate instructional objectives as well as appropriately evaluate the student.

Class procedures must also take into account the emotional aspects of learning styles. Fuhrmann (1980) eloquently summarized the work of Dunn, Dunn, and Price (1979) on these emotional elements: motivation, persistence, responsibility, and structure.

Highly motivated students may need only requirements and resources, but poorly motivated students may require special attention to bring out their interest and desire to learn. For example, a student who is poorly motivated by a traditional lecture class may be highly motivated by a programmed text or a small discussion group.

Characteristics

- Has difficulty writing answers on paper but may be able to give correct answers orally
- Written vocabulary much weaker than spoken vocabulary
- Handwritten work sloppy and disorganized
- Written ideas and concepts usually stronger than writing mechanics (for example, spelling, syntax, vocabulary level)
- Has trouble writing a sentence with a complete thought
- Demonstrates poor spelling skills
- Tests better on objective tests than on tests that require writing (essays and definitions)
- Frequently does not complete written assignments

Accommodations for all subject areas

- Allow students more time to complete written assignments.
- Allow students to give all short answers to questions (single word or phrase).
- Allow students to complete an assignment that calls for written sentences by doing half in sentences and half in short phrases. Gradually students can move toward writing sentences for each question.
- Stress accuracy, not speed. Emphasize the importance of content and legibility.
- Give students some class time to work on written reports. This will enable the teacher to lend needed assistance.
- Be specific in your comments about written work. For example, instead of writing "poor grammar," write "use *doesn't* instead of *don't*." Whenever possible, also give individual feedback.
- Avoid comments that reflect value judgments. Instead of "messy," write "erase mistakes fully before rewriting."
- Allow students to check and correct their own work sheets against a model (individually or in a group). This gives students accurate and complete written information needed for improvement.
- Permit students to use pictures, drawings, and diagrams as part of their written products.
- Post a proofreading checklist in class for students.
- Ask students to skip every other line when writing a rough draft.
- Allow students to do taped or live oral reports instead of written reports. An outline or short written summary may still be required.
- Allow students to answer fewer questions or problems on work sheets requiring written statements—for example, every other problem or asterisked questions.

(continued)

FIGURE 10.6

Written/motor problems and accommodations.

Note: From *Promoting Successful Mainstreaming: Reasonable Classroom Accommodations for Learning Disabled Students* by S. A. Fagen, D. L. Graves, and D. Tessier-Switlick, n.d., Rockville, MD: Montgomery County Public Schools. Adapted with permission.

The same length and type of assignment is probably not appropriate for all students because both attention span and persistence vary greatly. Furthermore, persistence is related to motivation; the more motivated a student is to achieve in a particular learning experience, the more persistent the student is likely to be in completing the task. Sequenced learning tasks, with clearly defined steps and a final goal, offer the teacher some flexibility in meeting the needs of students with differing degrees of persistence.

Accommodations for all subject areas — *continued*

- Consider making work sheets that reduce writing requirements—for example, multiple choice, short answer, matching, or fill-in-the-blank.

- Allow students to check math problems on calculators after working a set number of problems rather than having all problems completed before checking. This reduces writing fatigue while providing more immediate feedback.

- Permit students to work independently in an area free of distractions (away from windows, doors, or traffic areas). Intense concentration is often necessary for students with learning disabilities to write their best.

- Try assigning a different type of task or a modification of the original task as an alternative to asking students to do a poorly completed assignment over again. For example, instead of insisting that sentences be written within the lines, provide wide-lined paper or a typewriter.

- Encourage students to revise, edit, and proofread drafts before making final copies of their reports. Feedback will help students write better final copies. It also gives students the chance to do their own proofing.

- Use journals and diaries as an informal means for encouraging interest and fluency in writing.

- Try using all-student response cards in small-group settings. All students would have the same set of index cards, with each card containing a specific answer. In response to a question posed by the teacher, each student finds the card with the answer he or she believes is correct and holds up the card to the teacher. The teacher gives the correct answer and an explanation to the group if anyone has responded incorrectly. This type of activity could be used for math drills (cards would have numbers on them) or a homonym lesson (cards would have words on them, such as *pare, pair, pear*). Another use of response cards is for multiple-choice questions. Different-colored response cards can represent answer choices, such as blue = A, orange = B.

- Allow students to audiotape answers or work with peers, tutors, or volunteers who perform the writing tasks.

Accommodations for reading/literature

- Provide students with study guides for novels and units.

- Teach students to outline.

- Provide students with a purpose for reading. It is helpful for students to understand that we read differently for different purposes (to answer a specific question, to locate information, or for pleasure).

Accommodations for spelling/writing

- Provide a picture, title, topic sentence, or other prewriting activity to help students begin a creative story. Give students the opportunity to talk about their ideas and jot down key words before writing.

- Cut comic strips to help students organize ideas for writing. Students may be given the strips to sequence in the proper story order. These can serve as guides for writing.

FIGURE 10.6
Continued.

Like motivated students, responsible students require only clear assignments and resources to succeed. Irresponsible students, however, often experience failure and discouragement in such an environment. Usually, students lacking responsibility have historically failed to achieve in school and therefore lack the confidence to assume responsibility. Teachers must attend first to their lack of confidence by offering opportunities for them to experience small successes. Individualizing assignments, breaking objectives into smaller components, trying experimental assignments, and using all types of learning aids and resources may encourage such students.

Accommodations for spelling/writing — *continued*

- Give students guides for structuring creative writing stories by providing an organizational format.
- Give older students story starters (the first part of a story) to read before they are asked to write the story conclusion.
- Group students together to write round robin stories. Each student is responsible for an assigned portion of the whole story. One student may act as the recorder.
- Guide students' writing by giving them specifications or criteria sheets for the content and mechanics of written assignments. These can be valuable proofreading tools for students.
- Emphasize the importance of developing a topic sentence and then sentences of supporting detail when writing paragraphs.
- Provide a structure for writing reports or research papers by giving the class an outline of headings and subheadings to guide their paragraph development.
- Ask students to include the initial wording of the question that their sentence answers.

  Sample question: Why did Mrs. Smith lie to the police?

  Sample answer: Mrs. Smith lied to the police because she thought her brother was guilty.

- Ask older students to use the beginning margin line printed on notebook filler paper as a guide. If necessary, ask them to draw their own ending margin line on the right-hand side of the paper. Younger elementary students may need to draw, or have drawn for them, similar margin lines on both sides of the paper.
- Have students prenumber their answer sheets to ensure accurate matching of answers to question numbers.

Accommodations for math

- Turn lined paper vertically to help students organize math problems. This will help keep the ones, tens, and hundreds places lined up correctly.
- Use large graph paper if turning the paper vertically does not correct the problem. One numeral can be written in each square. Gradually make the transition to regular paper.

Accommodations for social studies/science

- Modify instructional materials that involve fine-motor skills (such as filling in charts, maps, diagrams) by
  1. Using sharp-colored pencils instead of crayons or wide markers
  2. Providing more space for color labeling
  3. Allowing extra time for completion
  4. Setting an index card at borders to prevent going out of bounds

FIGURE 10.6
Continued.

Students also differ in their response to structure—to the specific rules and directions they must follow to achieve certain objectives. More creative students often like a wide variety of options from which to choose, whereas those who are less creative may respond better to a single, well-defined method. Again, the emotional elements are related to one another because the more motivated, persistent, and responsible students require less structure than do the less motivated, less persistent, and less responsible ones (Fuhrmann, 1980).

Teachers, therefore, should make assignments, instruct, evaluate students, and carry out other class procedures on the basis of what they can determine about their students' learning styles and the emotional factors contributing to those styles.

Characteristics

- Does not enjoy discussions, oral presentations, or reading aloud
- Has difficulty explaining himself or herself clearly and coherently
- Displays poor speech—articulation, fluency, expressiveness
- Unable to vocalize thoughts rapidly
- Uses slang or colloquial terms instead of more precise words
- Spoken vocabulary that is much weaker than written vocabulary
- Reluctant to volunteer ideas or respond verbally to questions
- Remarks that are often irrelevant, confusing, or inaccurate
- Uncomfortable speaking in a group
- Has difficulty recalling a word he or she wants to use
- Uses grammatically incorrect sentences

Accommodations for all subject areas

- Give students a little extra time to respond. Many students have to struggle inwardly before being able to complete their thoughts verbally.
- If students are having difficulty, give them a hint to help them along.
- Urge students to use outlines or notes when presenting oral reports.
- Encourage students to use visual aids or handouts in conjunction with oral reports.
- Give students the opportunity to read silently before asking them to read orally.
- Structure opportunities for student verbal expression on a one-on-one basis and in small groups. Avoid calling on students to answer aloud in a group as punishment for inattentiveness during discussions.

FIGURE 10.7
Verbal problems and accommodations.

Note: From *Promoting Successful Mainstreaming: Reasonable Classroom Accommodations for Learning Disabled Students* by S. A. Fagen, D. L. Graves, and D. Tessier-Switlick, n.d., Rockville, MD: Montgomery County Public Schools. Adapted with permission.

Group Size

The group size most effective for instruction varies according to the learning styles of students and the content and purpose of the instruction. Some students learn better in small groups, some in large groups, and others one on one. Careful analysis of student performance helps the teacher select the most appropriate method. Most students with disabilities do not function well in large groups; instead, very small groups and one-on-one instruction are usually more effective.

Attention Span

Although each student has a different attention span, many students with mild disabilities have short ones. Thus, teachers in inclusive settings should vary teaching techniques and activities accordingly. In fact, teachers who match task to attention span find that students master tasks at a faster rate.

For example, a teacher can divide a math lesson for a student with a short attention span into (a) working problems at the desk, (b) completing additional problems at the

---

Accommodations for all subject areas— *continued*

- Limit the length of students' oral presentations. Gradually the length can be increased as students feel more comfortable in front of their peers.
- Actively involve students in listening during other students' presentations. This can be accomplished by deciding, as a group, on the important points of oral presentations. A rating sheet can be made. Students can then rate each other. This method also guides students as they do their own presentations and may avoid misunderstandings about grades.
- Sometimes permit students to use all-student response cards in small groups instead of giving verbal responses.
- Ask specific, structured questions. This will permit the students to use the elements of the question to organize their answers. For example, "Can you tell me one way that comets and meteors are alike?" instead of "compare comets and meteors."
- Arrange small discussion groups and paired talking activities that permit students to practice verbal skills in a smaller, more comfortable setting.
- Permit students to tape their oral presentations instead of doing them live in class.
- Allow students to do projects in lieu of oral reports occasionally, such as demonstrations or displays that demonstrate their understanding of new skills or knowledge.
- Encourage the use of notes, letters, messages, and journals as an alternative to verbal expression.
- Pass the microphone to each reader so that everyone can hear.
- Younger classes can post what day of the week they will be called on to read orally.
- Tell students a day ahead what they will be asked to read tomorrow.

FIGURE 10.7
Continued.

board, and (c) going to the learning center to continue with the same math skill but in a different setting. Teachers should first evaluate tasks according to the type of attention span required to complete them. Then they should adapt both their method of delivery and the tasks themselves to the variations of attention spans within the classroom.

Domains of Learning

After teachers understand students' various learning styles and how certain conditions affect those styles, they need to know about the three domains or taxonomies of learning: cognitive (Bloom, 1956), affective (Krathwohl, Bloom, & Masia, 1964), and psychomotor (Dave, 1970). Instruction falls into one of these three domains and then into one of several levels within each domain.

A teacher's instructional objectives fall into a specific level of one of the taxonomy structures. Usually, teachers teach in the cognitive domain. They should determine the student's present level within the cognitive domain and begin teaching at that level. For example, if an English teacher is presenting a unit on sentence writing (synthesis) and has a student with mild disabilities in the class who is learning the parts of speech (knowledge), the teacher must switch to the knowledge level for that student. The student's present level determines where the teacher should begin teaching. Table 10.2 explains how each level of the cognitive domain relates to students with mild disabilities.

TABLE 10.2
Cognitive domain and students with disabilities.

Level	Consideration for the Student
Knowledge	If the teacher uses a variety of teaching methods and adapts content, students with mild disabilities can succeed at this level. Long-term retention may be difficult.
Comprehension	Most students with mild disabilities can comprehend information. Repetition may be necessary. Concrete rather than abstract information is easier to comprehend. Children with comprehension problems need special assistance.
Application	Applying concrete rather than abstract information is easier for students. Hands-on teaching and functional uses of information make application easier for students.
Analysis	Use whole-part-whole teaching method. Make analysis concrete by letting students with mild disabilities see or touch the division of the whole into parts.
Synthesis	Use whole-part-whole teaching method. Make synthesis concrete by letting students with mild disabilities see or touch the combining of parts into a whole.
Evaluation	This is the most difficult level for many students with mild disabilities. Evaluation in life situations is a natural teaching approach here.

Note: From *Reaching the Hard to Teach* by J. W. Wood, 2004, Richmond, VA: Judy Wood, Inc. Reprinted with permission.

Learning Styles and Instruction

After assessing the learning styles of thousands of at-risk students, Carbo and Hodges (1988) concluded:

> The majority of these youngsters learn best in an informal, highly structured environment that contains soft light and has headsets available for those who learn best with quiet or music—such environments that seldom are provided in our schools. (p. 55)

Compared to achievers, at-risk youngsters also tend to be significantly less visual and auditory and have higher preferences for tactile/kinesthetic stimuli and greater needs for mobility and intake (food or drink). They tend to be unmotivated or strongly adult motivated, can concentrate and learn best with an adult or with peers, are most alert during the late morning or early afternoon hours, and most important, are global learners (p. 55).

Carbo and Hodges (1988) identified the following successful strategies used by teachers for at-risk students:

1. Identify and match student's learning style strengths, especially perceptual and global/analytic abilities.
2. Share information about learning styles with students.
3. De-emphasize skill work requiring a strong analytic learning style.
4. Begin lessons globally.
5. Use a variety of methods in reading.
6. Provide appropriate amounts of structure.
7. Allow youngsters to work with a peer, friend, teacher, or alone depending on their sociological preferences.
8. Establish quiet working sections sufficiently distant from noisy areas.

9. Create at least one special work area in the classroom by placing file cabinets or bookcases perpendicular to a wall.

10. Experiment with scheduling the most difficult subjects during the late morning and early afternoon hours.

Gardner's Frames of Mind

Let's review what we have studied so far in this chapter, and why. First, we looked at instructional structure, which is necessary for a random learner who does not have the natural tendency to impose structure or see logical connections. Second, we looked at learning styles and their importance to learning. The more we know about a student's learning style, the better match we can make between the child's style and the delivery system used to relay the content or subject matter. Now I would like to share Howard Gardner's theory of multiple intelligences (Gardner, 1999).

Understanding the nature of intelligence is just as important as understanding learning styles. Gardner has written numerous books about his philosophy of intelligence, the mind, and so on. His definition of intelligence "is the ability to solve problems, or to create products, that are valued within one or more cultural settings" (Gardner, 1993, p. x). It is important not to measure intelligence through paper and pencil tests. Instead, we should introduce someone to a task and see how well that person can progress beyond the novice stage with or without support. Gardner's multiple intelligences theory focuses on the "distinction among *intelligences, domains,* and *fields. . . .* At the level of the individual, it is proper to speak about one or more human intelligences, or human intellectual proclivities, that are part of our birthright" (1993, p. xvi). He continued:

> Domains, of course, involve human beings, [and] they can be thought of in an impersonal way—because the expertise in a domain can in principle be captured in a book, a computer program, or other kind or artifice. . . . The field—a sociological construct—includes the people, institutions, award mechanisms, and so forth that render judgments about the qualities of individuals' performances. . . . The trio of intelligence, domain, and field has proved not only useful for unraveling a host of issues raised by MI theory, but also particularly fruitful for studies of creativity. . . . The answer is that creativity should not be thought of as inhering principally in the brain, the mind, or the personality of a single individual. Rather, creativity should be thought of as emerging from the interactions of three nodes: the individual with his or her own profile of competencies and values; the domains available for study and mastery within a culture; and the judgments rendered by the field that is deemed competent within a culture. . . . The creative individual is one who regularly solves problems or fashions products in a domain, and whose work is considered both novel and acceptable by knowledgeable members of a field. (pp. xvi–xvii)

Gardner separates intelligence from single IQ scores and categorizes it into eight areas: linguistic, musical, logical-mathematical, spatial, bodily-kinesthetic, interpersonal, intrapersonal, and naturalist intelligence. Just as it is important to understand that students learn in different ways, it is important to know if a student excels in one of Gardner's intelligences. For example, I worked with a student who was extremely low linguistically yet excelled in logical-mathematical intelligence. The reading text was rewritten into a form of math logic, and we progressively moved the student into a standard reading book. Math remained the student's strength, however, and became the delivery system that encouraged the student to read.

Figure 10.8 presents Gardner's eight levels of intelligence with information related to teaching and learning. This figure helps link intelligence level, sensitivity, inclination, and ability (Silver, Strong, & Perini, 2000).

Disposition/ Intelligence	Sensitivity to:	Inclination for:	Ability to:
Verbal- Linguistic Intelligence	the sounds, meanings, structures, and styles of language	speaking, writing, listening, reading	speak effectively (teacher, religious leader, politician) or write effectively (poet, journalist, novelist, copywriter, editor)
Logical- Mathematical Intelligence	patterns, numbers and numerical data, causes and effects, objective and quantitative reasoning	finding patterns, making calculations, forming and testing hypotheses, using the scientific method, deductive and inductive reasoning	work effectively with numbers (accountant, statistician, economist) and reason effectively (engineer, scientist, computer programmer)
Spatial Intelligence	colors, shapes, visual puzzles, symmetry, lines, images	representing ideas visually, creating mental images, noticing visual details, drawing and sketching	create visually (artist, photographer, engineer, decorator) and visualize accurately (tour guide, scout, ranger)
Bodily- Kinesthetic Intelligence	touch, movement, physical self, athleticism	activities requiring strength, speed, flexibility, hand-eye coordination, and balance	use the hands to fix or create (mechanic, surgeon, carpenter, sculptor, mason) and use the body expressively (dancer, athlete, actor)
Musical Intelligence	tone, beat, tempo, melody, pitch, sound	listening, singing, playing an instrument	create music (songwriter, composer, musician, conductor) and analyze music (music critic)
Interpersonal Intelligence	body language, moods, voice, feelings	noticing and responding to other people's feelings and personalities	work with people (administrators, managers, consultants, teachers) and help people identify and overcome problems (therapists, psychologists)
Intrapersonal Intelligence	one's own strengths, weaknesses, goals, and desires	setting goals, assessing personal abilities and liabilities, monitoring one's own thinking	meditate, reflect, exhibit self-discipline, maintain composure, and get the most out of oneself
Naturalist Intelligence	natural objects, plants, animals, naturally occurring patterns, ecological issues	identifying and classifying living things and natural objects	analyze ecological and natural situations and data (ecologists and rangers), learn from living things (zoologist, botanist, veterinarian) and work in natural settings (hunter, scout)

FIGURE 10.8

Intelligences as dispositions.

Note: From *So Each May Learn: Integrating Learning Styles and Multiple Intelligences* (p. 11), by H. F. Silver, R. W. Strong, and M. J. Perini, 2000, Alexandria, VA: Association for Supervision and Curriculum Development. © 2000 by Silver Strong & Associates, L.L.C. Reprinted with permission.

To purchase this title, please call 800–962–4432 or visit www.ThoughtfulEd.com online.

ADAPTING TEACHING TECHNIQUES

A **teaching technique** or strategy is a method of imparting knowledge, skills, or concepts to a learner. Historically, colleges and universities have recommended various teaching techniques to educators, who in turn have used those techniques in public and private schools. How teachers teach and what types of strategies they employ depend greatly on previous training, models observed, areas of interest, value judgments, and common sense. According to Jarolimek and Foster (1981), "There is a great deal of disagreement, even among well-informed persons, about what constitutes good teaching and how teaching should take place" (p. 109).

This section, then, does not try to teach teachers how to teach but simply presents a variety of techniques that teachers can use in different situations or modify for particular students. Specifically, the section concerns ways of adapting instruction within teaching modes and techniques.

Teaching Modes

Jarolimek and Foster (1981) identified four major teaching modes: expository, inquiry, demonstration, and activity (see Figure 10.9). Each mode has specific teaching techniques common to it, and teachers can adapt or modify all these techniques for students in inclusive settings.

Expository Mode

Teaching in the expository mode centers around the "concept exposition, which means most simply to provide an explanation" (Jarolimek & Foster, 1981, p. 110). This mode, probably the most popular among educators, requires extensive directive teaching. The class focuses on the teacher, who explains or disseminates the information; students are involved only minimally. General education teachers report using this mode 53% of the time during instruction, whereas special education teachers use the expository mode

Expository	Inquiry	Demonstration	Activity
Lecture	Asking questions	Experiments	Role playing
Telling	Stating hypotheses	Exhibits	Constructing
Sound filmstrip	Coming to conclusions	Simulations	Preparing exhibits
Explanation	Interpreting	Games	Dramatizing
Panels	Classifying	Modeling	Processing
Recitation	Self-directed study	Field trips	Group work
Audio recording	Testing hypotheses		
Motion pictures	Observing		
Discussion	Synthesizing		

FIGURE 10.9

Specific techniques used in various teaching modes.

Note: From Jarolimek, J., & Foster, C. D. (1981). *Teaching and learning in the elementary school* (pp. 131–132). New York: Macmillan. Copyright 1981 by Macmillan, Adapted by permission.

TABLE 10.3
Expository mode: Alternative teaching techniques.

Teaching Techniques	Alterations or Modifications for Mainstreamed Students
Lecture	• Provide lecture outlines. • Provide copy of lecture notes. • Use transparencies to provide visual presentation simultaneously with lecture.
Telling	• Keep lecture short. • Be specific about information given. • Be sure you have students' attention. • For students with short attention spans, give information in small segments.
Sound filmstrip	• Provide visuals when possible. • Give earphones to students easily distracted by sounds.
Explanation	• Keep explanations simple and direct. • Give them in simple declarative sentences. • Provide outline of explanation.
Audio recording	• Present recordings with visuals. • Give earphones to students easily distracted by sounds.
Motion pictures	• Orient students to movie before showing. • Be sure length is appropriate. • Place students with auditory problems close to sound. • Review main points of film. • Provide brief outline of main points.
Discussion	• Ask questions you know students can answer. • Keep discussion short. • As points are made, list them on board or transparency. • Divide class into groups for brief discussions. • Keep students on topic. • Involve everyone on appropriate levels. • Use organizer to group ideas and show conclusion drawn.

Note: From *Reaching the Hard to Teach,* by J. W. Wood, 2004, Richmond, VA: Judy Wood, Inc. Reprinted with permission.

only 24% of the time. Table 10.3 presents the specific teaching techniques used in the expository mode, with suggested adaptations for each. In four of these techniques—lecture, telling, explanation, and discussion—the teacher orally delivers information. These four techniques account for 93% of the time that general education teachers teach in the expository mode and 87% for special education teachers (Wood, 1993).

Presenting new skills or concepts orally (lecturing, explaining, discussing, telling) can make learning extremely difficult for the student who cannot impose structure on learning. Educators can use the following suggestions for adapting these types of techniques:

1. *Multisensory input.* Visual aid materials that address a variety of learning styles should be an important instructional consideration. Because students learn through many sensory systems, educators need to use numerous modes to enhance oral presentations and provide multisensory input for students. Students need to be taught in the different perceptual styles—visually, auditorially, and tactually. Using the overhead projector to present main points or underline or circle main ideas is an excellent technique

ACCOMMODATING TECHNOLOGY

Overhead Projectors and Computer Projection Systems

The overhead projector is still a very common piece of equipment used by teachers, especially at the secondary level. The principles that are a foundation for the use of the overhead projector can be carried over to the use of computer-generated presentations. This section suggests ways of making and using adaptations for presentations that may involve the use of overhead projectors or computer projection systems, ideas for making transparencies or presentations more effective, tips for teaching with transparencies or computer projection systems, ideas for using the overhead or computer projection system according to subject area, teaching with transparencies or presentation slides, and computer technology in today's classroom.

USES AND ADAPTATIONS FOR OVERHEAD PROJECTORS AND COMPUTER PROJECTION SYSTEMS

Teachers can effectively use the overhead projector or a computer projection system in numerous ways. Here are a few examples:

- Provide a visualization to support the main points in a lecture. This visualization can be created through the development of a series of notes or drawings on transparencies or in a computer-generated presentation such as Power-Point or Claris Works.
- Introduce new concepts or new material by creating a "set" that highlights new terms or vocabulary with a drawing or picture that represents the concept.
- Encourage class discussions or full class participation by identifying key questions, drawings, or pictures that will stimulate discussion on the topics related to the instructional lesson. This strategy is particularly effective for presenting math concepts in a problem-solving scenario.
- Visually reinforce directions by displaying them on the overhead projector or the computer projection system.

IDEAS FOR MAKING TRANSPARENCIES OR PRESENTATIONS MORE EFFECTIVE

Participating in a class on how to prepare computer-based presentations will help you make effective use of computer projection systems and overhead projectors in the classroom.

Following are some general tips on presentations:

- Use a font size and type that can be read by anyone in the room. Generally a 24-point standard font will accomplish this goal.
- Use colors that provide a distinct contrast for easier viewing throughout the classroom.
- Be familiar with the type of lighting in the classroom. If the room maintains a high source of light, use a darker contrast in the background and in the print on the presentation or transparency.

(continued)

TIPS FOR TEACHING WITH TRANSPARENCIES OR COMPUTER PROJECTION SYSTEMS

- To orient students before your lecture, prepare a lecture outline on the overhead projector or computer presentation.
- Permit students to use these technologies for their presentations. This will help them organize their thoughts and ideas.
- Use a variety of colors to generate interest and emphasize or differentiate areas, content, and certain categories.
- Use only a few points or items per transparency or slide. Too much information on a transparency or slide lessens its impact.
- Prepare student handouts that provide information about materials shown on the overhead. This is an easy process when preparing presentations using a presentation software application.
- Use only boldface or a primary type when generating transparencies, slides, or computer presentations.

IDEAS FOR USING THE OVERHEAD PROJECTOR OR COMPUTER PROJECTION SYSTEM ACCORDING TO SUBJECT AREA

Art Evaluation

- Use cutout designs to demonstrate shapes or the basic principles of formal and informal balance.
- Cut headlines from newspapers and catalogs to demonstrate the differences among Roman, Gothic, and text lettering styles.
- Create a color-lift transparency or slide of a face. By using overlays and water-soluble pens, facial structures can be discussed.

English

- Use a transparency or slide to demonstrate the use of library card catalogs, or make excerpts from a reader's guide to explain research guidelines.
- Use transparencies or slides to construct different paragraphs to explain structure, grammar, spelling, and clarity. (Students could write paragraphs as well.)
- Use transparencies or slides to demonstrate the conjugation of verbs, sentence structure, speech, and the relationship of words.
- Demonstrate different styles of letters on a transparency or slide.
- Make a transparency or slide of excerpts from good papers you have collected to demonstrate the technique of good writing.

Math

- Use geometric shapes on transparencies to teach fractions.
- Make a transparency or slide of a graph grid. If the overhead is being projected onto the chalkboard, use chalk to plot the lines on the graph.
- Use newspaper clippings to present math word problems or exercises in probability.

Social Studies

- To discuss the function of our voting system, make transparencies or slides like sample ballots. Use them to discuss candidates, issues in policy, and amendments.
- Outlines of maps can be generated to teach the concepts of latitude and longitude. Maps can be generated to teach the recognition of states.

Science

- Before conducting experiments, prepare transparencies or slides that list the materials to be used.
- List the steps of an experiment on a transparency or slide. Demonstrate each step.

Career and Technical Education

- Use drawings to help students identify tools and their functions.
- Use the overhead to visualize the correct technique for sharpening tools.
- Use transparencies or slides and overlays to explain the parts and the function of a machine and machine safety devices.

TEACHING WITH TRANSPARENCIES OR PRESENTATION SLIDES

As you prepare to teach with transparencies or using a computer-generated presentation, you must plan for the use of these tools. Before you teach, during teaching, and after teaching are all times to use these tools. If your lesson plan involves a class discussion, develop a transparency or slide that presents the major points of the lesson. If you have a transparency or slide that contains detailed information, such as a diagram, a map, or parts of the digestive system, give the students a matching copy on which to record notes. Most of the computer-generated presentation applications include steps for printing handouts that can be used by students. Keep a file for transparencies or slides, and organize and label them under subject headings, titles, or lesson topics. Use a database to describe the transparency or slide contents and any accompanying activities. To learn more about how to appropriately use presentation tools in a classroom, classes and online tutorials are good ways to get started.

COMPUTER TECHNOLOGY IN TODAY'S CLASSROOM

Education is a responsibility and reflection of society. Education today is quickly reflecting the changes of the information age or our emerging "e-world." To prepare all students, especially those with disabilities, to be successful in this new age, teachers must understand the impact of technology. The information age creates a framework for change in how we learn, what we learn, how we apply what we know to society, and how we prepare for post–high school success. In this information age, students with disabilities can have unlimited opportunities, but if they are not prepared for this new technological/electronic global world and economy, these same students will face even greater challenges in accessing opportunities.

PRACTICAL APPLICATIONS

Creating a strong visual or auditory presence in the classroom through multimedia and technology strengthens the learning experiences for all students. Some strategies involving the power of bulletin boards for enhancing learning are as follows:

- A bulletin board shows a surfer on a wave that extends into the room. The surfer can be moved onto the wave, under the wave, around the wave, and so on. Can you guess what the teacher is teaching with this bulletin board? Prepositions! Prepositions are very abstract, but the surfer bulletin board turns this abstraction into a concrete learning experience.
- A bulletin board is an excellent place for exhibiting student work. While focusing on the ability to communicate a concept, students' writing samples about the concept or pictures that communicate the concept can be placed on the bulletin board. To provide an opportunity for all student work to be displayed, vary the topics or concepts and include a rotation list to ensure that no student has been overlooked when posting class work.
- A bulletin board makes an excellent student assignment. Create teams of students in the class that have the rotational responsibility of developing a bulletin board. This strategy can also be used to create a little healthy competition and creativity between teams of students.
- A bulletin board can come alive with the incorporation of a small portable CD or tape player. A bulletin board on the life of Dr. Martin Luther King can include a tape clip of one of his speeches. Review chapter 8 for additional suggestions about planning bulletin boards.

CHALKBOARD OR DRY ERASE BOARD

The chalkboard or dry erase board is a common support item found in almost every classroom. When using the chalkboard or dry erase board, be sure that it is clean and that the color of chalk or marker shows up from all angles of the classroom. Strategies for using the chalkboard or dry erase board for enhancing learning include the following:

- Organize your ideas and keep writing to a minimum. For example, if you are discussing explorers, what they discovered, and important dates, develop a table with three headings (explorers, what was discovered, important dates) and write it on the chalkboard or dry erase board. After the class discussion, each student will have a clear, organized picture of the day's lesson.
- Use one section of the board on a daily basis to identify the day's schedule, homework assignments, special events, etc.
- A calendar of upcoming assignments and checkpoints for those assignments can help students start to plan and organize their time effectively. For example, if a term paper is due in 30 days, the weekly reminder could state the component of the paper that should be completed by the end of the week in order to complete the entire paper within the 30 days.
- Use color to differentiate among key points of a lesson.
- Use freehand drawing to assist students in understanding key points or concepts.
- Have students work in pairs or small groups at the board on problem-solving activities.
- To strengthen all classroom activities, use the chalkboard or dry erase board in conjunction with additional media in the environment, such as bulletin boards, and overhead projectors, or computer presentations.

for orienting students to the material. Videotapes provide instant playback of information for reinforcement. Students who miss a portion of the class will also benefit from a video-tape. Audiotape recorders are excellent audiovisual aids for reinforcement of oral mate-rials. Graphic materials such as globes and maps reinforce both visually and tactually the material to be learned. Bulletin boards assist the teacher in presenting new informa-tion or providing reinforcement. Presenting information for multisensory input not only en-hances classroom instruction but also provides for and addresses the perceptual learning styles of students.

2. *Acquisition outlines.* Acquisition outlines present students with a graphic whole-part-whole method of learning. This method of adapting assists students in seeing the whole of the presentation and then hearing a discussion of the parts. The acquisition outline serves as a formative study guide. The teacher should provide an acquisition outline when presenting new information, concepts, or skills to be learned. Before the unit of study begins, a summative study guide is provided, which sets the stage for studying (see chapter 11). The teacher can place the acquisition outline on the overhead projector or give each student a copy to be completed. When introduc-ing the outline, the teacher should follow these steps:

(a) Introduce the topic.

(b) Explain how the topic for today continues yesterday's lesson and will extend into tomorrow's lesson.

(c) Introduce each of the major topics (points 1, 2, 3, and so on).

(d) Point out that related topics are listed beneath each major point.

(e) Return to point 1.

(f) Review the topics listed under point 1.

(g) Begin the discussion of point 1.

(h) When the lesson is over, return to the whole outline and review the topics.

(i) Have the student file the outline in the appropriate notebook section.

(j) Save a copy for the teacher's note-taking file.

Acquisition outlines keep students from guessing what will be coming next, help them perceive the organization of the presentation, and serve as a formative study guide for test review. Here are some general tips for using acquisition outlines:

(a) The acquisition outline can be developed into one of three formats: blank, partial, or completed. The more difficulty a student has in organizing and absorbing orally presented information, the more information should be provided on the outline.

(b) When covering a point that is further explained within a text or a handout, tell the students to write the page number from the text or the name of the handout in the left margin.

(c) If some points on the outline require extensive note taking, the teacher may provide a handout to promote accurate reception of information and save instructional time.

An example of an acquisition outline appears in Figure 10.10.

Mr. Able was teaching angles to his fifth-grade class. Prior to class he developed an acquisition outline to assist all learners, especially the learners at risk. Figure 10.11 presents the outline Mr. Able used. Mr. Able was able to complete the lesson quickly with little lesson repeat or reteach. The learners at risk quickly understood the concept of an angle, the definition, and the types.

Topic: Vertebrates

   I. Mammals—Textbook page 120
      A. Have hair or fur
      B. Feed babies with mother's milk

   II. Fish—Textbook page 122
      A. Have gills
      B. Live in water

   III. Amphibians—Textbook page 130
      A. Have scaleless skin
      B. Usually live part of life in water and part of life out of water

   IV. Reptiles—Textbook page 133
      A. Have dry, scaly skin
      B. Some live on land and some live in water

   V. Birds—Textbook page 140
      A. Have feathers, wings, and beaks
      B. Bones filled with air

FIGURE 10.10
Acquisition outline.

Note: From *Reaching the Hard to Teach* by J. W. Wood, 2004, Richmond, VA: Judy Wood, Inc. Reprinted with permission.

3. *Graphic organizers.* Information within classrooms is most often presented in a linguistic manner. We talk to students or have them read printed text. When nonlinguistic representation is coupled with linguistic, students are better able to think about and recall knowlege (Marzano, Pickering, & Pollock, 2001). Common concepts educators use may be developed into organizers (see Figure 10.12).

4. *Audiotaped presentations.* Frequently students are unable to write down all the important information provided. The student who is a strong visual learner may miss important facts. Letting students tape-record the presentations provides for additional reinforcement at a later time.

Inquiry Mode

The inquiry mode involves "asking questions, seeking information, and carrying on an investigation" (Jarolimek & Foster, 1981, p. 116). This mode of teaching follows five basic steps: "(a) defining a problem, (b) proposing hypotheses, (c) collecting data, (d) evaluating evidence, and (e) making a conclusion" (p. 116). The teacher's guidance is still important, but the inquiry mode allows for more teacher–pupil interaction and encourages a team approach to teaching. For many students, however, the teacher often needs to provide some additional structure. Table 10.4 suggests teaching techniques for the inquiry mode.

The inquiry mode is used 23% of the time by general educators and 35% by special educators. Of the techniques listed (see Table 10.4), general education teachers report asking questions 66% of the time, whereas special education teachers ask them 59% of the time. Asking questions of students with disabilities and those at risk can accomplish many things during the lesson. According to Davies (1981), questions help motivate students by getting their attention or gaining their interest, encourage students to think, involve more than one student in the instructional process, and provide feedback for the teacher on students' progress.

I. Angles
   A. Definition: Two rays with a common end point

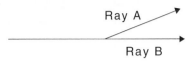

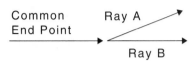

   B. Types of Angles
      1. Right Angle
         a. Definition: Exactly 90°
         b. Example

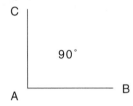

      2. Acute Angle
         a. Definition: Less than 90°
         b. Example

      3. Obtuse Angle
         a. Definition: Greater than 90° but less than 180°
         b. Example

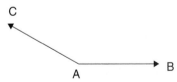

FIGURE 10.11
Acquisition outline.

Note: From *Reaching the Hard to Teach* by J. W. Wood, 2004, Richmond, VA: Judy Wood, Inc. Reprinted with permission.

Raphael (1982) suggested four types of questions, which can be placed into either of two categories: in-the-book questions and in-the-head questions. Helping students understand question types or marking the question type for them helps when they are attempting to answer questions orally or are looking in a text to find answers to written questions. Table 10.5 lists the four types of questions and their characteristics.

As teachers teach, they deliver information, require students to learn the information, and ask questions from one of the six levels of Bloom's cognitive taxonomy to

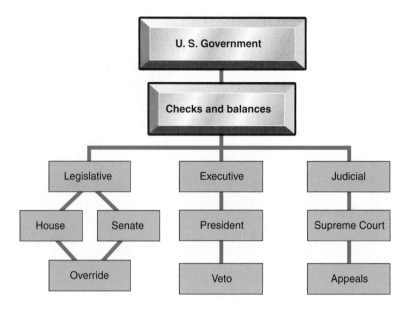

FIGURE 10.12
Acquisition outlines.

Note: From *Reaching the Hard to Teach* by J. W. Wood, 2004, Richmond, VA: Judy Wood, Inc. Reprinted with permission.

STUDENT KNOWLEDGE CHECK

The vignette at the beginning of this chapter described a problem with teaching angles that Mr. Able was experiencing. By now you have found within the chapter how Mr. Able solved the problem.

  1. Could you suggest other methods of delivery Mr. Able could use?
  2. How would knowledge of the students' styles of learning help Mr. Able?

see if students have retained the information. Asking questions is a natural part of instruction. Teachers ask questions to assess student attention and comprehension, but they need to realize that questions also reflect taxonomy levels. Adapting instruction for students in inclusive settings involves knowing the level of one's questions and changing that level if necessary. Questions directed at special needs students should relate to their specific levels of learning. Particular word choice can help teachers relate instruction to specific levels on Bloom's (1956) taxonomy. Figure 10.13 lists verbs to use for stating behavioral objectives.

The following general suggestions will help teachers determine how to ask questions of students with disabilities and those at risk:

1. Ask questions at the taxonomy level at which the student is functioning.

2. Provide wait time for responses. Extra time is necessary for responses to divergent questions (Kindsvatter, Wilen, & Ishler, 1988). Research shows that teachers usually allow about 1 second for a response, but students typically need 3 to 5 seconds (Rowe, 1974).

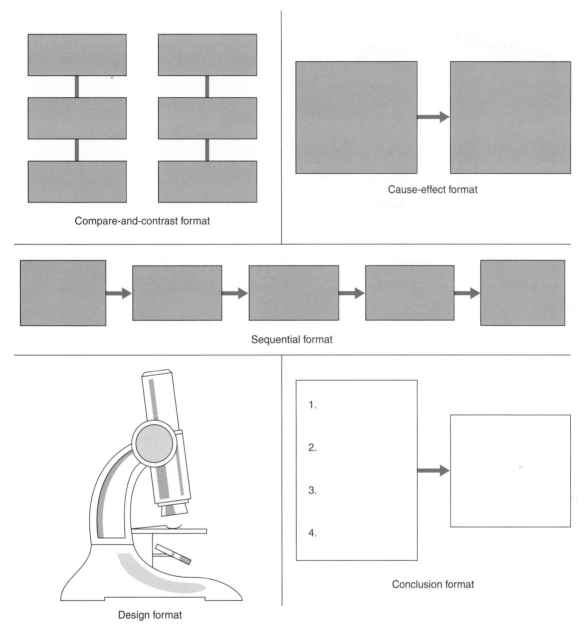

Compare-and-contrast format

Cause-effect format

Sequential format

Design format

Conclusion format

FIGURE 10.12
Continued.

3. Allow wait time for all students to think about an answer given by one student before proceeding to the next question.

4. Ask questions in a planned and patterned order or sequence. Factors that influence the choice of sequence include the lesson's objective, student's ability level, and student's understanding of the content covered (Kindsvatter et al., 1988).

TABLE 10.4
Inquiry mode: Alternative teaching techniques.

Teaching Techniques	Alterations or Modifications for Mainstreamed Students
Asking questions	• Use appropriate wait time. • Ask questions on appropriate level of taxonomy scale; vary questions to meet different taxonomy levels of students. • Call student's name before directing a question to him or her. • Do not embarrass students by asking questions they cannot answer.
Stating hypotheses	• Have students choose from two or three hypotheses instead of having to formulate their own. • Provide model for writing hypotheses.
Coming to conclusions	• Present alternative conclusions. • List information needed for conclusions.
Interpreting	• Assign peer tutor to help. • Present alternative interpretations.
Classifying	• Use concrete instead of abstract concepts. • Provide a visual display with models.
Self-directed study	• Give specific directions about what to do. • Make directions short, simple, and few. • Collect and place resources for study in one area.
Testing hypotheses	• Assign peer tutor.
Observing	• Give explicit directions about how and what to observe. • Provide sequential checklist of what will happen so that student sees steps. • Have student check off each step observed.
Synthesizing	• Assign peer tutor to help. • Provide model of whole.

Note: From *Reaching the Hard to Teach* by J. W. Wood, 2004, Richmond, VA: Judy Wood, Inc. Reprinted with permission.

5. Remember that some sequencing begins with lower level questions and progresses to higher level thinking. Some students will start with higher level questions and remain there (Kindsvatter et al., 1988).

6. Because responses to lower level questions determine student understanding of content, use those responses as an indication of starting points for reteaching.

7. Allow student to formulate questions to ensure active participation in the questioning process (Kindsvatter et al., 1988).

8. State questions clearly and specifically.

9. When asking a question, state the question, call the student's name, and repeat the question.

10. Encourage all students to participate in the questioning process by responding in a positive way to all student responses.

11. Avoid sarcasm, reprimand, personal attack, accusation, or no response at all as teacher responses to student answers (West, 1975).

TABLE 10.5
Question types.

Broad Categories	Question Type	Characteristics
In-the-book questions	1. Right-there questions	• Literal questions • Detailed in nature • Found *right* in text • *Example:* "What color are the girl's eyes?"
	2. Think-and-search questions	• Answer in text but not in one place. • *Example:* Putting events into sequence
In-the-head questions	3. Author-and-you questions	• Inferences/conclusions required • Involve learner's prior knowledge • *Example:* "Why did the man decide to wear black?"
	4. On-your-own-questions	• Cannot be answered from the text • Learner must use own experience • Questions asked before reading • Extensive questions • *Example:* "How are modern cars and the cars of the 1920s different?"

Note: Table adapted from Raphael, Taffy E. (1986, February). Teaching question and answer relationships, revisited. *The Reading Teacher, 39*(6), 516–522. Reprinted with permission of Taffy E. Raphael and the International Reading Association.

The teacher in this picture is using the overhead projector for delivery of instruction. The classroom is also very engaging for the learner. From looking at the picture, what do you see that is learner engaged?

1. *Knowledge:* remembering previously learned material

cite	know	pick	state
define	label	pronounce	underline
fill in	list	quote	write
find	match	recall	
group	memorize	recite	
identify	name	reproduce	

Answer who? what? when? where?

2. *Comprehension:* ability to grasp the meaning of material

account for	discover	manage	re-word
alter	expand	paraphrase	show
change	explain	relate	substitute
convert	extend	reorganize	summarize
define	give examples	rephrase	translate
demonstrate	group	represent	vary
depict	illustrate	restate	
describe	interpret	reward	

3. *Application:* ability to use learned materials in new and concrete situations

apply	employ	predict	select
choose	evidence	prepare	show
classify	experiment	present	solve
compute	interview	put into action	use
construct using	manage	put together	utilize
demonstrate	manifest	put to use	
direct	model	record	
discover	organize	relate	

Answer how many? what? what is? Write an example.

FIGURE 10.13
Verbs for stating behavioral objectives.

Note: From *Reaching the Hard to Teach* by J. W. Wood, 2004, Richmond, VA: Judy Wood, Inc. Reprinted with permission.

12. If students hesitate to raise their hands to ask questions in class, tape pockets to their desks containing cards (any color will do). Have students take out the cards and put them on the corner of their desks if they have questions or do not understand. Check for these cards as you walk around the room.

13. Have a question box on the teacher's desk for students who are hesitant to answer questions.

4. *Analysis:* ability to break down material into its component parts so that its organizational structure may be understood

analyze	determine	divide	search
ascertain	diagnose	examine	separate
associate	diagram	find	simplify
break down	difference	infer	sort
classify	discover	inspect	survey
compare	discriminate	outline	take apart
contrast	dissect	put into categories	uncover
designate	distinguish	reduce	

5. *Synthesis:* ability to put parts together to form a new whole

blend	develop	make up	rearrange
build	devise	modify	revise
combine	expand	originate	rewrite
compile	extend	plan	suppose
compose	form	pose	synthesize
conceive	generalize	predict	theorize
construct	imagine	produce	write
create	integrate	propose	
design	invent	project	

Answer how can we improve? what would happen if? how can we solve?

6. *Evaluation:* ability to judge the value of material for a given purpose

appraise	criticize	evaluate	rate
assess	critique	grade	recommend
award	decide	judge	weigh
compare	deduce	justify	
conclude	defend	measure	
contrast	determine	rank	

FIGURE 10.13
Continued.

14. Use color responses. All students will have three cards for responding. When a question is asked, each student will put a card at chest level. For example:

Green: Ask me; I know.

Yellow: Maybe I know; I'll try.

Red: Don't call on me; I don't know.

15. Have students respond to questions as follows:

Four fingers: I know the answer.

Three fingers: I know the answer, but I don't want to answer.

Two fingers: I don't know the answer.

One finger: Please rephrase the question.

16. Have a "ponder period" during which students sit in groups to ponder questions and answers before the question activity.

17. Give each student two chips. This gives them the opportunity to answer a question or contribute information. When chips are used, the student has made a contribution. This helps the teacher give many students the opportunity to contribute.

18. Tell a student who may not know answers to raise one hand and place the other hand on the desk. Skip that student. When one hand is up and the other hand is not on the desk, the student is signaling that he or she knows the answer to the question.

Demonstration Mode

Essential components of the demonstration mode are "showing, doing, and telling" (Jarolimek & Foster, 1981, p. 120). Like the expository mode, the demonstration mode depends on directive teaching. Because it presents information in a concrete way, this method is essential for teachers to use when instructing students with disabilities.

Table 10.6 presents techniques used in the demonstration mode, with suggested alterations for included students. The demonstration mode is used only 3% of the time by general educators and 6% by special educators. Of the techniques listed in Table 10.6, general educators use experiments 34% of the time, and special educators use modeling 36% of the time.

Modeling is an excellent technique to use for students who are having difficulty understanding the information presented. Models may be visual (such as a map, chart, or globe) or verbal (such as a language mode). Models may also be participatory, in which the teacher demonstrates a skill and the students become actively involved. Here are some suggestions for modeling:

1. Exaggerate the modeling presentation.
2. If the steps in the model are lengthy or difficult, use several short time spans rather than one long demonstration.
3. Videotape the modeling demonstration for students to replay and replicate.
4. When repeating the steps in a model, use the same sequence you used in the original presentation.
5. Provide a checklist of the steps in the model for students to follow as you demonstrate.
6. Provide auditory clues along with visual cues.
7. When a student is implementing a model, reward the student's behavior.
8. Use modeling for social, technical, or academic skills.
9. As a student models a desired skill, use the situation to point out the behavior to other students.

Activity Mode

The activity mode of teaching is "a set of strategies that involve pupils in learning by doing things that are, for the pupils, meaningfully related to the topic under study" (Jarolimek & Foster, 1981, p. 127). This method of teaching is best described by an old Native American proverb: "I hear and I forget, I see and I re-

TABLE 10.6
Demonstration mode: Alternative teaching techniques.

Teaching Techniques	Alterations of Modifications for Mainstreamed Students
Experiments	• Provide sequential directions. • Have student check off each completed step. If teacher demonstrates, let student assist. • Be sure student fully understands purpose, procedures, and expected outcome of experiment. • Set up incidental learning experiences. • Display materials. • Model the activity. • Provide an outline and a handout/checklist. • Make a list of lab procedures and assign a lab procedure. • Tape instructions and videotape demonstrations.
Exhibits	• Assign projects according to student's instructional level. • Have student select project topic from a short list. • Provide directions and list of materials needed. • Be sure project does not require skills student lacks. • Have student display his or her exhibits.
Simulations	• Do not embarrass the student by requiring him or her to do something that the student cannot do. • Make sure the student understands directions, terms used, and expected outcome.
Games	• Design games making skills, not winning, the priority. • Make directions simple. • Highlight important directions with color codes. • With peer tutor, let student prepare own game. • Design games; emphasize skills needed by student.
Modeling	• Model only one step at a time. • Use task analysis on steps. • Use visual models when possible. • Exaggerate the presentation to make the concept being modeled clear. • Use several short time spans rather than one long demonstration. • Model in hierarchical sequence. • Use video modeling for student to replay. Perform in same manner as the first presentation. • Provide a lecture outline on which the student may take notes.
Field trips	• Prepare students by explaining destination, purpose, expected behavior, and schedule. • Provide a checklist of expectations.

Note: From *Reaching the Hard to Teach* by J. W. Wood, 2004, Richmond, VA: Judy Wood, Inc. Reprinted with permission.

member, I do and I understand." By using the activity mode, teachers provide students with actual experience and thus a clearer understanding of concepts. The activity mode is used 21% of the time by general educators and 35% of the time by special educators. Table 10.7 suggests activities to accompany the techniques in the activity mode.

TABLE 10.7
Activity mode: Alternative teaching techniques.

Teaching Techniques	Alterations or Modifications for Mainstreamed Students
Role playing	• Be sure student understands role. • Short lines or no lines at all may be best. • Respect privacy of student who does not want role. • Let such a student assist another role player.
Constructing	• Select project for students or have them select from a short list. • Try to use projects that include special education objectives. • Provide sequential checklist.
Preparing exhibits	• Assign peer tutor to help. • Use alterations suggested for "constructing."
Dramatizing	• Respect privacy of those who do not want parts. • Let such students help others prepare sets, and so on.
Processing	• Clearly state steps. • Make steps sequential and short. • List steps on board.
Group work	• Assign peer tutor. • Select activity in which students can succeed. • Use variety of grouping procedures (see chapter 8).
Game/contest	• Be sure game matches lesson objective. • Check game to see if required decision-making skills match students' ability level. • List rules for engaging clearly on board. • Keep pace appropriate. • Assign a buddy. • Provide feedback for game skill as well as for social skills used.

Note: From *Reaching the Hard to Teach* by J. W. Wood, 2004, Richmond, VA: Judy Wood, Inc. Reprinted with permission.

The technique of group work is used 66% of the time by general educators and 72% of the time by special educators. Group work is a method of structuring a class so that students work together to achieve a shared academic goal. As you have learned, there are three kinds of group work: peer tutoring, group projects, and jigsaw. For details about each one, refer back to chapter 8.

Group work has several advantages:

1. Students are responsible for other group members, which encourages liking and learning among students.
2. Assignments can be individualized without working one on one.
3. Teachers can structure students' assignments so that each group member can succeed.
4. Mainstreamed students can be given a short, simple part of the assignment.
5. Group work reduces the time a teacher must spend in preparation.
6. It improves behavior control by minimizing the time focused on one student.
7. It motivates reluctant students through social interaction.

8. It prevents boredom through a variety of group assignments.

9. Students can contribute something from their area of expertise. For example, if they are good in art, they can volunteer (or be assigned) to do the art for the group.

10. Because all students are equally involved in the group's decision, mainstreamed students feel highly motivated.

Role playing is another useful technique in the activity mode. Here are several suggestions for incorporating it into your teaching:

1. Select the role-playing situation.

2. Warm up with some simple charades or another similar exercise.

3. Explain the general situation to participants and observers.

4. State the problem to be worked on, including the setting.

5. Explain the roles that participants will be playing.

6. Explain the roles that the audience will be expected to perform.

7. Start the role playing with a discussion.

8. Follow the role playing with a discussion.

9. Evaluate the exercise.

Role playing has several advantages:

1. Students can express their true feelings without risk.

2. Students can discuss private issues without embarrassment.

3. Students learn to empathize with others by taking on another identity.

4. Students practice alternative behaviors and attitudes.

5. Role playing brings academic subjects to life and thus makes them more meaningful.

6. Motivation and interest increase because they are based on an activity.

Additional Teaching Techniques

In addition to the teaching modes mentioned in Tables 10.3, 10.4, 10.6 and 10.7, other techniques are used for delivering instruction. It is important to remember that the techniques discussed next also use the specific techniques listed in the preceding section. For example, you could use scaffolding as you lecture (expository mode), ask questions (inquire mode), model (demonstration mode), or process (activity mode).

The following strategies are selected from an excellent work published in 2003, *Removing Barriers: Research-Based Strategies for Teaching Those Who Learn Differently,* by Anne Parkinson, Isabel Dulfano, and Carl E. Nink. The work was completed by the MTC Institute and funded by the Management and Training Corporation, which operates 23 Job Corps centers in 19 states for the U.S. Department of Labor.

Direct Instruction. Direct instruction uses a bottom-up approach of teaching subskills to master basic skills. This technique is not simply a lecture method in which students are passive learners, but instead actively involves students through frequent responding and participative activities. A positive, established student-teacher relationship enhances the effectiveness of this technique. Direct instruction segments a task into small parts, supplies repeated feedback, provides diagrammatic or pictorial presentations, uses teacher modeling of skills, allows students to learn at their optimal pace, uses

TABLE 10.8
Direct instruction model.

Task	Explanation
Provide objectives, establish expectations, and introduce the skill.	Activate background knowledge, involve all students, relate to real life, label the learning, and set goals.
Introduce and model the skill	• Teacher performs the skill (students use eyes and ears). • Teacher performs the skill, students help (students use eyes, ears, voices, and pencils). • Students perform the skill, teacher helps (students use eyes, ears, voices, and pencils). • Students perform the skill (students use pencils).
Use guided practice with feedback.	Students use their new skills under the teacher's supervision. Can use peer tutoring or cooperative learning.
Close the lesson.	Students tell someone what they have learned, show what they have learned, and practice once more.
Use independent practice and generalization.	Students practice independently, doing a problem every day. The teacher discusses how the skill can be used in other settings.

Note: Adapted from *Removing Barriers: Research-Based Strategies for Teaching Those Who Learn Differently* by A. F. Parkinson, I. Dulfano, and C. E. Nink, 2003, Centerville, UT: MTC Institute. Reprinted with permission of MTC Institute, Management & Training Corporation.

simple verbiage, and has the teacher ask skill-related questions (Swanson, 1999). Table 10.8 summarizes the main points of the direct instruction model.

With direct instruction, the goals and objectives of the lesson should be clearly stated at the beginning of class (Hammeken, 1995), tying the material to everyday life. Material presented in an organized manner with simple vocabulary assists the note-taking process, as does providing a written outline of the subject's main topics with room to take notes. Explicitly stating, "Please remember this," "This is important," and similar phrases can help students distinguish the most important lesson points. Comparing and discussing notes between students will help ensure all have the relevant details. Varying the difficulty of questions during discussion allows all students to participate.

Combining direct instruction with strategy instruction has proven effective in teaching students who learn differently, more so than either method alone or an alternative method (Corley & Taymans, 2002).

Contextual Teaching. The traditional model of educating students using basic skills segmented into discrete units with little direct application to practical life and minimal student interaction and involvement may not be the most effective method of teaching students in today's classrooms (Peterson, LeRoy, Field, & Wood, 1992). Instead, applying new information and skills to a realistic context may prove more productive. "Learning for all students involves determining what the learning means and how it fits into their understanding and experience. Students must be able to make sense of what is being taught if they are going to learn it well enough to be able to use it without the assistance of a teacher" (Ferguson & Jeanchild, 1992, p. 163). Instructors can apply skills learned in math, science, language, and other areas to everyday occurrences in the students' lives. This helps students who have struggled with school in the past connect learning to home and community. Once the practical applications are understood, the theory behind them (the abstract concepts) may be more easily grasped.

Integrating Material. Students need to integrate new material, or build on prior knowledge, in order to understand and easily remember new information. Teachers can enhance this process by explicitly linking new information to that previously learned. "Research has shown that coordinating the various components of instruction so that concepts are clearly and unambiguously communicated and then later combined has a positive effect on the learning of students with disabilities" (Grossen, Davis, Caros, & Billups, 2000, p. 33). Visually connecting previously learned and new information through graphic organizers like concept maps or trees can be especially effective (Dye, 2000).

Group Discussions. Class discussions encourage critical thinking in classrooms with students of varying ability and education. These discussions also "promote articulate speech and respectful, active listening" (Am. Ed. Research Assoc., 2002 p. 8). Participation in such discussion encourages students to organize their thoughts and clearly present their ideas. They also learn how to think critically about others' ideas and that alternative points of view always exist.

To have a productive discussion, instructors must plan an interesting topic and introduction. Thought-provoking hypothetical questions or questions asking the students to agree or disagree with a statement often work well. These discussions can be entertaining for the students as they actively support their points of view and debate with peers.

Review. Planning valuable review helps students master material. Effective review is sufficient, distributed over time, varied, and cumulative. Those who learn differently should apply previously taught knowledge to facilitate greater understanding, longer retention, and appropriate application (Burke, Hagan, & Grossen, 1998). Initially, review should occur frequently, with increasing periods between reviews (Grossen et al., 2000). Cumulative review helps prevent future confusion when students meet similar facts, concepts, principles, and strategies that follow different procedures, such as adding and multiplying fractions. Review can be especially vital in open-entry, open-exit classes since students will constantly be called upon to recall and use information in which they missed instruction.

Scaffolding. Scaffolded instruction uses what the student already knows to determine the next step for instruction (Corley & Taymans, 2002). Teachers model the processes and guide students as they practice. Gradually less and less support is necessary as students approach independent performance. Peers can also provide personal guidance, assistance, and support to students who learn differently (Burke et al., 1998). This method acts as a bridge between teacher- and student-centered learning (Grossen et al., 2000).

Self-Paced Learning. Student readiness is critical to successful self-paced learning. Some students who learn differently may not yet have the self-knowledge and determination critical to self-directed education (Corley & Taymans, 2002). As these students are unlikely to benefit from such a method, instructors should more heavily rely on other techniques. In addition, self-direction should only be used when instructors have the time required to attend to individual needs. Beder and Medina (2001) found,

"In classes in which individualized instruction was used to address mixed skill levels, it was often difficult for teachers to help learners when needed. When this help was not provided, learning became stalled" (p. 14). However, for students who are ready and in the right environment, self-paced educational programs can lead more easily to independent learning (McKee & Clements, 2000). The instructor in such environments becomes a monitor, motivator, evaluator, and reinforcer.

Teaching Materials. Diagrams, drawings, visual demonstrations, stories, rhymes, and mnemonics or other memory devices can help students understand and remember abstract concepts or other important content (Am. Ed. Research Assoc., 2002). Generally, the instructor introduces the material to be learned, then presents the device and ties it to the material. The teacher can use the device over the next few days to easily review or reinforce the information learned. Visual or graphic organizers, including concept maps, Venn diagrams, semantic webs, and genealogical trees, assist students in spatially organizing information to see relationships and linkages to previously learned material (Dye, 2000).

Using colored chalk or markers when teaching also enhances learning (Hammeken, 1995). Instructors can use color-coding when teaching place value in math or teaching parts of speech. Manipulatives aid some students' understanding and retention in math instruction. Rulebooks kept by the students for different subjects help them to be more independent. Students can easily reference grammar, math, or other guiding rules, answering many questions without relying on the instructor or peers. Rulebooks can also include terminology and diagrams.

Preteaching Strategies. Many students who learn differently experience success if they are somewhat familiar with material before it is presented in class (Hammeken, 1995). Providing in advance a weekly spelling list and/or a list of words in boldface type found in the text allows students to familiarize themselves before they must use them in class. Highlighting important information in the student's textbook or color-coding the textbook can also help. Simply providing an outline of main ideas and vocabulary words for each unit also serves this function. (pp. 6–8)

SUMMARY

Teaching is a complex issue. As we learned in chapter 8, the learning environment must be in place. In chapter 9 we saw the complex process of lesson planning. In this chapter we began to look at structure and the importance of structure on the learner. Understanding learning and learning styles is a prerequisite to the delivery of information. Lastly, educators must understand how they deliver information to help students receive it in an organized manner. Imposing structure to the delivery process and to information helps the learner assimilate and retain information. "Telling is not teaching, and told is not taught." How we deliver instruction becomes a carefully planned exercise.

RESOURCES

Association for Supervision and Curriculum Development (ASCD)
1703 North Beauregard Street
Alexandria, VA 22311–1714
Service center: (703) 578–9600
or (800) 933–2723, then press 2
Online store: http://shop.ascd.org

Council for Exceptional Children (CEC)
1110 North Glebe Road, Suite 300
Arlington, VA 22201–5704
(888) 232–7733

SUGGESTED READINGS

Kimball, J. W., Kinney, E. M., Taylor, B. A. & Stromer, R. C. (2002). Lights, camera, action! Using engaging computer-cued activity schedules. *Teaching Exceptional Children, 36*(1) 40–45.

Maroneyh, S. A., Finson, K. D., Beaver, J. B., & Jensen, M. M. (2003). Preparing for successful inquiry in inclusive science classrooms. *Teaching Exceptional Children, 36*(1) 18–25.

WEBSITES TO VISIT

Discovery Channel Online. A wealth of information and links to a variety of subjects. www.discovery.com.

The History Channel. Website where information can be searched by keyword or by date. www.thehistorychannel.com.

PBS Online. Website of the Public Broadcasting System showing program scheduling and other information. www.pbs.org.

U.S. News Classroom Program. Provides teachers' guides and other aids to teach current events and topics. www.usnews.com/classroom.

REFERENCES

American Educational Research Association. (2002, November). *Correctional Education Bulletin,* 6(2). Horshem, PA: LRP Publications.

Beder, H., & Medina, P. (2001). *Classroom dynamics in adult literacy education.* [NCSALL Reports No. 18a.] Boston: The National Center for the Study of Adult Learning and Literacy.

Bloom, B. S. (Ed.). (1956). *Taxonomy of educational objectives: The classification of educational goals. Handbook 1: Cognitive domain.* New York: Longman.

Burke, M. D., Hagan, S. L., & Grossen, B. (1998, September/October). What curricular designs and strategies accommodate diverse learners? *Teaching Exceptional Children.*

Carbo, M., & Hodges, H. (1988, Summer). Learning style strategies can help students at risk. *Teaching Exceptional Children,* 55–58.

Coles, R. (1997). *The moral intelligence of children: How to raise a moral child.* New York: Random House.

Corley, M., & Taymans, J. (2002). Adults with learning disabilities: A review of the literature. *Annual Review of Adult Learning and Literacy, 3,* 44–83. Boston: National Center for the Study of Adult Learning and Literacy.

Costa, A. L., & Kallick, B. (2000). *Discovering & exploring: Habits of mind.* Alexandria, VA: Association for Supervision and Curriculum Development.

Dave, R. H. (1970). *Taxonomy of educational objectives: Psychomotor domain.* New Delhi, India: National Institute of Education.

Davies, I. K. (1981). *Instructional techniques.* New York: McGraw-Hill.

Dunn, R., Dunn, K., & Price, G. E. (1979). *Learning styles inventory manual.* Lawrence, KS: Price Systems.

Dye, G. A. (2000, January/February). Graphic organizers to the rescue! Helping students link—and remember—information. *Teaching Exceptional Children.*

Ferguson, D., & Jeanchild, L. (1992). It's not a matter of method: Thinking about how to implement curricular decisions. In S. Stainback & W. Stainback (Eds.), *Curriculum considerations in inclusive classrooms: Facilitating learning for all students.* Baltimore: Brookes.

Feuerstein, R., Rand, Y., Hoffman, M. B., & Miller, R. (1980). *Instrumental enrichment: An intervention program for cognitive modifiability.* Baltimore: University Park Press.

Fuhrmann, B. S. (1980, August). *Models and methods of assessing learning styles.* Paper presented at a meeting of the Virginia Educational Research Association.

Gardner, H. (1983). *Frames of mind: The theory of multiple intelligences.* New York: Basic Books.

Gardner, H. (1993). Educating for understanding. *American School Board Journal, 180*(7), 20–24.

Gardner, H. (1999, July). *Multiple intelligences.* Speech delivered at Thinking for a Change Conference, 7th International Thinking Conference, Edmonton, Alberta, Canada.

Goleman, D. (1995). *Emotional intelligence: Why it can matter more than IQ.* New York: Bantam.

Griggs, S., & Dunn, R. (1996). Hispanic-American students and learning style. ERIC Digest ED393607. Urbana, IL: ERIC Clearinghouse on Elementary and Early Childhood Education.

Grossen, B., Davis, B., Caros, J., & Billups, L. (2000). *Promoting success in the general curriculum for high school students with disabilities: Instructional technology, media, and materials: A review of literature.* [Research Syntheses Series]. Lawrence: University of Kansas, Institute for Academic Access.

Guilford, J. P., & Hoeptner, R. (1971). *The analysis of intelligence.* New York: McGraw-Hill.

Hammeken, P. (1995). *Inclusion: 450 strategies for success.* Minnetonka, MN: Peytral.

Jarolimek, J., & Foster, C. (1981). *Teaching and learning in the elementary school* (2nd ed.). New York: Macmillan.

Johnson, G. R. (1976). *Analyzing college teaching.* Manchach, TX: Sterling Swift.

Keefe, J. W. (1979). *Student learning styles: Diagnosing and prescribing programs.* Reston, VA: National Association of Secondary School Principals.

Kindsvatter, R., Wilen, W., & Ishler, M. (1988). *Dynamics of ef-fective teaching.* New York: Longman.

Marzano, R. J., Pickering, D. J., & Pollock, J. E. (2001). *Classroom instruction that works: Researched-based strategies for increasing student achievement.* Alexandria, VA: Association for Supervision and Curriculum Development.

McKee, J., & Clements, C. (2000, September). The challenge of individualized instruction in corrections. *The Journal of Correctional Education, 51*(3), 270–281.

Parkinson, A. F., Dulfano, I., & Nink, C. E. (2003). *Removing barriers: Research-based strategies for teaching those who learn differently.* Centerville, UT: MTC Institute.

Perkins, D. N. (1995). *Outsmarting IQ: The emerging science of learnable intelligence.* New York: The Free Press.

Peterson, M., LeRoy, B., Field, S., & Wood, P. (1992). Community-referenced learning in inclusive schools: Effective curriculum for all students. In S. Stainback & W. Stainback (Eds.), *Curriculum considerations in inclusive classrooms: Facilitating learning for all students.* Baltimore, MD: Brookes.

Project Personnel. (2004). Strategies for teaching science to African American students. West Virginia University. Retrieved September 9, 2004, from www.as.wvu.edu/~equity/african.html.

Raphael, T. E. (1982). Question-answering strategies for children. *Reading Teacher, 36,* 186–190.

Rowe, M. B. (1974). Wait time and reward as instructional variables, their influence on language, logic, and fate control. Part 1: Wait time. *Journal of Research on Science Teaching, 11,* 81–94.

Silver, H. F., Strong, R. W., & Perini, M. J. (2000). *So each may learn: Integrating learning styles and multiple intelligences.* Alexandria, VA: Association for Supervision and Curriculum Development.

Sternberg, R. J., Torff, B., & Grigorento, E. (1998, May). Teaching for successful intelligence raises school achievement. *Phi Delta Kappan, 79,* 667–669.

Swanson, H. L. (1999). *Intervention research for adolescents with learning disabilities: A meta-analysis of outcomes related to high-order processing.* Retrieved November 11, 2002, from www.ncld.org/research/ncld_high_order.cfm.

Swisher, K. (1991). American Indian/Alaskan Native learning styles: Research and practice. ERIC Digest ED335175. Charleston, WV: ERIC Clearinghouse on Rural Education and Small Schools.

West, E. (1975). *Leading discussions.* Unpublished paper, University of Minnesota, St. Paul.

Wood, J. W. (1993). *Mainstreaming: A practical approach for teachers.* Upper Saddle River, NJ: Merrill/Prentice Hall.

11

Adapting the Format of Content

LEARNER OBJECTIVES

After you read this chapter, you will be able to:

- Discuss ways of giving directions.
- Provide more appropriate work sheets for students.
- Understand the note-taking process and tips for helping students.
- Teach notebooking to students.
- Develop study guides.
- Develop numerous interventions for presenting the format of content.
- Develop a task analysis.
- Adapt assignments.
- Understand the five components of whole language theory.

CHAPTER AT A GLANCE

```
                          ┌──────────────┐
                          │  Organizing  │
                          │   Content    │
                          └──────┬───────┘
      ┌──────┬────────┬──────────┼──────────┬──────────┬──────────┐
 ╭────────╮ ╭────────╮ ╭────────╮ ╭────────╮ ╭────────╮ ╭────────╮ ╭────────╮
 │Directions│ │  Work  │ │The Note-│ │Notebooks│ │ Study  │ │General │ │ Taped  │
 ╰────────╯ │ Sheet  │ │ Taking │ ╰────────╯ │ Guides │ │ Study  │ │ Books  │
            │Modifica-│ │Process │           ╰────────╯ │Tips for│ ╰────────╯
            │ tions  │ ╰────────╯                       │Secondary│
            ╰────────╯                                  │Students│
                                                        ╰────────╯
```

Directions | Work Sheet Modifications | The Note-Taking Process | Notebooks | Study Guides | General Study Tips for Secondary Students | Taped Books

Adapting the Presentation of Content

Modifications and Whole Language

Task Analysis

Adapting Assignments

Tips for Assignment Books | Assignment Assumptions | Types of Assignments

KEY TERMS

Mrs. Jimenez was teaching a lesson on maps. She started with explaining the class globe. As the class discussion continued, Mrs. Jimenez asked, "Where is the equator?" One student quietly walked to the back of the classroom, ripped the equator band from the globe and walked to the front of the class. Proudly he handed the equator band from the globe to the teacher and stated, "Here it is!" This is a wonderful example of how students take what the teacher says literally!

After teachers select the appropriate teaching technique to deliver the lesson, they may have to consider alternative ways of presenting the academic content. For example, teachers usually teach the subject of reading from a basal textbook and teach math using exercises and examples in a textbook. Assignments to prepare for tomorrow's class may be given at the end of today's class. Work sheets traditionally are used in classrooms across the country.

But what happens to the student who simply cannot achieve success with the strategies and formats used for teaching the content? Sometimes, even if techniques have been adapted, the student still may not understand the material. In such cases, the regular class teacher should ask the following questions:

1. Does the student have the skills to complete the required task?
2. If not, does the student have the prerequisite skills for beginning the required task?
3. Does instruction begin at the student's functioning level?
4. Was the teaching technique appropriate for delivering the instruction to the student?

After answering these questions, the teacher may see a need to modify the strategies and formats used for reorganizing instruction.

This chapter discusses and presents ideas for providing a clear understanding of the content for students. The content is the subjects being taught: reading, math, social studies, science, art, physical education, and so on. There are three major areas of focus when we are analyzing our content or subject: What organizational skills are needed to help the student understand the subject and be in a constant state of learning for test and review? What strategies can educators use to bring life (understanding) to the content of a subject? When the class is over and assignments are presented, our job is only beginning. How can educators adapt assignments to meet individual students' needs?

ORGANIZING CONTENT

Structure is an important component of content, or subject matter, as it is for other blocks of the SAALE model. Remember, when educators provide structure, students will eventually, and naturally, learn to impose their own. Organizing content has six important parts: directions, work sheets, note taking, notebooks, study guides, and taped texts.

Directions

Giving directions is one of the first things teachers do in class and also one of the tasks they do most frequently. If students have not heard, listened to, or understood the directions, they are lost from the start. There are three aspects of directions: before giving directions, giving oral directions, and providing written directions. Each part is crucial to the process.

Before Giving Directions

Teachers should think about the following suggestions before giving directions:

1. Be sure you have all students' attention. You can get their attention in many ways—wearing a funny hat, holding up a small directions flag, and so on.
2. Allow the class to select the direction clue to be used each month. This gives them ownership in the process.
3. Check to see that everyone has the necessary materials for recording directions (such as paper, pencils, and highlighters).
4. Try not to scold anyone before giving directions. Embarrassment may prevent students from paying attention.
5. Offer small prizes to sections of the class that focus on the direction clue first.
6. Number each direction if more than one is to be used.

Giving Oral Directions

Here are some tips for giving oral directions:

1. Get students' attention.
2. Eliminate unnecessary words.
3. Speak in short, simple sentences.
4. Give only one direction if possible.
5. Use a visual backup and speak slowly, stopping after each direction if more than one is given.
6. Remember, no matter how slowly you speak or how long you pause, some students can only process one direction and not a series of directions.
7. Ask for volunteers to repeat the directions.
8. Keep visual support present during the activity. In other words, do not erase the visual backup before the activity or assignment has been completed.
9. Have a system in place for students who do not understand directions. In other words, they should know what to do to find out. Do not tell them to raise their hands because some students are embarrassed about doing this. Develop a discreet way for them to get clarity.
10. If repeating directions, restate them exactly the same way (for students with auditory processing difficulties).

Providing Written Directions

I have several suggestions for providing written directions:

1. Use few words.
2. Provide an example.

3. Read the directions orally as the students highlight the written directions.

4. Keep directions on the page that a student is working on. If the assignment is more than one page long, the directions should appear on a card, the chalkboard, or another easily accessible place.

5. Be sure that the students understand all parts of, and all words in, the directions.

6. Have a backup system for students who do not understand the directions. Remember that students who do not understand the directions are usually those who do not want to raise their hands in front of their peers. Find a discreet way for them to get information.

Work Sheet Modifications

I have never been a big fan of work sheets. However, the reality is that work sheets are used frequently in schools. A work sheet should have a definite purpose related to the task at hand and should not be used as busy work.

One of my favorite stories regarding work sheets relates to an incident that occurred some years ago. I frequently visit schools and observe many wonderful, talented, creative educators. I also like to drop into the teacher's lounge, where you can truly feel the pulse of a school. This particular day I was having a Coke and visiting with the teachers. I noticed that one teacher was running off a stencil on a mimeograph machine. (Most of you probably have never seen a mimeograph machine. In the past, this was how teachers did their copying. Ask your professors. I bet they remember!) The teacher's stack of work sheets grew higher and higher. Curious (as usual!), I walked over to look at the stack of papers, wondering what was so important. When I found out, I'm sure the look on my face showed everyone my shock. All those papers were the same. Each sheet was filled with an enormous letter *C,* which students were supposed to trace with a crayon.

Observing my look of bewilderment, the teacher said, "These boys and girls certainly need lots of work on the letter *C.*" All I could think was, "It looks like they're going to get more than they want." But naturally, I remained professional, smiled politely, and returned to my chair.

My point is that work sheets must have a purpose. Teachers should think about that purpose when constructing, implementing, and evaluating them.

Construction

Here are some tips for constructing work sheets:

1. Limit the amount of material on each page.

2. Focus on only one concept at a time.

3. Provide large, readable print or type.

4. Make sure the work sheet teaches what you intend it to teach.

5. Do not use work sheets for busy work.

6. Keep directions simple.

7. Do not hand out numerous work sheets at one time.

8. When a student finishes one work sheet, do not just hand out another.

Implementation

Teachers should consider these suggestions before implementing work sheets:

1. Provide short, clear directions.
2. Present all directions both orally and visually.
3. Be sure students clearly understand directions.
4. Have students color code or highlight directions.
5. Present only one work sheet at a time.
6. Allow students to work with a buddy when completing the work sheet.
7. Allow students to complete part of the work sheet or odd/even sections.

Evaluation

Here are three tips for evaluating work sheets:

1. Provide self-correcting work sheets. Answer cards may be used for checking answers, or a completed work sheet may be used.
2. Permit students to correct their own work sheets.
3. If work sheets are turned in, be sure they are graded and returned.

The Note-Taking Process

Note-taking is a skill that requires instruction, structure, and practice, although teachers often assume that it is an easy task for students. Many students in inclusive settings have difficulty taking notes because of their inability to organize ideas or concepts, distinguish main points or ideas, or transfer information from written or oral formats. Some students also have deficits in processing or in motor skills.

Students must have the correct information in a format useful for study if we expect them to learn class information and pass class tests. The note-taking process serves as a study process for many students, especially if the class is organized and systematic. Learning how to take notes in difficult situations is a skill that may be carried not only into other classes but into adult life as well. Learning note taking, learning the method of adaptation that is required, and getting a complete set of notes provide instructional security for students. Their anxiety is reduced when they know that they have the proper information from which to organize their study.

Many students fail tests because of incomplete notes, not because they do not know the material. Test success is extremely dependent on having good notes. Thus, the point of intervention could be working on students' note-taking abilities.

Before providing adaptations for the note-taking process, educators need to consider the sources from which the notes will be given. Will the information be orally presented through lectures, movies, videotapes, or filmstrips? Or will it be in written format, using the chalkboard, an overhead projector, a textbook, newspapers, magazines, or PowerPoint? Students should also develop an awareness of the source of the notes and specific adaptations they need for each source.

Second, teachers should tell students about the type of test to expect from the notes, such as multiple choice, essay, or short answer. This helps the student focus on how the material will be presented in the testing situation.

Notes Taken from Oral Material

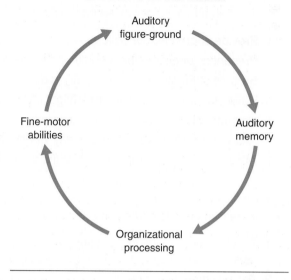

Notes Taken from Printed Material

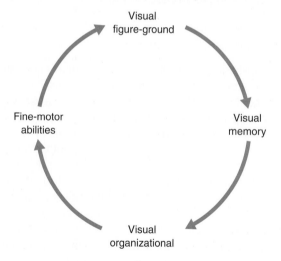

FIGURE 11.1
The note-taking process: Oral material and printed material.

We often think of note taking as a single skill that students use in the classroom. Actually, there are two distinct types of note taking, and each requires different skills. Figure 11.1 shows the process of note taking from both oral and printed presentations.

Taking Notes From Oral Material

Material given orally includes lecture, video, filmstrips, and so on. Think of this type of note taking as a four-step process. First, the student must auditorily pick up the information (figure-ground). (In this case, **figure-ground** means hearing a word and selecting it from a background of other words.) Second, the student must remember what was just said (auditory memory). Third, some sort of organizational processing takes place. Because all information is not equal, students must pinpoint the topic and determine the major and minor parts. Fourth, the student must transfer the material heard into written format. Fine motor abilities come into play here. The process is continuous, not as jerky as it seems in this discussion.

What kinds of trouble do special needs students have with this kind of note taking? Imagine that you are a student with poor auditory memory. By the time you write down part of what you heard and return your attention to the speaker, pockets of information are missing from your notes. I call this "Swiss cheese" note taking.

The lecture is one of the most common situations in which students take notes from oral information. Students have difficulty taking notes from a lecture for a number of reasons. These include an inability to impose structure, visual processing problems, deficient motor skills, and auditory processing problems. Many students are unable to listen to the teacher, extrapolate the major and minor concepts, and put this information on paper. For them, everything that the teacher says appears equally important. Students with visual processing deficits may not be able to move their eyes from one focal point (the teacher) to a new focal point (the paper) smoothly enough to take notes quickly. Deficient fine motor control may cause handwriting problems so that students cannot read their own notes. Auditory processing problems may cause students to be unable to hear the lecture clearly and accurately, resulting in incomplete or incorrect notes.

One suggestion for adapting the note taking process is to provide a lecture outline. An outline gives the student the major and minor parts of the coming lecture, either on a single page or on one or more pages, with space allotted for filling in notes. Chapter 10 offered suggestions for structured organizers, which can also help students who have trouble taking notes on oral material.

Before beginning the lecture, the teacher should follow these steps:

1. Present the topic or objective of the material to be covered.
2. Relate the material to the sequence of material taught yesterday and to the total course sequence.
3. Introduce the lecture outline by pointing out the major points (points 1, 2, 3, and so on).
4. Remind students that minor or supporting information will be listed under each major topic.
5. Give the page numbers where students can find the information in the text.
6. Begin the lecture and indicate noteworthy information.
7. Throughout the lecture or discussion, refer to the outline number to keep students on track.
8. If paper shortage is a concern, present the outline on the chalkboard or use an overhead projector.
9. At the conclusion of the lecture, briefly summarize the information covered.

Another adaptation for oral lectures is to use tape recorders for recording lectures or discussions. Students may bring their own recorders, or the teacher can record the lecture and allow students to check out tapes at a later date.

During class lectures teachers can also use the chalkboard to help students organize the information. They can start by developing a chart format with headings and then fill in key information during the lecture for students to copy. When the class is completed, students will have a set of notes organized by categories to make studying and review easier.

Good listening is essential for taking notes from lectures, class discussions, reviews, or other oral presentations. Students should be trained to listen. Teachers should remember that, after a while, everything begins to sound the same. Therefore, it is important to take an occasional "listening break." Pause for a stretch, tell a story that is related to the topic, or insert a joke. Breaking the constant flow of the lecture helps the listener attend to noteworthy information.

Teachers can also give signals to let students know what is important to write down. Students who have difficulty with structure may also have difficulty distinguishing major and minor details. When teachers come to parts of the lecture they know students must remember for a test or other reason, they can give a clue, such as, "This is noteworthy." Students should know what the clue words are. They should be instructed to either underline the noteworthy information or put a star in the margin. By giving clues, teachers can (a) keep students on track, (b) help students attend to the important information, and (c) teach the difference between major and minor information.

Taking Notes From Printed Material

Taking notes from printed matter can also be difficult for students. This kind of note taking falls into two areas: far-point copying and near-point copying. Far-point copying is required when copying from an overhead projector, chalkboard, flip chart, and so on. Near-point copying is required when, for example, copying math problems from a textbook onto paper or copying from one paper to another.

Figure 11.1 displays the four skills required for a student to be able to copy from printed matter. Some students have difficulty finding their place in printed material when they move their eyes from book to paper (visual figure-ground). With such a problem, taking notes can take forever. Because note taking requires many skills, just one breakdown point can throw the student significantly behind.

Taking notes from the chalkboard requires good skills in visual tracking, handwriting, and organization. If these skills are not fully developed, the student with disabilities may have great difficulty getting the notes. The arrangement of class seating is essential. The teacher should be sure that students are seated so they can see the chalkboard easily as well as to avoid distractions. Teachers who plan to provide a complete set of notes to students who are unable to copy from the board may require them to copy certain sections of the lecture. This will keep them working with the class but take away the stress of trying to get all of the notes. Students can then focus on the discussion, knowing that a complete set of notes will follow.

When giving notes from the overhead projector, teachers should make the same adaptations described for the chalkboard. In addition, they should keep covered any information they have not yet discussed so that students cannot see it until it is presented. Before discussing the information, teachers should allow time for students to copy it. Talking while students write will result in many of them missing the discussion. Teachers often ask students to take notes from preprinted material such as textbooks, magazines, and newspapers. If the notes are being written for future study and review, students may wish to use the format presented in Figure 11.2: If a student is copying material onto a note card, similar information may be placed on the card. The teacher should make sure to put the page number of the material on the card and number the cards when finished.

General Note-Taking Tips

The information in this section applies to note taking from any material, whether presented orally or in written form. Figure 11.3 offers a number of note-taking sugges-

PRACTICAL APPLICATIONS
ADAPTING VOCABULARY

1. Make a list of all boldfaced and italicized words and those presenting new concepts from the chapter. List the words in the order they occur within the chapter. Record the corresponding page number to the left of each word.
2. Beside each vocabulary word, provide a synonym or simplified definition.
3. Provide all students with the list of new vocabulary words before introducing the content of the chapter.
4. If students have difficulty looking up definitions or key words, provide the definition. This will cut down on their amount of work so they can spend time learning the definition of the word, which is the task we are asking them to do.
5. Instead of having the student copy vocabulary words and their definitions on notebook paper, have them write each word separately on the front of a 3″ × 5″ card and the corresponding definition on the back. These steps save time and will produce a set of flash cards for reinforcement activities. The cards can be filed in a box in order by chapter number.
6. When working with the flash cards, follow these steps:
   - The student holds the flash card and looks at the word.
   - Another student, a teacher, or a parent holds a list of the words and their definitions.
   - Another student looks at the word and supplies the definition.
   - The student immediately flips the card over, checking the definition on the card against his or her response.
   - Work on only 5 words at a time, adding another 5 after the first 5 are mastered. After learning the second 5 words, review all 10 words. Now add 5 more words. Then review all 15. This type of distributed practice is much better for memory load.
7. Be sure that the student knows what type of test you will use for vocabulary. For example, if the test will be a fill-in-the-blank without a word bank, the study process will be different from that required for a test with a word bank.
8. Tape-record the words for each chapter with each definition. This process will help students who cannot read the words initially to learn the words and their definitions. Be sure to number the words and read the number on the test.

tions. (I'd like to thank the following educators for their contributions: Cathy Wobser, Sandra Gilbert, Maureen Thomas, Cathy Perini-Korreck, Marshall Welch, and Ida Crandall.)

To help students improve their approach to note taking, teachers can show them how to format the paper they plan to take notes on. Here are some suggestions about formatting:

1. Teach students to use only two thirds of their paper for note taking and one third for study and review:
   a. Have students take notes in the right-hand column.
   b. As the notes are being given, point out important dates, facts, vocabulary, and so on; have the student put facts into the left-hand column.

Name: _____

Topic: _____   Class: _____

Source of material: _____   Period: _____

Page numbers: _____   Date: _____

As you develop the outline, put important facts, vocabulary, and dates in this column. The specific page number may also be listed.	Outline material in this section
	I.
	  A.
	  B.
	  C.
	II.
	  A.
	  B.
	  C.
	III.
	  A.
	  B.
	  C.

FIGURE 11.2
Format for taking notes from printed matter.

    c. When you have completed a section of notes, stop and ask students to review their notes and list in the left-hand column possible text questions.

    d. Review the questions presented and have the class complete missing information.

2. After note taking, students can work in pairs to study and review notes.

3. Have students develop a format for their notepapers. This will help them to organize, file, and retrieve for later review.

4. Loose-leaf paper means easier filing. However, commercial notebooks can be purchased if you prefer students to keep notes in a spiral-bound book.

Teachers can also help students after the note-taking process. Consider the following suggestions:

1. Teach students how to use the notes for study and review.

2. Assign buddies or study-and-review teams to work together using the notes.

3. Buddies can color code notes. Use three colors: one for vocabulary, one for facts to remember, and one for concepts to study. You can quickly check to see whether important information is highlighted.

4. Buddies can check one set of notes with another and, in the left-hand column, write missing information.

1. Save a set of notes from another class to give to the student.
2. Give the student a copy of the teacher's notes (see Figure 11.4).
3. Let one student copy his or her notes to give to the student who has difficulty taking notes.
4. Use an organizer for taking notes on poems. For example:

Title	Author	Type	Poetic devices used

Summary of poem:

Class discussion:
    What I learned from the discussion:
    Questions I have about the poem:

5. Seat the student appropriately to avoid auditory or visual distractions.
6. Provide structured organizers for note taking.
7. Provide a lecture outline for note taking.
8. Develop a who, what, when, where, how, and why outline for note taking.

Who ———— [_____]

What ———— [_____]

When ———— [_____]

Where ———— [_____]

How ———— [_____]

Why ———— [_____]

Who	What	When	Where	How	Why

9. When having students copy from the chalkboard or overhead projector, use various colors of chalk or pens. Each sentence should be written in a different color (blue, pink, green). This method is very useful for all students in finding information in a visual field. But be careful: too many colors overwhelm and distract.

(continued)

FIGURE 11.3
Note-taking suggestions for oral or written materials.

5. Teach students to file their notes in an organized manner. Work on this process for an extended period until students develop the structure themselves.
6. Before the test, refer to notes by dates or topics that should be reviewed. Tell the students the test type for specific notes.

10. After a film, divide the chalkboard into four sections and use words or pictures to review. This is an easy note-taking idea for young children.

11. When handing out study work sheets to be kept in a student folder, have students highlight the important information. Many students can never read all of the material, but will or can read the highlighted information.

12. Be sure all notes to be copied are typed or printed. Cursive writing is extremely hard to read.

13. Use the 1/3–2/3 folding method for note taking. This may be used for lecture notes or chapter notes. Put main idea or question on left side and answer or detail on right side. For example:

Felony	Crime for which the punishment is one year or longer.

14. Provide a classroom set of clipboards as an incentive for children to get physically involved in note taking from the chalkboard.

15. Provide a binder available to all students in one place in the room. Have two volunteers/ secretaries copy their notes and place them in the binder at the end of each class. The teacher makes 6 to 8 copies of the better set and places them back into the binder. The next day students with note-taking difficulties may get a complete set of notes from the day before.

16. Use a *KIM* sheet for note taking. It looks like this:

a. Students make their chart using any type of paper.

b. **K** is for key words. **I** is for information about the key word, which can be numbered or lettered. **M** is for a memo to help students remember the information, page, and so on.

c. This method is generic for any class. Students always have the outline when needed. When using the **KIM** sheet to study for a test, you can cover the **K** column and read clues from the **I** column and check answers, or cover the **I** column and use **K** as clues. If writing a report, **K** is your topic, and **I** is the information for each paragraph or sentence.

FIGURE 11.3
Continued.

17. Use the *T* note method. Divide your paper into a simple *T*. For example:

Main idea	1. detail 1 2. detail 2 3. detail 3

a. Take all main ideas down on the left side of the paper.

b. All details that go with the main ideas are placed on the right side of the *T* and are numbered.

c. Vocabulary words go to the left and definitions on the right.

d. *T* notes are easy to study by either folding the paper or overlapping papers as shown below.

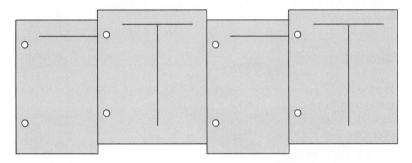

18. Use the note-taking–note-making method. For example:

Note taking	Note taking
Notes that the teacher gives in about 8-minute increments. Stop!	What the students make out of the notes given: • Rephrasing • Questions • Any type of response
Drawing	**Relating**
On the back of another sheet students draw their understanding of concepts from the lecture.	Students make associations and explain them in a paragraph. Share in class the next day.

Basic Water Conservation and Management Principles

1. Intercept the force of the running water
2. Slow it down
3. Control it
4. Reduce the amount of water leaving the land source
   - Sheet erosion moves the soil surface in a large usually unseen thin sheet
   - Erosion takes place anywhere there is bare soil
   - Water beats away at the soil, loosening soil particles and moving them short distances or even far away
   - Erosion causes sediment to fill reservoirs, lakes, and streams that kills aquatic life
   - Erosion can clog water delivery systems that bring water to cities
   - In cities where there is more pavement than soil, water runs off quicker and fills storm drains and sewer systems. This is what causes flooding.

Water and Conservation

Water can generally be managed and conserved as it becomes available through precipitation.

- Water management begins with soil management.
- Soil erosion begins with a drop of water blasting soil particles, like a bomb.

FIGURE 11.4

Student notes given by teacher prior to class.

Note: From Science, Spring Oaks Middle School, 2000. A special thanks to Ashly Tardif, Houston, Texas.

7. It is good practice to keep an extra set of class notes on file in the class. Students who are absent or who have missed sections of notes can refer to this set for assistance. File the notes by class date for easy retrieval.

8. When covering a large amount of material in class, provide students with a basic notes outline and encourage them to add more in-depth information as it is presented. See Figure 11.4 for an example.

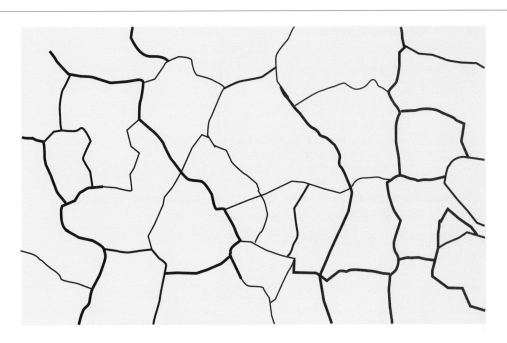

About Water

Water surrounds us. It is in the air as rain, ice, snow, steam, and fog. It is in lakes, streams, rivers, oceans, and glaciers.

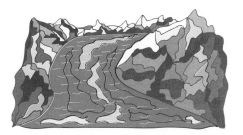

(continued)

Providing adaptations for notes is a crucial support for students. If students are unable to get a complete set of notes, how can we expect them to be successful on tests? The ideas I have presented help bridge the gap between notes and students. Let's look at a few tips that help students help themselves. Figure 11.5 presents note-taking tips that students can incorporate into their own skill base. These are also good ideas for the college student.

Before closing this section, I want to leave you with one thought:

It is not important that students *take* the notes. It is important that they *get* the notes.

Humans are about 65% water

    Blood = 80–90%

    Muscles = 75%

Water isn't ever new, it is recycled time and time again. No new water is being manufactured.

Water is 2 hydrogen molecules and 1 oxygen molecule. H_2O.

The Earth's surface is about 75% water but only 3% is fresh water.

Precipitation falls to Earth from clouds, rain, or snow.

The process then starts over again.

Key Processes of Hydrological Cycle

1. Evaporation: water goes from liquid to gas stage
2. Transpiration: water given off through leaves

FIGURE 11.4
Continued.

Notebooks

At the beginning of each school year, teachers across the United States announce, "In this class, you will keep a notebook." Some teachers provide the format for the notebooks, whereas others leave the format open. Here are suggestions for helping students organize and keep notes, checking notebooks, and reviewing notes for tests.

3. Precipitation: raining or snowing
4. Infiltration: fill the pore spaces between individual soil particles
5. Respiration: breathing
6. Combustion: burning

The Water Cycle—Nature's Recycling System

Recycling: to pass through a cycle or a part of cycle again

Hydrological cycle: a natural process of water molecules recycling from the land, to the air, and back to the land

Sun's energy warms the water and the vapor goes into the atmosphere.

In the atmosphere the vapor is formed into clouds.

Clouds are carried by weather patterns.

Organizing the Notebook

Before organizing the notebook, the teacher should examine the structure of the class. For example, how does the structure relate to the types of tests given? Does the class follow a certain structure each day? Notebook organization should reflect that structure. Table 11.1 shows the notebook organization for a class in geography.

By making students aware of the match between class structure and notebook format, and including the test item type for each section, teachers help students think

Prepare for the class by completing background reading prior to the class.

Get to class on time so that you don't miss the teacher's opening statements, which are often a statement of the purpose of the lecture.

Don't try to write down every word the teacher says. Focus instead on key phrases, important points, new terms, summary statements, names, dates, etc. Choose one example of a point to record rather than trying to write down each one in detail. Do record all the points in a list.

Keep your mind focused on what the teacher is saying. Try not to look around or think of other things.

Taking notes in outline form will help you focus on main ideas.

Develop your own short-hand system for commonly used words and phrases, for example: b/c for because, w/o for without, ≅ for approximately, ↑ for increased, ∴ for therefore, vs. for versus, ≠ for does not equal. Also create a course-specific set of abbreviations, such as: cong. for congressional, adm. for administration, gov't for government, dem/rep for democrats and republicans, etc.

Don't write down small words such as *a, the, is* that are not needed to understand the information.

Remember that your notes are for your own use. Don't be overly concerned about neatness or correct spelling.

If a word is used that you don't know or can't quite understand, write it down phonetically, circle it, and ask a classmate about it or look it up later.

When the teacher uses phrases such as, "This is important," "The main point . . . ," or "An important finding . . . ," prior to presenting the information, mark this information by putting a star in the margin of your notes.

When the teacher uses phrases such as "First . . . second . . . third . . . ," "At this stage . . . ," " Finally . . . ," recognize these as transitional words that signal a sequence of steps or events.

Notice when the teacher raises the volume of her voice or repeats a word or phrase. This probably signals important information.

Leave plenty of white space in your notes and wide margins for expanding your notes later.

Use a pen rather than a pencil for taking notes. A pen will slide across the paper more quickly and your notes won't smudge and fade like those taken in pencil.

Put the date and day on each set of notes. Draw a line after the last sentence you write and indicate "end."

If you have a question about what the teacher is saying or missed some information, wait until she has completed her thought before interrupting to request repetition or clarification.

If you consistently have difficulty copying lengthy information from overhead transparencies, ask if you can get copies of the transparencies or if you can look at them during a break or after class to fill in information you missed.

If you are going to tape-record a lecture let the teacher know that you plan on doing this. Always try to back up the tape with notes.

Review your notes as soon as possible after class, filling in information you missed.

Rewriting your notes right after you take them may help you learn the information and also gives you a chance to organize your notes for future study.

Arrange for another student to use carbon paper for a second set of notes. This is most helpful if you need to focus on the lecture and not split attention between listening and taking notes.

FIGURE 11.5

Note-taking tips for students.

Note: For practice on note taking, see Flemming, L, & Leet, J. (1994). *Becoming a Successful Student.* New York: HarperCollins College.

TABLE 11.1
Sample notebook organization.

Class Structure	Notebook Format	Reorganized Notebook Format	Test Item
Class opening	Class notes	Atlas notes/maps	Listing questions
Atlas questions from the overhead projector	Maps	Study questions/notes	Short-answer
Study questions from homework	Quizzes	Lecture outline/notes	Multiple-choice, true–false
Class lecture		Quizzes	
	Exams	Exams	
Tomorrow's assignment			
Class closing			

of the class from beginning to end. Other tips for organizing notebooks include using dividers for each subject and section and keeping separate notebooks in a loose-leaf binder for each subject. Figure 11.6 offers additional notebook organization ideas. (I'd like to thank Betty Powell and L. Wakefield for their contributions.)

Keeping the Notebook

Keeping notebooks can become a major problem for many students. For this reason, teachers should work with students during the first day or two of class as they build their notebooks. They should explain the overall format; provide an example of a completed notebook; and show students the relationship among class, notebook, and tests. Each student should compile the notebook in class, and teachers should review the final product. This may seem like wasted time, but you will find that it is time well spent. Directions are not sufficient for many students because they cannot follow through with structure without support. For the first two or three weeks, teachers should work with the class each day on keeping the notebook in order. Eventually, they can reduce the number of prompts. Remember, the student who would never get a notebook together alone is the one who benefits most from notebook building in class.

Figure 11.7 suggests more notebook-keeping tips. (Thanks to Suzi Lockamy, Gloria Robin, and Alice Jane Rouse for their contributions.)

Notebook Checkup

A checkup is an easy way to help students continue to keep their notebooks organized. Teachers should inform the class that they will have a notebook quiz from time to time. The quiz will consist of asking questions from different sections of the notebook by date of notes. This type of quiz will be an easy way to get an A. On the first quiz, teachers should record only the A's and remind the rest of the class that simple organization guarantees an A. The second quiz will count for all students. Personally, however, I like to give only positive grades for good notebooks and am opposed to marking students down for not having their notebooks.

The notebook is also used for test review. Teachers can tie together the study guide provided at the beginning of the unit (discussed in the next section) and the notes taken during the study period. Students should understand that studying and

1. Organize a "desk elf" for younger students. Use one basket per child for glue, scissors, crayons, books, pencils, and so on. Maintain a desk folder for papers to keep or work on and a home folder for things to go home. Keep desk elves on a shelf.

2. "Tub teaching" for young students helps keep students organized who change classes. Each student is given a Rubbermaid tub with built-in handles to transport books and materials. The tub slides easily under desks and can travel with the students as they move from room to room.

3. Students may keep a table of contents and a point sheet in their notebooks. For example:

Table of Contents

Date	Page number	Topic

Point Sheet

Date	Grade	Page	Test/quiz

4. Give student an activity sheet for keeping a record of activities.

5. Of greatest importance, organize the notebooks with the class. Divide the notebook sections based on your class structure.

6. Be sure each student has a buddy who cross-checks to see if the notebook is being set up properly.

7. Notebooks can be obtained through local businesses or organizations.

8. Put boxes in the halls at each year's end and have students put all items they don't want into the box. You will be surprised at the materials you will get.

9. Last, but certainly not least, organizing notebooks is part of instruction and not just a task assigned for an out-of-class activity.

FIGURE 11.6
Suggestions for organizing notebooks.

reviewing notes will improve their test scores significantly. They should be taught to distribute their studying over shorter periods of time.

Here is a notebook-checking tip: Instead of grading notebooks, have a notebook test at the end of a grading period or term. For example, ask, "Quiz number 2 (March 3) was about _____?" If the student has the quiz paper, he or she can easily get a perfect grade. If the student has lost the paper, he or she is free to make copies of

1. To help students keep study outlines in their notebooks, color code the outlines or other materials. Each chapter outline is printed on green paper. If students lose the outline (or other handout), they get another one (no questions asked). But the new handout will be yellow. If they lose the yellow one, they get another one, but it will be red. This helps the teacher eyeball organizational skills, and students truly don't want any yellow or red papers in their notebooks.

2. Periodically during the grading period, have a notebook cleaning party. Save materials that will be needed later in folders, which the teacher keeps. Tell students what may be thrown out or taken home for kitchen art.

3. Keep a monthly organizational chart at the front of the student's notebook. At the beginning of each month replace the old chart with a new one, with the student's record and significant events/tasks to remember. For example:

	Monday	Tuesday	Wednesday	Thursday	Friday
Week of May 1–5	Quiz in math		Science project due	Map quiz	English vocabulary test
Week of May 8–12		Social studies report: Mexico		Test on short story unit	
Week of May 15–19		Social studies test chapters 5–7	Science lab due		
Week of May 22–26		Math quiz	English paper due	P.E. test: tennis	
Week of May 29– April 3		Oral report P.E.			Math test

(continued)

FIGURE 11.7
Keeping a notebook.

another student's quiz before the notebook test. However, other simple notebook tests can involve checking to see that everyone has his or her notebook in class or having two students (or more) work together to catch up on missing papers.

Study Guides

A study guide helps students develop a plan for study and review. As teachers teach, study guides become instruments for improving structure both as the lesson develops and when the lesson is over and test review begins. Study guides benefit students in numerous ways:

1. Provide organization of information for studying purposes
2. Help students develop a whole-part-whole concept for the material
3. Present information in a sequential, logical manner
4. Tie together the information from yesterday to today and tomorrow
5. Impose structure on information
6. Impose a focal point for the teacher
7. Facilitate collaboration between special and general education teachers
8. Help parents assist their children in study and review

4. A subject time-organization chart also may be used weekly. For example:

Subject		Monday	Tuesday	Wednesday	Thursday	Friday	Saturday	Sunday
Social studies	Time							
	Task							
Science	Time							
	Task							
Language arts	Time							
	Task							
Math	Time							
	Task							
P.E./health	Time							
	Task							

5. When you are finished with a set of materials or an activity, put the materials into the appropriate section of the notebook and have a buddy cross-check. This process takes only seconds and saves great confusion down the line.

FIGURE 11.7
Continued.

9. Aid students in preparing for specific test types
10. Help students impose structure in other classes without guides
11. Provide a connection for the students from the lessen or unit to a standard or benchmark.

Types of Study Guides

There are two types of study guides: formative and summative. Each serves a specific function for imposing structure and organizing material.

A formative study guide organizes information in short, distributive segments. The guide focuses on specific details of the information covered. An example is the acquisition outline or lesson frame discussed in chapter 10. As a new concept or section of information is presented, students follow the class discussion and record important details in an organized manner. As we discussed in chapter 10, this outline may be on one page or on several pages, and it should have space for notes. The teacher may provide an incomplete outline for students to complete or an outline that has the details already completed. A second option is helpful for students who have difficulty taking notes. Each outline should list the page numbers for the specific information, the

Study Guide (Formative)

Subject: Science

Student Name:

Grade level: 5

Activity: Develop one acquisition outline and one organizer for the subject and grade
level listed above.

Subject: Science

Topic: Parts of a Seed

I. Embryo (page 10)

    A. Monocot

    B. Dicot

II. Food storage tissue (pages 11–12)

III. Seed coat (page 15)

    A. Function

    B. Appearance

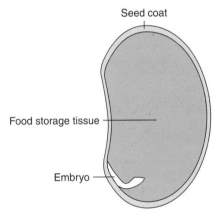

FIGURE 11.8

Sample formative study guide.

Note: Thanks to Luanne Berry.

title or objective for the lesson, and the lesson date. After the class, students should be instructed to place the outline in the appropriate notebook section. Figure 11.8 presents a sample formative study guide for grade 5.

Summative study guides help students prepare for a quiz or test. They are designed to provide general information about the notes to be quizzed, which lays the foundation for organizing the study effort. The teacher may direct students to put all formative study guides in sequential order by date and place the summative study guide first. The summative study guide provides structure for the student's study effort.

Figures 11.9 and 11.10 present sample summative study guides for secondary and elementary levels. The guides can be completed by the teacher or with the class.

Student: _____   Date of test: _____

Subject: _____   Date guide issued: _____

Teacher: _____

Study Guide

1. Lesson/test objective:

2. Textbook/workbook/manual pages to be covered:

3. Handouts/lectures/films/speakers/demonstrations/labs/maps/charts to be covered:

4. Key words/vocabulary to be learned/location:

5. Review questions for organizing study:

6. Type of test to be given:

	Number of items	Point value
_____ Multiple-choice	_____	_____
_____ Matching	_____	_____
_____ True–false	_____	_____
_____ Fill-in-the-blank	_____	_____
_____ Word bank included?	_____	_____
_____ Short answer	_____	_____
_____ Essay	_____	_____
_____ Diagrams/charts	_____	_____
_____ Maps	_____	_____
_____ Word bank for map?	_____	_____
_____ List of maps to review	_____	_____
_____ Practical tests	_____	_____

Math items:

	Number of items	Point value
_____ Computation/equations	_____	_____
_____ Word problems	_____	_____
_____ Formulas	_____	_____
_____ Graphing	_____	_____
_____ Proofs	_____	_____
_____ Other; please describe	_____	_____

7. Other suggestions for study and review:

Thank you for your help!   Student signature: _____

                                  Parent signature: _____

FIGURE 11.9

Summative study guide: Secondary level.

Note: From *Reaching the Hard to Teach* by J. W. Wood, 2004, Richmond, VA: Judy Wood, Inc. Reprinted with permission.

Important vocabulary:

_____

Review questions:

_____

Possible short-answer questions:

_____

Important topics:

_____

Parent signature: _____

FIGURE 11.10
Summative study guide: Elementary level.

Study Guide (Formative)

Subject: Science

Student Name: Betty Barger

Grade level: 1st

Important Vocabulary:

1. Eggs (page 2)

2. Larva (caterpillar) (page 3)

3. Pupa (chrysalis) (page 3)

4. Adult (butterfly) (page 4)

Review Questions:

1. Can you show the sequence of the life cycle of a butterfly? (Use prepared pictures)

2. Can you label the stages in the life cycle of a butterfly? (Prepared cards with words are used)

3. Label the prepared sheet showing the stages in the life cycle of a butterfly with a number 1, 2, 3, 4 showing the sequence in the stages.

FIGURE 11.11
Sample formative study guide for science.

Note: From *Reaching the Hard to Teach* by J. W. Wood, 2004, Richmond, VA: Judy Wood, Inc. Reprinted with permission.

Figures 11.11 through 11.13 present study guides for grades 1 and 5. These examples should give you an idea how formative and summary study guides may be developed for multilevel abilities and subjects.

Students are directed to the study guide to review the lesson or test objective, the textbook, workbook, or handouts to be covered, and key words or vocabulary to be learned. If the test includes short-answer or essay items, review questions are a must. These questions will help the student organize study and review essay questions. The type of test and number of items and point values must also be considered carefully. The type of test reflects the type of retention measure the teacher used while teaching the lesson. In other words, if the lesson focused on specific dates, people, and facts, then the test is a recognition measure. If the lesson focused on general concepts such as "How did the invention of irrigation affect the lives of the people?" then the test is a subjective measure. Just remember this advice:

> Study guides need to be given out to students before
> a unit of study or at the beginning of a new chapter.

Study Guide (Summary)

Subject: Science

Student Name: Betty Barger

Grade level: 1st

Topic: Life Cycle of the Butterfly

Four Stages

A. Egg

B. Larva (caterpillar)   Show pictures of each and label

C. Pupa (chrysalis)

D. Adult (butterfly)

Organizer: Design Format

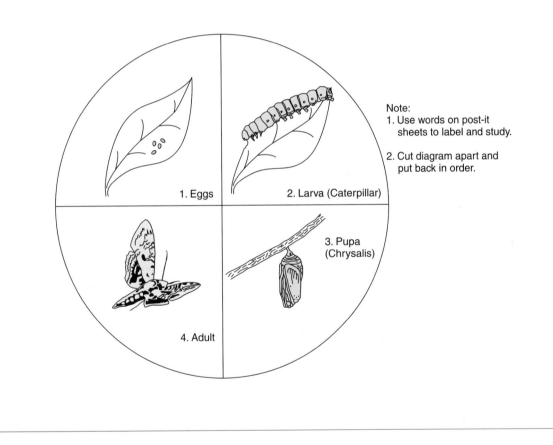

Note:
1. Use words on post-it sheets to label and study.

2. Cut diagram apart and put back in order.

FIGURE 11.12

Test review: Student will label each stage of the butterfly.

Note: From *Reaching the Hard to Teach* by J. W. Wood, 2004, Richmond, VA: Judy Wood, Inc. Reprinted with permission.

Study Guide

Student: _____ Date of test: _____

Subject: Reading _____ Date of study guide: _____

Teacher: _____

Study Guide
(Summary)

Needed study materials/pages:	Key points addressed:		
	_____		
	Test		
Key vocabulary words:	Type	Number of items	Point value
	Suggestions/Comments for study:		

Student signature: _____

Parent signature: _____

FIGURE 11.13

Sample study guide for reading.

Note: From *Reaching the Hard to Teach* by J. W. Wood, 2004, Richmond, VA: Judy Wood, Inc. Reprinted with permission.

Organizing for Study

After the student has completed the formative and summative study guides, organizing for study becomes the next focus. Many students still need the guided practice of planning for the study process. Using the monthly organization chart and the subject time-organization chart facilitates this process. The teacher may provide a chart form for students to complete by themselves or with the class. The monthly organization chart can be placed at the beginning of the notebook and completed daily. As tests, quizzes, projects, and papers are assigned, the student records each in the appropriate daily box for the month. To see a sample monthly organization chart, look back at Figure 11.7.

The subject time-organization chart provides structure for organizing the study time needed for each subject on a weekly basis. In planning the subject time-organization chart, the student refers to the monthly organization chart to be sure to include any important study items. These charts can be kept in the notebook or some other convenient place. Look back at Figure 11.7 to see a sample subject time organizer.

General Study Tips

Teachers can help students see the value of planned, organized study by offering the following general study tips:

- Keep notes and guides organized.
- Plan study time for each task.
- Review all class notes nightly.
- Develop flash cards for recognition of information.
- Plan a specific time and place for study.
- Develop a plan for reinforcement of study.

General Study Tips for Secondary Students

Secondary students can use the following ideas to help them begin their study and make the best use of their time:

- Develop a study schedule for 1 week to 1 month in advance.
- Always cross off an assignment when completed. This is an excellent self-motivator.
- Always use an assignment notebook.
- Plan to break up long assignments with a brief rest period, or work on a different subject.
- Schedule rewards for finishing your assignments.
- Sit close to the front of class.
- Make sure you have a complete set of notes.

Taped Books

All subject areas have texts that support the course. A major issue in our country is that students do not read "on grade level." This is the reality. Another reality is that students are presented or issued texts for subjects and the texts are on a subject-specific grade level. We expect students to read the texts (which are above their grade level) and pass the class. Although all of this does not make sense, it is a reality. However, we can teach students subject content *even* when they cannot read. If we are going to issue textbooks, all along knowing the student cannot read the material, then it is

1. Get the course syllabus from the student so that you will know when specific sections of the text are needed.

2. Ask the student to clarify which sections and pages are needed.

3. Be sure you have written permission from the publisher to record the text (the student or the taping service should supply this).

4. Secure an extra copy of the text. Sometimes complementary copies for the purpose of recording can be obtained from the publisher, instructor, or campus bookstore.

5. Allow 30 seconds of empty brown tape at the beginning.

6. Then announce cassette number and leave 15 seconds of tape silent (to go back later and add chapter and page numbers).

7. State title, author, publisher, copyright information, and your name.

8. At the beginning of each chapter, state the page number, chapter number, and name of the chapter.

9. Indicate "heading" or "subheading" as you read each one.

10. Read and spell out each name the first time it appears in a chapter. Do the same for foreign names or technical terms.

11. For long quotes, read as "quote . . . end quote."

12. For material in parentheses, read as "parenthesis . . . end parenthesis."

13. For graphs, tables, figures, and pictures, read the caption only. Read as "caption . . . end caption."

14. Read footnotes immediately following the sentence in which the footnote number appears. Read as "note (number) . . . end note" and then return to the text.

15. At the end of each side, state "End of cassette number (I, etc.) on page number _____."

16. Go back to the beginning of the tape and add the page numbers.

17. Label the tape. Include the title, author, edition, cassette number, side number, chapters, and pages.

FIGURE 11.14

Tip sheet for recording taped texts.

Note: From *Volunteer Reader/Taping Service Handbook* by C. Lendman, 1995, Columbus, OH: Association of Higher Education and Disability.

our professional responsibility to see that students receive the subject content in a manner in which they can learn.

I know that in the best of worlds everyone will be on grade level. However, this just is not the case in America's schools. The dilemma worsens as students move into higher grades. The gap between the reading and math levels of the student widens. So we *must* begin to tackle this issue. Yes, we keep working on the skills, but learning content is a major focus.

Figures 11.14 and 11.15 present ideas for recording texts and tips for using taped texts. The Accommodating Technology box provides sources from which to order recorded texts.

- Listen for short periods of time, stopping periodically to review and summarize what was said.

- Use the text as additional stimulus, to keep focused and to assist with pronunciation.

- Use headphone sets to eliminate outside noises and distractions, if necessary.

- Some students may need to close the text and their eyes in order to cut down on the amount of stimuli being received.

- Delineate the cassette's side and page changes using the printed cards enclosed with the tapes.

- Mark side and page changes with colored pens in order to clarify the text information.

- Find a quiet, distraction-free environment.

- Concentrate on listening and integrating the material. Auditory learning demands "active listening."

- Take notes while listening. Highlight the text and use the pause button when necessary.

- Adjust the tape recorder's speed control buttons to slow down or speed up the reading.

- Allow enough time to listen and relisten to the text. Listening to tapes takes time.

- Use the tape counter to mark important text information.

Note: Because of the time involved in ordering, taping, and receiving taped texts, students may need to preregister for courses and begin getting the needed texts prior to the first week of class.

FIGURE 11.15
Tips for students using taped texts.

Note: From *Volunteer Reader/Taping Service Handbook* by C. Lendman, 1995, Columbus, OH: Association of Higher Education and Disability

ACCOMMODATING TECHNOLOGY

BOOK/TAPE COMPANIES

Audio Book Contractors/Classic Books on Cassettes, P.O. Box 40115, Washington, DC 20016; 202-363-3429. Approximately 110 cassettes of children's and adult classics for sale or rent for one third the purchase price.

Books on Tape, Box 25122, Santa Ana, CA 92799-5122; 800-626-3333 (www.books-ontape.com/gif/rentalinfo.pdf). Publishes an annual catalogue and monthly updates. Rentals from $9.50 to $17.50 per box. Discount plans include 10% off for ordering three books at one time, 10% off plus a free selection for ordering 10 books. Interval shipment available. Gift certificates for $15.00 or more available. A current promotion allows a customer to order a book as a gift for a new customer for $5.00. If the recipient places an order, the giver receives a free rental.

(continued)

Recorded Books, P.O. Box 409, Charlotte Hall, MD 20622; 800-638-1304 (www.recordedbooks.com/index.cfm?fuseaction=basics.contact). Publishes a bimonthly catalogue. Rentals range from $7.50 to $20.50. Discount plans include 10% off for ordering three books at one time; free postage for ordering 10 books.

PUBLIC LIBRARIES

Libraries in the Washington, DC, area find it hard to keep shelves stocked for walk-in patrons, but are building their collections.

Library of Congress Talking Books Program, National Library Service for the Blind and Physically Handicapped, Washington, DC 20542, or contact your local library for information. Tapes and equipment lent free to people with disabilities who can't read conventional print materials. Eligibility must be certified by a physician. More than 40,000 recorded books available through the mail.

"On cassette 1987–1988," an annotated guide to audiocassettes, available in library references sections.

ACCOMMODATING DIVERSITY

Many options exist for presenting content that can help teachers of inclusive classrooms effectively instruct all of their students. Curriculum integration is one such method that holds promise for today's classrooms. With curriculum integration, subjects are not studied in isolation, but instead are used together to explore a particular topic or theme (Association for Supervision and Curriculum Development, 2004). For example, a class may use math, social studies, and science concepts to study the ocean.

Curriculum integration can lead to several positive outcomes for all students. Integration can allow educators to teach more because it reduces the duplication of skills and content (Drake, 1993). At-risk students don't always easily link what they are learning to other content or to the real world, but integration does both, leading to greater understanding and retention. This interdisciplinary approach also encourages the development of higher order thinking skills important in future learning.

The Association for Supervision and Curriculum Development (2004) stated that for effective interdisciplinary studies, educators must have a topic that lends itself to study from several points of view and two to five valuable themes they want the students to explore. After initiating an integration project, middle school teachers in Texas found that the process involved five stages: vision, curriculum development, professional development, implementation, and assessment (Bryan, Merchant, & Cramer, 1999). The result of curriculum integration can be "an approach and activities to further students' understanding more than is possible in a traditional, single-discipline unit" (Association for Supervision and Curriculum Development, 2004, p. 1).

ADAPTING THE PRESENTATION OF CONTENT

Student success may sometimes depend on the teacher's ability or willingness to adapt the presentation of content. The following activities provide a starting point for developing your own ideas. Many creative educators use inventive adaptations in the class, and the ideas in this chapter represent only a small number of the many possibilities. As much as possible, activities are organized into similar categories. In addition, they are coded *E* (elementary), *S* (secondary), or *E/S* (either elementary or secondary). Here is an example.

Activity (E/S):   Alternatives to writing book reports

Adaptations:

1. *Book jacket or bookmark:* Illustrate a cover for the book, or design a bookmark with characters or a setting from the book.
2. *News report:* Summarize the book by writing a news report as if the events in the story actually took place. Pretend to be a TV anchorperson and give the report.
3. *Ending rewrite:* Give the book a new ending. Pursue different ways the story could have ended.
4. *Advertisement:* Dress and act like a character from the book and "sell" the book to the class.
5. *Write to the author:* Write to the book's author in care of the publisher including comments about other books you have read.
6. *Poetry:* Summarize a book by retelling it in poetry form.
7. *Character journal:* Write a journal portraying a character from the book. The journal should be written in the first person and describe the character's thoughts, feelings, and ideas.
8. *Plays:* Rewrite the book in play form. For longer stories, take a chapter or chapters and write an act or scene of the play.
9. *Models:* Make a model of the setting or characters from the book.
10. *Bulletin board:* Use a classroom bulletin board to describe and display the setting, characters, and theme of the book.
11. *Map:* Draw a map of the story setting to show the story action. Use the map as a prop when discussing the book.
12. *Life-size posters:* Make life-size characters to use as props when presenting an oral book report.
13. *Letter:* Write a letter telling a friend about the book. Describe setting, characters, and plot.
14. *Comic book:* Summarize the book in the form of a comic book. This would be a good idea for unmotivated readers who are very interested in drawing and art.
15. *Oral and taped presentation:* This is an easy alternative to written reports. With taped reports, sound effects can be added to interest the audience.
16. *Condensed book:* Write and illustrate a short synopsis of the book. This is similar to what certain magazines do to advertise a book.
17. *Illustrations:* Draw main characters, the setting, or a climactic scene from the book.
18. *Panel discussion:* For students who are reporting on the same book, form a panel and have a question-and-answer period.
19. *Demonstration:* For how-to books, students can demonstrate what they learned. For example, for a book about cake decorating, a student could bring in a cake and show the steps in decorating.
20. *Time line:* Draw a time line of events as they happened in the story. Illustrations may be added to explain events.

21. *Popular music:* Write and perform (or record) rap songs about the book.

22. *Shoe box filmstrips.* Illustrate and summarize the books on cards and then put the cards into a shoe box. When a reader flips the cards, they look like a filmstrip. These filmstrips are kept in the class, and other students look at them and decide whether to read the books.

23. *Tape-recording stories.* Let students tape-record their book reports. You will be surprised how much students know orally that they can't express in a written format.

Frequently, students in inclusive settings can master the academic content presented in general education classes. However, learning will be easier when alternative ways of presenting content become standard procedure in general classrooms. For example, in a class on English grammar, success may depend on the teacher's ability to adapt or modify the presentation of content. A wonderful experience happened in one of my workshops, which clearly explains what I mean by adapting the presentation of content. This story was related to me by teacher A. One day teacher B came into teacher A's room, complaining that a young girl in the class simply could not learn how to do a certain skill. Teacher B said, "I have shown that student how to do the skill *seven* times, and she still cannot get it." Teacher A asked, "Did you show the student the same way each of the seven times?"

"Why, yes," replied teacher B.

Teacher A said, "The problem is that *you* don't get it!"

When a student cannot learn a skill one way, we need to adapt our teaching. This is adapting the format of content.

Activity (E/S):   Participating in oral classroom discussion

Adaptation: To help a student listen to questions and give appropriate answers, allow him or her to use a tape recorder. Tape questions with pauses for the student to respond. This gives the student a chance to play back the question and organize the answer. As the student becomes more comfortable with oral discussions, taping can be reduced.

Activity (E/S):   Giving oral reports

Adaptations: Allow students who are giving oral reports or speeches to use prompts, such as cards, posters, or visual models. Reports can also be presented using puppets or costumes.

Activity (E):   Storytelling

Adaptation: Provide story starters for students who have trouble with original ideas. Allow students to tape-record stories to help them formulate ideas or make presentations.

Activity (E/S):   Plays

Adaptation: Allow students with visual tracking difficulties to code or highlight their lines.

Joke and riddle books	Greeting cards
Album jackets	Comic books
Comic strips	Tongue twisters
Travel brochures	Transportation schedules
TV schedules	Catalogues
Advertisements	Classified ads
Telephone book, Yellow Pages	Cookbooks
Society columns, *Dear Abby*	Biographies
Sports page	How-to books
First-aid books	Driver's education manual
Magazines	The Internet

FIGURE 11.16
Motivation materials for reluctant readers.

Activity (E/S):   Comprehension

Adaptation: Highlight *who, what, where* questions in different colors. For example, highlight *where* questions in yellow, *who* questions in blue, and so on.

Activity (S):   Understanding idioms

Adaptation: Ask students to demonstrate using concrete illustrations.

Activity (E/S):   Understanding compound words

Adaptation: Provide cards with individual words on them and have the student select two. The student puts these two words together or exchanges with a friend. Nonsense words can be created and drawings or magazine pictures used to illustrate the new compound word.

Activity (E/S):   Motivating readers

Adaptations: After years of reading failure, students become turned off to reading. Therefore, it is up to the teacher to find reading material that interests them enough so that they find reading acceptable and enjoyable. Figure 11.16 offers a list of motivators for reluctant readers.

Activity (E/S):   Organizing and critical thinking

Adaptations: Figure 11.17 offers five tips. (Thanks to Froma Foner and Joan Sanders for their contributions.)

Activity (S):   Figurative language/learning parts of speech

Adaptation: Table 11.2 offers a suggestion.

1. Most needlework stores carry plastic sheets or strips that are easy on your eyes when working on a pattern (such as counted-cross stitch). The usual colors are yellow and blue. These strips or sheets may be placed on the reading material.

2. The gels (colored plastic sheets that are placed over theater lights) may be placed over reading material. Let the student select the color of choice and place over the page to be read. This helps for focus.

3. Place a Yellow Pages information guide in your classroom. Use a wide three-ring binder with tabs. After students have read a book they must complete an activity: sociogram, diorama, opinion/proof, cartoon, report, and so on. When each of the activities is explained, make an example and place it in the Yellow Pages behind the activity-labeled tab. You may place a student example behind your example with detailed requirements and directions. Thus, the teacher only has to explain once, and students have an ongoing prompt.

4. Here is a way to organize story elements:

S + Ch + Co + Pl + Cl + Th

Setting	**Ch**aracters	**Co**nflict	**Pl**ot	**Cl**imax	**Th**eme (lesson learned)
Time	People	Self			
Place	Animals	Others			
Mood	Others	Nature			
	(aliens, etc.)				

5. Here is a critical thinking tip:

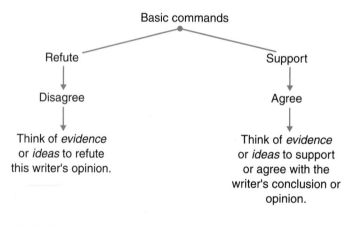

FIGURE 11.17
Reading tips.

Activity (S):   Antonyms and analogies

Adaptation: Figure 11.18 demonstrates a three-step process for prompting students' selection of antonyms and analogies.

Activity (E/S):   Making predictions and drawing conclusions

Adaptation: This skill may be modified by (a) reading the passage to the students and (b) presenting several choices of outcomes from which students select the correct answer.

TABLE 11.2
Figurative language prompt for short stories.

	Page Number	Column	Top third of page (T) Middle third of page (M) Bottom third of page (B)
Alliteration	27	1	T
	27	2	B
	28	2	M
	31	1	M
Metaphor	27	2	M
Simile	30	1	B
Personification	28	2	T
Hyperbole	31	1	T
	32	2	M

---

1. What you know
2. What you are reasonably sure of (an educated guess) through
   a. Association
   b. Prefixes
   c. Base words
   d. Personal creation within sentence
3. What you don't know
   Strategy for SWAG (*Scientific Wild-Donkey Guess*)
   a. If you know the prompt:
      • Pick answer you don't know.
         i. If more than one, choose B, C, or D.
         ii. If more than one in B, C, and D, pick longest.
   b. If you don't know the prompt, and don't know some choices
      • Pick as above or what you didn't know.
   c. If you don't know the prompt but know all choices, take the longest answer from B, C, and D. If longest is tied, then select least familiar.

If in doubt, guess the longest of B, C, and D. This has 33 to 40% accuracy.

FIGURE 11.18
Antonyms and analogy prompts.

Activity (E/S):   Reading graphs and maps

Adaptation: Use high-interest information on the graph or map such as favorite TV shows.

Activity (E/S):   Draw a chapter

Adaptation: As children read a novel, have them draw pictures of each chapter to help them remember events in the story. Drawings are kept in students' journals as a ready reference for sequence and events.

Activity (E/S):   Understanding the four kinds of sentences

Adaptation: Provide a basic sentence key: four cards with the type of sentence on one side and an example on the back.

Activity (E/S):   Sentence writing

Adaptation: Prepare substitution tables for teaching sentence structure (Anderson, Greer, & Odle, 1978). Begin with a simple sentence substitution table using the subject-predicate pattern.

1	2
Girls	play.
Boys	run.
Children	sing.

This activity can be extended from teaching simple agreement between subject and predicate to more complicated sentences.

1	2	3
I'm	going	to the White House.
You're	going	home.
He's	going	to school.
She's	going	to Frayser.
It's	going	to Dixiemart
We're	going	to the grocery.
You're	going	downtown.
They're	going	to the post office.

Activity (E):   Punctuation

Adaptation: Using newspaper cartoons, replace the cartoon bubbles with assigned sentences and allow the student to punctuate them. You may want to provide a choice of punctuation marks.

Activity (E/S):   Punctuation

Adaptation 1:   Tape-record sentences. Provide a work sheet that has the same sentences with punctuation marks omitted. As students listen to each sentence, they follow along on the work sheet and add the correct punctuation. You may want to include two or three choices of punctuation marks at the end of each sentence so students can circle correct responses. For example, "Is your house on fire (. ! ?)"

Adaptation 2: Give students a punctuation key to use when punctuating sentences. The key consists of four cards, each containing a punctuation mark and sample key words or sentences.

Adaptation 3: In preparing work sheets or listing sentences on the board, group sentences by punctuation types. For example, list all sentences requiring question marks or periods together. After students have acquired the skill, begin to mix the sentences, first using only two types of punctuation marks and then adding a third.

Activity (E/S): Compound words

Adaptation: Give students a word list with three columns. Tell students to select the first words from columns 1 and 2 and combine them in column 3. After students have learned the concept, mix the words in columns 1 and 2. Then have students select the appropriate word from column 1 and match with a word from column 2 to make a compound word in column 3.

1	2	3
after	noon	afternoon
some	one	someone
with	out	without
any	body	anybody

Activity (E/S): Spelling

Adaptation 1: Divide the spelling list into halves or fourths for students with mild disabilities. Often they can learn how to spell the words, but not as quickly as other students.

Adaptation 2: Provide "structure spellers" for students who have trouble remembering all of the words on the spelling list.

interesting I__ t __ __ e __ __ __ __ g

America __ m e __ i __ __

Activity (S): Pluralizing irregulars

Adaptation: Develop a format for making plurals on transparencies. Students can use the format over again for each new word. Figure 11.19 suggests one possible approach.

Activity (E/S): Creative writing

Adaptation: Don't be overly critical of grammatical errors in creative writing activities. Be concerned about the creativity, praise the efforts, and provide assistance with rewriting.

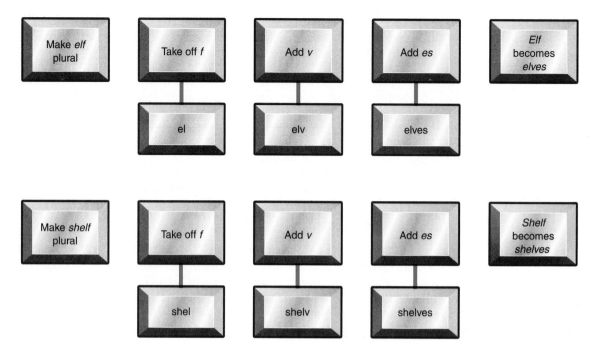

FIGURE 11.19
Pluralizing irregulars.

Activity (E/S):   Finding reference materials

Adaptation: Teach students to use a variety of reference materials. Provide a list and a map that shows the location of these items in the library.

Activity (E/S):   Collecting reference information

Adaptation: Give students a reference check work sheet to help keep track of reference information.

Activity (S):   Writing a business letter

Adaptation: Give students a visual model with lines to be filled in at appropriate parts of the letter. This prompt can be reduced by using dotted lines in place of solid lines.

Activity (E/S):   Writing multiparagraph papers

Adaptation: Figure 11.20 presents an organizational format for helping students develop a framework for writing multiparagraph papers. (Thanks to Tonya Evers for her contributions.)

Activity (E/S):   Proofreading checklists

Adaptation: Figures 11.21 and 11.22 suggest two types of checklists for use in the proofreading stage.

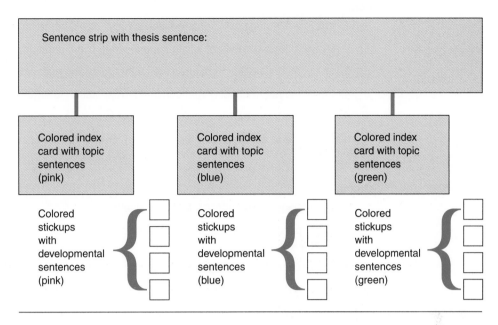

Directions:
1. Put up the organizer on the class wall as it is developing.
2. Before writing or organizing let students ask questions regarding topic or objective.
3. Students can move cards and stickups around to develop or change sequence of material.

FIGURE 11.20
Group activity for writing a multiparagraph paper.

Activity (S):   Organizing research material

Adaptation: Use a graphic organizer:

1. List the topic to be researched on the first line.
2. After reading or taking notes on the topic, divide information into major headings.
3. On index cards, list all words that represent the major headings.
4. Organize words into major areas.
5. Place words under appropriate subheading.
6. Place the words into the organizer format.

Figure 11.23 illustrates a graphic organizer.

Activity (E/S):   Vocabulary

Adaptations: Figure 11.24 presents 17 ways for modifying the teaching of vocabulary. (Thanks to the following educators for their contributions: Alyce Goolsby Kennard, Midway [TX] Independent School District, Saharli Cartwright, Andie Brown, Rodney Conrad, John W. Wilkie Jr., and Lisa Pharr.) Figures 11.25 through 11.27 suggest other ideas for vocabulary practice.

Form

____ 1. I have a title page with centered title, subject, class, name, and date.

____ 2. I have a thesis statement telling the main idea of my paper.

____ 3. I have an outline that structures the major topics and minor subheadings.

____ 4. I have footnoted direct quotations and paraphrased material.

____ 5. I have made a footnote page using correct form.

____ 6. I have made a bibliography, using correct form, of all reference materials.

Grammar

____ 1. I have begun all sentences with capital letters.

____ 2. I have put a period at the end of each sentence and a question mark at the end of each question.

____ 3. I have used other punctuation marks correctly.

____ 4. I have checked words for misspelling.

____ 5. I have reread sentences for correct noun-verb agreement and awkward phrasing.

____ 6. I have checked all sentences to be sure each is complete.

Content

____ 1. I have followed my outline.

____ 2. I have covered each topic from my outline thoroughly and in order.

____ 3. Each paragraph has a topic sentence.

____ 4. The paper has an introduction.

FIGURE 11.21
Proofreading checklist.

When you've finished writing, you should read your essay to make sure it's complete.
Use the checklist below to edit your work.

Check one

Yes **No**

_____ _____ I began with a topic sentence.

_____ _____ I provided details to support the topic sentence.

_____ _____ I finished with a summary statement.

_____ _____ All my sentences are complete.

_____ _____ My handwriting is legible.

_____ _____ My spelling is correct.

If you checked yes for all of the statements, you've mastered the steps in writing a good essay response!

FIGURE 11.22
Essay checklist.

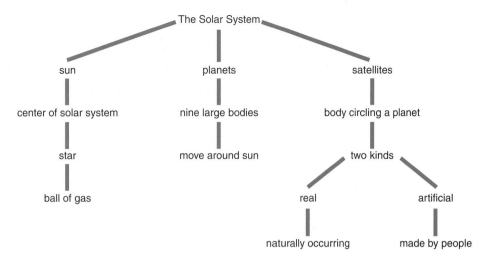

FIGURE 11.23
Graphic organizer.

Activity (E/S):   Understanding rules and laws

Adaptation: Students can role-play selected rules or law-breaking vignettes and then discuss what consequences are suitable for certain crimes. This is a good opportunity to discuss why certain rules and laws exist and look at their positive aspects.

Activity (E/S):   Understanding different cultures

Adaptation: Students with disabilities often have trouble visualizing life in other countries. When studying different cultures, allow students to "live" in that culture. Encourage them to dress, act, speak, eat, work, and play in the culture. Class periods could be devoted to experiences such as cooking and eating authentic meals, making costumes, or learning the languages. Discuss what is important to the culture and how it would feel to be a person from that setting.

Activity (E/S):   Using maps

Adaptation: Begin with something familiar to the students. Make a map of the school and have students label specific points. Then have them map out their neighborhoods. Eventually progress to states, sections of a country, and finally whole countries.

Activity (E/S):   Reviewing maps

Adaptation: Make an overhead transparency of a blank map. Project the map onto the chalkboard and have students write in specific information being reviewed, such as states, capitals, and rivers. Students can erase and repeat until they've learned the material.

1. Enlarge the diagram of a plant, or perhaps an animal cell. Place the correct vocabulary word on a sentence strip backed with tacky paper. Let the student place the correct word on the correct diagram part.

2. The same technique may be used in social studies. The correct CONTENT may be stuck on the correct place on the map: OCEAN, STATES, and so on.

3. Have students place a vocabulary word on one side of the page and the definitions on the other. The paper may be copied by the teacher and placed in the student's notebook or in a class notebook. The original paper can be cut into flash cards. For example:

Vocabulary Word	Definition
Vocabulary Word	Definition
Vocabulary Word	Definition
Vocabulary Word	Definition

4. Have students draw a picture to go with the vocabulary word as a clue. For example:

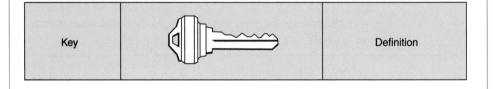

Key		Definition

FIGURE 11.24
Teaching vocabulary.

364

5. A wonderful and fun way to teach vocabulary and to keep all of those words and definitions in one place is to make a vocabulary booklet. For example:

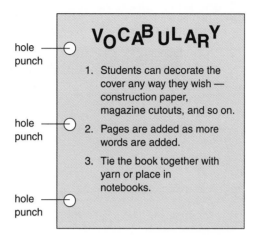

Now let's look inside.

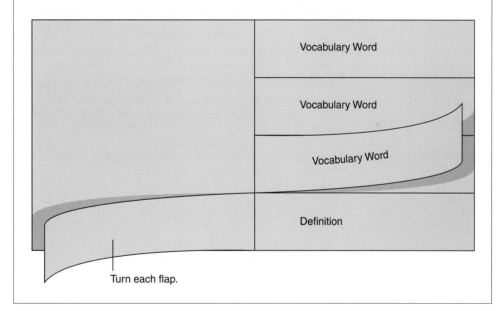

(continued)

6. Use color coding to keep track of vocabulary cards. The different colors represent different subjects: blue for history, pink for reading, and so on. Because the white cards are less expensive, use highlighter pens to color code or use small stick-on dots. In the corner of the card, write the chapter, number, and/or period.

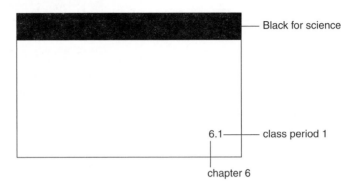

7. For storing vocabulary cards, use sports card holders. Punch holes and put into folders or notebooks. The cost is approximately $3.99 for 25 sheets. The 3″ × 5″ cards will have to be cut to the size of baseball cards.

8. Vocabulary cards may also be stored in baggies. Place tape on the baggie to label each set of cards.

9. In preparing vocabulary cards, write the word on the blank side and the definition and a sentence using the word in context on the lined side.

10. Tape-record words, definitions, and sentences. Listen while getting ready for school, before going to bed, while waiting for the school bus, or when riding in the car.

FIGURE 11.24
Continued.

Activity (E/S):   Understanding graphs and charts

Adaptation: Use high-interest information such as favorite TV shows, foods, and sports. Figure 11.28 gives an example.

11. Vocabulary cards can be typed and printed on construction paper, cut with a paper cutter, and made ready for students, with or without a buddy, to complete. For example:

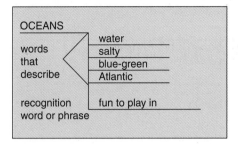

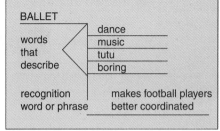

12. When flash cards (vocabulary or informational) go home, have the parents sign a note saying that the child has answered all cards correctly and give five bonus points to be added to the test score. Students with no parent in the home, or one who is having difficulty, may ask someone else to sign his note. The student still gets the five points and you have a measure of the student's ability level.

13. For flash cards, put the word on one card and the definition on a separate card (not on the back of the word card). This makes it easy to match the word to the definition. Also, put little numbers on the back of each card so that the student will get immediate feedback of response.

14. Make sure that you teach all vocabulary that is interchangeable and explain why it is interchangeable or use only one set of vocabulary and test it. For example:

    War between the States:

    North = Union = Yankees = Blue

    South = Rebels = Confederate = Gray

15. Watch the vocabulary tests that come with teacher guides. Frequently, the definitions we discuss in class look nothing like the definition in the test guide.

16. Some students do not know how to decode the words in the definition and thus do not understand the words even after looking up the definition. Go over the definition and decode all words.

17. Let students design Trivial Pursuit questions to share with each other and with their parents.

Activity (S):   Understanding a sequence of events on a time line

Adaptation: First, have students list important events in their lives and the approximate date when each occurred. Provide a time line and have students transfer the information onto it. Figure 11.29 gives an example.

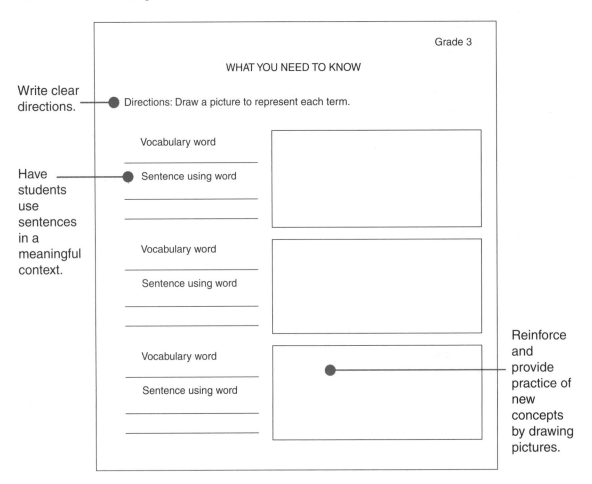

FIGURE 11.25
Vocabulary: Sentence and picture.

STUDENT KNOWLEDGE CHECK

In the vignette at the beginning of the chapter, Mrs. Jimenez was presenting a lesson on map skills.

1. What are some note-taking accommodations Mrs. Jimenez could make for the class?
2. What are three different assignments Mrs. Jimenez could give at the end of the assignment?

Activity (E):   Studying products made in different sections of the United States

Adaptation: On the bulletin board, draw an outline of the United States. Develop a series of transparencies with shading for different areas of the country. Pose a question such as "What are the major corn-producing states?" A student will select the correctly shaded transparency to project onto the U.S. outline on the bulletin board.

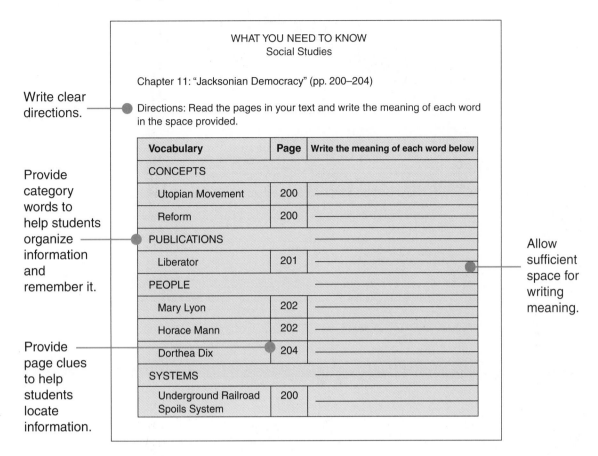

Write clear directions.

Provide category words to help students organize information and remember it.

Provide page clues to help students locate information.

Allow sufficient space for writing meaning.

FIGURE 11.26
Vocabulary: Word and meaning.

Activity (E/S): Solving word problems using structured organizers

Adaptation: Figure 11.30A offers two suggestions. (Thanks to Diane Damback for her contributions.)

Activity (E/S): Solving word problems

Adaptation: Use Figure 11.30B.

Activity (E/S): Steps in problem solving

Adaptation: See Figure 11.30C. (Special thanks to Helen Giestie.)

Activity (E): Money

Adaptation: Make the concept meaningful by using paper money. Begin by using several pretend paper one-dollar bills. To show that two half-dollars constitute one dollar, cut one paper dollar in half. Then place the two halves on the whole paper dollar and ask the student to put the cut paper dollar together. This activity functions just like putting parts of a puzzle together. The activity may be extended to other fractions of a dollar such as fourths or tenths.

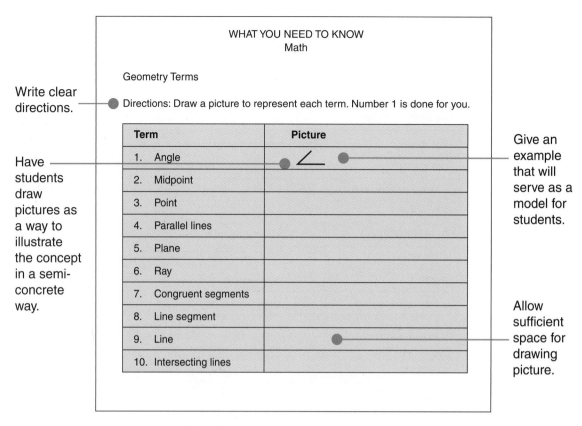

Write clear directions.

Have students draw pictures as a way to illustrate the concept in a semi-concrete way.

Give an example that will serve as a model for students.

Allow sufficient space for drawing picture.

FIGURE 11.27
Vocabulary: Word and picture.

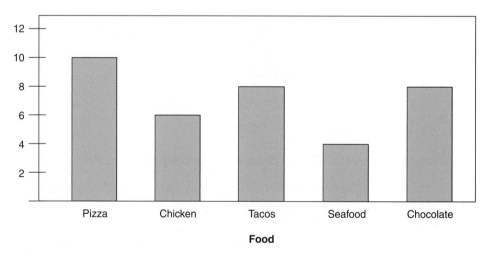

FIGURE 11.28
Favorite foods.

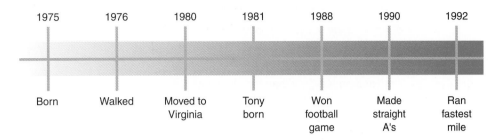

FIGURE 11.29
Time line.

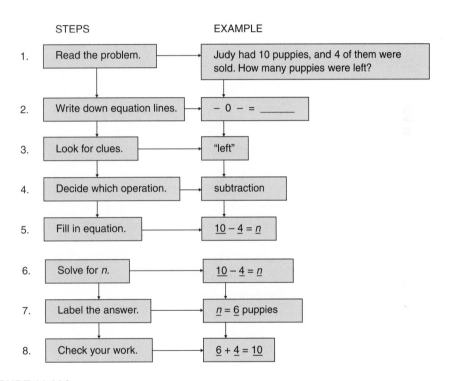

FIGURE 11.30A
Solving word problems using structured organizers.

Activity (E): Addition and subtraction

Adaptation: Block off each column of numbers so that students don't get distracted visually. Figure 11.31 gives an example.

Activity (E/S): Division

Adaptation: Use a model to teach division. Fade parts of the model as students begin to understand where each number belongs. Figure 11.32 gives an example.

1. [Write] down numbers putting big number on top.

2. [Read] the problem.

3. [Decide] if the answer is bigger than the big number.

4. [Refer] to chart:

If answer is *bigger*	If answer is *smaller*
$+$	$-$ (comparisons, buying)
$\times$ (times, every, each, same number over 2 over)	$\div$ (each, every, same number)

5. If there are more than two numbers, look at the question for the significant numbers and eliminate distractors.

FIGURE 11.30B
Solving word problems.

1. Read the question and *circle* what you are trying to find.
2. Determine the unit of measure in which your answer should be expressed.
3. Write down the values you know with the correct units of measure.
4. Choose the correct formula, one which includes what you know and what you are looking for with no other gaps.
5. Fill in the formulas with your values, being sure to include the correct units.
6. Isolate the unknown on one side of the equal sign.
7. Solve for the unknown and follow through with the units.

   Example: What mass of aluminum will have a volume of 15 cm^3? Aluminum has a density of 2.7g/cm^3.

   density = 2.7 g/cm^3 $D = m/v$

   volume = 15 cm^3

   mass = ?   2.7 g/cm^3 = m/15 cm^3

   (15 cm^3)(2.7g/m^3) = m

   40.5g = mass

   Answer Sheet for Prompt

   Looking for _____

   Know _____

   Formula Calculation _____

   Answer _____

FIGURE 11.30C
Steps in problem solving.

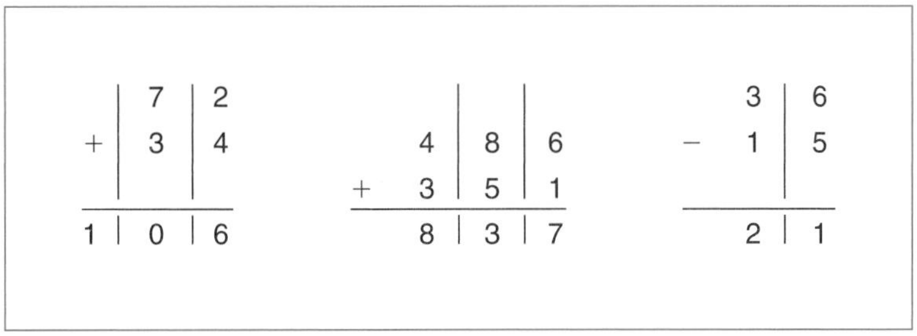

$$
\begin{array}{r}
7 \ | \ 2 \\
+ \quad 3 \ | \ 4 \\
\hline
1 \ | \ 0 \ | \ 6
\end{array}
$$

FIGURE 11.31
Blocking columns of numbers.

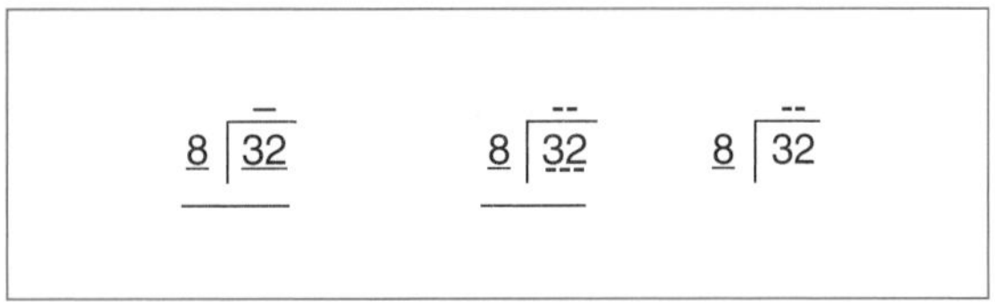

$$8\overline{)32} \qquad 8\overline{)32} \qquad 8\overline{)32}$$

FIGURE 11.32
Division model.

Activity (E/S):   How to study for a math exam

Adaptation: Give students the following advice (thanks to Lee Cairel):

1. Start early. Don't be afraid to ask review questions in class. Probably six more students have the same question.
2. Find out when your teacher is available for extra help out of class. Then go see him or her.
3. Scan the last chapter exam to review skills already learned.
4. Know exactly *what* the exam will cover and *when* it will be. (Chapter exam? definitions? solving problems? must show work? part credit given?)
5. Think about the name and objective of the chapter (What is the chapter talking about?). Draw pictures in your mind and think about them. Draw pictures on paper, too.
6. Review each section and do a few problems in each homework assignment. (Do some odd-numbered problems; they usually have answers in the back of the book.) Also, ask your teacher about problems that you forgot how to do or didn't get the right answers for.
7. Study important properties and vocabulary words and know how to use them.
8. Review any notes you have taken; go over any examples and quizzes from the chapter.
9. Look over the chapter review at the end of the chapter; go back again to sections that are fuzzy. Ask questions.
10. Take the chapter test at the end of the chapter as if it were an exam. For any problems that are difficult, ask your teacher.

1. Develop a "check off" chart for helping
    students divide.

$$\begin{array}{r} 25 \\ 3\overline{)75} \\ -64 \\ \hline 15 \\ -15 \\ \hline 00 \end{array}$$

$\div$ divide
$\times$ multiply
$-$ subtract
$\downarrow$ bring down

FIGURE 11.33
Graphics.

Note: From *Reaching the Hard to Teach* by J. W. Wood, 2004, Richmond, VA: Judy Wood, Inc. Reprinted with permission.

11. Finally, look over the chapter test again the night before, and get a good night's sleep.

12. Have a healthy breakfast in the morning and come ready to do a good job on the exam.

Activity (E/S):   Division

Adaptation: Develop a "check-off" chart for helping students divide.

Activity (E/S):   Sequential graphics (see Figure 11.33)

Adaptation: Use color coding (see Figure 11.34).

Activity (E/S):   Division

Adaptation: Use steps of assisting with division (see Figure 11.35).

Activity (E/S):   Math prompts for math vocabulary

Adaptation:

Multiplication	Division
Cue words:	Cue words:
multiply	divide
product	quotient
times	divided by
twice (32)	halved (divide by 2)
doubled (32)	quartered (divided by 4)
tripled (33)	equal parts
quadrupled (34)	

2. When using sequential graphics, add color. For example, *green* for the beginning step, *yellow* for the middle, and *red* for the end.

Example: Solving algebra equations

$$\boxed{2 \;+\; x \;=\; 8} \qquad \leftarrow \text{green}$$

$$\boxed{\begin{array}{ccc} 2 & + \; x & = \; 8 \\ -2 & & -2 \\ 0 & x & 6 \end{array}} \qquad \leftarrow \text{yellow}$$

$$1$$

$$\boxed{x = 6} \qquad \leftarrow \text{red}$$

FIGURE 11.34
Color coding.

Note: From *Reaching the Hard to Teach* by J. W. Wood, 2004, Richmond, VA: Judy Wood, Inc. Reprinted with permission.

Dividing

Steps:

1. Divide the dividend by the divisor in the greatest place value position possible.
2. Multiply.
3. Subtract.
4. Bring down the next digit or digits.

Repeat steps 1 to 4 until the remainder is less than the divisor.

To check, multiply the quotient and the divisor, add the remainder to get the dividend.

Examples

$$
\begin{array}{r}
58 \quad \leftarrow \text{quotient} \\
\text{divisor} \rightarrow 6\overline{)348} \quad \leftarrow \text{dividend} \\
-30\downarrow \\
\hline
48 \\
-48 \\
\hline
0 \quad \leftarrow \text{remainder}
\end{array}
$$

$$
\begin{array}{r}
158\text{R}3 \\
5\overline{)793} \\
5\downarrow \\
\hline
29 \\
25\downarrow \\
\hline
43 \\
40 \\
\hline
3 \quad \leftarrow \text{remainder}
\end{array}
$$

(continued)

FIGURE 11.35
Steps for division.

Note: From *Reaching the Hard to Teach* by J. W. Wood, 2001, Richmond, VA: Judy Wood, Inc. Reprinted with permission.

Think About It!

Answer the question and solve the equation.

(a) How many fives in 10? → $10 \div 5 = a$

(b) How many fours in 16? → $16 \div 4 = b$

(c) 30 students in the class.

    6 students on a team.

How many teams are there?

      $30 \div 6 = N$

Complete this table

Since	We know that
$6 \times 5 = 30$	$30 \div 5 = \underline{6}$
$7 \times 6 = 42$	$42 \div 6 = \underline{7}$
$24 \times 17 = 408$	$408 \div 17 = \underline{24}$
$52 \times 36 = 1872$	$1872 \div 36 = \underline{52}$

Mental Math

Try to move across each row without using pencil and paper.

If you do your work correctly, you will end with the starting number.

1. | 24 | ÷4 | 6 | ×2 | 12 | ÷3 | 4 | ×5 | 20 | +8 | 28 | ÷7 | 4 | ×6 | 24 |

2. | 40 | ÷5 | 8 | +7 | 15 | +5 | 20 | ÷4 | 5 | ×7 | 35 | +7 | 42 | −2 | 40 |

FIGURE 11.35
Continued.

Activity (E/S):   Choosing the correct operation

Adaptation: Use the four-step method:

    Step 1 Understand the problem.

    Step 2 Make a plan.

    Step 3 Carry out the plan.

    Step 4 Check the answer for reasonableness.

Activity (S):   Lab assignments

Adaptation: Many schools ask students to complete part of a lab assignment sheet before the teacher's demonstration and to finish the sheet after the demonstration. Table 11.3 shows how to adapt a lab assignment for the mainstreamed student.

Teachers also need to prepare the physical environment for a lab. They should (a) plan ahead to accommodate students with disabilities and (b) interview students

TABLE 11.3
Adapting a lab assignment.

Lab Assignment Outline	Standard Student Response	Adaptations for Mainstreamed Student
Title of lab	Student completes.	Fill in for student.
Materials	Student completes from observing teacher or reading text.	Complete for student or let peer tutor assist.
Purpose of lab	Student completes from text or lecture.	Complete for student.
Lab procedures	As teacher demonstrates, student records the procedure.	List procedures on the board so student can follow each step. Provide a check sheet and have student check off each step.
Observations	Student records the observed experiment.	Let student tape-record the observed demonstration.
Conclusion	Student records.	This step requires the evaluation level of Bloom's taxonomy, so the teacher may choose to omit it for a mainstreamed student.
Analysis/questions	Student responds.	Provide answers for the mainstreamed student.

concerning their needs, keeping communication open. Student needs may involve the following:

1. Adjustment of table height so that students using a wheelchair can pull up to the table
2. Accessible sinks for cleanup
3. Microscope stands at eye level and within arm's reach
4. Display models or chemistry sets at seat level
5. Adequate space around tables and entrances to allow access by wheelchairs, walkers, and so on
6. Flexible arrangement of lab space to allow changes when needed
7. Transition time to and from various activities to accommodate students who may take longer to move from one area to another

When preparing students for a lab, teachers should do the following:

1. Prepare materials being used in advance. (For example, open jars if screw tops are difficult for students with physical impairments.) Waiting for activities to begin can be frustrating for students with ADHD.
2. Encourage students to speak to you about directions that may be unclear to them, or state instructions several times throughout lab activities.

A multimodality approach to teaching content reaching all learner types. What suggestions would you have for teachers for multimodality instruction?

3. Keep lab activities structured and limit directions.

4. Be open to the use of tape recorders or other forms of backup support.

5. Summarize and review information covered at the end of each session.

6. Consider alternative test-taking and grading procedures.

7. Keep overhead transparencies or written materials simple and free of clutter.

Here are some lab tips for students:

1. Speak with your lab instructor concerning your individual needs and concerns.

2. Allow yourself extra time to get prepared and comfortable before the lab begins.

3. If you are using a tape recorder or any other device, discuss it with the instructor in advance.

4. Cue yourself using key terms or phrases if you have difficulty maintaining focus.

5. If information is unclear to you, speak with your instructor or ask questions.

6. Review your lab notes immediately after class to help retain information.

7. Limit distractions to help you focus on tasks and schedules in the lab.

8. If you have difficulty following the sequence of steps in a procedure, ask for a printed copy of the procedure prior to class so that you can familiarize yourself with the steps. As you complete each step, mark it off.

9. Supplement your notes with diagrams to illustrate concepts, procedures, etc. Develop and use a shorthand method for noting technical terms that appear often in your notes.

10. If you are aware of physical accommodations or technological adaptations that will enable you to use the lab more fully (e.g., a straight chair fastened to a platform on casters or foot-operated rather than hand-operated equipment), discuss these with your instructor.

Activity (S):   Teaching students with disabilities to drive

Adaptation: Here are some suggestions:

1. Our attitude toward persons with disabilities is their biggest handicap.
2. Sincerity is sensed easily by a person with a disability.
3. Find something to praise, no matter how small the accomplishment, especially during the early lessons. This builds rapport and relaxes the student.
4. Be honest. For example, if the student needs to stay off the expressway and out of rush-hour traffic, tell him or her to plan driving times during the least busy times of the day.
5. Students do not want sympathy; they want independence. Be objective and positive and expect their best performance.
6. Follow up on students to ensure that the correct vehicle modifications are made.
7. During the final phases of driving, encourage parents and other members of the family to observe the student's driving. Explain the purpose and importance of each piece of equipment.
8. It is very easy for us to help the student in his or her efforts to drive (for example, learning to use the key quad to turn the ignition), but the real reward is seeing the student successfully and independently achieve this goal. Don't rush to help. Be patient and look at the expression on the student's face when he or she finally succeeds. The time is worth it.
9. When you must tell a student you are unable to help him or her at a particular time, never say *never.* Tell the student, "I am placing your evaluation on file at the present time and will contact you as soon as I am able to help you." Research and modern technology are constantly changing. At the same time, if you truly sense that the person will never drive, don't give false hope. Be honest and explain in detail. At this time, the person's emotions will surface, so be gentle.
10. Ninety percent of driving depends on vision. If you detect a visual problem during the evaluation, require that a medical evaluation be sent to you to ensure that this can be corrected.

Before completing our section on activities and adaptations for teaching select subject matter, I would like to introduce you to one of seven *"Power Prompts"* created by Randy Larson with Judy W. Wood (2000), which is an example of assisting the student in turning an essay into a fun project.

Activity (E/S):   Writing a narrative essay

Adaptation: See Figure 11.36   .

Power Prompts

Narrative

Taking an essay test is like going to the dentist, except you don't get the lollipop when it's all over. You painfully open a test booklet, and you see long-winded questions requiring long, dreary answers about drippy topics like why rainforests are so rainy.

Boring!

Created by Randy Larson
with Judy W. Wood, Ph.D.

A **Power Prompt** is the part of an essay question that says what you have to do to answer correctly. Some prompts will say to PROVE or EVALUATE or DEFINE or DESCRIBE or ILLUSTRATE something about a topic like "justice" or "freedom."

Narrative

Narratives (brief stories) can often put some life into your essay answers and make them more to-the-point when writing about hard-to-explain concepts or ideas. For example, if the **Power Prompt** says, "*Define 'bravery' and illustrate how this concept relates to freedom,*" you might include in your answer a brief **NARRATIVE** (story) about a time when bravery was important to your own personal freedom; maybe you stood up to a bully or something. Whatever your story is, make sure it's to the point. Don't ramble for six pages. You have only a few moments to answer most essay questions, so if you decide to include a story in your answer, be brief when you respond to **Power Prompts** that command you to **Illustrate, Prove, Define, Evaluate**, or **Describe** a concept or an idea.

Power Prompts

To respond to **Power Prompts** correctly, you need to know what they mean. Any of these **Power Prompts** could be answered by using a brief NARRATIVE as part of your written response.

ILLUSTRATE: give *examples* to make your point clear and to give a clear picture of the topic. An example could be a STORY.

PROVE: give reasons, facts and *examples* to convince your reader that your ideas or viewpoints are true and right and valid.

DEFINE: provide the clear meaning of a term or concept. You can show how the term is different from other terms or has ideas that are similar. You could give an *example* of how the term works in real life: use a brief STORY.

EVALUATE: decide if an idea or concept or decision is good or bad, useful or useless. You could show how your evaluation of the topic is the best by giving a clear example: a STORY.

DESCRIBE: draw a word picture of how something is done, or how it should look. Pretend you are a reporter and tell the facts that you want the reader to SEE.

TEQ: Tricky Essay Question

Which **Power Prompt** above would be most easily answered using a brief, powerful NARRATIVE? WHY?

FIGURE 11.36
Power prompts: Narrative.

Note: From *Power Prompts: Narrative* by R. Larson and J. W. Wood, 2000, Midlothian VA: Judy Wood, Inc. Reprinted with permission of Judy Wood, Inc.

Get Your NARRATIVE Example Here!

Question: *Define* the term "friendship," and *illustrate* (show) the value of true friendship in all areas of human life.

POWER TIP!!!!

Good things come in three's: **Morning, Noon, and Night – Breakfast, Lunch, and Dinner – Beginning, Middle, and End**, especially the end of school!

When you write an answer to an essay question, use the last good thing listed above; use a three-part structure — have a clear **beginning**, a solid **middle**, and an interesting **ending**.

For example, in the essay answer next door, the beginning is the definition part of the answer. The middle is the story, the narrative, about the two boys who were friends. The end is the summary that wraps up the essay and ties the story into the definition.

Beginning: Define the term "friendship"

Middle: Story about "friendship"

End: Tie the story into the definition of "friendship." Make the ending as interesting as possible.

True friendship is a deal made between people that says, "We will not betray each other. We'll be there when one of us needs the other." This kind of social bargain is at the heart of human life. Without true friendship, life would be like a bird with one wing.

There is a story that illustrates this point. A boy named Manuel caught beautiful birds to sell to tourists who came through his mountain village. Manuel's best friend, Carlos, wanted to go along into the mountains to capture the soft-singing birds, but Carlos was blind and couldn't go.

Over time, Carlos became jealous of Manuel's good fortune, so one night he turned all his friend's birds loose and smashed the little wooden cages. Manuel was enraged and searched the village for the criminal who did this terrible deed.

Carlos hid and did not see Manuel for many days. Finally, Manuel went to Carlos and asked if he knew who did the destruction.

Carlos said, "I did it. I am sorry. I could not control my anger. You have freedom and you have money. You have a fine business. I have nothing."

Manuel said, "You have one thing more than money. You have my friendship, and always will. I am sorry I have left you out of things because of your blindness. From now on, I will go out to catch the birds, but when I return, you will help me build the cages and you will give the birds each of their names. We will split the money down the middle, like a ripe melon."

Friendship is being partners with someone in the deepest sense. It is based on forgiveness and on wanting the best for another person. Without friendship, the best parts of life would be impossible to experience. Like a bird with two wings, only when we are true friends with another person, can we truly "fly."

SEQ'S - SAMPLE ESSAY QUESTIONS

An essay is a long answer to a short question!

1. *Prove* the importance of music by *illustrating* how life would be without the presence of music in the world.

2. *Evaluate* the actions of Hansel and Gretel toward the witch in the cottage. Was it okay for them to stick her in the oven? Were they just trying to protect themselves, or was there another reason for their actions? Were they right or wrong in doing what they did?

3. *Describe* the effect of an alien from a distant galaxy dropping in on one of your Aunt Tilly's Tupperware parties that she has at her apartment every second Friday after every full moon.

4. *Define* the term "nerd" and *illustrate* how nerds are having a tremendous impact on the world around us, especially in the area of computer science.

5. *Evaluate* the performance of a Salad Shooter as compared to a cleaver-wielding Japanese chef at a high-speed restaurant in San Francisco or New York, then *describe* how the Salad Shooter has changed the way the world relates to vegetables.

6. *Describe* the game of "grammar polo" and *prove* that it is the world's most boring sport.

7. *Illustrate* how the absence of all fast-food restaurants in America would result in widespread starvation for teenagers from coast to coast.

8. *Define* "middle age" and *describe* what life will be like when you are a middle-aged human.

FIGURE 11.36
Continued.

MODIFICATIONS AND WHOLE LANGUAGE

"Whole language is an attempt to build curriculum based on what we know about natural language learning." It avoids using a skill-sequence approach that seems logical to adults. Breaking language into small parts to be learned in sequence "seems logical only until you watch how little kids are handling language" (Jerome Harste, personal communication).

According to the Association for Supervision and Curriculum Development, components of whole language theory include the following:

1. *Focus on meaning, not the component parts of language.* Children learn language from whole to part. Therefore, instruction in reading and writing should begin by presenting whole texts (engaging poems and stories) rather than zeroing in on the bits and pieces that make up language (words, syllables, and sounds in isolation). By keeping language whole, teachers focus on its purpose—to communicate meaning—rather than reduce language to a set of abstractions that children can't relate to. Teachers should teach skills in context, not in isolation. Children learn the subskills of language such as letter–sound relationships, spelling, punctuation, and grammar most readily when these skills are taught in the context of reading and writing activities. Teachers should coach children in skills as the need for skills arises rather than march children in lockstep through a sequenced-skills curriculum.

2. *Expose children to lots of good literature.* High-quality children's literature is the heart and soul of a whole language program. By acquainting children with stories and nonfiction works that capture their interest, teachers motivate children to become adept readers and writers and plant the seeds of a lifelong love for books. Shared literature also provides a meaningful context for teaching skills.

3. *Get children writing early and often.* Teachers should encourage young children to write as soon as they can hold a pencil rather than wait until they have learned to read. Reading and writing develop best in tandem. When children write, they master phonics relationships because they must constantly match letters with sounds to write what they want to say.

4. *Accept invented spelling.* Whole language teachers do not expect perfect spelling from the beginning. Instead, they encourage children to make their best efforts. Children's crude approximations reveal to what degree young writers have cracked the phonetic code. Over time, as children's spelling becomes more conventional, teachers can gradually insist on more correct spelling.

5. *Allow pupils to make choices.* Teachers should let children choose at least some of the books they read and topics they write on. When children have some control over their learning, they are more motivated and retain what they learn longer.

The concept of whole language works from the whole to the parts. This technique for teaching acquisition (whole-part-whole) was discussed in chapter 10. Within the context of teaching whole language, an educator can still make modifications that fit into the instructional process at any time.

When thinking of ways to adapt the presentation of content, teachers should not overlook teacher manuals. They contain many resources.

TASK ANALYSIS

Task analysis is the breakdown of skills within a task into sequential steps. When teachers teach specific content and realize that a student still does not grasp the concept, they should check to see whether the skill could be broken down into smaller steps. Then teach each step separately.

Task analysis can be used for the entire course by dividing all content into specific skills to be taught. As Anderson and colleagues (1978) pointed out, "At any point in the learning process, the child may have failed to acquire mastery of any skill or concept necessary for success at subsequent levels" (p. 168). Such gaps in acquiring a skill make it difficult for students to go beyond a certain point in an assignment.

Anderson and colleagues suggested three steps for teachers to follow in rearranging textbooks. First, the teacher studies the table of contents and identify the skills covered by the book. Second, the teacher divides those skills into major tasks and subtasks and arranges subtasks sequentially in order of planned instruction. Third, the teacher tabulates page numbers for examples of all the subtasks. The teacher can then use these examples in class as exercises, practice assignments, or test examples or questions. Table 11.4 uses task analysis to reorganize the content of a mathematics textbook.

TABLE 11.4
Task analysis of math book content.

Major Tasks and Subtasks	Instructional Examples on Page:	Text Examples On Page:
Addition		
Addition combinations	5–7	9–13, 462
Tens in addition	14	14–15
Hundreds in addition	14	16
Column addition	16–17	17–27, 56, 454, 458
Regrouping in addition	28	28–29
Estimating sums	30	31–34, 37, 55–56
Mental addition	35	35–36
Subtraction		
Subtraction combinations	7–9	9–13, 463
Tens in subtraction	14	15, 38
Hundreds in subtraction	14	15–16, 38
Regrouping in subtraction	40–41	42–47, 56, 455, 459
Expanded notation	42	42
Subtraction of fractions	48–49	49–51
Estimating differences	51	51–52, 53–56
Mental subtraction	53	53–55
Multiplication		
Multiplication combinations	57–59, 60, 62–63	59, 61, 464
Properties of multiplication	66	67
Number pairs and graphs	70–71	72–73, 76–77
Multiplying using tens	72, 74–75	72–73, 76–77, 456, 460
Multiplying using a machine	78–81	81
Mental multiplication	82, 86	82–83, 86–88
Estimating products	84	84–85, 88
Division		
Division combinations	65	65, 465
Properties of division	66	67
Division involving remainders	67	68–69, 92, 457, 461
Dividing a number by single digit	69, 92–93	68, 93, 103, 457, 461
Dividing using tens	72, 92	78, 89, 94–95, 103, 457, 461
Trial quotients	95–97	97–98
Estimating quotients	96–99	99–100, 102–103
Mental division	101	101–102

Note: From Anderson. R. M., Greer, J. G., & Odle, S. J. (Eds.). (1978). *Individualizing educational materials for special children in the mainstream* (p. 169). Baltimore: University Park Press. Copyright 1978 by Pro-Ed, Inc. Reprinted by permission.

TABLE 11.5
Reorganizing a table of contents.

Original Table of Contents	Sequentially Reorganized Table of Contents
Writing sentences	Learning parts of speech
Writing letters	Writing sentences
Learning parts of speech	Using correct punctuation
Writing paragraphs	Writing paragraphs
Using correct punctuation	Writing letters

Using task analysis to break down textbooks for students offers them more opportunities for success. They can acquire major skills more easily when the instructional material is organized for quick access to specific and smaller skills.

Teachers can also reorganize language arts texts so that they can sequentially teach the skills required at a specific level. Many times, the major subjects in a basal language arts text, as listed in the table of contents, are not in sequential order. To reorganize the table of contents, the teacher must first determine the prerequisite skills for each major area.

Table 11.5 presents excerpts from a basal language arts text and a sequential reorganization of the table of contents. The teacher does not deviate from the basic topics to be taught but simply redesigns the order of the material. By rearranging texts into small sequential skills, the teacher makes it possible for students to complete assignments.

In applying the task analysis model, the regular classroom teacher uses the principle underlying Bloom's domain of cognitive learning: identifying the specific skill being taught and breaking down the skill into steps, proceeding from the easiest to the most difficult. Figure 11.37 shows how learning to use the dictionary can be broken down into 14 steps. Students with no dictionary skills would have difficulty beginning with step TA-10 in Figure 11.37. However, because the task has been broken into such small steps, the teacher can begin where the student presently functions, whether it be step TA-1 or a higher level.

When teaching a concept or skill in a specific academic area, the teacher needs to analyze the skill and decide whether the student has the prerequisite skills for learning it. A teacher who thinks a student is ready to learn the new skill should then examine the skill further to see if it can be organized into sequential steps. Breaking a new task into small sequential steps makes learning easier for the student who may have learning difficulties.

ADAPTING ASSIGNMENTS

This section is divided into three parts: tips for assignment books, assignment assumptions, and types of assignments.

Tips for Assignment Books

Before any assignment is given, students need to establish an organization process for keeping assignments. Figure 11.38 suggests tips for assignment books.

TA-1	Given five books, including a dictionary, the student will point to and state the function of the dictionary.
TA-2	Given directions to say the alphabet, the student will recite it in proper sequence.
TA-3	Given a random selection of 10 letters, the student will arrange them in alphabetical order.
TA-4	Given a list of not more than 10 words, beginning with different letters, the student will write the words in alphabetical order.
TA-5	Given a list of not more than 10 words, beginning with the same first letter, the student will write the words in alphabetical order.
TA-6	Given a list of not more than 10 words beginning with the same first two letters, the student will write the words in alphabetical order.
TA-7	Shown a dictionary page, the student will point to and state the function of the guide words.
TA-8	Shown a dictionary page, the student will point to and state the function of the entry words.
TA-9	Given oral directions to state the meaning of the word *definition,* the student will do so.
TA-10	Given a list of two guide words and a list of entry words, the student will write those entry words that come between the two guide words.
TA-11	Given a list of entry words and a dictionary, the student will write the page number on which the entry word is found.
TA-12	Shown an entry word in a dictionary, the student will state the number of definitions listed for that word.
TA-13	Given a list of entry words and a dictionary, the student will find the words and write definitions for each word.
TA-14	Given a sentence containing a specific word, the student will write the definition of the word as used in that sentence.

FIGURE 11.37

Task analysis of dictionary skills.

Note: From Vermont State Department of Education, Division of Special Education and Pupil Personnel Services. "Reading competency #6a—Gets information from resource material: Dictionary." In *Basic skills sequence in English* (p. 10). Montpelier: Author. Copyright by Vermont State Department of Education, Division of Special Education and Pupil Personnel Services. Reprinted by permission.

COLLABORATION TIPS

In 1966 Wood developed intervention taxonomy levels designed to accomplish collaborative lesson planning in inclusive settings. Today's emphasis is on inclusion and helping all students achieve. The intervention taxonomy serves many purposes that facilitate decision making for professionals. Following are some of the benefits of this intervention taxonomy,

- Provides a framework that illustrates the process of collaboration among special and general educators as they provide appropriate instruction in the least restrictive environment
- Is a vehicle to help educators work collaboratively to analyze how to develop inclusive practices and modifications and decide who will develop and implement them
- Provides educators with the ability to clearly define roles and responsibilities for all service providers as they cooperatively decide who

will develop and deliver instructional modifications
- Is useful to campus and district administrators in assessing program needs, determining staff allocation, and identifying staff development needs
- Is available to educators in moving forward from the theory of inclusion to the successful practice of inclusion

The following taxonomy planning chart resulted from a national look at how educators perceived the practice of developing and implementing interventions. From "lighter" interventions (type 1) to "heavier" interventions (type 9), educators' perceptions of the intervention setting and who developed and implemented the intervention varied. Hopefully, this chart will encourage discussions on collaboration between general and special educators. Opinions will vary, but agreement is possible. (see Table 11.6.)

Assignment Assumptions

Educators make many assumptions about assignments. While I was visiting a sixth-grade social studies class, the teacher gave the assignment for the next day as the class was coming to a close: "Bring in one article that reflects what we studied in class today."

The bell rang and all the students, except for one young man, hurried out of class to the next one. The young man walked up to the teacher and said, "We don't have a newspaper for an article in my home."

TABLE 11.6
Intervention intensity taxonomy for lesson planning.

Type	Intervention Intensity	Setting	Developed By	Implemented By
1	Interventions which may be made to lesson format that are useful to all students	regular class	general education teacher	general education teacher
2	Interventions made to lesson plan format for student choice	regular class	general education teacher	general education teacher
3	Interventions specific to student mismatch that general education teacher can make independently	regular class	general education teacher	general education teacher
4	Interventions specific to student mismatch that are developed by special education teacher and implemented by general education teacher	regular class	special education teacher	general education teacher
5	Interventions specific to student mismatch that are developed by both general and special education teachers and implemented by general and/or special education teacher and/or support staff (i.e. instructional assistant or paraprofessional) in a regular class setting	regular class	general & special education teacher	general & special education teachers and/or support staff
6	Interventions specific to student mismatch that are developed by special education teachers and implemented by special education teachers and/or support staff in a regular class setting	regular class	special education teacher	special education teachers and/or staff
7	Interventions specific to student mismatch that are developed by special education teacher and implemented by special education teacher and/or support staff in alternative environments (outside the regular class setting)	alternative environment	special education teacher	special education teachers and/or staff
8	Parallel lesson that is developed by general and/or special education teacher and implemented in a regular education and/or alternative environment	regular class and/or alternative environment	general & special education teacher	general &/or special education staff
9	Alternative lesson that is developed by general and/or special education teacher and implemented in a regular education and/or alternative environment	regular class and/or alternative environment	general & special education teacher	general &/or special education staff

Note: From *Intervention Taxonomy Levels* by J.W. Wood, 1997, Richmond, VA: Judy Wood, Inc. Reprinted with permission.

Selecting/organizing assignment books

1. Many school supply sections in stores sell assignment books. When selecting a book:
   - Be sure the size is appropriate for the student's notebook or book bag.
   - Check the assignment book to see if the sections are appropriate for the student.
2. Many schools have assignment books preprinted for students. Here are some suggestions and a list of advantages:
   - All students will have the same assignment book.
   - Because everyone will be using an assignment book, no student will feel awkward.
   - Let students design the cover for the assignment book. Conduct an election to vote on the class choice. This introduces ownership in the assignment book.
   - The book could include a space for the yearly schedule.
   - Include a letter from the principal, student body president, or another "famous" person.
   - Each year the letter could come from a "mystery writer" to be held in strict confidence until the books are handed out.
   - A guessing contest with prizes could be used to see who this year's mystery writer will be.
   - The book could contain general information, school rules, services, activities, and a monthly calendar listing all important events.
   - The last section could provide weekly divided sections for assignments, due dates, class periods, and a special reminder section.
   - One benefit of a school-provided assignment book is that no one does without because of cost.
3. Use a teacher's plan book as an assignment notebook. Set it up for a student's individual schedule.

FIGURE 11.38
Tips for assignment books.

The teacher quickly replied, "Oh, just use a magazine article. Any article will do. Now hurry, or you will be late for your next class."

As I watched the young man walk down the hall, I imagined a zero for class tomorrow. I wanted to say to the teacher, "Don't you have ears?" That student was trying to tell his teacher that he was willing to complete the assignment but had no materials at home. The teacher's assumption? Students have at home what they need to complete assignments.

We simply cannot make assumptions about students. Figure 11.39 lists other assignment assumptions.

1. We assume that students can copy the assignment from the board correctly.
2. We assume that students can complete the assignment.
3. We assume that the assignment is not too difficult.
4. We assume that the assignment is not too long.
5. We assume that students understand the assignment because they do not raise their hand when we say, "Are there any questions?"
6. We assume that students have materials needed to complete the assignment.
7. We assume that students have the money necessary to buy the materials to complete the assignment.
8. We assume that the students' parents will help them with the assignment.
9. We assume that the students' parents can do the assignment.
10. We assume that the students have parents.
11. We assume that the parents are home.
12. We assume that the parents care.
13. We assume that students have a home.
14. We assume that students have time to complete the assignment.
15. We assume that the students care if they complete the assignment.
16. We assume that the students or parents have the language skills necessary to complete the assignment.
17. We assume that the students have proper places to complete the assignment.
18. We assume that we are the only teachers giving homework.

FIGURE 11.39
Assignment assumptions.

Types of Assignments

Assignments, the learning tasks that reinforce concepts taught during class instruction, are crucial to skill acquisition. However, for various reasons, some students may not be able to complete an assignment.

There are two types of assignments: control and no control. Control assignments include in-class assignments and other assignments over which the teacher has complete control. These include class discussions; problem solving; group experiments; group projects; and independent seatwork assignments such as reading from the text, answering questions, and completing work sheets. When students are working on these assignments, the teacher has the power to make any necessary adjustments for a student. The teacher can answer questions or observe a student's work. If an assignment is too difficult, lengthy, or confusing, the teacher can immediately remedy the situation.

When students take assignments home, the teacher begins to lose control. No-control assignments are those that are no longer under the supervision of the teacher.

PRACTICAL APPLICATIONS
ADAPTING CHAPTER QUESTIONS

1. Do not require that all questions be answered.
2. Reword questions to simplify vocabulary or sentence structure.
3. Avoid questions that require lengthy responses.
4. Allow students to answer questions without writing down the questions.
5. For students who have difficulty reading, make a study list of all questions the way they occur either within the context of the chapter or at the end of the chapter. Provide the correct answer and the page number where the answer can be found within the chapter.
6. Some students may need the questions and answers recorded on tape, allowing them to read along with the tape. With the recording, students who are poor readers would learn some information rather than no information.
7. Some students will benefit from having the page number where the answer can be found. This step will reduce busy work and help the slow reader focus on the question.
8. Remember to teach all students that the answers to questions usually occur sequentially within the text. For example, the answer to question 1 will appear in the text before the answer to question 2.
9. Allow students to copy each chapter question on a 3- by 5-inch card and number each question. As the students read the chapter, place the card with question 1 on the table beside the text. Tell them to read, looking for the answer to question 1. When they find the answer, they flip the card over and write the answer on the card, along with the page number in the text where they found the answer. They return to the text with the flash card for question 2 in front, again looking for the answer. This process assists slow readers by allowing them to read the text on time and finish with the answers to all the chapter questions. The set of cards can be used individually or with a buddy for review. This is a time saving idea that results in a set of flash cards. If you want to grade the questions, have the students turn in the cards.

Homework falls into this category. The teacher has now lost all control or power to provide direct assistance during students' work on the assignment.

Homework is assigned for a number of reasons (Turner, 1984):

1. Homework facilitates learning through practice and application.
2. Homework individualizes learning for all students.
3. Homework is assigned for work not completed during the school day.
4. Homework teachers independent study skills and helps develop good work habits.
5. Homework communicates to parents which concepts and skills are taught in class.

1. Student attends to oral directions.
2. Student processes oral information.
3. Student takes notes from oral directions.
4. Student attends to written directions.
5. Student processes visual information.
6. Student can far-point copy.
7. Student independently works on in-class assignment.
8. Student asks questions when necessary.
9. Student has organizational skills needed for keeping assignments in notebook.
10. Student remembers to place out-of-class assignment in book bag.
11. Student takes books from locker and puts into book bag.
12. Student takes book bag home.
13. Student has necessary materials to do assignment.
14. Student has skills to begin out-of-class assignment independently.
15. Student has skills to complete out-of-class assignment independently.
16. Student places out-of-class assignment into folder in book bag.
17. Student takes book bag to school.
18. Student takes assignment to proper class.
19. Student can ask questions if assignment is not understood.

FIGURE 11.40
Task analysis for completing in-class and out-of-class assignments.

Figure 11.40 presents a task analysis of in-class and out-of-class assignments. Figure 11.41 suggests tips for adapting assignments. (Thanks to Julie Duff for her contributions.)

For a no-control assignment, the teacher must be absolutely sure that the student has the skills necessary to be successful. Lee and Pruitt (1970) divided homework into four categories: preparation, practice, extension, and creativity. Table 11.7 shows each category and suggests adaptations for teachers to use with students experiencing difficulty with homework.

Salend and Schliff (1988) offerred several guidelines for implementing homework. These appear in Table 11.8.

1. Be sure that student has the correct information on the assignment (page numbers, date due, and so on).

2. Review the assignment and check for questions.

3. The assignment should be geared to the level of each student.

4. Structure each assignment so that all students can experience success.

5. Provide immediate feedback on all assignments.

6. If the assignment requires students to look up answers to questions, use an asterisk to distinguish implied fact from literal questions requiring a stated fact.

7. If the assignment is lengthy, provide class time to complete it partially or divide assignment time into two or more days.

8. Identify an assignment buddy for each student. The buddy may be another student within the class, a student in another class, or a friend or parent outside of class. This provides a support system for the student who may not know how to complete the assignment.

9. Assignments may be given to two or more students. It is suggested that class time be given for shared assignments and that split grading be used.

10. Teach students the concept of grade averaging with and without zeros. Many students do not realize the difficulty of trying to raise an average after just one zero on an assignment.

11. Allow students the option of dropping one or more low assignment grades per grading period.

12. Establish assignment passes earned for good work, which can be cashed in when an assignment is forgotten or a low grade is received.

13. Be consistent in placing the assignment for class or homework in the same place each day.

14. Provide written and oral directions for assignments.

15. If an assignment requires several steps or stages (such as projects), provide a checklist for the students.

16. If the assignment is to be copied from the board, provide a copy for the student who may have difficulty copying.

17. If the assignment is to be copied from the text, allow the student who has difficulty copying or who copies slowly to copy only the answers.

18. Work sheets should be clear and uncluttered. Watch for the overuse of work sheets. Don't make the reward for completing one work sheet another work sheet. Also, giving a stack of work sheets can be overwhelming.

19. Tell students to put books they need to take home in the locker with the spine to the back of the locker and on the right side of the locker. At the end of the day, the student reaches into the locker and retrieves all spine-back books to take home.

20. Require a method of recording assignments.

21. Make copies of the assignments for a week and give the student and the resource teacher a copy.

22. After the class assignment is completed, tell the student where to put the assignment and what to do next.

23. Do not punish the student by making him or her finish assignments during free time, recess, or after school.

24. For in-class assignments, give a warning when it is almost time to turn in the assignment.

(continued)

FIGURE 11.41
Tips for adapting assignments.

25. Orient students to the major points of the assignment.

26. Begin all assignments with a planned opening and a purpose.

27. Practice for assignments should be distributed instead of given in a mass.

28. Relate all activities within an assignment directly to the objective of the assignment.

29. Assess the assignment for the appropriate instruction level.

30. Use feedback from previously completed assignments to indicate the quality of the next assignment.

31. To assist students with organizing assignments, have every content area on a different color of paper. Each assignment will get placed in the appropriate section.

32. At the end of each class let students have 15 minutes to start on their homework. Circulate around the class to see who needs help. Just before the bell rings, ask each student to circle the last problem they completed. Assign everyone to do five more problems for homework. This allows for differences in the number of problems students can complete in a given period of time. Everyone doesn't have to do 1 through 30, but everyone gets independent practice.

33. Do you have trouble with students not being responsible for homework? Try giving them a clipboard with the assignment sheet and all homework sheets attached. It must be returned the next day and signed by a parent.

34. To make sure that students clearly understand assignments in class or out of class, have each student turn to a buddy and repeat what he or she thinks the assignment is and how to respond.

35. Allow students to do auditory homework.

36. Let students turn in homework early, then grade homework early, and return to student for correction before final grading.

37. Have one night during the school week for "no homework" night (K–12). This gives families a break or provides a catch-up time for students.

38. Have all major tests, projects, spelling tests, book reports, and so on due on Wednesday. This gives the weekend for catchup.

39. Start spelling units on Wednesday and test on the unit the following Wednesday. This really helps the child and parent. Weekends can be used for studying.

40. Each Monday provide an assignment grid with all assignments/tests indicated. Place on bulletin board. This helps organize study time. For example:

	Monday	Tuesday	Wednesday	Thursday	Friday
Social studies					
Science					
Reading					
Spelling					
Math					

41. Assign projects to be completed at school. Teacher may provide display boards, materials, help, and so on. Children have equal opportunity regarding socioemotional level. This also avoids parent project participation stress.

FIGURE 11.41
Continued.

TABLE 11.7
Types of homework and suggested adaptations

Type of Homework	Example	Suggested Adaptations
Preparation: homework assigned to assist students' preparation for the next day's lesson/class	• Reading a chapter • Reviewing a film	1. Provide recorded materials for materials to be read. 2. Review in class before the lesson to assist students who cannot prepare ahead of time. 3. Allow students to prepare with a buddy. 4. Provide a summary of material to be read. 5. Provide a checklist for steps on procedures to be reviewed.
Practice: homework assigned to reinforce the skills taught during the day's lesson	• Working on math problems • Answering questions about class lecture	1. Be sure that the student understands the assignment. 2. Review assignment directions. 3. Review the assignment. 4. Provide a model. 5. Provide guided practice before independent practice. 6. Check for student functional level and match assignment. 7. Provide alternative amounts of assignments to students who cannot complete the same quantity as others.
Extension: homework assigned to extend or transfer skills taught	• Book reports • Practicing computer skills	1. Provide models for required reports. 2. Provide a checklist of procedures. 3. Allow buddies to work together on a shared assignment. 4. Be sure that students have been taught for acquisition and retention before requiring transfer.
Creativity: homework that requires synthesis of skills and concepts previously taught	• Term papers • Research assignments	1. Allow partners on projects. 2. Provide a clearly explained checklist with examples for all projects. 3. Do class projects that model each step of an independent project before assigning the latter. 4. Remember that students who have difficulty with structure need guidance with assigned projects, papers, and research projects. 5. Consider alternative assignments for students who may not be at this level.

TABLE 11.8
Guidelines for implementing homework.

Homework Practice	Guidelines
1. Selecting the type of homework	• Consider the instructional purpose of the assignment as it relates to the type of homework. • Practicing material learned in class may require drill-oriented assignments. • Preparing students for future lessons should be structured to provide prerequisite information that will be necessary for a successful class lesson. • Extending or transferring types of homework takes what a student may have learned and applies it to a more complex situation. • Creating new ideas requires that students synthesize learned skills.
2. Deciding on the content of homework	• Consider the type of homework (preparation, practice, extension, creativity) in deciding on the content. • Have individual content for each student. • Parallel IEP objective and content of homework. • Realize that preparation of homework may be difficult for a student who cannot read or who traditionally has difficulty with assignments. • Relate practice homework directly to skills taught in class. • Evaluate the understanding level of concepts and skills taught before assigning practice homework.
3. Determining the amount of homework	• This depends on the student's age and educational placement. • Use homework sparingly in the early grades • Avoid weekend homework. • Consider level of understanding and completion of class assignments to indicate the amount of homework that can be completed. • Consider the specific disability of a student. • Consider the amount of homework in other subjects. • Consider homework already given in subject for the week.

4. Explaining homework to students	• Inform students of
	    the purpose of the assignment
	    the directions necessary for completion
	    the date due
	    the required format
	    the necessary materials needed for completion
	    the source for assistance if needed
	• Repeat all assignments orally and visually.
	• Provide a model of a completed assignment.
	• Provide examples that will be duplicated.
	• Check to see that students fully understand the assignment.

5. Assisting students with their assignments	• Teach the value of having a selected time and place for homework. • Review the materials that the students will need to complete the assignment. • Provide homework folders. • Establish a homework hotline or class network system for answering questions when a student is in trouble and at home. • Help students to remember books needed for homework.
6. Motivating students to complete homework	• Make homework assignments as interesting as possible. • Prevent homework from being punishment. • Help students to see the effects of zeros on grades by teaching the principle of averaging. • Praise students for completed homework. • Try to understand why a student does not do homework. Many times it may be related to home situations or lack of understanding. • Consider alternatives for students who do not complete homework.

Homework Practice	Guidelines
7. Evaluating homework	• Evaluate daily and provide immediate feedback. • Allow students to provide corrections for a grade change. • Let students have homework pass grades to be used to drop low homework grades. • Provide grade averaging based on correctness as well as for attempting assignment.
8. Involving parents in homework	• Keep communication open between teacher and parents. • Remember that many parents may not understand the homework well enough to assist their child. • Consider the fact that after a long day's work and extended family responsibilities, parents may be too tired to monitor homework. • Consider family-oriented activities that can serve as homework.

Note: From "The Many Dimensions of Homework" by S. J. Salend and J. Schliff (1988), *Academic Therapy, 23*(4), 397–403. Copyright 1988 by PRO-ED, Inc. Adapted with permission.

SUMMARY

This chapter has been developed to help you "uncover subject matter." We are assigned subjects, or content, to teach, and in conjunction with our teaching, we are constantly developing strategies for adapting the format. If a student cannot divide, the teacher should find an organizational strategy to help the student understand the skill.

RESOURCES

National Braille Association (NBA)
3 Townline Circle
Rochester, NY 14632
(716) 427-8260

National Braille Press
88 St. Stephen Street
Boston, MA 02115
(617) 266-6160; (800) 548-7323

SUGGESTED READINGS

Kuder, S. J., & Hasit, C. (2002). *Enhancing literacy for all students.* Upper Saddle River, NJ: Pearson Education.

McKenna, M. C. (2002). *Help for struggling readers.* New York: Guilford.

Tucker, B. F., Singleton, A. H., & Weaver, T. L. (2002). *Teaching mathematics to all children: Designing and adapting instruction to meet the needs of diverse learners.* Upper Saddle River, NJ: Merrill/Prentice Hall.

WEBSITES TO VISIT

Scholastic. A wide variety of resources and activities for kids, parents, teachers, administrators, and librarians. http://scholastic.com.

Wright Group. Resource products for pre-K to adult teachers and administrators. www.wrightgroup.com.

The National Council for the Social Studies. A site with a lot of resources for social studies content. www.socialstudies.org.

National Science Teachers Association. Features teacher resources, professional information, and a science store. www.nsta.org.

REFERENCES

Anderson, R. M., Greer, J. G., & Odle, S. J. (1978). *Individualizing educational materials for special children in the mainstream.* Baltimore: University Park Press.

Association for Supervision and Curriculum Development. (2004). The definition of curriculum integration. Retrieved September 14, 2004, from www.ascd.org/cms/index.cfm?TheViewID=995.

Bryan, J. K., Merchant, C., & Cramer, K. (1999). America calls: Technology-based interdisciplinary planning and instruction. *Classroom Leadership, 2*(5). Alexandria, VA: Association for Supervision and Curriculum Development.

Drake, S. M. (1993). *Planning integrated curriculum: The call to adventure.* Alexandria, VA: Association for Supervision and Curriculum Development.

Larson, R., & Wood, J. W. (2000). *Power prompts: Narrative.* Midlothian, VA: Judy Wood.

Lee, J. F., Jr., & Pruitt, K. W. (1970). Homework assignments: Classroom games or teaching tools? *Clearing House, 1,* 31–35.

Salend, S. J., & Schliff, J. (1988). The many dimensions of homework. *Academic Therapy, 23,*(4), 397–403.

Turner, T. (1984). The joy of homework. *Tennessee Education, 14,* 25–33.

12

Adapting Assessment, Evaluation, and Grading

LEARNER OBJECTIVES

After you read this chapter, you will be able to:

- Discuss standard high stakes testing.
- List three major testing types.
- List and discuss two major laws relating to student assessment.
- List accommodations allowed for statewide testing and district testing.
- Discuss alternative assessment.
- List classroom-embedded assessment measures.
- Discuss grading issues, alternative grading measures, and graduation requirements.
- Discuss the teaching–learning process.

CHAPTER AT A GLANCE

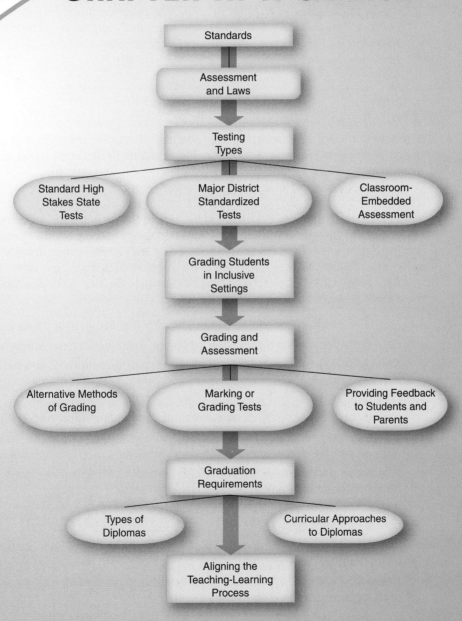

Standards

Assessment and Laws

Testing Types

Standard High Stakes State Tests

Major District Standardized Tests

Classroom-Embedded Assessment

Grading Students in Inclusive Settings

Grading and Assessment

Alternative Methods of Grading

Marking or Grading Tests

Providing Feedback to Students and Parents

Graduation Requirements

Types of Diplomas

Curricular Approaches to Diplomas

Aligning the Teaching-Learning Process

KEY TERMS

*S*ara *has been failing all assessments in her fourth-grade class. Sara's parents are extremely worried because the teacher at the last parent conference expressed concern that Sara may not be promoted to the fifth grade. Even though Sara has not been identified as a student with special needs, her teacher asked that the building intervention team provide suggestions for assessing her. The team suggested that other methods of assessment be used for Sara to evaluate her progress accurately. This chapter provides that information.*

*F*or the past 35 years, general and special educators have been working together to modify curricula, adapt lesson plans, and alter classroom environments to meet the needs of students with mild disabilities. Today, attention has been given to the evaluation of all students.

The emphasis in education and educational reform is accountability. "It is not an exaggeration to say that the core component of the educational reform movement of the 1990s [was] accountability. Education in the United States has been criticized for allowing students to leave school without the skills necessary to compete in a global economy, and increasing pressure is being applied to every level of the system to improve student achievement" (National Association of State Directors of Special Education, 1997).

As we move into this chapter, it may be helpful to develop an understanding of the most current issues relating to assessment:

- *School improvement.* Schools strive to improve all aspects of their system.
- *Standards.* Outcomes established by states. All students must achieve.
- **Statewide assessment.** State tests developed to determine whether students meet state standards.
- **High stakes.** The state tests represent high stakes for educators, students, and parents because they affect pass/fail rates, graduation rates, and funding.
- *School superintendents.* Must have high scores on state tests for their districts. High scores are tied to accreditation, funding,—and community pride.
- *Alternative assessment.* State tests for students with selected disabilities. Alternative assessments are established by each state.
- *School principals.* Are pressured to have their schools meet the standards to compete within their district.
- *Teachers.* High student scores on state tests reflect good teaching and sometimes determine job tenure.
- *Students.* Personal high scores on state tests are needed for grade advancement and high school graduation.

- *Parents.* Their children's high scores on state tests result in personal pride.
- *Community.* School districts with excellent student scores on state tests draw populations, have high real estate values, and have an overall sense of community pride.

Assessment or testing of K–12 students falls into four categories: classroom testing (referred to in this text as classroom-embedded assessments), district testing, state testing, and national testing. As students select postgraduation tracks, testing continues. Vocational students may take aptitude tests, and college-bound students take national tests for college admissions. This chapter will address each of these areas. Because assessment trickles from the top down, the chapter will first address state and national testing. The chapter will also present a model for aligning the teaching–learning process.

STANDARDS

School improvement is tied to accreditation, and accreditation is tied directly to funding and community pride. We continually hear about standards. Regardless of whether you are in Virginia, with their "standards of learning," or in another state, there is a state assessment of children and their achievement. Every state is more focused on outcome-based results. In the past, generally, students with special needs were excluded from participation in these assessments, or if they were allowed modifications, their scores were not included in the total picture for that district. Today, all students are assessed, and students with disabilities must be included in statewide testing.

A common saying in the education field is, "What gets measured gets taught." Much of the focus of the national reform movement has been in the area of general education because there was no systematic collection of data on the achievement results of students with disabilities. Therefore, monies to improve education were intended for general education purposes. With the reauthorization of IDEA and the reforms of the No Child Left Behind (NCLB) Act, students with disabilities are to be included in this state assessment, with accommodations if appropriate. Alternative assessments are provided for students who cannot participate in the state assessment.

Standards are a hot topic today, and they are important. They have helped unify the curriculum used across a state. In the past the curriculum in one part of the state could be very different from that in another part of the state. We are becoming a very transient population. If we want to prepare students to be a part of a global society, then curricula shouldn't be extremely different even from state to state. For this reason, we should view standards in a positive light.

A phrase used more consistently now in discussions on standards is that they apply to *all* students. This has been, and will continue to be, a major challenge for education. All students are a part of the accountability system, and they benefit from instructional changes and educational reforms that are implemented in response to information on assessment results.

The idea that all students should be included in the accountability process is based on three assumptions:

1. All students can learn.
2. Schools are responsible for measuring the process of learners.
3. The learning process of all students should be measured. (National Center on Education Outcomes [NCEO], 1996)

Assessment and Laws

Nationally, legal mandates are in place to ensure appropriate education and now assessment for students with disabilities as for all students served in American education systems. The two laws now on the surface of educational concern are the Individuals with Disabilities Education Act and the No Child Left Behind Act.

Individuals with Disabilities Education Act (IDEA, PL 105–117)

Since the reauthorization of IDEA in 1997, federal funds continue to support the education of students with disabilities. Changes that address assessment include the fact that "IEPs must now document how the student's disability affects involvement and progress in the general curriculum; individual modifications needed for students to participate in state and district assessments; and, if the student is unable to participate in the general assessment, why and how learning will be assessed. Public reporting requirements are also included in the reauthorization of IDEA" (Thurlow, Elliott, & Ysseldyke, 2003, p. 261).

No Child Left Behind Act (NCLB, PL 107–110)

On January 8, 2002, President Bush signed into law the No Child Left Behind Act, the latest reauthorization of the Elementary and Secondary Education Act. Stronger accountability for student results is a major emphasis of this law. Now states must do the following:

- Have strong academic standards for reading, math, and science.
- Administer tests in each grade from grades 3 through 8, and during high school.

ACCOMMODATING DIVERSITY

Under the No Child Left Behind Act (NCLB), all students must undergo annual statewide assessments in reading and math in grades 3 through 8 and at least once in high school (National Education Association, 2004). Students with disabilities must be included in these assessments, although the way they participate may be different. They can take the regular grade-level assessment with or without accommodations, as most students with disabilities do (Kleinert, Green, Hurte, Clayton, & Oetinger, 2002), or they can participate through an alternative assessment. Students participating in an alternative assessment generally have severe disabilities.

Individual states determine both who is eligible for an alternative assessment process and what constitutes an acceptable alternative assessment (Byrnes, 2004). Examples of such assessments include teacher observation, standardized performance tasks, and portfolios, or samples of student work demonstrating mastery of content standards (National Education Association, 2004). Most states use performance-based portfolios (Byrnes, 2004).

Teachers may worry about the time necessary to gather materials for a student's portfolio, but research and practitioners offer help. The extent to which an alternative assessment is integrated into daily instruction and the level of student involvement in the construction of their own portfolio is a stronger predictor of a student's score than is teacher time (Kleinert et al., 2002). Creating a system to gather student work on a regular basis (Byrnes, 2004) and using student planning, monitoring, and self-evaluation forms on a daily basis (Kleinert et al., 2002) can help the alternative assessment process be a success for the teacher and, more important, the student.

- Produce annual state and district reports that show results for each designated student group.
- Monitor the extent to which students in each group are making adequate yearly progress toward proficiency.
- Assign real consequences to districts and schools that fail to make progress. (Thurlow et al., 2003, p. 261)

TESTING TYPES

Testing falls into three major types: standard high stakes state tests, district tests, and classroom-embedded assessment. This section will address each test type, problems students have in each test type, and accommodations teachers may use. The section will conclude with six tips for helping students become better test takers.

Standards and High Stakes State Tests

Each state can determine what it considers to be "high stakes" tests or barrier tests. "High stakes accountability refers to decisions that are made on the basis of the results of the assessment" (Turnbull, Turnbull, Shank, & Smith, 2004, p. 49). These could include "whether the student is eligible to progress through the grades, attend a magnet school, or even graduate and, if graduated, the type of diploma awarded" (Turnbull et al., 2004, p. 49). Standardized high stakes testing is designed to measure general education achievement and the achievement of standards of learning in content areas. The National Center on Education Outcomes (1997) made the following findings:

- In the states where high stakes testing was required, more students were retained.
- Of those students retained, indirect evidence might suggest that more of the students drop out of school. (pp. 9–10)

Schools today are busy aligning standards to the curriculum, teaching students the curriculum, and hoping students will reach the standards and succeed on the state test. However, many problems prevent students from doing their best on state tests. Some of these issues are addressed by states during statewide testing; others are not. Figure 12.1 shows a model for assessment considerations for state testing.

Problems Students Encounter During Statewide Testing

Before putting pen to paper, many students encounter problems that can result in test failure. The teacher needs to understand the problems that can arise before students even enter a testing situation. Many states provide accommodations for some of these problems. Some accommodations are allowed for district assessment; however, teachers may provide any necessary accommodation for classroom-embedded assessments.

Thurlow and colleagues (2003) researched statewide accommodations allowed for students with disabilities and organized them into five categories: setting, schedule, timing, presentation, and response. Table 12.1 presents these five categories along with problems encountered by students in each.

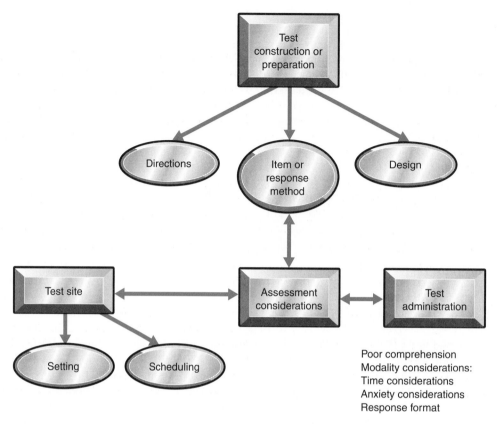

FIGURE 12.1
Assessment considerations for testing.

Note: From *Reaching the Hard to Teach* by J. W. Wood, 2004, Richmond, VA: Judy Wood, Inc. Reprinted with permission.

Accommodations Allowed for Statewide Testing

Thurlow and colleagues (2003) researched the accommodations allowed by states in the five categories outlined in Table 12.1. These are presented in the Tables 12.2 through 12.6.

Alternative Assessment

When students are unable to participate in the traditional district or state assessment, an **alternate assessment** measure is provided. Approximately 1% of the total student population, or 10% of the students with disabilities, may qualify for alternative assessments. Alternative assessments were required to be in place by July 1, 2000. Each state develops its own assessments, which are in continuous transition. "Students who participate in the alternative assessment should be those for whom regular assessment is not appropriate for two major reasons: (1) any and all accom-

ACCOMMODATING TECHNOLOGY

Many schools and districts struggle with the sometimes enormous task of tracking data for their special education students, and more and more are turning to technology for help. 4GL School Solutions, based out of Maryland, provides customized software that automates and streamlines data collection and special education management (4GL, 2003). 4GL's products can help districts operate efficiently and effectively. In addition, by eliminating redunant data entry and ensuring that forms are filled out correctly and compliantly, 4GL's products help reduce districts' vulnerability to legal challenges.

4GL has contracted with more than 80 school districts representing more than 1.3 million students. Winston-Salem/Forsyth County Schools in North Carolina uses the company's special education tracking system to automate its IEP process and all of its special education paperwork. Staff can track all aspects of the individualized education process from referral through delivery of services using electronic versions of district forms. Compliance requirements are automatically verified as data are entered, and staff can easily access current information. After integrating 4GL's products, the district achieved a 57% decrease in the length of IEP meetings and a decrease in the time needed to prepare IEPs from over an hour to 15 minutes, eliminated 95% of IEP procedural issues, and reduced staff turnover by 20% (4GL, 2004b). The Dallas Independent School District realized similar results after automating its special education procedures (4GL, 2004a). With products like those offered by 4GL, educators can use technology to help them not only in the classroom, but also in the behind-the-scenes processes that enable successful student outcomes.

modations that might be provided to students still do not enable them to participate, and (2) students are working on instructional goals that are not assessed by the assessment" (Thurlow et al., 2003, p. 78). Table 12.7 provides possible measurement approaches for an alternative assessment.

Major District Standardized Tests

Standardized state and national tests are a big issue everywhere in the country. By definition, "a standardized test consists of a set of items administered to all students, under the same conditions, scored in the same way, and with results interpreted in the same way" (Wilson, 2002, p. 28). Because every student is tested the same way, the test is said to be "standardized." These standardized conditions allow comparisons to be made among students and groups of students. Based on these tests, schools make major decisions regarding student placements in academic groups and yearly promotions or retentions. Teachers are under tremendous pressure for their classes to score high. Principals are pressured to have building scores in line with or better than those of other schools. School superintendents are pressured when local and state papers publish their districts' test scores. Colleges select prospective students from test scores.

TABLE 12.1
Problems encountered by students during statewide testing.

Accommodation Area	Definition	Student Problem
Setting	Changes in assessment place	Lack of focus Needs special equipment
Timing	Changes in duration or organization of time during testing	Needs extra time to use certain equipment Fatigues Processing difficulties Writing difficulties
Scheduling	Changes in when testing occurs	Need to coordinate assessment with the effects of medication Frustrates easily
Presentation	Changes in how an assessment is given	Need of assistive devices Modality needs Difficultly with directions Need for large print or braille Clarification of directions Difficulty with reading level
Response	Changes in how a student responds to an assessment	Has physical or sensory disabilities Process difficulties

Note: Adapted from M. L. Thurlow, J. L. Elliott, and J. E. Ysseldyke, 2003, *Testing Students with Disabilities: Practical Strategies for Complying with District and State Requirements* (pp. 51–69). Copyright © 2003 by Corwin Press, Inc. Reprinted by permission of Corwin Press, Inc.

TABLE 12.2
Examples of setting accommodations allowed by states.

State	Condition						Location		
	Small Group	Individual	Adaptive Furniture	Acoustics	Study Carrel	Separate Room	Seat Location	Hosp.	Student Home
AL	X	X	*	X	X		X		*
AK	X	X	X	X	X	X			
AR	X	X			X		X		
AZ	X	X	X	X		X			
CA	X	X				X			
CO	X	X	X	X	X	X	X	X	X
CT	*	*							
DE	X	X	X	X			X		
FL	X	X	X	X	X	X			
GA	X	X	X	X	X	X			
HI	X	X					X		
ID	X	X	X	X	X	X	X		
IL	X	X		X	X	X			
IN	X	X	X	X			X		
IA	X	X	X	X	X	X	X		X

State	Condition				Study Carrel	Separate Room	Location		
	Small Group	Individual	Adaptive Furniture	Acoustics			Seat Location	Hosp.	Student Home
KS	X	X		X	X	X			
KY						X			
LA	X	X			X	X	X		
ME	X	X			X	X	X		X
MD	X	X			X	X	X	X	X
MA	X	X			X	X	X		
MI	X	X	X	X				X	X
MN	X	X	X	X	X	X	X		
MS	X	X	X	X	X	X	X		*
MO	X	X							
MT	X	X				X			
NE	X	X	X	X	X	X	X		X
NV	X	X	X	X	X	X			*
NH	X	X			X	X	X		*
NJ	X	X	X	X	X	X	X	X	X
NM	X	X	X	X	X	X	X	X	X
NY	X	X	X	X	X	X	X		
NC	X	X					X	X	X
ND	X	X	X	X		X	X		
OH	X	X							
OK	X	X	X	X	X	X			
OR	X	X			X	X			*
PA	X	X	X	X	X	X	X		
RI	X	X	X	X		X	X		
SC	X	X	X	X		X			
SD	X	X	X	X		X	X	X	X
TN	X	X			X		X		*
TX	*	X							
UT	X		X	X	X		X		
VT					X	X	X		
VA	X	X	X	X	X		X	X	X
WA	X	X	X	X	X	X	X		X
WV	X	X	X	X		X	X		
WI	X	X	X	X	X	X	X		
WY	X	X	X	X	X	X			

X = acceptable * = not acceptable in some cases or score may not be aggregated or reported. Information in this table is adapted from Thurlow, Lazarus, Thompson, and Robey (2002). "State Polices on Assessment Participation and Accommodations," with permission from the National Center on Educational Outcomes.

Note: Adapted from M. L. Thurlow, J. L. Elliott, and J. E. Ysseldyke, 2003, *Testing Students with Disabilities: Practical Strategies for Complying with District and State Requirements* (pp. 53–54). Copyright © 2003 by Corwin Press, Inc. Reprinted by permission of Corwin Press, Inc.

TABLE 12.3
Examples of timing accommodations allowed by states.

State	Duration		Organization	
	Extended Time	Student Determined	Breaks During Testing	Multiple Sessions
AL	*	X	*	
AK			*	
AR			*	X
AZ			X	X
CA	*		*	*
CO	X	X	X	X
CT	X		X	X
DE	*	X	X	X
FL	*		X	X
GA	*		*	
HI			*	
ID	*		X	X
IL	X		X	X
IN	X	X	X	X
IA	X		X	X
KS			X	
KY	X			
LA	*		X	X
ME	X	X	X	X
MD	*		*	X
MA				X
MI	X		X	X
MN	X		*	X
MS	*	*		X
MO	*			X
MT	X		*	
NE	*		*	X
NV	*		*	
NH	X		X	
NJ	X	X	X	
NM	X		X	X
NY	X		X	X
NC	X		X	X
ND	X		X	X
OH	X			X
OK	*			
OR	X		X	X
PA	X		X	
RI	X		X	
SC	X		X	X
SD	*			X
TN	*			
TX			X	X
UT			X	X
VT	X		*	X
VA	X		X	X
WA	X	X	X	
WV	*		*	
WI	X		X	X
WY	X		X	X

X = acceptable * = not acceptable in some cases or score may not be aggregated or reported. Information in this table is adapted from Thurlow, Lazarus, Thompson, and Robey (2002). "State Policies on Assessment Participation and Accommodations," with permission from the National Center on Educational Outcomes.

Note: Adapted from M. L. Thurlow, J. L. Elliott, and J. E. Ysseldyke, 2003, *Testing Students with Disabilities: Practical Strategies for Complying with District and State Requirements* (pp. 57–58). Copyright © 2003 by Corwin Press, Inc. Reprinted by permission of Corwin Press, Inc.

TABLE 12.4
Examples of scheduling accommodations allowed by states.

Columns grouped as: **Timing** (Over Several Days; Specific Time of Day or Week) and **Organization** (Best Time for Student; Subparts in Different Order). Two blocks of states are shown side by side.

State	Over Several Days	Specific Time of Day or Week	Best Time for Student	Subparts in Different Order	State	Over Several Days	Specific Time of Day or Week	Best time for Student	Subparts in Different Order
AL			X		MT			X	X
AK	*				NE	X		X	
AR	X		X		NV	*		X	
AZ			X		NH			X	
CA	X			X	NJ				
CO	X	X	X		NM	X		X	
CT	*				NY	X		X	
DE					NC	X			
FL	*		X		ND	X			
GA			X	X	OH				X
HI	X		X		OK	X		X	
ID	X		X		OR			X	
IL	X		X	X	PA				
IN			X		RI	X	X	X	*
IA			X		SC	*	*	X	
KS					SD	X		X	
KY					TN			X	
LA	X		X		TX				
ME		X	X		UT	X		X	
MD	X		X		VT				
MA			X		VA	X		X	
MI			X	X	WA	*		X	
MN			X		WV			X	X
MS	X		X		WI	X		X	
MO					WY			X	

X = acceptable * = not acceptable in some cases or score may not be aggregated or reported. Information in this table is adapted from Thurlow, Lazarus, Thompson, and Robey (2002). "State Policies on Assessment Participation and Accommodations," with permission from the National Center on Educational Outcomes.

Note: Adapted from M. L. Thurlow, J. L. Elliott, and J. E. Ysseldyke, 2003, *Testing Students with Disabilities: Practical Strategies for Complying with District and State Requirements* (pp. 61–62). Copyright © 2003 by Corwin Press, Inc. Reprinted by permission of Corwin Press, Inc.

TABLE 12.5
Examples of presentation accommodations allowed by states.

State	Format			Procedure		Assistive Device			
	Braille Edition	Large Print	Read Test	Sign Directions	Read/Clarify Direction	Magnification	Amplification	Noise Buffer	Templates
AL	*	X	*	X		X	X	X	X
AK	X	X	*	*	X	X	X	X	X
AR	X	X	*	X		X		X	
AZ	*	*			*	X	X		X
CA	*	X	*	X	X	X	X		X
CO	X	X	*	*	X	X	X	X	
CT	X	X	*	X	X	X			
DE	X	X	*	X	X	X	X	X	X
FL	X	X	*	X	X	X			X
GA	*	X	*	*	X	X	X		
HI	X	*			*				
ID	X	X	*	X	X	X	X	X	X
IL	X	X	*						
IN	*	X	*	*	*	X	X	X	
IA	X	X	*	X	X	X			
KS	X	X	*	X		X			X
KY			X	X	X	X	X	X	X
LA	*	X	*	X	X	X			
ME	X	X	*	*	X	X	X	X	X
MD	*	X	*	X	X		X		
MA	X	X	X	X	X	X	X	X	X
MI	X	X	*	*	X		X	X	
MN	X	X	*	X	*	X	X		X
MS	*	X	*	X	X	X	X		X
MO	X	X	X	X		X	X		X
MT	*	X	*	*	*	X			X
NE	X	X	*	X	X	X	X	X	X
NV	X	X	*	X	X	X	X	X	X
NH	X	X	*	X	X	X	X	X	X
NJ	*	X	*	X	X				X
NM	X	X	*	X	*	X	X	X	X
NY	X	X	X	X	X	X	X	X	X
NC	X	X	*	X		X			
ND	X	X	*	X	X	X	X		X
OH	X	X							
OK	X	X	*	X	X	X	X	X	X
OR	X	X	*	X	*	X	X	X	X
PA	X	X	*	X	X	X	X		X
RI	X	X	*	X		X		X	X
SC	X	*	*	X	X	X	X	X	X

State	Format			Procedure		Assistive Device			
	Braille Edition	Large Print	Read Test	Sign Directions	Read/Clarify Direction	Magnification	Amplification	Noise Buffer	Templates
SD	*	X		*	*		X	X	X
TN	X	X	*	X	*	X	X	X	X
TX	*	X	*	X					
UT	*	X	*	X	X				
VT	*	X	X			X			
VA	*	X	*	X	X	X	X	X	X
WA	X	X	*	X	X	X	X	X	
WV	X	X	*	X	X		X	X	
WI	X	X	*	X	*	X	X	X	X
WY	X	X	*	X		X	X	X	X

X = acceptable * = not acceptable in some cases or score may not be aggregated or reported. Information in this table is adapted from Thurlow, Lazarus, Thompson, and Robey (2002). "State Policies on Assessment Participation and Accommodations," with permission from the National Center on Educational Outcomes.

Note: Adapted from M. L. Thurlow, J. L. Elliott, and J. E. Ysseldyke, 2003, *Testing Students with Disabilities: Practical Strategies for Complying with District and State Requirements* (pp. 64-65). Copyright © 2003 by Corwin Press, Inc. Reprinted by permission of Corwin Press, Inc.

TABLE 12.6
Examples of response accommodations allowed by states.

State	Format		Procedure		Assistive device	
	Mark on Test	Special Paper	Point to Response	Dictate to Tape	Proctor/ Scribe	Communication Device
AL	*		*		*	*
AK	X		X	X	X	X
AR	X				X	
AZ				X	X	
CA	X		*	X	*	X
CO	X		X		X	X
CT	X				*	*
DE	X		X	*	X	X
FL	X				X	
GA	X		X			
HI	X				*	
ID	X		X	X	X	X
IL	X			X	X	
IN	X				*	*
IA	X				X	X
KS			X	X	X	
KY			X	X	X	X
LA	X		X	X	*	*
ME		X			*	X
MD	X		X	*	X	*

(continued)

TABLE 12.6
Continued.

| State | Format | | Procedure | | Assistive Device | |
	Mark on Test	Special Paper	Point to Response	Dictate to Tape	Proctor/ Scribe	Communication Device
MA	X			X	X	X
MI	X		X	X	X	X
MN	X		X	*	*	
MS	X			X	X	X
MO			X	X	X	X
MT	X			X	X	X
NE	X		X	X	X	X
NV	X		*	*	*	*
NH					*	X
NJ	X				X	X
NM	X			X	*	*
NY	X		X	X	X	X
NC	X				X	
ND	X		X	X	X	X
OH					X	
OK	X		X	X	X	X
OR	X		X		*	X
PA	X			*	*	X
RI				*	X	X
SC	X			X	*	
SD				*	*	
TN	X				*	
TX	*			*	*	
UT						
VT				X	X	*
VA	X				X	X
WA	X		X		X	X
WV	X		X		X	X
WI	X		X	X	X	X
WY	X		X		X	X

X = acceptable * = not acceptable in some cases or score may not be aggregated or reported.
Information in this table is adapted from Thurlow, Lazarus, Thompson, and Robey (2002). "State Policies on Assessment Participation and Accommodations," with permission from the National Center on Educational Outcomes.

Note: Adapted from M. L. Thurlow, J. L. Elliott, and J. E. Ysseldyke, 2003, *Testing Students with Disabilities: Practical Strategies for Complying with District and State Requirements* (pp. 68–69). Copyright © 2003 by Corwin Press, Inc. Reprinted by permission of Corwin Press, Inc.

TABLE 12.7
Possible measurement approaches for an alternate assessment.

Observation	Interviews and Checklists
Marking occurrence of specific behaviors	Interviews: teachers, peers, parents, employers
Written narrative of what is observed	Rating scales or checklists: mobility and community skills, self-help skills, daily living skills, adaptive behavior, social skills
Notation of the frequency, duration, and intensity of behavior	Peer and/or adult rating scales or checklists
Videotape	
Audiotape	

Testing	Record Review
Performance events	School records
Portfolios	Student products
Curriculum-based measures	IEP objectives and progress

Note: Adapted from M. L. Thurlow, J. L. Elliott, and J. E. Ysseldyke, 2003, *Testing Students with Disabilities: Practical Strategies for Complying with District and State Requirements* (p. 79). Copyright © 2003 by Corwin Press, Inc. Reprinted by permission of Corwin Press, Inc.

Problems Students Have During District Testing

Problems experienced by students taking district standardized tests parallel those problems experienced during statewide tests. Please refer to the discussion in the preceding section on statewide assessment.

Accommodations Allowed for District Testing

According to Thurlow and colleagues (2003), districts and states have written policies on the use and type of accommodations allowed during testing. "These policies are quite general (e.g., allowing whatever the student uses during instruction) and other times quite specific (e.g., extended time may be used during one assessment, but not during another, and if used, the student's score will not be included in summaries of performances)" (p. 40). Everyone should become acquainted with their district's and state's requirements. Table 12.8 presents a list of norm-referenced tests and the accommodations allowed for each.

Classroom-Embedded Assessment

Because instruction and assessment are developed together, **classroom-embedded assessment** measures can help teachers evaluate their teaching methods while also serving as a grading measure. Although assessment and grading are often considered together, every assessment measure does not require a grade. On-demand assessments and extended-time assessments, discussed later, may serve as a method of assessing skills taught and may or may not be given a grade. As we walk through various methods of assessing, remember that all assessment is curriculum based. Initially, curriculum-based assessment (CBA) was designed to fill the need for an assessment process based on the student's progress through curriculum. A major goal of CBA was to eliminate the mismatch between low-achieving students and the sometimes unreasonable demands of the curriculum. Today, when planning instruction,

TABLE 12.8
Selected norm-referenced tests and accommodations allowed.

Norm-Referenced Test	Accommodations Allowed
Iowa Test of Basic Skills (ITBS) Iowa Test of Educational Development (ITED) (Riverside Publishing)	Individually or in small group; quiet environment; distraction free environment, special lighting; magnifying equipment; adaptive or special furniture; typewriter; communication device; pointing to answer; dictating answer; large-print edition; reduced number of items on page; signing of directions; markers to maintain place; papers secured with tape; directions reread as needed (except for Listening Test).
Metropolitan Achievement Test/8 (MAT/8) (Harcourt Educational Measurement)	Breaks between subtests; more frequent breaks; multiple test sessions over several days; extended time (up to twice the time); time of day; small group; individual setting; learning/study cards; special lighting; adaptive or special furniture; location with minimal distractions; noise buffers; preferential seating; hospital/home administered; large print; repeating directions; interpreting directions (via signing, cued speech); secure papers to work area with tape/magnets; provide cues (arrows and stop signs) on answer forms; visual aids (templates, masks or markers); amplification equipment (hearing aid, auditory trainer); large diameter pencil, pencil grip, special pencil or pen.
Stanford Achievement Test/9 (SAT 9) (Harcourt Educational Measurement)	Separate room; small group; large-print booklet; magnifying device; translations of words or phrases; windows or markers to frame text used by child; highlighter used by child.
Terra Nova 2 Terra Nova California Achievement Tests/6 Terra Nova California Test of Basic Skills/5 (CTBS/5) (CTB McGraw-Hill)	Use visual magnifying equipment; use large-print edition; use audio amplification equipment; use markers to maintain place; mark responses in test booklet; mark responses on large-print answer document; indicate responses to scribe (for selected-response items); record responses on audio tape (except for constructed-response writing items); use sign language to indicate response (for selected-response items); use computer, typewriter, Braille writer or other machine (e.g., communication board) to respond; use template to maintain place for responding; indicate response with other communication devices; take test alone or in a study carrel; take the test with small group or different class; take the test at home or in care facility (e.g., hospital) with supervision; use adaptive furniture; use special lighting or acoustics; take more breaks that do not result in extra time or opportunity to study information in a test already begun; have flexible scheduling (e.g., time of day, days between sessions) that does not result in extra time or opportunity to study information in a test already begun.

Note: Adapted from M. L. Thurlow, J. L. Elliott, and J. E. Ysseldyke, 2003, *Testing Students with Disabilities: Practical Strategies for Complying with District and State Requirements* (pp. 41–42). Copyright © 2003 by Corwin Press, Inc. Reprinted by permission of Corwin Press, Inc.

educators consider the student who may not respond to certain curricular demands and attempt to align the assessment with the instruction.

Classroom-embedded assessment is an important aspect in the big picture of educational assessment. Most assessment is provided by the classroom teacher day by day. These assessments must be aligned with standards, and standards must be aligned with the information taught. Standards-based assessment measures, then, validate the results of classroom assessments.

Reteaching or teaching to mastery relies heavily on classroom-embedded assessment. Thus, the assessment must measure not only what the student learned, but also the student's ability to respond to the assessment. If a student cannot respond

COLLABORATION TIPS

To work together to modify any test, general and special education teachers must find opportunities to meet, either during the day or after school. Elementary teachers generally do not have planning periods, so their only option is usually after school. However well intentioned the general and special education teachers may be, faculty meetings, school activities, family commitments, and parent conferences frequently prevent such joint work sessions. Similarly, general and special education teachers on the secondary level rarely share identical planning periods. In addition, planning periods and after-school hours often fill up with conferences and other school and family responsibilities. Alternatives to meeting after school might include the following:

1. General and special education teachers work together to familiarize the general teacher with each student's needs, with the ultimate goal of having the general teacher assume the major responsibility for intervention.

2. General and special education teachers work together to familiarize the general teacher with the ways the special education teacher modifies tests.

3. General and special education teachers work together for a longer period of time, with the ultimate goal of creating a bank of tests from which both can draw throughout the year and then make minor modifications depending on the amount of material covered.

in writing, an essay test would not be appropriate. The student would be better assessed through product development, recording answers on a tape recorder, answering the essay with voice-activated computer software, and so on. Most important is that the assessments provide the teacher with information on the student's understanding of the content. If the student has not mastered the content, then reteaching is essential. Therefore, thoughtful consideration should be given to classroom-embedded assessment.

Problems Students Encounter During Classroom-Embedded Assessments

As with statewide assessments and district assessments, students bring to the classroom testing situation numerous problems. These problems can determine whether the student passes or fails. Most important, these problems can prevent a teacher from truly assessing the student for content mastery. Student problems include poor comprehension, auditory and visual perception problems, time constraints, and anxiety.

Poor Comprehension. *Comprehension* means the ability to understand clearly what is said or explained. Students with mild disabilities often do not understand verbal directions. When the teacher gives a series of directions, they cannot recall each step correctly. Without a clear understanding of what to do or how to proceed, they might either proceed incorrectly or turn in papers with only their names on the page. Certainly, such responses do not accurately indicate the full extent of the student's knowledge. Similarly, written directions are often too lengthy or complicated for the student with mild disabilities. The reading level alone may be above the student's instructional level. Directions may contain words or phrases that the student does not know, may instruct the student to perform several operations, or may ask the student to follow more than one procedure. For example, a student with poor comprehension would have difficulty following and understanding these directions:

1. Write a sentence containing a gerund.
2. Draw a circle around the gerund.
3. Indicate whether the gerund is the subject, direct object, predicate nominative, or object of the proposition by writing S., D.O., P.N., or O.P. above the gerund.

A related difficulty involves abstractions. Some students with mild disabilities can recall facts and deal with concrete ideas but do not respond well to evaluative questions or those requiring inferences or deductive reasoning. For example, the student may understand how to write a paragraph but have trouble writing several paragraphs on an abstract topic such as "Ecology in Action in Our Community."

Auditory Perceptual Problems: Teacher Variables. Students with auditory perceptual problems cannot process auditory information quickly and easily. They can hear, but problems in learning occur when they try to process what they hear. However, auditory problems associated with teacher variables can be avoided. The teacher who administers tests orally, for example, greatly penalizes students with auditory deficits. Even simple spelling tests pose problems. Some teachers proceed too fast, not allowing the student enough time to sound out the words and transfer the sounds into their written forms. Some teachers simply call out the words without clearly delineating each syllable or sound.

Some students may experience minor difficulty with spelling tests but have major problems when the teacher administers quizzes or chapter tests orally. The student must not only process the question through the auditory system—a giant undertaking—but also transfer the information to paper. Sometimes this task is virtually impossible. In addition, the student with auditory disabilities simply cannot recall previously asked questions. Thus, a traditional technique prevents the student from demonstrating concept mastery.

Auditory Perceptual Problems: Environmental Variables. Although teachers can adjust the amount of information they present verbally or the number of tests they administer orally, they may have little control over certain environmental auditory distractions both inside and outside the classroom. Frequently, teachers grow accustomed to a reasonable amount of background noise and become oblivious to these distractions. Students with auditory problems, however, are not as fortunate. A variety of environmental variables may distract the students from their class work or from verbal information the teacher is presenting. These distractions include noise outside a window; conversations in an adjoining classroom; learning module distractions; announcements on the P.A. system; and incidental noise such as students asking questions, students whispering among themselves, and teachers reprimanding students for talking at unauthorized times.

Because many of these auditory distractions cannot be eliminated or modified, the teacher should realize that, even for a few seconds, these conditions create an environment hostile to learning and one not ideal for testing. The teacher must guard against assuming that, if students would just pay attention, they would be able to understand, or if they would just concentrate more, they could complete the assigned task or test. Students with auditory perceptual problems often have difficulty discriminating between the sounds coming from the front of the classroom (such as instructions from the teacher) and the sounds filtering into the room from elsewhere. For some, concentrating and remaining focused on the task become virtually impossible in a classroom with normal environmental sounds. For students experiencing auditory difficulties, alternative instructional methods or testing sites may be needed.

Visual Perceptual Problems: Teacher Variables. Many students experience problems when they receive information visually. Again, the problem for such students is not an inability to see but an inability to process information received visually. Teacher variables often contribute to students' visual problems.

For example, most teachers use the chalkboard as an instructional tool. They post spelling words, homework assignments, and other reminders on the board for students to copy into their notebooks. A number of teachers even write tests on the board, whereas others require students to work math problems, diagram sentences, or complete other tests at the chalkboard. Many teachers assume that information they write on the board will be copied correctly into notebooks.

The majority of students in the classroom succeed with ease, but any students with visual perceptual difficulties experience a variety of problems. Primarily, they have trouble transferring information from the board to their papers or notebooks. They may transpose numbers, such as page numbers assigned for homework, or interchange letters, such as spelling words or key terms for a new unit. Students then memorize the incorrect information, leading to a misrepresentation of their abilities or poor test scores. Copying homework assignments incorrectly leads to additional confusion. At night, students open their books to unfamiliar pages and problems they may not know how to solve; the following day, the teacher may be suspicious of the student's explanation for not completing the assignment. The student with visual perceptual problems encounters some of the same difficulties when attempting to take a test written on the board, such as trouble transferring information to paper, understanding written directions or questions, and copying correctly. As if these problems were not enough, visual distractions on or near the chalkboard clutter the students field of vision—for example, homework assignments on the same board as the test, spelling words in another corner, and bulletin boards adjacent to the chalkboard. The majority of teachers keep a clean chalkboard, but not all of them do.

The teacher's handwriting also affects how a student responds to any test. Although most teachers' printing or cursive handwriting ranges from average to excellent, not all teachers can claim such a distinction. Of course, typed tests are better than handwritten ones, but teachers cannot always have their tests typed. A good test does not require typing, but legibility is a must. Teachers with unusual cursive styles should print. If printing also presents problems, the teacher should ask someone else to write the test. The teacher must also ensure that all copies are legible. Not all schools possess the newest or most efficient duplicating equipment, but unreadable copies are inexcusable. Students must be able to decipher the questions to pass the test.

Most teachers use written tests in one form or another—multiple choice, true–false, matching, fill in the blank or completion, essay, and others. The student with visual perceptual problems will encounter many obstacles with such tests. For example, a teacher may give students a matching test with a long column of descriptive statements and an equally long column of answer choices. Although students may know the answer to the first descriptive statement, they must peruse the entire column of answer choices, from top to bottom, to locate the correct answer. Students spend unnecessary time searching for letter equivalents to answers, sometimes to the extent that they are unable to complete the test. Even more common, some students may be oblivious to time and consequently spend the allotted period on just the matching section, not even attempting the remaining sections.

Length can also become a psychological barrier to success on written tests. At-risk students usually have failed repeatedly. The majority of such students equate tests with unpleasantness. If the students were asked about previous tests or their ability to pass tests, their responses would probably be negative. A lengthy test of three or more pages can discourage students, especially those with visual problems. They may attempt the first page and stop when they realize they cannot finish, or they may feel defeated upon first examining the test. Teachers may overhear remarks such as, "I know I don't know the answers to that many questions" or "I know I'll never finish, so why should I even begin?" The number of questions or problems per page may visually overwhelm other students. Their eyes may busily scan and rescan the page; as a result, they cannot focus on individual questions or problems and thus cannot proceed.

Some students with visual problems have difficulty identifying, recognizing, or decoding symbols and abbreviations. Simple mathematical solutions such as $+$, $-$, $>$, $<$, and $=$ may cause visual turmoil for students with visual perceptual problems. They may confuse one symbol with another, or they may have trouble associating the symbol with its written equivalent—for example, $+$ with *plus.* Students with pronounced visual difficulties usually experience extreme anxiety when attempting to solve algebraic equations such as this one:

$$\frac{(2x + 4)}{2} - 4 = (2x + 6) + 3(2x + 3x)$$

Of course, not all students with disabilities will take algebra, but some will need to complete the course if their goal includes a college degree. Others may not take algebra but will encounter basic mathematical symbols throughout their academic and postacademic years.

Visual Perception Problems: Environmental Variables. Visual distractions and stimuli abound, both inside and outside the classroom. The degree of distraction varies from student to student. For some students, most visual distractions are momentary. For others, a single distraction can completely disrupt their present visual field, their ability to concentrate, and their ability to keep working. The distraction may originate outside the classroom window or inside the room, as a result of students moving at their desks or turning in their papers, from peers making motions or gestures, or from visitors entering the classroom. Whatever the source, these distractions cause students with minor visual problems to become temporarily nonfunctional and those with more serious visual problems to remain nonfunctional indefinitely.

Time Constraints. Teachers generally strive to develop a test to fit the time frame available for giving it. Most teachers attempt to allow extra time for students who worked more slowly than others. For students with disabilities, time often plays a major role in taking a test. Within that group of students with disabilities, individuals may have auditory or visual perceptual problems, motor coordination difficulties, and frequently, reading problems. Generally, these students are not intentionally slow or lazy, and they do not mean to aggravate the teacher or disrupt the test. Rather, they have real problems caused by identified learning modality deficits. The teacher needs to remember that students with auditory problems may not be able to answer oral questions in the same time frame as students without such a disability. Similarly, students with visual perceptual, motor coordination, or reading problems probably will not be able to complete most tests designed for the general education student. Teachers must try to avoid penalizing students with recognized exceptionalities and give them an opportunity to demonstrate their proficiency.

Anxiety.   Most teachers have experienced test anxiety at least once during their academic lives. Most admit that test anxiety exists and is very real to the person experiencing it. Teachers need to understand further that the degree of test anxiety varies considerably from student to student. When anxiety makes a student nonfunctional, the teacher should realize it as a disability similar to disabilities in comprehension, visual and auditory perception, and motor coordination. Anxiety differs from other disabilities, however, because it is usually temporary. Years of failure and negative responses from teachers, peers, and parents result in measurably lower self-concepts for students with mild disabilities. Because many students automatically associate taking a test with failure, they become fearful and anxiety ridden even at the thought. Fear and anxiety, along with a history of previous failures, may even cause test phobias for a few students. For all practical purposes, these students simply cannot function in a traditional test setting. Others feel anxiety but not to the same extent. For example, they may be extremely hesitant at the beginning of the test because they lack self-confidence, or they may stop midway through the test because they encounter one or two questions they do not know. Others stop working when they realize that their peers have finished and are turning in their papers. Such students want to at least appear normal. They do not want to be the last ones working or be called "dummies." Still other students allow their initial impression of the length or scope of the test to overwhelm them and, like students with test phobias, become nonfunctional for a while. Anxiety, although difficult to measure, influences a student's ability to take and pass a test. Teachers should consider anxiety level when evaluating a student's performance and attempt to reduce that level as much as possible by adapting the test.

Model for Assessment Considerations

A model for assessment consideration was presented in Figure 12.1. Looking at the big picture of assessment, there are three major places where accommodations can occur: test construction or preparation, test administration, and test site. As stated earlier, allowed accommodations for statewide and district assessments are very specific. However, for classroom-embedded assessments, accommodations are at the teacher's discretion.

Educators generally agree about the appropriateness of instructional accommodation. Issues arise, however, when testing accommodations are mentioned. Teachers should recognize the appropriateness of making accommodations for both instruction and testing.

Test Construction or Preparation.   Test construction or preparation is the first step in assessment considerations. This step includes writing test directions, choosing the test item or response method, and designing the test.

Test Directions.   Test directions that are not clear and understandable may cause failure for students before they even try to complete the test. Consider the following suggestions for making test directions clear for all students:

1. Keep directions short.
2. Keep directions simple; avoid unnecessary words.
3. Type directions.
4. If directions are not typed, print neatly.
5. Place all directions at the beginning of each separate test section.
6. When giving more than one direction, list them vertically.
7. List only one direction in each sentence.
8. Underline the word *directions* to focus students' attention.
9. Avoid using words such as *never, not, always,* and *except.* If you must use these words, underline and capitalize them.
10. Define any unfamiliar or abstract words.
11. Color code directions.
12. Avoid making oral directions the only means of communicating the purpose of the test to the students. Read directions orally and write them clearly on the test.
13. Tell students the reason for or purpose of the test.
14. Go over each direction before the test. Be sure that students understand what they should do.
15. Remember that students who do not clearly understand the directions will be the last to raise hands and ask for clarification.
16. While the test is in progress, walk around the room and check to see that students are following directions.
17. Teach students that they should only lose points for not knowing items on the test. They should avoid losing additional points for not following or understanding the test directions.
18. Teach students how to approach tests in a systematic manner. Look over the total test.
19. Read directions to the class at least twice.

Test Item or Response Method.   The second aspect of test construction is choosing a test item or response method. These methods can be divided into two categories as shown in Table 12.9: on-demand assessments and extended-time assessments. On-demand assessments require students to respond within a certain period of time. Extended-time assessments provide a longer period of time for completion.

On-demand assessments include forced choice and constructed items. Forced choice is used to assess student knowledge. Knowledge is the lowest level on Bloom's taxonomy (see chapter 10) and is a necessary measurement to ensure that students have the necessary knowledge to build a foundation for higher order responses. Items in this area include multiple choice, matching, true–false, and fill in the blank with or without a word bank (a list of words from which students select a response to place in the blank). All of these, with the exception of true–false, are *recognition tests* that require students to examine a group of choices and select a quick answer. Because the correct answer is presented within a list of distracters, recall can be prodded. The stu-

TABLE 12.9
Classroom-embedded assessments.

On-Demand Assessments	Extended-Time Assessments: Student Driven

Student Response: Forced Choice
  • Multiple choice
  • True–false
  • Fill in the blank with a word bank
  • Matching questions
	• Performance/products (individual or groups)
	• Oral reports
	• Student self-assessment
	• Portfolios

Student Response: Constructed Response
  • Brief essay
  • Expanded essay
  • Short written responses
  • Reading comprehension
  • Definition questions
  • Extended-response item
  • Computational problems
  • Work problems
  • Lab practicals
	Extended-Time Assessments: Teacher Driven
	
	• Observations
	• Interviews
	• Anecdotal records
	• Assignments
	• Homework
	• Multiple intelligences
	• Authentic assessment

Note: From *Reaching the Hard to Teach* by J. W. Wood, 2004, Richmond, VA: Judy Wood, Inc. Reprinted with permission.

dent may recall after seeing the correct choice. Class instruction should focus on retention of specific information such as facts and data. Study guides should require students to focus on specific ideas.

Structured recall requires the student to recall the answer to a question without a visual prompt. This type of recall is heavy on memory load. Class instruction should focus on general information such as broad topics or ideas. Study guides should include focus questions designed to help students organize the study process around the general area the test questions will cover. A true–false item requires structured recall.

Multiple-choice items are some of the most useful types of objective test questions. The following suggestions may prove helpful for teachers who are constructing them:

1. Avoid frequent use of fillers. For example:
   a. Either . . . Or
   b. All of the above
   c. None of the above

2. Let the student circle the correct answer rather than place the answer on an answer sheet or blank form. This reduces the possibility of copying errors when transferring letters to the blanks.

3. Arrange the correct answer and the distracters (incorrect answers) vertically on the page. Example: You have a board 48 inches long. If you cut off a 6-inch piece, how much is left?
   a. 38 inches
   b. 42 inches
   c. 48 inches

4. Be sure that all choices are grammatically consistent. Example: Because of poor land and a short growing season, the New England colonies were forced into the economic choice of:

   a. Exporting food

   b. Trading and shipbuilding

   c. Growing and exporting cotton

5. Avoid using more than 10 multiple-choice questions per test.

6. State question and answer choices clearly.

7. Avoid using unnecessary words.

8. Give credit to students if they marked out the choices they know are incorrect answers, even if they did not mark the correct answer. This is an alternative for multiple-choice items that involve thought. Perhaps students cannot determine what is correct, but they can process what's not possible. Both require knowledge of the material.

9. Mark out one or two choices (of four choices) with a black marker for some lower level students before handing out the test. Usually the choice eliminated is very close to the correct answer and involves thinking.

The matching exercise is designated to measure factual information based on simple association. It is a compact and efficient method of measuring simple relationships. The following suggestions may be helpful when selecting matching items for tests:

1. Place all matching items and choice selections on the same page.

2. Leave extra space between items in columns to be matched.

3. Use homogeneous material for each matching exercise.

4. Use small groups of matching questions. Avoid long matching lists.

5. Have one extra response in one of the columns. For example, if you have 10 items in column A, place 11 choices in column B. This statistically puts the question in the student's favor.

6. Have only one correct answer for each item.

7. Avoid having students draw lines to correct answers. This may be visually confusing.

8. Keep all matching items brief. The student who has comprehension and reading problems may not be able to process long, wordy items.

9. Place the responses, such as names of explorers, on 3″ × 5″ cards. These become a manipulative exercise. Students can match items to the correct answer by placing the card next to the item. (Thanks to Janice Mael for her suggestion.)

10. Place the list with more lengthy items, usually the descriptive items, in the left-hand column. This makes for less reading and will assist the slow reader.

11. Make a mini-letter bank under the blank to reduce the number of choices.

12. Place the blank for the response after each item in column A.

13. For tests with columns that are reversed, teach students to begin the test working from column B to column A.

14. Teach students to answer questions in reverse.

15. Place the blank before the number in column B.

16. Put responses to matching test items in alphabetical order on the left-hand side to facilitate location of the answer.

Here is an example of a matching test:

Column A	Column B
1. The island continent	a. Africa
2. Bordered by the Atlantic	b. Asia
3. Located north of the Mediterranean Sea	c. Atlantic Ocean
4. Bordered by Africa and Asia	d. Australia
5. The largest ocean	e. Europe
6. Bordered by the Atlantic and Pacific, north of the equator	f. Indian Ocean
7. The largest continent	g. North America
8. Bordered by the Atlantic and Pacific, south of the equator	h. Pacific Ocean

The most common use of the true–false test is to measure the student's ability to identify the correctness of statements of fact or definition. The following suggestions for modifications may help teachers construct these items:

1. Avoid stating questions negatively.
2. Avoid long, wordy sentences.
3. Avoid statements that are trivial or do not assess student knowledge.
4. Allow students to circle the correct answer.
5. Avoid using too many true–false questions at one time, preferably no more than 10 items per test.
6. Avoid using *never, not, always,* and *except.* If you must use these words, underline and capitalize them.
7. Avoid having students change false statements to true statements unless you have taught this skill.
8. Place the words *true* and *false* at the end of each sentence.

   Example: Imperialism was a cause of World War I. True False

Fill-in-the-blank or completion questions are suitable for measuring knowledge of items, specific facts, methods or procedures, and simple interpretation of data. Because this type of test requires structured recall, it is difficult for many inclusive students and should be used sparingly, if at all. In many cases, multiple-choice items may be more appropriate. If teachers still want to use fill-in-the-blank items, they can attempt to reduce their complexity by following these suggestions:

1. Write simple and clear test items.
2. Avoid using statements directly from the textbook. Taken out of context, they are frequently too general and ambiguous to be used as test questions.
3. Provide large blanks for students with poor handwriting or motor control problems.
4. Be sure that the blank size matches the response. If the blank is too long or too short, students may think that their response is incorrect.
5. Place the blank at the end of the sentence.
6. Provide word banks for the test.

7. Provide a mini-word bank immediately under the response blank. This reduces memory load and can be implemented on a test that is already constructed.

8. Allow students to circle the correct choice in the mini-word bank.

9. Before the test, tell students whether they will have a word bank on the test.

10. Use a floating word bank that is detached from the test. The student can move the word bank up and down the right side of the page to check for the correct word, placing the words close to the blanks.

11. Have another teacher read your test to check for clear understanding of each item.

12. Place one extra word in the word bank, which statistically puts the test in the student's favor.

13. If a word will be used as a response more than once, list it the appropriate number of times in the word bank.

14. Break the test section into two parts: five questions and a six-word word bank. Repeat for each section. For example:

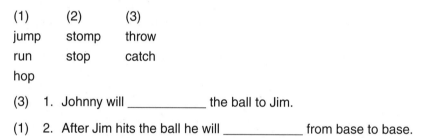

(1)   (2)   (3)
jump   stomp   throw
run   stop   catch
hop

(3)   1.   Johnny will _____ the ball to Jim.

(1)   2.   After Jim hits the ball he will _____ from base to base.

The second category of on-demand assessments is constructed response. These items require that a student create an answer. Forced choice items provide choices for student selection (i.e., multiple choice). In constructed item tests students have a prompt (a question or problem to answer) and must create an answer from recall of information previously learned, or develop a response from created information. Constructed items include brief or expanded essays, short written responses, reading comprehension, definition questions, extended-response items, computational problems, word problems, and lab practicals.

Teachers use brief or expanded essays and short written response questions to measure learning that cannot be evaluated by objective test items. These items may be used to assess higher order thinking. Most essay or short written response items require the student to recall relevant factual information, mentally organize ideas, and write an extensive or short response. Tests of this type may require skills that students with poor organization abilities, memory problems, or deficient writing skills do not have. The Practical Applications box on pages 427 and 428 offers a step-by-step process teachers can use to teach included students how to answer essay questions.

Reading comprehension tests require students to read a passage and respond to it in some way, either by answering questions about it or by giving their impressions or opinions of it. Students won't be able to study for the exact questions that will be asked on the test, but they can practice finding the important information in a passage.

Teachers can use reading comprehension questions to assess students' abilities to locate and retrieve information from the printed page. These questions are also a good way to find out how well students interpret what they read. Students may become frustrated if they haphazardly search for answers rather than use a systematic approach to recognize important information.

PRACTICAL APPLICATIONS
ESSAY QUESTIONS

Essay questions offer students a great opportunity to show what *they* know and what *they* think about a topic. They give students a chance to think creatively on paper, rather than ask them to come up with one right answer to a question.

Essay questions make some students nervous because they must fill a blank piece of paper with their own ideas. Other students like essay questions because they don't limit them to narrow choices. Instead, students can express themselves creatively.

Following is a step-by-step process students can follow when answering essay questions. These 15 tips will lead them down the path to success.

1. Essay questions on tests aren't always in the form of questions. They're more like directions that tell you what to do. The direction for an essay question is called a *prompt.* You should read the prompt word for word before you begin writing. Don't just skim it over—read every word.

2. Read the prompt a second time to make sure you understand what the direction is asking you to do.

3. Find and underline the command word. A command word is a verb in an essay prompt that tells you what to do to answer the question. Examples of command words are *list* and *discuss.* You should always identify the command word before you start to write your answer. Some prompts have more than one command word. Make sure you identify each one before you begin to answer so you don't leave out part of the answer.

4. Define the command word. What does the command word mean? What are you supposed to do or show in your answer? It's important to know the answer to these questions before you begin writing.

5. Determine the category or purpose of the command word. Command words can be divided into four categories, which tell you the goal you're trying to achieve in your answer:
   a. Describing (you list or name things)
   b. Outlining or explaining (you explain information and give details)
   c. Persuading (you prove, support, or criticize your answer)
   d. Ordering (you put events in the order they happened)

6. Some prompts are in the form of questions. If a prompt asks you to answer a question, change the question into a statement with a command word before you begin answering. Here's an example.
   Prompt: What is the natural resource?
   Statement with a command word: Define natural resource.

7. Decide whether your answer can be completed in one paragraph. Sometimes you'll need more than one paragraph to answer an essay prompt. If you're not sure, check the number of command words to give you a clue. Generally, you'll need one paragraph for each command word.

8. Form a topic sentence. The first sentence of your essay is the topic sentence. You may restate the prompt to form your topic sentence. Here's an example.
   Prompt: Discuss your favorite sport.
   Topic sentence: My favorite sport is football.

(continued)

9. Write the main idea. The main idea is the most important idea—it's what you're going to write about in your essay. After you've formed the topic sentence, write the main idea of your essay. Here's an example.
Topic sentence: My favorite sport is football.
Main idea: Tell why I like football.

10. Add details to your main idea. Details tell about your main idea. You may list one or more details under your main idea. Here's an example:
Main idea: Tell why I like football.
   Detail: I meet new friends.
   Detail: It's good exercise.
   Detail: It's a thinking game.

11. Use the main idea and details to develop a visual organizer. A visual organizer is a chart, outline, list, or word map to follow when writing your answer. Before you begin writing, use the main idea and details from your outline to develop a visual organizer. It's important to do this so you organize your ideas on paper before you begin writing your answer. Here's an example:

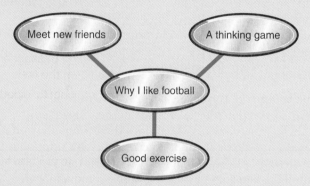

12. Check the time remaining to answer the question. Prewriting steps are all the things you do to organize your thoughts before you begin writing out your answer. Tips 8 through 11 are the *prewriting steps*. After you've completed the prewriting steps, check the clock to see how much time you have left to answer the question. As you're writing, occasionally check the time remaining to answer the question. You'll want to save enough time to write a summary statement and read through your essay before turning it in.

13. Now you're ready to write your answer to the essay prompt. Follow the information from your prewriting work to write your answer on a separate piece of paper. Be sure to include the topic sentence and details in your essay.

14. Close your essay with a summary statement. A summary statement is a sentence that briefly retells the main idea and details of your essay. It may be helpful to begin your summary statement with words that signal closure, such as *In conclusion, To summarize,* and *In closing.* Here's an example.
In closing, I've chosen football as my favorite sport for several reasons—I meet new friends, it's good exercise, and it gives me a mental challenge.

15. Read your essay to make sure it's complete. When you've finished writing, check your answer for the topic sentence, details, and summary statement. You'll also want to read through your essay to make sure all the sentences are complete, all the words are spelled correctly, and your handwriting is legible.

Following are suggestions for teaching reading comprehension to elementary students:

1. Read the story twice. Underline words that tell <u>who</u> and <u>what</u>.
2. Read the story twice. Underline words that tell <u>when</u> and <u>where</u>.
3. The main idea tells what the story is mostly about. Ask yourself what big idea the sentences in the story tell about.

If the emphasis in daily classroom activities is on word recall, students will have even greater difficulty with reading comprehension tests that require them to make inferences or draw conclusions. Classroom activities should include both oral and written practice with the same question-and-answer formats that students will find on tests.

To help students perform better on reading comprehension questions, teachers should consider the following when writing tests:

1. Ask a reasonable number of questions per paragraph. Too many items results in questions that are repetitive or irrelevant. Too few items results in overlooking important points.
2. Mix question types for each paragraph.
3. Use a consistent format on all reading tests.
4. Avoid introducing new vocabulary in reading passages. If you do, provide a definition key and type key words in boldface on the test.
5. Space passages so students have enough room to underline important information.

Following are seven suggestions to help secondary students answer reading comprehension questions:

1. Read the passage over quickly. The first time you read through a passage, try to get a general idea of what it's about.
2. Read the passage a second time. You'll probably be asked questions about the *who, what, where,* and *when* information in the reading passage. To help you remember this important information, read the passage slowly and carefully the second time. Circle or underline the names of all the people and places, and the times, dates, and numbers in the passage. Remember, "Once is not enough!"
3. Try to answer multiple-choice questions by looking at the stem only. Here's a strategy to follow when answering multiple choice questions about a reading passage:
   • Read the passage twice.
   • Circle or underline the names of all the people, places, times, dates, and numbers in the passage.
   • Try to answer the question without looking at the choices.
   • If you don't know the answer, look at the choices and try to eliminate some of them.
   • Look at the passage again to decide which answer to choose.
4. Look back at the passage if you're unsure of the answer. Not all of the answers to reading comprehension questions can be found in the paragraph, but it's a good place to start if you're unsure of an answer. Even if the answer isn't stated in the paragraph, looking back at it will remind you of the key points and help you form your answer.
5. Look for the main idea. The main idea is the most important idea. It tells you what the paragraph is about. Some test questions will ask you to read a paragraph and find the main idea. If a word or phrase isn't used in the passage, or if it's used only once, it's probably not the main idea.

6. Back up your answer with an explanation or a reason. Sometimes you'll be asked to read a passage and tell about your reaction to it or give your opinion. There usually aren't any wrong answers to these types of questions, especially if you back up your answer with a good explanation or reason. Here are some examples of how these kinds of questions start:

How do you think . . .

Why do you think . . .

Do you think . . .

An easy way to begin your answer is to repeat the question.

7. Double-check your answers. You'll get a better grade if you check your answers before handing in your paper. The answers to most reading comprehension questions are somewhere in the reading passage. As you answer each question, look back at the paragraph to make sure you've answered it correctly (Lazzari & Wood, 1994, pp. 105–106).

Defining words and using words in context is an expectation of teachers across all content areas. Some teachers use definition tests for weekly spelling vocabulary assessment. Others require students to respond to definition items in social studies, literature, or science.

Although popular with teachers, definition tests can be difficult for many students because they require structured study and memorizing. The format itself is very flexible; however, it can vary from requiring simple recognition responses to structured recall formats. Matching, true–false, multiple choice, sentence completion with or without word banks, and sentence dictation are the most popular formats for definition tests.

Teachers can help their students by explaining about the importance in real life of understanding definitions and why teachers across all content areas expect their students to define words and use words in context. Definition items may appear in various test formats, but they all require extensive study and memorization.

The key to success on definition tests is studying and memorizing. The following 21 study tips will help students prepare for definition tests:

1. Practice a three-step approach to learning definitions. Write the words and definitions you want to learn on a sheet of notebook paper. Divide the paper into three vertical sections. Put the word in section 1 and the definition in section 2. Fold section 3 over section 2 while you're studying.

2. Use flash cards to study. Put the word on one side of an index card and its definition on the other side. Use the cards to study by yourself or with a partner.

3. Use a memory strategy for remembering words and definitions. Use the Look, Say, and Write strategy for learning definitions:

- Look at the word and study the definition.
- Say the word and its definition.
- Write the word.

4. Study words and definitions in groups of five. Study five words and definitions at a time. After you've learned the first five words and definitions, study another group of five. Then, review all ten words. Continue studying groups of five words and definitions at a time. After studying each group of five, go back and review all the words you've studied before adding any new word groups.

5. Find a study partner. After you've used the Look, Say, and Write strategy for studying the words, have someone say the words and you give the definitions.

6. Vary the study technique you use with your partner. You might also want to have someone give you the definitions and you name the words.

7. Think of short definitions for words. Try to think of a one- or two-word definition for a word rather than a long phrase or sentence. For example, instead of memorizing *to accumulate gradually* for the word *gather,* use the word *collect* as your definition.

8. Highlight prefixes, suffixes, and root words. When you learn the meanings of common prefixes, suffixes, and root words, this will help you define words you're unsure of. Look at the following example for the word *preexistence.*

- *Pre* is the prefix. It means "before."
- *Exist* is the root word. It means "to come into being."
- *Ence* is the suffix. It means "a state of being."

By looking at the prefix, suffix, and root word, you can figure out that *preexistence* means "to come into being before something else."

9. Learn basic root words. Learning root words can help you figure out the meanings of words you're unsure of. For example, the root word *magni,* means "great" or "big." If you know this, it can help you figure out the meanings of words like *magni*fy, *magni*ficent, and *magni*tude.

10. Learn prefix meanings. Even if you don't know the meaning of the root word, knowing its prefix can give you a clue to the word's meaning. For example, what do you think the word *dissatisfied* means? If you know the prefix *dis* means "not," you can guess the meaning of this word as "not satisfied."

11. Learn suffix meanings. Even if you don't know the meaning of the root word, knowing its suffix can give you a clue to the word's meaning. For example, what do you think the word *reliable* means? If you know the suffix *able* means "able to," you can guess the meaning of this word as "able to rely on."

12. Use visualization and association to help recall definitions. When you visualize something, you try to picture it in your mind. When you associate something, you try to link it to something it's like. For example, you might use visualization and association to remember the meaning of the word *cowl,* which is a monk's hood. To do this, picture the hood coming down in a point over the monk's forehead, like the markings on an owl's face.

13. Make up jingles to help you learn definitions. For example, you can think of a jingle for the word *separate,* which means "to keep apart." You might think, "The crowd will sepa*rate* if a *rat* appears."

14. Look for small words within words. Long words are often made up of two or three smaller words. Looking for the small words can help you learn to spell the long words. For example, the word *separate* has the words *par* and *ate* in it.

15. Match your study techniques to the type of test. Will the test be a sentence completion test? Will it have a word bank? Will you be asked to take dictation? Will you be asked to provide an antonym or a synonym for a word? Always ask your teacher how the test will be given so you'll know how to study.

16. Complete the definitions you know first. Then you'll know how much time you have to answer the ones you don't know.

17. Use the number and length of blanks as a clue to the answer. If the definition is given as an incomplete sentence, check the number and length of the blanks. Sometimes this is a clue to the size and the number of words.

18. Look for *a* or *an* right before the blank. If the definition is given as an incomplete sentence, check the word right before the blank. This can be a clue to the word you are looking for. *A* usually comes before a word that starts with a consonant. *An* usually comes before a word that starts with a vowel.

19. Decide which part of speech is missing from an incomplete sentence. If the definition is given as an incomplete sentence, check the part of speech that's missing. Subjects and verbs must agree. Look at these examples:

A <u>pilot</u> <u>is</u> the person who flies the plane.

<u>Pilots</u> <u>are</u> people who fly planes.

20. Use context clues. All of the words in a sentence depend on the others. If you don't know the meaning of a word, look at the words around it for a clue. This kind of clue is called a *context clue.* There are five types of context clues:

- Synonyms
- Definition or description
- Association
- Tone and setting
- Cause and effect

21. Ask your teacher if there's a penalty for incorrect answers. If there isn't a penalty, always guess at definitions you're unsure of. (Lazzari & Wood, 1994, pp. 89–92)

Extended-response items are becoming more frequent on state assessment measures. This response item may appear in different domain areas and require higher order thinking skills. An effective solution requires that the student complete all parts of the task and clearly communicate and justify the answer. In some cases, writing skills are evaluated. General tips for helping students respond to constructed-response items are helpful when practicing for extended-response items. Following is an example of an extended-response item for the domain area of math:

Solve the Problem   Rhonda has 23 CDs in her music collection. She gives away 8 of them.

    a. Write a number sentence that shows one way to find the number of CDs she has left in her collection.

    b. What is the solution to your number sentence?

    c. Write a story problem of your own that could be solved by the master sentence shown below.

       $15 - ? = 8$

    d. Show how to find the solution to your number sequence.

Computation problems usually require the student to apply an algorithm or a formula to find a numerical answer. Consider the suggestions in Figure 12.2.

Word problems can be very difficult for students with disabilities. The suggestions in Figure 12.3 are helpful during evaluation.

Lab practicals can be used to assess students with mild disabilities. If students have been learning how to operate Bunsen burners, for example, a test could involve giving them a checklist to work on throughout the lab (see Figure 12.4). Students who need individual help can work with a lab partner or in a small group. Teachers can follow up with more specific questions, which students should complete with the burner turned off. Teachers can write similar checklist tests for the use of other lab equipment, such as balances, graduated cylinders, and microscopes.

1. Provide manipulative objects that make the problems more concrete.

2. Avoid mixing different problem formats in the same section. For example, a student with organizational or visual tracking difficulties may be able to solve problem A but may not be able to align the numbers in problem B.

   Problem A
   ```
     468
      83
   + 1894
   ```

   Problem B

   $670 + 40 + 2861 =$ _____

3. Avoid mixing vertical and horizontal problems in the same section. For example, for the student with visual tracking problems or one who has difficulty changing gears from one process to another, the shift in presentation from problem C to problem D may be confusing. It would be better to test the student's knowledge of the two processes in two separate sections of the test.

   Problem A
   ```
       8
   ×   5
   ```

   Problem B

   $5 \times 6 =$ _____

4. Give formulas and meanings of symbols.

   $<$ means *less than*

5. Give a set of written steps for applying algorithms.

   Long Division
   1. Divide
   2. Multiply
   3. Subtract
   4. Check
   5. Bring down

FIGURE 12.2

Adaptations for computation problems.

Note: Adapted with permission from "Adapting Test Construction for Mainstreamed Mathematics Students" (*Mathematics Teacher*), copyright May 1988 by the National Council of Teachers of Mathematics. All rights reserved.

1. Use simple sentences. Avoid words that may cause confusion.
2. Use a problem context that is relevant to the student's arsenal of experience.
3. Underline or circle key words—for example, *less, more.*
4. Use no more than five word problems per test because they require greater effort to read and understand.
5. Give formulas as reminders of operations to be used.
6. Be sure that the reasoning skills being tested are appropriate to the student's comprehension level. Avoid the use of word problems (with some students) because this may be testing language and measuring skills above the student's level. For example, a student with a mild disability who has poor reading and comprehension skills may not be able to understand a complex word problem without assistance.

The following example incorporates many of these suggestions:
   John lives 3 and ⁷⁄₁₀ miles from Fair Oaks elementary school.
   Trish lives 2 and ¾ miles from school.
   Which one lives farther from school? _____
   How much farther? _____

FIGURE 12.3

Adaptations for word problems.

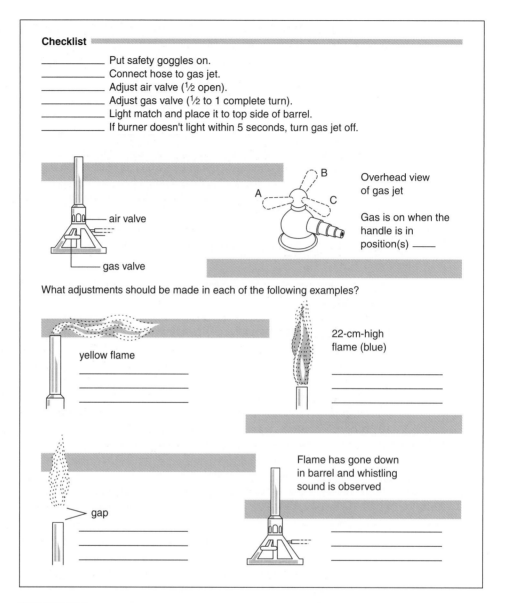

Checklist

_____ Put safety goggles on.
_____ Connect hose to gas jet.
_____ Adjust air valve (½ open).
_____ Adjust gas valve (½ to 1 complete turn).
_____ Light match and place it to top side of barrel.
_____ If burner doesn't light within 5 seconds, turn gas jet off.

air valve

gas valve

B

A   C

Overhead view
of gas jet

Gas is on when the
handle is in
position(s) _____

What adjustments should be made in each of the following examples?

yellow flame

_____
_____
_____

22-cm-high
flame (blue)

_____
_____
_____

gap

_____
_____
_____

Flame has gone down
in barrel and whistling
sound is observed

_____
_____
_____

FIGURE 12.4
Lab practical for the Bunsen burner.

Note: Adapted with permission of NSTA publications from "Stress the Knowledge, Not the Student," by Wood et al., from *The Science Teacher,* November 1988, published by the National Science Teachers Association, Arlington, Virginia.

Many students can answer questions better orally than in writing. To test students' safety knowledge, teachers can make slides of people using improper safety procedures. They can then show these slides and ask students to describe orally which rules are being broken. Another adaptation is to read tests aloud to students with reading disabilities.

For students who learn best through hands-on experiences, teachers can design tests that evaluate students in a hands-on manner. For example, instead of labeling a diagram of an atom on a test, students can construct a three-dimensional model of an atom using plastic foam balls. The students can indicate on the model the location and charge of neutrons, protons, and electrons.

Wilson (2002) presented five constructed-response pitfalls students may encounter.

1. All section of the question must be answered. Some problems have more than one step. Therefore, the student must reread the question after answering the question. Extended-response item is an example of a multiple-step question.
2. Be sure and show all of your work. Some problems are graded on a point system and a step omitted could result in a loss of points.
3. Provide all evidence to support your answer. Younger children may assume that the grader knows the answer and therefore, there is no need to provide details. Have students reread their answer from another student's point of view.
4. Practice with class using scoring rubrics so that students begin to construct in their minds the characteristics of a good response.
5. Look ahead at the questions to be answered so as not to become bogged down on one question, not allowing time to respond to all of the questions. (pp. 44–45)

The second category of classroom-embedded assessment is extended-time assessment. This category allows the student a longer period of time for completing the assessment measure and allows the teacher more time for collecting data for student evaluation. Extended-time assessment may be student driven or teacher driven.

Student-driven assessments are products students create over an extended time frame. They include performance assessments or products, oral reports, self-assessments, and portfolios.

A popular form of student-driven assessment is performance or product based. These may be developed by an individual student or by a group. Jacobs (1997) in her work on curriculum mapping matched learner developmental characteristics and assessment genres by grade level. (see Figure 12.5).

Types of student products or performances are presented in Table 12.10, which lists resources for learning (human, print, and nonprint) and evidence of learning. The types of products or performances include written work, visual presentations, hands-on experiences, oral presentations, dramatizations and performances, conversations and conferences, and reflections. This excellent list, provided by the Hawaii Office of Curriculum, provides a wide range of ideas for teachers to use to evaluate students' achievement of standards.

Many students avoid oral reports because of stage fright. The Practical Applications box on pages 439 and 440 provides tips for each of the basic components of an oral report: introduction, beginning, middle, and conclusion.

Student self-assessment, according to Marzano (2000), is well suited to the grading aspects of informational topics, process topics, thinking and reasoning, communication, and nonachievement factors (p. 87). "Although the most underused form of classroom assessment, student self-assessment has the most flexibility and power as a combined assessment and learning tool" (p. 102).

Portfolios have been in existence for a long time and are used by such professionals as artists, architects, and photographers. In education, portfolios can do the following:

- Engage students in learning content
- Help students learn the skills of reflection and self-evaluation
- Document student learning in areas that do not lend themselves to traditional assessment
- Facilitate communication with parents (Danielson & Abrutyn, 1997)

K–2 Developmental Characteristics

Cognitive level is concrete operations; sensory-motor modalities dominate; egocentric; parallel play still dominates with the beginning signs of social interaction with other peers; strong need for primary affiliation with a key adult at school and parental surrogates; willingness to experiment and take risks; verbal skills generally more pronounced in girls; spatial-motor generally more pronounced in boys; evident disparities between various areas of development as in fine motor/gross motor differences; uneven development in speaking skills; reading and writing emerges at this level with the learner's fascination with sound–symbol relations.

Examples of K–2 Genres

Captions	Story boards
Labels	Story lines
Simple research	Graphs/charts
Maps	Joke telling
Interview with a key question	Observational drawing

Grades 3–5 Developmental Characteristics

Cognitive operations are moving through concrete functions with early signs of simple abstract thinking; students are able to combine several concepts and perceive cause-and-effect relationships; fascination with the world; excellent "reporters" and seekers of interesting information; social skills related strongly to peers and to teachers; enjoy large group projects; social concern for others emerging; physical stability and agility.

Examples of Grade 3–5 Genres

Simple research report	Extended research report
Note cards	Interview: questions series
Short stories	Photo essay with text
Artifact analysis	Comparative observations
Newspaper articles	

Grades 6–8 Developmental Characteristics

Labile period of development; surge into formal operations; quest for personal identity; fascination with issues of fairness, justice, and trust; pronounced surges in physical development; uneven development among peers; self-consciousness about physical presence; concern for others conflicting with concern for self.

Examples of Grade 6–8 Genres

Persuasive essays	Descriptive essays
Analytical essays	Personal essays
Hypothesis testing	Issue-based forums
Blueprints and modeling	Original play writing
Museum text/captions	Four note-taking forms

Grades 9–10 and 11–12 Developmental Characteristics

Significant differences among 9th and 12th graders progressing from mid-adolescent concerns to pre-adult education; formal operations involving abstract concepts; projections; social life focused on smaller groupings and pairings; sexuality is an issue; physical maturity rapidly paces; focus on future and next steps.

Examples of Grades 9–10 and 11–12 Genres

Position papers	Legal briefs
Business plans	Anthologies
Choreography	Game book
Film and literary criticism	Senior project and defense
Work study analysis	Interview simulations
Case studies	Original musical
Compositions	

FIGURE 12.5

Matching learners and assessment genres.

Note: From *Mapping the Big Picture: Integrating Curriculum and Assessment K-12* (pp. 36–37) by H. H. Jacobs. Copyright © 1997 by the Association for Supervision and Curriculum Development. Reprinted by permission. The Association for Supervision and Curriculum Development is a worldwide community of educators advocating sound policies and sharing best practices to achieve the success of each learner. To learn more, visit ASDC at www.ascd.org.

TABLE 12.10
Resources and examples of products.

Resources for Learning

Human	Print	Nonprint
Business leaders	Advertisements	Apprenticeships
Church members	Anthologies	Art work
Coaches	Bibliographies	Artifacts
Community members	Biographies	Audiotapes
Content-area experts	Books, textbooks	Community centers
Counselors	Brochures, pamphlets	Computer software
Cultural experts	Charts, tables, diagrams	Debates
Family members	Dictionaries	Demonstrations
Friends	Encyclopedias	Exhibits
Industry experts	Guidebooks, manuals	Experiments
Librarians	Historical novels	Festivals, celebrations
Media representatives	Journals	Field trips, excursions
Military experts		
Parents		
Politicians, elected officials		
Professionals		
Public service workers		
School staff		
Senior citizens		
Service providers		
Students		
Teachers		
Tutors		

Evidence of Learning Products/Performances

Written Work

Assignment	Essay	Newspaper article	Recipe
Autobiography	Flowchart	Notes/notebook	Report
Bibliography	Glossary	Outline	Research paper
Book	Guide	Pamphlet	Script
Book review	Instructions	Paragraph	Short story
Booklet	Inventory	Poem	Summary
Characterization	Letter	Position paper	Survey
Chronology	List	Proposal	Table
Critique	Magazine article	Protocol	Vocabulary list
Crossword puzzle	Manual	Questionnaire	Worksheet
Editorial	Newsletter		

Visual Presentations

Activity	Chart	Flip book	Photo essay
Advertisement	Collage	Graph	Picture book
Animation	Data table	Illustrated story	Portfolio
Banner	Diagram	Map	Poster
Blueprint	Display	Mask	Scrap book
Book jacket	Drawing	Movie	Slide presentation
Bulletin board	Exhibit	Mural	Story board
Cartoon	Family tree	Painting	Timeline

Oral Presentations	Hands-on Experience	Conversations & Conferences	Dramatization & Performances
Audiotapes	Art project	Class meeting	Dance
Choral reading	Craft project	Panel discussion	Language dialogue
Class report	Diorama	Small or large group	Musical performance

(continued)

TABLE 12.10
Continued.

Resources for Learning		Evidence of Learning Products/Performances			
Print	**Nonprint**	**Hands-on Experience**	**Oral Presentations**	**Dramatization & Performances**	**Conversations & Conferences**
Magazines	Interviews	Experiment	Commentary	Pantomime	Teacher/student conference
Maps	Job shadowing	Festival	Debate	Play	Teacher/parent/student
Newsletters	Labs	Game	Demonstrations	(Poetry) interpretation	Team debrief
Newspapers	Lectures	Invention	Documentary	Puppetry	Writers workshop
Nonfiction works	Movies	Lab work	Group discussion	Rap	
Position papers	Music	Mobile	Interview	Recital	**Reflections**
Posters	Observations	Model	Lecture	Role play	Diary
Primary documents	Performances, plays, concerts	Movie production	Multimedia	Simulation	Freewrite
Reference books	Photographs	Shop project	Oral report	Skit	Journal
Reports, reviews	Presentations		Panel presentation	Song	Learning log
Research papers	Public events		Speech	Storytelling	Observation log
Thesaurus	Research project			Teach a lesson	Self-report
Websites	Televised events				
	Video tapes				

Note: From Hawaii Department of Education, Office of Curriculum, Instruction and Student Support, Special Education Services, Carolyn Hamoda, Educational Specialist. Reprinted with permission.

PRACTICAL APPLICATIONS
SUGGESTIONS FOR STUDENTS' ORAL REPORTS

INTRODUCTION

An oral report is a composition with legs—your legs. You have to get up in front of a group of people and provide them with information about a certain subject with your voice, not your pen. (Hint: Do not crawl to the front of the room. People might think you are frightened, and they won't respect you as an authority on the subject you are presenting.)

Walk up to the front with dignity. Do not be afraid. You have something the rest of the folks in the room should hear.

An oral report is like a composition because it has a beginning, a middle, and a conclusion.

BEGINNING

Your beginning statements should put your listeners (not readers) at ease, as well as present your topic. This can be done using a three step process called "the look, the hook, and the delivery."

Step 1: The Look: Look around at the audience. Look to the left. Look to the right. Then look to the center of the group. Those are people out there. They are a lot like you. So don't panic and race out of the room at the sight of them.

Step 2: The Hook: Introduce yourself (if only a few of the people know you), then make some statements that might interest your listeners in hearing more about your topic. You might say, "According to statistics, half of you sitting in the audience have had a very serious situation occur in your life in the past 3 years. This situation has changed your life completely. Things will never be the same again." The audience is wondering what in the world you are referring to! Then you fill them in.

Step 3: The Delivery: Here is where you deliver the punch line. You can say, "The event that has struck many of you is the splitting of the family. In essence, I mean divorce. Divorce in America is the most serious social problem of our generation."

You LOOK, you HOOK, then you DELIVER the punch line, or thesis.

Oral reports are built the same way compositions are built—sentence after sentence, paragraph after paragraph, connector after connector—HOOK, LINE, AND SINKER!

Oral reports are compositions with legs—and voices.

MIDDLE

The middle of your oral report is exactly like the middle of a composition. It gives the listener (not the reader) information about the thesis. Here you can either explain or tell.

(continued)

Explain: Why more men are going into nursing; why a good mechanic will never go hungry in the United States; why toddlers are more intelligent today because of television.

Tell: What things about the snow leopard make it so exciting; what information indicates that water skiing is America's favorite sport.

(Hint: You may have to do some research in magazines and encyclopedias to fully explain your thesis.)

Make notes on index cards the way you do for your written reports.

REINFORCE YOUR THESIS

You guessed it! After you locate some information on your thesis (topic), write out a paragraph or two like you would for a composition. Then connect your first paragraph in this middle section to the beginning section and speak these two sections to the class.

Try not to read your report off the paper word for word. If you have to glance at the paper now and then, well, nobody's going to yell at you. After all, even the men and women on the six o' clock news glance once in a while.

You need to be cool, calm, and collected during an oral report. People are watching you. Don't stutter or stammer. Be confident. Read your report to yourself five times before presenting it to a class. This can help you look in control.

Speak up! Don't hide behind the speaker's stand (podium). Look people in the eye as if to say, "I've got some good information here if you folks are interested." Present a good speech or report, and they'll be interested!

CONCLUSION

The end of your report is as important as the beginning. People remember the last thing they hear! End your report with a restatement of your thesis (the main point of your report). Say it again, Sam!

Note: Thanks to Randy Larson.

Portfolios may be "used as an assessment framework. Portfolios are systematic collections by students and teachers that serve as the basis to examine 'effort, in improvement, processes, and achievement as well as to meet the accountability demands usually achieved by more formal testing procedures' " (Johns, as cited in Danielson & Abrutyn, 1997, p. vi). Examples of assessment portfolios are listed in Figure 12.6.

Extended-time assessment measures that are teacher driven include observations, interviews, anecdotal records, assignments, homework, multiple intelligences assessment, and authentic assessment measures. Teacher observations and interviews are closely related. According to Marzano (2000), "one of the most straight forward ways to collect classroom assessment data is through informal observations of students" (p. 99). Educators need to be aware of the skills they are observing. Marzano continued, "teacher observation is probably the perfect assessment tool for the nonachievement factors—effort, behavior, and attendance" (p. 99). One type of observation is the interview, in which teachers probe students for information learned.

Reading
- Audiotape or oral reading of selected passages
- Original story grammar map
- Transcript of story retelling
- Log of books read with personal reactions, summaries, vocabulary
- Representative assignments; responses to pre-/post-reading questions
- Favorite performance
- Journal entries, including self-evaluation

Science
- Representative work samples
- Student-selected best performance
- Report from hands-on investigation
- Notes on science fair project
- Journal entries, including self-evaluation

Writing
- Scrapbook of representative writing samples
- Selected prewriting activities
- Illustrations/diagrams for one piece
- Log/journal of writing ideas, vocabulary, schematic maps, compositions, evaluations
- Conference notes, observation narratives
- Student-selected best performance
- Self-evaluation checklists and teacher checklists

Social studies
- Representative work samples
- Student-selected best performance
- Design of travel brochure, packet, or itinerary of trip
- Notes on history fair project
- Journal entries, including self-evaluation

Mathematics
- Reports of mathematical investigations
- Representative assignments
- Teacher conference notes
- Descriptions and diagrams of problem-solving processes
- Video, audio, or computer-generated examples of work
- Best performance
- Journal entries including self-evaluation

Arts
- Best performance
- Favorite performance
- First, middle, and final renderings of projects
- Tape of performance
- Journal entries, including self-evaluation

Generic
- Learning progress record
- Report cards
- Personal journal
- Tests
- Significant daily assignments
- Anecdotal observations
- Photographs
- Awards
- Personal goals

FIGURE 12.6
Examples of assessment portfolios.

Note: From "What Makes a Portfolio a Portfolio?" by F. L. Paulson, P. R. Paulson, and C. A. Meyer, *Educational Leadership, 48*(5), 60–63. Copyright © 1991 by the Association for Supervision and Curriculum Development. Adapted by permission. The Association for Supervision and Curriculum Development is a worldwide community of educators advocating sound policies and sharing best practices to achieve the success of each learner. To learn more, visit ASDC at www.ascd.org.

Anecdotal records are notes teachers keep on an ongoing basis regarding a student's work. These brief notes record the student's work progress and skill development, and where the student may need to be retaught.

Assignments and homework are also types of teacher-driven assessments. Like other response assessments, assignments and homework provide feedback on student learning and may or may not be given a grade. Ideas for assignment and homework interventions may be found in chapter 11.

Authentic assessment requires realistic demands in a real-life setting. It is sometimes used interchangeably with performance assessment, which requires a student to use the knowledge learned. Educators using authentic or performance assessment are able to provide multiple opportunities for students to perform and show work mastery.

Frequently, authentic assessments, or performance tasks, are confused with essay questions. According to Marzano (2000),

> Essay items that require the application of knowledge, then, are types of performance tasks. However, not all performance tasks are essays. Some performance tasks do not require written responses, whereas all essays do. For example, a performance task requiring students to apply their knowledge and skill in playing the violin would not require the student to write (or say) anything.
>
> Like essay items, one of the most powerful aspects of performance tasks is that they can be used to assess a variety of forms of knowledge. (p. 97)

Examples of authentic assessment are given in Figure 12.7.

Howard Gardner's eight multiple intelligences provide educators yet another way to assess students. Table 12.11 presents each of the eight dispositions or intelligences and lists what a child with each intelligence may be sensitive to, how the child may be inclined, and what the child's abilities are. Lazeur (1998) presented an assessment menu for each of the eight intelligences (see Table 12.12).

Reading
- Actual or audio/videotape of reading to peer
- Log and critiques of books read
- Book review
- Book jacket design

Science
- Scientific experiment to prove theory
- Original investigation and a report of findings
- Journal of observations of moons, stars
- Solutions to local environment problems

Oral Expression
- Transmission of message to several classes
- Phone call to request information
- Debate about current issues
- Persuasive speech

Social studies
- Map of school or community
- Design of museum exhibit on topic of interest
- Advertising campaign for political candidate
- Identification of social problem for co-op group

Written expression
- Student interviews
- Article for school paper
- Written resume and job application
- Invitation to party
- Letter to editor

Arts
- Design and decoration of bulletin board
- Submission of art to contest
- Artwork design for public building
- Performance in a play

Mathematics
- Solving real-life problems using math knowledge
- Solving a puzzle using logic and reasoning
- Monitoring a savings account
- Personal budget

Generic
- Reflective journal of learning progress
- Competition for "grant" money
- Planning and teaching a lesson to peer
- Laser disc storage of assessment information

FIGURE 12.7

Examples of authentic assessment.

Note: From "Performance Assessment and Special Education: Practices and Prospects" by J. A. Poteet, J. S. Choate, and S. C. Steward, 1993, *Focus on Exceptional Children, 26*(1), 7. Adapted with permission.

TABLE 12.11
Intelligences as dispositions.

Disposition/Intelligence	Sensitivity to:	Inclination for:	Ability to:
Verbal-linguistic intelligence	The sounds, meanings, structures, and styles of language	Speaking, writing, listening, reading	Speak effectively (teacher, religious leader, politician) or write effectively (poet, journalist, novelist, copywriter, editor)
Logical-mathematical intelligence	Patterns, numbers, and numerical data, causes and effects, objective and quantitative reasoning	Finding patterns, making calculations, forming and testing hypotheses, using the scientific method, deductive and inductive reasoning	Work effectively with numbers (accountant, statistician, economist) and reason effectively (engineer, scientist, computer programmer)
Spatial intelligence	Colors, shapes, visual puzzles, symmetry, lines, images	Representing ideas visually, creating mental images, noticing visual details, drawing and sketching	Create visually (artist, photographer, engineer, decorator) and visualize accurately (tour guide, scout, ranger)
Bodily-kinesthetic intelligence	Touch, movement, physical self, athleticism	Activities requiring strength, speed, flexibility, hand–eye coordination, and balance	Use the hands to fix or create (mechanic, surgeon, carpenter, sculptor, mason) And use the body expressively (dancer, athlete, actor)
Musical intelligence	Tone, beat, tempo, melody, pitch, sound	Listening, singing, playing an instrument	Create music (songwriter, composer, musician, conductor) and analyze music (music critic)
Interpersonal intelligence	Body language, moods, voice, feelings	Noticing and responding to other people's feelings and personalities	Work with people (administrators, managers, consultants, teachers) and help people identify and overcome problems (therapists, psychologists)
Intrapersonal intelligence	One's own strengths, weaknesses, goals, and desires	Setting goals, assessing personal abilities and liabilities, monitoring one's own thinking	Mediate, reflect, exhibit self-discipline, maintain composure, and get the most out of oneself
Naturalist intelligence	Natural objects, plants, animals, naturally occurring patterns, ecological issues	Identifying and classifying living things and natural objects	Analyze ecological and natural situations and data (ecologists and rangers), learn from living things (zoologists, botanists, veterinarians) and work in natural setting (hunters, scouts)

Note: From *So Each May Learn: Integrating Learning Styles and Multiple Intelligences* (p. 11), by H. F. Silver, R. W. Strong, and M. J. Perini, 2000, Alexandria, VA: Association for Supervision and Curriculum Development. ©2000 by Silver Strong & Associates, L.L.C. Reprinted with permission. To purchase this title, please call 800-962-4432 or visit www.ThoughtfulEd.com online.

TABLE 12.12
Multiple intelligences assessment menu.

Verbal-Linguistic Intelligence (Language arts–based assessment instruments)	Logical-Mathematical Intelligence (Cognitive patterns–based assessment instruments)	Visual-Spatial Intelligence (Imaginal-based assessment instruments)	Bodily-Kinesthetic Intelligence (Performance-based assessment instruments)
Written essays	Cognitive organizers	Murals and montages	Lab experiments
Vocabulary quizzes	Higher-order reasoning	Graphic representation and visual illustrating	Dramatization
Recall of verbal information	Pattern games	Visualization and imagination	Original and classical dance
Audiocassette recordings	Outlining	Reading, understanding, and creating maps	Charades and mimes
Poetry writing	Logic and rationality exercises	Flowcharts and graphs	Impersonations
Linguistic humor	Mental menus and formulas	Sculpting and building	Human tableaux
Formal speech	Deductive reasoning	Imaginary conversations	Invention projects
Cognitive debates	Inductive reasoning	Mind mapping	Physical exercise routines and games
Listening and reporting	Calculation processes	Video recording and photography	Skill demonstrations
Learning logs and journals	Logical analysis and critique	Manipulative demonstrations	Illustrations using body language and gestures

Musical-Rhythmic Intelligence (Auditory-based assessment instruments)	Interpersonal Intelligence (Relational-based assessment instruments)	Intrapersonal Intelligence (Psychological-based assessment instruments)	Naturalist Intelligence (Environment-based assessment instruments)
Creating concept songs and raps	Group "jigsaws"	Autobiographical reporting	Hands-on labs/demonstrations
Illustrating with sound	Explaining to or teaching another	Personal application scenarios	Species/natural pattern classification
Discerning rhythmic patterns	"Think-pair-share"	Metacognitive surveys and questionnaires	Nature encounters/ field trips
Composing music	"Round robin"	Higher-order questions and answers	Environmental feedback
Linking music and rhythm with concepts	Giving and receiving feedback	Concentration tests	Nature observations
Orchestrating music	Interviews, questionnaires, and people searches	Feelings, diaries, and logs	Care for plants and animals
Creating percussion patterns	Empathic processing	Personal projection	Sensory stimulation exercises
Recognizing tonal patterns and quality	Random group quizzes	Self-identification reporting	Conservation practices
Analyzing musical structure	Assess your teammates	Personal history correlation	Archetypal pattern recognition
Reproducing musical and rhythmic patterns	Test, coach, and retest	Personal priorities and goals	Natural world simulations

Note: From Lazear, D. (1988). *The rubrics way* (p. 37). Chicago, IL: Zephyr Press. Reprinted with permission.

Test Design.   Test design is the third aspect of test construction that can be easily adapted. Adaptations in test design include the following:

1. Use test items that reflect the techniques used in teaching. For example, if the students were taught only to recall facts, avoid essay questions.

2. Type or print legibly. Use large type when available. If you prepare the test in longhand, be sure to list items clearly, concisely, and neatly.

3. Prepare a study guide that matches the design of the test.

4. Adjust the readability level of the test to meet the students' needs.

5. Prepare the test in short sections that you can administer individually if necessary.

6. Place one type of question on each page. For example, use one page for multiple-choice questions and another for essay questions.

7. After consulting students privately about personal testing needs, adapt the test to meet those needs.

8. If you use the chalkboard for a test, clear other material from the board, then print or write in large, legible letters. Avoid lengthy tests for students with copying difficulties.

9. Avoid using only oral tests and quizzes.

10. Plan to allow students with disabilities to take tests in a separate setting to overcome problems with time, reading ability, or embarrassment.

11. Clearly duplicate the test using black ink, if available.

12. Use a large sheet of dark construction paper under the test to act as a border. Provide a sheet of paper with a "window frame" cut into it to help in reading the test. This helps students with visual acuity and visual perception problems.

13. If a student has difficulty finishing on time, administer an adapted, shortened version of the test. Another option is split-halves testing, in which half the test is administered on one day and the other half on the next day.

14. If a modified test is necessary for an included student, design it to resemble the general test to avoid embarrassment.

15. Arrange tests so that questions that count the most come first. Some students generally work in order and may not finish the test.

16. If possible, use canary yellow paper with black print for the test.

17. Write the point value for each section on the test.

18. Draw a line between math problem rows to help a student finish each row and not get mixed up while moving through the problems.

19. Place a heading for each test section with directions if the directions have changed.

20. Make sure handwriting is neat and legible.

21. If typing is not possible, print the test.

22. Number all pages of the test.

23. Use a felt marker to divide sections of the test so that the student knows when to move to another set of directions.

24. Watch the complexity of sentences so that the test does not become a language test and content is lost.

25. For reading sections, put the reading selection on one page and the questions on a second page. The student can then place the reading selection and the questions side by side.

Accommodations During Test Administration

The second component of the model for adapting classroom tests (see Figure 12.1) involves the administration of the test. Many students with disabilities may need alternative modes of administration when taking the test. Adaption of test administration relates directly to the problems that students encounter in the test situation as discussed at the beginning of this chapter. These include poor comprehension, modality considerations, time considerations, anxiety considerations, and response format.

Students with comprehension problems need special considerations during testing. Following are suggestions for test administration for such students:

1. Give test directions both orally and in written form. Make sure all students clearly understand.
2. Avoid long talks before the tests.
3. Allow students to tape-record responses to essay questions or the entire test.
4. Allow students to take the test in an alternative test site, usually the resource classroom.
5. Correct for content only, not for spelling or grammar.
6. Provide an example of the expected correct response.
7. Remind students to check tests for unanswered questions.
8. When the test deals with problem-solving skills, allow the use of tools, such as multiplication tables or calculators during math tests.
9. Read test aloud for students who have difficulty reading.
10. Give a written outline for essay questions.
11. Tape-record instructions and questions for a test.
12. Use objective rather than essay tests.

Modality difficulties may require accommodations during test administration. The difficulties may occur in auditory or visual perception. Suggestions for auditory perception problems are as follows:

1. For oral spelling tests, go slowly, enunciating each syllable and sound distinctly.
2. Avoid oral tests.
3. Seat student in a quiet place for testing.
4. Allow students to take tests in an alternative test site, such as the resource classroom.
5. Place a TESTING sign on the classroom door to discourage interruptions.

Suggestions for students with visual perception problems include the following:

1. Give directions orally as well as in written form.
2. Check students discreetly to see if they are on track.
3. Give the exam orally or tape-record it.
4. Seat students away from distractions (such as windows or doors). Use a carrel or face the desk toward a wall.
5. Avoid having other students turn in papers during the test.
6. Meet visitors at the door and talk in the hallway.

7. Hang a DO NOT DISTURB—TESTING sign on the door.

8. Use an alternative test site if the student requests it.

Many students have difficulty with time constraints in testing situations. Frequently, we associate time difficulties with standardized tests. Actually, all tests are timed. Think about it. When a teacher hands out the test papers, an assumption is made that the test will be turned in by the time class is over. Technically, all tests are timed unless considerations are provided during test administrations. For standardized tests, certain accommodations are allowed. For classroom testing, consider the following:

1. Allow enough time for students to complete the test. Inclusive students may require longer periods of time.

2. Provide breaks during lengthy tests.

3. Allow split-halves testing. Give half the test on one day and the remaining half on the second day.

4. Allow students to take the test in the resource room if necessary.

5. Allow students to complete only the odd- or even-numbered questions. Circle the appropriate questions for students who may not understand the concept of odd and even.

6. Use untimed tests.

7. Give oral or tape-recorded tests. Students with slow writing skills can answer orally or on tape.

Test anxiety is very real for many students. Many students even become physically ill prior to a test. Sometimes the anxiety results from the embarrassment many students feel when presented with a testing situation. We always want students to do their very best. Consider the following suggestions for test administration for students experiencing test anxiety or embarrassment:

1. Avoid adding pressure to the test setting by admonishing students to "hurry and get finished" or "do your best; this counts for half of your six-weeks' grade."

2. Avoid threatening to use a test to punish students for poor behavior.

3. Give a practice test.

4. Give a retest if needed.

5. Don't threaten dire consequences for failure.

6. Grade on the percentage of items completed.

7. Have students take the regular test with the class and an adapted test in the resource room.

8. Make a modified test closely resemble the regular test to avoid embarrassing self-conscious students.

9. Avoid calling attention to inclusive students as you help them.

10. Confer with students privately to work out accommodations for testing.

Response accommodations may be required for students with fine motor problems, written expression problems, or visual or verbal deficits. In addition, students with physical and sensory disabilities require accommodations during test administration. Students with memory problems who cannot recall multiplication facts may need a calculator. Sequencing and memory issues, such as in spelling, may require a spell checker. Some students have difficulty responding to "bubble" answer sheets. Following are suggestions for response accommodations during test administration:

1. Prepare students to respond to the test format prior to the test situations.

2. Assist students in checking the time allowed for the test. If the test is timed, response time becomes important.

3. Review with students the penalty, if any, for guessing or leaving questions unanswered.

4. Check to see that students have the necessary materials needed for the test.

5. Encourage students to check their work if time is left over.

6. Review tips for taking selected tests items or responses prior to test day.

7. Provide necessary accommodations for students with physical and sensory disabilities.

8. Provide a ruler for students who have difficulty answering on a "bubble" answer sheet. The ruler can be placed under the number answered and slid down after each response.

9. Have students make a mark after every five "bubble" items. When they come to the mark, they should be on number 5 then number 10, etc. This prevents students from completing the answer sheet with items left over, which indicates that they have misaligned the questions and answers.

   If marks are not allowed on answer sheets, the same procedure can be used in the test booklet.

Test Sites

Students may need an alternative test site such as a change of place for the test (setting) or a change in the test scheduling. A change in test setting may include going to the resource room to take the test. Many students with disabilities do better when the test is given with the special education teacher, who knows the student's unique strengths and weaknesses. Students with reading difficulties (slow readers and those with low vocabulary or low comprehension) can benefit from having the test read orally, having more time to complete the test, having questions clarified and new vocabulary explained, and feeling less pressure. The test may also be recorded on a tape recorder. When students are embarrassed by taking a test that is different from the one given to peers in the regular class, a different test setting is a helpful solution. Some students are easily confused by verbal or written directions and, in a different setting, have more opportunities to ask questions. This may help them feel less frustrated. Students who are distracted by the activity within the regular classroom may find that an alternative setting contains fewer distractions. For students experiencing test anxiety and frustration, different settings can reduce anxiety because they are no longer competing with peers, can work at their own pace, and have resource support. Alternative test settings may also include small groups within the classroom, a different general education classroom, and so forth.

According to Thurlow and colleagues (2003), "scheduling accommodations are changes in when testing occurs" (p. 56). Any time a student takes a test at a time other than when the test is regularly scheduled, a scheduling accommodation has been made. Reasons for a scheduling change include avoiding the effects of medication and reducing frustration. Other reasons include avoiding scheduling too many tests

COLLABORATION TIPS

General education teachers often fear that general education students will resent inclusive students for making better grades when they take tests in the resource room. This fear is based on the false assumption that students with mild disabilities will always make better grades because their tests are "easier." In fact, although some students with disabilities may score significantly higher, many are fortunate if they pass. General education students usually do not resent their peers who take their tests in a resource setting. Instead, they exhibit compassion: They are pleased when their friends can pass and do well; they realize that their friends have problems in school; and they often understand that their disabled peers function below grade level, take different tests, and have reasons for being tested in the resource setting. Usually, when teachers handle resource programming and testing appropriately, both general and special education students view the program positively. Even average and above-average students sometimes ask to attend resource classes for temporary assistance or to complete a test, and the majority of slow learners not eli-

gible for special education services would gladly attend resource classes.

The dilemma revolves around equality of evaluation. Teachers who evaluate by traditional testing methods generally express the results of their evaluation via the use of traditional letter grades (A, B, C, D, F) or numerical grades (95, 90, 85, 80). To teachers, students, parents, and the general public, these symbols generally represent a certain standard. When students take different tests but still receive traditional grades, some believe a standard has been violated. This issue has not been resolved; however, the following points should be noted:

1. Students with mild disabilities have definite learning problems, as their placement in special education attests.
2. Authorities recommend alternative site testing.
3. School systems across the nation use alternative grading systems.

For the present, general and special education educators should strive to develop equitable grading policies that will reward students with disabilities for their efforts and encourage all students to work toward their potential.

on one day, skipping a day between tests for preparation, reducing test anxiety, and accommodating students who do better in smaller testing sessions.

Determining the least restrictive testing environment is the responsibility of the IEP committee and is closely tied to the student's instruction and unique learning need. According to Jayanthi, Epstein, Polloway, and Bursuck (1996), nationally, educators perceived that the three most helpful testing accommodations are assisting with test directions, reading test questions or items to students, and rewording or simplifying test question wording. As with any accommodation, the educator strives to move the student from the use of an accommodation to the removal of the accommodation. For example, a student may initially need a note-taking accommodation, but eventually move to taking notes without an accommodation. The same stands for testing accommodations. Educators plan to move students from the present level of adaptations to ones that more closely approximate the testing environment of their nondisabled peers.

Student Preferences for Test Adaptations

Nelson, Jayanthi, Epstein, and Bursuck conducted a study reported in *Remedial and Special Education* (2000, pp. 41–52) in which they attempted to discover the specific testing adaptations of seventh- and eighth-grade students with high-incidence disabilities (such as learning disabilities) and general education students with low, average, high, and very high achievement. They found that adaptations most preferred by the entire sample were as follows:

- Open-note tests
- Open-book tests
- Practice questions for study
- Multiple choice instead of short answer or essay
- Use of dictionary or calculator
- A copy of the test to study
- Extra answer space

Testing adaptations that were least preferred by students in the sample were as follows:

- Teacher reading questions to students
- Tests with fewer questions than given other students
- Tests covering less material than tests given other students
- Tests written in larger print
- Oral responses instead of written ones
- Use of computer to write answers
- Individual help with directions during the test
- Learning test-taking skills

The study looked further into whether students' academic status related to their preferences for testing adaptations. Two other of the most liked adaptations were take-home tests and working in a small group. This study deserves more explanation than space allows here. However, it appears that some of the most preferred adaptations required the least amount of extra teacher time and that all groups of students acknowledged that adaptations are of benefit. Students do not want to be singled out, or made to feel "stupid" or "different" in front of their peers. Teachers need to be sensitive to this as they make adaptations.

GRADING STUDENTS IN INCLUSIVE SETTINGS

The problems inherent in evaluating students and assigning grades can become even more complex for students in inclusive settings. Here, the integration of students with disabilities into regular education classes has created a dilemma for teachers in terms of assigning grades fairly and objectively. On the one hand, questions arise about the equity of using different standards to evaluate students in the same classroom. For example, is it fair to the other students in the classroom to award the same letter grades and course credit to a student who has not met the class performance standards? On the other hand, proponents of individualized grading point out that to do otherwise places an added burden on students already at a disadvantage for competing fairly with their peers and does not provide useful information to students and parents. For example, a grade of "satisfactory" or C does not reveal what new knowledge students have gained or how they have performed relative to their individual strengths and weaknesses. Nor does it provide information on the effectiveness of instructional adaptations. Other questions arise concerning who should assign grades and which criteria and grading process they should use.

A preliminary question to answer when considering the issue of grading a student is whether alternative grading procedures are necessary for that individual. In many cases, making appropriate adaptations of the learning environment, format of content, teaching techniques, and testing procedures will enable the student with special needs to be graded according to the same methods used for other students in the classroom. When accommodations in grading procedures are needed, they should be noted on the student's IEP along with any other adaptations that are necessary. In addition to identifying the grading procedures, the IEP should specify if a grade reporting schedule other than the standard school schedule is to be used and should identify which teacher will be responsible for determining the student's grades.

GRADING AND ASSESSMENT

Grading is clearly tied to assessment, although not every assessment must receive a grade. Grading establishes criteria for success on assessment measures and also provides feedback for reteaching. Additionally, in practice, grades also serve several other functions (Jacobsen, Eggen, & Kauchak, 1989):

- Providing feedback to parents as an indicator of their children's achievement
- Providing data for grouping students
- Guiding decisions about promotion and graduation
- Providing a basis for making awards and scholarships
- Determining a student's eligibility for extracurricular activities
- Helping determine college eligibility and participation in collegiate athletics

Traditionally, the practice of assigning grades helped the administration differentiate among groups of students rather than providing useful information to students and parents. Everyone was graded on the same outcomes, and the same measures were used for each student.

Today, we still have outcomes and measures. However, education is becoming broader in focus—outcomes, and how these outcomes are reached, may vary for certain individuals.

Letter grades are still used, but more and more predictors of future success are seen as factors, not just one grade. Students who leave school to enter the workplace need feedback that more closely resembles the type they will receive on the job. It is important for educators to continue to strive to develop grading procedures that can more appropriately meet the needs of all students.

According to Marzano (2000), teachers usually consider four factors to include in grades: academic achievement, effort, behavior, and attendance. There is value in reporting student feedback on the nonachieving factors of effort, behavior, and attendance. Effort is perceived as participation in class and work completion. Behavior is defined as following rules and being able to work in teams. Attendance is divided into the areas of absenteeism and tardiness. These factors can be assessed accurately. However, the most important factor in grading is student academic achievement.

Alternative Methods of Grading

Although the development of alternative grading criteria for students with disabilities may not be an easy task, it is an extremely important adaptation that must be made if students with special needs are to have any chance of success in the general educational environment. Table 12.13 displays 10 alternative evaluation approaches, which are discussed in detail in this section.

Pass/Fail

The establishment of general criteria for passing or failing an assignment or a course is a common modification of traditional grade criteria. Because determination of acceptable work is judged according to broad-based criteria, the student in the inclusive setting has a greater chance of success in reaching the minimum course competencies. Like any measurement procedure, there are advantages and disadvantages to using a pass/fail system. Vasa (1981) identified the following advantages:

- Students feel less pressure to compete.
- Students feel less anxiety.
- Students need not cheat or butter up the teacher.
- Students know what the teacher expects of them and work toward a goal.
- The teacher can increase a student's achievement or aspiration level.
- The teacher can carefully examine the student's relative abilities and disabilities.
- The teacher does not have to compare students' work.

However, the pass/fail system does have disadvantages (Vasa, 1981):

- The teacher may not provide corrective feedback in weak areas.
- The passing grade does not distinguish among students of differing abilities.
- Some students do less work when freed of traditional grade pressure.
- Students close to failing feel the same pressures they do with traditional grades.
- Teachers sometimes find minimum standards arbitrary and difficult to define.

IEP Grading

This approach bases grading on the student's attainment of the goals and objectives specified in the IEP. Because the IEP must specify target accuracy levels or minimally acceptable levels of competence for specific skills or knowledge, built-in criteria for grading exist. Teachers can determine grades by translating the competency levels on a student's IEP into the school district's performance standards. If, for example, the

TABLE 12.13
Alternative approaches to evaluation.

Approach	Example
1. *Traditional grading:* Letter grades or percentages are assigned.	Students earning 94% or greater of the total points available will earn an A.
2. *Pass/fail system:* Broad-based criteria are established for passing or failing.	Students who complete all assignments and pass all tests will receive a passing grade for the course.
3. *IEP grading:* Competency levels on student's IEP are translated into the school district's performance standards.	If a student's IEP requires a 90% accuracy level and the range of 86–93 equals a letter grade of B on the local scale, then the student receives a B if he or she attains target accuracy level.
4. *Mastery- or criterion-level grading:* Content is divided into subcomponents. Students earn credit when their mastery of a certain skill reaches an acceptable level.	Students who name 38 of the 50 state capitals will receive a passing grade on that unit of the social studies curriculum.
5. *Multiple grading:* The student is assessed and graded in several areas, such as ability, effort, and achievement.	Student will receive 30 points for completing the project on time, 35 points for including all of the assigned sections, and 35 points for using at least four different resources.
6. *Shared grading:* Two or more teachers determine a student's grade.	The regular education teacher will determine 60% of the student's grade, and the resource room teacher will determine 40%.
7. *Point system:* Points are assigned to activities or assignments that add up to the term grade.	The student's science grade will be based on a total of 300 points: 100 from weekly quizzes, 100 from lab work in class, 50 from homework, and 50 from class participation.
8. *Student self-comparison:* Students evaluate themselves on an individual basis.	If a student judges that he or she has completed the assignment on time, included the necessary sections, and worked independently, then the student assigns himself or herself a passing grade for this assignment.
9. *Contracting:* The student and teacher agree on specific activities required for a certain grade.	If the student comes to class regularly, volunteers information at least once during each class, and turns in all required work, then he or she will receive a C.
10. *Portfolio evaluation:* A cumulative portfolio is maintained of each student's work, demonstrating achievement in key skill areas from kindergarten to 12th grade.	Cumulative samples of the handwriting show progress from rudimentary manuscript to legible cursive style from grades 1 to 4.
11. *Rubrics:* Establishing a point scale for students to use to evaluate their work.	Establishing clear boundaries for successful performance on a specific assessment task. The rubric may be designed for the task required of the student, and all student required tasks are not necessarily the same.

IEP requires 80% accuracy, and 80 equals a letter grade of C on the local scale, then the student receives a C.

Mastery- or Criterion-Level Grading

This approach divides content into various subcomponents, with pre- and posttest measures required for each step. Students earn credit only after their proficiency or mastery of a certain skill reaches an acceptable level. One disadvantage of this approach is that students are rewarded or passed for minimum, rather than optimum, performance.

Multiple Grading

This approach rewards the student in several areas, such as ability, effort, and achievement. Another approach to multiple grading is to separate the process and product when grading students who are working diligently to master a concept or process, such as arithmetic computation, but cannot complete the work accurately (Gloeckler & Simpson, 1988). By assigning a separate grade for each of these "major messages," teachers can maintain school and district standards of grading while acknowledging individual student progress that may not result in their reaching mastery level for a particular skill or subject area.

Shared Grading

Here, two or more teachers determine a grade—for example, when a student in a regular classroom receives assistance from the resource room teacher.

Point System

In this approach, teachers assign points to activities or assignments that add up to the term grade. Because teachers can give equal weights to activities other than tests, they are able to individualize their instruction and evaluation much more easily than with traditional grading systems.

Student Self-Comparison

Here, students evaluate themselves on a strictly individual basis on whether they have met the goals and objectives of their instructional program. Many students with disabilities and those at risk have a history of academic failure. This often results in low self-esteem and an inability to recognize their own strengths and achievements. For this reason, it is helpful to give all students opportunities to evaluate their own work, enabling them to recognize their individual progress as well as target areas for improvement. Self-evaluation can help students notice error patterns that they can later strive to avoid, a valuable skill to acquire before leaving school for the workplace. In addition, the technique can free the teacher's time for planning and instruction.

Self-comparison can be used with even the youngest students. Kindergarten and primary-level students can be asked to compare three or four of their own projects or papers done during the school week and then tell which one they like best and why. In lieu of letter grades, upper elementary students can be asked to apply one of several descriptive statements to their work (such as "terrific," "good try," and "oops!"). More in-depth evaluations can be used with middle- and secondary-level students, changing the criteria to match the type of assignment.

If a decision is made to let students evaluate their own work, the teacher must be prepared to accept the students' judgments, even if they do not correspond with the teacher's own evaluation of their work. Most often, if a discrepancy exists, it will be in the direction of students' underestimating their own merits in comparison to the teacher's evaluation.

A number-line or Likert-scale approach can be used to let students compare their evaluation of an assignment to that of the teacher. After the teacher has evaluated the assignment on the graph, students are given a chance to mark their own evaluation on the same graph, or the judgments can be made independently and compared later. The final grade on the assignment is then derived from averaging the two scores.

Contracting

In this approach, the student and teacher agree on specified activities or assignments required for a certain grade. Contracts allow teachers to individualize both grading requirements and assignments.

Contracting is a special education technique that has been successfully adopted by many regular educators. A contract is a written agreement between student and teacher about the quantity, quality, and time lines required to earn a specific grade (Hess, Miller, Reese, & Robinson 1987). A good contract also includes statements about the types of work to be completed and about how the student's grade will be determined. Often, a contract is a direct extension of the IEP, reflecting the performance outcomes for the specific objectives written in the IEP.

One distinct advantage of contracting is that a well-written contract leaves little question about what is expected of the student to earn a passing grade. Another advantage of contracting is that it helps students prepare for the expectations of the workplace: If they perform specified job tasks, meeting a certain standard within a given amount of time, they will receive a reward in the form of wages. A disadvantage is that, if the contract is not carefully written, the quality of students' work can be overshadowed by the quantity.

Portfolio Evaluation

This alternative to traditional grading is now used in many statewide testing programs. Cumulative samples of students' work based on specific educational program goals are gathered periodically. At the end of each school year, approximately four pieces of the student's work representing key skills are selected for inclusion in the student's portfolio. The teacher and the student decide which pieces they will put into the portfolio. The remaining pieces could be compiled in booklet form and given to the student's parents as a permanent record. For each key subject area, the portfolio provides evidence of a student's growth and achievement. For example, for the skill area of writing, a student's portfolio might include samples of descriptive, persuasive, and expository writing developed over the course of several years. Because portfolio evaluation compares students' current work with their work in previous years, it eliminates the need to use letter grades in comparing students with others. This makes portfolio evaluation especially useful for those students who have unique talents or strengths in particular skill areas, yet do not perform well on graded tasks (D. Wilkin, personal communication, December 17, 1990).

Rubrics

A rubric is a popular evaluating measure that is designed on a point system. For each task to be performed, clear boundaries are established. The rubric for one student may be different from the rubric for another student. For example if a student is asked to respond to a question, provide information from the material, share his or her experience and prior knowledge, and expand on the concept, four points would be given for a complete answer. The following would be used as a rubric evaluation:

1. Student is barely able to answer the question. (1 point)
2. Student is able to formulate a complete answer and provide information from the material, but has difficulty explaining his or her related experience and prior knowledge and is unable to expand on the concept. (2 points)

3. Student is able to formulate a complete answer, provide information from the material, and explain his or her related experience and prior knowledge, but is unable to expand on the concept. (3 points)

4. Student is able to formulate a complete answer, provide information from the material, explain his or her related experience and prior knowledge, and expand on the concept. (4 points)

Marking or Grading Tests

Teachers may use the following suggestions when marking or grading tests for students with disabilities or those at risk:

1. When students make low grades, let them tell you why. Give extra points if they can tell you where they need to improve.

2. Give extra points on tests when students include information that you taught but did not cover in test questions.

3. Be careful about letting students check one another's papers. This procedure can prove to be embarrassing.

4. Let students keep a graph of their grades.

5. Return all graded papers folded to respect privacy.

6. Place the grade on the second page of the test or at the bottom of the front page.

7. Write "see me" instead of a grade on papers with low marks.

8. Allow students to turn in projects early for teacher review before the due date. This practice encourages students to complete work early and provides the reward of teacher feedback before final grading.

9. If the grade on a project is low, allow the student to redo it for a higher grade.

10. If the test is a short quiz, let the student retake it for a higher grade. Students who receive a low grade will learn that they still need to learn the material.

11. If students can justify an answer on a test, give full or partial credit.

12. If a test question is worth 3 points and a student misses 1 point, write the score as +2 instead of −1.

STUDENT KNOWLEDGE CHECK

You believe Noah has mastered the skills you have taught, but he is having difficulty demonstrating his mastery. The assessment used was writing an essay.

1. What alternative assessment measures to writing an essay would you select to accurately reflect what Noah has learned?

2. After you select alternatives, what advice would you provide to Noah's teacher?

Providing Feedback to Students and Parents

Regardless of the criteria or procedure selected for awarding grades, the final step in grading any student's work should be to provide feedback to the student and parents. Many teachers are required to report student progress using traditional report card formats. Report cards are concerned with general expectations for the whole class. For this reason, some schools may recommend or require that a notation be made to indicate those grades for which the program content has been adjusted to meet an individual student's ability. Teachers may choose to supplement report cards with narrative reports or checklists that more accurately reveal information about the student's progress and current status, such as skills that the student has or has not mastered; the student's ability to work with others; the student's readiness for future units of instruction; and the success of adaptations that have been made in format, content, or classroom environment. This practice may be more widespread at the elementary level, where most report cards continue to be handwritten, as opposed to the middle and high school levels, where students usually receive computer-generated report statements that do not provide space for teacher narratives.

An example of a parent feedback sheet is shown in Figure 12.8. The student is given a report card at the end of each grading period with traditional grading (A, B, C, D). The sheet in Figure 12.8 is sent with the report card so that the parent knows the exact skills (according to the standards) the child has mastered, progressed toward mastering, or not mastered at grade level. This method aligns the traditional report card to the standards.

A narrative letter is another helpful means of sharing child-specific information with parents. This format enables teachers to communicate more of the qualitative aspects of a student's work than report cards or checklists can do. Used more widely in early childhood and elementary programs, narrative letters can include a description of a student's learning style and pattern of interaction with others as well as lists of books read, projects completed, or materials used. The letter may also include descriptions of specific incidents that reflect an individual student's progress (Spodek, Saracho, & Lee 1984).

In addition to report card grades or other standard reporting formats, students should receive feedback about their classroom behavior, participation, and study habits. If the only type of feedback given to students is a quantitative reporting of a score or a letter grade, they may not be able to realize the error patterns in their work or generalize a successful approach to a problem from one situation to another. Without understanding what their grade means in terms of the way they approached a problem or assignment, the students may continue to repeat the same erroneous pattern of problem solving in future work. Another disadvantage of presenting only scores or letter grades without constructive or supportive feedback is that it trains students to focus only on the end result of an assignment—the grade—rather than on the learning process.

An issue regarding report cards in many areas is whether to indicate by the grade whether the student received interventions during the instruction. This issue runs the continuum across the country. This author believes that interventions are a natural part of curriculum and instruction, and an indication that an intervention was made is not necessary. Interventions are a natural process. Using outlines for the total class is good practice. Giving a student who cannot use the dictionary the definitions of words is okay. Remember, we must decide what we want students to learn and take the path

Student's Name _____

Grade _____

Reading/Language Arts Skills

	1	2	3	4
Vowels				
Consonants				
Digraphs/Blends				
Contractions				
ABC Order				
Phonemic Awareness				
Nouns				
Verbs				
Sight Words				
Synonyms				
Antonyms				
Syn/Ant. Combination				
Prefixes & Root Words				
Suffixes & Root Words				
Story Elements				
Plurals				
Analogies				
Guide Words				
Sequence Pictures/Sentences				
Cause and Effect				
Main Idea				
Predict Outcomes				
Identify Details				
Compare/Contrast				
Classify Pictures/Words				
Fact/Opinion				
Literal Meaning				
Context Clues				
Charts & Graphs interpretation				
Charts & Graphs Creation				
Parts of a Book				
Dictionary Skill Usage				
Reference Books				
Real Life Applications				

Evaluation Key

M = Mastery
Indicates success in learning all skills which are appropriate at this time.

P = Progress
Indicates success in learning most skills which are appropriate at this time.

N = Non-Mastery
Indicates no success in learning skills which are appropriate at this time.

Asterisk (*)
Indicates skill instruction above grade level.

Minus Sign (−)
Indicates skill instruction below grade level.

Check mark (√)
Indicates skill instruction is on-going.

Math Skills

	1	2	3	4
Addition				
Subtraction				
Multiplication				
Division				

Math Skills

Perform/Apply Word Problems

	1	2	3	4
Addition				
Subtraction				
Multiplication				
Division				
Patterns/Algebraic Thinking				
Geometric Concepts				

Measurement/Standard & Non/Standard

	1	2	3	4
Measurement				
Time				
Money				
Conversions				
Temperature				
Calendar				
Data Analysis/Prediction				
Graphs				
Estimation				

Number Sense/Explain & Explore

	1	2	3	4
Fractions				
Place Value				
<, >, =				
Number Sense Recognition				
Rounding				
Skip Counting				
Roman Numerals				
Ordinal Positions/Numbers				
Number Line				
Ratio				

FIGURE 12.8

Parent report card feedback sheet.

Note: From Raymond Elementary School, Raymond, Mississippi.

Traditional grading poses significant problems when working with learning-disabled students:

- A low grade reinforces failure.
- Grades do not describe strengths and weaknesses.
- Grades do not reflect each student's level of functioning.

Many of these problems may be eliminated by adapting variations of traditional grading and evaluation procedures. The following alternatives suggest a variety of ways that the grading problem may be addressed.

1. Grade by achievement level
   - The student is graded as above average or below average on each level of functioning.
   - A variation may include student self-grading on a daily basis.
2. Grade by progress (the level of performance is not as important as the rate of learning)
   - Grading is based on how much learning has occurred during a given time.
3. Multiple grades (measures achievement, ability, and attitude)
   - A grade of C would mean the student has average achievement, has progressed further than expected for his or her ability, and has a good attitude with high interest.
4. Alternative grades
   - The pass/fail and satisfactory/unsatisfactory system may be useful.
   - The teacher may allow for one free grade to be substituted for any one grade during the quarter or semester.
5. Extra credit
   - Allow special projects or assignments for extra credit to improve the grade. For example, if the student makes a poor grade on a test, he or she may be allowed to do a project on the same course content for credit to supplement the test score.
6. Task mastery grading
   - The student must attain a certain level of mastery to receive a grade.
   - A contract may be set between the student and teacher before beginning the course of work.

FIGURE 12.9
You don't have to give an F if you don't want to: Alternative grading techniques.

of least resistance for teaching. If the grade given is on work that is not at grade level, however, this must be indicated to parents and future teachers.

A final consideration for educators when reporting grades is the meaning that grades take on when they are entered in a student's permanent record. Teachers in subsequent years use grades as an indication of a student's ability levels. For this reason, if grades are based on individual ability, a note to this effect should be made on the student's permanent record so that teachers will not hold unrealistic expectations for students. Six other grading alternatives appear in Figure 12.9.

GRADUATION REQUIREMENTS

Before the passage of PL 94-142 and section 504 of the Rehabilitation Act of 1973, a limited number of options existed for the education of students with disabilities at the secondary level. Unable to meet the demands of the regular curriculum, many students with disabilities or those at risk dropped out of high school and joined the workforce or, more likely, the ranks of the unemployed. Although more secondary-level special education programs began to be developed in response to the mandates of the legislation, many states increased the number of credits required for graduation in an effort to improve the quality of secondary education. Educators faced new dilemmas about awarding diplomas to students with disabilities.

The questions that surround this issue are similar to those surrounding the issue of grading. The basic argument against awarding diplomas to students in special education programs is that a diploma represents a certain level of achievement to the community and to prospective employers, certifying that any student who holds a diploma has met minimum standards in the approved course of study. Opponents view the awarding of diplomas to special education students, who may have completed an adapted or modified version of the approved course of study, as a misrepresentation of a long-standing symbol of accomplishment. Proponents of awarding diplomas to students with disabilities and those at risk point out that participants in a number of different courses of study such as college preparatory, vocational education, and general education traditionally have been awarded the same diplomas and that this practice has been readily accepted by the community and prospective employers alike. Completion of a course of study in special education represents yet another variation in the courses of study represented by the diploma. Another compelling

Graduation is an exciting day for all. More and more students with special needs and students at-risk are receiving high school diplomas. How could we better serve all students to reach this goal?

argument in favor of awarding diplomas to all students without regard to the nature of their individual course of study is that to do otherwise discriminates against students with disabilities, denying them the same recognition for their efforts that is provided to their nondisabled peers. According to Thurlow and colleagues (2003):

> Tests with high stakes for students, such as determining whether they move from one grade to the next or whether they earn a diploma, create special difficulties for students with disabilities because states have differing guidelines about the use of accommodations during these assessments. Although most states do allow accommodations to be used, these are not always the ones that individual students need.

> Because of the high stakes for students, there is generally some procedure for making special accommodations requests. This should be done for individual students when it is evident that the use of an accommodation is essential to the accurate measurement of a student's skills. If approval is not possible, and if passing the test is the only way to be promoted or to graduate, it is essential that the student's instruction be focused on ways to compensate for the unavailable accommodation. (p. 40)

Types of Diplomas

Regardless of the arguments for or against the awarding of uniform diplomas to all students, states have developed a variety of types of diplomas. Depending on state or local policy, one of three types of diplomas may be awarded to special education students. *Regular diplomas* are awarded to students in special education if they have earned the required units of credit, passed a literacy test or minimum competency test, and met other regulations prescribed by the local school board. Typically, participation in a literacy test or minimum competency testing program is an opt-out rather than opt-in program. That is, it is assumed that all students will take the test unless a decision is made to the contrary and is clearly spelled out on the student's IEP. *Special diplomas* or *modified diplomas* are awarded to students in special education who may not have earned the necessary units of credit or passed a literacy test or minimum competency test, but who have satisfactorily met the requirements of their IEPs. *Certificates of attendance* are awarded to students who have not earned units of credit or completed the requirements of their IEPs, but who have completed a prescribed course of study as defined by the local school board. In many districts, the certificate of attendance signifies merely that a student has attended school and does not indicate the level of attendance or amount of participation.

Curricular Approaches to Diplomas

Weintraub and Ross (1980) pointed out that, unless all students have access to a program of study that leads to a diploma, equal educational access is denied to students in special education. One means of minimizing discrimination against inclusive students is the use of a curricular approach to awarding diplomas. In this method, all students are provided with curricula to meet their individual needs. Teachers then can tailor the requirements for graduation to each curriculum, developing minimum competency tests or setting other standards of achievement as needed. One advantage of this approach is that students with disabilities can realistically be expected to earn a diploma upon successful completion of their curricula. A drawback is that educators have to develop and validate competencies for each curriculum. Another concern is that IEP teams might funnel students into existing curricula, a practice that is contradictory with the PL 94-142 requirement of developing individualized education programs to meet each student's unique needs.

The possible misuse of the curricular approach is cause for concern among some educators. For example, Wimmer (1981) noted that entire portions of some curricula are inappropriate for students with disabilities. She recommended that an alternative curriculum be available for some students with mild disabilities, which should include social and vocational preparation with an emphasis on career development.

Several viable alternatives to the broad-scale adoption of standardized curricula for students with disabilities exist. The majority of these students can participate successfully in the regular education curriculum if the necessary adaptations and accommodations are made. One such option is an approach whereby *special education parallels the general curriculum:* Alternative special education courses are developed that parallel courses in the regular curriculum in terms of course content but have adaptations in the pace of instruction, level of details presented, and materials used. Another option involves using an *alternative special education curriculum:* A special education curriculum is developed that departs from the academic orientation of the regular curriculum, focusing instead on functional life skills. Another approach is the *work-study program,* which allows students to earn credits while they explore various career options. This has been a traditional curricular option for students in general education. It may be an ideal approach for many students with disabilities or those at risk because it enables them to earn credits while focusing on functional skills pertinent to their lives after high school (Hess et al., 1987).

The many controversial issues regarding awarding credits and diplomas underscore the need for careful, long-range planning for students with disabilities. Many states require that issues related to a student's graduation be addressed on the student's IEP, which must state the anticipated date of graduation, the criteria that the student must meet to qualify for graduation, and whether the student's right to participate in the minimum competency testing program is to be exercised or waived. The requirement of PL 101–476 that transition services be addressed on each secondary student's IEP also supports the need for advance planning to promote a student's movement from school to postschool activities.

ALIGNING THE TEACHING–LEARNING PROCESS

Students cannot learn what we don't teach. Assessment helps us to know if students have learned what we have taught. Teaching is linked to learning; student learning reflects teaching, and classroom assessment must be appropriate and ongoing, measure learning, and therefore be a continuous process. Instruction and assessment are almost one. Figure 12.10 presents a model of the teaching–learning process.

To successfully align teaching with learning, teachers should keep the following points in mind:

1. Children learn in different ways and in different amounts.
2. Student learning reflects teaching
3. Classroom assessment must be appropriate, be ongoing, and measure learning.

Teaching is a continuous process that includes planning for instruction and assessment, implementing instruction, assessing instruction, and reteaching and reassessing when necessary. This is the process measured by standardized testing.

FIGURE 12.10
The teaching–learning process.

Note: From *Reaching the Hard to Teach* by J. W. Wood, 2005, Richmond, VA: Judy Wood, Inc. Reprinted with permission.

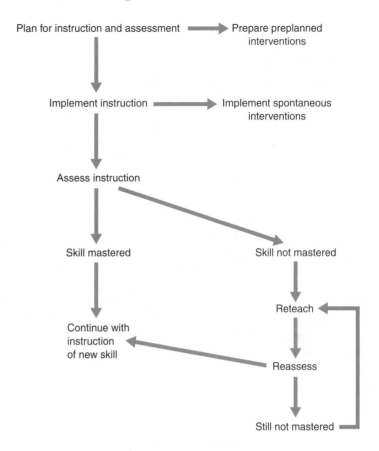

When planning for instruction, standards, benchmarks, indicators, and curricular alignment must be addressed. Lesson plans are developed, activities are selected, and interventions are planned and developed. Assessment is designed and implemented by the teacher and measures what the student has learned (refer to Table 12.9 for assessment ideas). The assessment measures selected must be aligned with information taught. Assessment measures might differ depending on student abilities. The decision to reteach is based on assessment results, and reassessment must follow reteaching. If the first assessment reveals that the student has mastered the material, reteaching is not necessary. Remember, not every assessment measure must be tested.

SUMMARY

Issues surrounding assessment, evaluation, and grading are emotionally charged and continue to be issues of concern for all students. With the emphasis on national and state standards and high stakes testing, educators are increasingly becoming concerned with curricula, instruction, and test scores. This chapter provided an overview of standards, high stakes testing, testing types, numerous ways to embed classroom assessment, grading students, grading and assessment, graduation requirements, and a process for aligning the teaching–learning process.

RESOURCES

Office of Educational Research and
Improvement (OERI)
U.S. Department of Education
555 New Jersey Avenue NW
Washington, DC 20208-5500
Fax: 202-219-2135

National Center on Education Outcomes
University of Minnesota
350 Elliot Hall
75 East River Road
Minneapolis, MN 55455
Telephone: 612-626-1530
Fax: 612-624-0879
Web: http://education.umn.edu/nceo

National Center for Research on Evaluation, Standards,
and Student Testing
CRESST UCLA
GSE & IS Building
Box 951522
300 Charles E. Young Drive, N
Los Angeles, CA 90095-1522
Telephone: 310-794-9148
Fax: 310-825-3883
Web: www.cse.ucla.edu

SUGGESTED READINGS

Arllen, N. L., Cable, R. A., & Hendrickson,
J. M. (1996). Accommodating students
with special needs in general education
classrooms. *Preventing School Failure, 41*(1), 7–13.
ASCD Infobrief, November, 2004. *What Does NCLB Mean to
Teachers?* http://www.ascd.org/cms/index.cfm?TheViewID=
372

National Education Association. A pdf file on *Balanced As-
sessment: The Key to Accountability and Improved Stu-
dent Learning* (23 pages). www.nea.org/accountability/
images/balanced.pdf.
Elliot, J., & Roeber, E. (1996). *Assessment accommodations
for students with disabilities.* (Videotape recording).
Alexandria, VA: National Association of State Directors of
Special Education.
National Center for Research on Evaluation Standards and
Student Testing. A pdf page entitled "Requirements for
Measuring Adequate Yearly Progress", (4 pages).
http://cresst.org/products/newsletters/policybrief6.pdf.

WEBSITES TO VISIT

Education Trust. Discussion of ESA (Elementary and Secondary Education Act). http://www2.edtrust.org/edtrust/
ESEA.

Education Commission of the States (ECS). This page provides links to other relevant resources related to NCLB,
both inside ECS and from other external sources. http://nclb2.
ecs.org/Projects Centers/index.aspx.

REFERENCES

4GL School Solutions, Inc. (2003). *Related solutions.* Retrieved
September 16, 2004, from www.4glschools.com/4glp.htm.
4GL School Solutions, Inc. (2004a). *A data-driven solution for
Dallas Independent School District.* Towson, MD: Author.
4GL School Solutions, Inc. (2004b). *Winston-Salem/Forsyth
meets demands of managing special education programs.*
Towson, MD: Author.
Byrnes, M. (2004). Alternate assessment FAQs (and answers).
Teaching Exceptional Children, 36(6), 58–63.
Danielson, C., & Abrutyn, L. (1997). *An introduction to using
portfolios in the classroom.* Alexandria, VA: Association for
Supervision and Curriculum Development.
Gloeckler, T., & Simpson, C. (1988). *Exceptional students in
regular classrooms.* Mountain View, CA: Mayfield.
Hess, R., Miller, A., Reese, J., & Robinson, G. A. (1987).
*Grading-credit-diploma: Accommodation practices for

students with mild disabilities.* Des Moines: Iowa State
Department of Education, Bureau of Special Education.
Jacobs, H. H. (1997). *Mapping the big picture: Integrating, curriculum and assessment K-12.* Alexandria, VA: Associa-
tion for Supervision and Curriculum Development.
Jacobsen, D., Eggen, D., & Kauchak, D. (1989). *Methods for
teaching.* Upper Saddle River, NJ: Merrill/Prentice Hall.
Jayanthi, M., Epstein, M. M., Polloway, E. A., & Bursuck, W. D.
(1996). A national survey of general education teachers'
perceptions of testing adaptations. *Journal of Special Education, 30*(1), 99–115.
Johns, J. (1992). How professionals view portfolio assessment.
Reading Research and Instruction, 32(1), 1–10.
Kleinert, H. Green, P., Hurte, M., Clayton, J., & Oetinger, C.
(2002). Creating and using meaningful alternate assessments. *Teaching Exceptional Children, 34*(4), 40–47.

Lazeur, D. (1998). *The Rubrics way.* Tucson, AZ: Zephyr Press.

Lazzari, A. M., & Wood, J. W. (1994). *125 ways to be a better test taker.* East Moline, IL: LinguiSystems.

Marzano, R. J. (2000). *Transforming classroom grading.* Alexandria, VA: Association for Supervision and Curriculum Development.

National Education Association. (2004). *What testing is allowed under the Elementary and Secondary Education Act (ESEA/NCLB) for students with disabilities?* (IDEA Brief No. 2). Retrieved September 22, 2004, from www.nea.org/specialed/ideabrief2.html.

Nelson, J. S., Jayanthi, J., Epstein, M. H., & Bursuck, W. D. (2000). Student preferences for adaptations in classroom testing. *Remedial and Special Education, 21*(1), 41–52.

1997 state special education outcomes. (1997). Minneapolis: University of Minnesota, National Center on Educational Outcomes.

Spodek, B., Saracho, O. N., & Lee, R. C. (1984). *Mainstreaming young children.* Belmont, CA: Wadsworth.

Thurlow, M. L., Elliott, J. L., & Ysseldyke, J. E. (2003). *Testing students with disabilities: Practical strategies for complying with district and state requirements.* Thousand Oaks, CA: Corwin.

Turnbull, R., Turnbull, A., Shank, M., & Smith, S. J. (2004). *Exceptional lives: Special education in today's schools.* Upper Saddle River, NJ: Merrill/Prentice Hall.

Vasa, S. F. (1981). Alternative procedures for grading handicapped students in the secondary schools. *Education Unlimited, 3*(1), 16–23.

Weintraub, F. J., & Ross, J. W. (1980). Policy approaches regarding the impact of graduation requirements on handicapped students. *Exceptional Children, 47,* 200–203.

Wilson, L. W. (2002). *Better instruction through assessment: What your students are trying to tell you.* Larchmont, NY: Eye on Education.

Wimmer, D. (1981). Functional learning curricula in the secondary schools. *Exceptional Children, 47,* 610–616.

13

Transition

CHAPTER AT A GLANCE

Transition
in the
Early Years

- Legal Foundations and Requirements
- Transition from Hospital to Home and Early Intervention
- Transition from Early Intervention to Preschool Programs
- Transition to and Within the K-12 System

Transition
from School
to Adulthood

- Legal Foundations and Requirements
- Key Principles for Transition from School to Adulthood
- Preventing Dropout of Students with Disabilities
- Transition from School to Careers
- Transition from School to Post-Secondary Education
- Understanding and Involving Adult Services

KEY TERMS

*T*erry, who has cerebral palsy, graduated from high school 15 years ago. Although he was always in regular education classes, he and his parents were constantly frustrated with his school system. Every move from one classroom, grade, or school to the next brought adjustment problems for Terry and his teachers, mostly regarding physical accommodation needs, required test modifications, his preferred learning methods, and more.

He spent the first 5 years after graduation trying to get into college or find a job the way his friends were able to do, but his high school grades weren't that impressive and his cerebral palsy made transportation to and from a job problematic. His main problem, though, was that he just didn't know what he wanted to do with his life, and so he did pretty much nothing except stay at home, watch television, and play computer games. Terry's parents helped him get on Social Security disability benefits to help support himself.

After 5 years of this unproductive lifestyle, Terry and his family were able to locate an office of their state's vocational rehabilitation (VR) agency. His VR counselor was able to get Terry enrolled in a 2-year training program for computer repairs and provided funds for both the program and transportation to and from the training center. When Terry completed the program, he interviewed at several computer shops in his area and answered ads for computer technicians, but wasn't able to get hired. After 2 more years of inactivity, Terry's VR counselor then helped Terry start a small business out of his parents' home so that his customers could bring work to him.

After 6 years, Terry's fledgling business doesn't support him completely, but between his income and his disability benefits, he has enough monthly income to plan for moving to a rental home with space for his business. He would like his business to grow and to eventually become financially independent, but he's glad that he was able to make a start—a start that he and his family wish had happened years ago.

*T*erry's story illustrates a critical issue that many students with disabilities face, lack of continuity and preparation for the transitions from one life stage or educational phase to the next. At the very least, poor transitional planning can disrupt a student's progress and lead to frustration for the teacher and the student.

In the early years of special education, many students with disabilities exited the school systems without a plan for how they would support themselves as adults, how or where they would live, or where to locate assistance and other critical needs. Since 1990, this planning has been mandated for all students with disabilities, but for students like Terry, this mandate came too late.

Periods of **transition** from one life phase to another are exciting for most children, adults, and families, but they can also cause stress and anxiety (Berliner, 1993). Transitions often bring about new responsibilities, uncertainties, and demands to which individuals must adjust. Transitions can be especially stressful for families with a child with disabilities, because they face new sets of rules and regulations, eligibility requirements, financial and lifestyle scrutiny, and other issues far beyond those that families of children who don't have special needs experience.

This chapter will discuss how early intervention and school personnel can help children with disabilities and their families make smoother transitions across the life span. The primary focus will be on the transition from the educational environment to adulthood. This area of transition is the most critical for lifelong independence and fulfillment, and entails the greatest levels of federal regulation and guidance.

TRANSITION IN THE EARLY YEARS

Legal Foundations and Requirements

Although transitional planning is considered "best practice" as the family and child move through each developmental stage, the only legal requirements relate to transition from early intervention to early childhood education. Early intervention services are authorized under Part C of the Individuals with Disabilities Education Act (IDEA) for children with disabilities from birth to age 3 (i.e., the Infants and Toddlers Program). **Early Childhood Special Education (ECSE)** refers to the preschool programs for children ages 3 to 5 authorized under Part B of IDEA. Part C of IDEA requires that when a child transitions from an early intervention to ESCE, transitional planning must occur. The time line requirements for this planning are as follows:

- The planning process must be initiated at least 6 months prior to a child's third birthday.
- A transition plan must be developed at least 3 months prior to the child's third birthday.

Further, the **individual family service plan (IFSP)** described in chapter 1 must address the procedures to be implemented to initiate the transition, and describe how families will be supported throughout the transition process. IDEA contains procedural safeguards to ensure that parents are provided with written notice and that their consent is obtained.

Transition from Hospital to Home and Early Intervention

Many types of childhood disabilities are evident at birth or even before birth, such as in cases of impairments caused by genetic disorders that are identified in prenatal screenings. In addition, many known risk factors for development of childhood disabilities may be known to medical practitioners, such as prematurity, low birth weight, use of alcohol or drugs by the mother, exposure to toxic substances, family histories, and many others.

When a child is born with an impairment or serious risk of impairment, the parents are often unprepared and ill informed. They may have fears and doubts about their child's future and their capabilities to parent a child with special needs. They may have received contradictory advice from family members, friends, doctors, professionals, and others.

Getting accurate information to these parents is an essential step to transitioning from the hospital to the home and, ultimately, to early intervention services. Fact sheets and brochures that target specific impairments or risk factors should provide parents with information on the following:

- Developmental expectations for a child who has the specific impairment or risk factor, both now and during their early years
- An overview of the IFSP process
- The types of early intervention services that meet the needs common to the specific impairment or risk factor
- Family support services, such as respite and counseling
- Support groups for families of children with disabilities
- The name and contact information for a single point of contact, such as a case manager

This information will enable the family to seek out early intervention services as quickly as possible. To protect the confidentiality of the family, these materials should be provided to neonatal units to distribute as needs arise.

Transition from Early Intervention to Preschool Programs

Several key transitional issues must be addressed in movement from an IFSP to an **individualized education program (IEP).** For one, the IEP is required for children ages 3 and over, but many children's birthdays fall in the middle of the school year. In such cases, IDEA allows the IFSP to remain active beyond the child's third birthday through the school year if the planning team deems it appropriate. Parents should be informed of the differences between the IFSP and the IEP, and must provide written consent to continue the IFSP.

The primary focus of the IFSP is the needs of the family, but the focus of the IEP is the needs of the child. As a result of this shift in focus, supports that families accessed under Part C, such as respite care and home therapies, may no longer be available. The locations of services and service providers may also change. These changes may be disruptive to the daily routines of the child and family and are often a cause of increased stress to the family system (Rosenkoetter, Hains, & Fowler, 1994). Parents should be informed of these potential changes and, if needed, assisted in locating alternatives.

Another key consideration when moving from early intervention to preschool programs is the provider of services. In many localities, the school system is not the provider of early intervention services; these services are often delivered through private providers contracted by the school system. Family members must address changes in eligibility requirements and in the types and location of services and supports. Because of these changes, they may feel that they are receiving less attention or that the quality of services from the early intervention provider to the school system has decreased (Hamblin-Wilson & Thurmon, 1990).

Transition to and Within the K–12 System

Although federal legislation requires transition plans for children moving from the Part C Infants and Toddlers Program into Part B preschool programs, specific transition plans are not required for children transitioning from preschool Part B programs into general kindergarten or first-grade classrooms. This is also, unfortunately, an area that is not widely addressed in practice. As evidence, a survey of over 3,500 kindergarten teachers by La Paro, Pianta, and Cox (2000) found that few school systems engaged in planning for students with disabilities entering kindergarten beyond or different from that provided to families of nondisabled children, such as open houses, letters, brochures, and the like. They also reported that the frequency of transition activities declined sharply from kindergarten to first grade.

Like the transition from early intervention to preschool programs, transition to the K–12 system requires collaboration and coordination among services personnel and administrators to facilitate the transition process for children and families. As La Paro and colleagues (2000) explained, some of the transition practices used infrequently, such as home visits to families with children with disabilities, often require time and travel outside general work hours.

Even though transition plans are not required for children in this age group, school systems and teachers should use them anyway. If schools systematically develop and follow transition plans, not only does the implementation of transition practices become part of the personnel's general responsibilities and incorporated in their schedules, but also more individualized transition practices may become possible. Kohlberg, Gustafson, and Ekblad (1999) described areas that the school system can address in this transition plan. These are listed in Figure 13.1.

Social/survival skills acquisition
- Social behaviors and classroom conduct
- Communication with peers and teacher
- Task-related behaviors
- Self-help behaviors

The new classroom environment
- Teacher, aide, student ratios
- Levels of attention and reinforcement
- Physical arrangement of the new classroom
- Changes in the daily schedule

New classroom rules and routines
- Requesting permission to speak
- Speaking to classmates
- Access to the bathroom
- Managing the child's own materials

Academics
- Minimum competency requirements
- Subjects taught
- Large-group, small-group, and individual instruction
- Response mechanisms typically required (written, oral)

FIGURE 13.1
Considerations in transition planning from preschool to K–12.

These same areas can be addressed as students with disabilities transition be-tween classrooms, grades, and schools. The most dramatic change will likely be from elementary to middle school, where the student will likely face many new classrooms and teachers because of subject area specialization. However, the principle remains the same: Planning for transition requires first gaining an understanding of the new school environments and necessary skills, and then preparing students for those new environments through instruction and support services.

TRANSITION FROM SCHOOL TO ADULTHOOD

Legal Foundations and Requirements

Dissatisfaction with postschool outcomes of former recipients of special education services resulted in a national focus on transition in the late 1970s and early 1980s. In a series of seminal articles, Lou Brown and his colleagues (1979, 1980) developed a model for providing ecologically based functional skills training for students with se-vere disabilities who would soon exit special education. The central theorem of this model was that training in skills that would be necessary or useful in postschool envi-ronments would be more meaningful and beneficial to students and their families than a continuation of the student's academic program.

Madeleine Will, director of the federal Office of Special Education and Rehabilita-tive Services (OSERS) during the Reagan administrations, championed transition as a national priority by calling for an "outcome oriented process encompassing a broad array of services and experiences that lead to employment" (Will, 1984). Since 1983, special education and vocational rehabilitation legislation has been modified to facili-tate transition. The Education of the Handicapped amendments of 1983 (PL 98–199) allowed state and local education agencies (SEAs and LEAs) to provide transitional services within a student's educational program, and also provided funding for transi-tion demonstration projects to identify best practices. The 1990 amendments, which changed the name of the legislation to IDEA, mandated that SEAs and LEAs provide transitional planning services beginning at least by the time the student reaches age 16 (20 U.S.C. 1401 [a][19]).

Changes were made in the 1997 amendments to these requirements. First, the age requirement for beginning transitional planning was lowered to 14 for the purpose of identifying the student's needs related to his or her future course of study. This could in-clude, for example, deciding the student's diploma goal, course work to achieve the diploma goal, or participation in vocational education. By age 16, transitional planning should identify needed postschool services for achieving the student's transitional goals.

Another change related to the recognition that students with disabilities who remain in school past age 18 are legal adults (with the exception of those who may be under guardianship or other legal restrictions). When students reach the age of 18, the due process rights that were afforded to the parents are transferred to the student. Thus, at least one year before the age of majority, the student must be informed of his or her rights under Part B of IDEA and the delivery of this information must be documented in the IEP.

Involvement in transition is also required for state vocational rehabilitation (VR) agencies funded under the Rehabilitation Act, for those students who are expected to need VR services as adults. This allows these agencies to work collaboratively with the schools to serve students who are nearing exit from school. However, each state is different with regard to legislation and policy on the involvement of VR staff in the transition planning process and funding of services for transition-age students.

IDEA defines transition as "a coordinated set of activities for a student with a disability that

- is designed within an outcome-oriented process that promotes movement from school to post-school activities, including post-secondary education, vocational training, integrated employment (including supported employment), continuing and adult education, adult services, independent living, or community participation;
- is based on the individual students needs, taking into account the students preferences and interests; and
- includes (1) instruction; (2) related services [see chapter 1]; (3) community experiences; (4) the development of employment and other post-school adult living objectives; and (5) if appropriate, acquisition of daily living skills and functional vocational evaluation.

As mentioned previously, IDEA requires that the educational areas of planning be a part of the IEP beginning by the time the student is 14, and that by age 16 the IEP and IEP team must document the student's adult service needs. However, this planning can be initiated at an earlier age if a student's IEP team believes it would be appropriate to do so.

Key Principles for Transition from School to Adulthood

Transition planning includes a focus on such postschool activities as employment, recreation, postsecondary education, self-determination, and community living and participation. Yet, despite this focus and the mandates in laws, research studies describe postschool outcomes for adults with disabilities that remain abysmal. For example, Blackorby and Wagner (1996) found that only 25% of students with mental retardation were employed 2 years after leaving high school. That number rose only slightly to 37% in the third to fifth years after high school.

In addition to poor employment outcomes, the literature reports postsecondary education outcomes that are sobering. There is a clear relationship between one's level of education and successful adult employment outcomes for adults with disabilities (e.g., Benz, Yovanoff, & Doren, 1997; Blackorby & Wagner, 1996). Completion of postsecondary education, including vocational education, significantly improves employment outcomes for individuals with disabilities. Despite this evidence, the enrollment of people with disabilities in postsecondary education institutions is still 50% lower than enrollment among the general population (Getzel, Stodden, & Briel, 2001).

If the promise of transition planning is to be fulfilled rather than simply institutionalized, the following foundational principles of effective transition planning must be in place: (a) expanded partnerships, (b) person-centered transition planning, (c) relevant curriculum experiences, (d) self-determination, and (e) seamless transitions to desired postschool outcomes.

Expanded Partnerships

In virtually all conceptualizations of effective transition planning, dynamic partnerships involving students, families, educators, rehabilitation counselors, adult service agencies, and others are considered to be foundational practices (Kohler, DeStafano, Wermuth, Grayson, & McGinty, 1994). Federal transition legislation makes it very clear

COLLABORATION TIPS

Community Resource Mapping

One method for gathering information about adult services, and thus improving collaboration, is community resource mapping. A resource map is a collection of information about agencies, services, and community supports that can be used in transition planning and adjustment. This information can be organized into a resource guide, manual, or electronic database.

Resource maps can be constructed at the student level or the school level, depending on who will use it and how. A student-level map would be designed around the unique needs of a student and his or her family, and identify resources within or close to their home community that can be accessed. A school-level map would be designed to be used by many students and families within a school, and would probably include multiple localities.

In addition to adult services, resource maps can include recreational outlets and other adult needs as well, such as restaurants, movie theaters, libraries, banks, shops, gyms—whatever needs are identified by the transition planning team. Resource mapping can be used as a community-based learning experience for students with disabilities to learn more about their communities. Graphical maps and symbols can be used to aid comprehension.

that postschool service agencies are to be involved as part of a collaborative partnership with students, their families, and school resources. However, the composition of most IEP transition teams does not represent these broad-based partnerships.

For most students with disabilities, and in particular for those with severe disabilities, involvement in adult services is critical in most areas of life. For example, school personnel can provide a student with community-based work experiences leading to job placement and training prior to school exit. However, this effort may go to waste if school personnel make no attempt to involve adult employment services agencies that can continue support services to the student and the employer.

Person-Centered Planning

Many school systems have incorporated **person-centered planning (PCP)** into the transitional planning process to some degree. Person-centered transition planning is a process for identifying a student's preferences and interests in the context of clarifying that student's vision for the future (Wehman, Everson, & Reid, 2001). There are several different methods for conducting PCP, but the basic principle behind each is to focus on the goals, needs, and choices of the individual and not on the services that are available to him or her at the current time. In other words, PCP shapes services and supports to match the person, not vice versa.

PCP meetings usually involve teachers, the immediate family, and school personnel, but may also include extended family, friends, neighbors, and others who will be a part of the student's adult life. According to Storms, O'Leary, and Williams (2000), a student's desired postschool goals or vision for the future is the first step in the transition planning process. The team (including the student) uses these goals to identify

PRACTICAL APPLICATIONS

Who were the people who helped you make the difficult transitions required to become an adult? The list might include immediate and extended family members; teachers; your guidance counselor; a boyfriend or girlfriend; neighbors; an employer; best friends; a minister, rabbi, or other spiritual leader; and perhaps many others. Students with disabilities are no different. Many people have played and will continue to play key roles in their lives, and can contribute to transition planning.

ACCOMMODATING DIVERSITY

A recent study by Geenan, Powers, Vasquez, and Bersani (2003) found that families of minority transition-age youth often encountered racial and ethnic insensitivity, disrespect, disregard, and ignorance regarding family and community beliefs, language, and culture. Many of the families surveyed described lack of cultural sensitivity as the most formidable barrier to effective transition planning.

Effective transition planning with students and families begins with the teacher understanding the world in which students will live and function as adults.

long- and short-term goals and needs, potential barriers, and other people who should be brought into the planning process. Ideally, those goals, needs, barriers, and additional people become the basis for developing IEPs throughout the remainder of the student's school experiences.

Relevant Curriculum Experiences

A student's curriculum experiences should match his or her vision for the future. There needs to be consistency and congruence between what students want to do when they leave high school and what they are doing in high school. Students' dreams and aspirations for the future must be matched with rich and varied experiences that allow them to determine whether their transition goals are right for them. In general, the secondary curriculum needs to value doing real things in real places.

If a student wants to work in the community immediately after exiting school, community-based work experiences should be a part of his or her daily curriculum, in areas that match career interests. If a student wants to pursue postsecondary education opportunities, he or she should be engaged in inclusive general education academic experiences or concurrently enrolled in some postsecondary curriculum offerings. Of course, if postsecondary education is a transitional goal, the planning team should ensure that the student is on an appropriate diploma track and is participating in standards testing as required by the SEA and by the No Child Left Behind Act of 1991.

Student and Family Self-Determination

Self-determination and **self-advocacy** are perhaps the most basic and fundamental of all the foundational pieces of effective transition planning. The self-determination capability of individuals with disabilities must be respected, and every attempt must be made to expand their opportunities to exercise their control over their own transition planning. Basically, people will do what is best for them; they make decisions based on what is right for them. By enriching students' experiences, we contribute to their understanding of what works for them, in the workplace, in the classroom, and in their community life as well.

For those students with disabilities who attain successful employment and employment-related postsecondary education outcomes, early and comprehensive transition planning with a strong emphasis on student self-determination throughout the process remains the key (Thoma, Rogan, & Baker, 2001; Wehmeyer, 2001). Wehmeyer and Schwartz (1997) found that students with disabilities who had self-determination skills were more likely to have better employment outcomes as well as community living options with which they were satisfied. In addition, Izzo and Lamb (2002) found that students with self-determination skills were more likely to transition to postsecondary education, to complete their education, and to find employment.

However, self-determination skills alone were not sufficient to ensure these outcomes. Thoma and colleagues (2001) found that other factors affected a student's use of self-determination skills, including the ability of parents and teachers to listen to the student, the ability of the transition planning process to be flexible enough to meet student visions, and the ability of adult services providers to support adult lifestyles that match the student's visions for the future.

Although far from mandating self-determination as a guiding principle, IDEA does require that a student's preferences and interests be taken into account when considering postschool goals and options. To ensure that students effectively participate in their own planning meetings, teachers should make sure that the following rules are followed:

- Students are allowed to select individuals to participate.
- Students are prepared to participate (refer to Table 13.2 on page 479).
- Students are given opportunities to ask questions and are encouraged to do so.
- Students are prompted for their opinions and ideas.
- When the student talks, everyone else listens.

Of course, in order to participate in the meeting, the student has to first be present. Although IDEA requires that the student be invited, many students still fail to attend their own meetings. Similarly, parental attendance is supported by federal mandates requiring parental notification and communication regarding parental rights as part of the IEP process, yet many parents choose not to attend or are passive participants (Abery & Stancliffe, 1996; Collett-Lingenberg, 1998; deFur, Todd-Allen, & Getzel, 2001; Hasazi, Furney, & Destefano, 1999; Morningstar, 1997; Powers, Turner, Martuszewski, Wilson, & Loesch, 1999; Salembier & Furney, 1997; Thoma et al., 2001; Wehmeyer & Lawrence, 1995; Zhang & Stecker, 2001). Although educational personnel often bemoan the lack of family involvement in this critical process, it may be more likely that educators have failed to communicate to students and parents just how critical this process will be for their future, or to effectively accommodate parents' work schedules or other barriers to attendance.

For many students and parents to be effective self-advocates in the planning process, they may require premeeting preparation. Table 13.1 provides lists of questions that can be provided to students and parents prior to the meeting. Role-playing activities can also assist students with disabilities to feel comfortable expressing their preferences.

TABLE 13.1
Preparing students and parents for transition planning meeting.

Questions for Students	Questions for Parents
1. What kind of job would you like to have?	1. Where do you envision your child living when he or she is no longer in school?
2. Where do you want to live? Alone or with other people?	2. What qualities about a home are most important from your child's perspective?
3. How much money will you need to live on?	3. What do you envision your child doing with his or her days after he or she is no longer in school?
4. What kind of things do you like to do for fun at home? In the community?	4. What additional training or education do you envision during your child's adult years?
5. Where do your friends live?	5. What do you envision your child doing for enjoyment during his or her adult life?
6. Do you have any goals for marriage or family?	6. Who will be the most important people to your child during his or her adult years? What help do you envision your child will need throughout his or her life in making decisions and protecting his or her self-interest?
7. What kind of help do you think you will need as an adult?	7. What do you envision to be your child's chief means of financial support throughout his or her life? If your child will need assistance managing his or her resources, who will do that?
	8. What other areas of your child's life, such as medical issues, transportation, and religious concerns, may also need special planning?

Seamless Transition

Finally, the success of transition planning must be judged by the outcomes attained by participants in the process. When students cross the stage at graduation, this matriculation should result in a continuation and/or expansion of opportunities for community inclusion rather than the end of such opportunity. If graduation is to represent a relatively seamless transition to desired postschool outcomes, a student's transition plan must be built around that individual's desired future, and personalized postschool supports (if needed) must have been secured through collaborative partnerships. The transition planning process has been found to be most successful when students' curriculum experiences match their desired outcomes and they are given increasing responsibility for all decisions that affect their life beyond high school.

In effect, these five principles of transition planning provide a foundation to assisting persons with significant disabilities to move from public school to postschool employment and/or postsecondary education. The question then is: What special education services are most effective? Successful transition planning practices have included the proactive identification of desired courses and curriculum content, the formation of collaborative partnerships between school and community resources, and participation in community-based experiences of direct relevance to desired outcomes.

STUDENT KNOWLEDGE CHECK

You have a student, Valerie, who has severe cerebral palsy and uses a wheelchair and lift van for mobility. She is in general education classes and has not had any problems passing her classes. She is turning 14 next year.

1. What requirements must you meet this year with regard to transitional planning? What will the requirements be when she turns 16?
2. Who will you invite to her transitional planning meeting this year? When she is 16?
3. What postschool goals can you foresee for Valerie?
4. How can you help Valerie and her family prepare to meet those postschool goals other than academic preparation?

Preventing Dropout of Students with Disabilities

Far too many students, disabled or not, leave secondary schools before completing their education. Exactly what percentage drop out is a subject of debate because of the different methods used to measure dropout rates. Table 13.2 presents three common methods for measuring dropout rates, which produce highly disparate results. The cohort rate, which looks at school enrollment over time, such as over the course of the school years, produces the highest estimate but is probably the method that best shows the extent of the dropout problem. To show how different the findings from these methods can be, data from one state for the 2002 school year showed an event dropout rate just over 2% for all students, but also reported a cohort dropout rate of 22%.

However dropout rates are measured, students with disabilities have a much higher rate than students without disabilities. For the school year ending in 2000, the U.S. Department of Education (2002) reported an overall dropout rate of 29.4% of students with disabilities using the cohort method (yielding the lowest estimate), with the dropout rate for students with emotional disturbance at over half—51.4%.

The National Longitudinal Transition Studies (NLTS) conducted by SRI International have recently shown that increasing numbers of students with disabilities are staying in school and earning diplomas (Wagner, Cameto, & Newman, 2003). This is encouraging because higher wages for working adults with disabilities are frequently tied to both (a) receipt of a high school diploma and (b) participation in postsecondary education experiences. These opportunities rarely come to individuals who have not graduated from high school (Getzel et al., 2001). Even for those students who are not expected to graduate with a diploma, completion of their secondary program provides the school system time to deliver the maximum amount of educational services, including functional skills training, collaboration with adult services, and job placement assistance.

Research on students with disabilities who leave school early has found that they do so for the same reasons as students without disabilities, such as (a) frustration with school and academic demands, (b) alienation from other students and teachers, (c) their friends drop out, (d) the student prefers or needs to work, and (e) impending parenthood (Thurlow, Sinclair, & Johnson, 2002).

TABLE 13.2
Commonly used methods for estimating dropout rates.

Method	Description	Relative Effect on Rate
Event rate (annual rate, incidence rate)	Proportion who enroll at the beginning of the school year but do not complete the year	Smallest rate
Status rate (prevalence rate)	Proportion who are out of school at any point in time	Between event and cohort rates
Cohort rate (longitudinal rate)	Proportion who enter high school but leave before completing their program of study	Highest rate

How can school personnel help keep students with disabilities in school? First, we should understand that dropping out of school is usually a process and not an event. Academic frustration can lead students to feel that they don't "belong" in school, and thus cause them to withdraw from friends, teachers, and school activities. They may begin to skip classes, which leads not only to poor grades but also to further alienation and possibly engagement in risky behaviors. The only connections that students may feel are to their friends who have left school to work, and this option looks increasing attractive. Finally, the student experiences the proverbial last straw, and doesn't return to school.

Recognizing that dropping out is a process has a very distinct advantage for school personnel: The process can be interrupted. In the case of students with disabilities who are at risk for dropping out, the school can closely monitor risk behaviors, such as excessive tardiness and absences, and communicate these behaviors to parents on a daily basis. Educators can also help students develop more school and peer affiliations through school-based and community-based clubs and activities. The school can provide supplemental services such as tutoring, counseling, and mentors (other students and adults) who can provide encouragement to stay in school. Problem-solving skills can be taught, which will help the student address the problems he or she is having in ways that are not self-destructive. Finally, the school can adjust the student's curriculum or diploma track to a vocational program that will hopefully motivate the student to finish school.

One method for addressing dropout is through **service learning,** or volunteering. Service learning involves volunteering in service tasks with structured opportunities for self-reflection; self-discovery; and the acquisition and comprehension of values, skills, and knowledge. For example, a student with an interest in environmental issues can be linked to volunteer opportunities to help clean streams, beaches, or parks. Saddler, Thoma, and Whiston (2002) found that when high school students participated in volunteer and/or service learning activities, they were more likely to stay in school.

Transition from School to Careers

Preparing students with disabilities for careers may seem like an imposing task. However, the process can begin, as it does with nondisabled children, in the elementary school years, by such means as (a) providing classroom activities for exploring different types of jobs, (b) giving students with disabilities class chores and responsibilities, and (c) encouraging parents to provide their child with disabilities the opportunities to perform chores at home.

ACCOMMODATING TECHNOLOGY

Assistive Technology and Transition

The Individuals with Disabilities Education Act defines an assistive technology (AT) device as "any item, piece of equipment, or product system, whether acquired commercially off the shelf, modified, or customized, that is used to increase, maintain, or improve the functional capabilities of a child with a disability." AT can be used to help students meet the academic demands required for transition to work or postsecondary education. AT devices can be used to control the environment, communicate with others, read or write, perform self-help tasks, and perform many other functions.

Following are some guidelines for testing and selecting AT devices to meet a particular student's needs:

1. Assess AT needs and test devices in real-life settings in which the device will ultimately be used.
2. Solicit and use input from the student and family in the assessment and testing process.
3. Consider low-tech options before high-tech options.
4. To the maximum extent possible, AT should be durable, adaptable to multiple environments, and unobtrusive.

Students with special needs can be gainfully employed after graduation. What may we do as educators to assist our students in moving from school to work?

The National Longitudinal Study of Youth with Disabilities (Wagner, Blackorby, Cameto, Hebbeler, & Newman, 1993) confirmed several of the positive benefits of work experience while in school. After all other variables were controlled, students who had taken vocational education during their last year in high school were more likely to be competitively employed. If youths' secondary vocational experiences involved work experience, the likelihood of employment was 14% higher than for students who had not engaged in work experience. School personnel can progressively focus students' job preferences and interests through the following means:

- In-school work experiences during a portion of the day
- Community-based work experience either in small groups or individually
- Job shadowing or mentoring
- Summer or after-school employment opportunities
- Participation in vocational education
- Volunteering
- Job placement and training prior to school exit

Community-based vocational education (CBVE) experiences can be an important step for students with disabilities and particularly for those with severe disabilities who may have had no real prior work experience. Typically, teachers locate businesses that are willing to allow them to bring students with disabilities onsite for vocational exploration and instruction in a variety of work tasks and behaviors. These experiences are typically unpaid, or, at most, the business might pay a stipend to a classroom fund.

In 1992, the U.S. Departments of Labor and Education issued policy guidelines regarding CBVE agreements between schools and businesses (Cobb, Halloran, Simon, Norman, & Bourexis, 1999). When communicating and developing agreements, it is critical that the school and the host business understand that the arrangement is for instructional purposes to benefit the student and not a manpower agreement to benefit the business. The educational purposes of the arrangement (i.e., career exploration, job training) should be defined in each student's IEP, and work tasks must be clearly delineated in a written agreement with the business. Although employees of the business can be used to monitor, supervise, or teach students, their activities must be under the direction of the teacher. The business cannot use the students to meet day-to-day work needs, displace current employees, avoid filling vacancies, or cover for absentee employees. This would constitute an exploitative situation and not an instructional arrangement.

Another critical issue in setting up CBVE sites is that of disclosure of students' disabilities, problems, or other private information. Without the permission of the parents (or, if age 18 or older, the student), teachers do not have the right to disclose this information to business owners to gain an agreement. If the family or the student does not wish this information disclosed, the teacher should state simply that the children are in need of a place to learn work skills and behaviors.

School-to-careers experiences and activities clearly include employment experiences (paid jobs, volunteer work, internships, community service, and service learning activities). They also include services such as receiving information about colleges or postsecondary training, assistance in writing essays and filling out applications for postsecondary education, assistance in filling out financial aid forms, help in finding a job, instruction in preparing resumes and cover letters, and instruction in filling out job applications (Saddler et al., 2002). Although all of these services and experiences increase a student's ability to prepare for work and/or postsecondary education, all but paid work experience also are linked to lower dropout rates for students with and without disabilities.

Transition from School to Postsecondary Education

Involvement in colleges and universities has been limited for young people with disabilities (National Council on Disability, 2003), even though these connections can be as important as those in business and industry. Movement into postsecondary education is critical for improving the employment outlook for students and adults with disabilities. Greater efforts should be made to educate faculty, staff, and other students regarding disabilities, accommodations, services, and the legal rights of students with disabilities.

Postsecondary options can include 4-year colleges and universities, 2-year colleges, or specialized training programs leading to certification in a career area. Many 2-year colleges offer certification programs that are geared specifically toward students with disabilities, such as the Program for Adults in Vocational Education (PAVE) at J. Sargeant Reynolds Community College in Virginia. PAVE is a vocational training program for adults with mental disabilities, including mild mental retardation, severe learning disabilities, and emotional disabilities. PAVE provides postsecondary training that incorporates functional academic instruction, job skills training, and community-based internships in four career areas: child care assistant, food service assistant, clerical assistant, and health care assistant.

Section 504 of the Rehabilitation Act prohibits organizations receiving federal funds, which would include publicly funded postsecondary schools and privately funded schools that accept Pell Grants or other federal financial assistance, from discriminating against otherwise qualified individuals with disabilities. Section 504 prohibits schools from the following:

- Limiting the number of otherwise qualified students admitted that have a disability
- Making preadmission inquiries as to whether an applicant has a disability
- Excluding an otherwise qualified student with a disability from any course of study
- Providing less financial assistance to students with disabilities than is provided to other students, or limiting eligibility for scholarships on the basis of disability
- Counseling students with disabilities into more restrictive career paths based solely on their disability
- Measuring student achievement using modes that adversely discriminate against a student with a disability
- Establishing rules and policies that have the effect of limiting participation of students with disabilities in educational programs or activities

Almost all publicly funded postsecondary schools, and many of the privately funded ones as well, have staff members who coordinate and deliver services for their students with disabilities. These individuals certify that a student is eligible for accommodations based on disability, work with the student to determine appropriate accommodations, and assist the student in obtaining accommodations. Some typical accommodations include the following:

- *Program modifications.* Waiving course or program requirements that would adversely affect a student because of a disability, such as allowing substitutions in elective courses
- *Alternative assessments.* Allowing a student with disabilities to be tested in a mode that best reveals his or her mastery of course content, such as substituting oral exams for written exams

- *Modified environments.* Moving classes to rooms or buildings that are more easily accessible to students with physical or mobility disabilities, or testing in a secluded setting
- *Auxiliary aids.* Allowing and/or providing tape recorders, calculators, laptop computers, or other equipment
- *Human assistance.* Providing students with sign language interpreters, note takers, library assistants, or other personal assistance

It is important for secondary students and their families to understand that at the postsecondary level, responsibilities shift from the school to the student. Whereas secondary schools are required to seek out students with disabilities, there is no similar obligation on postsecondary schools. Students must self-identify and disclose their disabilities to obtain accommodations, and may also be financially responsible for assessments to prove eligibility for accommodations.

As the student and family are narrowing their postsecondary choices, they should be encouraged to visit each school under consideration and speak with the coordinator of services for students with disabilities. These site visits will help them gain a better feel for how accommodating a school really is. When a final decision is reached, the coordinator of services for students with disabilities at the postsecondary school can be invited to participate on the transition planning team, either in person or via teleconference. Students should be encouraged to disclose their disabilities to the postsecondary school early, perhaps even in the application. If the student's disability is such that it may affect acceptance, such as poor grades in specific subject areas or taking longer to earn the high school diploma, a letter can be included in the application that (a) states that the student has a disability, (b) states which admission requirement(s) it affects and how, (c) includes alternative or additional information the student would like to have considered in the application, and (d) provides documentation of the student's disability by an appropriate professional.

Understanding and Involving Adult Services

For many students with disabilities, and particularly for those with severe disabilities, transitional planning and implementation models rely on the adult services system for achieving residential, recreational, and vocational outcomes. Yet it is often this component of the transitional process that precludes or delays competitive employment opportunities because of two systemic barriers: (a) already overburdened adult services systems and (b) limited competitive employment opportunities for individuals with severe disabilities in adult services.

The poor outcomes for students exiting special education services are not confined by geographic area, race, sex, community types, or other factors. Postschool outcome studies such as the National Longitudinal Transition Study (NLTS) show that a number of groups have made gains in comparison to their nondisabled peers in recent years; however, students with disabilities continue to lag far behind in terms of entering the competitive workforce or postsecondary education, earnings, achievement of full-time work with benefits, career movement, and economic and social dependence, with those having severe disabilities faring the worst (Blackorby & Wagner, 1996).

Special education instructors, their students, and students' families often lack understanding of the adult services system, the resources that are available, or the demands and expectations they will encounter (Benz, Lindstrom, & Latta, 1999). Collaboration with postschool entities, although critical for smooth transition, is an area that is often over-looked in teacher training programs (Roessler & Peterson, 1996). As a result, most school systems do not involve adult services to the extent that they could or should.

Effective planning for postschool needs requires that adult services agencies be involved early in the planning process and remain involved throughout. Specific adult services will vary according to each student's postschool goals and anticipated support needs. It is also incumbent upon special educators who teach students of transition age to investigate the types of adult services that are available in their area, the locations of those services, contact persons, eligibility criteria, and other information that can be used for planning the transition from school to adulthood.

SUMMARY

This chapter has discussed the different transitions that students with disabilities and their families experience across the life span, and how educators can assist in those transitions. The ultimate goal of transition is to ensure continuity of services that meet the needs of students and their families. Although the transitions described here occur at various ages, developmental stages, and intensities, the guiding principles are similar: Effective transition requires collaboration among educators, related services, family members, students, and, in some instances, nonschool services. Family members should be enlisted and treated as equal partners in transition processes. Finally, assisting students in adjusting to new environments and expectations requires an ecological approach, including an assessment of the skill demands and expectations of the new environments.

RESOURCES

National Center on Secondary Education and Transition (NCSET), University of Minnesota. NCSET coordinates national resources, offers technical assistance, and disseminates information related to secondary education and transition for youth with disabilities to create opportunities for youth to achieve successful futures. www.ncset.org.

National Early Childhood Transition and Training Center (NECTC), University of Kentucky. NECTC is funded by the U.S. Department of Education, Office of Special Education Programs. The center's mission is to examine factors that promote successful transitions between infant/

toddler programs, preschool programs, and public school programs for young children with disabilities and their families. www.ihdi.uky.edu/nectc/.

Transition Research Institute (TRI), University of Illinois, Urbana-Champaign. TRI identifies effective practices, conducts intervention and evaluation research, and provides technical assistance activities that promote the successful transition of youth with disabilities from school to adult life. TRI also serves as an information resource for teachers, service providers, and researchers statewide, nationally, and internationally. www.ed.uiuc.edu/SPED/tri/institute.html.

SUGGESTED READINGS

Cobb, B., Halloran, W., Simon, M.., Norman, M., & Bourexis, P. (1999). *Meeting the needs of youth with disabilities: Handbook for implementing community-based vocational education programs according to the Fair Labor Standards Act* (2nd ed.). Minneapolis: University of Minnesota, National

Transition Network. Available online at http://ici2.umn.edu/ntn/pub/hdbk/flsahdbk.html.

Wehman, P. (Ed.). (2001). *Life beyond the classroom: Transition strategies for young people with disabilities* (3rd ed.). Baltimore: Paul H. Brookes.

Wehman, P., & Targett, P. S. (1999). *Vocational curriculum for individuals with special needs: Transition from school to adulthood.* Austin, TX: Pro-Ed.

WEBSITES TO VISIT

National Early Childhood Transition Center (NECTC). Provides a searchable database of early childhood research, policy, and practice. www.ihdi.uky.edu/nectc/DATABASES/search.aspx.

The Arc. National organization of and for people with mental retardation and related developmental disabilities and their families. Includes article "Individuals with Disabilities Education Act: Transition from School to Work and Community Life," containing valuable information for parents and teachers regarding IDEA requirements and best practices in school-to-adult transition. www.thearc.org/faqs/qa-idea-transition.html.

National Center on Secondary Education and Transition (NCSET). Includes article "Community Resource Mapping: A Strategy for Promoting Successful Transition for Youth with Disabilities" (Crane & Skinner), that describes theory and practice in resource mapping. www.ncset.org/publications/viewdesc.asp?id=939.

Western Regional Resource Center, University of Oregon. Includes article "Transition Requirements: A Guide for States, Districts, Schools, Universities and Families," with FAQs, sample letters, and much more. interact.uoregon.edu/wrrc/trnfiles/trncontents.htm.

REFERENCES

Abery, B., & Stancliffe, R. (1996). The ecology of self-determination. In D. Sands & M. Wehmeyer (Eds.), *Self-determination across the life-span: Independence and choice for people with disabilities* (pp. 111–146). Baltimore: Brookes.

Benz, M. R., Lindstorm, L., & Latta, T. (1999). Improving collaboration between schools and vocational rehabilitation: The youth transition program model. *Journal of Vocational Rehabilitation, 13,* 55–63.

Benz, M. R., Yovanoff, P., & Doren, B. (1997). School to work components that predict postschool success for students with and without disabilities. *Exceptional Children, 63,* 151–166.

Berliner, B. (1993). *Adolescence, school transitions, and prevention: A research-based primer.* ERIC Document Reproduction Service No. ED 387746.

Blackorby, J., & Wagner, M. (1996). Longitudinal postschool outcomes of youth with disabilities: Findings from the National Longitudinal Transition Study. *Exceptional Children, 62,* 399–413.

Brown, L., Branston, M. B., Hamre-Nietupski, S., Pumpian, I., Certo, N., & Gruenewald, L. (1979). A strategy for developing chronological age appropriate and functional curricular content for severely handicapped adolescents and young adults. *Journal of Special Education, 13*(1), 81–90.

Brown, L., Falvey, M., Vincent, L., Kaye, N., Johnson, F., Ferrara-Parrish, P., et al. (1980). Strategies for generating comprehensive, longitudinal and chronological age appropriate individual educational plans for adolescent and young adult severely handicapped students. *Journal of Special Education, 14*(2), 199–215.

Cobb, B., Halloran, W., Simon, M., Norman, M., & Bourexis, P. (1999). *Meeting the needs of youth with disabilities: Handbook for implementing community-based vocational education programs according to the Fair Labor Standards Act (2nd ed.).* Minneapolis: University of Minnesota, National Transition Network.

Collett-Lingenberg, L. L. (1998). The reality of best practices in transition: A case study. *Exceptional Children, 65,* 67–78.

deFur, S., Todd-Allen, M., & Getzel, E. (2001). Parent participation in the transition planning process. *Career Development for Exceptional Individuals, 24,* 71–88.

Education for All Handicapped Children Act of 1975, PL 94–142, 20 U.S.C. 1410(i), 1412(2), (a)(i)(C), (1982).

Education for the Handicapped Act Amendments of 1983, PL 98–199, 97 Stat., 1357–1377.

Geenen, S., Powers, L., Vasquez, A. L., & Bersani H. (2003). Understanding and promoting the transition of minority adolescents. *Career Development for Exceptional Individuals, 26,* 27–46.

Getzel, E. E., Stodden, R. A., & Briel, L. W. (2001). Pursuing postsecondary education opportunities for individuals with disabilities. In P. Wehman (Ed.), *Life beyond the classroom: Transition strategies for young people with disabilities.* Baltimore: Brookes.

Hamblin-Wilson, C., & Thurmon, S. K. (1990). The transition from early intervention to kindergarten: Parental involvement and satisfaction. *Journal of Early Intervention, 14,* 55–61.

Hasazi, S. B., Furney, K. S., & Destefano, L. (1999). Implementing the IDEA transition mandates. *Exceptional Children, 65,* 555–566.

Individuals with Disabilities Education Act Amendments of 1997, 20 U.S.C. § 1400 (1997).

Individuals with Disabilities Education Act of 1990 (IDEA), PL 101–476, §602a, 20 U.S.C. 1401.

Izzo, M., & Lamb, M. (2002). Self-determination and career development: Skills for successful transitions to postsecondary education and employment. Unpublished manuscript.

Kohler, P. D., DeStefano, L., Wermuth, T. R., Grayson, T. E., & McGinty, S. (1994). An analysis of exemplary transition programs: How and why are they selected? *Career Development for Exceptional Individuals, 17,* 187–201.

La Paro, K. M., Pianta, R. C., & Cox, M. J. (2000). Teachers' reported transition practices for children transitioning into kindergarten and first grade. *Exceptional Children, 67,* 7–20.

Morningstar, M. (1997). Critical issues in career development and employment preparation for adolescents with disabilities. *Remedial and Special Education, 18,* 307–320.

National Council on Disability. (2003). *People with disabilities and postsecondary education.* Washington, DC: Author. Available online at www.ncd.gov.

Powers, L., Turner, A., Martuszewski, J., Wilson, R., & Loesch, C. (1999). Qualitative analysis of student involvement in transition planning. *Journal of Vocational Special Needs, 21*(3), 18–26.

Roessler, R. T., & Peterson, R. L. (1996). An exploratory analysis of parental satisfaction with transition services. *Rural and Special Education Quarterly, 15*(2), 29–35.

Rosenkoetter, S. E., Hains, A. H., & Fowler, S. A. (1994). *Bridging early services for children with special needs and their families: A practical guide for transition planning.* Baltimore: Brookes.

Saddler, S., Thoma, C. A., & Whiston, S. (2002). School-to-career services and experiences: Are they linked with lower dropout rates for high school students in Nevada? *Workforce Education Forum, 29*(1), 41–50.

Salembier, G., & Furney, K. S. (1997). Facilitating participation: Parents' perceptions of their involvement in the IEP/transition planning process. *Career Development for Exceptional Individuals, 20*(1), 29–42.

Storms, J., O'Leary, E., & Williams, J. (2000). *Transition requirements: A guide for states, districts, schools, universities, and families.* Minneapolis: University of Minnesota, Institute on Community Integration.

Thoma, C. A., Rogan, P., & Baker, S. R. (2001). Student involvement in transition planning: Unheard voices. *Education and Training in Mental Retardation and Developmental Disabilities, 36*(1), 16–29.

Thurlow, M. L., Sinclair, M. F., & Johnson, D. R. (2002). *Students with disabilities who drop out of school: Implications for policy and practice. Issue Brief: Examining current challenges in secondary education and transition.* ERIC Document Reproduction Service No. ED 468582.

U.S. Department of Education. (2002). *Twenty-Fourth annual report to Congress on the implementation of the Individuals with Disabilities Education Act.* Washington, DC: U.S. Government Printing Office.

Wagner, M., Blackorby, J., Cameto, R., Hebbeler, K., & Newman, L. (1993). *The transition experiences of young people with disabilities: A summary of findings from the National Longitudinal Transition Study of Special Education Students.* Menlo Park, CA: SRI International.

Wagner, M., Cameto, R., & Newman, L. (2003). *Youth with disabilities: A changing population: A report of findings from the National Longitudinal Transition Study (NLTS) and the National Longitudinal Transition Study-2 (NLTS2).* Menlo Park, CA: SRI International.

Wehman, P., Everson, J. M., & Reid, D. H. (2001). Beyond programs and placements: Using person-centered practices to individualize the transition process and outcomes. In P. Wehman (Ed.), *Life beyond the classroom: Transition strategies for young people with disabilities* (pp. 91–124). Baltimore: Brookes.

Wehmeyer, M. L. (2001). Self-determination and transition. In P. Wehman (Ed.), *Life beyond the classroom: Transition strategies for young people with disabilities* (pp. 35–60). Baltimore: Brookes.

Wehmeyer, M., & Lawrence, M. (1995). Whose future is it anyway? Promoting student involvement in transition planning. *Career Development for Exceptional Individuals, 18*(2), 69–83.

Wehmeyer, M. L., & Schwarz, M. (1997). Self-determination and positive adult outcomes: A follow-up study of youth with mental retardation or learning disabilities. *Exceptional Children, 63,* 245–255.

Will, M. (1984). *OSERS programming for the transition of youth with disabilities: Bridges from school to working life.* Washington, DC: U.S. Department of Education.

Zhang, D., & Stecker, P. (2001). Student involvement in transition planning: Are we there yet? *Education and Training in Mental Retardation and Developmental Disabilities, 36,* 293–303.

GLOSSARY

Academic Inclusion   Refers to the extent of involvement in learning activities with general education students.

Acceleration   Providing students with a curriculum that takes them from their current level of learning and moves them forward.

Acquisition   Original learning; learning a new skill, idea, or concept.

Adaptive Behavior Skills   The diverse abilities that a person needs to function independently in everyday life at home, work, school, or in the community.

Alternative Assessment   A state test for students with selected disabilities. An alternative test to the regular state test. The test is established by each state.

Assistive Technology   Any item, piece of equipment, or product system, whether acquired commercially off the shelf, modified, or customized, that is used to increase, maintain, or improve the functional capabilities of individuals with disabilities. An assistive technology service directly assists an individual with a disability in the selection, acquisition, or use of an assistive technology device.

Attention Deficit/Hyperactivity Disorder (AD/HD)   A disorder "characterized by symptoms of inattention, hyperactivity, and/or impulsivity that are developmentally inappropriate and are not the result of other conditions. Symptoms must have occurred before age 7 and exist in two or more settings. Students may be classified with one of three types: predominantly inattentive, predominantly hyperactive-impulsive, or combined" (Turnbull, Turnbull, Shank & Smith, 2004, p. 10).

Autism   The DSM-IV (*Diagnostic and Statistical Manual of Mental Disorders*—4th Edition) lists autism as one of five disorders under Pervasive Developmental Disorders (PDD), a category of neurological disorders characterized by "severe and pervasive impairment in several areas of development," including social interaction and communication skills (DSM-IV-TR) (Neisworth & Wolfe, 2005). Also included are Rett's disorder, Childhood Disintegrative Disorder, Asperger's Disorder and PDD-Not Otherwise Specified (PDD_NOS). All five categories experience multiple impairments; however, Asperger's Syndrome sets itself apart from the other disorders because there are no significant delays in language development or cognitive levels.

Behavioral Inclusion   Refers to the student with disabilities having behavioral expectations that are consistent with others in the class.

Benchmarks   Standards grouped by scope and sequence; what needs to be taught in each grade; and what within the grade level will be taught first, second, etc. (see Figure 9.1).

Child Study Team   A team composed of faculty from the building, and if necessary, outside personnel. They may provide additional suggestions for interventions to be tried by the general education teacher or recommend that further evaluations are necessary.

Classroom-Embedded Assessment   Ongoing assessment completed by the classroom teacher. These include projects, observations, interviews, etc.

Collaboration   How people work together, not what they do.

Cognitive Style   "Each of us develops a typical approach in our use of our cognitive characteristics to perceive, to think, and to remember. This approach constitutes our cognitive learning style" (Fuhrman, 1980, p. 2).

Collaborative Consultation   "An interactive process that enables people with diverse expertise to generate creative solutions to mutually defined problems" (Idol, Paolucci-Whitcomb, & Nevin, 1987, p. 1).

Communication   The verbal and nonverbal expressions a person makes. Also, the exchange of ideas, information, and suggestions.

Community   School districts with excellent scores on standardized state assessments draw populations, experience high real estate values, and have an overall sense of community pride.

Comorbidity   The co-occurrence of two or more conditions within the same individual.

Consultation   The key to the successful integration of students at risk and those with disabilities into the general education environment. Special education teachers provide support to teachers within general education classes.

Co-Teaching   A model for integrating students with disabilities into general education classrooms. The special educator participates in instruction.

Curriculum-Based Assessment   An assessment method that measures growth in basic skills (e.g., reading, mathematics, writing, and spelling) on short, curriculum-based "probes" or quizzes.

Direct Consultation   The special education teacher carries out some direct instruction within the general classroom setting in addition to providing the technical assistance of indirect consultation.

Due Process   The Education for All Handicapped Children Act (PL 94–142) required that states implement a process for ensuring parental rights and resolving disputes between the schools and parents or guardians of special education students. These requirements include appropriate notice for meetings, testing, changes in placement, etc.; the right to attend and contribute to edcuational planning meetings; and the right to appeal decisions related to placement and services.

Early Childhood Special Education (ECSE)   Preschool programs for children ages 3 to 5 authorized under Part B of the Individuals with Disabilities Education Act (IDEA).

Eligibility Determination   The process of determining, based on criteria, whether a child has a disability.

Emotional or Behavioral Disorder   A high-incidence disability category characterized by inappropriate emotions and/or behaviors.

Emotional Inclusion   Refers to the student with disabilities feeling that he or she has purpose and value within the class and therefore is "connected" to others.

Enrichment   An instructional approach that provides students with information, materials, and assignments that enable them to elaborate on concepts being presented as part of the regular curriculum.

Externalizing Behavior   Behavior that is directed outwardly at others; aggressive, disruptive behaviors that are observable to others.

Figure-Ground   Hearing an important word and selecting it from a background of other words.

Formal Assessment   An assessment used to obtain information that will be useful in determining if a child is a child with a disability. Test data on the student's intellectual, perceptual, language, and academic functioning are gathered for educational planning.

Free Appropriate Public Education (FAPE)   FAPE means special education and related services that (a) are provided at public expense, under public supervision and direction, and without charge; (b) meet the standards of the SEA; (c) include preschool, elementary school, or secondary school education in the state; and (d) are provided in conformity with an individualized education program (IEP).

Frequency Modulation System   The use of either classroom speakers or an individual headset to amplify the teacher's voice to increase comprehension and retention of information.

Full Inclusion   All students, regardless of disabling condition or severity, are in a general education classroom or program full time. All services must be taken to the child in that setting.

Functional Assessment   An assessment which "identifies specific relationships between a student's behavior and the circumstances that trigger those behaviors" (Turnbull, Turnbull, Shank, & Smith, 2004, p. 290).

Functional Curriculum   A curriculum concerned with teaching practical skills, such as adaptive behavior objectives, that are directly applicable to everyday life and promote independence. Examples include instruction in vocational skills, community mobility, money use, safety, and health maintenance.

Generalization (or Transfer)   Taking a learned skill, idea, or concept and using it in another location.

Gifted and Talented   Students identified by professionally qualified persons who by virtue of outstanding abilities are capable of high performance.

High Stakes   State tests have high stakes for educators, students, and parents because they affect pass/fail rates, graduation rates, and funding.

High-Incidence Disabilities   Disabilities that occur most often.

Inclusion   A term that expresses a commitment to educate each child in the school and classroom he or she would otherwise attend if he or she did not have a disability.

Indicators   Established to measure outcomes. They act as a stop sign to show when a student exhibits the indicated behavior or desired behavior.

Indirect Consultation   The special educator provides technical assistance to the general class teacher. No direct instruction is provided by the consultant.

Individual Family Service Plan (IFSP)   The legally mandated document for planning and delivering services to infants and toddlers with disabilities and their families (refer to chapter 1 for additional information).

Individualized Education Program (IEP)   A written statement for a child with a disability that is developed, reviewed, and revised in a team meeting. The IEP specifies the individual educational needs of the child and what special education and related services are necessary to meet the needs.

Informal Assessment   Assessments made by personnel other than a psychologist and consists of teacher-made tests, observations. curriculum-based tests, student work samples, student interviews, or self-reports.

Instruction   A continuous process of presenting information, adapting information, representing information, and testing for concept mastery.

Instructional Support Teams   Teams that ensure academic success for every student by providing immediate and coordinated support to classroom teachers and their students.

Internalizing Behavior   Behavior that is reflective of an individual's internal state; behaviors associated with anxiety, depression, fear, and social withdrawal.

Intervention/Transition Checklist   A helpful and practical instrument for identifying where adaptations or interventions in the learning environment may be needed.

Intraindividual Differences   A characteristic of learning disabilities in which an individual achieves significantly lower in one or more particular academic domains (e.g., reading) but not in others.

Mainstreaming   The selective placement of special education students in one or more general education classes with commensurate expectations for the special education students.

Language Disability   One aspect of speech-language disabilities (a high-incidence disability) that affects the ability to use language to communicate.

Learned Helplessness   A sense of helplessness, or dependence on others, as a result of having learned that circumstances are out of one's control. Learned helplessness leads to decreased initiative, motivation, and self-esteem.

Learning Disability   A high-incidence disability charaterized by average or above-average intelligence and low performance in one or more specific areas (e.g., reading).

Learning Styles   Students' individual approaches to learning.

Least Restrictive Environment (LRE)   LRE is the legal requirement from EAHCA for integration of students with educational handicaps in regular education classrooms. To the maximum extent appropriate, children with disabilities are educated with nondisabled children. Special classes, separate schooling, or other removal of handicapped children from the regular education environment occurs only when the nature or severity of the handicap is such that education in regular classes with the use of supplementary aids and services cannot be achieved satisfactorily.

Mental Retardation   A disability characterized by significant limitations in both intellectual functioning and adaptive behavior as expressed in conceptual, social, and practical adaptive skills. This disability originates before age 18. Five assumptions essential to the application of the definition are (1) limitations in present functioning must be considered within the context of community environments typical of the individual's age peers and culture; (2) valid assessment considers cultural and linguistic diversity as well as differences in communication, sensory, motor, and behavioral factors; (3) within an individual, limitations often coexist with strengths; (4) an important purpose of describing limitations is to develop a profile of needs supports; and (5) with appropriate personalized supports over a sustained period, the life functioning of the person with mental retardation generally will improve.

Meta-Cognition   The mental strategies used to approach and accomplish new learning tasks. In a broader sense, it is the awareness of one's own thought processes and the ability to monitor and control those processes.

Mild Cognitive Disabilities   A high-incidence disability that involves lower than average intelligence and deficits in adaptive behavior. The IQ range for mild cognitive disabilities is typically between 50 and 75.

Norm Group   An age or grade group that is used for test standardization purposes.

Novelty   An approach in which teachers give students opportunities to explore traditional curriculum content in alternative and unusual ways.

Orthopedic Impairments   By statutory definition, orthopedic impairments are severe physical or motor disabilities caused by disease, congenital anomalies, or trauma (excluding brain trauma, which is a distinct educational classification) that adversely affect a student's educational performance.

Other Health Impairments   Acute or chronic health problems that limit a student's strength, vitality, or alertness.

Paraprofessionals   Noncertified personnel who are assigned to assist teachers and other certified personnel in developing and implementing educational programs for a student.

Percentile Rank   A score in relationship to the position within a group of 100 scores. For example, a percentile rank of 34 would indicate that a person scored as well as or better than 34% of the people in the norm sample.

Person-Centered Planning   A generic term for a number of processes for identifying a student's preferences and interests and clarifying that student's vision for his or her future.

Preplanned Interventions   Interventions preplanned by the educator during lesson plan development.

Raw Score   The sum of the total number of correct responses; typically, each correct response receives one point.

Physical Inclusion   The placement of children with disabilities in general education classrooms; it demands that the student with disabilities be separated from the classroom and classmates as infrequently as possible, and support services, such as speech and language therapy or tutoring, be provided in the general education classroom.

Positive Reinforcement   Giving a reward to increase or maintain a behavior.

Related Services   Supplemental services that may be required to assist a child with a disability to benefit from special education. Eligibility for related services is linked to eligibility for special education, and is individually determined. EAHCA and IDEA list some possible related services, including speech-language pathology and audiology services, psychological services, physical and occupational therapy, therapeutic recreation, social work services, counseling services, orientation and mobility services, and diagnostic medical services.

Resiliency   An ability to rise above adverse circumstances.

Response-To-Intervention Model   A model of identifying learning disabilities based on students' response to increasingly intensive interventions.

Retention   Remembering a skill, idea, or concept already learned.

Risk-Free Environment   An environment in which students are not afraid to take chances; a safe place for students in which mistakes are seen as stepping-stones to success.

SAALE Model   A systematic approach for adapting the learning environment for students at risk. A process for differentiating instruction and assessing for inclusion.

Section 504   The section of the Rehabilitation Act of 1973, as amended, designed to eliminate discrimination on the basis of disability in any program or activity receiving federal financial assistance.

Self-Advocacy   Knowledge of one's rights afforded under law and the capability of expressing and defending those rights.

Self-Determination   Acting as the primary causal agent in one's life free to make choices and decisions about one's quality of life, free from undue influence or interference.

Sensory Impairments   Individuals with sensory impairments (i.e., hearing and visual impairments) comprise a heterogeneous group of people with challenging transition needs. The functional limitations associated with visual or hearing impairments—coupled with the frequent coexistence of other physical, cognitive, perceptual, or medical disabilities—present significant obstacles for young people in both educational and work arenas. People who are considered legally blind have a visual acuity of less than 20/200 with the best correction (i.e., they can see at 20 feet what a normal person with normal vision can see at 200 feet) or a field loss of at least 20 degrees. Although a person whose visual acuity is 20/200 has difficulty distinguishing fine details, he or she can typically recognize gross objects and may learn a great deal through vision. A person who is deaf has a loss of hearing ranging from severe to profound, and he or she does not generally learn speech and language through the auditory mode, with or without the use of hearing aids.

Service Learning   Volunteering in service tasks with structured opportunities for self-reflection, self-discovery, and the acquisition and comprehension of values, skills, and knowledge; a proven method for preventing dropout.

Sophistication   A strategy in which teachers help students to see the principles or systems that underlie the content the rest of the class is learning.

Special Education   Specially designed instruction, at no cost to parents, to meet the unique needs of a child with a disability, including instruction conducted in a classroom, at home, in hospitals, in institutions, and in other settings; includes physical education.

Speech Disabilities   One aspect of speech-language disabilities (a high-incidence disability) that affects the actual mechanism of speech production, the oral and nasal cavity, and/or respiration.

Social Inclusion   Refers to the nature and number of personal interactions with classmates.

Spontaneous Interventions   Interventions implemented by an educator when a student's needs for alternative instruction become evident during instruction implementation.

Standards   Broad concept established by states of what students should know (see Figure 9.1).

Standard Score   A statistical representation of the percentile rank used to determine a student's group standing. Most standard scores are based on a mean of 100 and a standard deviation of 15.

Statewide Assessment   State tests developed to determine whether students meet state standards.

Surface Behaviors   Behaviors that merit attention but do not demand total management programs.

Task Analysis   The breakdown of skills within a task into sequential steps.

Teaching Techniques   Methods of imparting knowledge, skills, or concepts to learner's; how teachers teach and what types of strategies they employ depend greatly on previous training, models observed, areas of interest, value judgments, and common sense.

Teams   Groups of professionals working together to serve students.

Technology   Assistive devices such as text-to-speech software for reading, writing, and test taking; speech recognition and word prediction software for writing; electronic organizers for time management and organization; and electronic graphic organizers for reading comprehension, writing, and studying that can be used to address the learning needs of students and strengthen the learning skills of others.

Transition   Progression from one life stage or educational phase to another, such as from teenager to adult or middle school to high school.

Universal Design   "The design of instructional materials and activities that makes the learning goals achievable by individuals with wide differences in their abilities to see, hear, speak, move, read, write, understand English, attend, organize, engage, and remember" (Danielson, 1999, p. 2).

Wraparound Service   When school staff and personnel from community agencies collaborate to provide services that "wrap around" the student and his or her family.

Zero Reject   A concept that states that students can't be excluded from educational services based on their disability, the severity of their disability, contagious conditions, or the costs of services.

INDEX